# Effective Management of Long-Term Care Facilities

## SECOND EDITION

**Douglas A. Singh, PhD, MBA**

Associate Professor of Management
School of Business and Economics
Indiana University–South Bend
South Bend, Indiana

JONES AND BARTLETT PUBLISHERS

*Sudbury, Massachusetts*

BOSTON    TORONTO    LONDON    SINGAPORE

*World Headquarters*

Jones and Bartlett Publishers
40 Tall Pine Drive
Sudbury, MA 01776
978-443-5000
info@jbpub.com
www.jbpub.com

Jones and Bartlett Publishers Canada
6339 Ormindale Way
Mississauga, Ontario L5V 1J2
Canada

Jones and Bartlett Publishers International
Barb House, Barb Mews
London W6 7PA
United Kingdom

Jones and Bartlett's books and products are available through most bookstores and online booksellers. To contact Jones and Bartlett Publishers directly, call 800-832-0034, fax 978-443-8000, or visit our website, www.jbpub.com.

Substantial discounts on bulk quantities of Jones and Bartlett's publications are available to corporations, professional associations, and other qualified organizations. For details and specific discount information, contact the special sales department at Jones and Bartlett via the above contact information or send an email to specialsales@jbpub.com.

This publication is designed to provide accurate and authoritative information in regard to the Subject Matter covered. It is sold with the understanding that the publisher is not engaged in rendering legal, accounting, or other professional service. If legal advice or other expert assistance is required, the service of a competent professional person should be sought.

**Production Credits**
Publisher: Michael Brown
Editorial Assistant: Catie Heverling
Editorial Assistant: Teresa Reilly
Senior Production Editor: Tracey Chapman
Senior Marketing Manager: Sophie Fleck
Manufacturing and Inventory Control Supervisor: Amy Bacus
Composition: Publishers' Design and Production Services, Inc.
Cover Design: Kristin E. Parker
Cover Image: © Comstock Images/Alamy Images; © Marafona/ShutterStock, Inc.
Printing and Binding: Malloy, Inc.
Cover Printing: Malloy, Inc.

**Library of Congress Cataloging-in-Publication Data**
Singh, Douglas A., 1946-
    Effective management of long-term care facilities / Douglas A. Singh. — 2nd ed.
        p. ; cm.
    Includes bibliographical references and index.
    ISBN-13: 978-0-7637-7403-5 (pbk.)
    ISBN-10: 0-7637-7403-0 (pbk.)
    1. Long-term care facilities—Administration. 2. Nursing homes—Administration. I. Title.
    [DNLM: 1. Nursing Homes—organization & administration. 2. Facility Design and Construction. 3. Homes for the Aged—organization & administration. 4. Long-Term Care—organization & administration.
    WT 27.1 S617e 2010]
    RA999.A35S56 2010
    362.16068—dc22
                                                                            2009010455

6048
Printed in the United States of America
13  12  11  10  09     10 9 8 7 6 5 4 3 2 1

# Table of Contents

**Foreword** . . . . . . . . . . . . . . . . . . . . . . . . . . . . . . . . . . . . . . . . . . . . . . . . . . . . **xvii**

**Preface** . . . . . . . . . . . . . . . . . . . . . . . . . . . . . . . . . . . . . . . . . . . . . . . . . . . . . . . **xix**

**Acknowledgments** . . . . . . . . . . . . . . . . . . . . . . . . . . . . . . . . . . . . . . . . . . . . . **xxvii**

**About the Author** . . . . . . . . . . . . . . . . . . . . . . . . . . . . . . . . . . . . . . . . . . . . . . **xxix**

**List of Abbreviations** . . . . . . . . . . . . . . . . . . . . . . . . . . . . . . . . . . . . . . . . . . . **xxxi**

**Part I      Introduction to Long-Term Care** . . . . . . . . . . . . . . . . . . . . . . . . . . . . **1**

**Chapter 1   Overview of Long-Term Care** . . . . . . . . . . . . . . . . . . . . . . . . . . . . **3**

The Nature of Long-Term Care . . . . . . . . . . . . . . . . . . . . . . . . . . . . . . . . . . . . 3
    *Variety of Services* . . . . . . . . . . . . . . . . . . . . . . . . . . . . . . . . . . . . . . . . . 4
    *Individualized Services* . . . . . . . . . . . . . . . . . . . . . . . . . . . . . . . . . . . . . . 8
    *Well-Coordinated Total Care* . . . . . . . . . . . . . . . . . . . . . . . . . . . . . . . . . 8
    *Promotion of Functional Independence* . . . . . . . . . . . . . . . . . . . . . . . . . . 9
    *Extended Period of Care* . . . . . . . . . . . . . . . . . . . . . . . . . . . . . . . . . . . . 9
    *Use of Current Technology* . . . . . . . . . . . . . . . . . . . . . . . . . . . . . . . . . . . 9
    *Use of Evidence-Based Practices* . . . . . . . . . . . . . . . . . . . . . . . . . . . . . 10
    *Holistic Approach* . . . . . . . . . . . . . . . . . . . . . . . . . . . . . . . . . . . . . . . . 10
    *Maximizing Quality of Care* . . . . . . . . . . . . . . . . . . . . . . . . . . . . . . . . . 10
    *Maximizing Quality of Life* . . . . . . . . . . . . . . . . . . . . . . . . . . . . . . . . . 11
Clients of Long-Term Care . . . . . . . . . . . . . . . . . . . . . . . . . . . . . . . . . . . . . 12
    *Older Adults* . . . . . . . . . . . . . . . . . . . . . . . . . . . . . . . . . . . . . . . . . . . . 12
    *Children and Adolescents* . . . . . . . . . . . . . . . . . . . . . . . . . . . . . . . . . . 13
    *Young Adults* . . . . . . . . . . . . . . . . . . . . . . . . . . . . . . . . . . . . . . . . . . . 14
    *People with HIV/AIDS* . . . . . . . . . . . . . . . . . . . . . . . . . . . . . . . . . . . . . 14
    *People Requiring Subacute or High-Tech Care* . . . . . . . . . . . . . . . . . . . . 15
The Long-Term Care Delivery System . . . . . . . . . . . . . . . . . . . . . . . . . . . . . 15
    *The Informal System* . . . . . . . . . . . . . . . . . . . . . . . . . . . . . . . . . . . . . . 16
    *The Community-Based System* . . . . . . . . . . . . . . . . . . . . . . . . . . . . . . . 17
    *The Institutional System* . . . . . . . . . . . . . . . . . . . . . . . . . . . . . . . . . . . 18
The Non-Long-Term Health Care System . . . . . . . . . . . . . . . . . . . . . . . . . . . 20
Rational Integration of Long-Term Care and Complementary Services . . . . . . . . 20
For Further Thought . . . . . . . . . . . . . . . . . . . . . . . . . . . . . . . . . . . . . . . . . . 22
For Further Learning . . . . . . . . . . . . . . . . . . . . . . . . . . . . . . . . . . . . . . . . . 23
References . . . . . . . . . . . . . . . . . . . . . . . . . . . . . . . . . . . . . . . . . . . . . . . . . 23

**Chapter 2   Long-Term Care Policy: Past, Present, and Future** .................. **25**
  Policy Overview ....................................................... 26
    *Forms and Sources of Policy* ....................................... 26
    *Policymaking* ...................................................... 28
    *Policy and Politics* ............................................... 28
  Long-Term Care Policy: Historical Perspectives ......................... 29
    *Welfare Policies and Long-Term Care* ............................... 29
    *Financing and Growth of Nursing Homes* ............................. 30
    *Financing of Community-Based Services* ............................. 31
    *Deregulation Averted* .............................................. 32
    *Efforts to Address Quality Issues* ................................. 32
    *Oversight for Other Services* ...................................... 34
  Current State of Long-Term Care Policy ................................. 34
    *Financing* ......................................................... 35
    *Utilization* ....................................................... 37
    *Quality* ........................................................... 38
  Policy for the Future .................................................. 39
    *Prevention* ........................................................ 40
    *Financing* ......................................................... 41
    *Workforce* ......................................................... 41
    *Health Information Technology* ..................................... 42
    *Mental Health* ..................................................... 42
    *Evidence-Based Practices* .......................................... 42
  For Further Thought .................................................... 42
  For Further Learning ................................................... 43
  References ............................................................. 43

**Chapter 3   The Long-Term Care Industry** ............................... **47**
  Scope of the Industry .................................................. 48
  The Provider Sector .................................................... 48
    *Community-Based Service Providers* ................................. 48
    *Quasi-Institutional Providers* ..................................... 50
    *Institutional Providers* ........................................... 52
  The Insurance Sector ................................................... 57
    *Commercial Insurance* .............................................. 57
    *Managed Care* ...................................................... 58
  Long-Term Care Professionals ........................................... 59
    *Administrative Professionals* ...................................... 59
    *Clinicians* ........................................................ 61
    *Paraprofessional Caregivers* ....................................... 65
    *Ancillary Personnel* ............................................... 66
    *Social Support Professionals* ...................................... 66
  The Ancillary Sector ................................................... 67
    *Case Management Agencies* .......................................... 67

  *Long-Term Care Pharmacies*. . . . . . . . . . . . . . . . . . . . . . . . . . . . . . . . . . 67
  *Long-Term Care Technology* . . . . . . . . . . . . . . . . . . . . . . . . . . . . . . . . . . 67
 For Further Thought. . . . . . . . . . . . . . . . . . . . . . . . . . . . . . . . . . . . . . . . . 70
 For Further Learning . . . . . . . . . . . . . . . . . . . . . . . . . . . . . . . . . . . . . . . . 70
 References . . . . . . . . . . . . . . . . . . . . . . . . . . . . . . . . . . . . . . . . . . . . . . 71

**Part II  External and Internal Environments. . . . . . . . . . . . . . . . . . . . . . 75**

**Chapter 4 Responding to the External Environment . . . . . . . . . . . . . . . . . . . . 77**
 The Closed and Open Systems. . . . . . . . . . . . . . . . . . . . . . . . . . . . . . . . . 78
  *Closed System* . . . . . . . . . . . . . . . . . . . . . . . . . . . . . . . . . . . . . . . . . 78
  *Open System*. . . . . . . . . . . . . . . . . . . . . . . . . . . . . . . . . . . . . . . . . . 78
 Stakeholders. . . . . . . . . . . . . . . . . . . . . . . . . . . . . . . . . . . . . . . . . . . . . 79
 Role of Governance . . . . . . . . . . . . . . . . . . . . . . . . . . . . . . . . . . . . . . . . 80
 Cycle of Exchanges . . . . . . . . . . . . . . . . . . . . . . . . . . . . . . . . . . . . . . . . 80
  *Resource Inputs* . . . . . . . . . . . . . . . . . . . . . . . . . . . . . . . . . . . . . . . . 80
  *Clients and Payments*. . . . . . . . . . . . . . . . . . . . . . . . . . . . . . . . . . . . 81
  *Production of Outputs* . . . . . . . . . . . . . . . . . . . . . . . . . . . . . . . . . . . . 81
  *Returns to the Environment* . . . . . . . . . . . . . . . . . . . . . . . . . . . . . . . . 81
 Open-System and Strategic Management . . . . . . . . . . . . . . . . . . . . . . . . . 82
 Understanding the Environment. . . . . . . . . . . . . . . . . . . . . . . . . . . . . . . . 84
  *Environmental Domains*. . . . . . . . . . . . . . . . . . . . . . . . . . . . . . . . . . . 84
  *Environmental Proximity* . . . . . . . . . . . . . . . . . . . . . . . . . . . . . . . . . . 86
 Building Exchange Relationships . . . . . . . . . . . . . . . . . . . . . . . . . . . . . . . 89
  *A Systems Model of Value Exchanges* . . . . . . . . . . . . . . . . . . . . . . . . . 89
  *Mission-Driven Partnerships*. . . . . . . . . . . . . . . . . . . . . . . . . . . . . . . . 90
 Focus on Outputs . . . . . . . . . . . . . . . . . . . . . . . . . . . . . . . . . . . . . . . . . 95
  *Facility Outputs as Key Ingredients*. . . . . . . . . . . . . . . . . . . . . . . . . . . 96
  *Expectations from the Exchanges* . . . . . . . . . . . . . . . . . . . . . . . . . . . . 96
 For Further Thought. . . . . . . . . . . . . . . . . . . . . . . . . . . . . . . . . . . . . . . . 96
 For Further Learning . . . . . . . . . . . . . . . . . . . . . . . . . . . . . . . . . . . . . . . 97
 References . . . . . . . . . . . . . . . . . . . . . . . . . . . . . . . . . . . . . . . . . . . . . . 97

**Chapter 5 Legal Environment. . . . . . . . . . . . . . . . . . . . . . . . . . . . . . . . . . . 99**
 Purpose of Laws. . . . . . . . . . . . . . . . . . . . . . . . . . . . . . . . . . . . . . . . . . 100
 Nursing Home Litigation . . . . . . . . . . . . . . . . . . . . . . . . . . . . . . . . . . . . 100
 Classifications of Laws . . . . . . . . . . . . . . . . . . . . . . . . . . . . . . . . . . . . . 101
  *Federal, State, and Local Laws* . . . . . . . . . . . . . . . . . . . . . . . . . . . . . 101
  *Constitutional, Statutory, Administrative, and Common Law* . . . . . . . . . . . 102
  *Public and Private Laws* . . . . . . . . . . . . . . . . . . . . . . . . . . . . . . . . . . 102
  *Civil and Criminal Law*. . . . . . . . . . . . . . . . . . . . . . . . . . . . . . . . . . . 103
  *Tort and Contract Law*. . . . . . . . . . . . . . . . . . . . . . . . . . . . . . . . . . . 103
 Personal and Corporate Liability . . . . . . . . . . . . . . . . . . . . . . . . . . . . . . 105
  *Personal Liability*. . . . . . . . . . . . . . . . . . . . . . . . . . . . . . . . . . . . . . 105
  *Corporate Liability* . . . . . . . . . . . . . . . . . . . . . . . . . . . . . . . . . . . . . 107

Corporate Law . . . . . . . . . . . . . . . . . . . . . . . . . . . . . . . . . . . . . . . . . . . . . . . 109
   *Types of Ownership* . . . . . . . . . . . . . . . . . . . . . . . . . . . . . . . . . . . . . . 109
Licensure, Certification, and Accreditation . . . . . . . . . . . . . . . . . . . . . . . . . . 111
   *Licensure* . . . . . . . . . . . . . . . . . . . . . . . . . . . . . . . . . . . . . . . . . . . . . 111
   *Certification* . . . . . . . . . . . . . . . . . . . . . . . . . . . . . . . . . . . . . . . . . . 112
   *Accreditation* . . . . . . . . . . . . . . . . . . . . . . . . . . . . . . . . . . . . . . . . . 114
Patient Rights . . . . . . . . . . . . . . . . . . . . . . . . . . . . . . . . . . . . . . . . . . . . . . . 114
   *Right to Self-Determination* . . . . . . . . . . . . . . . . . . . . . . . . . . . . . . . . 115
   *Right to Nondiscrimination* . . . . . . . . . . . . . . . . . . . . . . . . . . . . . . . . 117
   *Right to Freedom from Abuse, Neglect, and Misappropriation of Property* . . . 117
   *Right to Privacy and Confidentiality* . . . . . . . . . . . . . . . . . . . . . . . . . . 118
For Further Thought . . . . . . . . . . . . . . . . . . . . . . . . . . . . . . . . . . . . . . . . . . 121
For Further Learning . . . . . . . . . . . . . . . . . . . . . . . . . . . . . . . . . . . . . . . . . 121
References . . . . . . . . . . . . . . . . . . . . . . . . . . . . . . . . . . . . . . . . . . . . . . . . . 121

**Chapter 6   Regulation and Enforcement** . . . . . . . . . . . . . . . . . . . . . . . . . . . **123**
Purpose of Regulation and Enforcement . . . . . . . . . . . . . . . . . . . . . . . . . . . 124
Nursing Home Oversight . . . . . . . . . . . . . . . . . . . . . . . . . . . . . . . . . . . . . . 124
Requirements of Participation . . . . . . . . . . . . . . . . . . . . . . . . . . . . . . . . . . . 125
Survey and Enforcement . . . . . . . . . . . . . . . . . . . . . . . . . . . . . . . . . . . . . . 125
   *Types of Survey* . . . . . . . . . . . . . . . . . . . . . . . . . . . . . . . . . . . . . . . . . 125
   *Survey Process and Protocols* . . . . . . . . . . . . . . . . . . . . . . . . . . . . . . . 126
   *Plan of Correction* . . . . . . . . . . . . . . . . . . . . . . . . . . . . . . . . . . . . . . 130
   *Enforcement and Remedies* . . . . . . . . . . . . . . . . . . . . . . . . . . . . . . . . 135
*Life Safety Code* . . . . . . . . . . . . . . . . . . . . . . . . . . . . . . . . . . . . . . . . . . . . 136
General Accessibility Standards . . . . . . . . . . . . . . . . . . . . . . . . . . . . . . . . . 140
OSHA and Workplace Safety . . . . . . . . . . . . . . . . . . . . . . . . . . . . . . . . . . . 141
   *OSHA Standards and Enforcement* . . . . . . . . . . . . . . . . . . . . . . . . . . . 142
   *OSHA Recordkeeping Requirements* . . . . . . . . . . . . . . . . . . . . . . . . . . 143
For Further Thought . . . . . . . . . . . . . . . . . . . . . . . . . . . . . . . . . . . . . . . . . . 144
For Further Learning . . . . . . . . . . . . . . . . . . . . . . . . . . . . . . . . . . . . . . . . . 144
References . . . . . . . . . . . . . . . . . . . . . . . . . . . . . . . . . . . . . . . . . . . . . . . . . 145

**Chapter 7   Financing and Reimbursement** . . . . . . . . . . . . . . . . . . . . . . . . . . **147**
Financing and Its Importance . . . . . . . . . . . . . . . . . . . . . . . . . . . . . . . . . . . 148
Private Financing . . . . . . . . . . . . . . . . . . . . . . . . . . . . . . . . . . . . . . . . . . . . 149
   *Out-of-Pocket Financing* . . . . . . . . . . . . . . . . . . . . . . . . . . . . . . . . . . 149
   *Private Insurance* . . . . . . . . . . . . . . . . . . . . . . . . . . . . . . . . . . . . . . . 150
Medicare . . . . . . . . . . . . . . . . . . . . . . . . . . . . . . . . . . . . . . . . . . . . . . . . . . 151
   *Part A of Medicare* . . . . . . . . . . . . . . . . . . . . . . . . . . . . . . . . . . . . . . 151
   *Part B of Medicare* . . . . . . . . . . . . . . . . . . . . . . . . . . . . . . . . . . . . . . 154
   *Part C of Medicare* . . . . . . . . . . . . . . . . . . . . . . . . . . . . . . . . . . . . . . 155
   *Part D of Medicare* . . . . . . . . . . . . . . . . . . . . . . . . . . . . . . . . . . . . . . 155
Medicare Prospective Payment System . . . . . . . . . . . . . . . . . . . . . . . . . . . . 157
   *Case-Mix-Based Reimbursement* . . . . . . . . . . . . . . . . . . . . . . . . . . . . 157
   *Patient Assessment and Reimbursement* . . . . . . . . . . . . . . . . . . . . . . . 157

Medicaid. . . . . . . . . . . . . . . . . . . . . . . . . . . . . . . . . . . . . . . . . . . . . . . 158
Program of All-Inclusive Care for the Elderly . . . . . . . . . . . . . . . . . . . . . . . . . 160
Managed Care and Health System Partnerships . . . . . . . . . . . . . . . . . . . 161
   *Managed Care Financing* . . . . . . . . . . . . . . . . . . . . . . . . . . . . . . . . . . 161
   *Hospital and Health System Partnerships* . . . . . . . . . . . . . . . . . . . . . . . 162
   *Veterans Health Administration Contracts*. . . . . . . . . . . . . . . . . . . . . . . 163
Fraud and Abuse. . . . . . . . . . . . . . . . . . . . . . . . . . . . . . . . . . . . . . . . . 163
   *Federal Fraud and Abuse Law* . . . . . . . . . . . . . . . . . . . . . . . . . . . . . . . 164
   *False Claims Act* . . . . . . . . . . . . . . . . . . . . . . . . . . . . . . . . . . . . . . . . 164
For Further Thought . . . . . . . . . . . . . . . . . . . . . . . . . . . . . . . . . . . . . . . 166
For Further Learning . . . . . . . . . . . . . . . . . . . . . . . . . . . . . . . . . . . . . . . 166
References . . . . . . . . . . . . . . . . . . . . . . . . . . . . . . . . . . . . . . . . . . . . . . 166
Appendix 7-1 Minimum Data Set (MDS) 3.0 . . . . . . . . . . . . . . . . . . . . . . 168

**Chapter 8   Internal Environment and Culture Change** . . . . . . . . . . . . . . . . . . . . . **199**
Evolution of Nursing Home Internal Environments . . . . . . . . . . . . . . . . . . 200
Philosophy of Care Delivery . . . . . . . . . . . . . . . . . . . . . . . . . . . . . . . . . . 201
Challenges to a Full Integration. . . . . . . . . . . . . . . . . . . . . . . . . . . . . . . . 203
   *Primacy of Clinical Care*. . . . . . . . . . . . . . . . . . . . . . . . . . . . . . . . . . . 204
   *Economic Constraints* . . . . . . . . . . . . . . . . . . . . . . . . . . . . . . . . . . . . 204
   *Patient-Related Constraints*. . . . . . . . . . . . . . . . . . . . . . . . . . . . . . . . 204
   *Regulatory Burden*. . . . . . . . . . . . . . . . . . . . . . . . . . . . . . . . . . . . . . 204
   *Need for Balance* . . . . . . . . . . . . . . . . . . . . . . . . . . . . . . . . . . . . . . . 205
Clinical Organization . . . . . . . . . . . . . . . . . . . . . . . . . . . . . . . . . . . . . . 205
   *Nursing Units*. . . . . . . . . . . . . . . . . . . . . . . . . . . . . . . . . . . . . . . . . 205
   *Nursing Station* . . . . . . . . . . . . . . . . . . . . . . . . . . . . . . . . . . . . . . . 206
Socio-Residential Environment . . . . . . . . . . . . . . . . . . . . . . . . . . . . . . . 208
   *Personal Domain* . . . . . . . . . . . . . . . . . . . . . . . . . . . . . . . . . . . . . . 208
   *Public Domain* . . . . . . . . . . . . . . . . . . . . . . . . . . . . . . . . . . . . . . . . 211
Modern Architectural Designs . . . . . . . . . . . . . . . . . . . . . . . . . . . . . . . . 212
   *Cluster Design* . . . . . . . . . . . . . . . . . . . . . . . . . . . . . . . . . . . . . . . . 213
   *Nested Single-Room Design* . . . . . . . . . . . . . . . . . . . . . . . . . . . . . . . 213
Aesthetics. . . . . . . . . . . . . . . . . . . . . . . . . . . . . . . . . . . . . . . . . . . . . . 217
   *Lighting* . . . . . . . . . . . . . . . . . . . . . . . . . . . . . . . . . . . . . . . . . . . . 217
   *Color* . . . . . . . . . . . . . . . . . . . . . . . . . . . . . . . . . . . . . . . . . . . . . . 217
   *Furnishings* . . . . . . . . . . . . . . . . . . . . . . . . . . . . . . . . . . . . . . . . . . 218
Enriched Environments . . . . . . . . . . . . . . . . . . . . . . . . . . . . . . . . . . . . . 218
   *Theoretical Foundations* . . . . . . . . . . . . . . . . . . . . . . . . . . . . . . . . . . 219
   *Principles of Enrichment*. . . . . . . . . . . . . . . . . . . . . . . . . . . . . . . . . . 219
Culture Change. . . . . . . . . . . . . . . . . . . . . . . . . . . . . . . . . . . . . . . . . . 220
Contemporary Models of Culture Change. . . . . . . . . . . . . . . . . . . . . . . . . 222
   *The Eden Alternative* . . . . . . . . . . . . . . . . . . . . . . . . . . . . . . . . . . . . 222
   *The Green House Project*. . . . . . . . . . . . . . . . . . . . . . . . . . . . . . . . . . 224
Environment for Patients With Dementia. . . . . . . . . . . . . . . . . . . . . . . . . 228
For Further Thought . . . . . . . . . . . . . . . . . . . . . . . . . . . . . . . . . . . . . . . 229

For Further Learning . . . . . . . . . . . . . . . . . . . . . . . . . . . . . . . . . 229
References . . . . . . . . . . . . . . . . . . . . . . . . . . . . . . . . . . . . . . . . . 229
Appendix 8-1 Artifacts of Culture Change . . . . . . . . . . . . . . . . . . . . . 233

**Part III      Organization and Delivery of Services** . . . . . . . . . . . . . . . . . . . . . . . **245**

**Chapter 9    Social Services, Admission, and Discharge** . . . . . . . . . . . . . . . . . . . . **249**
Overview of Social Services . . . . . . . . . . . . . . . . . . . . . . . . . . . . . . . 250
Social Services Department . . . . . . . . . . . . . . . . . . . . . . . . . . . . . . . . 250
*Staffing* . . . . . . . . . . . . . . . . . . . . . . . . . . . . . . . . . . . . . . . . . 250
*Qualifications* . . . . . . . . . . . . . . . . . . . . . . . . . . . . . . . . . . . . 251
Knowledge of Aging and the Elderly . . . . . . . . . . . . . . . . . . . . . . . . . . 252
*Understanding Aging* . . . . . . . . . . . . . . . . . . . . . . . . . . . . . . . . 252
*Theories of Aging* . . . . . . . . . . . . . . . . . . . . . . . . . . . . . . . . . . 252
*Inaccurate Views of Aging* . . . . . . . . . . . . . . . . . . . . . . . . . . . . . 253
Diversity and Cultural Competence . . . . . . . . . . . . . . . . . . . . . . . . . . 255
*Cultural Accommodations* . . . . . . . . . . . . . . . . . . . . . . . . . . . . . 256
Skills and Competencies . . . . . . . . . . . . . . . . . . . . . . . . . . . . . . . . . 258
*Engagement Skills* . . . . . . . . . . . . . . . . . . . . . . . . . . . . . . . . . . 258
*Assessment Skills* . . . . . . . . . . . . . . . . . . . . . . . . . . . . . . . . . . 258
*Communication Skills* . . . . . . . . . . . . . . . . . . . . . . . . . . . . . . . 259
*Conflict Resolution Skills* . . . . . . . . . . . . . . . . . . . . . . . . . . . . . 259
*Interviewing Skills* . . . . . . . . . . . . . . . . . . . . . . . . . . . . . . . . . 261
*Documentation Skills* . . . . . . . . . . . . . . . . . . . . . . . . . . . . . . . 261
Social Service Roles . . . . . . . . . . . . . . . . . . . . . . . . . . . . . . . . . . . . 261
*Informational Role* . . . . . . . . . . . . . . . . . . . . . . . . . . . . . . . . . 262
*Case Manager Role* . . . . . . . . . . . . . . . . . . . . . . . . . . . . . . . . . 262
*Coordination Role* . . . . . . . . . . . . . . . . . . . . . . . . . . . . . . . . . 262
*Enabler Role* . . . . . . . . . . . . . . . . . . . . . . . . . . . . . . . . . . . . . 262
*Intervention Role* . . . . . . . . . . . . . . . . . . . . . . . . . . . . . . . . . . 263
*Advocacy Role* . . . . . . . . . . . . . . . . . . . . . . . . . . . . . . . . . . . . 263
Admission and Discharge . . . . . . . . . . . . . . . . . . . . . . . . . . . . . . . . 264
*Preadmission Inquiry* . . . . . . . . . . . . . . . . . . . . . . . . . . . . . . . . 264
*Admission and Orientation* . . . . . . . . . . . . . . . . . . . . . . . . . . . . 267
*Discharge Planning* . . . . . . . . . . . . . . . . . . . . . . . . . . . . . . . . . 269
Resident Council . . . . . . . . . . . . . . . . . . . . . . . . . . . . . . . . . . . . . . 270
Family Management . . . . . . . . . . . . . . . . . . . . . . . . . . . . . . . . . . . . 271
Death and Terminal Illness . . . . . . . . . . . . . . . . . . . . . . . . . . . . . . . 272
For Further Thought . . . . . . . . . . . . . . . . . . . . . . . . . . . . . . . . . . . 273
For Further Learning . . . . . . . . . . . . . . . . . . . . . . . . . . . . . . . . . . . 274
References . . . . . . . . . . . . . . . . . . . . . . . . . . . . . . . . . . . . . . . . . . 274

**Chapter 10   Medical Care, Nursing, and Rehabilitation** . . . . . . . . . . . . . . . . . . . **277**
Medical Care . . . . . . . . . . . . . . . . . . . . . . . . . . . . . . . . . . . . . . . . 278
*Attending Physicians* . . . . . . . . . . . . . . . . . . . . . . . . . . . . . . . . 278
*Medical Director* . . . . . . . . . . . . . . . . . . . . . . . . . . . . . . . . . . . 279

Nursing Services . . . . . . . . . . . . . . . . . . . . . . . . . . . . . . . . . . . . . . . . . . . . 283
   *Nursing Administration* . . . . . . . . . . . . . . . . . . . . . . . . . . . . . . . . . . 283
   *Director of Nursing* . . . . . . . . . . . . . . . . . . . . . . . . . . . . . . . . . . . . . . 283
   *Nursing Organization* . . . . . . . . . . . . . . . . . . . . . . . . . . . . . . . . . . . 285
Patient Assessment and Care Planning. . . . . . . . . . . . . . . . . . . . . . . . . 286
   *Plan of Care*. . . . . . . . . . . . . . . . . . . . . . . . . . . . . . . . . . . . . . . . . . . . 287
Infection Control . . . . . . . . . . . . . . . . . . . . . . . . . . . . . . . . . . . . . . . . . . 288
   *Policies and Procedures*. . . . . . . . . . . . . . . . . . . . . . . . . . . . . . . . . . 289
   *Screening* . . . . . . . . . . . . . . . . . . . . . . . . . . . . . . . . . . . . . . . . . . . . . 289
   *Infection Control Practices* . . . . . . . . . . . . . . . . . . . . . . . . . . . . . . . 289
   *Surveillance*. . . . . . . . . . . . . . . . . . . . . . . . . . . . . . . . . . . . . . . . . . . . 290
   *Education*. . . . . . . . . . . . . . . . . . . . . . . . . . . . . . . . . . . . . . . . . . . . . . 290
   *Control of Infectious Outbreaks*. . . . . . . . . . . . . . . . . . . . . . . . . . . . 291
Special Areas of Nursing Care Management . . . . . . . . . . . . . . . . . . . . 291
   *Falls and Fall Prevention*. . . . . . . . . . . . . . . . . . . . . . . . . . . . . . . . . 291
   *Pressure Ulcers* . . . . . . . . . . . . . . . . . . . . . . . . . . . . . . . . . . . . . . . . 292
   *Use and Misuse of Physical Restraints* . . . . . . . . . . . . . . . . . . . . . 294
   *Urinary Incontinence and Catheters* . . . . . . . . . . . . . . . . . . . . . . . 294
   *Mental and Cognitive Disorders* . . . . . . . . . . . . . . . . . . . . . . . . . . 295
Pharmacy Services. . . . . . . . . . . . . . . . . . . . . . . . . . . . . . . . . . . . . . . . . 297
   *Controlled Substances* . . . . . . . . . . . . . . . . . . . . . . . . . . . . . . . . . . 298
   *Emergency Kit* . . . . . . . . . . . . . . . . . . . . . . . . . . . . . . . . . . . . . . . . 299
   *Psychotropic Drugs* . . . . . . . . . . . . . . . . . . . . . . . . . . . . . . . . . . . . 299
Rehabilitation. . . . . . . . . . . . . . . . . . . . . . . . . . . . . . . . . . . . . . . . . . . . . 300
   *Restorative Rehabilitation* . . . . . . . . . . . . . . . . . . . . . . . . . . . . . . . 300
   *Maintenance Rehabilitation*. . . . . . . . . . . . . . . . . . . . . . . . . . . . . . 301
For Further Thought . . . . . . . . . . . . . . . . . . . . . . . . . . . . . . . . . . . . . . . . 301
For Further Learning . . . . . . . . . . . . . . . . . . . . . . . . . . . . . . . . . . . . . . . 301
References . . . . . . . . . . . . . . . . . . . . . . . . . . . . . . . . . . . . . . . . . . . . . . . . 302

**Chapter 11   Recreation and Activities**. . . . . . . . . . . . . . . . . . . . . . . . . . **307**
Activities: Their Goals and Purpose. . . . . . . . . . . . . . . . . . . . . . . . . . . . 308
Activity Department. . . . . . . . . . . . . . . . . . . . . . . . . . . . . . . . . . . . . . . . 309
   *Staffing*. . . . . . . . . . . . . . . . . . . . . . . . . . . . . . . . . . . . . . . . . . . . . . . 309
   *Qualifications* . . . . . . . . . . . . . . . . . . . . . . . . . . . . . . . . . . . . . . . . . 309
Skills and Competencies . . . . . . . . . . . . . . . . . . . . . . . . . . . . . . . . . . . . 310
Program Development . . . . . . . . . . . . . . . . . . . . . . . . . . . . . . . . . . . . . . 310
   *Basic Considerations* . . . . . . . . . . . . . . . . . . . . . . . . . . . . . . . . . . . 310
   *Meeting a Variety of Needs*. . . . . . . . . . . . . . . . . . . . . . . . . . . . . . . 313
   *Scheduling* . . . . . . . . . . . . . . . . . . . . . . . . . . . . . . . . . . . . . . . . . . . 314
   *Active and Passive Stimulation* . . . . . . . . . . . . . . . . . . . . . . . . . . . 315
   *Intergenerational Appeal* . . . . . . . . . . . . . . . . . . . . . . . . . . . . . . . . 315
Intervention Approaches . . . . . . . . . . . . . . . . . . . . . . . . . . . . . . . . . . . . 315
   *Sensory Stimulation* . . . . . . . . . . . . . . . . . . . . . . . . . . . . . . . . . . . . 316
   *Reality Orientation* . . . . . . . . . . . . . . . . . . . . . . . . . . . . . . . . . . . . 316

*Reminiscence* . . . . . . . . . . . . . . . . . . . . . . . . . . . . . . . . . . . . . . . 316
*Validation Therapy* . . . . . . . . . . . . . . . . . . . . . . . . . . . . . . . . . . 316
*Multisensory Stimulation* . . . . . . . . . . . . . . . . . . . . . . . . . . . . 316
Activities for Dementia Patients . . . . . . . . . . . . . . . . . . . . . . . . . . 317
Program Planning and Implementation . . . . . . . . . . . . . . . . . . . . . 318
*Identifying Suitable Programs* . . . . . . . . . . . . . . . . . . . . . . . . . 319
*Planning Programs* . . . . . . . . . . . . . . . . . . . . . . . . . . . . . . . . . 319
*Conducting Activities* . . . . . . . . . . . . . . . . . . . . . . . . . . . . . . . 320
Program Evaluation . . . . . . . . . . . . . . . . . . . . . . . . . . . . . . . . . . . . 320
Volunteer Support . . . . . . . . . . . . . . . . . . . . . . . . . . . . . . . . . . . . . 321
For Further Thought . . . . . . . . . . . . . . . . . . . . . . . . . . . . . . . . . . . 322
For Further Learning . . . . . . . . . . . . . . . . . . . . . . . . . . . . . . . . . . . 323
References . . . . . . . . . . . . . . . . . . . . . . . . . . . . . . . . . . . . . . . . . . . 323

**Chapter 12   Dietary Services** . . . . . . . . . . . . . . . . . . . . . . . . . . . . . **325**
Food Service Principles . . . . . . . . . . . . . . . . . . . . . . . . . . . . . . . . . 326
Dietary Department . . . . . . . . . . . . . . . . . . . . . . . . . . . . . . . . . . . . 326
*Supervision* . . . . . . . . . . . . . . . . . . . . . . . . . . . . . . . . . . . . . . . 326
*Food Service Assistants* . . . . . . . . . . . . . . . . . . . . . . . . . . . . . 327
*Dietary Consultation* . . . . . . . . . . . . . . . . . . . . . . . . . . . . . . . 328
*Dietary Screening* . . . . . . . . . . . . . . . . . . . . . . . . . . . . . . . . . . 328
Menu Planning . . . . . . . . . . . . . . . . . . . . . . . . . . . . . . . . . . . . . . . 328
*Meal Plans* . . . . . . . . . . . . . . . . . . . . . . . . . . . . . . . . . . . . . . . . 329
*Menu Choice* . . . . . . . . . . . . . . . . . . . . . . . . . . . . . . . . . . . . . . 329
*Menu Cycle* . . . . . . . . . . . . . . . . . . . . . . . . . . . . . . . . . . . . . . . 330
*Menu Development* . . . . . . . . . . . . . . . . . . . . . . . . . . . . . . . . . 330
*Standardized Recipes and Portions* . . . . . . . . . . . . . . . . . . . . . 332
Purchasing Food and Supplies . . . . . . . . . . . . . . . . . . . . . . . . . . . . 332
*Vendor Arrangements* . . . . . . . . . . . . . . . . . . . . . . . . . . . . . . . 332
*Food Ordering* . . . . . . . . . . . . . . . . . . . . . . . . . . . . . . . . . . . . . 333
*Dietary Supplies* . . . . . . . . . . . . . . . . . . . . . . . . . . . . . . . . . . . 333
Food Storage and Inventory . . . . . . . . . . . . . . . . . . . . . . . . . . . . . 333
*Receiving* . . . . . . . . . . . . . . . . . . . . . . . . . . . . . . . . . . . . . . . . . 333
*Storage* . . . . . . . . . . . . . . . . . . . . . . . . . . . . . . . . . . . . . . . . . . 334
*Inventory Control* . . . . . . . . . . . . . . . . . . . . . . . . . . . . . . . . . . 334
Food Cost . . . . . . . . . . . . . . . . . . . . . . . . . . . . . . . . . . . . . . . . . . . 335
Food Production . . . . . . . . . . . . . . . . . . . . . . . . . . . . . . . . . . . . . . 336
*Production Planning* . . . . . . . . . . . . . . . . . . . . . . . . . . . . . . . . 336
*Production Methods* . . . . . . . . . . . . . . . . . . . . . . . . . . . . . . . . 336
Therapeutic Diets and Nourishments . . . . . . . . . . . . . . . . . . . . . . . 338
*Modified Diets* . . . . . . . . . . . . . . . . . . . . . . . . . . . . . . . . . . . . 338
*Nourishments and Food Intake* . . . . . . . . . . . . . . . . . . . . . . . . 339
Intensive Nutrition . . . . . . . . . . . . . . . . . . . . . . . . . . . . . . . . . . . . 339

*Enteral Feeding* . . . . . . . . . . . . . . . . . . . . . . . . . . . . . . . . . . . . . . . . . . . . . 340
*Parenteral Feeding* . . . . . . . . . . . . . . . . . . . . . . . . . . . . . . . . . . . . . . . . . . . 340
Food Service . . . . . . . . . . . . . . . . . . . . . . . . . . . . . . . . . . . . . . . . . . . . . . . . . . 341
*Centralized and Decentralized Systems* . . . . . . . . . . . . . . . . . . . . . . . . 341
*Food Service Station* . . . . . . . . . . . . . . . . . . . . . . . . . . . . . . . . . . . . . . . . 341
*Accuracy* . . . . . . . . . . . . . . . . . . . . . . . . . . . . . . . . . . . . . . . . . . . . . . . . . . 342
*Food Transportation Systems* . . . . . . . . . . . . . . . . . . . . . . . . . . . . . . . . 342
*The Dining Experience* . . . . . . . . . . . . . . . . . . . . . . . . . . . . . . . . . . . . . . 343
Food Safety and Sanitation . . . . . . . . . . . . . . . . . . . . . . . . . . . . . . . . . . . . . 343
For Further Thought . . . . . . . . . . . . . . . . . . . . . . . . . . . . . . . . . . . . . . . . . . . 344
For Further Learning . . . . . . . . . . . . . . . . . . . . . . . . . . . . . . . . . . . . . . . . . . 344
References . . . . . . . . . . . . . . . . . . . . . . . . . . . . . . . . . . . . . . . . . . . . . . . . . . . 345

**Chapter 13   Plant and Environmental Services** . . . . . . . . . . . . . . . . . . . . . . . . **347**
Functions and Objectives . . . . . . . . . . . . . . . . . . . . . . . . . . . . . . . . . . . . . . . 348
Organization of Environmental Services . . . . . . . . . . . . . . . . . . . . . . . . . . 348
*Maintenance Department* . . . . . . . . . . . . . . . . . . . . . . . . . . . . . . . . . . . . . 348
*Housekeeping and Laundry Departments* . . . . . . . . . . . . . . . . . . . . . . 349
*Security and Safety Functions* . . . . . . . . . . . . . . . . . . . . . . . . . . . . . . . . 349
Maintenance Operation . . . . . . . . . . . . . . . . . . . . . . . . . . . . . . . . . . . . . . . . 350
*Urgent Service Calls* . . . . . . . . . . . . . . . . . . . . . . . . . . . . . . . . . . . . . . . . . 350
*Routine Repairs* . . . . . . . . . . . . . . . . . . . . . . . . . . . . . . . . . . . . . . . . . . . . . 350
*Preventive Maintenance* . . . . . . . . . . . . . . . . . . . . . . . . . . . . . . . . . . . . . 350
*Contract Work* . . . . . . . . . . . . . . . . . . . . . . . . . . . . . . . . . . . . . . . . . . . . . . 352
Housekeeping Operations . . . . . . . . . . . . . . . . . . . . . . . . . . . . . . . . . . . . . . 352
*Cleaning, Reconditioning, and Floor Care* . . . . . . . . . . . . . . . . . . . . . . 353
*Sanitizing* . . . . . . . . . . . . . . . . . . . . . . . . . . . . . . . . . . . . . . . . . . . . . . . . . . 353
*Infection Control* . . . . . . . . . . . . . . . . . . . . . . . . . . . . . . . . . . . . . . . . . . . . 353
Laundry Operations . . . . . . . . . . . . . . . . . . . . . . . . . . . . . . . . . . . . . . . . . . . 354
*Microbicidal Washing* . . . . . . . . . . . . . . . . . . . . . . . . . . . . . . . . . . . . . . . 354
*Standard Precautions* . . . . . . . . . . . . . . . . . . . . . . . . . . . . . . . . . . . . . . . 354
*Linen Inventory* . . . . . . . . . . . . . . . . . . . . . . . . . . . . . . . . . . . . . . . . . . . . . 355
Security Operations . . . . . . . . . . . . . . . . . . . . . . . . . . . . . . . . . . . . . . . . . . . 355
*Physical Security* . . . . . . . . . . . . . . . . . . . . . . . . . . . . . . . . . . . . . . . . . . . . 355
*Procedural Security* . . . . . . . . . . . . . . . . . . . . . . . . . . . . . . . . . . . . . . . . . 357
Fire and Disaster Planning . . . . . . . . . . . . . . . . . . . . . . . . . . . . . . . . . . . . . 358
*Fire Safety Plan and Steps* . . . . . . . . . . . . . . . . . . . . . . . . . . . . . . . . . . . . 358
*Emergency Evacuation* . . . . . . . . . . . . . . . . . . . . . . . . . . . . . . . . . . . . . . . 359
*Simulation Drills* . . . . . . . . . . . . . . . . . . . . . . . . . . . . . . . . . . . . . . . . . . . . 360
Waste Management . . . . . . . . . . . . . . . . . . . . . . . . . . . . . . . . . . . . . . . . . . . . 360
*General Waste* . . . . . . . . . . . . . . . . . . . . . . . . . . . . . . . . . . . . . . . . . . . . . . 360
*Hazardous Waste* . . . . . . . . . . . . . . . . . . . . . . . . . . . . . . . . . . . . . . . . . . . 361
Environmental Safety . . . . . . . . . . . . . . . . . . . . . . . . . . . . . . . . . . . . . . . . . . 361

For Further Thought . . . . . . . . . . . . . . . . . . . . . . . . . . . . . . . . . . . . . . . . . . . . . 362
For Further Learning . . . . . . . . . . . . . . . . . . . . . . . . . . . . . . . . . . . . . . . . . . . . 362
References . . . . . . . . . . . . . . . . . . . . . . . . . . . . . . . . . . . . . . . . . . . . . . . . . . . . 362

**Chapter 14   Administrative and Information Systems** . . . . . . . . . . . . . . . . . . . . . . **365**
The Business Office and Its Functions . . . . . . . . . . . . . . . . . . . . . . . . . . . . . . . 366
*Reception* . . . . . . . . . . . . . . . . . . . . . . . . . . . . . . . . . . . . . . . . . . . . . . . . . . 367
*Secretarial and Clerical* . . . . . . . . . . . . . . . . . . . . . . . . . . . . . . . . . . . . . . . 368
*Accounting and Bookkeeping* . . . . . . . . . . . . . . . . . . . . . . . . . . . . . . . . . . . 368
Payroll and Compensation . . . . . . . . . . . . . . . . . . . . . . . . . . . . . . . . . . . . . . . 368
*Exempt and Nonexempt Employees* . . . . . . . . . . . . . . . . . . . . . . . . . . . . . . 369
*Minimum Wage* . . . . . . . . . . . . . . . . . . . . . . . . . . . . . . . . . . . . . . . . . . . . . 370
*Overtime Compensation* . . . . . . . . . . . . . . . . . . . . . . . . . . . . . . . . . . . . . . 370
*Limits to FLSA's Jurisdiction* . . . . . . . . . . . . . . . . . . . . . . . . . . . . . . . . . . 371
*Payroll Withholdings* . . . . . . . . . . . . . . . . . . . . . . . . . . . . . . . . . . . . . . . . 371
Other Bookkeeping Tasks . . . . . . . . . . . . . . . . . . . . . . . . . . . . . . . . . . . . . . . . 372
*Accounts Payable* . . . . . . . . . . . . . . . . . . . . . . . . . . . . . . . . . . . . . . . . . . . 372
*Petty Cash Fund* . . . . . . . . . . . . . . . . . . . . . . . . . . . . . . . . . . . . . . . . . . . . 373
*Billing, Accounts Receivable, and Collection* . . . . . . . . . . . . . . . . . . . . . . 373
*Patient Trust Fund* . . . . . . . . . . . . . . . . . . . . . . . . . . . . . . . . . . . . . . . . . . 375
*Cash Receipts and Deposits* . . . . . . . . . . . . . . . . . . . . . . . . . . . . . . . . . . . 376
Medical Records . . . . . . . . . . . . . . . . . . . . . . . . . . . . . . . . . . . . . . . . . . . . . . . 376
*Staffing* . . . . . . . . . . . . . . . . . . . . . . . . . . . . . . . . . . . . . . . . . . . . . . . . . . . 376
*Functions* . . . . . . . . . . . . . . . . . . . . . . . . . . . . . . . . . . . . . . . . . . . . . . . . . 376
*Medical Record Content* . . . . . . . . . . . . . . . . . . . . . . . . . . . . . . . . . . . . . . 377
*Purpose of Medical Records* . . . . . . . . . . . . . . . . . . . . . . . . . . . . . . . . . . . 377
Information Systems . . . . . . . . . . . . . . . . . . . . . . . . . . . . . . . . . . . . . . . . . . . . 378
*Integrated Networks* . . . . . . . . . . . . . . . . . . . . . . . . . . . . . . . . . . . . . . . . . 379
*National Data* . . . . . . . . . . . . . . . . . . . . . . . . . . . . . . . . . . . . . . . . . . . . . . 380
*Security Issues* . . . . . . . . . . . . . . . . . . . . . . . . . . . . . . . . . . . . . . . . . . . . . 381
*System Development* . . . . . . . . . . . . . . . . . . . . . . . . . . . . . . . . . . . . . . . . . 381
For Further Thought . . . . . . . . . . . . . . . . . . . . . . . . . . . . . . . . . . . . . . . . . . . . . 382
For Further Learning . . . . . . . . . . . . . . . . . . . . . . . . . . . . . . . . . . . . . . . . . . . . 382
References . . . . . . . . . . . . . . . . . . . . . . . . . . . . . . . . . . . . . . . . . . . . . . . . . . . . 382
Appendix 14-1 Common Abbreviations Used in Patient Documentation . . . . . . . 384

**Part IV      Governance and Management** . . . . . . . . . . . . . . . . . . . . . . . . . . . . . . . **387**

**Chapter 15   Effective Governance, Leadership, and Management** . . . . . . . . . . . . **389**
Governance and Corporate Compliance . . . . . . . . . . . . . . . . . . . . . . . . . . . . . 390
*The Board's Composition* . . . . . . . . . . . . . . . . . . . . . . . . . . . . . . . . . . . . . . 390
*The Board's Functions* . . . . . . . . . . . . . . . . . . . . . . . . . . . . . . . . . . . . . . . . 391
*Role of the Nursing Home Administrator* . . . . . . . . . . . . . . . . . . . . . . . . . . 392
*Corporate Compliance* . . . . . . . . . . . . . . . . . . . . . . . . . . . . . . . . . . . . . . . 392

The Executive Roles. . . . . . . . . . . . . . . . . . . . . . . . . . . . . . . . . . . . . . . . . . . . . . . 393
   *The Roles of CEO and COO* . . . . . . . . . . . . . . . . . . . . . . . . . . . . . . . . . . . 394
   *The Administrative Officer Role*. . . . . . . . . . . . . . . . . . . . . . . . . . . . . . . . . 395
The Effective Administrator. . . . . . . . . . . . . . . . . . . . . . . . . . . . . . . . . . . . . . . . 395
   *Managing the Business Aspect*. . . . . . . . . . . . . . . . . . . . . . . . . . . . . . . . . . 396
   *Managing Work and Workers* . . . . . . . . . . . . . . . . . . . . . . . . . . . . . . . . . . 397
   *Managing the Facility in Community and Society*. . . . . . . . . . . . . . . . . . . 398
Leadership . . . . . . . . . . . . . . . . . . . . . . . . . . . . . . . . . . . . . . . . . . . . . . . . . . . . . 398
   *The Meaning and Purpose of Leadership* . . . . . . . . . . . . . . . . . . . . . . . . . 398
   *Leadership Attitudes and Styles*. . . . . . . . . . . . . . . . . . . . . . . . . . . . . . . . . 399
   *Implications of Leadership Theories* . . . . . . . . . . . . . . . . . . . . . . . . . . . . . 401
Management. . . . . . . . . . . . . . . . . . . . . . . . . . . . . . . . . . . . . . . . . . . . . . . . . . . . 403
   *Management Roles*. . . . . . . . . . . . . . . . . . . . . . . . . . . . . . . . . . . . . . . . . . . 403
   *Management Functions* . . . . . . . . . . . . . . . . . . . . . . . . . . . . . . . . . . . . . . . 405
Tools for Effective Management . . . . . . . . . . . . . . . . . . . . . . . . . . . . . . . . . . . . 407
   *Vision and Mission*. . . . . . . . . . . . . . . . . . . . . . . . . . . . . . . . . . . . . . . . . . 407
   *Values*. . . . . . . . . . . . . . . . . . . . . . . . . . . . . . . . . . . . . . . . . . . . . . . . . . . . 408
   *Managerial Decision Making* . . . . . . . . . . . . . . . . . . . . . . . . . . . . . . . . . . 409
   *Effective Meetings* . . . . . . . . . . . . . . . . . . . . . . . . . . . . . . . . . . . . . . . . . . 410
   *Conflict Management*. . . . . . . . . . . . . . . . . . . . . . . . . . . . . . . . . . . . . . . . . 413
   *Relationship with Superiors*. . . . . . . . . . . . . . . . . . . . . . . . . . . . . . . . . . . 414
   *Risk Management*. . . . . . . . . . . . . . . . . . . . . . . . . . . . . . . . . . . . . . . . . . . 416
For Further Thought . . . . . . . . . . . . . . . . . . . . . . . . . . . . . . . . . . . . . . . . . . . . . 416
For Further Learning . . . . . . . . . . . . . . . . . . . . . . . . . . . . . . . . . . . . . . . . . . . . 417
References . . . . . . . . . . . . . . . . . . . . . . . . . . . . . . . . . . . . . . . . . . . . . . . . . . . . . 417


**Chapter 16    Effective Human Resource and Staff Development** . . . . . . . . . . . . . . . **419**
Human Resources and Their Importance. . . . . . . . . . . . . . . . . . . . . . . . . . . . . 420
Human Resource Management . . . . . . . . . . . . . . . . . . . . . . . . . . . . . . . . . . . . 420
Goals, Main Functions, and Challenges. . . . . . . . . . . . . . . . . . . . . . . . . . . . . . 421
   *Human Resource Goals*. . . . . . . . . . . . . . . . . . . . . . . . . . . . . . . . . . . . . . . 421
   *Human Resource Functions*. . . . . . . . . . . . . . . . . . . . . . . . . . . . . . . . . . . . 421
   *Human Resource Challenges*. . . . . . . . . . . . . . . . . . . . . . . . . . . . . . . . . . . 422
Human Resource Planning. . . . . . . . . . . . . . . . . . . . . . . . . . . . . . . . . . . . . . . . 422
   *Staffing Levels* . . . . . . . . . . . . . . . . . . . . . . . . . . . . . . . . . . . . . . . . . . . . . 422
   *Scheduling* . . . . . . . . . . . . . . . . . . . . . . . . . . . . . . . . . . . . . . . . . . . . . . . . 424
Staff Recruitment and Compensation . . . . . . . . . . . . . . . . . . . . . . . . . . . . . . . 424
   *Creative Recruitment*. . . . . . . . . . . . . . . . . . . . . . . . . . . . . . . . . . . . . . . . 424
   *Compensation* . . . . . . . . . . . . . . . . . . . . . . . . . . . . . . . . . . . . . . . . . . . . . 425
Staff Licensure, Certification, and Registration. . . . . . . . . . . . . . . . . . . . . . . . 425
Managing Absenteeism and Turnover . . . . . . . . . . . . . . . . . . . . . . . . . . . . . . . 426
   *Absenteeism*. . . . . . . . . . . . . . . . . . . . . . . . . . . . . . . . . . . . . . . . . . . . . . . 426
   *Turnover and Retention* . . . . . . . . . . . . . . . . . . . . . . . . . . . . . . . . . . . . . . 426

Staff Development . . . . . . . . . . . . . . . . . . . . . . . . . . . . . . . . . . . . . . . . . . . 430
    *Staff Development Goals* . . . . . . . . . . . . . . . . . . . . . . . . . . . . . . . . . . . 430
    *Staff Development Content* . . . . . . . . . . . . . . . . . . . . . . . . . . . . . . . . 430
Performance Appraisal . . . . . . . . . . . . . . . . . . . . . . . . . . . . . . . . . . . . . . . . 431
Self-Managed Work Teams . . . . . . . . . . . . . . . . . . . . . . . . . . . . . . . . . . . . 432
Counseling, Disciplining, and Terminating . . . . . . . . . . . . . . . . . . . . . . . 433
    *Counseling* . . . . . . . . . . . . . . . . . . . . . . . . . . . . . . . . . . . . . . . . . . . . . . 434
    *Disciplining* . . . . . . . . . . . . . . . . . . . . . . . . . . . . . . . . . . . . . . . . . . . . . 434
    *Terminating* . . . . . . . . . . . . . . . . . . . . . . . . . . . . . . . . . . . . . . . . . . . . . 436
Labor Relations and Unionization . . . . . . . . . . . . . . . . . . . . . . . . . . . . . . 437
    *Election for Collective Representation* . . . . . . . . . . . . . . . . . . . . . . . 437
    *Unfair Labor Practices* . . . . . . . . . . . . . . . . . . . . . . . . . . . . . . . . . . . 438
    *Collective Bargaining* . . . . . . . . . . . . . . . . . . . . . . . . . . . . . . . . . . . . 439
    *Union Contract Administration* . . . . . . . . . . . . . . . . . . . . . . . . . . . . 439
    *Strikes and Picketing* . . . . . . . . . . . . . . . . . . . . . . . . . . . . . . . . . . . . 440
Employment Laws . . . . . . . . . . . . . . . . . . . . . . . . . . . . . . . . . . . . . . . . . . . 440
    *Employment-at-Will* . . . . . . . . . . . . . . . . . . . . . . . . . . . . . . . . . . . . . 440
    *Equal Employment Opportunity* . . . . . . . . . . . . . . . . . . . . . . . . . . . 441
For Further Thought . . . . . . . . . . . . . . . . . . . . . . . . . . . . . . . . . . . . . . . . . . 443
For Further Learning . . . . . . . . . . . . . . . . . . . . . . . . . . . . . . . . . . . . . . . . . 443
References . . . . . . . . . . . . . . . . . . . . . . . . . . . . . . . . . . . . . . . . . . . . . . . . . . 444

**Chapter 17    Effective Marketing and Public Relations** . . . . . . . . . . . . . . . . . . . . . **447**
The Importance of Marketing . . . . . . . . . . . . . . . . . . . . . . . . . . . . . . . . . . 448
Marketing: Its Philosophy and Essence . . . . . . . . . . . . . . . . . . . . . . . . . . 448
    *Value Perceptions* . . . . . . . . . . . . . . . . . . . . . . . . . . . . . . . . . . . . . . . 449
    *Influencing Value Perception* . . . . . . . . . . . . . . . . . . . . . . . . . . . . . . 449
    *Value Creation* . . . . . . . . . . . . . . . . . . . . . . . . . . . . . . . . . . . . . . . . . . 449
The Marketing Function and Its Goals . . . . . . . . . . . . . . . . . . . . . . . . . . . 450
    *Functional Activities* . . . . . . . . . . . . . . . . . . . . . . . . . . . . . . . . . . . . . 451
    *Organizational Attitudes and Orientation* . . . . . . . . . . . . . . . . . . . . 451
    *Marketing Goals* . . . . . . . . . . . . . . . . . . . . . . . . . . . . . . . . . . . . . . . . 451
Marketing Strategy . . . . . . . . . . . . . . . . . . . . . . . . . . . . . . . . . . . . . . . . . . 452
    *Segmentation and the Target Market* . . . . . . . . . . . . . . . . . . . . . . . . 452
    *Market Targeting* . . . . . . . . . . . . . . . . . . . . . . . . . . . . . . . . . . . . . . . . 455
    *Positioning* . . . . . . . . . . . . . . . . . . . . . . . . . . . . . . . . . . . . . . . . . . . . . 456
    *Marketing Mix* . . . . . . . . . . . . . . . . . . . . . . . . . . . . . . . . . . . . . . . . . . 458
Implementing the Marketing Mix . . . . . . . . . . . . . . . . . . . . . . . . . . . . . . 458
    *Product* . . . . . . . . . . . . . . . . . . . . . . . . . . . . . . . . . . . . . . . . . . . . . . . . 458
    *Price* . . . . . . . . . . . . . . . . . . . . . . . . . . . . . . . . . . . . . . . . . . . . . . . . . . 459
    *Place* . . . . . . . . . . . . . . . . . . . . . . . . . . . . . . . . . . . . . . . . . . . . . . . . . . 460
    *Promotion* . . . . . . . . . . . . . . . . . . . . . . . . . . . . . . . . . . . . . . . . . . . . . . 461
Competitive Differentiation . . . . . . . . . . . . . . . . . . . . . . . . . . . . . . . . . . . 462
    *Differentiation Strategy* . . . . . . . . . . . . . . . . . . . . . . . . . . . . . . . . . . 462
Personal Selling . . . . . . . . . . . . . . . . . . . . . . . . . . . . . . . . . . . . . . . . . . . . . 463

Customer Relations . . . . . . . . . . . . . . . . . . . . . . . . . . . . . . . . . . . . . . . . . . 465
Promotion and Public Relations Tools . . . . . . . . . . . . . . . . . . . . . . . . . . . . 466
    *Advertising* . . . . . . . . . . . . . . . . . . . . . . . . . . . . . . . . . . . . . . . . . . . 466
    *Publicity* . . . . . . . . . . . . . . . . . . . . . . . . . . . . . . . . . . . . . . . . . . . . . 467
    *Personal Contact* . . . . . . . . . . . . . . . . . . . . . . . . . . . . . . . . . . . . . . 467
    *Promotional Materials* . . . . . . . . . . . . . . . . . . . . . . . . . . . . . . . . . . 468
    *Event Promotion* . . . . . . . . . . . . . . . . . . . . . . . . . . . . . . . . . . . . . . 468
For Further Thought . . . . . . . . . . . . . . . . . . . . . . . . . . . . . . . . . . . . . . . . . . 469
For Further Learning . . . . . . . . . . . . . . . . . . . . . . . . . . . . . . . . . . . . . . . . . 469
References . . . . . . . . . . . . . . . . . . . . . . . . . . . . . . . . . . . . . . . . . . . . . . . . . . 469

**Chapter 18   Effective Budgeting and Financial Controls** . . . . . . . . . . . . . . . **471**
Financial Management and Its Importance . . . . . . . . . . . . . . . . . . . . . . . . . 472
Accounting and Financial Statements . . . . . . . . . . . . . . . . . . . . . . . . . . . . 473
    *The Income Statement* . . . . . . . . . . . . . . . . . . . . . . . . . . . . . . . . . . 473
    *The Balance Sheet* . . . . . . . . . . . . . . . . . . . . . . . . . . . . . . . . . . . . . 474
    *The Cash Flow Statement* . . . . . . . . . . . . . . . . . . . . . . . . . . . . . . . 474
Management Reports . . . . . . . . . . . . . . . . . . . . . . . . . . . . . . . . . . . . . . . . . 475
The Technique of Variance Analysis . . . . . . . . . . . . . . . . . . . . . . . . . . . . . 476
Managing Revenues . . . . . . . . . . . . . . . . . . . . . . . . . . . . . . . . . . . . . . . . . . 476
Controlling Costs . . . . . . . . . . . . . . . . . . . . . . . . . . . . . . . . . . . . . . . . . . . . 479
    *Types of Costs* . . . . . . . . . . . . . . . . . . . . . . . . . . . . . . . . . . . . . . . . 479
    *Controlling Labor Costs* . . . . . . . . . . . . . . . . . . . . . . . . . . . . . . . . 481
Controlling Nonlabor Expenses . . . . . . . . . . . . . . . . . . . . . . . . . . . . . . . . 485
    *Accounts Payble Report* . . . . . . . . . . . . . . . . . . . . . . . . . . . . . . . . 485
    *Inventory Management* . . . . . . . . . . . . . . . . . . . . . . . . . . . . . . . . . 485
Managing Receivables . . . . . . . . . . . . . . . . . . . . . . . . . . . . . . . . . . . . . . . . 488
    *Minimizing Lost Charges and Reimbursement* . . . . . . . . . . . . . . 489
    *Minimizing Write-offs* . . . . . . . . . . . . . . . . . . . . . . . . . . . . . . . . . 489
    *Minimizing the Collection Cycle* . . . . . . . . . . . . . . . . . . . . . . . . . 490
Budgeting . . . . . . . . . . . . . . . . . . . . . . . . . . . . . . . . . . . . . . . . . . . . . . . . . 492
    *Budgeting Revenues* . . . . . . . . . . . . . . . . . . . . . . . . . . . . . . . . . . . 492
    *Budgeting Expenses* . . . . . . . . . . . . . . . . . . . . . . . . . . . . . . . . . . 495
    *Budgeted Margin* . . . . . . . . . . . . . . . . . . . . . . . . . . . . . . . . . . . . . 496
For Further Thought . . . . . . . . . . . . . . . . . . . . . . . . . . . . . . . . . . . . . . . . . . 496
For Further Learning . . . . . . . . . . . . . . . . . . . . . . . . . . . . . . . . . . . . . . . . . 496
References . . . . . . . . . . . . . . . . . . . . . . . . . . . . . . . . . . . . . . . . . . . . . . . . . . 496

**Chapter 19   Effective Quality and Productivity Management** . . . . . . . . . . . . . **497**
Some Common Misperceptions . . . . . . . . . . . . . . . . . . . . . . . . . . . . . . . . . 498
Productivity and Quality . . . . . . . . . . . . . . . . . . . . . . . . . . . . . . . . . . . . . . 498
What Is Quality? . . . . . . . . . . . . . . . . . . . . . . . . . . . . . . . . . . . . . . . . . . . . 500
    *Consistency* . . . . . . . . . . . . . . . . . . . . . . . . . . . . . . . . . . . . . . . . . . 500
    *Holistic Well-Being* . . . . . . . . . . . . . . . . . . . . . . . . . . . . . . . . . . . . 501
    *Desirable Outcomes* . . . . . . . . . . . . . . . . . . . . . . . . . . . . . . . . . . . 501
    *Prevention of Undesirable Consequences* . . . . . . . . . . . . . . . . . . 501

Technical and Consumer-Defined Quality . . . . . . . . . . . . . . . . . . . . . . . . . . . . . . 502
Framework of Quality . . . . . . . . . . . . . . . . . . . . . . . . . . . . . . . . . . . . . . . . . . . . . 503
    *Structures* . . . . . . . . . . . . . . . . . . . . . . . . . . . . . . . . . . . . . . . . . . . . . . . . . . . 504
    *Processes* . . . . . . . . . . . . . . . . . . . . . . . . . . . . . . . . . . . . . . . . . . . . . . . . . . . . 504
    *Outcomes* . . . . . . . . . . . . . . . . . . . . . . . . . . . . . . . . . . . . . . . . . . . . . . . . . . . 505
Regulatory Minimum Standards . . . . . . . . . . . . . . . . . . . . . . . . . . . . . . . . . . . . 505
Measurement and Evaluation of Quality . . . . . . . . . . . . . . . . . . . . . . . . . . . . . 506
    *Focus on Outcomes* . . . . . . . . . . . . . . . . . . . . . . . . . . . . . . . . . . . . . . . . . . . 506
    *Measuring Customer Satisfaction* . . . . . . . . . . . . . . . . . . . . . . . . . . . . . . . 507
    *Evaluation and Interpretation* . . . . . . . . . . . . . . . . . . . . . . . . . . . . . . . . . . 507
    *Measuring Quality of Life* . . . . . . . . . . . . . . . . . . . . . . . . . . . . . . . . . . . . . 508
Quality Improvement . . . . . . . . . . . . . . . . . . . . . . . . . . . . . . . . . . . . . . . . . . . . 508
    *Meeting Customer Needs* . . . . . . . . . . . . . . . . . . . . . . . . . . . . . . . . . . . . . . 508
    *Leadership and Culture* . . . . . . . . . . . . . . . . . . . . . . . . . . . . . . . . . . . . . . . 512
    *Data-Driven Process Improvement Cycle* . . . . . . . . . . . . . . . . . . . . . . . . 513
    *Encompassing All Departments* . . . . . . . . . . . . . . . . . . . . . . . . . . . . . . . . 515
    *Interdisciplinary Work Teams* . . . . . . . . . . . . . . . . . . . . . . . . . . . . . . . . . 515
    *Continuous Learning* . . . . . . . . . . . . . . . . . . . . . . . . . . . . . . . . . . . . . . . . . 515
Quality Culture . . . . . . . . . . . . . . . . . . . . . . . . . . . . . . . . . . . . . . . . . . . . . . . . . 516
The Wellspring Model . . . . . . . . . . . . . . . . . . . . . . . . . . . . . . . . . . . . . . . . . . . 517
For Further Thought . . . . . . . . . . . . . . . . . . . . . . . . . . . . . . . . . . . . . . . . . . . . . 518
For Further Learning . . . . . . . . . . . . . . . . . . . . . . . . . . . . . . . . . . . . . . . . . . . . 519
References . . . . . . . . . . . . . . . . . . . . . . . . . . . . . . . . . . . . . . . . . . . . . . . . . . . . . 519

**Part V    Case Studies** . . . . . . . . . . . . . . . . . . . . . . . . . . . . . . . . . . . . . . . . . . **521**

**Case  1    A Central American Immigrant Couple** . . . . . . . . . . . . . . . . . . . . **523**

**Case  2    A Legal and Ethical Dilemma** . . . . . . . . . . . . . . . . . . . . . . . . . . . . **525**

**Case  3    Abusive Spouse** . . . . . . . . . . . . . . . . . . . . . . . . . . . . . . . . . . . . . . . . **529**

**Case  4    Advance Directives** . . . . . . . . . . . . . . . . . . . . . . . . . . . . . . . . . . . . . **533**

**Case  5    Wound Care at Mountainview Nursing Center** . . . . . . . . . . . . . . **535**

**Case  6    Implementing Culture Change in Food Service** . . . . . . . . . . . . . **539**

**Case  7    Evacuation of Angel Care Center** . . . . . . . . . . . . . . . . . . . . . . . . . **545**

**Case  8    Tug-of-War with the Director of Nursing** . . . . . . . . . . . . . . . . . . **557**

**Case  9    Corporate Compliance at Mid-Atlantic Care Centers** . . . . . . . . **561**

**Case 10    Chapel Square Health Care Center: Workforce Diversity** . . . . . . **565**

**Case 11    Start-up of Blissful Gardens** . . . . . . . . . . . . . . . . . . . . . . . . . . . . . **571**

**Case 12    Implementation of the Wellspring Model** . . . . . . . . . . . . . . . . . . **575**

**Glossary** . . . . . . . . . . . . . . . . . . . . . . . . . . . . . . . . . . . . . . . . . . . . . . . . . . . . . . **585**

**Index** . . . . . . . . . . . . . . . . . . . . . . . . . . . . . . . . . . . . . . . . . . . . . . . . . . . . . . . . **607**

# Foreword

I welcome the second edition of *Effective Management of Long-Term Care Facilities* because it makes a timely contribution in the critical area of long-term care administration. It takes into account the altered health care environment and updates the tools we need to prepare long-term care managers to discharge their awesome responsibility of ensuring quality of life for 1.1 million of our elders in over 16,000 nursing homes. As leaders, long-term care administrators guide and mentor 650,000 CNAs, 300,000 RNs and LPNs, and 400,000 other staff in the art of caring for seniors. In long-term care, more than in most other settings, quality blossoms or withers by the commitment of its managers; managers are the creators and nurturers of the culture of quality in a nursing facility. This culture of quality is the core of person-centered care emphasized in this book. The philosophy of person-centered care must permeate our long-term care facilities.

You may read this book as a student of health care administration while you prepare for the professional licensure examination, when you need a ready reference, or when you consider a career in long-term care administration. You will not be disappointed. Dr. Singh provides a compendium of information needed for successful administration in long-term care.

This book clearly defines an administrator's scope of responsibility in these four dimensions of care: physical, social, mental, and spiritual. Although regulations require that you create a "home-like" environment in the nursing home, elders and their families yearn for it to be a "home." By using the physical design judiciously, empowering the staff, and engaging the community as partners in care, the leader-administrator creates an environment that both elders and caregivers want.

Dr. Singh frames many of these issues in a manner that familiarizes the reader with important theories and models, such as theories of aging and quality improvement models. He demonstrates to the reader the importance of functioning in an "open system" that is integrally linked to the external environment. The text clearly points out that using models, systems, and processes is essential for excellent outcomes in all areas of quality of life and quality of care.

Leaders must understand the realities of today while envisioning the possibilities of tomorrow. While detailing what you must know to deal with today's standards, the author also points to models that contain the seeds of future realities.

The challenges of managing long-term care are numerous. Our society demands near perfection in care, but does not support an adequate reimbursement system. Although regulation is highly prescriptive, it mandates maximum autonomy and choice. Students and candidates in health care professions are frequently discouraged from working in long-term care by those oblivious to its many rewards. Being a leader in long-term care is one of the most rewarding and challenging positions in health care.

The American College of Health Care Administrators, the professional association for administrators in long-term care, conducted a survey of administrators in the fall of 2002. Their written comments were voluminous. This quote from one of those surveyed speaks to the reason that people working in the field find such rewards: *This is more than a job. I am in a position to affect change, to improve lives, to touch hearts. As administrators we should revel in the chance to make major differences in lives, patients, families, and staff. It is our privilege and our responsibility. Done correctly, the rewards are immeasurable.*

This edition will serve you as a source book that gives an overall feel for the evolving world of long-term care, as well as a ready reference for related issues you wish to pursue.

Mary Tellis-Nayak, RN, MSN, MPH
Vice President—Quality Initiatives,
My InnerView, Inc.
Past President/CEO, American College of
Health Care Administrators

# Preface

## To My Readers

Successful reception of the first edition, feedback from several users, and my own recognition of needed improvements as I used the book to teach my students prompted the major revisions, additions, and streamlining presented in this second edition. Throughout this process, the driving objective has been to furnish much-needed knowledge and skills to prepare the next generation of long-term care administrators and also, to put into the hands of practicing administrators, corporate officers, and governing board members an in-depth reference source. In a nutshell, my aim has been to make a good book even better.

This book differentiates itself from others on the market by giving you the most comprehensive, yet concise, understanding of how to effectively manage a long-term care facility. In that respect, the book goes much beyond a mere discussion of the long-term care continuum and policy issues. It explores laws, regulations, and financing; enlightens you on what is necessary for creating a person-centered environment in which six distinct types of services must be delivered; and furnishes skills necessary to manage it all. Further value is added by furnishing a brand-new section that contains 12 cases, each with assignment questions to apply the concepts and skills learned and to think be-

yond what any textbook can furnish. That's what you will be called upon to do in real life. This book can help you respond to that calling with a degree of self-confidence.

In the book's title, I have used the term "long-term care facilities" rather than "skilled nursing facilities" or "nursing homes" because, for the most part, the same or very similar skills are employed to effectively manage any other type of operation in the institutional long-term care continuum. If a person can learn how to manage a skilled nursing facility, he or she can easily make the transition into managing other, less complex and less challenging, environments such as assisted-living facilities or residential care facilities. Actually, both clinical and regulatory demands in these facilities will continue to grow. On the other hand, tomorrow's administrators must realize that effectively managed facilities will go beyond mere compliance with what regulations require.

## What You Will Learn from This Book

This edition progresses quite smoothly from understanding long-term care, to detailing the external and internal environments, to organizing and delivering services, to developing leadership and management skills, and finally, to applying knowledge and skills to cases. Hence, the book has five sections.

## Part I: Introduction to Long-Term Care

It is critical for any administrator in the field to first understand what long-term care is. I have finally developed the most complete definition and explanation by incorporating 10 essential dimensions that help explain what long-term care is, why it is needed, who needs it, and how it should be delivered. These dimensions are also the essential characteristics that will be found in an ideal delivery system. As a subset within a larger health care delivery environment, long-term care encompasses a variety of service options and can be referred to as a system in its own right, but it must also interface with the broader health care environment to meet the total care needs of the clients it serves. Hence, the first chapter builds this necessary foundation.

In Chapter 2, you will go back in history to the beginnings of long-term care in the United States. After a discussion of what policy is, what purpose it serves, and how policy is made, it is easy to understand that policy has been the driving force behind the evolution of long-term care services as they exist today. The future will be shaped by both government policy and private innovation, but policy will continue to play the dominant role.

Chapter 3 is based on the premise that efficient delivery of services to a nation's population necessitates a long-term care industry. First, the industry requires numerous types of providers—both community-based and institutional—because people's needs differ quite substantially. Nursing homes and other institutions operate within this larger context—and will continue to be influenced by it. Second, the industry cannot function without insurers; professionals who have the desired qualifications; and the ancillary sector that includes case management agencies, long-term care pharmacies, and technology.

## Part II: External and Internal Environments

An understanding of open systems, sensitivity to stakeholders' needs, and creation of value-based exchange partnerships often makes the difference between success and failure. But, has the governing board espoused their importance? Read Chapter 4 to find out why effective governance means supporting the open-system philosophy and to find out how it can be implemented.

Unrelenting litigation against long-term care providers is here to stay. But, does the long-term care administrator have the basic knowledge about malpractice, misconduct, contracts, personal versus corporate liability, patient rights, and privacy-related mandates imposed by the Health Insurance Portability and Accountability Act (HIPAA)? You will find these and other issues discussed in Chapter 5.

Regulatory oversight will also keep its unyielding pace. The Requirements of Participation are being enforced through the new Quality Indicator Survey. The well-prepared nursing home administrator must understand not only the survey and enforcement procedures, but also comply with the *Life Safety Code*®[1], the Americans with Disabilities Act, and the Occupational Safety and Health Act. Chapter 6 focuses on how to achieve regulatory compliance.

No health care administrator can survive without an understanding of financing and reimbursement. Chapter 7 attempts to simplify the complexities of both public and private sources of financing for long-term care services.

---

[1]*Life Safety Code*® and 101® are registered trademarks of the National Fire Protection Association, Quincy, Ma.

The internal structures, living environments, and ways of delivering care in the vast majority of nursing facilities date back more than 25 years. Now, there is a growing movement toward person-centered care, enriched environments, and staff empowerment. Loosely referred to as culture change, Chapter 8 will help you understand what this is all about.

## Part III: Organization and Delivery of Services

Long-term care institutions must organize their services into six departments or functions. These functions will be needed regardless of the adoption of culture change. Quality of care and quality of life must be the common themes that govern the delivery of these services.

First and foremost, a long-term care facility must enable the residents to cope and adapt to a major change in their lives when they move into a facility. It requires an understanding of aging and how to dispel the myths associated with aging. In addition, issues of cultural diversity, resident and family empowerment, planning for admission and discharge, and family support when death and terminal illness occur are all covered in Chapter 9.

Most administrators do not have background or training in clinical care. Yet, the primary reason that patients utilize a long-term care facility is to have their medical, nursing, and rehabilitation needs addressed. Along with other chronic and comorbid conditions, residents commonly suffer from depression, delirium, and dementia. An understanding of these and other areas of special attention are discussed in Chapter 10.

In Chapter 11, you will discover that activity programming is not simply a matter of putting together a recreational agenda to comply with regulatory requirements. Meaningful activities call for a great deal of skill and resourcefulness.

Chapter 12 explains that dietary services must be designed to meet individual nutritional needs, sensory gratification, and social interaction. Menu planning, ordering and receiving, food production, cost control, emergency plans, and close attention to sanitation and food temperatures all play an important role in achieving those objectives.

Maintenance and repairs, housekeeping, laundry, linen supplies and cost control, building security, fire and disaster planning, waste disposal, and environmental safety are the main topics found in Chapter 13.

In Chapter 14, you will learn that business office functions go beyond basic reception and bookkeeping. Payroll and compensation practices, handling of the patient trust fund, and medical records are all governed by laws and regulations. Information systems are essential for effective management.

## Part IV: Governance and Management

Chapter 15 emphasizes that the governing board has the primary responsibility for ensuring corporate compliance. The administrator is responsible for managing the business aspects of the operation, managing work and workers and making both more productive, and discharging responsibility toward the community and society. The task requires leadership skills and an understanding of management roles and functions.

Apart from the well-defined human resource functions and labor laws, in Chapter 16 you will pick up helpful tips on meeting the special challenges of long-term care in staffing, confronting absenteeism and turnover, and establishing self-managed work teams.

In addition to the typical themes in marketing and public relations, you will discover in Chapter 17 that perhaps the most challenging aspect of long-term care marketing is its personnel, the 5th P of the marketing mix.

Chapter 18 focuses on budgeting and financial controls and has been designed with the aim of dispelling the myth that financial management is difficult to grasp.

Chapter 19 should help you get a clear picture of not only what quality is, but also how quality can be improved.

## Part V: Case Studies

In case analysis, multiple factors generally need to be brought to bear on the issues. They require thinking beyond what may appear to be obvious from reading some section of a given chapter. Hence, a separate section instead of incorporating cases with individual chapters.

After studying the first three chapters, you should be able to address Case 1, in which an elderly immigrant couple needs long-term care services. The next three cases deal with legal and ethical issues in which patient rights must play an important role. Case 5 is about medical malpractice. Case 6 deals with both strategy and logistics that will often be necessary for implementing culture change. Evacuation of a facility (Case 7) is not common, but the administrator must be prepared to take action for various kinds of emergencies. In Case 8, you will find that leadership styles and actions can create conflicts that effective administrators must learn to prevent, but they must also address the conflict when it has already occurred. Corporate compliance is the theme in Case 9. There are many facilities today in which staff-

related problems will appear insurmountable. Case 10 challenges you to apply your ingenuity. Some administrators will face the challenge of opening new facilities. See if you are up to the challenges presented in Case 11. Culture change may be a buzzword today, but it is the wave of the future. Will you be deterred by what you encounter in Case 12?

## Tools That Will Enhance Learning

- Read the brief overview at the beginning of each of the five parts of the book.
- Go through the *What You Will Learn* summaries at the beginning of each chapter.
- Study the chapters, keeping in mind the main themes that divide each chapter.
- Use the Glossary when you encounter an unfamiliar technical term.
- Stop and review the numerous illustrations (figures, tables, exhibits, etc.) you will find throughout the book.
- Think through the *For Further Thought* assignments at the end of each chapter.
- Pick some area of interest to build on what you have learned by using the Internet resources in the *For Further Learning* sections.

Throughout the text, certain terms have been used interchangeably. Examples include: nursing home, nursing facility, facility, and long-term care facility; patient, resident, and elder; and employee, associate, staff member, and worker.

## For Instructors

Please contact your Jones and Bartlett representative to get access to the complete Instructor's Manual, PowerPoint presentations, a TestBank, and Excel materials. Also, if you would like to share your thoughts, I would be delighted to hear from you. See my contact information at the end of this Preface.

## Transition Guide and New Materials

If you used the first edition, this transition guide should help you locate materials that have been reorganized. This section also highlights what is new in this edition.

## Chapter 1: Overview of Long-Term Care

Pertinent materials from the previous edition's Chapters 1 and 2 are combined here. Long-term care has been explained by incorporating four additional domains in the six components that appeared in the old edition. The following have been moved to Chapter 4: open and closed systems, external environment (previously in Chapter 1), and exchange relationships (previously in Chapter 2).

## Chapter 2: Long-Term Care Policy: Past, Present, and Future

This is a brand-new chapter that reviews the past, present, and future of long-term care from a policy perspective. The main themes of financing, utilization, and quality from a current policy perspective are incorporated here (previously in the Introduction).

## Chapter 3: The Long-Term Care Industry

This chapter is brand new. First, it gives a detailed overview of the continuum of providers

(some of these, such as continuing care retirement communities, assisted-living facilities, and subacute care providers, were previously in Chapter 1). A detailed overview of providers includes home health care, homemaker and personal services, adult day care, hospice, government-assisted and private-pay housing, and custodial care providers such as adult foster care homes. The insurance sector includes managed care. A full section is devoted to professionals that include administrators in home health agencies, assisted living, and nursing homes and clinicians such as physicians, nurses, nonphysician providers, rehabilitation professionals, dietitians, paraprofessionals, and social support professionals. The specialized role of long-term care pharmacies is included. The chapter concludes with an overview of seven categories of long-term care technology according to what these technologies are designed to do.

## Chapter 4: Responding to the External Environment

Pertinent materials from former Chapters 1 and 2 are incorporated here. The SWOT model appropriately belongs here and has been moved from former Chapter 13.

## Chapter 5: Legal Environment

Much of the materials from former Chapter 3 are found here. Two mini-cases are embedded in the narrative, one old and one new. The section on patient rights, which also includes HIPAA, has been expanded. Requirements of Participation and survey and enforcement have been moved to Chapter 6. Materials on governance and the role of the nursing home administrator have been moved to Chapter 14.

## Chapter 6: Regulation and Enforcement

This is essentially a new chapter. It retains the regulatory parts of former Chapter 3, but it now incorporates brand-new materials on the *Life Safety Code*®, accessibility standards under the Americans with Disabilities Act, and OSHA standards and recordkeeping requirements.

## Chapter 7: Financing and Reimbursement

The previous edition's Chapter 4 has been expanded to include Medicare Part D, and all data have been updated. New materials include the Program of All-Inclusive Care for the Elderly (PACE), minimum data set (MDS) 3.0 (even though it was not yet launched at the time the book manuscript was completed), and resource utilization group classifications (RUG-53).

## Chapter 8: Internal Environment and Culture Change

This chapter was created by combining pertinent materials from former Chapters 5 and 6 and removing some of the extraneous materials. The chapter was reorganized for a smoother flow. Beginning with the adoption of hospital layout and the sick-role model in earlier nursing homes, the chapter transitions to the application of person-centered philosophy. Modern architectural designs, culture change, and Eden Alternative and Green House models make up the latter half. The traditional clinical structure from former Chapter 5 has been retained because the vast majority of nursing facilities are still organized that way. A new section includes environ-

ments for patients with dementia. Discussion of Snoezelen has been moved to Chapter 11 on activities, and the Wellspring Model has been moved to Chapter 19.

## Chapter 9: Social Services, Admission, and Discharge

New sections include diversity and cultural competence, cultural accommodation, conflict resolution skills, Preadmission Screening and Resident Review (PASRR) compliance, and death and terminal illness.

## Chapter 10: Medical Care, Nursing, and Rehabilitation

A new section has been added on mental and cognitive disorders that include depression, delirium, and dementia. The section on controlled substances has been expanded.

## Chapter 11: Recreation and Activities

The section on multisensory stimulation has been expanded. A new section, *Activities for Dementia Patients*, has been added.

## Chapter 12: Dietary Services

The 2005 Dietary Guidelines for Americans, jointly published by the U.S. Department of Health and Human Services and the U.S. Department of Agriculture, replace the former Food Guide Pyramid.

## Chapter 13: Plant and Environmental Services

The former Chapter 11 needed only minor updates.

## Chapter 14: Administrative and Information Systems

Compensation and job categories under the new Fair Labor Standards Act (FLSA) guidelines have been revised, and minimum wage information has been updated. Because this law can be confusing, a new section clarifies areas in which FLSA does not apply. The section on information systems has been tweaked a little, but overall it is considered adequate.

## Chapter 15: Effective Governance, Leadership, and Management

Governance, board composition, board functions, and corporate compliance are new materials. Some of the material was moved from former Chapter 3. Students had some difficulty relating the discussion on bureaucracy (in former Chapter 13) to management. That section is eliminated and replaced with management—and its roles and functions.

## Chapter 16: Effective Human Resource and Staff Development

The section on turnover and retention has been updated and expanded. The section on unionization includes the Employee Free Choice Act, which did not pass but is likely to be resurrected in the future. A section on alcohol and drug abuse has been added under the Employment Laws section. Students found that the calculation of staffing levels by determining weights and relative values was difficult to follow. The concept behind this has been retained, but the details on the calculations and accompanying exhibit have been deleted. Unfortunately, to my knowledge, there is currently no other practical model available for tying staffing levels to patient acuity. The exhibit from the old edition is included in the Excel files available to instructors.

## Marketing, Finance, and Quality

Chapters 17, 18, and 19 on marketing, financial management, and quality, respectively (former Chapters 15, 16, and 17), did not require any substantive changes, except that the Wellspring Model is now consolidated in Chapter 19. Additional information on Wellspring is contained in Case 12.

I continue to dedicate this book to all those who have decided to serve the noble profession of long-term care as caregivers or leaders in the field and to the educators who are preparing the next generation of these caregivers and leaders.

With my best wishes,

Douglas A. Singh
School of Business and Economics
Indiana University–South Bend
E-mail: dsingh@iusb.edu

# Acknowledgments

The addition of a much-needed section on cases was made possible only with the help of several collaborators. I would like to gratefully acknowledge the assistance of nursing home administrators Lynn Binnie, Anthony Ughetti, and others who wished to remain anonymous, and medical director, Dr. Patrick Claudius, for providing invaluable information and materials that were used in developing several of the cases. Other cases were made possible through partnerships with Jullet Davis (and the assistance of Paul Davis), University of Alabama; Jeffrey A. Kramer, University of Connecticut; Cindy K. Manjounes, Lindenwood University; Lisa E. Sliney, Barry University; Alan S. Whiteman, Barry University; and Paul R. Willging, Johns Hopkins University. These individuals independently developed and contributed cases for this edition, and their work is greatly appreciated.

Comments from the readers and users of the first edition prompted some of the revisions and additions incorporated in this edition. I appreciate their thoughtfulness. I am also very grateful to Mary Tellis-Nayak, former president/chief executive officer of the American College of Health Care Administrators, who provided valuable insight and assistance for the first edition, which remains the foundation for making this second edition a reality. Of course, all errors and omissions in this book remain my responsibility.

Douglas A. Singh

# About the Author

Dr. Douglas Singh teaches graduate and undergraduate courses in health care delivery, policy, finance, and management in the School of Business and Economics and in the Department of Political Science at Indiana University–South Bend. He has authored/co-authored four books and has been published in several peer-reviewed journals.

He spent more than 15 years as a licensed long-term care administrator in four states. He also held the positions of regional manager, vice-president, and consultant and supervised both skilled nursing care and independent living operations. His doctoral work at the School of Public Health, University of South Carolina, broke new ground in understanding nursing home performance on certification surveys, for which he was awarded the Long-Term Care Research award in 1995 by the Foundation of the American College of Health Care Administrators.

# List of Abbreviations

| | |
|---|---|
| AAC | Activity Assistant, Certified |
| AAHSA | American Association of Homes and Services for the Aging |
| AARP | Formerly known as the American Association of Retired Persons |
| ACHCA | American College of Health Care Administrators |
| ADA | Americans with Disabilities Act; American Dietetic Association |
| ADEA | Age Discrimination in Employment Act (1967) |
| ADC | Activity Director, Certified |
| ADL | Activities of daily living |
| ADN | Associate's degree in nursing |
| ADON | Assistant director of nursing |
| AFC | Adult foster care home |
| AFL-CIO | American Federation of Labor-Congress of Industrial Unions |
| AHCA | American Health Care Association |
| AHIMA | American Health Information Management Association |
| AI | Adequate intake |
| AIDS | Acquired immunodeficiency syndrome |
| AIT | Administrator-in-training |
| ALFA | Assisted Living Federation of America |
| AMDA | American Medical Directors Association |
| ASHA | American Speech-Language-Hearing Association |
| BBA | Balanced Budget Act of 1997 |
| BSN | Bachelor of science degree in nursing |
| BSW | Bachelor's degree in social work |
| CADE | Commission on Accreditation for Dietetics Education |
| CAPS | Certified aging-in-place specialist |
| CBO | Congressional Budget Office |
| CCRC | Continuing care retirement community |
| CDC | Centers for Disease Control and Prevention |
| CDM | Certified dietary manager |
| CDR | Commission on Dietetic Registration |
| CEO | Chief executive officer |
| CFO | Chief financial officer |
| CFR | Code of Federal Regulations |
| CMS | Centers for Medicare & Medicaid Services |

| | |
|---|---|
| CNA | Certified nursing assistant |
| CON | Certificate of need |
| COTA | Certified occupational therapy assistant |
| CPOE | Computerized provider order entry (system) |
| CQI | Continuous quality improvement |
| CSA | Controlled Substances Act (1970) |
| CSRA | Community Spouse Resource Allowance |
| CTRS | Certified therapeutic recreation specialist |
| DD | Developmentally disabled |
| DHHS | U.S. Department of Health and Human Services |
| DMA | Dietary Managers Association |
| DME | Durable medical equipment |
| DNR | Do-not-resuscitate (order) |
| DO | Doctor of osteopathic medicine |
| DON | Director of nursing |
| DPOA | Durable power of attorney |
| DRG | Diagnosis-related groups |
| DRI | Dietary Reference Intake |
| DTR | Dietetic Technician, Registered |
| EEOC | Equal Employment Opportunity Commission |
| EPA | U.S. Environmental Protection Agency |
| FCA | False Claims Act (1863) |
| FDA | U.S. Food and Drug Administration |
| FICA | Federal Insurance Contributions Act |
| FIFO | First-in first-out |
| FLSA | Fair Labor Standards Act |
| FMLA | Family and Medical Leave Act (1993) |
| FSES | Fire Safety Evaluation System |
| FUTA | Federal Unemployment Tax Act |
| GAAP | Generally accepted accounting principles |
| GNP | Geriatric nurse practitioner |
| HCBS | Home and Community Based Services |
| HHA | Home health agency |
| HI | Hospital Insurance (Part A of Medicare) |
| HIPAA | Health Insurance Portability and Accountability Act (1996) |
| HIT | Health information technology |
| HIV | Human immunodeficiency virus |
| HMO | Health maintenance organization |
| HUD | U.S. Department of Housing and Urban Development |
| IADL | Instrumental activities of daily living |
| ICF | Intermediate care facility |
| ICF/MR | Intermediate care facility for the mentally retarded |
| ICP | Infection control practitioner |

| | |
|---|---|
| IOM | Institute of Medicine |
| IRF | Inpatient rehabilitation facility |
| IRS | Internal Revenue Service |
| IT | Information technology |
| JCAHO | Joint Commission on Accreditation of Healthcare Organizations |
| LAN | Local area network |
| LPN | Licensed practical nurse |
| LSC | *Life Safety Code®* |
| LTC | Long-term care |
| LTCH | Long-term care hospital |
| LVN | Licensed vocational nurse |
| MA-PD | Medicare Advantage Prescription Drug Plan (under Part C of Medicare) |
| MBO | Management by objectives |
| MCCA | Medicare Catastrophic Coverage Act (1988) |
| MCO | Managed care organization |
| MD | Doctor of medicine |
| MDRO | Multi-drug resistant organism |
| MDS | Minimum data set |
| MIA | (Community Spouse) Monthly Income Allowance |
| MMA | Medicare Prescription Drug, Improvement, and Modernization Act (2003) |
| MR/DD | Mentally retarded/developmentally disabled |
| MRSA | Methicillin-resistant *Staphylococcus aureus* |
| MSBT | Multisensory behavior therapy |
| MSD | Musculoskeletal disorder |
| MSE | Multisensory environment |
| MSS | Multisensory stimulation |
| MSW | Master's degree in social work |
| NAB | National Association of Long Term Care Administrator Boards |
| NASPAC | National Association of Subacute/Post Acute Care |
| NBCOT | National Board for Certification in Occupational Therapy |
| NCCAP | National Certification Council for Activity Professionals |
| NCTRC | National Council for Therapeutic Recreation Certification |
| NF | Nursing facility (referring to a federal certification category) |
| NFPA | National Fire Protection Association |
| NHA | Nursing home administrator |
| NLRA | National Labor Relations Act (1935) |
| NLRB | National Labor Relations Board |
| NP | Nurse practitioner |
| NPP | Nonphysician practitioner |
| OAA | Old Age Assistance |
| OBRA-87 | Omnibus Budget Reconciliation Act of 1987 |
| OSCAR | On-line Survey Certification and Reporting (system) |
| OSHA | Occupational Safety and Health Administration |

| | |
|---|---|
| OT | Occupational therapist or occupational therapy |
| OTR | Occupational Therapist, Registered |
| P&L | Profit and loss statement (Income statement) |
| PA | Physician assistant |
| PACE | Program of All-Inclusive Care for the Elderly |
| PASRR | Pre-admission Screening and Resident Review |
| PDP | Prescription Drug Plan (under Part D of Medicare) |
| PDSA | Plan, do, study, act |
| PERS | Personal emergency response systems |
| PHI | Protected health information |
| PHP | Prepaid health plan |
| POA | Power of attorney |
| POC | Plan of correction |
| PPD | Per-patient-day; purified protein derivative |
| PPS | Prospective payment system |
| PT | Physical therapist or physical therapy |
| PTA | Physical therapy assistant |
| QCI | Quality of care indicator |
| QIS | Quality Indicator Survey |
| QM/QI | Quality measure/quality indicator (report) |
| QoL | Quality of life |
| RAI | Resident Assessment Instrument |
| RC/AL | Residential care/assisted living (administrator's license) |
| RD | Registered dietitian |
| RDA | Recommended daily allowances |
| RHIA | Registered health information administrator |
| RHIT | Registered health information technician |
| RN | Registered nurse |
| RUG | Resource utilization group |
| SLP | Speech/language pathologist |
| SMI | Supplementary Medical Insurance (Part B of Medicare) |
| SMWT | Self-managed work team |
| SNF | Skilled nursing facility |
| SPs | Standard precautions |
| SSI | Supplemental Security Income |
| TB | Tuberculosis |
| TCU | Transitional care unit |
| TPN | Total parenteral nutrition |
| TQM | Total quality management |
| USDA | U.S. Department of Agriculture |
| VHA | Veterans Health Administration |
| VRE | Vancomycin-resistant enterococci |

# PART I

# Introduction to Long-Term Care

As a major component of the health care delivery system, long-term care (LTC) is receiving increasing attention in both developed and developing countries. LTC is closely associated with disabilities emanating from chronic conditions that are mostly related to human aging. Developed countries have seen a steep rise in chronic conditions, and the trend will continue. A rise in chronic conditions and functional limitations will create a growing demand for LTC services in the developing world as well. Thanks to better sanitation, nutrition, and medical care, longevity is increasing in developing countries. The social environment in these countries is also changing. Both men and women are increasingly being drawn into the workforce to improve their standards of living. Their lifestyles are becoming hectic but sedentary.

A broad understanding of long-term care as a distinct segment of the health care delivery system, LTC clients and services, policy perspectives, and industry perspectives lay the foundation for managing any LTC orga-

nization. The three chapters in this section address these areas:

- Chapter 1 explains what long-term care is, why it is needed, what type of health care and social services constitute LTC, who are the clients served by long-term care, and how LTC should interface with the broader health care system.

- Chapter 2 focuses on policy as the driving force behind the evolution of LTC services. Financing, quality, and access to community-based services have shaped some of the recent developments. The future remains challenging and requires a number of policy initiatives to meet the challenges.

- Chapter 3 furnishes details of the long-term industry, which is necessary for the efficient delivery of services. The chapter covers community-based and institutional providers, insurers, LTC professionals, case management agencies, long-term care pharmacies, and seven categories of LTC technology.

# Chapter 1

# Overview of Long-Term Care

## What You Will Learn

- Long-term care, as a distinct part of the health care delivery system, is best understood through 10 main dimensions that characterize long-term care as a set of varied services. The diverse services fulfill a variety of needs.

- The clients of long-term care are diverse in terms of age and clinical needs. The elderly, however, are the major users of long-term care services.

- Enabling technology reduces the need for long-term care services for many people. But, those who need assistance obtain long-term care services through three systems of care: informal, community based, and institutional.

- Informal care is the largest of the three systems of long-term care. Community-based services have four main objectives and can be classified into two groups: intramural and extramural. The institutional system forms its own continuum of care to accommodate clients whose clinical needs vary from simple to complex.

- Non-long-term care services are often needed by long-term care patients. The long-term care system cannot function without these services. Hence, the long-term care and non-long-term care systems of health care delivery must be rationally linked.

## The Nature of Long-Term Care

Long-term care (LTC) is often associated with care provided in nursing homes, but that is a narrow view of LTC. Several types of noninstitutional LTC services are provided in a variety of community-based settings.

Family members and surrogates actually provide most of the long-term care that is unseen to outsiders and often unpaid. Another common misconception is that LTC services are meant only for the elderly. Many younger people, and even some children, require LTC services. The elderly, however, are the predominant users of these services, and most LTC services have been designed with the elderly client in mind.

There is no simple definition that can fully capture the nature of long-term care. This is because a broad range of clients and services are involved. Yet, certain characteristics are common to all LTC services, regardless of whether they are delivered in an institution or in a community-based setting.

***Long-term care*** can be defined as a variety of individualized and well-coordinated total care services that promote the maximum possible independence for people with functional limitations and that are provided over an extended period of time, using appropriate current technology and available evidence-based practices, in accordance with a holistic approach while maximizing both the quality of clinical care and the individual's quality of life. This comprehensive definition emphasizes 10 essential dimensions, which apply to both institutional and noninstitutional long-term care. An ideal LTC system will incorporate these 10 characteristics.

1. Variety of services.
2. Individualized services.
3. Well-coordinated total care.
4. Promotion of functional independence.
5. Extended period of care.
6. Use of current technology.
7. Use of evidence-based practices.
8. Holistic approach.
9. Maximizing quality of care.
10. Maximizing quality of life.

## Variety of Services

The delivery of most types of medical services is based on what is called the ***medical model***, according to which health is viewed as the absence of disease. When a patient suffers from some disorder, clinical interventions that are widely accepted by the medical profession are used to relieve the patient's symptoms. Prevention of disease and promotion of optimum health are relegated to a secondary status. By contrast, in long-term care, medical interventions are only a part of an individual's overall care. Emphasis is also placed on nonmedical factors such as social support and residential services.

Long-term care encompasses a variety of services for three main reasons: (1) to fit the needs of different individuals, (2) to address changing needs over time, and (3) to suit people's personal preferences. Needs vary greatly from one individual to another. Even the elderly, who are the predominant users of LTC services, are not a homogeneous group. For example, some people just require supportive housing, whereas others require intensive treatments. The type of services an individual requires is determined by the nature and degree of his or her functional disability and the presence of any other medical conditions and emotional needs that the individual may have.

Even for the same individual, the need for the various types of services generally changes over time. The change is not necessarily progressive, from lighter to more intensive levels of care. Depending on the change in condition and functioning, the individual may shift back and forth among the various levels and types of LTC services. For example, after hip surgery, a patient may require extensive rehabilitation therapy in a nursing facility for two or three weeks before returning home, where he or she receives continuing care from a home health care agency. After that, the individual may continue to live independently but require a daily meal from ***Meals On Wheels***, a home-delivered meals service. Later, this same person may suffer a stroke and, after hospitalization, have to stay indefinitely in a LTC facility. Hospice care may become necessary at the end of a person's life.

People's personal preferences also play a role in the determination of where services are received. Experts generally agree that, to the extent possible, people should be able to live and receive services where they want. Almost always, people prefer to live in the community, the first choice being their own home. Home- and community-based services have increasingly become available so that people can age in the community. Severe declines in health, however, may necessitate institutional services, particularly for people who need care around the clock. Again, a variety of long-term care facilities are now available.

LTC services are an amalgam of five distinct types of services:

- Medical care.
- Mental health services.
- Social support.
- Residential amenities.
- Hospice services.

Understanding the distinctive features of these services is important. In actual practice, however, they should be appropriately integrated into the total package of care in accordance with individual needs.

## Medical Care

Medical interventions in long-term care are primarily governed by the presence of two main health conditions that are closely related: chronic illness and comorbidity. First, as opposed to the care for acute conditions, LTC focuses on chronic ailments, particularly when they have already caused some physical or mental dysfunction. ***Acute conditions*** are episodic; require short-term but intensive medical interventions; generally respond to medical treatment; and are treated in hospitals, emergency departments, or outpatient clinical settings. ***Chronic conditions***, on the other hand, persist over time and are generally irreversible, but must be kept under control. If not controlled, serious complications can develop. In order of their prevalence among the aged population, the most common chronic conditions are hypertension, arthritis, heart disease, cancers, and diabetes (Federal Interagency Forum, 2004). The mere presence of chronic conditions, however, does not indicate a need for long-term care. When chronic conditions are compounded by the presence of ***comorbidity***—coexisting multiple health problems—they often become the leading cause of an individual's disability and erode that individual's ability to live without assistance. This is when LTC is needed. The prevalence of comorbidity and disability rise dramatically in aging populations.

Medical care in the LTC environment generally focuses on three main areas:

1. Continuity of care after treatment of acute episodes in hospitals.
2. Clinical management of chronic conditions and prevention of potential complications.
3. Hospitalization when necessary.

### Continuity of Care after Hospitalization

Long-term care generally involves continuity of care after discharge from a hospital. Patients are hospitalized for acute episodes. Post-acute LTC often consists of ***skilled nursing care***, which is physician-directed care provided by licensed nurses and therapists. Post-acute care may be provided in a patient's own home through home health care, or in a LTC facility. *Home health care* brings services such as nursing care and rehabilitation therapies to patients in their own homes because such patients do not need to be in an institution and yet are generally unable to leave their homes safely to get the care they need. A *long-term care facility* is an institution, commonly referred to as a nursing home, that is duly licensed to provide long-term care services.

### Clinical Management and Prevention

Because chronic conditions cannot be cured, they must be managed. Left unmanaged, chronic conditions often lead to severe medical complications over time. For example, untreated diabetes can lead to heart problems, nerve damage, blindness, and kidney failure. The onset of complications arising from chronic conditions can be prevented or postponed through preventive medicine that includes adequate nutrition, therapeutic diets, hydration (fluid intake), ambulation (moving about), vaccination against pneumonia and influenza, and well-coordinated primary care services. Ongoing monitoring and timely interventions are generally necessary.

### Hospitalization when Necessary

Onset of an acute episode requires medical evaluation and treatment in a hospital. Patients in LTC settings may encounter acute episodes, such as pneumonia, bone fracture, or stroke, and require admission to a general hospital. For the same medical conditions, the elderly are more prone to be hospitalized compared with people in younger age groups who may be treated as outpatients.

## Mental Health Services

Long-term care patients frequently suffer from mental conditions, most notably depression, anxiety disorders, delirium, and dementia. Approximately two-thirds of nursing home residents suffer from mental disorders (Burns et al., 1993). Mental disorders range in severity from problematic, to disabling, to fatal. Research shows that depression, although common in nursing homes and assisted living facilities, often goes undetected (Smalbrugge et al., 2006; Watson et al., 2006). Under-diagnosis and under-treatment of depression is also a serious problem among community-dwelling older adults. The risk of depression in the elderly increases with other illnesses and when ability to function becomes limited (NIMH, 2007). *Dementia* is another common mental disorder. Characterized by memory loss, patients with dementia find it difficult to do things that they used to do with ease. Patients with dementia are also likely to become aggressive and undergo mood changes.

It is erroneous to believe that mental disorders are normal in older people or that older people cannot change or improve their mental health. But major barriers must be overcome in the delivery of mental health care. Efforts to prevent mental disorders among older adults have been inadequate because present knowledge about effective prevention techniques is not as extensive as our understanding of the diagnosis and treatment of physical disorders. On the other hand, treatment of many elderly people may be inadequate because assessment and diagnosis of mental disorders in older people can be particularly difficult: the elderly often focus on physical ailments rather than psychological problems (DHHS, 1999). Another drawback is that many elder care providers, including primary care physicians, are often not adequately trained in the diagnosis and treatment of mental health problems.

Mental health services are generally delivered by specialized providers in both outpatient and inpatient facilities. Because LTC facilities are responsible for a patient's total care, nursing home employees must be trained to recognize the need for mental health care, and the facility must arrange to obtain needed services from qualified providers in the community.

## Social Support

*Social support* refers to a variety of assistive and counseling services to help people cope with situations that may cause stress, conflict, grief, or other emotional imbalances. The goal is to help people make adjustments to changing life events.

Various stressors commonly accompany the aging process itself and create such adverse effects as frailty, pain, increased medical needs, and the inability to do common things for oneself, such as obtaining needed information or running errands. Other stressors are event driven. Events that force an unexpected change in a person's lifestyle or emotional balance—such as moving to an institution, loss of a loved one, or experiencing social conflict—require coping with stress or grief. Even the thought of change brings on anxiety. Many people go through a period of "grieving" when coming to terms with change, which is a normal part of the transition process. Grieving may manifest in reactions such as anger, denial, confusion, fear, despondency, and depression (McLeod, 2002). Social support is needed to help buffer these adverse effects (Feld & George, 1994; Krause & Borawski-Clark, 1994).

Social support includes both concrete and emotional assistance provided by families, friends, neighbors, volunteers, staff members within an institution, organizations such as religious establishments and senior centers, or other private or public professional agencies. Such assistance may also include coordination of simple logistical problems that may otherwise become "hassles" of daily life, providing information, giving reminders, counseling, and offering spiritual guidance. Simply remaining connected with the outside world is an important aspect of social support for many people.

## Residential Amenities

*Supportive housing* is a key component of LTC because certain functional and safety features must be carefully planned to compensate for people's disabilities to the maximum extent possible in order to promote independence. Some simple examples include access ramps that enable people to go outdoors, wide doorways and corridors that allow adequate room to navigate wheelchairs, railings in hallways to promote independent mobility, extra-large bathrooms that facilitate wheelchair negotiation, grab bars in bathrooms to prevent falls and promote unassisted toileting, raised toilets to make it easier to sit down and get up, and pull-cords in the living quarters to summon help in case of an emergency.

Congregate housing—multi-unit housing with support services—is an option for seniors and disabled adults. *Support services* are basic assistive services. They may include meals, transportation, housekeeping, building security, social activities, and outings. However, not all housing arrangements provide all of these services.

In LTC institutions, adequate space, privacy, safety, comfort, and cleanliness are basic residential amenities. In addition, the institutional environment must feel home like, it must encourage social activities, it must promote recreational pursuits, and the décor must be both pleasing and therapeutic.

## Hospice Services

Hospice services, also called end-of-life care, are regarded as a component of long-term care. The focus of hospice, however, differs considerably from other LTC services. *Hospice* incorporates a cluster of special services for the terminally ill with a life expectancy of six months or less. It blends medical, spiritual, legal, financial, and family support services. However, the emphasis is on comfort, palliative care, and social support over medical treatment. *Palliation* refers to medical care that is focused on relieving unpleasant symptoms such as pain, discomfort, and nausea.

The hospice philosophy also regards the patient and family together as one unit of care. The option to use hospice means that temporary measures to prolong life will be suspended. The emphasis is on maintaining the quality of life and letting the patient die with dignity. Psychological services focus on relieving mental anguish. Social and legal services help with arranging final affairs. Counseling and spiritual support are provided to help the patient deal with his or her death. After the patient's death, bereavement counseling is offered to the family or surrogates.

The services are generally brought to the patient, although a patient may choose to go to a freestanding hospice center if one is available. Hospice care can be directed from a hospital, home health agency, nursing home, or freestanding hospice.

## Individualized Services

Long-term care services are tailored to the needs of the individual patient. Those needs are determined by an assessment of the individual's current physical, mental, and emotional condition. Other factors used for this purpose include past history of the patient's medical and psychosocial conditions; a social history of family relationships, former occupation, community involvement, and leisure activities; and cultural factors such as racial or ethnic background, language, and religion. An individualized plan of care is developed so that each type of need can be appropriately addressed through customized interventions.

## Well-Coordinated Total Care

Long-term care providers are responsible for managing the total health care needs of an individual client. *Total care* means that any health care need is recognized, evaluated, and addressed by appropriate clinical professionals. Coordination of care with various medical providers such as the attending physicians, dentists, optometrists, podiatrists, dermatologists, or audiologists is often necessary to prevent complications or to deal with the onset of impairments at an early stage. The need for total care coordination can also be triggered by changes in basic needs or occurrence of episodes. Transfer to an acute care hospital or treatment for mental or behavioral disorders may become necessary. Hence, long-term care must interface with non-LTC services.

## Promotion of Functional Independence

LTC becomes necessary when there is a remarkable decline in an individual's ability to independently perform certain common tasks of daily living. Among children, disabilities can result from birth defects, brain damage, or mental retardation. Younger adults may lose functional capacity as a result of an accident or a crippling disease such as multiple sclerosis.

The goal of LTC is to enable the individual to maintain functional independence to the maximum level practicable. Restoration of function may be possible to some extent through appropriate rehabilitation therapy, but, in most cases, a full restoration of normal function is an unrealistic expectation. The individual must be taught to use adaptive equipment such as wheelchairs, walkers, special eating utensils, or portable oxygen devices. Staff members must render care and assistance whenever the patient is either unable to do things for him- or herself or absolutely refuses to do so.

In keeping with the goal of maximizing functional independence for the patient, nursing home staff members should concentrate on maintaining whatever ability to function the patient still has and on preventing further decline of that ability. For example, a patient may be unable to walk independently but may be able to take a few steps with the help of trained staff members. Assistance with mobility helps maintain residual functioning. Progressive functional decline may be slowed by appropriate assistance and ongoing maintenance therapy, such as assisted walking, range of motion exercises, bowel and bladder training, and cognitive reality orientation. However, in spite of these efforts, it is reasonable to expect a gradual decline in an individual's functional ability over time. As this happens, services must be modified in accordance with the changing condition. In other words, LTC must "fill-in" for all functions that can no longer be carried out independently. For instance, a comatose patient who is totally confined to bed presents an extreme case in which full assistance from employees is required. In most other instances, staff members motivate and help the patient do as much as possible for him- or herself.

## Extended Period of Care

For most LTC patients, the delivery of various services extends over a relatively long period because most recipients of care will at least require ongoing monitoring to note any deterioration in their health and to address any emerging needs. Certain types of services—such as professional rehabilitation therapies, post-acute convalescence, or stabilization—may be needed for a relatively short duration, generally less than 90 days. In other instances, LTC may be needed for years, perhaps indefinitely. In either situation, the period during which care is given is much longer than it is for acute care services, which generally last only for a few days. Because patients stay in nursing care facilities over an extended time, holistic care and quality of life (discussed later) must be integrated into every aspect of LTC delivery.

## Use of Current Technology

Use of technology varies according to the type of LTC setting. Certain types of safety technologies, such as nonslip footwear and hip protectors that protect the hip from injury during a fall, can be used in almost all settings. Other technologies, such as call systems to summon assistance, bathing systems, and wander management systems, are designed for specific applications. Chapter 3 covers LTC technology in greater detail.

## Use of Evidence-Based Practices

*Evidence-based care* relies on the use of best practices that have been established through clinical research. Increasingly, clinical processes that have been proven to provide improved therapies are being standardized into *clinical practice guidelines*. These guidelines become evidence-based standardized protocols that are indicated for the treatment of specific health conditions. They have been developed to assist practitioners in delivering appropriate health care for specific clinical circumstances. An increasing number of standard guidelines have been developed for use in nursing homes. Some of these same guidelines can also be used in other LTC settings such as home health and assisted living.

## Holistic Approach

In sharp contrast to the medical model, the *holistic model* of health proposes that health care delivery should focus not merely on a person's physical and mental needs, but should also emphasize well-being in every aspect of what makes a person whole and complete. In this integrated model, a patient's mental, social, and spiritual needs and preferences should be incorporated into medical care delivery and all aspects of daily living.

By its very nature, effective LTC is holistic. Once the need for LTC has been established, a holistic approach must be used in the delivery of care. The following are brief descriptions of the four aspects of holistic caregiving:

1. *Physical.* This refers to the technical aspects of care, such as medical examination, nursing care, medications, diet, rehabilitation treatments, etc. It also includes comfort factors such as appropriate temperature and cozy furnishings, cleanliness, and safety in home and institutional environments.

2. *Mental.* The emphasis is on the total mental and emotional well-being of each individual. It may include treatment of mental and behavioral problems when necessary.

3. *Social.* Almost everyone enjoys warm friendships and social relationships. Visits from family, friends, or volunteers provide numerous opportunities for socializing. The social aspects of health care include housing, transportation services, information, counseling, and recreation.

4. *Spiritual.* The spiritual dimension operates at an individual level. It includes personal beliefs, values, and commitments in a religious and faith context. Spirituality and spiritual pursuits are very personal matters, but for most people they also require continuing interaction with other members of the faith community.

## Maximizing Quality of Care

*Quality of care* is maximized when desirable clinical- and satisfaction-related outcomes have been achieved. Maximization of quality is an ongoing pursuit, and is never fully achieved. Hence, maximizing quality requires a culture of continuous improvement. It requires a focus on the other nine dimensions encompassing the nature of LTC discussed in this section. It requires emphasis on both clinical and interpersonal aspects of caregiving. To improve quality, standards such as regulatory standards and evidence-based clinical practice guidelines must be implemented. Quality must be evaluated or measured to discover areas needing improvement, and processes should be changed as necessary. This becomes an ongoing effort.

## Maximizing Quality of Life

*Quality of life* refers to the total living experience, which results in overall satisfaction with one's life. Technology that enables people to live independently generally enhances the quality of life. Quality of life is a multifaceted concept that recognizes at least five factors: lifestyle pursuits, living environment, clinical palliation, human factors, and personal choices. Quality of life can be enhanced by integrating these five factors into the delivery of care.

1. Lifestyle factors are associated with personal enrichment and making one's life meaningful through activities one enjoys. For example, almost everyone enjoys warm friendships and social relationships. Elderly people's faces often light up when they see children. Many residents in institutional settings may still enjoy pursuing their former leisure activities, such as woodworking, crocheting, knitting, gardening, and fishing. Many residents would like to engage in spiritual pursuits or spend some time alone. Even patients whose functioning has decreased to a vegetative or comatose state can be creatively engaged in

something that promotes sensory awakening through visual, auditory, and tactile stimulation.

2. The living environment must be comfortable, safe, and appealing to the senses. Cleanliness, décor, furnishings, and other aesthetic features are critical.

3. Palliation should be available for relief from unpleasant symptoms such as pain or nausea.

4. Human factors refer to caregiver attitudes and practices that emphasize caring, compassion, and preservation of human dignity in the delivery of care. Institutionalized patients generally find it disconcerting to have lost their autonomy and independence. Quality of life is enhanced when residents have some latitude to govern their own lives. Residents also desire an environment that promotes privacy. For example, one field study of nursing home residents found that dignity and privacy issues were foremost in residents' minds, overshadowing concerns for clinical quality (Health Care Financing Administration, 1996).

5. As pointed out earlier, people overwhelmingly choose to be independent. However, even institutions should make every effort to accommodate patients' personal choices. For example, food is often the primary area of discontentment, which can be addressed by offering a selective menu. Many elderly resent being awakened early in the morning when nursing home staff begin their responsibilities to care for patients' hygiene, bathing, and grooming. Patient privacy is compromised when a facility can offer

only semi-private accommodations. But, in that case, the facility can at least give the patients some choice in deciding who their roommates would be.

# Clients of Long-Term Care

More than 10 million Americans are estimated to need LTC services. The majority (58%) are elderly, but a significant proportion (42%) are under the age of 65. Among those who need LTC, 14% are in nursing homes and 86% reside in the community (Kaiser, 2007). LTC clients can be classified into five main categories:

1. Older adults.
2. Children and adolescents.
3. Young adults.
4. People with HIV/AIDS.
5. People needing subacute or high-tech care.

## Older Adults

The elderly, people 65 years of age or older, are the primary clients of long-term care. Most of the elderly, however, are in good health. According to household interviews of the elderly civilian noninstitutionalized population, only 25% described their health as fair or poor (DHHS, 2008a). It is reasonable to assume that the segment of the elderly population in fair-to-poor overall health is likely to require LTC at some point. Even for those in good or excellent health, short-term LTC (needed for 90 days or less) may become necessary after an accident, surgery, or acute illness. Also, important differences in health exist according to population characteristics. Those in fair or poor health are more likely to be black, Hispanic, or American Indian rather than white or Asian; financially poor or near poor; and rural rather than urban residents.

A person's age, or the presence of chronic conditions, by itself does not predict the need for long-term care. However, as a person ages, chronic ailments, comorbidity, disability, and dependency tend to follow each other. This progression is associated with increased probability that a person would need long-term care (Figure 1–1). In 2007, approximately 7% of civilian, noninstitutionalized elderly in the United States needed help with personal care from other individuals (DHHS, 2008b).

Disability is commonly assessed in terms of a person's ability to perform certain key everyday activities. Although chronic mental impairments are often assumed to eventually manifest in physical dysfunction, that is not always the case. Individuals with certain chronic mental illnesses may be able to perform most everyday activities but may require supervision and monitoring. Severe dementias, on the other hand, which are mostly confined to older people, are commonly accompanied by physical functional limitations.

Two standard measures are available to determine a person's level of dependency. The first, the ***activities of daily living (ADL)*** scale, is used to determine whether an individual needs assistance in performing six basic activities: eating, bathing, dressing, using the toilet, maintaining continence, and transferring into or out of a bed or chair. Grooming and walking a distance of eight feet are sometimes added to evaluate self-care and mobility. The ADL scale is the most relevant measure for determining the need for assistance in a long-term care facility. Therefore, ADLs are a key input in determining a facil-

**Figure 1–1** Progressive Steps Toward the Need for Long-Term Care Among the Elderly

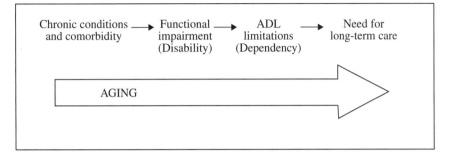

ity's aggregate patient acuity level. *Acuity* is a term used to denote the level of severity of a patient's condition and, consequently, the amount of care the patient would require.

The second commonly used measure is called *instrumental activities of daily living (IADL)*. This measure focuses on a variety of activities that are necessary for independent living. Examples of IADLs include doing housework, cooking, doing laundry, grocery shopping, taking medication, using the telephone, managing money, and moving around outside the home (Lawton & Brody, 1969). The measure is most helpful when a nursing home patient is being discharged for community-based LTC or independent liv-

ing. It helps in assessing how well the individual is likely to adapt to living independently and what type of support services may be most appropriate to ensure that the person can live independently.

## Children and Adolescents

In children, functional impairments are often birth related, such as brain damage that can occur before or during childbirth (Figure 1–2). Examples of birth-related disorders include cerebral palsy, autism, spina bifida, and epilepsy. These children grow up with physical disability and need help with ADLs. The term *developmental disability* describes the

**Figure 1–2** Common Conditions Creating the Need for Long-Term Care Among the Nonelderly

| | |
|---|---|
| Children/adolescents (ages birth to 17): | Birth defects<br>Brain damage<br>Mental retardation |
| Young adults (ages 18–64): | Major injury<br>Serious illness<br>AIDS<br>Complications from surgery |

general physical incapacity such children may face at a very early age. Those who acquire such dysfunctions are referred to as developmentally disabled, or DD for short. *Mental retardation*, that is, below-average intellectual functioning, also leads to developmental disability in most cases. The close association between the two is reflected in the term MR/DD, which is short for mentally retarded/developmentally disabled. Thus, some children and adolescents can have the need for LTC services that are generally available in special pediatric long-term care and MR/DD facilities.

## Young Adults

Permanent disability among young adults commonly stems from neurological malfunctions, degenerative conditions, traumatic injury, or surgical complications. For example, multiple sclerosis is potentially the most common cause of neurological disability in young adults (Compston & Coles, 2002). Severe injury to the head, spinal cord, or limbs can occur in victims of vehicle crashes, sports mishaps, or industrial accidents. Other serious diseases, injuries, and respiratory or heart problems following surgery can make it difficult, or even impossible, for a patient to breathe naturally. Such individuals, who cannot breathe (or ventilate) on their own, require a ventilator. A *ventilator* is a small machine that takes over the breathing function by automatically moving air into and out of the patient's lungs. Ventilator-dependent patients also require total assistance with their ADLs.

Many MR/DD victims are entering adulthood. The aging process begins earlier in people with mental retardation, and the age of 50 has been suggested to demarcate the elderly segment in this population (Altman, 1995). An increasing number of people with

MR/DD are now living beyond the age of 50. Hence, this population will manifest not only severe mental and physical impairments but also the effects of chronic conditions and comorbidity.

Evidence suggests that MR/DD patients may function better in community-based residential settings than in traditional nursing homes. Studies of patients who had moved out of nursing homes to community settings demonstrated that these patients had higher levels of adaptive behavior, lifestyle satisfaction, and community integration than residents who remained in nursing homes (Heller et al., 1998; Spreat et al., 1998). Opportunity to make choices, small facility size, attractive physical environment, and family involvement were associated with higher levels of adaptive behavior and community integration (Heller et al., 1999; Heller et al., 2002).

## People with HIV/AIDS

When it first gained national attention in the early 1980s, AIDS was a fatal disease that resulted in a relatively painful death shortly after HIV infection. Since then, the introduction of protease inhibitors, antiretroviral therapy, and antibiotics for the treatment of AIDS-related infections has vastly improved the health condition of HIV/AIDS patients. Consequently, AIDS has evolved from an end-stage terminal illness into a chronic condition. With reduced mortality, the prevalence of HIV in the population has actually increased, including among the elderly.

Over a period of time, people with AIDS are subject to a number of debilitating conditions, which create the need for assistance. Hence, the demand for LTC services is increasing, particularly because at least 25% of all known people with HIV/AIDS are age 50 and older (New York City Department of

Health and Mental Hygiene, 2004) and mortality rates from HIV/AIDS have decreased.

Care of HIV/AIDS patients presents special challenges, especially because this population has characteristics that are quite dissimilar to the rest of the LTC population. HIV/AIDS patients have a significantly higher prevalence of depression, other psychiatric disorders, and dementia associated with AIDS. HIV/AIDS patients also have a significantly higher prevalence of weight loss and incontinence of bladder and bowel (Shin et al., 2002).

## People Requiring Subacute or High-Tech Care

A growing number of nursing facilities have developed subacute and technology-intensive services. The term *subacute care* applies to post-acute services for people who require convalescence from acute illnesses or surgical episodes. These patients may be recovering but are still subject to complications while in recovery. They require more nursing intervention than what is typically included in skilled nursing care. The patients are transferred from the hospital to a nursing home after the acute condition has been treated, or after surgery. Some common orthopedic episodes include hip and knee replacement. Other subacute and high-tech services are needed for patients who require ventilator care, head trauma victims, comatose patients, and those with progressive Alzheimer's disease.

## The Long-Term Care Delivery System

The LTC system is sometimes referred to as the *continuum of long-term care*, which means the full range of long-term care services that increase in the level of acuity and complexity from one end to the other—from informal and community-based services at one end of the continuum to the institutional system at the other end.

The long-term care delivery system has three major components:

- The informal system.
- The community-based system.
- The institutional system.

The first component, informal care, is the largest, but it generally goes unrecognized. For the most part, it is not financed by insurance and public programs, but it includes private-duty nursing arrangements between private individuals. The other two components have formalized payment mechanisms to pay for services, but payment is not available for every type of community-based and institutional service. In many situations, people receiving these services must pay for them out of their personal resources.

Although institutional management is the focus of this book, the other two components, informal care and community-based service, also have important implications for administrators who manage LTC institutions. The community-based services and informal systems compete with the institutional system in some ways, but are also complementary.

The three subsystems that form the LTC continuum are illustrated in Figure 1–3. The patients' levels of acuity and the complexity of services they need increase from one end of the continuum to the other, for the most part. Informal care provided mainly by family members or friends involves basic assistance and is at one extreme of the continuum. Next on the continuum are the various community-based in-home services and

**Figure 1–3** The Continuum of Long-Term Care

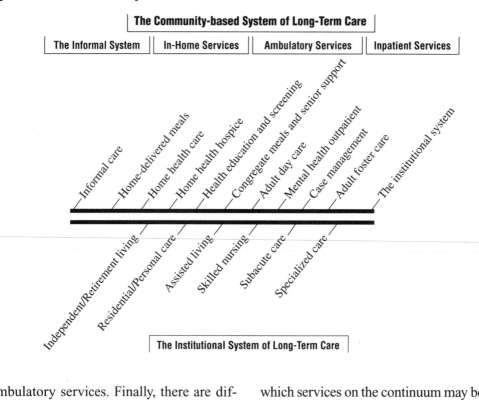

ambulatory services. Finally, there are different levels of institutional settings.

Given the complexity of the LTC system, case management (also called care management) fills in a key role. *Case management* is a centralized coordinating function in which the special needs of older adults are identified and a trained professional determines which services would be most appropriate, determines eligibility for those services, makes referrals, arranges for financing, and coordinates and monitors delivery of care to ensure that clients are receiving the prescribed services. Case management helps link, manage, and coordinate services to meet the varied and changing health care needs of elderly clients. Case management provides a single entry point for obtaining information about and accessing services. The extent of disability and personal needs primarily determine

which services on the continuum may be best suited for an individual. However, client preferences, availability of community-based services, and ability to pay for services also play a significant role.

In recent years, numerous public and private health care organizations have proliferated—organizations that offer information to consumers on how to care for someone at home, how to find and pay for community-based services, and how to find an appropriate institutional setting.

## The Informal System

The informal long-term care system is very large. An accurate estimate of its size is difficult, mainly because the system is not formally organized and it cannot even be called a system in the true sense. However, there are perhaps more than 7 million Americans who provide care to more than 4 million elderly persons with functional limitations. The economic value of such care may be as high as $96 billion a year (O'Keeffe & Siebenaler, 2006). For the most part, services rendered are believed to be basic, such as general supervision and monitoring, running errands, dispensing medications, cooking meals, assistance with eating, grooming and dressing, and, to a lesser extent, assistance with mobility and transfer.

The extent of informal care that an individual receives is highly dependent on the extent of the social support network the individual has. People with close family, friends, neighbors, or surrogates (such as members of a religious community) can often continue to live independently much longer than those who have little or no social support. For those who do not have an adequate informal support network, community-based services can become an important resource for allowing an individual to continue to live independently.

## The Community-Based System

Community-based LTC consists of formal services provided by various health care agencies. These services can be categorized as intramural and extramural. Community-based LTC services have a fourfold objective:

1. To deliver LTC in the most economical and least restrictive setting whenever appropriate for the patient's health care needs.
2. To supplement informal caregiving when more advanced skills are needed than what family members or surrogates can provide to address the patients' needs.

3. To provide temporary respite to family members from caregiving stress.
4. To delay or prevent institutionalization.

## Intramural Services

***Intramural services*** are taken to patients who live in their own homes, either alone or with family. The most common intramural services include home health care and Meals On Wheels. Limited support programs that provide services such as homemaker, chores and errands, and handyman assistance also exist, but the funding to pay for such services is not well established and varies from community to community.

## Extramural Services

***Extramural services*** are community-based services that are delivered outside a patient's home. They require that patients come and receive the services at a community-based location. This category mainly includes ambulatory services, such as adult day care, mental health outpatient clinics, and congregate meals provided at senior centers. Respite care is another type of service that can be classified as extramural.

***Adult day care*** enables a person to live with family but receive professional services in a daytime program in which nursing care, rehabilitation therapies, supervision, and social activities are available. Adult day care centers generally operate programs during normal business hours five days a week. Some programs also offer services in the evenings and on weekends. ***Senior centers*** are local community centers where seniors can congregate and socialize. Many centers offer a daily meal. Others sponsor wellness programs, health education, counseling services, information and referral, and some limited health care services. ***Respite care*** can include any kind of LTC service (adult day care, home health, or temporary institutionalization) when it allows family caregivers to take time off while the patient's care is taken over by the respite care provider. It allows family members to get away for a vacation or deal with other personal situations without neglecting the patient.

## The Institutional System

A variety of LTC institutions form the institutional continuum, with facilities ranging from independent living facilities or retirement centers at one extreme to subacute care and specialized care facilities at the other extreme (see the lower section of Figure 1–3). On the basis of the level of services they provide, institutional LTC facilities may be classified under six distinct categories:

- Independent or retirement living.
- Residential or personal care.
- Assisted living.
- Skilled nursing.
- Subacute care.
- Specialized care.

For most people, the array of facilities that often go by different names can be remarkably confusing. This is particularly true because distinctions between some of them can be blurry. For example, what is defined as board-and-care (i.e., residential and personal care) in one state may be called assisted living in another. This is because services provided by these facilities can overlap. Brief descriptions of these facilities follow. Additional details are found in Chapter 3.

## Independent or Retirement Housing

Independent housing units and retirement living centers are not LTC institutions in the true sense because they are meant for people who can manage their own care. These residences do not deliver clinical care but emphasize privacy, security, and independence. Their special features and amenities are designed to create a physically supportive environment to promote an independent lifestyle. For example, the living quarters are equipped with emergency call systems. Bathrooms have safety grab bars. Rooms are furnished with kitchenettes. Congregate housing units have handrails in the hallways for stability while walking. Other housing units offer detached cottages with individual garages that allow residents to come and go as they please. ***Hotel services*** such as meals, housekeeping, and laundry may or may not be available.

## Residential or Personal Care Homes

Facilities in this category go by different names such as domiciliary care facilities, adult care facilities, board-and-care homes, and foster care homes. In addition to providing a physically supportive environment, these facilities generally provide light assistive care such as medication use management and assistance with bathing and grooming. Other basic services such as meals, housekeeping, laundry, and social and recreational activities are also generally included. Because personal care homes are located in residential neighborhoods, they are sometimes regarded as a community-based rather than an institutional service.

## Assisted Living Facilities

An ***assisted living facility*** can be described as a residential setting that provides personal care services, 24-hour supervision, scheduled and unscheduled assistance, social activities, and some nursing care services (Citro & Hermanson, 1999). The services are specially designed for people who cannot function without assistance and therefore cannot be accommodated in a retirement living or residential care facility.

The range of services in assisted living facilities is similar to that in personal care homes, except that the level of frailty among the residents is generally higher. Hence, assistance with some ADLs is often furnished. Common types of ADL help include assistance with eating, bathing, dressing, toileting, and ambulation. Most residents also require help with medications.

## Skilled Nursing Facilities

These are the typical nursing homes at the higher end of the institutional continuum. Compared with the types of residences discussed earlier, the environment in skilled nursing facilities is more institutionalized and clinical. Yet, many facilities have implemented creative ideas in layout and design to make their living environments as pleasant and homelike as practicable. Some of these innovations are discussed in Chapter 8.

These facilities employ full-time administrators who must understand the varied concepts of clinical and social care and have been trained in management and leadership skills. The facility must be adequately equipped to care for patients who require a high level of nursing services and medical oversight, yet the quality of life must be maximized. A variety of disabilities—including problems with ambulation, incontinence, and behavioral episodes—often coexist among a relatively large number of patients. Compared with other types of facilities, nursing homes have a significant number of patients who are cognitively impaired, suffer from other mental ailments such as depression, and have physical disabilities and conditions that often require professional intervention. The social functioning of many of these patients has also severely declined. Hence, the nursing home setting presents quite a challenge to administrators in the integration of the four service domains discussed earlier—medical care, mental health services, social support, and residential amenities.

## Subacute Care Facilities

Subacute care, defined earlier, has become a substitute for services that were previously provided in acute care hospitals. It has grown because it is a cheaper alternative to hospital stay. Early discharge from acute care hospitals has resulted in a population that has greater medical needs than what skilled care facilities were earlier able to provide.

## Specialized Care Facilities

By their very nature, both subacute care and specialized care place high emphasis on medical and professional nursing services. Some nursing homes have opened specialized care units for patients requiring ventilator care, treatment of Alzheimer's disease, intensive rehabilitation, or closed head trauma care. Other specialized facilities include intermediate care facilities for the mentally retarded (ICF/MR). The key distinguishing feature of the latter institutions is specialized programming and care modules for patients suffering from mental retardation and associated disabilities. Another type of specialized facility provides pediatric LTC to children with developmental disabilities.

## The Non-Long-Term Health Care System

Health care services described in this section are complementary to long-term care. Even though these services fall outside the LTC domain, they are often needed by long-term care patients. Hence, ideally, the two systems—long-term care and non–long-term care—should be rationally linked. The following are the main non-LTC services that are complementary to long-term care:

• *Primary care*, which is defined as medical care that is basic, routine, coordinated, and continuous over time. It is delivered mainly by community-based physicians. It can also be rendered by mid-level providers such as physician's assistants or nurse practitioners. Primary care is brought to the patients who reside in nursing homes, whereas those residing in less institutionalized settings such as retirement living communities or personal care homes commonly visit the primary care physician's office.

• Mental health care delivered by community-based mental-health outpatient clinics and psychiatric inpatient hospitals.

• Specialty care delivered by community-based physicians in specialty practices, such as cardiology, ophthalmology, dermatology, or oncology. Certain services are also delivered by freestanding chemotherapy, radiation, and dialysis centers. Other services are provided by dentists, optometrists, opticians, podiatrists, chiropractors, and audiologists in community-based clinics or mobile units that can be brought to a long-term care facility.

• Acute care delivered by hospitals and outpatient surgery centers. Acute episodes in a LTC setting require transfer of the patient to a hospital by ambulance.

• Diagnostic and health screening services offered by hospitals, community-based clinics, or mobile medical services. Some common types of services brought to LTC facilities include preventive dentistry, X-ray, and optometric care.

## Rational Integration of Long-Term Care and Complementary Services

The LTC delivery system cannot function independently of other health care services. Hence, the LTC system must be rationally linked to the rest of the health care delivery system (Figure 1–4). In a well-integrated system, patients should be able to move with relative ease between needed services. At least some streamlining and coordination of services can be achieved through information technology, such as electronic health records.

Types of services comprising the broader health care continuum are summarized in Table 1–1. Long-term care patients, regardless of where they may be residing, frequently require a variety of services along the health care continuum, dictated by the changes in the patient's condition and episodes that occur over time. As an example, a person living at home may undergo partial mastectomy for breast cancer, return home under the care of a home health agency, require hip surgery after a fall in the home, and subsequently be admitted to a skilled nursing facility for rehabilitation. This individual will need recuperation, physical therapy, chemotherapy, and follow-up visits to the oncologist. Once she is able to walk with assistance and her overall condition is stabilized, she may wish to be

**Figure 1–4** Key Characteristics of a Well-Designed LTC System

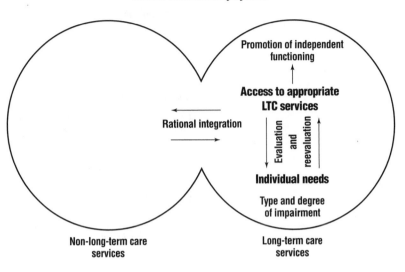

**Table 1–1** The Continuum of Health Care Services

| Types of Health Services | Delivery Settings |
| --- | --- |
| Preventive care | Public health programs |
| | Community programs |
| | Personal lifestyles |
| Primary care | Physician's office or clinic |
| | Self-care |
| | Alternative medicine |
| Specialized care | Specialist provider clinics |
| Chronic care | Primary care settings |
| | Specialist provider clinics |
| | Home health |
| | Long-term care facilities |
| | Self-care |
| | Alternative medicine |
| Long-term care | Long-term care facilities |
| | Home health |
| Subacute care | Special subacute units (hospitals, long-term care facilities) |
| | Home health |
| | Outpatient surgical centers |
| Acute care | Hospitals |
| Rehabilitative care | Rehabilitation departments (hospitals, long-term care facilities) |
| | Home health |
| | Outpatient rehabilitation centers |
| End-of-life care | Hospice services provided in a variety of settings |

## For Further Thought

1. How does long-term care differ from other types of medical services?

2. How can a nursing home facilitate the delivery of total care?

3. Why is it important that caregivers in long-term care settings not perform every task of daily living for the patient? How much should caregivers do for patients who have functional impairments?

4. For nursing home residents, dignity and privacy issues are often more important than clinical quality. Identify some staff practices that will promote each individual's privacy and dignity.

---

# For Further Learning

Administration on Aging: A federal agency established under the Older Americans Act.

www.aoa.gov/

Family Caregiver Alliance: A nonprofit organization set up to provide information and resources to address the needs of families and friends providing long-term care at home.

http://www.caregiver.org

The George Washington Institute for Spirituality and Health: Affiliated with the George Washington University, the Institute is a leading organization on educational and clinical issues related to spirituality and health.

http://www.gwish.org/

The Meals On Wheels Association of America: This organization represents those who provide congregate and home-delivered meal services to people in need.

http://www.mowaa.org/index.asp

National Council on Aging: A private, nonprofit organization providing information, training, technical assistance, advocacy, and leadership in all aspects of care for the elderly. It provides information on training programs and in-home services for older people. Publications are available on topics such as lifelong learning, senior center services, adult day care, long-term care, financial issues, senior housing, rural issues, intergenerational programs, and volunteers serving the aged.

www.ncoa.org

National Mental Health Association: The country's oldest and largest nonprofit organization that addresses all aspects of mental health and mental illness.

www.nmha.org

---

## REFERENCES

Altman, B.M. 1995, July. *Elderly Persons with Developmental Disabilities in Long-Term Care Facilities*. AHCPR Pub. No. 95-0084. Rockville, MD: Agency for Health Care Policy and Research (now Agency for Healthcare Research and Quality).

Burns, B. et al. 1993. Mental health service use by the elderly in nursing homes. *American Journal of Public Health* 83: 331–337.

Citro, J., & Hermanson, S. 1999. Fact sheet: Assisted living in the United States. Washington, DC: American Association of Retired Persons.

Compston, A., & Coles, A. 2002. Multiple sclerosis. *Lancet* 359, no. 9313: 1221–1231.

DHHS. 1999. Mental health: A report of the Surgeon General. Rockville, MD: U.S. Department of Health and Human Services.

DHHS. 2008a. Trends in health and aging. Respondent-assessed health by age, sex, and race/ethnicity: United States, 1982–2006. Available at: http://205.207.175.93/aging/TableViewer/tableView .aspx (accessed September 2008).

DHHS. 2008b. Early release of selected estimates based on data from the 2007 National Health Interview Survey. Available at: http://www.cdc.gov/nchs/data/nhis/earlyrelease/earlyrelease 200806.pdf (accessed September 2008).

Federal Interagency Forum on Aging-Related Statistics. 2004. *Older Americans 2004: Key Indicators of Well-Being*. Washington, DC: U.S. Government Printing Office.

Feld, S., & George, L.K. 1994. Moderating effects of prior social resources on the hospitalizations of elders who become widowed. *Journal of Aging and Health* 6: 275–295.

Health Care Financing Administration. 1996. Nursing home quality of life study spotlights residents' concerns. *Health Care Financing Review* 17, no. 3: 324.

Heller, T., et al. 1998. Impact of age and transitions out of nursing homes for adults with developmental disabilities. *American Journal of Mental Retardation* 103, no. 3: 236–248.

Heller, T., et al. 1999. Autonomy in residential facilities and community functioning of adults with mental retardation. *Mental Retardation* 37, no. 6: 449–457.

Heller, T., et al. 2002. Eight-year follow-up of the impact of environmental characteristics on well-being of adults with developmental disabilities. *Mental Retardation* 40, no. 5: 366–378.

Kaiser (Kaiser Commission on Medicaid and the Uninsured). 2007. *Medicaid Facts*. The Henry J. Kaiser Family Foundation. Available at: http://www.kff.org/medicaid/upload/2186_05.pdf (accessed September 2008).

Krause, N., & Borawski-Clark, E. 1994. Clarifying the functions of social support in later life. *Research on Aging* 16: 251–279.

Lawton, M.P., & Brody, E.M. 1969. Assessment of older people: Self-maintaining and instrumental activities of daily living. *Gerontology* 9: 179–186.

McLeod, B.W. 2002. *And Thou Shalt Honor: A Caregiver's Companion*. Wiland-Bell Productions, distributed by Rodale at www.rodalestore.com.

New York City Department of Health and Mental Hygiene. 2004. *HIV Surveillance and Epidemiology Program Quarterly Report*, 2, no. 1. New York: New York City Department of Health and Mental Hygiene.

NIMH (National Institute of Mental Health). 2007. *Older Adults: Depression and Suicide Facts*. Available at: http://www.nimh.nih.gov/health/publications/older-adults-depression-and-suicide-facts.shtml (accessed September 2008).

O'Keeffe, J. & Siebenaler, K. 2006. *Adult Day Services: A Key Community Service for Older Adults*. Washington, DC: U.S. Department of Health and Human Services.

Shin, J.K. et al. 2002. Quality of care measurement in nursing home AIDS care: A pilot study. *Journal of the Association of Nurses in AIDS Care* 13, no. 2: 70–76.

Smalbrugge, M., et al. 2006. The impact of depression and anxiety on well-being, disability and use of health care services in nursing home patients. *International Journal of Geriatric Psychiatry* 21, no. 4: 325–332.

Spreat, S., et al. 1998. Improve quality in nursing homes or institute community placement? Implementation of OBRA for individuals with mental retardation. *Research in Developmental Disabilities* 19, no. 6: 507–518.

Watson, L.C., et al. 2006. Depression in assisted living is common and related to physical burden. *American Journal of Geriatric Psychiatry* 14, no. 10: 876–883.

# Chapter 2

# Long-Term Care Policy: Past, Present, and Future

## What You Will Learn

- Public policy can take many different forms and can come from different governmental sources.

- There is no single process or model that can describe how policies are made, except that legislative policymaking follows a well-defined process.

- Policies do not always achieve their intended objectives and sometimes produce unintended side effects that can be positive or negative.

- In the United States, long-term care policy and general welfare have been closely intertwined. The Social Security Act of 1935 and the creation of Medicare and Medicaid in 1965 were landmark policies that indirectly started the nursing home industry. Regulation of the industry soon followed.

- Quality of care issues in nursing homes took center stage during the 1980s. The Nursing Home Reform Act of 1987 provides current nursing home regulations dealing with patient care, but the regulations also have some serious drawbacks.

- Most of the current activity in long-term care policy is at the state level. Community-based services and purchase of private insurance are receiving various degrees of state-level attention.

- The complex interaction of financing, access, utilization, and expenditures is critical to current and future long-term care policy.

- Future policy initiatives are necessary in the areas of prevention, financing, workforce development, health information systems, mental health, and evidence-based practices.

## Policy Overview

Long-term care (LTC) policy is specifically crafted to address issues pertaining to access, financing, delivery, quality, and efficiency of LTC services. Long-term care policy is a subset of broader health policies that fall within the domain of public policy.

*Public policy* refers to decisions made and actions taken by the government that are intended to address current and potential issues that the government believes are in the best interest of the public. As with other types of decisions, policy is intended to accomplish certain defined purposes. However, the intended objectives of public policy are not always achieved. On the other hand, public policy can produce some unintended consequences, even though such unintended results are not always bad.

When the intended goals of public policy pertain to health care, the government's decisions and actions are referred to as *health policy*. Health policies pertain to health care in all aspects, including production, delivery, and financing of health care services. Health policies affect groups or classes of individuals, such as physicians, the poor, the elderly, or children. They can also affect various types of organizations, such as medical schools, managed care organizations, nursing homes, manufacturers of medical technology, or employers in the American industry. Health policy can have a major effect on access to services, shifts in utilization, market competition, availability of an adequate and qualified workforce, and development and use of technology.

Long-term care policies particularly affect the recipients of services such as the elderly or disabled; provider organizations such as nursing homes, home health agencies, and senior centers; caregivers such as physicians and certified nursing assistants; managers such as nursing home administrators; manufacturers and purveyors of technology and medical supplies; and, sometimes, potential consumers of long-term care. For example, favorable tax policies adopted by many states are intended to provide financial incentives so that more consumers can buy long-term care insurance to enable them to cover high LTC expenses later on. However, research shows that tax incentives have not induced the purchase of LTC insurance any more than other factors such as income, health status, and family support (Nixon, 2007). This is one example in which public policy may not produce the intended effects.

The term *policy* is sometimes also used in the context of private policy. More appropriately, however, private policies are strategic decisions that various private organizations make to better serve their markets. In the health care sector, public policy is often an important consideration when private organizations make strategic decisions. For example, a strategic decision by a skilled nursing facility to convert some of its beds to deliver subacute care may be driven by a public policy to increase reimbursement for subacute care. This would be an important consideration in addition to market demand factors.

## Forms and Sources of Policy

Commonly, policy takes the form of laws passed by legislative bodies such as the U.S. Congress or state legislatures. Administrative bodies, such as the Centers for Medicare and Medicaid Services (CMS) or state health boards, interpret the legislation and formulate rules and regulations to implement the laws. In the process of interpretation and implementation, the administrative bodies also end up creating public policy. The term ***policymakers*** is generally applied to legislators and decision makers in regulatory agencies who become actively involved in crafting laws and regulations to address health care issues. The two sources of policymaking just mentioned are the most common. Less frequently, certain decisions rendered by the courts and executive orders issued by the President of the United States or state governors also become public policy. The president often plays an important role in policymaking by generating support of his agenda in Congress, by appealing to the American people as to why certain issues are important, and by proposing legislation. Hence, all three branches of government—legislative, judicial, and executive—can make policy. The executive and legislative branches can establish health policies; the judicial branch can uphold, strike down, or modify existing laws affecting health and health care. Examples in all three areas follow. (1) Legislation contained in the Balanced Budget Act of 1997 required Medicare to develop a prospective payment system (PPS) to reimburse skilled nursing facilities. This legislative policy triggered several rounds of policymaking. First, the Health Care Financing Administration (now called Centers for Medicare and Medicaid Services) developed and implemented a new payment methodology in 1998. Subsequently, to address concerns from nursing home operators, Congress instituted a series of temporary payment increases through two pieces of legislation—the Balanced Budget Refinement Act of 1999 and the Medicare, Medicaid, and SCHIP Benefits Improvement and Protection Act of 2000 (MedPAC, 2002). (2) A 1999 decision by the U.S. Supreme Court in *Olmstead v. L.C.* directed states to provide community-based services for persons with disabilities—including persons with developmental disabilities, persons with physical disabilities, persons with mental illness, and the elderly—when such services were determined to be appropriate by professionals responsible for rendering health care to these people. (3) The 2004 Executive Order 13335 provided incentives for the use of health information technology (HIT) and established the position of a National Health Information Technology Coordinator. One of the main objectives of this executive order was to develop a nationwide HIT infrastructure that would allow a patient's electronic health records to be portable and available to different health care providers (i.e., make electronic health records ***interoperable***). The LTC profession has been actively participating to ensure that it is included in this national policy. These examples also illustrate that public policy can take many different forms that can have far-reaching consequences. When policies require that certain individuals or organizations perform or behave in a certain manner, the policies carry the force of law. Violations can result in various kinds of penalties that can include monetary fines, expulsion from participation in public programs, and prison terms for criminal offences.

Health policy may be made at the national, state, or local level of government. For example, national building and fire safety codes govern the construction, design, and safety features for LTC facilities. State policies govern licensure of facilities and health care professionals. States also establish guidelines that insurance companies must follow in the design and sale of LTC insurance. Local governments establish zoning laws specifying where LTC facilities may be built. Local governments may also decide on the availability of certain community-based services on the basis of budget constraints.

## Policymaking

There is no single process or model that can describe how policies are made because there are different sources of policy. Hence, policymaking is difficult to describe, and the process can be obscure (Cockrel, 1997). On the other hand, policymaking does not occur in a vacuum. In a representative democracy, the policymaking process must insure that all relevant viewpoints are heard and that the rights of individuals are protected. The larger and more diverse the constituency, the more difficult policymaking becomes (MRSC, 1999).

The formation and implementation of legislative policy generally occurs in a policy cycle that has six main stages: (1) issue raising, (2) policy design, (3) building of public support, (4) building of policy support, (5) legislative decision making, and (6) policy implementation. The enactment of a new policy is generally preceded by a variety of actions that first create a widespread sense that a problem exists and that it must be addressed. The actions are intended to bring issues to the forefront with some degree of importance and urgency. At the second stage, specific policy proposals are designed in the form of a *bill*, which is simply a proposed piece of legislation. If the bill is crafted at the federal level, the proposal is reviewed by various committees and subcommittees in Congress. Amendments may be added. At the third stage, to build public support, policy proposals are sent to organizations and interest groups that may be affected by them. *Interest groups* are an organized sector of society—such as a business association, citizen group, labor union, or professional association—whose main purpose is to protect its members' interests through active participation in the policymaking process.

Hearings are held and testimonies, both in favor of and in opposition to the proposed policy, are given by citizens, business representatives, labor groups, interest groups, professional associations, and experts in the field. At the fourth stage, internal support of the policy becomes critical for it to pass. Influential members of Congress meet with members of their own party, influential leaders from the opposition, and with the president in an effort to gain support. At the fifth stage, the issues are debated on the congressional floor. In the end, a majority vote is needed, and subsequently the bill becomes law if the president signs it. At the sixth stage, once legislation has been signed into law, it is forwarded to the appropriate administrative agency, such as the CMS, for implementation. The agency publishes proposed regulations in the *Federal Register* and holds hearings on how the law would be implemented.

Policymaking can be triggered by events such as natural disasters, growing social problems such as crime, severe economic shocks such as the Great Depression (started in 1929 and ended in the late 1930s), increasing burden on taxpayers such as the rising cost of health care services, demand from consumers such as product safety, etc. For example, the Social Security Act of 1935 was passed during the Great Depression. Widely reported events such as fires and cases of food poisoning in nursing homes during the early 1970s prompted development of nursing home regulations in 1974.

## Policy and Politics

Policymaking and politics are often closely intertwined because most policymakers are politicians. The danger is that policymaking often becomes highly politicized and becomes hostage to the ideologies of a political party. The primary concern of politicians is to get elected or reelected. Hence, certain public policies are driven by the desire to keep campaign promises or to please some powerful constituent group. For example, politicians pay attention to powerful organizations, such as the AARP, that represent the growing population of the elderly. It was in this political context that the Medicare Prescription Drug, Improvement, and Modernization Act of 2003 was passed. Going against the wishes of the elderly would have been political suicide for some.

The policy-for-politics approach generally does not ask for or consider the cost benefit of a proposed policy. It is pushed through mainly for ensuring votes. For example, no one cared to inquire what impact the new prescription drug program would have on reducing future disability among the elderly.

# Long-Term Care Policy: Historical Perspectives

Policy evolution in the United States did not progress according to some planned design. This follows the general pattern of American health policymaking. Health care policymaking has followed an ad hoc approach to incrementally address issues as they have cropped up.

## Welfare Policies and Long-Term Care

The history of LTC policy in the United States goes back to the building of poorhouses (or almshouses) in the late 17th century. A *poorhouse* was a government-operated institution during colonial and post-colonial times where the destitute of society, including the elder-

ly, the homeless, the orphan, the ill, and the disabled, were given food and shelter, and conditions were often squalid. The first poorhouse in the United States is recorded to have opened in 1660 in Boston (Wagner, 2005, p. 10). The poorhouse program was adopted from the Elizabethan system of public charity based on English Poor Laws. In the United States, cities, counties, and states operated these facilities, which were often located on farms and, hence, referred to as poor farms. The poorhouses were part of a very limited public relief system that was financed mainly by local governments. These facilities admitted poor and needy persons of all kinds, including those released from prison, and the ill who did not have family or relatives to take care of them. In response to the growing concerns about abuse and squalid living conditions, some states created state-run Boards of Charities in the mid-1800s to oversee and report on the local poorhouse operations. The Boards' efforts led to some improvement in living conditions and to separation of the insane from the sane and the dependent elderly from the able bodied (Stevenson, 2007). The tireless efforts of Dorothea Lynde Dix (1802–1887), a social reformer, were particularly instrumental in convincing Massachusetts' legislature to pass laws that would put the mentally ill in separate facilities. These reform efforts spread to other states and even abroad to Canada and Europe.

Passage of the Social Security Act in 1935 was a landmark piece of legislation. The elderly were particularly hard hit during the Great Depression as many of them saw their lifetime savings disappear. Hence, the federal government specifically addressed the needs of America's elderly. Simultaneously, deplorable conditions in the poorhouses fueled a reform movement that favored community-based care over institutionalization.

An Old Age Assistance (OAA) program was included in the Social Security Act. However, instead of providing direct community-based services, the OAA program made federal money available to the states to provide financial assistance to needy elderly persons. The Social Security program, even though it left out a relatively large number of Americans (including many elderly and disabled people) was instrumental in putting an end to the poorhouse system (Wagner, 2005, pp. 132–133). For the fiscal year that ended on June 30, 1936, Congress authorized the sum of $49,750,000 under Title I of the Act in the form of matching grants, meaning the states participating in the program would share in the total cost of the program (Social Security Administration, undated). Prior to this, several states had their own old age assistance programs. The new law purposely prohibited payments to anyone living in a public institution (i.e., a poorhouse). An unintended side effect of this policy was that it started a private nursing home industry in the United States because many elderly now were able to pay for services in homes for the aged and boarding homes (Eustis et al., 1984, p. 17).

The Hospital Survey and Construction Act of 1946, commonly known as the Hill-Burton Act, provided federal funds to states for the construction of new hospital beds. An unplanned result of the Hill-Burton legislation was that many of the old hospitals that were being replaced were converted to nursing homes (Stevenson, 2007).

Policies during the 1950s provided federal funds for the construction of nursing homes while, at the same time, OAA payments were increased, and a 1950 Social Security Amendment required payments for medical care to be made directly to nursing homes rather than to the recipients of care. Nursing homes could now contract directly with the state governments and get reimbursed for services delivered to the elderly poor. Also, at this time, nursing homes were required to be licensed by the states. The legislation contained no specific standards for licensure; hence, each state set its own standards (Phillips, 1996).

## Financing and Growth of Nursing Homes

The creation of Medicare and Medicaid in 1965 as Title 18 and Title 19 amendments, respectively, to the Social Security Act brought about the most transforming changes on the American health care landscape. Medicare and Medicaid are two major public insurance programs. *Medicare* covers health care services for the elderly, certain disabled people, and those who have end-stage renal disease (kidney failure). *Medicaid* covers health care services for the poor. These programs are more fully discussed in Chapter 7.

With the creation of Medicare and Medicaid, LTC became a part of the health care delivery system in the United States. Also, the federal and state governments became the largest payers for LTC services, and the politics of long-term nursing home care took roots. Medicare and Medicaid funding for nursing homes also attracted Wall Street investors and real estate developers to a fast-growing nursing home industry dominated by chains—that is, multifacility systems that own and operate nursing homes in several states (Hawes et al., 2007). Medicare and Medicaid policies favored payments to nursing homes that lawmakers could regulate rather than payments for community-based services that would be difficult to regulate. These policies led to the institutionalization of a large number of people, many of whom did not belong in nursing homes.

Nursing home utilization and government expenditures exploded shortly after Medicare and Medicaid went into effect. The massive infusion of dollars into the nursing home industry, which had already acquired a tarnished image, prompted regulations to hold individual nursing homes accountable for meeting minimum standards of care. In 1968, Congress passed legislation, commonly known as the Moss Amendments (named after Senator Frank Moss), that paved the way for comprehensive regulations to improve care in the nation's nursing homes. It was not until 1974, however, that final regulations for skilled nursing facilities were promulgated, and their enforcement began in earnest. Compliance with standards such as staffing levels, staff qualifications, fire safety, and delivery of services now became a requirement for participation in the Medicare and Medicaid programs. Later, these regulations were widely criticized that they concentrated on a facility's capacity to give care, not on the quality of services actually delivered (DHEW, 1975).

Interestingly, licensing of health care professionals and hospitals was initiated by the professionals themselves and by the institutional providers, respectively. In contrast, licensing of nursing homes and of nursing home administrators (NHAs) came about through federal laws. As mentioned earlier, the 1950 amendments to the Social Security Act required that states license nursing homes in order to participate in the OAA program. Licensing of NHAs was a major exception to the general trend of requests from professionals that anyone practicing in their respective professions be licensed. The demand for qualified persons to manage nursing homes was not initiated by the industry, but came

about as a result of public outcry over fraud and abuse. As a result, the 1967 amendments to the Social Security Act included a provision that, for states to participate in the Medicaid program, they had to pass laws to govern the licensing of NHAs. In contrast, hospital administrators were not required to be licensed. One key characteristic of licensure is that it is a responsibility of each state, not the federal government. Licensure by the state permits an institution to begin and continue operations and health care professionals to begin and continue to practice (Eustis et al., 1984, pp. 143–145).

## Financing of Community-Based Services

Social Security amendments in 1974 authorized federal grants to states for various types of social services. These programs included protective services, homemaker services, transportation services, adult day care, training for employment, information and referral, nutrition assistance, and health support (Lee, 2004). The Social Security Amendment of 1975 created Title 20, which consolidated the federal assistance to states for social services into a single grant. Under Title 20, one of the goals for the states was to prevent or reduce "inappropriate institutional care by providing for community-based care, home-based care, or other forms of less intensive care."[1] In 1981, Title 20 was amended to create Social Services Block Grants. The single block grants actually reduced federal funding to the states for social services. Also, Title 20 covered services for all ages, not just the elderly. Consequently, block grants have provided relatively little money for LTC services.

---

[1]Title XX appears in the United States Code as §§1397-1397f, subchapter XX, chapter 7, Title 42.

Also in 1981, the Home and Community Based Services waiver program was enacted under Section 1915(c) of the Social Security Act. The 1915(c) waivers, as they are commonly referred to, allow states to offer LTC services that are not otherwise available through the Medicaid program, which had authorized payments for institutional care only. The waivers have been particularly successful, and states have increasingly used them to expand community-based LTC services, thus saving money on institutional care. Today, all states provide waiver services to the elderly, working-age people with disabilities, and those with developmental disabilities. Some states also serve people with AIDS and those with serious mental health problems (Miller et al., 2006). Between 1987 and 1997, spending on waiver programs soared from $451 million to $8.1 billion (Coleman, 1999), an increase of 1,696%. By 2006, there were 329 waivers, and the expenditures amounted to $25.6 billion in state and federal Medicaid dollars (Acosta & Hendrickson, 2008).

## Deregulation Averted

In the early 1980s, nursing home regulations came under the broader sweep to deregulate industry and downsize the federal bureaucracy. Rumors leaked out that a task force on regulatory reform in the Reagan administration was planning to downgrade sanitation standards, eliminate staff development requirements, reduce physician visits, delete medical director requirements, reduce social work programs, and ignore certain staff qualifications (Trocchio, 1984). Various interest groups such as consumer advocates and professional associations representing medical directors, social workers, and activity personnel lobbied Congress. In the end, interest group politics and congressional opposition derailed any attempts to deregulate the nursing home industry.

## Efforts to Address Quality Issues

The nursing home industry remained fraught with scandals about severely substandard quality of care and an ineffective regulatory system to enforce compliance with standards. At the request of Congress, the Institute of Medicine (IOM) conducted a comprehensive study that culminated in a scathing report on the state of nursing homes in the United States. The study found that residents of nursing homes were being abused, neglected, and given inadequate care. Sweeping reforms were proposed (IOM, 1986). The IOM's prestige lent scientific credibility to its recommendations, and the report triggered the most comprehensive revision of the federal standards, inspection process, and enforcement system for nursing homes since the creation of Medicare and Medicaid in 1965 (Hawes et al., 2007). National organizations representing consumers, nursing homes, and health care professionals worked together to create consensus positions on major nursing home issues and supported them before Congress. Their consensus positions on most IOM recommendations laid the foundation for a new federal law (Turnham, 2001). Although the IOM report has been widely credited to be the impetus for the Nursing Home Reform Act of 1987, it has also been observed that the *Estate of Smith v. Heckler* (1984) class-action lawsuit in Colorado may have played a role. The suit was brought on behalf of all the Medicaid beneficiaries in the state's nursing homes. In essence, the suit charged that the constitutional rights of the nursing home residents were violated because the federal and state governments failed to enforce its laws and regulations. The district court judge, Richard T. Matsch, ruled against the plaintiffs, but his decision was later overturned on appeal. The appeals court ruled that the Secretary of the Department of Health and Human Services (DHHS) did have a duty to establish a system that could determine whether a nursing facility was providing the high-quality care required by the Social Security Act (Phillips, 1996, pp. 10–14).

In 1987, President Reagan signed into law the Omnibus Budget Reconciliation Act of 1987 (OBRA-87), which contained the Nursing Home Reform Act. OBRA-87 brought enormous changes to nursing home operations. The most important provisions of the law are summarized (Castle, 2001; Turnham, 2001) as follows:

- Emphasis on a resident's quality of life as well as quality of care.

- New expectations that each resident's ability to walk, bathe, and perform other activities of daily living will be maintained or improved absent medical reasons.

- A resident assessment process leading to development of an individualized care plan.

- 75 hours of training and testing of paraprofessional staff, such as nursing assistants.

- Right to remain in the nursing home absent nonpayment, dangerous resident behaviors, or significant changes in a resident's medical condition.

- New opportunities for services inside and outside a nursing home to address the needs of residents with mental retardation or mental illnesses.

- Right to safely maintain or bank personal funds with the nursing home.

- Right to return to the nursing home after a hospital stay or an overnight visit with family and friends.

- Right to choose a personal physician and to access medical records.

- Right to organize and participate in a resident or family council.

- Access to an ombudsman to resolve disputes and grievances.

- Right to be free of unnecessary and inappropriate physical and chemical restraints.

- New remedies to be applied to certified nursing homes that fail to meet minimum federal standards.

OBRA-87 also changed the way state inspectors approached nursing home inspections. Inspectors were to no longer spend their time exclusively with staff or with facility records, as was the case in the past. Conversations with residents and families and observation of dining and medication administration became critical steps in the inspection process (Turnham, 2001).

Ironically, OBRA-87 reforms were nearly repealed in 1995 as part of a larger attempt to reform Medicaid. This time, part of the nursing home industry supported repeal of the OBRA reforms, particularly the enforcement provisions. But consumer advocates, aided by researchers, were able to use empirical evidence about the positive effects of OBRA provisions to effectively oppose the dilution of federal regulations. Once consumer advocates redefined the issue as one of quality of care, Congress opposed the repeal of the Nursing Home Reform Act (Hawes et al., 2007).

OBRA-87 altered the regulatory landscape in a significant way. Even though substantial funds were allocated to carry out the legislative mandate, it was a complex piece of legislation, and numerous hurdles were encountered in developing regulations. The final rules were published at the end of 1994 to be effective in July 1995, more than eight years after the law had been passed (Phillips, 1996, p. 35).

## Oversight for Other Services

It is interesting to note that while the nursing home industry has been under the spotlight from federal policymakers for more than half a century now, the same policymakers have shown little interest in the assisted living industry. The latter has been one of the fastest growing areas of LTC delivery in recent years, and the aging-in-place philosophy has raised the level of clinical acuity of residents in these facilities. The absence of direct federal reimbursement to assisted living facilities is perhaps the reason any federal regulatory oversight is unlikely, unless at some point crises and failure of care similar to those encountered during the long history of nursing homes become apparent (Edelman, 2003). Most regulatory efforts for assisted living facilities have occurred at the state level. Similar variations in state regulations exist for adult day care centers. Medicaid-funded adult day care services must meet applicable state licensing and regulatory requirements such as minimum staff-to-participant ratios. The majority of states have instituted inspections (O'Keeffe & Siebenaler, 2006).

A 1988 court ruling on a class-action lawsuit, *Duggan v. Bowen*, opened up broad access to Medicare-covered home health services, and for some time, home health had become the fastest growing health care service in the United States. In August 1997, Congress enacted the Balanced Budget Act (BBA) of 1997, which mandated that Medicare's cost-based, retrospective reimbursement policy for home health agencies as well as skilled nursing facilities be replaced by a prospective payment system (PPS). This policy was part of a broader financial reform to slow down the growth of Medicare spending. A prospective reimbursement method for skilled nursing facilities was implemented in July 1998 and a home health PPS reimbursement was implemented in October 2000.

## Current State of Long-Term Care Policy

The national stage for LTC policy has been largely silent as other pressing issues preoccupy politicians. Long-term care is not expected to see any major changes in the near future. States, on the other hand, continue to forge incremental policy initiatives to expand the purchase of private LTC insurance and reduce the level of institutional care in favor of community-based services. Both initiatives are intended to curtail the states' burden of nursing home expenditures and to save money overall in the LTC delivery system. A third area of state-level policymaking encompasses ongoing efforts to license alternative housing and care facilities. As pointed out in Chapter 1, the institutional continuum of LTC includes various types of living and care arrangements other than traditional nursing homes.

Public policy in long-term care has evolved in three main directions: financing, utilization, and quality. Almost all health care policy can be classified into these categories.

Financing, access, and utilization go hand in hand. *Utilization* is the actual use of health care occurs when people needing services have access to them. *Access* is the ability of a person needing services to obtain those services. Two main factors drive access: financing and availability of services. If *financing* (i.e., the ability to pay for services) is adequate but availability is limited, the services get rationed and access is restricted. On the other hand, if services are available but financing is not, access becomes restricted for those who cannot afford the services. Also, increased utilization negatively affects financing. Increased utilization makes total expenditures rise, and financing becomes constrained.

## Financing

Financing is the means by which patients pay for the services they receive. Financing varies by the type of service, and there can be different sources of financing even for the same service. For example, care in a skilled nursing facility can be financed through Medicaid, Medicare, private insurance, Veterans Health Administration, or one's own personal funds. Hence, LTC financing is quite fragmented because no single source can be tapped on to pay for services. Consequently, access and utilization become uneven. People face financial obstacles in a system that is complex and nonintegrated. Complexities arise when people have to move from one type of service to another, such as from nursing home to the community or vice versa, or even when they have to stay within one LTC sector. For example, many who require nursing home care for a long period of time can face a financing nightmare. Medicare pays only for post-acute short-term stays, and Medicaid requires people to exhaust their financial resources to become eligible. Many elders who do not qualify for either program have to pay on a private basis either through private LTC insurance or out of personal savings. In 2005, 44% of the financing for nursing home care was derived from Medicaid, and only 16% came from Medicare. Private out-of-pocket payments financed 26%, and 7% was paid through privately purchased LTC insurance. The remainder was paid through miscellaneous private and public sources (Kaiser, 2007).

## Expansion of Community-Based Services

Medicaid remains the largest source of funding for LTC services. It finances 41% of the total spending for LTC services of all types. Spending on Medicaid home- and community-based services (HCBS) has been growing, but states vary greatly in financing HCBS. In 2006, spending on HCBS accounted for 41% ($44.9 billion) of total Medicaid LTC services spending, up from 13% in 1990 (Kaiser, 2007). As mentioned earlier, lawsuits such as *Duggan v. Bowen* and *Olmstead v. L.C.* played an important role in shifting utilization from institution-based care to community-based services. More recently, the Deficit Reduction Act of 2005 provided federal funding to states to expand community-based care. As part of this legislation, Congress granted $1.8 billion over five years for states to provide 12 months of LTC services in a community setting to individuals who currently receive Medicaid services in nursing homes (Kasper & O'Malley, 2006). This legislation may be a turning point in national LTC policy because it makes rebalancing between institutional and community-based services a national priority (Mor et al., 2007) under a federal–state joint initiative referred to as Money Follows the Person. Under this program, when a person transfers from a nursing home to the community, funds that had previously paid for nursing home care are transferred to community-based services for that person.

HCBC has been viewed as a potentially more cost-effective option than nursing home care, but research evidence remains inconclusive that expanding community-based care lowers overall LTC spending (Grabowski, 2006; Long et al., 2005). It reduces expenditures for nursing home services, but opens up access to HCBS for many who previously did not have access. On the other hand, studies do show that community-based services significantly improve the quality of life of clients. People prefer less restrictive noninstitutional settings over services received in LTC facilities.

## Reimbursement to Providers

Other policy issues related to financing surround the levels of reimbursement to providers from Medicare and Medicaid. Nursing home operators have long contended that payments from public payers have been inadequate to support quality services. Independent experts have also voiced opinions that reimbursement levels should be raised. However, Medicaid and Medicare administrators have been concerned about rising expenditures, while the public is not inclined to pay more in taxes. The paradox is that, unlike many other industries, nursing home care is highly labor intensive because caregivers have to render services one on one. Hence, few options are available to increase productivity or slash operating costs.

## Incentives for Private Insurance

Coverage for nursing home care from private LTC insurance has increased slightly in recent years, but fewer than 10% of people 50 years of age and older have purchased private insurance for long-term care (Seff, 2003). The elderly population most likely to benefit from private LTC coverage also has a lower average income than the general population.

Hence, LTC insurance is difficult to market because premiums must be high enough to cover costs but low enough to attract clients. Insurance is based on the principle of adequately spreading risk among a large segment of the population. However, younger healthy groups have shown little interest in buying LTC insurance because they see the need for LTC only as a remote possibility.

A few states offer tax deductions or credits for purchasing private insurance, but the incentives appear to be too small to induce many people to purchase LTC plans (Wiener et al., 2000). Another state-based policy initiative that is designed to increase the number of middle-income people who buy private insurance is the Partnership for Long-Term Care program. The program was designed by the Robert Wood Johnson Foundation, a private nonprofit organization, through a demonstration project in California, Connecticut, Indiana, and New York. Currently, about half the states have implemented the program. The Partnership program encourages individuals to purchase insurance, and, if these individuals require LTC services, they can apply for Medicaid after their insurance benefits have been exhausted. To qualify for Medicaid, these individuals would be allowed to keep all or some of their financial assets. Otherwise, under Medicaid policy, people have to first use up their income and assets before they can qualify for benefits. Under the Partnership program, exceptions are made to this rule. States have been permitted to do this under the Deficit Reduction Act of 2005. Some experts believe that the Partnership program has made progress toward meeting its goals. For example, the original four states have been modestly successful in promoting quality insurance products. As of mid-2006, about 240,000 Partnership insurance plans had been sold, and about 194,000 were being used to obtain services. There are critics, but the program was not intended to be a comprehensive solution to all LTC needs; it was designed to fill a financial gap (Alliance for Health Reform, 2007).

Another area in which progress has been made is information to consumers. Long-term care, with its many service and financing options, is confusing for most people. People have also assumed that the government will somehow pay for their LTC needs. Government resources, however, have been shrinking and it is unlikely that public resources will be enough to meet the needs of a burgeoning elderly population. The DHHS has created the National Clearinghouse for Long-Term Care Information (see For Further Learning). The website is designed to help people understand why planning for LTC is important and how they can plan for it.

## Utilization

Table 2–1 provides capacity and utilization data for nursing homes. During the 1990s, nursing home beds in the United States continued to increase while their utilization continued to decrease. Between 2000 and 2006, both the number of nursing homes and beds decreased. As a result, there was some improvement in capacity utilization as reflected in the occupancy rates. On the other hand, the utilization of nursing homes by the population, as reflected in the resident rates, has continued to decline at a rather dramatic rate.

During the 1980s, nursing homes entered the subacute and rehabilitation markets, mainly as a result of the DRG-based (diagnosis-related group) prospective payment system implemented in hospitals, which created incentives for early discharge of patients from hospitals. The trend accelerated during the 1990s because the proliferation of managed care put further pressures on reducing the length of stay in hospitals. While these trends should have increased nursing home utilization, other factors in play since the 1980s promoted the use of alternative settings such as home health care, other community-based LTC services, and assisted living facilities.

It is estimated that 5 to 12% of residents in nursing homes require low levels of care according to their functional and clinical characteristics (Mor et al., 2007). Their needs

**Table 2–1** Nursing Home Utilization (Selected Years)

|  | 1992 | 1995 | 2000 | 2006 |
|---|---|---|---|---|
| Number of nursing homes | 15,846 | 16,389 | 16,886 | 15,899 |
| Number of beds | 1,692,123 | 1,751,302 | 1,795,388 | 1,716,102 |
| Occupancy rates[a] | 86.0% | 84.5% | 82.4% | 83.5% |
| Resident rates[b] | 444.4 | 404.5 | 349.1 | 270.6 |

*Sources:* Data from *Health, United States* 1996–97, p. 248; *Health, United States* 2007, pp. 370–371.

[a]Percent of beds occupied (number of residents per 100 available beds).

[b]Number of nursing home residents of all ages per 1,000 population 85 years of age and over.

could be met with appropriate community-based LTC services. However, HCBS programs, being part of the state-administered Medicaid programs, have not developed uniformly across states. Also, states vary in their enthusiasm for nursing home transition programs. Some states, for example, have transitioned residents to assisted living facilities instead of home- and community-based services. Motivation of individuals and their families and the availability of a community support system to supplement formal services are viewed as key factors in determining who transitions back to the community from nursing homes. Logistical barriers may also hamper transitions. For example, hospital discharge planners find it easier to move patients from the hospital to nursing homes. Arranging for appropriate community-based services is generally time consuming and complex because it requires coordination and determination of how services will be financed. Other obstacles include shortage of housing alternatives (Mor et al., 2007) and waiting lists for community-based care in some states (Kasper & O'Malley, 2006).

Some efforts are being made at the state level to carry out evaluations of HCBS to improve the programs. In the meantime, policymakers are hesitant to broadly implement new initiatives because they have not been validated for quality and evaluated for how much they would end up costing (Acosta & Hendrickson, 2008).

Private paying patients have found the residential and social lifestyles in assisted living facilities to be much more appealing than those in skilled nursing facilities. Many people have figured that they might as well spend their personal savings in an upscale assisted living home and later apply for Medicaid if they need care in a skilled nursing facility.

## Quality

Quality has been a well-recognized issue in LTC for some time. Because Medicare and Medicaid finance more than half of the nation's nursing home care, government regulations play a major role in establishing standards to ensure at least the minimum level of quality. Research has demonstrated that the overall effects of this regulation have been positive. On the other hand, little has been done to ensure quality of care in assisted living facilities and for community-based services.

From the standpoint of quality of care delivered to nursing home residents, OBRA-87 was revolutionary. For example, the sharp decline in the use of physical and chemical restraints has been attributed to the requirements of OBRA-87. Other positive care practices since the implementation of OBRA-87 standards include improved staffing levels, more accurate medical records, comprehensive care planning, increased use of incontinence training programs and a decrease in the use of urinary catheters, and increased participation of residents in activity programs (Hawes et al., 1997; Marek et al., 1996; Teno et al., 1997; Zhang & Grabowski, 2004). OBRA-87 also mandated a comprehensive patient assessment process, which led to the development of a standardized Resident Assessment Instrument (RAI). The assessment protocols are designed to help nursing homes identify and treat or manage chronic conditions, the onset of acute illnesses, adverse effects of medications, or other factors that caused or contributed to a clinical problem (Hawes, 2003).

Although substantial progress has been made, OBRA-87 remains controversial for several reasons:

- In 2006, nearly one-fifth of the facilities were cited for violations that caused harm or presented immediate jeopardy to residents. Improvements appear to have reached a plateau (Wiener et al., 2007).

- Regulations continue to be inconsistently applied both within and across regions (Miller & Mor, 2006). Over a decade ago, Phillips (1996) had pointed out that there were significant differences in how inspectors applied the regulations and gave citations for noncompliance with the regulations. The oversight process is reliable only for assessing aggregate results, but inspectors frequently disagree on the scope and severity of problems uncovered (Lee et al., 2006).

- Phillips (1996) concluded that only 16% of the OBRA-87 regulations actually focused on clinical care and therefore did not primarily focus on high-quality care.

- Enforcement of OBRA-87 regulations takes on a punitive rather than a remedial tone. Nonflagrant violations can be better addressed with a focus on improvement rather than punishment (Willging,[2] 2008).

- Staffing levels have been relatively stable for many years, despite the increased clinical acuity in the patient population (Wiener et al., 2007).

- There is practically no available quantitative data on quality of life, which is an important component of LTC (Wiener et al., 2007).

---

[2]Dr. Willging was president of the American Health Care Association (AHCA) at the time OBRA-87 was passed. The AHCA was heavily involved in representing the for-profit nursing home sector, which supported the legislation.

## Policy for the Future

The future of LTC will be shaped by both policy and innovation, but policy will continue to play the dominant role. Long-term care faces many serious challenges ahead. Much will depend on (1) the health status of Americans and the prevalence of disability in the population; (2) birth and mortality rates; (3) quality of education for the younger generation, innovations that generate national wealth, and quality of immigration that would be necessary for a strong economy; and (4) availability of financial resources as well as priorities for their use. These factors are critical from a broad policy perspective. The future need for LTC services is just one part of the equation; much will depend on the nation's ability to actually finance and deliver the needed services. For example, if the infrastructure for delivery (such as a skilled workforce) is inadequate, many people may have to do without the services they may otherwise need.

The complex interaction among financing, access, and utilization for LTC services would play out within a broader context of health policy for two main reasons: (1) The aging of the population will have far-reaching repercussions beyond LTC, with spillover effects for retirement, Social Security, primary health care, acute care in hospitals, and numerous other health care services. With aging, the utilization for all types of health care services increases, not just the need for LTC. (2) Financing for LTC services is an integral part of the Medicare and Medicaid programs, which also cover various types of other health care services.

Life expectancy for a newborn in the United States has risen from 68.2 years in

1950 to 78.1 years in 2006, the highest ever recorded (Heron et al., 2008). During the same time period, birth rates[3] dwindled from 24.1 to 14.2 (Martin et al., 2009). More than 75 million baby boomers are about to enter retirement age in 2011 and beyond. Between 2005 and 2050, the nation's elderly population is projected to more than double, while the number of working-age Americans and children will grow more slowly than the elderly population (Passel & Cohn, 2008).

Future growth of one population group at the expense of another group (in this case, growth of the elderly population while at the same time a contraction of the working population) is called the ***demographic imperative***. It has potentially serious consequences at two main fronts: (1) With fewer working people and a burgeoning elderly population, the financial burden for LTC on future generations is expected to be enormous. This is an impending dilemma that policymakers have been reluctant to bring up for public policy debates. (2) A labor force crisis for LTC delivery is already beginning to emerge because a smaller proportion of people from a shrinking pool of new workers are choosing employment in health care delivery settings (Stone & Wiener, 2001). Commissions have been organized at both federal and state levels to recommend solutions to address the issue of labor shortages (Friedland, 2004).

The future need for LTC will be closely associated with health and disability trends in an aging population. Actually, some research has shown that there are positive trends in the health of older Americans, thanks to advances in medical treatments. The bad news, however, is that obesity and diabetes have both increased among older people as it has in the younger age groups, and hypertension has increased in older women (Kramarow et al., 2007). Nevertheless, at least according to one source, the rise in the number of people with activity limitations is expected to moderate over time. Acosta and Hendrickson (2008) projected the number of people with activity limitations to rise 14% between 2010 and 2020, but the rate of increase would moderate to 10.5, 7.9, and 5.8%, respectively, during the subsequent 10-year periods between 2020 and 2050. Even according to this scenario, the aging demographic lends urgency to how best to restructure federal and state budgets to pay for more than 12 million older Americans who will probably need LTC services starting in 2010 (Acosta & Hendrickson, 2008). On the other hand, policymakers will continue to explore new ways for providing cost-effective LTC services without turning LTC into an expanded social program because both Medicare and Medicaid face serious cost challenges in the future. As part of these efforts, funding for community alternatives will continue, but many recipients of care in the home- and community-based settings will eventually need to be institutionalized. In addition to policies that promote community-based care, other policies can help strengthen the LTC system.

## Prevention

LTC policy issues tend to focus on receiving and delivering care, rather than on actions that can prevent or delay the need for care. Enhancing community environments that can promote walking—such as repairing or building sidewalks, ensuring safety from traffic, protecting older adults from crime, and promoting leisure activities—can improve physical activity and promote better health. Other

---

[3]Birth rate is number of live births per 1,000 population.

preventive measures include a balanced diet, obesity control, smoking cessation, and vaccinations against influenza and pneumonia. Both community-based and institution-based fall prevention programs are critical because they result in high medical costs, disability, functional limitations, and diminished quality of life (CDC/Merck, 2007).

## Financing

Currently, most middle-class families are unprepared to meet LTC expenses. Most people think that Medicare would pay for their LTC needs, but Medicare covers only short-term post-acute care after discharge from a hospital. Less than 10% of the elderly have private LTC insurance (Burke et al., 2005). Without a strong reliance on private LTC insurance coverage, the public sector will see its expenditures grow rapidly. Purchasing LTC insurance is both expensive and confusing. Also, current tax policies provide greater incentives to business owners and older adults than to younger people when they purchase LTC insurance. The Congressional Budget Office (CBO, 2004) recommended improving the way private markets for LTC insurance currently function, but policy initiatives are needed to expand purchase of private insurance.

## Workforce

It is estimated that between 2000 and 2010 alone, when the baby boomers are about to reach retirement age, an additional 1.9 million direct care workers would be needed in LTC settings (DHHS, 2003). Stone (2003) believes that shortage of a stable and qualified workforce may be the most important and most neglected policy concern. The infrastructure can be severely restricted in its ca-

pacity to provide services without an adequate number of qualified workers. Experts in LTC rate workforce issues at par with the aging of the population itself (Miller et al., 2008). An inadequate supply of qualified workers hinders recruitment efforts. Once recruited, retention becomes equally challenging. Some health care workers have low preferences about caring for elderly people who have physical and mental incapacities. Hard work without adequate pay is another factor that makes people leave employment in the LTC sector (see Chapter 16 for details on effective recruitment and retention).

Another issue that must be addressed is training deficits in geriatrics among physicians, nurses, therapists, social workers, and pharmacists. Ironically, all 125 U.S. medical schools have a pediatrics department, but only three have a geriatrics department. Evidence shows that care of older adults by health care professionals prepared in geriatrics yields better physical and mental outcomes without increasing costs (Cohen et al., 2002). It is estimated that only about 9,000 practicing physicians in the United States (2.5 geriatricians per 10,000 elderly) have formal training in geriatrics. This number is expected to drop down to 6,000 in the near future. Among nurses, less than 0.05% have advanced certification in geriatrics (CDC/Merck, 2004).

There are also not enough well-trained administrators to provide leadership in the LTC field. Recruitment and retention of NHAs is a growing problem nationwide (Maine Department of Professional and Financial Regulation, 2004). Lack of appropriate educational standards as a requirement for licensure of NHAs no doubt contributes to the problem. In turn, the shortage of NHAs prevents the raising of national educational standards to a minimum of a bachelor's degree in health care administration.

## Health Information Technology

Leaders in the LTC field tend to look to the government for direction in health information technology (HIT) adoption (Hudak & Sharkey, 2007). Interoperable HIT can enable providers to track patients' care across hospitals, nursing homes, home health agencies, pharmacies, and physicians' offices. Interoperability is essential for an integrated system of health care that interfaces with LTC services. Long-term care needs to be fully represented in all future interoperable electronic health records. Such systems are particularly critical because the elderly frequently make transitions between LTC and non-LTC settings. Currently, such transitions rarely occur smoothly because of high rates of missing or inaccurate information (Miller & Mor, 2006). HIT can also help reduce isolation among seniors and caregivers through electronically enabled social networks and online training for caregivers (Martin et al., 2007). HIT applications can also improve staff efficiency, interface with quality measures, reduce billing errors, improve clinical accuracy, and improve communication among providers.

## Mental Health

The quality of mental health services in LTC settings remains a challenge. There are concerns that patients are not receiving the mental health care they need or that they are receiving inappropriate, and sometimes unnecessary, mental health services. Even though certain aspects of mental health and psychiatric care are addressed in the OBRA-87 legislation, outcome evaluations have presented challenges (Streim et al., 2002).

## Evidence-Based Practices

As pointed out earlier, quality improvement in LTC has come to a standstill. Also, there is little evidence that merely increasing the amount of spending improves quality. To the contrary, quality improvement often reduces costs. Evidence-based practices will drive the future of quality improvement in all types of health care delivery settings. Best practices in the form of clinical practice guidelines have been developed for long-term care. However, no policy initiatives have emerged to provide incentives for their use.

## For Further Thought

1. Why is it important for administrators in the long-term care field to understand policy and policymaking?

2. What lessons in U.S. policymaking can be learned from the passage of the Nursing Home Reform Act in 1987 and its near-repeal in 1995?

3. Do interest groups help or hinder the policymaking process?

4. Should policy be made only after due consideration of its cost-benefit?

## For Further Learning

Clearinghouse for the Community Living Exchange Collaborative: A joint effort of the Institute for Rehabilitation and Research and Rutgers Center for State Health Policy. The Exchange is a vital hub of information collection, sharing, and dissemination.

http://www.hcbs.org

National Clearinghouse for Long-Term Care Information. U.S. Department of Health and Human Services

http://www.longtermcare.gov/LTC/Main_Site/index.aspx

Overview of the Nursing Home Reform Act

http://www.ltcombudsman.org/uploads/OBRA87summary.pdf

## REFERENCES

Acosta, P., & Hendrickson, L. 2008. *Discussion Brief: Advancing Medicaid HCBS Policy: From Capped Consumer to Consumer-Directed*. Rutgers Center for State Health Policy. Retrieved September 2008 from http://www.hcbs.org/files/136/6774/ConsumerChoice.pdf.

Alliance for Health Reform. 2007. *Long-Term Care Partnerships: An Update*. Washington, DC: Alliance for Health Reform.

Burke, S.P., et al. 2005. *Developing a Better Long-Term Care Policy: A Vision and Strategy for America's Future*. Washington, DC: National Academy of Social Insurance.

Castle, N.G. 2001. Citations and compliance with the Nursing Home Reform Act of 1987. *Journal of Health and Social Policy* 13, no. 1: 73–95.

CBO. 2004. *Financing Long Term Care for the Elderly*. Washington, DC: Congressional Budget Office.

CDC/Merck. 2004. *The State of Aging and Health in America, 2004*. Centers for Disease Control and Prevention and Merck Company Foundation. Retrieved October 2008 from http://www.cdc.gov/aging/pdf/State_of_Aging_and_Health_in_America_2004.pdf.

CDC/Merck. 2007. *The State of Aging and Health in America*. Centers for Disease Control and Prevention and Merck Company Foundation. Retrieved October 2008 from http://www.cdc.gov/aging/pdf/saha_2007.pdf.

Cockrel, J. 1997. *Public Policymaking in America*. Retrieved September 2008 from http://www.ca.uky.edu/agc/pubs/ip/ip19/ip19.pdf.

Cohen, H.J., et al. 2002. A controlled trial of inpatient and outpatient geriatric evaluation and management. *New England Journal of Medicine* 346, no. 12: 906–912.

Coleman, B. 1999. *Trends in Medicaid Long-Term Care Spending*. Research report, AARP Public Policy Institute. Retrieved September 2008 from http://www.aarp.org/research/assistance/medicaid/aresearch-import-646-DD38.html#community.

DHEW (Department of Health, Education, and Welfare). 1975. *Long Term Care Facility Improvement Study: Introductory Report*. Washington, DC: Department of Health, Education, and Welfare.

DHHS (Department of Health and Human Services). 2003. *The Future Supply of Long-Term Care Workers in Relation to the Aging Baby Boom Generation, Report to Congress*. Washington, DC: Department of Health and Human Services.

Edelman, T.S. 2003. Enforcement in the assisted living industry: Dispelling the Industry's Myths. *NAELA Quarterly* 3, no. 2: 9–12.

Eustis, N., et al. 1984. *Long-Term Care for Older Persons: A Policy Perspective*. Monterey, CA: Brooks/Cole Publishing.

Friedland, R.B. 2004. *Caregivers and Long-Term Care Needs in the 21st Century: Will Public Policy Meet the Challenge*. Washington, DC: Health Policy Institute, Georgetown University.

Grabowski, D.C. 2006. The cost-effectiveness of noninstitutional long-term care services: Review and synthesis of the most recent evidence. *Medical Care Research and Review* 63, no. 1: 3–28.

Hawes, C. 2003. Ensuring quality in long-term care settings. In D. Blumenthal et al. (eds.). *Long-term Care and Medicare Policy: Can We Improve the Continuity of Care?* (pp. 131–143). Washington, DC: National Academy of Social Insurance.

Hawes, C., et al. 1997. The impact of OBRA-87 and the RAI on indicators of process quality in nursing homes. *Journal of the American Geriatrics Society* 45, no. 8: 977–985.

Hawes, C., et al. 2007. *The RAI and the Politics of Long-Term Care: The Convergence of Science and Politics in U.S. Nursing Home Policy*. Report published by the Milbank Memorial Fund. Retrieved September 2008 from http://www.milbank.org/reports/footnotes/US.html.

Heron, M.P., et al. 2008. Deaths: Preliminary data for 2006. *National Vital Statistics Reports*, Vol. 56, no. 16. Hyattsville, MD: National Center for Health Statistics.

Hudak, S., & Sharkey, S. 2007. *Health Information Technology: Are Long Term Care Providers Ready?* Oakland, CA: California HealthCare Foundation.

IOM. 1986. *Improving the Quality of Care in Nursing Homes*. Washington, DC: National Academy Press, Institute of Medicine.

Kaiser (Kaiser Commission on Medicaid and the Uninsured). 2007. *Medicaid Facts*. The Henry J. Kaiser Family Foundation. Retrieved September 2008 from http://www.kff.org/medicaid/upload/2186_05.pdf.

Kasper, J., &. O'Malley, M. 2006. *Nursing Home Transition Programs: Perspectives of State Medicaid Officials*. Kaiser Commission on Medicaid and the Uninsured. Retrieved September 2008 from http://www.kff.org/medicaid/upload/7484.pdf.

Kramarow, E., et al. 2007. Trends in the health of older Americans, 1970–2005. *Health Affairs* 26, no. 5: 1417–1425.

Lee, J. 2004. *Aging Policy and Policy in U.S.* Center for Human Resource Research, Ohio State University (PowerPoint slides, June 2004). Retrieved September 2008 from www.kspa.org/multy_board/bbs_files/20060406041206.ppt.

Lee, R.H., et al. 2006. Reliability of the nursing home survey process: A simultaneous survey approach. *The Gerontologist* 46, no. 6: 772–780.

Long, S.K., et al. 2005. Getting by in the community: Lessons from frail elders. *Journal of Aging and Social Policy* 17, no. 1: 19–44.

Maine Department of Professional and Financial Regulation. 2004. Report of the Board of Nursing Home Administrators. Retrieved February 2009 from http://www.maine.gov/pfr/legislative/documents/nursingh.pdf.

Marek, K.D., et al. 1996. OBRA '87: Has it resulted in positive change in nursing homes? *Journal of Gerontological Nursing* 22, no. 12: 32–40.

Martin, J.A., et al. 2009. Births: Final data for 2006. *National Vital Statistics Reports*, Vol. 57, no. 7. Hyattsville, MD: National Center for Health Statistics.

Martin, R.D., et al. 2007. *Essential but Not Sufficient: Information Technology in Long-Term Care as an Enabler of Consumer Independence and Quality Improvement*. Report to the National Commission for Quality Long-Term Care. Mclean, VA: BearingPoint Management and Technology Consultants.

MedPAC. 2002. *Report to Congress: Medicare Payment Policy*. Washington, DC: Medicare Payment Advisory Commission.

Miller, E.A., & Mor, V. 2006. *Out of the Shadows: Envisioning a Brighter Future for Long-Term Care in America*. Providence, RI: Brown University.

Miller, E.A., et al. 2008. Assessing experts' views of the future of long-term care. *Research on Aging* 30, no. 4: 450–473.

Miller, N.A., et al. 2006. Strengthening home and community-based care through Medicaid waivers. *Journal of Aging and Social Policy* 18, no. 1: 1–16.

Mor, V., et al. 2007. Prospects of transferring nursing home residents to the community. *Health Affairs* 26, no. 6: 1762–1771.

MRSC. 1999. *Local Government Policy-Making Process* (Report No. 45). Seattle, WA: The Municipal Research Services Center of Washington.

Nixon, D.C. 2007. *State Programs to Encourage Long Term Care Insurance: Worthwhile or Wasted?* Paper presented at the annual meeting of the Midwest Political Science Association. Palmer House Hotel, Chicago, April 12, 2007. Retrieved September 2008 from http://www.allacademic.com/meta/p198586_index.html.

O'Keeffe, J., & Siebenaler, K. 2006. *Adult Day Services: A Key Community Service for Older Adults*. Washington, DC: U.S. Department of Health and Human Services.

Passel, J.S., & Cohn, D. 2008. *U.S. Population Projections: 2005–2050*. Washington, DC: Pew Research Center.

Phillips, R.E. 1996. *Crises in the Regulation of Long-Term Care*. Doctoral dissertation: Western Michigan University, April 1996.

Seff, M.K. 2003. Clearing up health care myths. *Golden Lifestyles* (Jan. Feb. Mar.): 7.

Social Security Administration. Undated. Legislative history: Social Security Act of 1935. Retrieved September 2008 from http://www.ssa.gov/history/35acti.html.

Stevenson, K. 2007. *History of Long-Term Care*. Retrieved September 2008 from http://www.elderweb.com/home/main.

Stone, R. 2003. Reality of caring for the long-term care population. In *Long-term Care and Medicare Policy: Can We Improve the Continuity of Care?*, D. Blumenthal et al. (eds.) (pp. 40–47). Washington, DC: National Academy of Social Insurance.

Stone, R., & Wiener, J. 2001. *Who Will Care for Us? Addressing the Long-term Care Workforce Crisis*. Washington, DC: Urban Institute and the American Association of Homes and Services for the Aging.

Streim, J.E., et al. 2002. Regulatory oversight, payment policy, and quality improvement in mental health care in nursing homes. *Psychiatric Services* 53, no. 11: 1414–1418.

Teno, J., et al. 1997. The early impact of the Patient Self-Determination Act in long-term care facilities: Results from a ten-state sample. *Journal of the American Geriatrics Society* 45, no. 8: 939–944.

Trocchio, J. 1984. Nursing home deregulation: Regulatory reform efforts. *Nursing Economics* 2, no. 3: 185–189.

Turnham, H. 2001. *Federal Nursing Home Reform Act from the Omnibus Budget Reconciliation Act of 1987*. National Long Term Care Ombudsman Resource Center. Retrieved September 2008 from http://www.ltcombudsman.org/ombpublic/49_346_1023.cfm.

Wagner, D. 2005. *The Poorhouse: America's Forgotten Institution*. Lanham, MD: Rowman & Littlefield Publishers.

Wiener, J.M., et al. 2000. Federal and state initiatives to jump start the market for private long-term care insurance. *Elder Law Journal* 8, no. 1: 57–102.

Wiener, J.M., et al. 2007. *Nursing Home Care Quality: Twenty Years After the Omnibus Budget Reconciliation Act of 1987*. Menlo Park, CA: The Henry J. Kaiser Family Foundation.

Willging, P. 2008. Personal electronic communication. September 23, 2008.

Zhang, X., & Grabowski, D.C. 2004. Nursing home staffing and quality under the Nursing Home Reform Act. *The Gerontologist* 44, no. 1: 13–23.

# Chapter 3

# The Long-Term Care Industry

## What You Will Learn

- The primary component of the long-term care industry consists of various providers in community-based settings, quasi-institutions, and institutional facilities. The industry cannot function without other key partners.

- Home health care is a prime example of community-based long-term care providers. Others include homemaker and personal care service providers, adult day care providers, and hospice service providers.

- Independent living and retirement centers and custodial care providers such as adult foster care facilities can be referred to as quasi-institutions.

- Institutional providers are the most visible sector of the long-term care industry. They range from assisted living facilities to a variety of providers that are commonly referred to as nursing homes. Some institutional long-term care services are based in hospitals.

- Commercial insurance companies and managed care organizations play a critical role in the financing of long-term care services.

- A variety of health care personnel are involved in the delivery of long-term care. They can be classified as administrative professionals, clinicians, paraprofessional caregivers, ancillary personnel, and social support professionals.

- The ancillary sector includes case management agencies that assist clients with identifying and obtaining appropriate long-term care services, long-term care pharmacies that provide drug management and pharmaceuticals to facilities, and developers of long-term care technology.

# Scope of the Industry

Efficient delivery of services to a nation's population necessitates a long-term care (LTC) industry. The industry in the United States has been shaped primarily by LTC policy. But, the government's role has been mainly indirect—as a financier and regulator. The government plays a very small role in the direct delivery of LTC services. The LTC industry mainly consists of providers of services other than informal caregivers and government agencies that deliver social services. Among the providers are hospital-based LTC services that emerged in the late 1980s. Hospice services provide end-of-life care and are regarded as a component of long-term care. The industry cannot function without other key partners. These partners include the insurance industry, managed care organizations, professionals employed in the LTC industry, case management agencies, long-term care pharmacies, and developers of technology.

# The Provider Sector

*Providers* are organizations or individuals that deliver LTC services and get paid for the services delivered. The health care industry is replete with examples of providers, including hospitals, nursing homes, home health agencies, hospices, physicians, pharmacists, and laboratories. Various private organizations and facilities, both for-profit and nonprofit, are part of the LTC industry. Most of these organizations deliver institutional care, but the private sector that delivers community-based services has also grown. A prime example is home health care, which

has been a growing industry in itself. The LTC industry is predominantly funded by the government, and certain sectors of the industry are more stringently regulated than others.

## Community-Based Service Providers

Four main types of providers constitute the community-based sector of the LTC industry: (1) certified home health providers, (2) homemaker and personal care service providers, (3) adult day care providers, and (4) hospice service providers.

## Certified Home Health Providers

Home health care is consistent with the philosophy of maintaining people in the least restrictive environment possible. Without the availability of skilled nursing care and rehabilitation services in patients' own homes, the patients would have to be in hospitals or nursing homes to receive the same services at a much higher expense.

As pointed out in Chapter 2, the 1988 class-action lawsuit of *Duggan v. Bowen* was instrumental in expanding home health benefits under Medicare. The new rules that took effect in 1989 (1) removed the requirement of a three-day hospital stay before home health visits would be covered under Medicare, (2) abolished the maximum limit of 100 visits, and (3) included coverage for skilled observation with stable health needs rather than expectations of improvement, as the former criterion had specified. In spite of these changes, Medicare criteria continue to focus on recovery from acute illness, not long-term maintenance or assistance with functional disability (Hughes & Renehan, 2005). Although visits continue until the client's plan of care is addressed, this period is short, often a few weeks in length for most clients (Dieckmann, 2005).

Between 1990 and 1996 alone, the number of home health care providers grew from 5,800 to 9,900 (Liu et al., 1999). In 2007, there were 9,284 Medicare-certified home health agencies. Of these, 17% were affiliated with an institution such as a hospital or nursing facility and 83% were freestanding (NAHC, 2008). Medicare is the largest single payer for home health services. For Medicaid beneficiaries, states pay for the same services that Medicare does. Private insurance also includes skilled home care benefits.

In addition to Medicare-certified agencies, there are numerous noncertified home care agencies, home care aide organizations, and hospices. Often, such agencies do not provide the breadth of services that Medicare requires. For example, home health aide organizations do not provide skilled nursing care (NAHC, 2008).

## Homemaker and Personal Care Service Providers

Various private agencies offer services for in-home assistance. Some of these agencies are also Medicare-certified to deliver skilled nursing and rehabilitation care. Homemaker and personal care services, however, are not covered under the Medicare program. To varying degrees, states pay for homemaker and personal care for Medicaid beneficiaries. Personal funds are used to pay for these services by those who do not qualify for Medicaid. Homemaker and personal services include assistance with personal hygiene (such as bathing), light housework, laundry, meal preparation, transportation, and grocery shopping.

## Adult Day Care Providers

Adult day care is a nonresidential, community-based extramural service. It enables people to live with their families and fulfills family caregivers' need for respite so they can go to work during the day. These centers may be located in senior centers, nursing facilities, churches or synagogues, or hospitals. Many centers also provide transportation from home to the center and back. On the other hand, lack of transportation and the high cost of transportation are also major impediments to the use of adult day services (O'Keeffe & Siebenaler, 2006).

Based on their focus, there are three main models of adult day services (NADSA, 2008): (1) the social model emphasizes recreation and furnishes meals and some basic health-related services; (2) the medical/health model provides nursing care and rehabilitation therapies in addition to social activities; and (3) the specialized model provides services only to specific care recipients, such as those with dementia or developmental disabilities. Many programs combine the first two models. Among those using adult day services nationwide, 52% have some cognitive impairment and are the largest users of this type of service. Other users are frail elderly who need supervision and those with mental retardation/developmental disabilities (PIC, 2003).

In 2002, more than 3,400 adult day centers were operating in the United States, and they provided care to 150,000 adults each day (PIC, 2003). The vast majority were operated by a parent organization, such as a hospital or nursing facility, on a nonprofit basis. Adult day care has become a growth industry because of rising demand, and an increasing number of for-profit centers are being opened.

The national average for adult day care cost is around $56 per day (Feldstein, 2008). Costs often vary by the type of service, particularly the extent of health care services the participant requires. Medicare does not pay for adult day care, but expenses can be covered through a variety of other sources. Under the home- and community-based services (HCBS) waiver program, introduced in Chapter 2, Medicaid is the leading source of payment for adult day care. Other sources of funding include Title III of the Older Americans Act, Veterans Health Administration, private long-term care insurance, and private out-of-pocket funds. Some rehabilitation therapies may be covered under Medicare.

## Hospice Service Providers

Hospice services were introduced in Chapter 1. Medicare added hospice benefits in 1983, 10 years after the first hospice opened in the United States. For a patient to receive hospice benefits, a physician must certify that the patient is terminally ill and that the patient's life expectancy is six months or less. Benefit payments by Medicare, however, are not limited to six months. The patient must also agree to waive the right to benefits for the medical treatment of the terminal illness.

People most commonly served by hospice have cancer, heart disease, unspecified debility, dementia, or lung disease. Cancer accounts for approximately 41% of all diagnoses. In 2007, 39% of all deaths in the United States occurred in hospices (NHPCO, 2008).

Hospice can be a part of home health care when the services are provided in the patient's home. In other instances, services are taken to patients in nursing homes, retirement centers, or hospitals. Services can be organized out of a hospital, nursing home, freestanding

hospice facility, or home health agency. In 2007, there were roughly 4,700 hospice providers located in all 50 states, the District of Columbia, Puerto Rico, Guam, and the U.S. Virgin Islands. The majority of hospices are independent, freestanding agencies (Figure 3–1). These hospices served 1.4 million patients in 2007 (NHPCO, 2008).

Medicare is the primary source of payment (83.6% in 2007) for hospice care (NHPCO, 2008). Other sources include private insurance and Medicaid.

## Quasi-Institutional Providers

As noted in Chapter 1, the institutional continuum of LTC includes a range of facilities that often do not have clear-cut distinctions. Yet, these facilities can be classified into three main categories: (1) independent living

**Figure 3–1** Types of Hospice Agencies, 2007

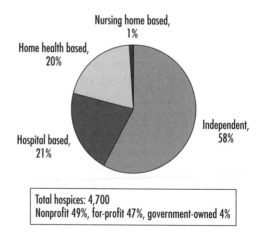

*Sources:* Data from National Hospice and Palliative Care Organization, 2008; and *NHPCO Facts and Figures: Hospice Care in America,* retrieved October 2008 from http://www.nhpco.org/files/public/Statistics_Research/NHPCO_facts-and-figures_2008.pdf.

facilities, which are not truly institutions because they do not generally deliver health care; (2) custodial care providers that limit their services to social support and personal care; and (3) assisted living facilities and nursing homes. Here, the first two categories are referred to as quasi-institutions because clinically oriented services are either nonexistent or minimum in these facilities.

## Independent Living and Retirement Centers

The variety of community-based LTC services that are now available have enabled many older and disabled adults to live independently in supportive housing units. The residents can come and go as they please. Facilities include designated parking spaces.

The two main independent living categories are (1) government-assisted housing and (2) private-pay housing. These dwellings differ from other institutional settings in that staff are generally not present 24 hours a day. A business manager generally maintains office hours five days a week and may be available on-call for emergencies.

### Government-Assisted Housing

The U.S. Department of Housing and Urban Development (HUD) administers three different housing programs:

1. Under the Public Housing program, HUD administers federal aid to local housing agencies that manage the housing for low-income residents at rents they can afford. Anyone with low income, including the elderly and disabled persons, can apply for the program.

2. The Section 8 program offers vouchers or certificates that allow people to choose any housing in the private market that meets certain requirements and apply the voucher or certificate toward rent. Section 8 program is also managed by local public housing agencies.

3. The Section 202 Supportive Housing for the Elderly program is specifically meant for low-income people who are at least 62 years old at the time of initial occupancy.

HUD provides interest-free capital advances to private, nonprofit sponsors to finance the development of supportive housing for the elderly. HUD also provides rent subsidies for the projects to help make them affordable. The capital advance does not have to be repaid for 40 years as long as the project serves very-low-income elderly persons. A similar program is Section 811 Supportive Housing for Persons with Disabilities. Additional supportive services such as Meals On Wheels, homemaker services, and transportation are arranged from community-based providers.

### Private-Pay Housing

Many upscale retirement centers abound, in which one can expect to pay a fairly substantial entrance fee plus a monthly rental or maintenance fee. These complexes have various types of recreational facilities and social programs. The fees often include the evening meal. Cleaning services, transportation, and other types of basic assistance may be provided at an extra charge. Many of these facilities provide monthly blood pressure and vision screenings, and many organize local outings for shopping and entertainment. Nursing or rehabilitation services, when needed, can be arranged with a local home health agency.

## Custodial Care Providers

*Custodial care* is nonmedical care that includes routine assistance with the activities of daily living (ADLs), but does not include active nursing or rehabilitative treatments. Such care is provided to maintain function because the person's overall condition is not likely to improve. It is the focus of residential or personal care. Custodial services are rendered by *paraprofessionals*, such as aides, rather than licensed nurses or therapists. The facilities in this sector go by various names: adult foster care homes, board-and-care homes, personal care homes, sheltered care homes, and domiciliary care homes. Each state has established its own standards to license these facilities. Funding typically comes from Medicaid, private insurance, and personal sources. Medicare does not pay for custodial care alone. Depending on temporary needs, home health care can be called in to deliver skilled nursing and rehabilitation services.

*Adult foster care (AFC) homes* (also called adult family homes or adult family care) are family-run homes that provide room, board, supervision, and custodial care. The homes are modified to accommodate people with disabilities and prevent unsupervised wandering because many residents have some degree of dementia or psychiatric diagnosis. There is 24-hour supervision in the homes. Typically, the caregiving family resides in part of the home. To maintain the family environment, most states license fewer than 10 beds per family unit. However, many people have made a business of AFC by buying several houses and hiring families to live in them and care for the residents. A skeleton staff is employed to provide assistance with ADLs, to clean, and to cook meals.

Some states are trying to boost capacity of custodial care providers. Under the Money Follows the Person program, states see a greater need for quasi-institutional alternatives. However, in some states, such facilities are declining in numbers. Low reimbursement rates relative to assisted living are seen as one factor in the declining number of persons willing to be AFC providers (Mollica et al., 2008).

## Institutional Providers

Institutional providers are the most visible sector of the LTC industry. Most people equate LTC with long-term care institutions. Institutional care generally connotes some degree of confinement to an institution because of a relatively high level dependency.

## Assisted Living Facilities

For lack of clear-cut distinctions, there can be considerable overlap among personal care, custodial care, and assisted living. Here, assisted living facilities are regarded as those facilities that provide services that range between custodial care and skilled nursing care. Most assisted living residents require assistance with some ADLs, such as bathing, dressing, and toileting, but do not need intensive medical and nursing care. Flexible services that meet residents' scheduled and unscheduled needs and allow residents to age in place are key elements of the philosophy of assisted living (Hawes, 2001).

Assisted living has been the fastest growing type of LTC institution in the United States. These facilities generally have a skeleton staff of licensed nurses, mostly licensed practical (or vocational) nurses, who perform admission assessments and deliver basic nursing care. Advanced nursing care and rehabilitation therapies can be arranged through a home health agency.

There are an estimated 39,500 assisted living facilities serving more than 900,000 residents in the United States (AAHSA, 2008). Assisted living is paid for on a private basis for the most part. The average monthly charges are approximately $3,200, which is about half of what a private room would cost in a skilled nursing facility (Prudential, 2008). Costs, however, vary considerably among states. Costs also vary according to amenities, room size and type (e.g., shared versus private), and the services required by the resident. Most facilities charge a basic monthly rate that covers rent, board, and utilities. Additional fees are charged for nursing and personal care services. Many facilities also charge a one-time entrance fee, which may be equal to one month's basic rent. In some states, assisted living care may be covered under the Medicaid program for the recipients of Supplemental Security Income (SSI) or may be funded through Title XX Social Services Block Grants or 1915(c) HCBS waivers. The main purpose of these grants and waivers is to extend Medicaid services to people who otherwise would have to reside in nursing homes at a much higher cost to the Medicaid program. Upscale facilities, however, do not participate in public payment programs.

Although most states license assisted living facilities, the trend is toward increasing the regulatory oversight of these facilities. This is mainly because there is a general trend for assisted living providers to expand services to keep their residents as long as they are able to stay. For example, many assisted living facilities are providing specialized care for the elderly who have dementia and Alzheimer's disease. On the other hand, moderate to severe cognitive impairment and behavioral problems in particular are often the most common reason for discharging a resident from an assisted living facility (Mead et al., 2005).

## Nursing Homes

In the minds of many people, long-term care is synonymous with nursing homes. The appellation "nursing home," however, has no specific meaning. In health care literature, the term "nursing home" is generally used for facilities that are licensed as nursing homes and are often certified by the federal government. Licensing of nursing homes is mandatory in every state. In addition to licensing, certification enables a nursing home to participate in the Medicare and Medicaid programs. Details on licensure and certification of nursing homes are covered in Chapter 5.

### Skilled Nursing Facilities

A skilled nursing facility (SNF) provides a full range of clinical LTC services, from skilled nursing care to rehabilitation to assistance with all ADLs. ***Skilled nursing care*** is medically oriented care provided by a licensed nurse. Examples of skilled nursing care include monitoring of unstable conditions; clinical assessment of needs; and treatments such as intravenous feeding, wound care, dressing changes, or clearing of air passages. Examples of skilled rehabilitation include post-surgical orthopedic care after knee or hip replacement, cardiopulmonary rehabilitation that is necessary after heart surgery or heart catheterization, and improvement of physical strength and balance. A variety of disabilities—including problems with ambulation, incontinence, and behavior—often coexist among a relatively large number of patients in need of skilled care. Compared with other types of facilities, nursing homes have a significant number of patients who are cognitively impaired because of depression, delirium, or dementia. The social functioning of many of the patients is also severely impaired.

A physician must authorize the need for skilled care. An attending physician must approve the plan of treatment. Delivery of care is also periodically monitored by the attending physician who makes rounds and follows up on the course of various treatments being given. Rehabilitation services are provided by registered therapists—physical therapists, occupational therapists, and speech/language pathologists—who may be employed in-house or contracted from a therapy services provider. The majority of direct care with ADLs is delivered by paraprofessionals, such as certified nursing assistants and therapy assistants, but under the supervision of licensed nurses and therapists.

In June 2006, there were 15,899 nursing homes in the United States (National Center for Health Statistics, 2007). According to a 2008 industry survey, 17% of skilled nursing facilities had an assisted living unit or wing and 30% had an Alzheimer's unit or wing (MetLife, 2008). Between 1995 and 2006, the number of nursing home beds declined by 2%, and the number of residents receiving care in these facilities declined by 3% (see Table 2–1 in Chapter 2). This is mainly because government policy has increasingly supported utilization of community-based LTC alternatives. On the other hand, there is some evidence that occupancy rates in nursing homes may be gradually creeping up (Kramer, 2003). This trend is expected to continue as the community-based LTC industry matures. A growing population with chronic conditions, comorbidities, and subsequent disability along with increased lifespans will eventually need nursing home care.

The nursing home industry in the United States is dominated by private, for-profit nursing home chains that operate a group of nursing homes under one corporate ownership. Approximately 54% of all nursing home beds in the United States are chain affiliated because chains have acquired an increasing number of independent facilities. In 2007, the 10 largest nursing home chains operated at least 100 nursing homes each (Sanofi-Aventis, 2008a). About 62% of all nursing home beds are operated by proprietary (for-profit) nursing homes, and 29% are operated by private nonprofit entities (U.S. Census Bureau, 2008, Table 183). The remaining 9% are government owned (most of which are owned and operated by local counties; approximately 135 are operated by the Veterans Health Administration). The average size of a nursing home (108 beds) has changed little over time.

Although the charges for services vary quite substantially among states, the national average for a private room in 2008 was $217 per day (Prudential, 2008). Medicaid is the largest single source of payment for nursing home services. Coverage under Medicare is for a short duration subsequent to a hospital stay. Less than 8% of institutional LTC services are paid through private insurance. Some LTC insurance policies may cover only a portion of the total expenses—especially when care in a nursing home is needed over several years.

## Subacute Care Facilities

Subacute care includes post-acute services for people who require convalescence from acute illnesses or surgical episodes. These patients may be recovering but are still subject to complications while in recovery. They require more nursing intervention than what is typically included in skilled nursing care. According to the National Association of Subacute/Post Acute Care (NASPAC), the severity of a patient's condition often requires active physician contact, professional nursing care, involvement of an interdisciplinary team in total care management, and complex medical or rehabilitative care (NASPAC, 2005). The patients may still have an unstable condition that requires active monitoring and treatment, or they may require technically complex nursing treatments such as wound care, intravenous therapy, blood transfusion, dialysis, ventilator care, or AIDS care.

Subacute services are generally found in three types of locations:

1. ***Transitional care units (TCUs)***, which are skilled nursing units located within hospitals. Hospitals entered into this service after they started facing severe occupancy declines because of payment restrictions from the government, starting in the mid-1980s. They generally have higher staff-to-patient ratios and can provide more intensive rehabilitation and nursing therapies than freestanding skilled care facilities.

2. Unlike TCUs that are certified as skilled nursing facilities, long-term care hospitals (LTCHs) are certified as acute care hospitals. Here, LTCHs are classified as nursing homes because they compete with other types of LTC institutions. LTCHs treat patients with subacute or multiple chronic problems requiring long-term, hospital-level care. Many LTCH patients are admitted directly from short-stay acute-care hospital intensive care units with complex medical needs. Not surprisingly, LTCHs are the most expensive of the three types of subacute settings. Skilled nursing facilities are often a more cost-effective alternative, and at least some physicians think that the level and intensity of care in the two settings is comparable. LTCHs play an important role in providing high-level continuity of care to Medicare patients. Nationwide, the number of LTCHs has grown rapidly from 105 facilities in 1993 to 392 in 2006 (MedPAC, 2004, 2008).

3. Many skilled nursing facilities have developed subacute units by offering technology intensive services and by raising the staff skill-mix by hiring additional registered nurses and having therapists on staff. Some subacute type services are also rendered by community-based home health agencies.

## Specialized Facilities

Specialized facilities generally provide special services for individuals with distinct medical needs. For example, inpatient rehabilitation facilities (IRFs) provide intense therapies, an intermediate care facility for the mentally retarded (ICF/MR) has specialized programs for the mentally retarded and/or developmentally disabled populations, and Alzheimer's facilities have developed a specialized niche within the institutional continuum of LTC.

### Inpatient Rehabilitation Facilities

IRFs are either freestanding facilities, sometimes called rehabilitation hospitals, or they may be rehabilitation units located within acute care hospitals. These specialized facilities provide intensive rehabilitation therapies that can last three hours or more per day, five days per week. The most common rehabilitation diagnoses include spinal cord and traumatic brain injuries, orthopedic conditions, stroke, and complex arthritis-related conditions.

### Intermediate Care Facilities for the Mentally Retarded

Federal regulations provide a separate certification category for LTC facilities classified as ICF/MRs. In 1971, Public Law 92–223 authorized Medicaid coverage for care in ICF/MR facilities. States have been required by federal law to provide appropriate services to each person with MR/DD in an ICF/MR or in a community-based setting outside of institutional care (see *Olmstead v. L.C.* in Chapter 2). However, all 50 states have at least one ICF/MR facility for those who cannot be housed in community settings. This program serves approximately 129,000 people with mental retardation and other related conditions. Most have other disabilities in additional to mental retardation. Many of the individuals are nonambulatory and have seizure disorders, behavior problems, mental illness, visual or hearing impairments, or a combination of these. All beneficiaries must qualify for Medicaid assistance financially (CMS, 2006).

### Alzheimer's Facilities

*Alzheimer's disease* is a progressive degenerative disease of the brain, producing memory loss, confusion, irritability, and severe functional decline. The disease becomes progressively worse and eventually results in death. Alzheimer's facilities provide special programming and have special security features because the residents tend to wander.

Carefully designed lighting, color, and signage are used to orient the residents (Skaggs & Hawkins, 1994).

## Continuing Care Retirement Communities

Full-service continuing care retirement communities (CCRCs)—also called life-care communities—integrate and coordinate the independent living and other institution-based components of the LTC continuum. Different levels of services are generally housed in separate buildings, all located on one campus. The range of services is based on the concept of *aging-in-place*, which accommodates the changing needs of older adults while living in familiar surroundings. The range of services includes housing, health care, social services, and health and wellness programs. The residents' independence is preserved, but assistance and nursing care are available when needed. Approximately 1,900 CCRCs operate in the United States (AAHSA, 2008).

The CCRC living option is directed at middle- and upper-middle-income clientele. Communities are operated by both for-profit and nonprofit organizations. Residents typically choose to enter these communities when they are in their late 70s and are still relatively healthy. A CCRC commonly has the following levels of LTC services available:

- Independent living units may be in the form of cottages or apartments. Generally, various size options are available from studio apartments to two- or three-bedroom apartments.
- Custodial care and assisted living are available in an adjoining facility.
- A skilled nursing facility is located in a separate building. Residents of the CCRC receive priority in admission.

CCRCs, for the most part, require private financing, with the exception of services delivered in a Medicare-certified SNF. To become a resident in a CCRC, customarily the client must pay an entrance fee that can range between $60,000 and $120,000 (AAH-SA, 2008). In addition, a monthly accommodation fee is charged (average monthly cost is about $2,700). The monthly charges are adjusted when a resident needs personal or nursing care. A contract, called a continuing care agreement, which lasts for more than one year and that describes the service obligations of the CCRC and the financial obligations of the resident, must be signed. The contract often has a cancellation clause that specifies the amount of refund a resident may be entitled to upon leaving the community.

Three types of CCRC contracts are common in the industry: extensive, modified, and fee-for-service. Extensive contracts include a complete package of services and a commitment to provide unlimited future LTC services when needed. A modified contract promises to offer future LTC services at a discounted fee. The fee-for-service contract has the lowest entrance fee, but future LTC services are billed at the full rates applicable at the time.

# The Insurance Sector

The insurance sector plays an important role in the financing of LTC services. It includes numerous commercial insurance companies. Companies that have the largest market share are Genworth Life Insurance Company, John Hancock, and Metropolitan Life Insurance Company, although there are many others that offer LTC insurance. These companies offer individual and group LTC insurance. Employees of the federal government can purchase LTC insurance at group rates through the Federal Long-Term Care Insurance Program.

Individual insurance is purchased by people directly through insurance companies or insurance brokers very much like they would purchase auto insurance or home insurance. *Group insurance* is made available to individuals through their employers, unions, professional organizations, or consumer organizations such as the AARP. Generally, group premiums are lower than those for individually purchased insurance because a large number of people band together to purchase insurance through a group sponsor. Managed care organizations (MCOs) are also involved in LTC insurance.

## Commercial Insurance

Approximately 8 million Americans have LTC insurance; 400,000 people obtained coverage in 2007 alone. In 2007, 180,000 individuals received insurance benefits, and the insurance industry paid out $3.5 billion in claims for the three main types of covered LTC services (Figure 3–2). Alzheimer's is the primary reason for claim payment; 27% of Alzheimer's-related claims are paid for nursing home care and 18% for home health care.

Half the people who apply to purchase insurance are between the ages of 55 and 64; the average age is 57 (American Association for Long-Term Care Insurance, 2008). Purchase of insurance becomes increasingly unaffordable later in life, and the denial rates of people applying to purchase insurance increase because of the presence of chronic conditions. Besides a person's age, premium costs also vary according to the type of coverage and the state in which a person resides. A typical plan may offer $150 in daily benefits with a 5% compounded increase in benefits each

**Figure 3–2** Claims For Services Paid Under Long-Term Care Insurance Coverage, 2007

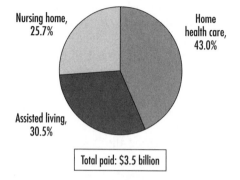

Total paid: $3.5 billion

*Sources:* Data from American Association for Long-Term Care Insurance. 2008; and *The 2008 Sourcebook for Long-Term Care Insurance Information.* Westlake Village, CA: AALTCI.

year, a coverage period of 36 months, and a 90-day *elimination period*, which is the initial waiting period during which LTC services are used but not covered by insurance.

Commercial insurance companies are risk underwriters. They determine the level of premiums necessary to cover potential claims in the future. They collect premiums and pay claims arising from the utilization of LTC services when the covered beneficiaries use the services in accordance with the insurance contract. Commercial insurance companies, however, do not select the providers of services. That choice is left to the beneficiaries.

## Managed Care

*Managed care* is an approach to delivering a comprehensive array of health care services to a defined group of enrolled members through efficient management of service utilization and payment to providers. The most common type of MCO that is active in the delivery of LTC services is health mainte-

nance organizations (HMOs). HMOs enter into financial contracts with Medicaid and Medicare to deliver health care services to the beneficiaries enrolled in these programs.

HMOs are also insurance entities that underwrite risk. In contrast with commercial insurance companies, however, HMOs select the providers of services. The selected providers are those with whom the HMO has payment contracts. Under the Medicaid program, the Balanced Budget Act of 1997 gave states the authority to enter into contracts with two broad types of managed care entities: HMOs and Prepaid Health Plans (PHPs). HMOs take the responsibility to provide a comprehensive package of health care services included in the Medicaid benefits. PHPs offer a less comprehensive package of Medicaid benefits. For example, a PHP may only deliver services covered under an HCBS waiver program.

Both HMOs and PHPs employ a utilization management function in which a primary care physician or some other managing entity authorizes medically necessary services before care is delivered. Beneficiaries must use approved providers for receiving various health care services.

In 2007, all states except Alaska, Mississippi, and Wyoming had Medicaid recipients enrolled in HMOs. Approximately 15 states had 80% or more of their Medicaid beneficiaries enrolled in HMOs. Of all Medicaid beneficiaries nationwide, 63.5% received health care services through HMOs in 2007 (Sanofi-Aventis, 2008b).

The Balanced Budget Act of 1997 also authorized the Medicare+Choice program, which was renamed Medicare Advantage in 2003. Medicare gives its beneficiaries the choice to either remain in the traditional Medicare program or enroll in Medicare

Advantage, in which services are provided through various MCOs. In 2007, almost 20% of the beneficiaries were enrolled in Medicare Advantage (Sanofi-Aventis, 2008b).

# Long-Term Care Professionals

A variety of health care professionals are involved in the delivery of long-term care. They can be classified as (1) administrative professionals, (2) clinicians, (3) paraprofessional caregivers, (4) ancillary personnel, and (5) social support professionals. The types of personnel involved vary according to the level of LTC services delivered in a given setting. For example, independent living and retirement centers may employ one or two administrative professionals and a small staff of ancillary personnel. A nursing home has all five categories of LTC professionals. Certain clinicians may be found only in specialized facilities. Growth of the LTC industry will continue to create jobs in all areas, many of which already have critical shortages.

## Administrative Professionals

Every agency or organization requires at least one administrative professional to manage the organization. The number and types of administrative professionals increase with the organization's size and complexity.

## Administrators

Administrators are needed to manage the organization. They must also oversee compliance with federal and state regulations and ensure that services are delivered in accordance with the organization's policies and established standards. Administrators must have a good understanding of financing and reimbursement systems pertinent to their organization. They must be knowledgeable about legal and ethical constraints. Administrators who manage larger organizations must also be skilled in managing human resources, marketing the facility's services, and overseeing the facility's quality improvement program. Leadership, communication, financial management, and problem-solving skills are also essential for effective management of LTC organizations.

The title for the administrator's position may vary, such as administrator, executive director, director, manager, or general manager. This section mainly focuses on administrators of home health agencies, assisted living facilities, and nursing homes.

### Home Health Agency Administrators

According to Medicare Conditions of Participation for home health agencies, the administrator must either be a licensed physician, a registered nurse, or someone who has training and experience in health services administration and at least one year of supervisory or administrative experience in home health care or related health programs (CMS, 2005). Agencies often employ a registered nurse or someone with a business degree as administrator.

### Assisted Living Administrators

A number of states now require administrators of assisted living facilities to be licensed. Education, experience, and examination requirements vary from state to state. On the other hand, the National Association of Long Term Care Administrator Boards (NAB) has established requirements for licensure as a residential care/assisted living (RC/AL) administrator. To be licensed, individuals must complete a 40-hour state-approved course covering the domains of practice and pass the NAB's licensure examination. To take the NAB's licensure exam, an individual must have a combination of education and experience (NAB, 2007): (1) a high school diploma and two years of experience in assisted living, including one year in a management position; or (2) an associate's degree and one year of experience in assisted living, including six months in a management position, or (3) a bachelor's degree and six months of management experience in assisted living. The NAB examination for RC/AL covers five main areas, referred to as the domains of practice: resident care management, human resource management, organizational management, physical environment management, and business/financial management. A state may also require working experience with a trained preceptor. A *preceptor* is a nursing home or assisted living administrator who meets prescribed qualifications and has been certified to mentor interns in an administrator-in-training (AIT) program. Generally, licensed nursing home administrators are allowed to manage assisted living facilities without any further training. Continuing education requirements are also becoming common for license renewal.

## Nursing Home Administrators

A nursing home administrator (NHA) must be licensed by the state. Qualifications required for licensure vary widely from one state to another. The first step toward becoming a licensed NHA is to contact the particular state's licensing agency and obtain a copy of the state's licensure requirements. The prospective administrator must meet the minimum educational qualifications. Most states require a college degree; some states also require completion of a short course in long-term care. A common requirement by all states is passing the national examination administered by the NAB. In addition to the NAB examination, candidates must pass a shorter examination on state nursing home regulations. Some states may also require an internship with a state-certified preceptor who is also a practicing NHA. Many states have reciprocity agreements, meaning that an administrator licensed in one state can obtain a license in another state if that state has a reciprocity agreement with the other state.

Nursing homes are complex organizations to manage and have been the target of much regulatory oversight and public criticism. The NHA position is, in many respects, similar to that of a general manager in a complex human services delivery organization. The NHA must have a 24/7 commitment to an organization that must meet the patients' clinical needs, ensure their social and emotional well-being, preserve their individual rights, promote human dignity, and improve their quality of life. The NHA must have adequate understanding of the clinical, social, and residential aspects of care delivery.

The nursing home must also operate as an efficient business. The NHA must manage staff relations, budgets and finances, marketing, and quality. Hence, NHAs typically have a broad range of managerial responsibilities and are closely involved in day-to-day operational details.

Nursing home administration entails much more than overseeing the various functions in an organization or following set routines. Over time, effectively managed nursing facilities achieve acceptable levels of organizational stability and have predictable outcomes in patient care quality and financial performance. In the long run, success is achieved by managing six critical areas:

1. The community must come to view the nursing home as a vital service organization. One of the NHA's primary roles should be to serve the community in partnership with other public and private health agencies and care delivery organizations.

2. NHAs must understand and operate within the confines of what reimbursement will allow.

3. The LTC industry has evolved over time, and it will continue to change. The NHA must adapt to new trends and new demands as they become established.

4. Compliance with legal and regulatory requirements is essentials. The organization must also be managed according to the highest standards of ethical conduct.

5. The internal operations must be streamlined to deliver services in a seamless fashion.

6. NHAs must manage the operation through effective leadership, human resource development, strategic marketing, financial control, and data-driven quality improvement.

Risk taking and innovation will mark successful administrators of the future. Being an NHA is a rewarding career, both financially and professionally. The psychological rewards that can come from delivering quality care to patients, helping family members, supporting community initiatives, coaching the staff, and building excellence into the organization often exceed the financial rewards.

## Department Directors

Department directors constitute the middle-management stratum of a nursing home. The organization of nursing homes is well established. The main department directors include the director of nursing, food service director or dietary manager, social worker or director of social services, activity director, business office manager, housekeeping/laundry supervisor, and maintenance supervisor. They report to the administrator and carry out supervisory functions in their respective departments. Their main role is to ensure adequate staffing, availability of supplies and materials, and coordination of service delivery that complies with established standards. Required qualifications are established by state nursing home regulations. Qualifications for the various department directors are covered in Part III of the book.

## Other Administrative Personnel

Depending on the size and type of organization, administrative personnel may include assistant administrators, office managers, bookkeepers, and receptionists. Very large LTC organizations may also employ human resource or personnel directors, admissions coordinators, and marketing directors. At a minimum, most organizations need (1) a receptionist to greet visitors, provide information, and handle basic office tasks and (2) a bookkeeper whose main responsibility is to handle all billings and collections. Additional help is generally needed for payroll and accounts payable functions.

## Clinicians

Various types of clinicians are employed in home health agencies, nursing homes, and assisted living facilities. They mainly include physicians, nurses, rehabilitation professionals, dietitians, and assistants and technicians who work under the direction of these professionals. With the exception of nurses, most others are generally contracted.

## Physicians

Only very large and specialized facilities can afford to employ a full-time physician. Most organizations contract with a physician in the capacity of a medical director, which is typically a part-time position and is discussed in Chapter 10. It is not uncommon for the medical director to also provide medical services to many of the patients in nursing homes. The patient, however, has the right to choose his or her attending physician provided that the physician is willing to follow up on the patient's medical care while he or she is in the nursing home. The patient's physician is also involved in the plan of care for services provided by a home health agency. Admission to a nursing facility or care by a home health agency is also authorized by a physician. Physicians play a central role in the medical care of patients. Other clinicians follow physicians' orders for prescribed medical, nursing, rehabilitation, and dietary interventions. Most physicians practicing in the LTC field are generalists or family practitioners rather than specialists.

All states require physicians to be licensed in order to practice. The licensure requirements include graduation from an accredited medical school that awards a doctor of medicine (MD) or doctor of osteopathic medicine (DO) degree, successful completion of a licensing examination governed by either the National Board of Medical Examiners or the National Board of Osteopathic Medical Examiners, and completion of a supervised internship/residency program. Residency is graduate medical education in a specialty that takes the form of paid on-the-job training. Most physicians serve a one-year rotating internship after graduation from medical school and before entering a residency program. Both MDs and DOs use traditionally accepted methods of treatment, including drugs and surgery. The two differ mainly in their philosophies and approach to medical treatment. *Osteopathic medicine*, practiced by DOs, emphasizes the musculoskeletal system of the body such as correction of joints or tissues. In their treatment plans, DOs emphasize preventive medicine such as diet and the environment as factors that might influence natural resistance. MDs are trained in *allopathic medicine*, which views medical treatment as active intervention to produce a counteracting reaction in an attempt to neutralize the effects of disease. MDs trained as generalists may also use preventive medicine along with allopathic treatments (Shi & Singh, 2008).

## Nurses

The two main categories of nurses in LTC settings are registered nurses (RNs) and licensed practical (or vocational) nurses (LPNs or LVNs). All nurses must be licensed by the state in which they practice. The two main educational programs today for RNs are associate's degree (ADN) programs offered by community colleges and bachelor of science degree (BSN) programs offered by four-year colleges and universities. Regulations require the delivery of skilled nursing services to be under the supervision of RNs. In LTC settings, RNs compose only a small percentage of the workforce. They mostly hold administrative and supervisory positions such as director of nursing or head nurse. A number of studies have shown that an adequate number of RNs in nursing homes positively affects quality outcomes.

The majority of nurses in LTC settings are LPNs/LVNs who are graduates of one-year practical nursing programs offered at community colleges or vocational technical schools. LPNs/LVNs render treatments and administer medications. LPNs also function as charge nurses and team leaders and supervise the work of paraprofessional caregivers.

## Nonphysician Practitioners

*Nonphysician practitioners (NPPs)* are clinical professionals who practice in many of the areas in which physicians practice but who do not have an MD or DO degree. The two main types of NPPs who practice in LTC settings are nurse practitioners and physician assistants.

*Nurse practitioners (NPs)* are advanced practice nurses who provide health care services similar to those of primary care physicians. They can diagnose and treat a wide range of health problems. Some physicians employ NPs to follow up on the medical care of their patients. Studies of NPs in nursing homes suggest that they enhance the medical services available to residents and prevent unnecessary hospital admissions (IFAS, 2005). NPs receive advanced graduate-level education and clinical training beyond what is required for RN preparation. Most have master's degrees; some specialize in geriatrics (American Academy of Nurse Practitioners, 2007).

*Physician assistants (PAs)* are increasingly employed to provide LTC services under the direction of a physician. Both NPs and PAs are sometimes referred to as physician extenders because they enable physicians to see more patients and make better use of their skills and time. Admission to a PA training program requires roughly two years of science-based college coursework. After enrolling in a PA program, students study the basic medical sciences and physical examination techniques, followed by clinical training that includes classroom instruction and clinical rotations in primary care and several medical and surgical specialties. Overall, the PA student completes more than 2,000 hours of supervised clinical practice prior to graduation. The didactic and clinical training takes an average of 26 months. Their scope of practice includes performing physical examinations, diagnosing and treating illnesses, ordering and interpreting laboratory tests, and making rounds at LTC facilities (American Academy of Physician Assistants, 2007). Both NPs and PAs can prescribe drugs when authorized to do so under state law. Their generalist training and emphasis on patient relationships make them particularly valuable in LTC caregiving.

## Rehabilitation Professionals

Rehabilitation therapies enable patients to regain lost functioning and improve current functioning. The most common rehabilitation services are provided by physical therapists, occupational therapists, and speech/language pathologists. Certain treatments can be provided by assistants under the direction and supervision of therapists. Services of a physiatrist are common in facilities that provide intensive rehabilitation.

### Physiatrists

A *physiatrist* is a physician who has specialized in physical medicine and rehabilitation. Physiatrists can treat a variety of problems from pain to work- and sports-related injuries.

Diagnoses may include severe arthritis, brain injury, spinal cord injury, stroke, multiple sclerosis, amputations, and various conditions requiring post-surgical recovery. Physiatrists may prescribe drugs or assistive devices and direct therapists to carry out various types of treatments to help restore, improve, or maintain function.

## Physical Therapists and Assistants

***Physical therapists (PTs)*** specialize in the treatment of musculoskeletal disorders (loss of function associated with bones, joints, spine, and soft tissue), neuromuscular disorders (loss of function associated with the brain and nervous system, such as stroke), patients recovering from cardiopulmonary problems, and severe wounds. They specialize in the restoration of various ADL functions.

PTs need a master's degree from a physical therapy program accredited by the Commission on Accreditation in Physical Therapy Education. Of the 209 accredited physical therapy programs in 2007, 43 offered master's degrees and 166 offered doctoral degrees. Master's degree programs typically last two years, and doctoral degree programs last three years. In the future, a doctoral degree might be the required entry-level degree. All states require PTs to pass national and state licensure exams before they can practice (BLS, 2007). The Federation of State Boards of Physical Therapy develops and administers the national examinations for both PTs and physical therapy assistants (PTAs).

PTAs can provide part of a patient's treatment under the direction and supervision of a PT. In many states, PTAs are required by law to have at least an associate's degree (BLS, 2007). Most states also require PTAs to be licensed.

## Occupational Therapists and Assistants

***Occupational therapists (OTs)*** are involved in a broad range of therapies that help patients recover or maintain the daily living and work skills. Their goal is to help patients achieve independence and satisfaction in all facets of their lives. For example, OTs can help patients learn how to use a computer or care for their daily needs such as dressing, cooking, and eating.

A master's degree or higher in occupational therapy is the minimum requirement for entry into the field. In 2007, 124 master's degree programs offered entry-level education, 66 programs offered a combined bachelor's and master's degree, and 5 offered an entry-level doctoral degree. OTs must be licensed to practice. To obtain a license, applicants must graduate from an accredited educational program and pass a national certification examination. Those who pass the examination are awarded the title "Occupational Therapist, Registered (OTR)" (BLS, 2007). OTR is a registered trademark of the National Board for Certification in Occupational Therapy (NBCOT), which administers the national certification examination.

Occupational therapy assistants help patients with rehabilitative activities and exercises outlined in a treatment plan developed in collaboration with an OT. An associate's degree or a certificate from an accredited community college or technical school is generally required to qualify as an occupational therapy assistant. To be licensed in most states, occupational therapy assistants must pass a national certification examination administered by NBCOT after they graduate. Those who pass the examination are awarded the title "Certified Occupational Therapy Assistant (COTA)" (BLS, 2007).

## Speech/Language Pathologists

***Speech/language pathologists (SLPs)***— informally referred to as speech therapists— assess, diagnose, and treat speech, language, and cognitive disorders. ***Dysphagia***, that is, swallowing difficulty, is another common problem that SLPs are called upon to treat in LTC settings.

A master's degree is commonly required for licensure in most states; it is mandatory for receiving the Certificate of Clinical Competence from the Council of Clinical Certification of the American Speech-Language-Hearing Association (ASHA). In 2007, more than 230 colleges and universities offered graduate programs in speech/language pathology accredited by the Council on Academic Accreditation in Audiology and Speech-Language Pathology of ASHA (BLS, 2007).

## Clinical Dietitians and Technicians

Clinical ***dietitians***, sometimes referred to as nutritionists, provide nutritional information and diet-related services to patients. They assess patients' nutritional needs, develop and implement nutrition programs, and evaluate the results. They also confer with physicians and other health care professionals to coordinate medical and nutritional needs. Clinical dietitians often develop diet plans for patients who have renal problems, diabetes, heart disease, and weight loss or weight gain issues.

Minimum qualifications for clinical dietitians include a bachelor's degree from a program approved by the Commission on Accreditation for Dietetics Education (CADE) of the American Dietetic Association (ADA), completion of a CADE-accredited and super-vised practicum at a health care facility that can be 6 to 12 months in length, and passing a national examination administered by the Commission on Dietetic Registration (CDR) of the ADA (ADA, 1997a). Those who complete these requirements are awarded the title "Registered Dietitian (RD)." As of 2007, there were 281 bachelor's degree programs and 22 master's degree programs approved by CADE (BLS, 2007).

Dietetic technicians assist dietitians in the delivery of food service in accordance with nutritional guidelines. Under the supervision of dietitians, they may plan and produce meals based on established guidelines, teach principles of food and nutrition, or counsel individuals. Becoming a Dietetic Technician, Registered (DTR), requires completion of at least a two-year associate's degree from a program accredited or approved by CADE, completion of 450 hours of supervised practicum, and passing a national examination administered by CDR (ADA, 1997b).

## Paraprofessional Caregivers

Long-term care services heavily rely on paraprofessional caregivers, who give most of the hands-on personal care and assist patients with all ADLs. They also change bed linens and serve meals to patients. These paraprofessionals include certified nursing assistants (CNAs), therapy aides, personal care attendants, and home health aides. They constitute the largest group of health care workers in the LTC industry. Paraprofessional positions are at the bottom of the organizational hierarchy. These workers typically carry heavy workloads, are poorly paid, and are often treated with little respect.

In most LTC organizations, such as nursing homes, assisted living facilities, and home health agencies, paraprofessionals work under the direction of licensed nurses. CNAs are also trained to take vital signs; watch for and report any changes in the patients' condition to nurses; and do simple urine tests for sugar, acetone, and albumin. The 1987 Nursing Home Reform Act mandated that CNAs receive a minimum of 75 hours of training. The training program must include 16 hours of hands-on training in which the trainee demonstrates knowledge while performing tasks for an individual under the direct supervision of a nurse. CNA students must also pass a state certification exam and skills test, and subsequently complete 12 hours of in-service or continuing education each year (Wright, 2006). CNAs can received further training to become rehabilitation aides who provide basic therapies such as walking and range of motion exercises under the supervision of licensed therapists and nurses. CNAs can also become medication aides after further training to safely give medications to patients.

## Ancillary Personnel

A variety of ancillary personnel provide hotel services such as meals, cleaning, laundry, and maintenance of physical plant and equipment in LTC facilities. Food service personnel such as cooks and cook's helpers prepare meals. Dietary aides wash dishes and cooking utensils. Building cleaning workers include janitors and housekeepers. Laundry washers sort and wash linens. Others fold, store, and deliver clean linens to patient care areas. Maintenance personnel handle basic repairs and groundskeeping.

## Social Support Professionals

Social support professionals include social workers and activity professionals. In LTC settings, social workers engage in diagnostic assessment of patients' cognitive, behavioral, and emotional status; counseling; and conflict resolution. They help people cope with various types of issues in their everyday lives. They also have community resource expertise that is often called upon to obtain professional services available in the community. A bachelor's degree in social work (BSW) is the minimum requirement for social work positions in nursing homes and assisted living facilities. The Council on Social Work Education accredits educational programs in social work. In 2008, there were 463 accredited bachelor's degree programs and 191 accredited master's social work programs (Council on Social Work Education, 2008).

Activity professionals provide a variety of recreational programs for groups and individuals to improve and maintain the patients' physical, mental, and emotional well-being. Programs include arts and crafts, games, music, movies, dance and movement, social celebrations, and community outings. Passive activities such as reading and working with puzzles are prescribed for those who prefer solitude. Although no specific degrees are specified for activity professionals, the National Certification Council for Activity Professionals (NCCAP) offers four different tracks, based on education and experience, for the credential, Activity Director, Certified (ADC). NCCAP also offers three different tracks for the credential, Activity Assistant, Certified (AAC). Another organization, the National Council for Therapeutic Recreation Certification (NCTRC) offers the Certified Therapeutic Recreation Specialist (CTRS) credential based on education, experience, and a certification examination.

# The Ancillary Sector

The ancillary sector produces services and products that help people locate the right kind of services, facilitate caregiving, improve people's quality of life, or improve organizational efficiencies.

## Case Management Agencies

Case management was discussed in Chapter 1. The myriad LTC services can present daunting challenges for most people who either need services for themselves or for those who need to help family or friends find appropriate services. Case management agencies do not provide actual LTC services. They assist clients in navigating the system by assessing client needs, identifying sources of payment, matching client needs with available services that are likely to best address those needs, making referrals to appropriate services, and providing ongoing follow-up and coordination as circumstances change over time. Services are often coordinated both within and outside the LTC system.

Case management agencies employ experienced nurses and social workers as case managers. These professionals have specialized training in patient need assessment and a comprehensive knowledge of both financing and service resources.

## Long-Term Care Pharmacies

Historically, LTC facilities have experienced numerous challenges in providing pharma-ceutical services to their residents. Medication errors, preventable adverse drug events, and delivery of pharmaceutical services, in general, have posed the main challenges (Stevenson et al., 2007). The Omnibus Budget Reconciliation Act of 1990 required pharmacies to review Medicaid recipients' entire drug profile and to evaluate therapeutic duplication, drug-disease contraindications, drug interactions, incorrect dosage, duration of drug treatment, drug–allergy interactions, and evidence of clinical abuse or misuse. In part because of this regulatory requirement, certain pharmacy providers have specialized in LTC pharmacy practice. Through their consultant pharmacists, LTC pharmacies offer comprehensive drug management services and often coordinate related quality improvement activities (Stevenson et al., 2007). Such comprehensive services, round-the-clock attention to critical and emergency medications, and dispensing of intravenous medication solutions are generally not available through retail community pharmacists.

Long-term care pharmacies are estimated to serve three out of every five residents in LTC facilities (LTCPA, 2006). In 2007, there were 1,125 LTC pharmacies in the United States that derived at least half of their revenue from LTC facilities (Sanofi-Aventis, 2008a).

## Long-Term Care Technology

Technology has been playing an increasing role in all aspects of health care delivery. Adoption of technology for LTC use has been slow, but it will continue to grow in homes, other residential settings, and LTC institutions. Innovative products are being brought to the market all the time. For example, various types of **domotics** technology, that is, "smart home" technology, can enable a growing number of elderly people live in their own homes. Long-term care technology can be classified into seven main categories:

1. *Enabling technology.* Also referred to as assistive technology, this includes various devices and equipment that enable people to do things independently despite functional impairments. Examples include hearing aids, simple self-feeding aids such as specially designed eating utensils, and custom-fitted mobility scooters that improve people's quality of life regardless of whether they are living independently in their own homes or in LTC institutions. Some newer technologies enable people to live independently. These technologies include reminder systems that are particularly useful for those with mild cognitive impairments. Automatic enunciators remind people of tasks they must do that day, such as keeping a doctor's appointment. Enunciators are also being integrated with medication administration systems to remind people when certain medications must be taken. Talking blood sugar monitors, thermometers, blood pressure monitors, and automated pill dispensers are now available for use in the home (Cheek et al., 2005). The National Association of Home Builders has developed an aging-in-place certification specialist program. A Certified Aging-in-Place Specialist (CAPS) has specialized skills in home remodeling solutions to enable older adults live in their own homes as they age. Various products and devices are used to promote accessibility and safety in the bathroom, bedroom, or kitchen. For example, clapper lighting systems turn on the lights at the sound of clapping.

2. *Safety technology.* Personal emergency response systems (PERS) are now widely available for people living alone to summon help in an emergency. Technology that uses signals, alarms, and wireless transmitters can be installed in nursing facilities to notify staff when a wandering patient opens a door to go out. Wireless sensors to ensure patient safety are also being developed. Fall detection devices can signal the staff when an at-risk resident attempts to leave a bed, wheelchair, or toilet unattended.

3. *Caregiving technology.* Feeding and nutritional therapies—such as enteral and parenteral feeding (discussed in Chapter 12)—have been around for a long time. Other technologies such as in-home dialyzers for people with kidney failure are more recent. Caregivers are now increasingly using automated medication dispensing systems that improve accuracy and efficiency. A variety of beds and overlays are available to reduce pressure to promote healing of pressure ulcers. Ultrasound bladder scanners are used for the management of urinary incontinence. Barcode technology has been adopted to verify patient identification and dispense medications. **Home telehealth systems** use telecommunication technology for the distance monitoring of patients and delivery of health care with or without the use of video technology. They have the potential to

improve access and reduce costs by minimizing the need for the patient to make trips to physicians' offices or for home health nurses to make frequent visits to the patient's home. Interactive technology enables "virtual visits" between clinicians and patients. It enables distance monitoring of the patient and promotes self-management of chronic conditions. Remote patient monitoring systems collect data on vital signs and blood pressure and allow a nurse to also observe any behavior changes.

4. *Labor-saving technology.* Introduction of labor-saving technology is designed to improve worker efficiency and reduce physical injuries by decreasing the need for heavy transfers and lifting. Electrically operated ceiling-suspended dining tables can convert a dining room to a multipurpose room at the flip of a switch. Ceiling-mounted patient lifting and transfer equipment and labor-saving bathing systems are other examples of labor-saving technology. Computerized medical records that replace handwritten charting can save caregivers time that can be spent in delivering patient care.

5. *Environmental technology.* Products and fibers that have greater fire resistance; improved fabrics for upholstered furniture that resist soil and fluid absorption; new fibers for carpeting that resist soil, stains, and odors; and nonskid floor coverings are some examples that enhance the aesthetics and safety of living environments. Computerized controls for hot water systems are designed to save en-

ergy and prevent the supply of overheated water that can cause severe burns. Sensorial signals, such as color and textured materials, are employed to support orientation of cognitively impaired individuals in their own homes and in institutions (Cheek et al., 2005).

6. *Staff training technology.* Interactive tools, CD-ROMs, and remote video teleconferencing are available to provide training and continuing education on a large variety of topics.

7. *Information technology.* Information technology (IT) deals with the transformation of data into useful information and is covered in more detail in Chapter 14. IT is a broad area. In health care organizations, application of IT falls into four main categories:

- ***Clinical information systems*** are designed to be used by various clinicians to support the delivery of patient care. Electronic medical records, for example, can provide quick and reliable information necessary to guide clinical decision making and to produce timely reports on quality of care delivered. Computerized provider order entry (CPOE) systems enable electronic transmission of medication orders to the pharmacy and help reduce errors. Clinical information systems also support patient assessment, care planning, and clinical documentation. These systems can be integrated with other applications such as administrative and financial systems, menu planning, and food ordering.

- ***Administrative information systems*** are designed to assist in carrying out financial and administrative support activities such as payroll, patient accounting, billing, accounts receivable, materials management, budgeting and cost control, and management of residents' personal funds.

• *Decision support systems* provide information and analytical tools that support effective management. For example, the system can help analyze performance indicators, staffing adequacy, staff productivity, rates of infections and patient incidents such as falls, and staff injuries.

• *The Internet*, or the Web as it is commonly called, is now widely used by clients and providers to access information. A vast amount of clinical and caregiving information can be accessed online. Various IT applications, however, have also become Web-based. In this manner, updated software applications can be accessed and used on the Internet at all times. Various LTC providers increasingly use the Web for advertising their services and provide other client-related information.

## For Further Thought

1. In what ways is the long-term care industry likely to evolve in the future?
2. Are hospitals likely to play a bigger role in the future delivery of long-term care?

## For Further Learning

Assisted Living Federation of America: A group that offers basic consumer-oriented information on assisted living and gives a directory of assisted living facilities. This trade organization represents assisted living and other senior housing facilities.

www.alfa.org

Home Care Research Initiative: This organization supports research projects to address issues in long-term care. Research articles and fact sheets can be downloaded.

http://www.vnsny.org/hcri/index.html

Hospice Foundation of America: A nonprofit organization that provides leadership in the development and application of hospice and its philosophy of care.

http://www.hospicefoundation.org

National Adult Day Services Association: This organization represents the adult day care industry and also furnishes consumer information.

http://www.nadsa.org

National Association for Home Care and Hospice: The nation's largest trade association representing the interests and concerns of home care agencies, hospices, home care aide organizations, and medical equipment suppliers.

http://www.nahc.org

National Association of Long Term Care Administrator Boards (NAB). This organization administers the national licensure examinations for assisted living and nursing home administrators. It has publications available to prepare for the examination. The website also provides links to the licensing agencies in all states.

http://www.nabweb.org

National Association of Subacute and Post-Acute Care. The association was formed in 1995 through a consolidation of the International Subacute Healthcare Association and the American Subacute Care Association.

http://www.naspac.net/faq.asp

National Hospice Foundation: A nonprofit, charitable organization affiliated with the National Hospice and Palliative Care Organization that provides support and information about hospice care options.

www.nationalhospicefoundation.org

## REFERENCES

American Academy of Nurse Practitioners. 2007. *Frequently Asked Questions: Why Choose a Nurse Practitioner as Your Healthcare Provider*. Retrieved November 2008 from http://www.npfinder .com/faq.pdf.

American Academy of Physician Assistants. 2007. *Physician Assistant Practice in Long-Term Care Facilities*. Retrieved November 2008 from http://www.aapa.org/gandp/issuebrief/long-term-care.htm.

AAHSA. 2008. *Aging Services: The Facts*. American Association of Homes and Services for the Aging. Retrieved December 2008 from http://www.aahsa.org/article.aspx?id=74#GeneralFacts.

American Association for Long-Term Care Insurance. 2008. *The 2008 Sourcebook for Long-Term Care Insurance Information*. Westlake Village, CA: AALTCI.

ADA. 1997a. *Becoming a Registered Dietitian*. American Dietetic Association. Retrieved November 2008 from http://www.eatright.org/ada/files/RD_Check_it_Out.pdf.

ADA. 1997b. *Becoming a Dietetic Technician, Registered*. American Dietetic Association. Retrieved November 2008 from http://www.eatright.org/ada/files/DTR_Check_it_Out(1).pdf.

BLS. 2007. *Occupational Outlook Handbook, 2008–09 Edition*. Bureau of Labor Statistics. Retrieved November 2008 from http://www.bls.gov.

CMS. 2005. *State Operations Manual: Appendix B—Guidance to Surveyors: Home Health Agencies*. Centers for Medicare and Medicaid Services. Retrieved November 2008 from http://cms.hhs.gov/manuals/Downloads/som107ap_b_hha.pdf.

CMS. 2006. *Intermediate Care Facilities for the Mentally Retarded*. Centers for Medicare and Medicaid Services. Retrieved October 2008 from http://www.cms.hhs.gov/Certificationand Complianc/09_ICFMRs.asp.

Cheek, P., et al. 2005. Aging well with smart technology. *Nursing Administration* 29, no. 4: 329–338.

Council on Social Work Education. 2008. *Commission on Accreditation, June 2008 Decisions*. Retrieved November 2008 from http://www.cswe.org/NR/rdonlyres/9F229762-8A02-4C3C-8E6C-FDC33B946F6B/0/Actions_2008_June.pdf.

Dieckmann, J.L. 2005. Home health administration: An overview. In M.D. Harris (ed.), *Handbook of Home Health Care Administration*, 4th ed. (pp. 3–15). Sudbury, MA: Jones and Bartlett Publishers.

Feldstein, M.J. 2008. Companies moving steadily in adult day care business. *St. Louis Post-Dispatch*. Retrieved October 2008 from http://www.stltoday.com/stltoday/business/stories.nsf/story/02D1846F93FE494F862573D4000E735E?OpenDocument.

Hawes, C. 2001. In S. Zimmerman et al., (eds.), *Assisted Living: Needs, Practices, and Policies in Residential Care for the Elderly*. Baltimore: The Johns Hopkins University Press.

Hughes, S.L., & Renehan, M. 2005. Home health. In C.J. Evashwick, (ed.), *The Continuum of Long-Term Care*, 3rd ed. (pp. 87–111). Clifton Park, NY: Thomson Delmar Learning.

IFAS. 2005. *The Long-Term Care Workforce: Can the Crises be Fixed?* Washington, DC: Institute for the Future of Aging Services.

Kramer, R.G. 2003. Financial benchmarks: Signs of struggle and hope. *Nursing Homes Long Term Care Management* 52, no. 9: 68–69.

Liu, K., et al. 1999. *Medicare's Post-Acute Care Benefit: Background, Trends, and Issues to be Faced*. Retrieved October 2008 from http://aspe.hhs.gov/daltcp/reports/mpacb.htm#secIII.

LTCPA. 2006. Mission. Long-Term Care Pharmacy Alliance. Retrieved February 2009 from http://www.ltcpa.org/mission/default.asp.

Mead, L.C. et al. 2005. Sociocultural aspects of transitions from assisted living for residents with dementia. *The Gerontologist* 45, special issue 1: 115–123.

MedPAC. 2004. *New Approaches in Medicare: Report to the Congress*. Washington, DC: Medicare Payment Advisory Commission.

MedPAC. 2008. *Long-Term Care Hospitals Payment System*. Washington, DC: Medicare Payment Advisory Commission.

MetLife. 2008. *The MetLife Market Survey of Nursing Home and Assisted Living Costs, October 2008*. New York: Metropolitan Life Insurance Company.

Mollica, R., et al. 2008. *Adult Foster Care: A Resource for Older Adults*. New Brunswick, NJ: Rutgers Center for State Health Policy.

NAB. 2007. *Residential Care–Assisted Living Administrators Licensing Examination: Information for Candidates*. National Association of Long-Term Care Administrator Boards. Retrieved October 2008 from http://www.nabweb.org/NABWEB/uploadedFiles/Examinations/2008 CandHand-RCAL.pdf.

NAHC. 2008. *Basic Statistics About Home Care*. National Association of Home Care and Hospice. Retrieved October 2008 from http://www.nahc.org/facts/08HC_Stats.pdf.

NADSA. 2008. *Adult Day Services: Overview and Facts*. National Adult Day Services Association. Retrieved October 2008 from http://www.nadsa.org/adsfacts/default.asp.

NASPAC. 2005. What is the definition of subacute care? Retrieved March 2009 from http://www.naspac.net/faq.asp.

National Center for Health Statistics. 2007. *Health, United States, 2007*. Hyattsville, MD: U.S. Department of Health and Human Services.

NHPCO. 2008. *NHPCO Facts and Figures: Hospice Care in America*. National Hospice and Palliative Care Organization. Retrieved October 2008 from http://www.nhpco.org/files/public/Statistics_Research/NHPCO_facts-and-figures_2008.pdf.

O'Keeffe, J., & Siebenaler, K. 2006. *Adult Day Services: A Key Community Service for Older Adults.* Washington, DC: U.S. Department of Health and Human Services.

PIC. 2003. *National Study of Adult Day Services: 2001–2002.* Winston-Salem, NC: Wake Forest University School of Medicine, Partners in Caregiving.

Prudential. 2008. *Research Report 2008: Long-Term Care Cost Study.* Newark, NJ: The Prudential Insurance Company of America.

Sanofi-Aventis. 2008a. *Managed Care Digest Series, 2008: Senior Care Digest.* Bridgewater, NJ: Sanofi-Aventis US, LLC.

Sanofi-Aventis. 2008b. *Managed Care Digest Series, 2008: Government Digest.* Bridgewater, NJ: Sanofi-Aventis US, LLC.

Shi, L., & Singh, D.A. 2008. *Delivering Health Care in America: A Systems Approach*, 4th ed. Boston: Jones and Bartlett Publishers.

Skaggs, R.L., & Hawkins, H.R. 1994. Architecture for long-term care facilities. In S.B. Goldsmith (ed.), *Essentials of Long-Term Care Administration* (pp. 254–284). Gaithersburg, MD: Aspen Publishers.

Stevenson, D.G., et al. 2007. *Medicare Part D, Nursing Homes, and Long-Term Care Pharmacies.* Retrieved February 2009 from http://www.medpac.gov/documents/Jun07_Part_D_contractor.pdf.

U.S. Census Bureau. 2008. *Statistical Abstract of the United States, 2008.* Washington, DC: U.S. Government Printing Office.

Wright, B. 2006. In brief: Training programs for certified nursing assistants. *AARP: Policy and Research for Professionals in Aging.* Retrieved November 2008 from http://www.aarp.org/research/longtermcare/nursinghomes/inb122_cna.html.

# PART II

---

# External and Internal Environments

After giving the reader an understanding of the broad field of long-term care, this and subsequent sections of the book focus mainly on nursing home administration. A logical point of departure to discuss effective management of long-term care facilities is to recognize that no organization can be self-contained. Organizations are not self-sufficient and cannot function effectively in isolation from their external environments. In modern management, the open-system theory has found a strategic role in operating an organization in a changing environment. To be successful, an organization must adapt to external forces.

The internal environments of nursing homes have been traditionally influenced by hospitals. However, a culture change based on person-centered care has been underway and is gaining momentum. Thirty years from now, most nursing homes will probably be quite different from what they are today.

This section of the book covers the major environmental components that effective nursing facility administrators must recognize, understand, and deal with for their organization's success in the long run:

- Chapter 4 explains that operating a successful long-term care facility requires an open-system approach to manage-

ment. It explains how a nursing home administrator can establish exchange relationships with the organization's main external constituents.

- Chapter 5 centers on the legal environment and how different classes of laws apply to nursing home administration. The chapter also discusses the concept of malpractice, circumstances when criminal law may apply, situations in which administrators may be personally liable, and when corporations may be liable. Administrators frequently have to deal with contracts and agreements. It is also critical for them to understand licensure and certification of facilities, patient rights, and confidentiality requirements under the Health Insurance Portability and Accountability Act.

- Chapter 6 details regulations and their enforcement. It covers the Nursing Home Reform Act, the survey process, types of deficiencies and the critical elements of a plan of correction, the *Life Safety Code*®, accessibility requirements under the Americans with Disabilities Act, and

---

*Life Safety Code*® is a registered trademark of the National Fire Protection Association, Quincy, MA.

safety standards and recordkeeping required by the Occupational Safety and Health Act.

- Chapter 7 focuses on financing and reimbursement for nursing homes. It covers private out-of-pocket and insurance financing, the four parts of Medicare, the prospective payment system, Medicaid, the PACE program, managed care, and hospital partnerships. The chapter also covers the federal fraud and abuse law and False Claims Act as they apply to financing and reimbursement.

- Chapter 8 addresses the internal environment and organization of a nursing facility. The chapter begins with the evolution of the internal environment. It details the key elements necessary for creating an environment of person-centered care and the challenges that nursing facilities face in creating such an environment. It discusses the details of the clinical and the socio-residential environments. The latter half of the chapter is devoted to modern architectural designs, aesthetical features, enriched environments that incorporate the theories of biophilia and thriving, and contemporary models of enriched environments as found in the Eden Alternative® and Green House® concepts.

---

Eden Alternative® is a registered trademark of The Eden Alternative.

Green House® is a registered trademark.

# Chapter 4

# Responding to the External Environment

## What You Will Learn

- A closed-system approach to management is important, but it has serious drawbacks for attaining long-range success.
- An open-system approach to management recognizes the importance of establishing exchange relationships with external constituents, the stakeholders.
- Strong governance is essential for open-system management.
- The give-and-take exchange relationships between a nursing facility and its external constituents follow a cycle of exchanges. The facility needs resource inputs that are used to serve its clients. It receives payments for the services rendered. In the process, certain outputs are produced that benefit the external environment.
- The open-system approach is essential for strategic planning.
- The external environment is best understood by recognizing changes occurring in social, political, economic, technological, informational, and ecological domains.
- The concept of environmental proximity determines the methods for environmental scanning, the nature of exchange relationships, the administrator's role in addressing environmental demands, and the type of strategic plans.
- A facility has numerous options for building exchange partnerships. The facility's broad objectives should include establishing and maintaining value-based exchange relationships that must be sustained through commitment, continuity, and consistency.
- A nursing facility's outputs—care quality, client satisfaction, staff loyalty, and profits—are the essential ingredients necessary for creating and maintaining meaningful exchanges.

# The Closed and Open Systems

A system can be defined as "a set of elements standing in interrelation among themselves and with the environment" (Von Bertalanffy, 1972). Whether or not an organization's internal systems are effectively linked to the external environment is what differentiates between closed and open systems. Here the term "external environment" refers to the composite of forces that are external to the organization—such as demographic changes, competition, and laws and regulations—that can influence an organization in significant ways. Without appropriate adaptation to these outside influences, the long-term survival of the organization could be at stake.

## Closed System

Organizations that function as a *closed system* emphasize only the interrelationships among the various internal components, while the interaction with the external environment is largely ignored. The organization essentially becomes an island to itself. A closed system typically focuses on procedures for monitoring outputs, comparison of outputs with preset standards, evaluation of discrepancies between actual outputs and preset standards, and mechanisms for taking action to rectify negative variances between actual outputs and preset standards (Brown, 1977). Closed-system management is essentially focused on organizational structures, productivity, effectiveness, cost control, profitability, and quality. In a closed system, administrative energies are directly solely toward making the various departments of a nursing facility work together cohesively, support each other, and develop processes to improve quality and efficiency. Clearly, management must focus on improving the internal operations. However, even though these aspects of management are extremely important, a closed-system functions as a self-contained entity in which management does not have specific plans to steer the operations to satisfy external demands. Valuable resources and management efforts can actually be wasted if internal operational improvements are not directed toward satisfying external demands. No matter how efficient the internal systems of an organization may become, without the open-system approach a nursing facility will stagnate and eventually lose any competitive advantage it may have once enjoyed.

## Open System

According to the open-system theory, organizations are viewed as living entities that exist within, and are part of, a larger environment. An *open system* approach to management recognizes the effects of external factors and views internal operations in relation to changes in the external environment. The open-system approach is based on the premise that "no organization can survive for long if it ignores government regulations, supplier relations, or the myriad external constituencies upon which the organization depends" (Robbins, 2000, p. 606).

The open-system approach is necessary because organizations do not function in a stable and predictable environment. External forces impose new demands, compelling the organization to respond, conform, adapt, and innovate. Internal operations must be evaluated in terms of the new demands, and strategies must be crafted to meet new challenges or to take advantage of new opportunities. Appropriate responses to external demands result in interactions that can benefit the organization as well as the constituencies the organization serves. Hence, long-term care (LTC) administrators who understand and are attuned to external factors and their potential effect on the organizations they manage are likely to outperform those who do not pay attention to the changes or do not grasp their implications for the facility. Open-system theory suggests that an organization's interface with its external environment should be viewed as an exchange relationship—a give-and-take relationship—between the organization and its environment.

## Stakeholders

An organization benefits from its relationship with certain constituencies called stakeholders. A *stakeholder* can be any constituent group that has an interest in what a nursing facility stands for and what outcomes it produces. Administrators of successful LTC organizations view the stakeholders as exchange partners. A critical stakeholder is the community at large from which the organization derives clients and major resources such as associates (i.e., staff members) who provide services to the organization's clients.

Dill (1958) identified four main constituents in the environment that are particularly relevant for organizational goal setting and goal attainment:

- Clients.
- Suppliers of labor, materials, capital, etc.
- Competitors for both markets and resources.
- Regulators.

Patients and their families as clients become the most important stakeholders. They are the organization's primary exchange partners. Expectations of LTC clients differ considerably from those in other health care delivery settings. Long-term care clients are not looking for medical cures. Above all, they expect a safe and comfortable environment, preservation of privacy and dignity, timely delivery of individualized services, coordination of total care, and prevention of undue complications that can arise from the patients' chronic conditions.

Next to clients, the employed associates as service providers are the second most important exchange partners. Because of the nature of LTC in which care delivery involves a long period of time, clients and caregivers often form special bonds. The associates should also recognize that the client–associate relationship is built on effective delivery of services on which the long-term success of both the associates and their organizations depends. As employees of the organization, associates expect fairness in work assignments and compensation, respect from supervisors, a safe and enjoyable work environment, opportunities for professional development, and recognition for their contributions to the organization.

A variety of secondary exchange partners include various other health care providers such as hospitals, physicians, rehabilitation service providers, imaging and laboratory services, home health agencies, and other LTC facilities. These stakeholders play a critical role in enabling a nursing facility to obtain services that it does not provide. Competition from other LTC providers promotes innovation and improves quality. Exchange relationships with vendors of medical supplies, equipment, food, cleaning supplies, etc., help ensure that products meet specified quality standards, are delivered in a timely manner, and are competitively priced. Government regulatory agencies are primarily interested in ensuring that nursing facilities comply with established regulatory standards. The community at large expects the LTC facility to conduct its business in accordance with the highest standards of ethical behavior. It also expects the facility to be a socially responsible citizen and provide certain benefits to the community.

## Role of Governance

Strong governance is essential for open-system management. ***Governance***, or governing, refers to trusteeship and stewardship of an organization's resources and capabilities to benefit its stakeholders. It implies that an organization's resources—both material and intangible resources such as knowledge and skills of its staff—are to be used primarily for carrying out stakeholder wishes as effectively as possible.

Nursing homes are required by law to have a ***governing body***, which is also referred to as the board of directors, board of trustees, or simply "board," for short. The board bears ultimate authority and accountability for the organization's affairs (Pointer & Orlikoff, 2002). From the open-system perspective, the governing body has two main responsibilities:

1. Defining the nursing facility's mission in the community.
2. Providing direction and authorizing resources so that the facility can develop and maintain exchange partnerships. One critical resource the board must authorize is funds in the annual budget that are specifically earmarked for exchange relationships.

In many nursing home organizations, the open-system approach is either nonexistent or assigned a back seat with only "lip service" given to recognizing the importance of stakeholders and engaging in forming exchange partnerships. This is a symptom of ineffective governance. Governance should be a shared responsibility between the administrator and the facility's governing body. This is because the administrator has a better understanding of the local community and is in a better position to form exchange relationships with local stakeholders. The governing body, on the other hand, is in a better position to do the same at the state and national levels.

## Cycle of Exchanges

The relationship between an organization and its environment goes through a complete cycle of exchanges, which has four identifiable phases, as illustrated in Figure 4–1. The cycle of exchanges gives an overview of the exchange relationships that occur between the facility and its key stakeholders.

### Resource Inputs

At the receiving end, the organization obtains from its environment various inputs in the form of resources such as a license to operate the facility, federal certification, human resources, capital financing, supplies and equipment, technology, fire and police protection, and complementary services needed by the organization's clients. These basic inputs are critical to a LTC facility's ability to deliver appropriate levels of patient care. An organization that is capable of pulling resources from its environment remains dynamic. Over time, it builds internal strengths that enable it to attract clients, serve them

**Figure 4–1** Organizational Interface with the External Environment

well, improve profitability, and develop its associates. Such an organization gains a certain momentum, enabling it to meet new challenges and profit from new opportunities when other organizations may remain inert and suffer from atrophy.

## Clients and Payments

The nursing facility must attract clients who will benefit from the services provided by the organization. Clients establish the primary exchange whereby the organization produces services: clients receive services tailored to meet their individual needs, and the facility gets paid for the services it has rendered. This exchange relationship among the facility, its clients, and payers generates revenues that make an indispensable contribution to a nursing facility's profitability.

## Production of Outputs

As they deliver services to clients, nursing care organizations transform the resources

obtained from the environment into critical outputs such as clinical quality, client satisfaction, staff loyalty, and profits. Effectiveness and consistency in producing these outputs determine the long-range success of a nursing facility.

## Returns to the Environment

At the giving end, organizations provide jobs, pay taxes, contribute to cost-efficiency within the health care system by actively competing in the marketplace, engage in community outreach by providing education and information, and positively influence a community's health and well-being. Thus, the organization creates external benefits through what it produces and returns to the environment. Finally, the cycle is completed as external agencies take into account a facility's outputs and benefits returned to the community when the facility needs resources to sustain its operations. A facility's ability to attract desirable resource inputs is often conditional upon its outputs and contributions to the environment. For example, an LTC facility that produces poor-quality outputs will find it difficult to attract the most qualified associates, a key resource the facility must obtain from the external environment. Such a facility is also likely to face difficulties attracting clients. Other health care providers, such as hospitals and physicians, may stop referring their patients. In extreme cases, the facility may risk losing its license and certification, which may put it out of business. An organization builds its reputation and image on the basis of what it delivers to the environment. When a facility fails to meet community expectations, it jeopardizes its prospects for attracting quality resource inputs and further weakens its ability to stay competitive.

## Open-System and Strategic Management

There is an inextricable link between the open-system approach and strategic management. The terms **strategy** and *strategic planning* refer to major decisions that an organization's top managers must periodically make to steer the organization in a direction that is in response to changes in the external environment. Strategic plans are driven by an understanding of the needs, expectations, and demands placed on the organizations by the external environment. The main purpose of strategy is to ensure that any changes in the internal operations of the organization are in harmony with the expectations of external stakeholders.

When a nursing facility administrator adopts the open-system approach to management, he or she will monitor changes in the environment, decide on the type of strategic response that would be in the organization's best interest according to organizational mission and values, plan a course of action, and carry out the plan. Using various formal and informal processes to identify significant trends and events on an ongoing basis is called **environmental scanning**. A formal analysis and evaluation of environmental trends to understand their potential implications for a facility's long-term success is called **environmental assessment**. This is the most important step in strategic management because adoption of strategic plans is costly and risky. A wrong decision can waste resources and jeopardize the operations.

Periodically, all health facility administrators must confront external threats, take action to meet new environmental challenges, or take advantage of some opportunity to gain market share. For example, when new competition enters the market, new regulations take effect, or payment methods are changed, the facility must be prepared to address these challenges. On the other hand, opportunities can emerge when a nursing home administrator is able to identify an unserved LTC need in the community or when a home health agency closes its doors.

To pursue opportunities or to confront threats, the organization needs to have internal strengths in leadership, human resources, finance, quality, and marketing. Therefore, an honest assessment of the organization's strengths and weaknesses is important.

Conceptually, strategic planning requires management to evaluate external opportunities and threats against the organization's internal strengths and weaknesses. The model commonly used to help such an analysis is referred to as the SWOT analysis. The acronym SWOT (or TOWS) stands for strengths, weaknesses, opportunities, and threats (Figure 4–2).

**Figure 4–2** The SWOT Matrix

|  | **Strengths** | **Weaknesses** |
|---|---|---|
| **Opportunities** | Pursue opportunities | Fix internal operations |
| **Threats** | Confront threats | Explore retrenchment |

Strategic management requires a high level of conceptual skills. It requires administrators to be active in their local communities, exchange ideas with managers in other health care organizations, and actively participate in professional associations representing the LTC industry to understand changes that may affect the organization or the industry. Figure 4–3 gives an overview of the strategic planning process and includes examples of strategic plans.

**Figure 4–3** Strategic Planning Process

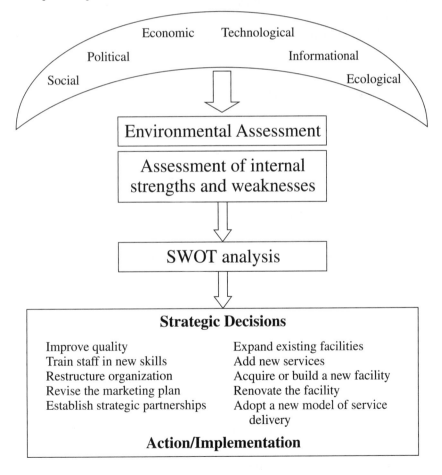

## Understanding the Environment

Environmental scanning and assessment activities are greatly facilitated by a conceptual model that classifies the macroenvironment of an LTC facility into six main domains: social, political, economic, technological, informational, and ecological (Figure 4–4). Forces in these domains have varying degrees of influence on an entire industry and its member organizations. The nursing home industry is no exception. Over time, the LTC industry in the United States has been shaped by such factors as innovations in medical care and technology, government regulations, national health policy, consumer advocacy groups, people's attitudes and commitments at work and home,

and changes in consumers' expectations. Such external influences will continue to pressure the industry to change. While broad forces influence the whole industry, individual LTC facilities are affected by their local environment. Examples include market competition, shifts in local demographics, and makeup of the labor force in the area.

### Environmental Domains

#### Social Factors

Social factors include demographic trends, social change, cultural factors, and lifestyle preferences. The demand for LTC and the type of services are influenced by changes in the population's demographic composition,

**Figure 4–4** Environmental Influences in the Primary and Secondary Proximities of an Organization

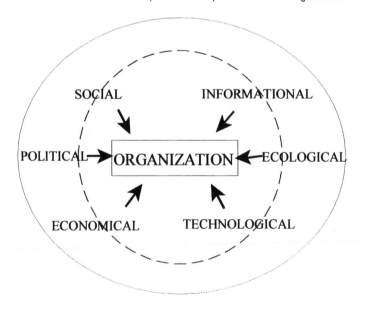

_ _ _ _        Primary Proximity (local community and county)

──────        Secondary Proximity (state and national)

such as age, gender, and prevalence of disability. Greater longevity has given rise to the "sandwich generation" of middle-aged families who must take responsibility for their teenage and college-age children on the one hand and for elderly parents on the other. An increasing number of women in the workforce implies that married couples may need formal help to care for their elderly parents. Strong family and social support enables people with disabilities to continue to live independently. Other trends, such as job mobility, often require making appropriate arrangements for the elderly parents who are left behind as close family members move away. Migration of retired people to areas of the country that offer a more temperate climate has important implications for the development of LTC services in those areas. Lifestyle preferences of baby boomers are giving rise to a new demand for nursing care settings that emphasize personal independence and lifestyle choices. Consequently, a growing movement of culture change in nursing homes (discussed in Chapter 8) is gaining momentum.

## Political Factors

The policy agenda that sets priorities for political action, tax policy, the appropriation of tax dollars to various programs, and laws and regulations have a tremendous impact on the management of LTC facilities. For instance, high corporate taxes chip away profit margins in for-profit businesses. Federal and state funding appropriations for the Medicare and Medicaid programs determine how much nursing facilities will get paid for serving patients covered by these programs. New sources of funding give rise to new sectors within the LTC industry. New laws and regulations demand compliance, which often requires changing the ways things were done

before. The political clout of the LTC industry can influence how state and federal funds are appropriated or how the industry is regulated. Administrators can participate in the political process by establishing contacts with their state and federal representatives, by voicing their opinions, and by becoming members of professional associations representing their interests.

## Economic Factors

Economic growth or recession, industrial development, and unemployment create demographic shifts that can bring people into an area or make them leave. Economic factors may also dictate whether people can afford to pay for LTC, especially when public financing does not cover certain services. Changes in the labor market affect the availability of skilled workers and hence a facility's ability to recruit qualified associates. Tight labor markets, for example, make it easier to recruit nursing assistants, cooks, and housekeepers because those workers have difficulty finding jobs in restaurants, hotels, motels, and other low-skilled service industries in tough times. The job market also governs wages and benefits necessary to attract and retain qualified associates. Competition from other facilities, and from substitute services such as home health care, presents challenges that nursing home administrators must not ignore. Other major economic events, such as the growth of managed care since the late 1980s, have an enormous impact on every aspect of health care delivery, including long-term care.

## Technological Factors

Technological innovation in medical sciences will continue to revolutionize health care. It also has social implications as people live longer and healthier lives and as the elderly seek more independent lifestyles. Technology has enabled many individuals to receive LTC services in less restrictive or noninstitutional settings instead of getting that care in traditional nursing homes. Home health care, for instance, is not only a cheaper alternative to nursing homes but is also preferred by clients when services such as intravenous antibiotics, oncology therapy, hemodialysis, and parenteral and enteral nutrition can be provided by home health agencies. On the other hand, technology has enabled nursing care facilities to provide specialized services and has allowed these facilities to care for acutely ill patients who previously could receive such services only in a hospital. Examples include AIDS care, ventilator care, head trauma services, and post-orthopedic rehabilitation.

## Informational Factors

Computer-based information systems and the Internet have numerous applications. Adoption of information technology (IT) is changing many of the processes of health care delivery. IT has become indispensable for managing today's health care organizations. As discussed in Chapter 3, areas of application where IT has made a positive difference include clinical records, patient assessment and care planning, patient care protocols, inventory management, data collection and analysis, advertising, and computer support systems for both clinical and management decision making. The proliferation of electronic health records will make it necessary for nursing homes to adopt them in the near future. The Internet has also opened access to a barrage of information for practitioners and consumers alike.

## Ecological Factors

New infections and diseases, as well as a carry-over of certain medical conditions into older populations, will affect LTC delivery. The potential of infections from the human immunodeficiency virus (HIV) and hepatitis C virus have shown the need for staff training in precautionary measures and practice of stringent infection-control procedures in nursing facilities. Also, new treatments have delayed the onset of acquired immune deficiency syndrome (AIDS). As people infected with HIV live longer, AIDS is likely to become more prevalent among older people. People with developmental disabilities are also living longer and need specialized care. Other ecological factors such as natural disasters (earthquakes, floods, hurricanes, snowstorms, tornadoes, etc.) require that facilities develop adequate plans and prepare for unforeseen eventualities, particularly if they are located in areas that may be prone to such events. The possibility of bioterrorism has raised new concerns for patient safety. It also requires that health care facilities work in close collaboration with local civil defense and public health agencies to address potential threats.

## Environmental Proximity

Environmental proximity is a concept that helps one understand how closely certain influences surround the organization. An organization's relationship to its environment and the degree of control it may have over environmental issues is often governed by proximity. For instance, a facility administrator generally has much more control over managing relationships with the local hospital than he or she does over state or national policy that affects nursing home regulations and reimbursement. The methods of environmental scanning, the nature of exchange relationships, the administrator's role in addressing environmental demands, and the type of strategic plans will be governed by the proximity.

First, in rather broad terms, we can think of primary and secondary proximities (Figure 4–4). The primary proximity is closer to the organization, and the six environmental domains operate in a local environment such as the community, which can be a neighborhood, a local district, or an entire metropolitan area. In other instances, such as facilities serving rural areas, an entire county would constitute the primary proximity. The secondary proximity consists of environmental domains operating at the state and national levels. Primary proximity offers the administrator opportunities for direct involvement in the community, it helps identify local agencies with which exchange relationships should be established, it creates heightened expectations for the organization's social re-

sponsibility toward the community, and it influences the market's competitiveness.

Another way to illustrate the interplay of external factors is through four proximal levels shown in Figure 4–5. In this four-level model, the first three levels comprise the primary proximity; the fourth level forms the secondary proximity.

## Level 1 Proximity

The most proximal influence surrounding a nursing home is other similar facilities and substitute services that directly or indirectly compete against the organization. **Substitute services** are other LTC options that clients may choose from. For example, home health can be a substitute for institutional care. Three-fourths of all elderly patients receiving home health care require nursing services, and almost 30% need physical therapy (U.S. Bureau of the Census, 2003). These same services are also provided by nursing care facilities. Competition is generally viewed as a threat, but it may also drive the

**Figure 4–5** Four Levels of Environmental Proximity

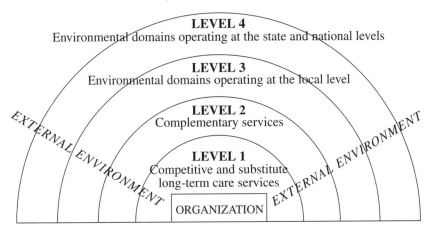

organization to innovate and expand its range of services. For example, a nursing home may open an outpatient rehabilitation center or expand into delivering home health care. Well-thought-out strategic plans can maintain or enhance a facility's competitive advantage.

## Level 2 Proximity

Level 2 proximity includes a wide variety of *complementary services*. These are services that are not directly rendered by the facility in which the patient resides but that are necessary to address the total health care needs of a patient. As pointed out in Chapter 1, a nursing home must assume responsibility for the total care of all patients. When evaluation and treatment of a health condition are beyond the nursing home's scope of services, a timely referral to an outside provider is necessary. For example, a skilled care facility is not a mental health institution. It must, however, recognize mental health needs when they arise and coordinate the delivery of appropriate mental health care. In some cases, it may be necessary to move a patient temporarily to an acute care hospital. In other instances, a patient may need to be referred to a dentist, optometrist, or podiatrist.

Community outreach efforts, marketing decisions, and liaisons with complementary service providers that would facilitate ready access to services needed by a facility's patients can only be undertaken with a keen understanding of the level 2 proximity. Administrators must forge meaningful relationships with external providers with the goal of establishing a two-way patient referral system. Skilled nursing facilities can also make informal agreements with retirement centers, assisted living facilities, and home health agencies to transfer patients among them to accommodate the changing needs of their clients.

## Level 3 Proximity

At level 3, we can think of environmental factors that operate in a facility's primary proximity. These are local environmental factors and various community and civil services that are not directly associated with health care delivery. Examples include the local economy, demographic shifts in the county, local job conditions, local ordinances, and local police and fire protection services.

## Level 4 Proximity

Level 4 environmental factors affect the nursing home industry at the state and national levels. But, in many instances, these changes also affect local nursing homes. Examples are changes in the government's payment methods for patients on public assistance, changes in rules and regulations, reports on nursing homes by state or national media, and major industry trends that may eventually become more localized (such as the spread of managed care or growth of substitute services). These influences often shape decisions that administrators must make. Administrative decisions in response to state or national influences often have long-range consequences for the nursing facility, and the type of response is generally quite different from what would be appropriate for the previous three levels of proximity. The first three levels of proximity primarily call for establishing community exchanges and involvement and for adapting facility services to meet local needs. Level 4 proximity generally requires changes in internal operations to respond to broader issues. Level 4 proximity also requires active participation in the professional and trade associations that represent the industry. Some of the major long-term care associations include the American Health Care Association (AHCA), the American Association of Homes and Services for the Aging (AAHSA), the Assisted Living Federation of America (ALFA), and the American College of Health Care Administrators (ACHCA). These organizations closely follow major economic and political developments, and they keep their members informed about these developments. These organizations maintain active lobbying efforts at the state and national levels in order to influence LTC policy. From time to time, they also engage in mobilizing grassroots campaigns by directing their members to contact their elected representatives and to educate those representatives about specific nursing home issues.

# Building Exchange Relationships

## A Systems Model of Value Exchanges

Exchange relationships are founded on value received by each partner in the exchange. Conceptually, an organization creates value when it produces benefits that exceed, or at least equal, the inputs brought by outsiders into the input-output exchange relationships illustrated in Figure 4–1. More generally, value is perceived when a party expects to receive more than it gives up in an exchange. Miller (1986) argued that seeking any value-based objectives by an organization requires some sacrifice or paying a price. If the organization desires value but is not committed to paying the price, then the value is no more than a wish. A facility's long-range commitment requires paying a price that is set aside in the annual budget. In addition, time commitments by the administrator and key nursing home personnel are required. Conversely, a facility may eventually pay a price through the erosion of its standing in the community if it does not make sacrifices to build community partnerships.

A systems model built on value exchanges (Figure 4–6) is a basic operating model that governs a total pattern of values received, generated, and distributed through the facility's ongoing relationships with its clients and stakeholders. Allee (2000) has called such a pattern of value exchanges a "value network," which can be applied to almost any type of organization. The values flowing mainly to primary exchange partners—patients and family members—can be regarded as primary service values, which are generated by building and managing the delivery of LTC services (covered in Part III of the book) and by managing these resources effectively (covered in Part IV of the book). Clients assess the value received through clinical outcomes and their satisfaction with the services. Values return from clients to the nursing facility in the form of revenue and increased profitability. However, there are also intangible benefits that go beyond those accounted for in traditional financial measures (Allee, 2000). For example, satisfaction with services builds customer loyalty. The facility benefits from word-of-mouth marketing when satisfied clients say positive things about the facility to people they know. Caregivers obtain personal gratification (psychic wage) and find their jobs more satisfying when they receive positive feedback from clients. Some loyal family members choose to become volunteers for the facility and serve in areas that enrich the lives of residents. Over time, the facility's enhanced image can produce immeasurable benefits for all major stakeholders in the value network.

**Figure 4–6** Systems Model of Value Exchanges

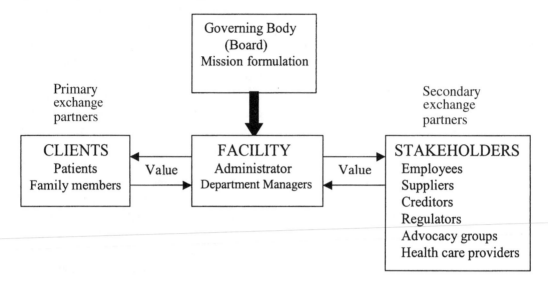

The relationship between the facility and its secondary exchange partners is also interdependent because value can be exchanged with mutual advantage to each individual partner. The entire system must be maintained in equilibrium (homeostasis) through management decisions and actions.

## Mission-Driven Partnerships

Although a facility's primary mission is to provide appropriate LTC services to members of the community who need those services, its role in the community extends beyond that. In accordance with the facility's formal mission, the administrator must also set up other types of exchanges and partnerships with the community. This broader mission is driven by the facility's social accountability to the community that is met by engaging in various activities to benefit the community. That establishing such partnerships is in the facility's own best interest should be evident from the open-system model discussed earlier. But, the question arises, "What kind of partnerships should the facility establish?"

## Premises for Partnership

Four main partnering principles can help guide the administrator in establishing appropriate community relationships:

- Become a community resource for long-term care.
- Form linkages along the continuum of health care services.
- Establish value-based partnerships.
- Build trust and commitment.

### Becoming a Community Resource for Long-Term Care

Allee (2000) considers knowledge to be an important medium of exchange in a value network. Every LTC administrator can find some avenue by which the facility can become a valuable resource because most facilities have expertise in caring for the elderly. A facility can garner expertise by hiring, retaining, and training the most qualified professionals in key positions and by forming alliances with well-positioned professionals in the community. A six-point plan for community outreach is presented in Exhibit 4–1.

The effective LTC administrator constantly evaluates what expert resources the facility possesses, how the existing resources can be enhanced and supplemented as necessary, and how they can be deployed to benefit the community. Depending on the extent of its planned outreach, the facility can establish partnerships with numerous agencies such as hospitals, physicians, local Area Agencies on Aging, local chapters of organizations such as the American Cancer Society, insurance and managed care organizations, etc. The following list of examples will help administrators recognize various opportunities for the facility to become an active community resource:

- Participation in community health fairs or a fair held at the facility.
- Blood pressure and blood sugar screenings for community residents.
- Seminars on caring for chronically disabled family members at home.
- Seminars on using adaptive equipment at home.

**Exhibit 4–1** Six-point Outreach Plan

1. Inventory current resources and level of expertise.
2. Begin small programs using existing resources.
3. Evaluate success.
4. Plan programs for further outreach.
5. Establish partnerships with appropriate external agencies. Evaluate the need for staff training.
6. Implement. Evaluate. Modify as necessary.

- Seminars on creating safe home environments.
- Support groups for dementia-related problems.
- Support groups on handling personal guilt and anxiety associated with institutional placement.
- Educational seminars on nutritional needs of the elderly.
- Educational seminars on Medicare, Medicaid, and private long-term care insurance.
- Information on managed care and its role in long-term care delivery.
- Information on the role of long-term care ombudsmen.
- Information on respite care.
- Fund-raising events for nonprofit groups or foundations.
- Fund-raising events for local charity.
- Other events to benefit the community.

Sharing expertise with the community is a goodwill gesture. In almost all instances, the programs should be offered free to the public, except to cover the cost of any materials the facility may provide to the participants. Light refreshments are often served to promote social bonding. By sponsoring such programs, the facility creates name recognition for itself and builds a positive image. Many of these events also allow the public to visit the facility and see the premises first-hand.

## Forming Linkages along the Continuum of Health Care Services

Partnerships can be established with the various LTC and non-LTC service sectors. Such linkages also rationally integrate the system to best address patient needs.

### Linking with the Informal System

Some of the community exchanges discussed earlier help establish linkages with the informal sector of long-term care. Informal caregivers often need support and assistance with their personal stress and burnout. Many are seeking answers on how to cope with parents or relatives who suffer from memory loss, depression, behavioral episodes, or incontinence. Although the facility establishes such exchanges with no expectation of immediate returns, over time the partnerships become inconspicuous sources of patient referral. The facilities that have forged effective community relationships over time stand a better chance of attracting new clients than competitors who have not forged such relationships. As Figure 4–7 shows, roughly 30% of all new admissions to nursing homes come from private residences.

### Linking across the Long-Term Care Continuum

Different types of linkages can be formed with the formal LTC sector for participating in the continuum of services. Examples include becoming a food preparation center for the local Meals On Wheels program, developing an adult day care center or participating in one at another site, establishing partnerships with retirement homes or personal care homes to lend expert assistance to their residents when needed, and formalizing transfer arrangements with these institutions to best accommodate the changing needs of their residents.

### Linking with Advocacy Agencies

An often-overlooked area for meaningful exchanges is the local Area Agency on Aging and the ombudsman. Area Agencies on Aging were established in local communities under the 1973 amendments to the federal Older Americans Act of 1965 to address the needs of Americans aged 60 and over. Among other services, these agencies assess clients' needs and determine eligibility for services best suited to meet their needs. Amendments to the Older Americans Act in 1978 mandated that each state have an ombudsman program,

**Figure 4–7** Living Quarters Before Nursing Home Admission for People 65 Years Old and Over

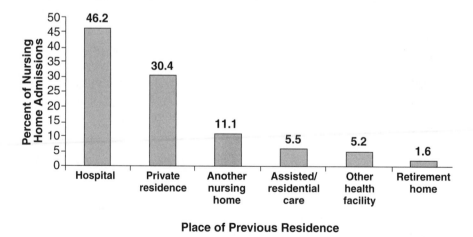

Place of Previous Residence

*Source:* Data from *Statistical Abstract of the United States: 2003,* p. 129 U.S. Census Bureau (Based on the 1999 National Nursing Home

which is administered by the Agencies on Aging. An *ombudsman* is a trained professional who works independently with nursing home residents and their families to resolve concerns they may have about their lives in a facility. As an advocate for residents of nursing homes, board-and-care homes, and assisted living facilities, the ombudsman investigates and resolves complaints on behalf of facility residents and informs consumers on how to obtain quality care. For instance, an ombudsman helps educate the public and facility staff on complaint filing, new laws governing facilities, and the best practices used in improving quality of care and evaluating LTC options (IOM, 2001). The ombudsman also informs public agencies about the problems of older adults residing in nursing facilities. A facility can form positive working relationships with its local ombudsman by inviting him or her to the facility for the purpose of giving the ombudsman a first-hand overview of the facility's amenities, its social and cultural atmosphere, the services provided, and how the residents are taken care of. The ombudsman may also be given periodic involvement, as an external resource, in the facility's resident council and family-council programs.

**Linking with the Non-Long-Term Sector**
The non-LTC sector is complementary to long-term care. Complementary services enable an LTC facility to address the total care needs of a patient. Therefore, it is incumbent upon the facility administrator to establish linkages with community physicians and hospitals. Physicians often struggle with questions from family members about nursing home placement. They may or may not be inclined to make a direct recommendation but are likely to suggest two or three facilities for a family member to check out before making

a decision. Hospital discharge planners may also find themselves in similar situations where family members may depend on them for suggestions. Also, some communities have a shortage of nursing home beds, and hospitals often struggle to find LTC beds at short notice. At a minimum, a facility's relationship with the hospitals would include a daily or periodic phone call or e-mail message updating the discharge planners on the availability of beds.

Savvy nursing facility administrators are also working with acute care providers, positioning themselves to meet the needs of managed care organizations looking for high-quality, low-cost health care. Beck (1996) recommended three different ways (discussed in Chapter 7) in which hospitals and nursing facilities can establish partnerships: through sponsorship agreements, bed reserve arrangements, or shared service agreements.

*Establishing Value-Based Partnerships*

Value-based exchanges between any two or more entities require win–win opportunities for the parties to the exchange. All too often, facility administrators focus only on how to get more patients to fill empty beds. Such thinking is short sighted because the administrator seeks to benefit only the facility and often exhibits little regard for what is in the patient's best interest. The first type of exchange discussed earlier—in which the facility becomes a community resource for LTC and provides helpful services to the community—may appear to be a one-sided exchange that benefits only the community. In the long run, however, such exchanges often benefit the facility as well. Administrators who have established ongoing exchanges with the community generally have little reason to worry about future patient referrals to the facility.

Partnerships with the formal LTC sector and with the non-LTC sector are also based on the mutual-value concept. A win–win situation adds value for all partners, so value is potentially lost when the same exchange relationship is not formed. Added value also benefits the patients. For example, collaboration between a nursing home and hospice adds value because research documents superior outcomes for residents who enroll in hospice for end-of-life care (Miller & Mor, 2002). One in four Americans who reach the age of 65 will probably spend their last days in a nursing home (Hanson et al., 2002); thus, linking nursing home and hospice services can deliver added value to patients. Value creation in LTC is often founded on such patient service initiatives.

The implication of value-added partnerships for administrators is that they need to think about how a potential exchange relationship can add value for the other partner and for the patients. What each party will put into the exchange and the potential benefits to be derived should be openly discussed in order for such exchanges to materialize. A simple question the other party will ask itself is, "What is in it for my agency?" Before they agree to formalize any relationships, the other parties have to be convinced that "there is something in it for them." This type of a value-based proposition can be called win–win. For example, nursing facilities depend on the local police and fire services for emergency situations. These civil agencies in turn benefit when the facility takes adequate preparatory steps to safeguard its property, residents, and staff against possible eventualities. On the other hand, potential future rewards are often accompanied by certain risks. Partnerships are built on an open discussion of possible risks and rewards and a willingness to share both.

One caveat must be kept in mind while building partnerships. The facility must refrain from any activities that may be interpreted as payment for referral of patients. Anti-kickback legislation (discussed in Chapter 7) makes it illegal to knowingly and willfully offer, pay, solicit, or receive remuneration to induce referrals for which payment may be made by Medicare or Medicaid, the two major public financing programs that pay for nursing home services.

## Building Trust and Commitment

Trust is built over time in an environment of mutual understanding and respect. It requires open and frequent communication, congruent goals and objectives, and joint problem solving (Kaluzny & Zuckerman, 1999). A win–win proposition is the first step toward building trust, but it requires a long-range strategy driven by commitment, continuity, and consistency, the "3 Cs" that are indispensable for sustaining partnerships over time.

1. *Commitment* requires three things:

   a. Determining where the greatest needs are. Evaluate the expertise the facility is able to provide and decide on programs that will optimize mutual benefits for the community, other exchange partners, and the facility.

   b. Funding appropriate expenditures in the annual budget to carry out the community-oriented programs. The budget may also require salary appropriations for a full-time or part-time staff position responsible for coordinating the programs and getting the word out into the community. Large nursing facilities, for example, may employ a marketing director who will shoulder the major coordinating and follow-up responsibilities.

c. Time commitments by the administrator and key managers. Besides the administrator who will have the primary responsibility for building and sustaining exchange partnerships, the facility's key departmental managers (such as the social worker, the director of nursing, and activity director) may also have some external involvement within their respective areas of responsibility. For example, the social worker has to work closely with the discharge planner at the local hospital, the director of nursing maintains contact with community physicians, and the activity director establishes liaisons with community volunteers and social organizations such as churches and schools. By building a professional team through coaching and support, eventually the administrator can rely on subordinate members of the team to carry out most routine engagements and community contacts.

2. *Continuity* is based on long-range commitment. It also requires time commitments to manage the relationship on an ongoing basis and to handle details as they arise. The administrator needs to be involved in monitoring and nurturing the relationships through periodic contact.

3. Once a facility has made the commitment to engage in goodwill exchanges, they must be carried out with *consistency*. Occasional exchanges do not form sustainable relationships. Consistency is based on written policies that are used as a basis for understanding between two parties. Written policies also provide continuity despite turnover of administrators or key staff members. These policies must be incorporated in the training and orientation of new associates.

Once trust is established, community stakeholders can be the facility's "eyes and ears." They can be included in discussions for improving existing services and in strategic decisions such as adding a new service or, if necessary, discontinuing an existing program.

A community advisory board consisting of key stakeholders can be instrumental in helping the facility fulfill its ongoing mission. A *community advisory board* is distinct from the main governing body. Unlike the governing body, the advisory board does not oversee facility operations or evaluate the administrator's performance. Composed of key community leaders, the advisory board functions as the "eyes and ears" for the facility. Through their influence, the advisory board members can also help the administrator form meaningful partnerships discussed in this section.

## Focus on Outputs

In completing the cycle of exchanges (Figure 4–1), the facility must focus on the efficient production of outputs. It is these outputs that enable a nursing care organization create and maintain meaningful exchanges.

## Facility Outputs as Key Ingredients

Long-term care facilities produce four major outputs:

- Care quality.
- Client satisfaction.
- Staff loyalty.
- Profits.

The first three—care quality, client satisfaction, and staff loyalty—are essential for creating the goodwill necessary to make the facility attractive to potential exchange partners. Once the exchange relationships have been established, they often function as powerful avenues through which the facility can market its services to the community. But for such marketing strategies to succeed, the facility must pay utmost attention to the first three outputs; they will become the determining factor in shaping the facility's reputation and image in the community. The fourth output, profits, provides the financial resources necessary for achieving the other three outputs. Profits also provide the means for funding the community-oriented programs carried out as a goodwill gesture by the facility when it functions as an expert resource on various LTC issues.

## Expectations from the Exchanges

At this point, the facility administrator may ask the question, "What is in it for my facility if I have to initiate all the exchanges?" The answer is, the facility generally realizes no direct and immediate reward. The establishment of exchange relationships should be viewed as an investment in the facility's future. Like any other investment, this is a long-range proposition. But, over a period of time, the facility can expect to gain some healthy indirect returns on the investment. The facility is dependent on the community to get patients who need its services. The exchanges established by the facility help build its reputation, not only among the general public but also among professional agencies that are part of the exchange. Whenever these agencies come across clients who need nursing home services, these entities will be more inclined to refer those clients to a facility that is in an exchange relationship with them than to one that is not. Creation of referral sources is one marketing strategy the facility can employ.

---

## For Further Thought

1. Is the open-system approach needed only when the organization faces challenges or tries to take advantage of emerging opportunities? Explain.

2. W.R. Dill identified four external constituents that are necessary for organizational goal achievement: (a) customers; (b) suppliers of labor, materials, capital, etc.; (c) competitors for both markets and resources; and (d) regulators. What contribution, if any, do each of these factors make in enhancing the organizational effectiveness of a nursing facility? What is the interrelationship among these four factors?

3. Both formal and informal processes can be employed to carry out environmental scanning. Discuss some of the formal and informal means that a nursing home administrator can employ to identify significant environmental trends.

4. Identify the various entities in a nursing facility's primary proximity. What influences might each have on the organization? Again, using the four-level model of proximities, discuss the influences various entities may have on a nursing facility.

## For Further Learning

Become familiar with the two main organizations that represent the nursing home industry:

American Health Care Association

    www.ahca.org

American Association of Homes and Services for the Aging

    www.aahsa.org

National Long Term Care Ombudsman Resource Center

    http://www.ltcombudsman.org/

## REFERENCES

Allee, V. 2000. Reconfiguring the value network. *Journal of Business Strategy* 21, no. 4: 36–39.

Beck, D.C. 1996. Partnerships may tame subacute rivalry. *Contemporary Long-Term Care* 19, no. 7: 72.

Brown, W.B. 1977. Systems theory, organizations, and management. In S. Levey and N.P. Loomba (eds.), *Long-Term Care Administration: A Managerial Perspective*, Vol. I. New York: Spectrum Publications.

Dill, W.R. 1958. Environment as an influence on managerial autonomy. *Administrative Science Quarterly* 2: 409–443.

Hanson, L.C., et al. 2002. As individual as death itself: A focus group study of terminal care in nursing homes. *Journal of Palliative Medicine* 5, no. 1: 117–125.

IOM. 2001. *Improving the Quality of Long-Term Care*, eds. G.S. Wunderlich and P.O. Kohler. Washington, DC: National Academy Press, Institute of Medicine.

Kaluzny, A.D., & Zuckerman, H.S. 1999. Alliances in a changing industry. In R.W. Gilkey (ed.), *The 21st Century Health Care Leader* (pp. 149–157). San Francisco: Jossey-Bass Publishers.

Miller, R.L. 1986. Toward a more complete theory of objectives: A systems model of corporate value exchanges. *American Business Review* 4, no. 1: 1–13.

Miller, S.C., & Mor, V.N. 2002. The role of hospice care in the nursing home setting. *Journal of Palliative Medicine* 5, no. 2: 271–277.

Pointer, D.D., & Orlikoff, J.E. 2002. *Getting to Great: Principles of Health Care Organization Governance*. San Francisco: Jossey-Bass Publishers.

Robbins, S.P. 2000. *Managing Today*, 2nd ed. Upper Saddle River, NJ: Prentice Hall.

U.S. Bureau of the Census. 2003. *Statistical Abstract of the United States: 2003*. Washington, DC: U.S. Government Printing Office.

Von Bertalanffy, L. 1972. The history and status of general systems theory. *Academy of Management Journal* 15, no. 4: 407–427.

# Chapter 5

---

# Legal Environment

## What You Will Learn

- In general, laws serve a protective purpose. A wronged party can seek damages through litigation. Litigation against nursing homes has been on the rise.
- There are different ways of classifying laws. Nursing homes must comply with all applicable federal, state, and local laws and regulations.
- Civil law encompasses tort law and contract law. Malpractice falls under the broad umbrella of tort law. Certain tortious acts can result in punitive damages in addition to compensatory damages.
- There are circumstances in which criminal law applies to misconduct on the part of nursing home administrators and corporations.
- An offer and its acceptance and a stated consideration are the two main conditions that must be met for a contract to be legally enforceable.
- Nursing home administrators and other professionals can be held personally liable under certain conditions when negligent or intentional misconduct occurs.
- Corporations can be held liable for the tortious conduct of their employees under the doctrine of *respondeat superior*. Clear differentiation between an employee and a contractor is important. An agent is not held liable when acting within the scope of his or her authority.
- Three main types of ownership can be formed under corporate law. Type of ownership has tax and other implications.
- All nursing facilities must be licensed to legally conduct business. Certification and accreditation are voluntary, but most nursing homes are certified to admit patients covered under public assistance programs.

- Patient rights, advance directives, and patient privacy under the Health Insurance Portability and Accountability Act (HIPAA) are vital areas for nursing home administrators to understand. The facility must have privacy policies and enforce procedures required under HIPAA.

The legal environment is vast and complex. The purpose of this chapter is to provide basic legal knowledge necessary for day-to-day management of nursing care facilities. When issues arise that could have potentially substantial legal ramifications, the administrator should have access to expert legal counsel. Large multi-facility corporations generally have their own corporate attorneys. Small corporations and independent facilities should engage a reputable law firm to help the administrator deal with legal and regulatory issues when they crop up. A basic understanding of the law to prevent potential legal actions and seeking legal counsel before minor issues turn into major problems are vital elements of effective management.

## Purpose of Laws

As Chapter 2 amply illustrated, public policy is often formulated and carried out through laws. This is because laws provide a basic mechanism to ensure the enforcement of public policy. Hence, laws are intended to safeguard a society's best interests. An organized society formulates laws to prescribe rules of conduct that are enforced by public authority under threat of punishment for violating the laws. In business transactions, laws and regulations serve a protective purpose. They are designed to protect all parties involved. For instance, laws have been written to protect businesses, agencies, and individuals that may

have business dealings with an organization. Laws protect the employees working for an organization, the clients receiving services from the organization, suppliers furnishing goods and services to the organization, and the community in which the organization conducts business. Further, the organization itself is protected against illegal activities of others. Finally, in a free society, private organizations are also protected against unlawful government action. Like other organizations, health care providers can use laws to protect their own interests. For example, in some states, nursing homes have sued to stop proposed cuts in payment from government sources.

## Nursing Home Litigation

*Litigation* is legal action brought before a court of law. Litigation involves two main parties. A *plaintiff* is one who brings legal action by filing a complaint with a court to seek damages or other legal remedies. The other party is called a *defendant*, against whom a lawsuit is brought.

By seeking legal redress against a nursing home, the plaintiff wishes to obtain compensation for pain and suffering or death. Legal action may also get the public's attention through media reports. The main drawback of litigation as a method of nursing home oversight is that it provides remedies for harm that has already occurred. It may, however, be effective in changing management's future behavior and may prevent harm to others. Another downside of litigation is that it increases health care costs.

Nursing home malpractice has become an area ripe for litigation. During the 1990s, the nursing home industry became the fastest growing area of litigation in health care, and the pace of litigation has picked up (Stevenson & Studdert, 2003). Nursing home litigation has become a major area of practice for many law firms. Attorney Charles Huber (2006) gave three main reasons for increased nursing home litigation:

1. Parents of baby boomers are reaching the age when they may need nursing home care. Compared with previous generations, the baby boomers appear to be more litigious and have a greater sense of entitlement.

2. People who have to admit their loved ones to a nursing home often feel guilty for doing so. They may also have unreasonable expectations both in terms of the care provided and the potential outcomes. This is also the mindset of many jurors.

3. Physicians contribute to the problem by taking a wait-and-see approach in communicating their prognoses instead of clearly telling the family what is to be reasonably expected.

# Classifications of Laws

Laws can be classified in several different ways. Figure 5–1 provides a simple classification arrangement.

## Federal, State, and Local Laws

Laws are formulated at the federal, state, and local levels of government. Generally, federal laws supersede state and local laws. This is called *federal preemption*. Accordingly, states and local jurisdictions can enact and enforce only those laws that do not conflict with

**Figure 5–1** Classifications of Laws

| | |
|---|---|
| **By the level of government**<br>(level of government at which a law is formulated) | **Federal, state, and local laws** |
| **By the source of law**<br>(source from where the law is derived) | **Constitutional law**<br>**Statutory law**<br>**Administrative law**<br>**Common law** |
| **By the law's application**<br>(to whom it applies) | **Public law**<br>**Private law** |
| **By the nature of litigants**<br>(private parties or a private party v. the public) | **Civil law**<br>**Criminal law** |
| **By the type of wrong committed**<br>(a civil wrong or a breach of contract) | **Tort law**<br>**Contract law** |

federal law (Pozgar, 2002, p. 5). On the other hand, the United States is governed under the principle of *federalism*, which gives the states considerable power in matters of governance. Certain matters have been specifically delegated to the states. For example, states have the authority to regulate long-term care insurance, establish Medicaid reimbursement for nursing homes, and license health care facilities and personnel. In other areas, both federal and state laws may apply. For example, federal law requires the payment of a minimum wage to workers and specifies the hourly minimum wage. A state may establish its own minimum wage that is higher than the federal minimum wage. Laws passed by the local governments (counties, cities, and municipalities) are generally referred to as *ordinances*. For example, local zoning ordinances prescribe land use for commercial or residential purposes.

## Constitutional, Statutory, Administrative, and Common Law

The judicial system in the United States relies on four main sources of law: constitutional law, common law, statutory law, and administrative law. *Constitutional law* is based on the Constitution of the United States, which is the supreme law of the nation. The U.S. Constitution defines the structure and powers of government and the rights of individuals. The Supreme Court of the United States is the final arbiter in constitutional matters. *Statutory law* comprises statutes passed by legislative bodies, such as the U.S. Congress, state legislatures, or legislative bodies of local governments. *Administrative law* is formulated by the departments or agencies of the executive branch of government. It consists of rules and regulations, which are generally used to implement statu-

tory laws crafted by the legislative branch. *Common law* (also referred to as case law) is the body of legal principles and precedents that have been handed down in the form of court decisions. In rendering a decision, a court must review the merits of the case before it. However, it is also obligated to apply settled principles of law from previous cases embracing similar facts and involving similar principles (Landry, 1997). Common law is the only source available when statutory and administrative law are silent about a matter before a court.

Rules and regulations established by an agency must be consistent with the statute under which they are promulgated (Pozgar, 2002, p. 6). They provide administrative interpretations of the statutes and contain details for carrying them out. For example, state regulations prescribe the conditions under which a nursing facility may be licensed or the qualifications a person must have to be licensed as a nursing home administrator (NHA). Regulations also govern facility certification under Medicare and Medicaid rules (discussed later in this chapter). Administrative agencies, such as the Department of Health and Human Services (DHHS), first issue proposed regulations. Comments from concerned organizations such as hospitals and nursing homes and from the general public are received and reviewed. Changes are commonly made before final rules are issued.

## Public and Private Laws

Constitutional, statutory, and administrative laws are public laws. *Public laws* affect society as a whole. For example, criminal law deals with wrongs committed against society. *Private laws* affect an individual, family, or small group. For example, a contract between two parties falls in the category of private law because the contract affects only the parties who entered into the contract. Harm caused to an individual or damage to one's property by another also fall under private law. Thus, private law deals with civil matters.

## Civil and Criminal Law

*Civil law* is the body of laws governing private legal affairs, such as private rights and duties, contracts, and commercial relations. In civil law, a private party (individual or corporation) files the lawsuit and becomes the plaintiff (Standler, 1998). Civil penalties in the form of monetary damages—as opposed to jail terms—ensue from a breach of what the law prescribes.

The second category of law, *criminal law*, defines crimes and provides punishments for them. A *crime* is an offense committed against the general public, regardless of the number of individuals wronged. Jail terms, fines, or both may be imposed for criminal offenses. Examples of crime include theft, murder, disorderly conduct, and sexual abuse. In addition to such common criminal acts, other types of actions particular to health care may also constitute crimes. Billing the Medicare program for services that are not medically necessary, billing for services that were not performed, or gross violation of commonly recognized standards of care may constitute Medicare fraud, which is a criminal offense. (Federal fraud and abuse law and the False Claims Act are covered in Chapter 7.) A reckless disregard for the safety and well-being of patients may constitute criminal negligence. Crimes are ranked as felonies and misdemeanors. A crime classified as a *felony* is of a serious nature and is subject to a jail term of more than one year. A *misdemeanor* is a less serious crime that

is punishable by a jail term of less than one year.

The wrongdoer who commits a crime is subject to prosecution by the state. Often a public prosecutor, not a private party, brings the case before a court. Prosecution of an action that has been deemed a crime may still allow the wronged party to pursue civil action when the same conduct violates both criminal and civil laws.

## Tort and Contract Law

Civil law distinguishes between tort and breach of contract. Generally, injury must be sustained to claim damages. *Injury* can be in the form of physical, financial, or emotional harm.

### Tort Law

A *tort* is defined as a civil wrong—other than a breach of contract—committed against a person or a corporation. Tort may also involve interference with another's rights, either intentionally or otherwise.

In broad terms, a tort almost always constitutes the violation of some duty. It can be in the form of wrongdoing—that is, something was done incorrectly or something that should have been done was omitted (Miller & Hutton, 2000, p. 361). Malpractice falls under the broad umbrella of tort law. *Malpractice* is defined in terms of negligence or carelessness in the delivery of services according to accepted standards of care so that harm is caused to the recipient of care.

On admitting a patient, the facility becomes duty bound to meet the patient's total care needs. If the facility is not equipped to meet all of the patient's needs because of staff shortages, lack of training, or any other reason, the patient should not be admitted. If an admitted patient's condition deteriorates so that a higher level of care—perhaps available only in a hospital—would be more appropriate, the facility must make the needed transfer arrangements, including safe transportation to another facility.

In tort law, **compensatory damages** are generally awarded to "make the person whole again." However, the court may also award punitive damages in excess of the actual losses suffered. **Punitive damages** are also called *exemplary damages* because their intent is to make a public example of the defendant, supposedly to deter future wrongful conduct by others. Punitive damages are generally awarded when the defendant's conduct is determined to be egregious. Such conduct may also be prosecuted under criminal law. Egregious or blatant conduct generally falls into four categories:

1. *Malicious intent.* Also called **malice**, it involves knowingly doing something with the desire to cause harm. The plaintiff is required to demonstrate that the defendant carried some ill-will toward the plaintiff and that the defendant acted on that ill-will to cause serious injury (Thornton, 2006).

2. *Gross negligence.* This is more than simple negligence (discussed later). The defendant must have acted with conscious indifference to the rights, safety, or welfare of another and should have known of the potential harm he or she might cause.

3. *Blatant disregard for the rights of others.* Punitive damages are particularly important in torts involving harm to the plaintiff's dignity (e.g., invasion of privacy) or other breaches of civil rights, where the actual monetary injury to the plaintiff may be small (Standler, 1998).

4. *Fraud.* This is a knowing disregard of the truth that results in harm. It involves deception and an intent to defraud someone.

A landmark 2001 verdict from Texas, *Fuqua v. Horizon/CMS Healthcare Corporation*, illustrates the kind of circumstance in which punitive damages may be warranted. In one of the largest-ever jury verdicts in a nursing home malpractice lawsuit, brought by Cecil Fuqua on behalf of the estate of his mother, Wyvonne Fuqua, the plaintiff was awarded $2.7 million in compensatory damages and an additional $310 million in punitive damages. The suit was filed after the death of 76-year-old Wyvonne Fuqua in 1997. Fuqua had been admitted to a nursing home in Fort Worth, Texas, in 1994, following a stroke. In late 1996, Fuqua began developing severe pressure ulcers. As her condition deteriorated, the nursing home staff allegedly did not apprise the family of Fuqua's condition and did not discharge her to a facility that could adequately treat her pressure ulcers. In April 1997, Ms. Fuqua's adult children moved her to a local hospital. She arrived in a state of malnutrition, with 16 pressure ulcers, of which 9 were Stage III and 5 were Stage IV (the most severe type in which bone or muscle may be exposed). Two months after she left the nursing home, Fuqua died (Schabes, 2002).

## Contract Law

A civil wrong involving the violation of a specific agreement between two parties constitutes a **breach of contract**, not a tort. In a civil case, the remedy is often in the form of recovery of damages. However, the injured party has the duty to mitigate (i.e., reduce) potential damages. For example, an employee who is separated from an organization in breach of a contract that existed between the employee and the organization has the duty to try to find other employment. Punitive damages are not available in breach of contract cases.

Many business relationships are governed by contracts. Contracts may concern patients or parties responsible for them, certain employees, independent providers of services to the facility's patients, construction contracts, lease contracts, loan agreements, purchasing contracts, etc. A *contract* is a legally binding agreement between two or more parties to carry out a legal purpose. For instance, two parties cannot enter into a contract to commit fraud. Although most contracts are executed in writing, certain verbal agreements can also be legally viewed as contracts. A contract essentially represents a mutual assent or "meeting of the minds."

For most contracts to be legally enforceable, two main conditions must be met:

1. Making of an offer and its acceptance should have occurred, indicating that an agreement has actually been reached. Generally, all parties to a contract sign a written document to affirm the agreement.

2. Promise of a price or benefit—called consideration—should be stated. A *consideration* is something of value promised to another in exchange for something else of value. The party that is being required to perform under the contract will receive the consideration upon performance.

Only contracts executed between competent parties are considered legal. To be considered *competent*, the parties must be of sound mind and of legal age. Thus, agreements with minors or those who do not have the mental capacity to enter into a contract because of mental illness, mental retardation, dementia, or substance abuse are not enforceable. In most cases, competence can be determined by a physician. In more difficult situations, the matter is referred to a court. Agreements reached under duress may also be unenforceable. Unless a court determines a contract to be invalid, and therefore unenforceable, the parties must perform according to its provisions. Otherwise, the aggrieved party can bring a complaint before a court for breach of contract and recover damages.

When admitting a patient, a nursing home enters into a contract with the patient or someone acting on behalf of the patient, such as a family member. The *admission agreement* is a contract that spells out the services the nursing home will provide and the cost of those services. The nursing home can be sued for breach of contract if a patient is harmed and if the harm is determined to have resulted because services promised in the contract were not delivered. On the other hand, the patient or a responsible party who signed the admission agreement may be sued for nonpayment.

# Personal and Corporate Liability

*Liability* refers to the potential damages ensuing from legal action. In health care, liability commonly occurs as a result of malpractice. Liability may be ascribed to an individual or a corporation.

## Personal Liability

As a general rule, both tort law and criminal law ascribe personal liability to an individual who commits wrongful acts. For example, falsification of medical or business records may be grounds for criminal prosecution. The administrator and other employees of a long-term care facility can be held liable when their actions result in injury to someone else. To incur personal liability, an individual must do something wrong or fail to do something he or she should have done. The administrator would be held personally responsible only when he or she has acted on his or her own behalf, has engaged in a tortious act (i.e., behavior that constitutes a tort), or has remained passive about something that results in a tort when he or she knew or should have known but failed to take action.

Maggie Hazelton, who was 33 years old, was admitted to Driftwood Nursing Center on April 9 and was discharged on May 30. She was readmitted in June of the same year and then discharged to a hospital in August. Two days later Maggie died in the hospital. Darlene Hester, administratrix of the decedent's estate, filed suit against the nursing home and its administrator, Richard Smith. The lawsuit alleged personal injuries and wrongful death. Hester alleged that the patient was a victim of neglect and, as a result, had suffered pneumonia, falls, unexplained injuries, urinary and kidney infections, weight loss, and ultimately death. Hester asserted that the nursing home's negligent conduct caused the patient to lose her dignity and caused her death to be preceded by extreme and unnecessary pain, degradation, anguish, unnecessary hospitalization, and emotional trauma. In his defense, Smith filed a motion for *summary judgment*, that is, a prompt disposition of the case without a trial. The trial court granted the motion for summary judgment and entered final judgment of dismissal in favor of Smith. In essence, the court held that Smith could not be held personally liable for any alleged negligence on the part of any of the employees of the nursing home. Later, the Court of Appeals of Mississippi affirmed the summary judgment in favor of Smith (Tammelleo, 2007).

In addition to earlier discussions, individuals may be held liable for unlawful acts, whether or not those acts result in injury to others. An example of this kind of unlawful act would be possession or use of illegal drugs.

Personal tort liability may result from either negligent or intentional acts.

## Negligence

*Negligence* is the failure to exercise the degree of care that a reasonable person would have exercised in similar circumstances. It is generally associated with a breach of duty. A nursing facility has a duty to exercise due care. For instance, it must have adequate equipment and staff to provide services as required by the needs of its patients.

An act of negligence is not sufficient for establishing liability unless it has resulted in injury. An administrator who fails to install an alarm system to monitor patients who may wander out of the facility is not liable unless a patient has actually wandered away and sustained injury. For a plaintiff to establish injury from negligence, four conditions must be present:

- A duty must be owed. For instance, nursing facilities have the duty to maintain a safe environment and provide services that meet acceptable standards.
- There must be a breach of duty.
- An injury must be sustained.
- A direct cause-and-effect relationship must be present between the breach of duty and the injury sustained.

In health care, *duty* is commonly defined in terms of standards of care. Judgments about standards of care are often based on established regulations, evidence-based practices, written procedures or policies of the facility, best professional judgment (expert opinion), or what a reasonable person would do on the basis of common sense. The duty that is breached can be in the form of an act of commission, such as a nurse giving the wrong medication, or it can be an act of omission, such as a nurse failing to give the prescribed medication.

## Intentional Torts

An *intentional tort* is a willful act that violates the rights or interests of others. *Willful* means that a person knows and desires the consequences of his or her acts. Actions commonly regarded as intentional torts are assault, battery, false imprisonment, invasion of privacy, defamation of character, fraud, and intentional infliction of mental distress.

- An *assault* creates a threatening environment in which a person fears being touched in an offensive, insulting, provoking, or potentially injurious manner. No physical contact has to occur, but the assaulted individual must reasonably believe that the aggressor has the ability to carry it out presently. If the aggressor actually touches the other individual without consent, that action results in *battery*. In this context, restraining a patient without a physician's order or the patient's consent may amount to battery.

- *False imprisonment* is the unlawful restriction of freedom. Unlawful use of restraints may constitute false imprisonment in addition to battery. Restraints are regarded as an intervention, and harm caused by medical intervention can make the nursing home liable (Yorker, 1988). Also, generally accepted medical procedures and the state health code must be followed when isolating patients who have a contagious disease.

- Invasion of privacy concerns both privacy and confidentiality. A patient's name, pictures, or private affairs should not be made public without proper authorization. Unreasonable search or intrusion, such as opening personal mail without consent, is a violation of a patient's privacy rights. Patients' medical records belong to the long-term care facility, but these records are confidential. Release of information to persons not involved in patient care requires the patient's authorization, or its release may be governed by law.

- Defamation of character involves making false reports that result in damage to someone's reputation. The false reports may be in written form (constituting a *libel*), or they may be communicated verbally (constituting a *slander*).

- *Fraud* occurs when harm or loss is incurred because of a knowing disregard of the truth. Fraud is almost always an egregious act and a crime.

- Intentional infliction of mental distress is considered intentional tort when some outrageous conduct results in mental or emotional trauma. Patients and their families must be treated in a civil manner. Health care professionals can be held liable when outbursts of anger, abusive language, or other irrational behavior results in mental distress.

## Corporate Liability

The ultimate legal responsibility for the facility's operations and for their outcomes is vested in the governing body or board. Responsibility for daily management is delegated to the administrator. Generally speaking, individual members of the governing body are not held personally liable for negligence amounting to errors of judgment. They may, however, be held liable for gross or willful negligence. Hence, board members acting in good faith can have wide latitude in fulfilling their roles and responsibilities. Acting in **good faith** (Latin: *bona fide*) generally means how a reasonable person would have acted under similar circumstances. On the other hand, board members may be held criminally liable in cases involving fraud or engaging in activities for personal gain.

The law regards corporations as individuals and as entities separate from their owners. The corporation is often held liable for actions of its directors, officers, and employees, notwithstanding the personal liability of individuals. The doctrine of *respondeat superior* and the concept of agency are two main areas with which health facility administrators should become familiar.

## Respondeat Superior

All people are responsible for their own tortious conduct. At times, however, the law will hold liable for a tort not only the tortfeasor (i.e., person who commits the tort) but also the organization that hired the tortfeasor. In most instances, the nursing facility is held liable for the wrongful acts of its employees when such acts are committed during the course of their employment. It does not matter if the organization takes all reasonable steps in selecting, training, and supervising its employees.

A corporation's liability for the acts of its officers or employees is known as **vicarious liability**, which is founded on the legal doctrine of **respondeat superior** (let the master respond). A supervisor is not regarded as an employer and is not held liable except for his or her own personal acts, as described in the previous section. Also, *respondeat superior* does not absolve the employee of personal liability, nor does it obligate the employer to provide liability protection to its employees.

The doctrine of *respondeat superior* does not apply to the wrongful acts of an independent contractor, who is responsible for his own acts. Hence, it is important to differentiate between an employee and a contractor, but this distinction is not always clear in law. For instance, it is a common practice in long-term care facilities to contract rehabilitation services. Generally, a facility would not be liable for the wrongful acts of contracted therapists treating patients in the facility. However, if the facility exercises some measure of control over the therapists (such as patient scheduling, billing, and compliance with the facility's policies) and if the therapists are represented to clients as employees of the facility, they may not qualify as independent contractors under law. On the other hand, a facility is not liable for the actions of a nonemployed attending physician who generally is not under the control of the facility's staff.

Often, whether or not someone should be regarded as a contractor does not become clear until a case is brought to trial before a court. However, NHAs can minimize legal exposure by adhering to the following practices:

- Review and document the qualifications and credentials of providers who may be rendering services to the facility's residents as independent contractors.

- Verify and document that all personnel providing services to patients are duly licensed if they are required to be licensed under state laws.

- Ensure that licensed professionals do not provide services outside their scope of practice.

- Investigate, document, and report any professional misconduct to the appropriate licensing authority.

## Agency

An *agent* is someone who is authorized to act on behalf of another, called a *principal*. For example, the NHA is, in many instances, an agent of the corporation that employs him or her. The corporation (i.e., the principal) would generally be liable for the acts of commission or omission of its agent when the latter acts within its authority. For example, when the administrator enters into a contract with a third party within the scope of his or her authority, any liability ensuing from a breach of contract will fall on the corporation. The administrator will not have personal liability. On the other hand, if the third party has been led to believe that the agent is a principal, the agent would be liable if a breach of contract occurs. Individual partners in a partnership, or institutions in a joint venture, are considered each others' agents. For example, partners are liable for tortious actions of other partners.

---

# Corporate Law

Statutes concerning the rights and responsibilities of private corporations may be loosely referred to as *corporate law*.

## Types of Ownership

An organization's ownership structure defines, in a broad sense, its rights and responsibilities. This structure has implications for how the organization and the owners are taxed, whether the organization or the owners have liability for civil offenses, and what rights and responsibilities the organization and its owners have. There are three main classes of ownership (national data for nursing homes and beds for the three types of ownership are shown in Figure 5–2):

- Public.
- Private nonprofit.
- Private for-profit (proprietary).

## Public Facilities

A *public facility* is owned by the government. It may be operated under a specific statute enacted by a city or county. That statute would include the specific duties and limitations for the organization. Often, such statutes specifically outline the charity mission for which the institute may have been created. In some instances, the statute may prohibit leasing of the facility to a private corporation. Other aspects of facility management may be governed by statute. In a broad sense, then, the rights and responsibilities of a government-owned nursing home are subject to the statute that created the organization.

## Private Nonprofit Facilities

A privately owned facility incorporated as a *nonprofit* (also called not-for-profit) entity is prohibited from distributing its profits to individuals. A nonprofit nursing facility is not prohibited from earning a profit, but the facility must serve a charitable purpose. Nonprofit corporations are exempt from federal taxation under Section 501(c)(3) of the Internal Revenue Code. The law provides for federal exemption from taxation to any organization operated exclusively for "religious, charitable, scientific or educational purposes." These organizations are also exempt from state income and sales taxes and may be exempt from local taxes, such as property taxes. Tax law also enables nonprofit entities to obtain private donations, for which the donors

**Figure 5–2** Percentage Distribution of Nursing Homes and Beds by Ownership

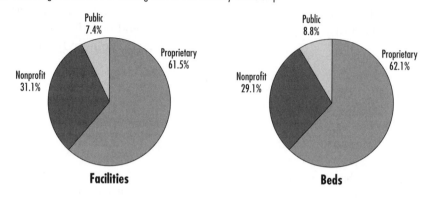

*Sources:* Data from the National Nursing Home Survey, 2004; and U.S. Census Bureau, *Statistical Abstract of the United States, 2009,* Table 187.

can claim a charitable deduction on their income tax returns.

The owners and administrators of non-profit facilities must be particularly careful that the privileges afforded under the law are not abused. "Charity" does not mean that the facility is required to provide free care to anyone. It does mean that the facility must make its services available at the lowest feasible cost and that it should not force anyone who cannot pay for services to move out. To provide care to residents who are unable to pay, the facility may participate in government funding programs such as Medicaid, obtain private donations, or cover such costs out of its own profits.

## Private For-Profit Facilities

A privately owned for-profit (also called proprietary) facility is operated to generate a profit that can be distributed to its owners or shareholders. Proprietary enterprises are also required to pay all federal, state, and local taxes. There are three types of proprietorships:

- Corporations.
- Partnerships.
- Sole proprietorships.

A *corporation* is formed as a legal entity that is entirely separate from its owners. For-profit corporations may be owned by a group of private investors or by a parent corporation, such as a nursing home chain or a proprietary hospital. The parent corporation may also be publicly owned, in which case the company's stock is available to any investor through the stock market.

A *partnership* is another type of private ownership described as an association of two or more individuals or organizations for the purpose of conducting business for profit. A partnership is specifically created for the purpose of sharing profits among the partners. They also share the expenses and liabilities of the partnership. In a *general partnership*, there is no limit on the potential liability of the partners. On the other hand, a *limited partnership* can be established to limit the individual liability of partners. Limited partners are liable only to the extent of their investment, as long as they do not participate in the management and control of the operations (Miller & Hutton, 2000, p. 25). Thus, limited partners can be viewed as mere investors in a business enterprise.

A *sole proprietorship* consists of a single owner who has not incorporated the business. All income of the business is taxed as personal income of the owner, and the owner's potential liability is unlimited. Because of the many complex tax and legal issues they entail, nursing facilities are rarely operated as sole proprietorships.

# Licensure, Certification, and Accreditation

*Licensure*, *certification*, and *accreditation* carry different meanings, but all three serve at least one main purpose—to establish minimum standards of quality and to enforce compliance with those standards. Exhibit 5–1 provides a summary of the main distinctions between licensure and certification.

## Licensure

A license is a legal requirement without which it will be unlawful to operate a nursing facility. License to operate a nursing facility is issued by the state in which the facility is located.

The licensure process starts at the planning stage, before a new facility can even be built. If an existing facility is acquired, it must be relicensed. Once a facility has been built or acquired, its licensure status must be maintained, generally through an annual renewal process. Many states have *certificate of need (CON)* laws that require a state planning agency to approve building of a

**Exhibit 5–1** Differences between Nursing Home Licensure and Certification

| Licensure | Certification |
|---|---|
| • State function | • Federal function |
| • Mandatory | • Optional |
| • Basic requirement for operating a nursing home | • A facility must first be licensed before it can apply for certification |
| • Does not make a facility eligible for public funds | • Required for receiving public funds |
| • There is one licensing category for nursing care facilities | • There are three categories depending mainly on the source of government funding and types of patients served: |
|  |   1. SNF—Medicare, post-acute, short stay |
|  |   2. NF—Medicaid, long stay (if the patient qualifies) |
|  |   3. ICF/MR—Medicaid, long stay, MR/DD patients only |
| • With the exception of the Life Safety Code, licensing standards differ between states | • Uniform federal standards for all states |

new facility or expansion of an existing one. In some states, transfer of ownership must also go through the CON approval process. State CON requirements define several aspects of building or acquiring a facility:

- The type of expenditures that are subject to review. A state may allow a certain number of beds to be built without the CON review.
- The criteria for evaluating need for additional beds or services.
- The procedures for review, which include public hearings.

The licensure function generally falls within the purview of each state's health department. A license is granted on the condition that the facility meets standards that specify minimum thresholds for staffing, adequacy of services, building construction specifications, and compliance with fire and safety regulations mandated by the *Life Safety Code*. The *Life Safety Code* standards are national (see Chapter 6 for details). Standards in the remaining areas are developed by each state, and they vary from one state to another.

Licensure also requires that the facility supply information about the professional credentials of the principal owners and key employees, such as the administrator and the director of nursing. If a principal owner or key officer has had a criminal conviction, facility license may be denied or revoked.

## Certification

All facilities must be licensed, but *certification* is not mandatory. Certification is required for admitting patients enrolled in the Medicaid or Medicare programs. In contrast to licensure, which is a state function, certifi-

cation is a federal function. The Centers for Medicare and Medicaid Services (CMS), a federal agency, promulgates certification standards (discussed in Chapter 6) with which nursing facilities must comply to retain their certification status.

Until 1989, federal statutes classified nursing homes into two types: skilled nursing facilities (SNFs), for residents enrolled in either Medicare or Medicaid, and intermediate care facilities (ICFs), for those covered by Medicaid only. Patients needing a higher level of care were eligible for admission to a SNF that was required to have a licensed nurse on duty 24 hours a day and a registered nurse (RN) on the day shift. By contrast, ICFs were required to have a licensed nurse on duty only on the day shift.

The Nursing Home Reform Act as part of the Omnibus Budget Reconciliation Act of 1987 (OBRA-87) removed the distinctions between ICFs and SNFs for both Medicare and Medicaid. The new law created two categories of nursing homes, but for certification purposes only.

A nursing home certified to admit Medicare patients is now certified as *SNF (skilled nursing facility)*. Such a facility can be freestanding or a *distinct part*—that is, a section of a nursing home that is certified apart from the rest of the facility. When SNF certification applies to a distinct part, Medicare patients can be admitted only to that particular section of the facility. SNF certification conforms to the original intent of the Medicare legislation (Social Security Amendment of 1965), according to which Medicare would cover only post-hospital services in a nursing facility.

An LTC facility serving only Medicaid patients (but not Medicare patients) is certified as *NF (nursing facility)*. SNF and NF are both legal terms associated with certification, not necessarily with the level of services. A facility may be dually certified as both SNF and NF. Facilities that have ***dual certification*** can admit both Medicare and Medicaid patients.

The federal standards for the delivery of care in SNFs and NFs are the same. For federal certification purposes, the former ICF category has been abolished. However, because the Medicaid program is administered by each state, some states distinguish among levels of care within the NF category. The state of Tennessee, for example, created level I NF (NF-1) and level II NF (NF-2) categories. In the NF-1 category, services are less intensive than they are at the NF-2 level. Other states maintain the ICF category to provide services to Medicaid patients who do not require the degree of care and treatment that a skilled nursing facility is designed to provide. These states pay nursing homes a lesser amount for the ICF level of care. National data on the distribution of facilities and beds according to certification appear in Figure 5–3.

A third certification category is ***ICF/MR*** (Intermediate Care Facility for the Mentally Retarded) discussed in Chapter 3. To qualify for Medicaid reimbursement, ICF/MRs must be licensed by the state and must comply with federal standards. The Conditions of Participation—found in the Code of Federal Regulations at 42 CFR Part 483, Subpart I, Sections 483.400 to 483.480—specify eight areas in which standards must be met: management, client protections, facility staffing, active treatment services, client behavior and facility practices, health care services, physical environment, and dietetic services. ICF/MR services may be furnished in a distinct part of a facility, provided the distinct part is ICF/MR certified.

According to certification regulations, the term "facility" does not necessarily imply a separate physical structure. The term can be used for the facility as a whole or, within the context of certification, it may apply to a distinct part.

A few facilities have elected not to participate in the Medicaid and Medicare programs and are ***noncertified***. These facilities can admit only those patients who have a private source of funding for nursing home care. Although Medicare and Medicaid patients

**Figure 5–3** Percentage Distribution of Nursing Homes and Beds by Type of Certification

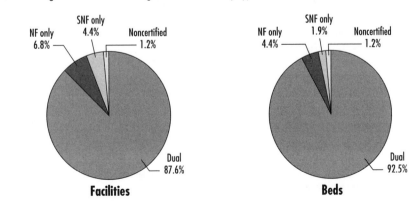

*Sources:* Data from the National Nursing Home Survey, 2004; and U.S. Census Bureau, *Statistical Abstract of the United States, 2009*, Table 187.

cannot be admitted to noncertified facilities, *private-pay patients*—those who have a private source of funding—are not restricted to noncertified facilities. Such patients may be admitted to SNF or NF certified beds as well. Hence, most nursing homes are certified because they can serve private-pay patients as well as those on public assistance. Figure 5–4 illustrates how a facility can have distinctly certified sections.

## Accreditation

In contrast to licensure and certification, which are government functions, *accreditation* is a private function. Hence, accreditation is totally voluntary. The Joint Commission on Accreditation of Healthcare Organizations (JCAHO)—a private nonprofit organization—accredits hospitals, nursing homes, and other types of health care sites and has issued its own standards for the purpose of accreditation. Compared with hospitals, relatively few nursing facilities have opted to seek accreditation. From its inception, Medicare regulations have conferred deemed status on hospitals accredited by JCAHO. *Deemed status* is a Medicare rule that a hospital accredited by the JCAHO is deemed to have met the Medicare certification criteria. Nursing facilities, however, are not given deemed status on the basis of accreditation. Accreditation does have its advantages: accreditation status is highly correlated with a facility's ability to comply with certification standards. Compared with nonaccredited facilities, accredited ones also perform better on various quality measures and have lower exposure to risk, such as malpractice lawsuits (Grachek, 2002). On the other hand, many facilities find that accreditation fees are high in relation to the benefits reaped.

## Patient Rights

Patient rights are founded on both legal and ethical principles. Patient autonomy is the ethical principle governing patient rights. Autonomy includes notions such as self-determination and independence of choice and action without outside coercion. In

Figure 5–4 Distinctly Certified Units in a Nursing Home

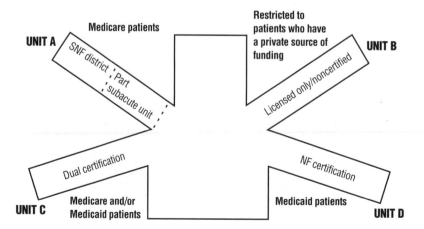

addition, patients have the right to nondiscrimination; freedom from abuse, neglect, and misappropriation of property; and privacy and confidentiality.

## Right to Self-Determination

In health care facilities, patients must be informed of their rights. The Patient Self-Determination Act of 1990 also requires health care providers to protect and promote patient rights. Many states require that health care facilities develop a patient's bill of rights. Other states have taken the initiative in proposing these rights (see Exhibit 5–2 for an illustration of the rights proposed by North Carolina). Whether or not required by state law, facilities should have a bill of rights in printed form to inform residents and family members of these rights.

The Patient Self-Determination Act of 1990 also governs a patient's right to make decisions about treatment and covers issues regarding advance directives, which are briefly discussed below. All documents pertaining to patients' rights should be appropriately maintained in their medical records.

## Informed Consent

*Informed consent* is the right of a patient to make an informed choice about medical care. Express consent may, however, be waived or implied under certain circumstances, such as emergency situations in which a physician may determine that delay incurred in the process of obtaining consent may result in harm to the patient.

To make an informed choice, the resident must be given sufficient information to make a decision. A resident has the right to refuse treatment, even when the treatment is medically advisable. Legal consent, however, requires that the patient has actually understood whatever he or she is consenting to. So, if a resident is not legally competent to give consent, another individual who has legal authority to act on the patient's behalf must give consent. Obtaining consent from family members is a widely accepted practice, but it may give rise to legal issues, especially if the family consents to withhold treatment against medical advice. Sometimes, a patient who is legally incompetent may have a *guardian* who is legally empowered and responsible for making decisions in the patient's best interest. The legal guardian's decisions overrule those of family members. Substitute decision making (i.e., decision by someone other than the patient) is not generally a simple matter. Clear communication between the decision makers and clinicians about the benefits and risks of expected clinical interventions, participation of decision makers in the deliberations of ethics committees, and joint decisions regarding what the patient would have desired given the circumstances are some of the means employed for making decisions on behalf of a patient. An *ethics committee* is a multidisciplinary forum that is generally called upon to make decisions in the patient's best interest, particularly when legal avenues are not clear cut. Other alternatives available when the patient loses the capacity to make decisions and indicate consent are discussed in the next section.

## Advance Directives

When a patient lacks decision-making capacity, an *advance directive* provides an avenue for the patient to convey his or her wishes about medical treatment in the event of cognitive impairment. Advance directives must be prepared before a person loses his or her competency for making decisions. Three

**Exhibit 5–2**  North Carolina's Bill of Rights for Nursing Home Residents (condensed version)

EVERY RESIDENT SHALL HAVE THE FOLLOWING RIGHTS:

(1) To be treated with consideration, respect, and full recognition of personal dignity and individuality.

(2) To receive care, treatment, and services that are adequate and appropriate, and in compliance with relevant federal and State statutes and rules.

(3) To receive at the time of admission and during stay, a written statement of services provided by the facility, including those required to be offered on an as-needed basis, and of related charges. Charges for services not covered under Medicare and Medicaid shall be specified. The patient will sign a written receipt upon receiving the above information.

(4) To have on file physician's orders with proposed schedule of medical treatment. Written, signed evidence of prior informed consent to participation in experimental research shall be in patient's file.

(5) To receive respect and privacy in his medical care program. All personal and medical records are confidential.

(6) To be free of mental and physical abuse. Except in emergencies, to be free of chemical and physical restraint unless authorized for a specified period of time by a physician according to clear and indicated medical need.

(7) To receive from the administration or staff of the facility a reasonable response to all requests.

(8) To associate and communicate privately and without restriction with persons and groups of the patient's choice at any reasonable hour. To send and receive mail promptly and unopened. To have access to a telephone where the patient may speak privately. To have access to writing instruments, stationery and postage.

(9) To manage his/her own financial affairs unless other legal arrangements have been implemented. The facility may also assist the patient, but is required to follow stringent guidelines.

(10) To have privacy in visits by the patient's spouse, and if both are patients in the same facility, they shall be given the opportunity, where feasible, to share a room.

(11) To enjoy privacy in his/her room.

(12) To present grievances and recommend changes in policies and services personally, through other persons or in combination with others, without fear of reprisal, restraint, interference, coercion, or discrimination.

(13) To not be required to perform services for the facility without personal consent and the written approval of the attending physician.

(14) To retain, to secure storage for, and to use his personal clothing and possessions, where reasonable.

(15) To not be transferred or discharged from a facility except for medical, financial, or their own or other patient's welfare, nonpayment for the stay or when mandated by Medicare or Medicaid. Any such transfer shall require at least five days' notice, unless the attending physician orders immediate transfer, which shall be documented in the patient's medical record.

(16) To be notified within ten days after the facility's license is revoked or made provisional. The responsible party or guardian must be notified as well.

*Source:* North Carolina Division of Aging http://www.dhhs.state.nc.us/aging/rights.htm.

types of commonly used advance directives include a living will, a do-not-resuscitate order, and a durable power of attorney. A *living will* specifies a person's wishes regarding medical treatment in the event this person becomes incompetent. The main drawback with this approach is that it cannot possibly conceive all possible situations in which the advance directive may become necessary. A *do-not-resuscitate order (DNR)* specifies that the person does not wish to have heartbeat or breathing restored in the event of a cardiac or respiratory arrest. By executing a *durable power of attorney (DPOA)*, a person appoints another individual to make decisions on his or her behalf after the person becomes incompetent. A DPOA should not be confused with a power of attorney (POA). A POA is an agreement in which a person (called the principal) gives another person (called the attorney-in-fact, not to be confused with an attorney or a lawyer who practices law) the authority to make decisions on behalf of the principal. A POA is generally drawn for the purpose of handling the principal's financial affairs. Health care decisions can be included, but such authority must be specified in the POA. It is important to note that an attorney-in-fact can make medical decisions on behalf of a principal only if the principal is incompetent to make his or her own decisions. An attorney-in-fact cannot make decisions contrary to the wishes of the patient to the extent that the patient is able to indicate what he or she wants.

## Right to Nondiscrimination

From the legal perspective, patients in nursing facilities and those seeking admission to a facility have all the rights of citizenship that are guaranteed to every American by the Constitution of the United States. Additional protections against discrimination are included in federal and state laws. Title VI of the Civil Rights Act of 1964 applies to programs receiving federal funds. The law prohibits denial of benefits on the basis of race, color, or national origin. Denial of benefits may be construed to mean discrimination in admission, segregation by race or ethnicity, and unequal treatment in other respects. Section 504 of the Rehabilitation Act of 1973 prohibits any facility receiving federal funds from discriminating on the basis of physical or mental handicap. Admission to a facility may be denied only if that facility does not provide the level of services that a patient in a protected category requires. Individuals with HIV/AIDS are also protected under the Rehabilitation Act. The Americans with Disabilities Act (ADA) of 1990 goes beyond the requirements of the Rehabilitation Act. It specifically states that "no individual shall be discriminated against on the basis of disability in the full and equal enjoyment of the goods, services, facilities, privileges, advantages, or accommodations of any place of public accommodation." Accessibility requirements and use of the facilities by the disabled are explained in Chapter 6.

## Right to Freedom from Abuse, Neglect, and Misappropriation of Property

OBRA-87 added further rights regarding freedom from resident abuse, neglect, and misappropriation of resident property in nursing homes. *Abuse* is defined as "willful infliction of injury, unreasonable confinement, intimidation or punishment with resulting physical harm, pain or mental anguish." *Neglect* means "failure to provide goods and services necessary to avoid physical harm, mental anguish, or mental illness." *Misappropriation of resident property* means "deliberate misplacement, exploitation, or wrongful, temporary, or permanent use of a resident's belongings or money without the resident's consent."

The Balanced Budget Act of 1997 calls for denial of payment under Medicare and Medicaid to facilities charged with abuse and mistreatment of patients. The law also directed the states to establish nurse aide registries. Part of the information contained in the registry pertains to findings of abuse, neglect, and misappropriation of resident property. This information is designed to ban nurse aides who have been abusive in the past from employment in nursing facilities.

## Right to Privacy and Confidentiality

Facilities are required to preserve patients' privacy in the delivery of care and treatments. It is important for nursing home associates to realize that the facility is considered the patients' home. Facility administration should institute practices such as knocking before entering a patient's room, drawing privacy curtains for personal care, and ensuring appropriate dressing and grooming of residents. Facilities are also required to keep patient information confidential. The responsibilities of nursing homes, however, go far beyond ensuring the basic rights to privacy, dignity, and confidentiality.

The Health Insurance Portability and Accountability Act (HIPAA) of 1996 makes it incumbent upon facilities to develop policies and procedures to protect patient privacy. The legislation provides for some of the strongest safeguards to maintain the confidentiality of patient information. Final rules, referred to as the *Privacy Rule*, were issued by the DHHS and became effective April 14, 2003. HIPAA makes it illegal to gain access to personal medical information for reasons other than

health care delivery, operations, and reimbursement. To the extent it is necessary to promote quality of health care, information can be shared among physicians, nurses, and other professionals. It can also be used for getting reimbursement for services delivered and to facilitate operations such as transfer of a patient from one facility to another. However, the legislation mandates the exercise of strict controls on the transfer of personally identifiable health data between two entities.

The Privacy Rule applies to all medical records and other identifiable health information regardless of whether the information is electronic, on paper, or orally transferable. Patients have significant rights to understand and control how their health information is used:

- Health care organizations are required to provide a notice to patients detailing the ways in which the facility will use or disclose the patient's *protected healthcare information (PHI)*, which is defined as individually identifiable health information that relates to the past, present, or future physical or mental health of, or the provision of health care to, a patient (Battaglia, 2003).

- Patients generally have the right to examine their medical records. They can obtain copies of their records, but the medical establishment can charge a fee for copying and sending the information. Patients also have the right to request corrections of any errors in their records.

- Patients have the right to request restrictions on the uses and disclosures of their information. Releasing individual medical information for any purpose other than patient care should only be done with the patient's express written consent. In addition, the patient's authorization must be made with informed consent; the patient must be aware, in a general way, what information will be released and what use will be made of the information. The information released should be strictly limited to that required to fulfill the purpose of the authorization. Authorizations should be retained as a part of the official medical record (Huffman, 1990).

- The Privacy Rule sets restrictions and limits on the use of patient information for marketing purposes. Pharmacies, health plans, and other entities must first obtain an individual's specific authorization before disclosing patient information for marketing.

To comply with HIPAA, a nursing facility must have a detailed privacy policy in place (see Exhibit 5–3 for guidelines on developing a policy statement). At the time of admission, a copy of the policy should be given to the patient or guardian, and receipt of the privacy notice must be acknowledged in writing. The policy must also be posted at a prominent location within the facility, and on the facility's website, if one exists.

Violations of the Privacy Rule can result in civil as well as criminal penalties. The DHHS Office of Civil Rights enforces civil violations of the Privacy Rule, and the Department of Justice enforces criminal violations. Civil penalties are $100 per violation, up to $25,000 per person per year for each requirement or prohibition violated. Criminal penalties apply when patient privacy is knowingly violated. For example, for knowingly disclosing the PHI, the penalty is up to $50,000 in fines and one year in prison. The penalty is up to $100,000 in fines and up to five years in prison for obtaining PHI under false pretenses. For obtaining or disclosing PHI for commercial use, the penalty is up to $250,000 in fines and up to 10 years in prison.

**Exhibit 5–3** Elements to be Included in a Facility's Privacy Policy under HIPAA

- **A statement as a header and prominently displayed must declare: THIS NOTICE DESCRIBES HOW MEDICAL INFORMATION ABOUT YOU MAY BE USED AND DISCLOSED AND HOW YOU CAN GET ACCESS TO THIS INFORMATION. PLEASE REVIEW IT CAREFULLY.**

This requirement is easily followed, but note that the statement must be in all caps and worded exactly as set forth above.

- **Information relating to the uses and disclosures of the individual's PHI (protected healthcare information), including a description and one example for each of the types of uses and disclosures that the facility is permitted to make for the purposes of treatment, payment, and healthcare operations; a description of each of the other purposes that the facility is permitted or required to perform without consent, such as public health, governmental health oversight, judicial and administrative proceedings, law enforcement, and work-related illness or injury; and enough detail to clarify the uses and disclosures that are permitted or required by the Privacy Rule or other applicable laws.**

(continues)

**Exhibit 5–3**  Elements to be Included in a Facility's Privacy Policy under HIPAA (Continued)

This section may be lengthy because it will list the multiple ways that PHI is used and disseminated. You may want to consider for inclusion in the privacy policy: treatment purposes including creation of the healthcare records at the facility and for referrals to other healthcare providers, payment purposes, or healthcare operations such as quality improvement, business associates, facility directory, notifications to family members, marketing, fundraising, public health requirements, law enforcement requirements, and reports required by health oversight agencies, including your survey and certification office.

- **Information that other disclosures and uses will be made only with the resident's written authorization and that he or she may revoke this authorization.**

This information can be placed anywhere in the document and can state that revocation is possible, and the request for revocation must be in writing.

- **Statement that describes the resident's rights concerning his or her PHI and how those rights may be exercised, such as (i) to request restrictions concerning certain uses and disclosures of PHI, (ii) to receive confidential communications of PHI, (iii) to inspect and copy PHI, (iv) to amend PHI, (v) to receive an accounting of disclosures of PHI, and (vi) to obtain a paper copy of the privacy notice on request even if the individual has agreed to receive the notice electronically.**

Again, this provision will result in a lengthy disclosure. Under section i, the facility wants to make clear that while the resident can request that PHI not be disclosed, the facility is under no obligation to grant the request. Medicare and Medicaid facilities can state that there are times when the request cannot be honored—including emergencies, if the resident is being transferred to another healthcare facility, or the disclosure is required by law. Under section iii, remember to indicate that if the resident wants copies of his/her medical record, HIPAA allows the facility to charge a reasonable copying fee. Section iv indicates that amending PHI is allowed, and requests for amendment should be made in writing with information to support the requested change. The accounting provisions listed under section v should be conditioned, and the policy should state that an accounting can only go back six years, and that no accounting will be given for disclosures for reason of treatment, payment, or healthcare operations; for disclosures made to the resident, the resident's legal representative, or any other individual involved in the resident's care; for disclosures to law enforcement officials; or for disclosures for national security purposes.

- **The facility is required by law to maintain the privacy of the resident's PHI with a list of the duties and practices of the facility with respect to PHI; and further, the facility is required to abide by the terms of the notice currently in effect. The notice should state that the facility reserves the right to change the terms of its notice and to make new notice provisions effective for all PHI that it maintains. The facility must also describe how it will provide residents with a revised notice.**

Facilities can choose to use a "layered notice," where this information is included on a summary page (or first layer) along with a summary of the resident's rights, then have a "second layer" that contains all of the elements required by the Privacy Rule.

*Source:* Excerpted from Battaglia SK. HIPAA compliance requires facilities to have privacy policy. *Nursing Homes Long Term Care Management* 2003; 52, no. 3:30–31. Used with permission of Medquest Communications LLC.

## For Further Thought

1. What specific lessons can a nursing home administrator learn from *Fuqua v. Horizon/ CMS Healthcare Corporation*? What do you think may have been the basis for award-ing huge punitive damages in this case?

2. On what basis did both the trial court and the appellate court rule in favor of Richard Smith? Who should be held liable? Discuss the liability in this case from the per-spective of both personal liability and corporate liability.

## For Further Learning

Legal definitions and explanations of legal terms are found at:

   http://definitions.uslegal.com

## REFERENCES

Battaglia, S.K. 2003. HIPAA compliance requires facilities to have privacy policy. *Nursing Homes Long Term Care Management* 52, no. 3: 30–31.

Grachek, M.K. 2002. Reducing risk and enhancing value through accreditation. *Nursing Homes Long Term Care Management* 51, no. 11: 34–36.

Huber, H. (Interview with). 2006. Baby boomer values drive growth in nursing home litigation. *Of Counsel* 25, no. 4: 18–19.

Huffman, E.K. 1990. *Medical Record Management*. 9th ed. Berwyn, IL: Physicians' Record Company.

Landry, P. 1997. The common law: tradition and stare decisis. A Blupete essay. Retrieved December 2008 from http://www.blupete.com/Literature/Essays/BluePete/LawCom.htm.

Miller, R.D., &. Hutton, R.C. 2000. *Problems in Health Care Law*. 8th ed. Gaithersburg, MD: Aspen Publishers.

Pozgar, G.D. 2002. *Legal Aspects of Health Care Administration*. 8th ed. Gaithersburg, MD: Aspen Publishers.

Schabes, A.E. 2002. Liability: Hints of "sweet reason" from the Midwest. *Nursing Homes Long Term Care Management* 51, no. 9: 52–53.

Standler, R.B. 1998. Differences between civil and criminal law in the USA. Retrieved December 2008 from http://www.rbs2.com/cc.htm.

Stevenson, D.G., & Studdert, D.M. 2003. The rise of nursing home litigation: Findings from a na-tional survey of attorneys. *Health Affairs* 22, no. 2: 219–229.

Tammelleo, A.D. 2007. Officers of nursing home not liable for nurse's negligence. Retrieved De-cember 2008 from http://www.entrepreneur.com/tradejournals/article/169824266.html.

Thornton, R.G. 2006. Medicolegal issues. Malice/gross negligence. *Baylor University Medical Center Proceedings* 19, no. 4: 417–418.

Yorker, B.C. 1988. The nurse's use of restraint with a neurologically impaired patient. *Journal of Neuroscience Nursing* 20: 390–392.

# Chapter 6

# Regulation and Enforcement

## What You Will Learn

- Long-term care is heavily regulated because the government is a major payer and the recipients of services are among the most vulnerable.

- The Nursing Home Reform Act continues to play a major role in regulatory oversight by enforcing substantial compliance with the Requirements of Participation through the survey and enforcement process.

- A new Quality Indicator Survey (QIS) is being gradually phased in.

- The seriousness of each deficiency is indicated by its severity and scope. Three categories of remedies are based on the seriousness of the deficiencies.

- An acceptable plan of correction must address five elements for each deficiency cited.

- Compliance with the Requirements of Participation incorporates compliance with the *Life Safety Code*. A facility has three options to address *Life Safety Code* deficiencies. Administrators must become thoroughly familiar with the Requirements of Participation and the main requirements of the *Life Safety Code*.

- Nursing homes are required to comply with the accessibility standards for the disabled under the Americans with Disabilities Act.

- Under the Occupational Safety and Health Act of 1970, OSHA is responsible for ensuring the safety and health of nursing home employees. Nursing homes are legally required to comply with OSHA standards. Administrators should take advantage of the instructional and consultancy resources available from OSHA. Nursing homes must also comply with OSHA's recordkeeping rules.

## Purpose of Regulation and Enforcement

The health care sector has been the object of numerous regulations, for two main reasons: (1) The government is a major payer for individuals receiving health care services under Medicare, Medicaid, and other public programs (discussed in Chapter 7). By committing a significant amount of tax dollars to the delivery of health care, the government retains a vested interest in how the money is spent by private organizations that deliver health care. (2) Health care in general, and long-term care in particular, provides services to the frailest and most vulnerable individuals in society. Many of them are physically or mentally incapacitated and have no one else to act on their behalf. The regulatory system is deemed obligated to protect vulnerable populations against negligence and abuse, to ensure that they receive needed services for which they are eligible, and to ensure that the services provided meet at least certain defined minimum standards of quality. Administrative agencies have the power to enforce the rules and regulations that they formulate. The most important federal agency regulating nursing facilities certified as SNF (skilled nursing facility) or NF (nursing facility; see Chapter 5) is the Centers for Medicare and Medicaid Services (CMS), an administrative agency under the U.S. Department of Health and Human Services (DHHS). The U.S. Department of Justice enforces compliance with the accessibility standards for the disabled. Workplace safety rules are enforced by the Occupational Safety and Health Administration (OSHA), an agency of the U.S. Department of Labor.

## Nursing Home Oversight

As pointed out in Chapter 2, regulatory policies have played a major role in nursing home oversight. The Nursing Home Reform Act of 1987 updated nursing home standards and required states to enforce better oversight to verify compliance with those standards in nursing homes that care for Medicare and Medicaid patients. States can use their enforcement powers to take action against facilities that do not comply with the standards. Regulatory oversight, however, has its weaknesses. Monitoring for compliance is based on periodic inspections and complaint investigations. Inspections of a nursing home may take place as much as 15 months apart. This sporadic system of monitoring does not guarantee that compliance with standards is continuous. Complaint investigations can be conducted any time, but they take place only when a complaint is filed against the nursing home by someone, such as a patient, family member, friend, or employee.

Nursing home oversight begins with state licensing regulations discussed in Chapter 5. Compliance with state regulations is essential for a facility to remain in business. Secondly, compliance with federal certification regulations is necessary to admit Medicaid and Medicare beneficiaries and to receive payments from the government for providing services to these beneficiaries. The regulations governing federal certification are referred to as *Requirements of Participation* and are prescribed by the Nursing Home Reform Act. Although the CMS is responsible for overseeing compliance, the actual task of monitoring for compliance is delegated to each state. The agency responsible in each state to carry out monitoring and compliance with the state licensure standards and the federal Requirements of Participation is referred to as the *State Survey Agency*. Monitoring is carried out through an annual inspection, called a *survey*, of the facility.

## Requirements of Participation

The Requirements of Participation are standards that are widely regarded as minimum standards of quality for nursing facilities. There are roughly 185 different standards, which are classified under 15 major categories. A summary of the broad requirements appears in Exhibit 6–1, which is meant for illustrative purposes only. The actual regulations can be found in the Code of Federal Regulations (CFR), Title 42, Part 483 (short form is stated as 42 CFR 483). The regulations and their application are periodically clarified by the CMS. The Guidance to Surveyors is contained in the current edition of the State Operations Manual produced by the CMS (see the Internet resources listed at the end of this chapter for accessing the State Operations Manual online). It is imperative for nursing home administrators to become thoroughly familiar with the regulations and their application.

Enforcement of the requirements of participation is based on substantial compliance rather than "zero tolerance" because perfect compliance sets expectations that are unrealistic in most instances. Enforcement of zero tolerance could disqualify most nursing facilities from providing services to Medicare and Medicaid patients. The law defines *substantial compliance* as "a level of compliance with requirements of participation such that any identified deficiencies pose no greater risk to patient health and safety than the potential for causing minimal harm." In simple language, it means that violation of a certification standard should not endanger the health and safety of a patient. If a facility meets this criterion, it is deemed to be in substantial compliance. The law also emphasizes the need for continued rather than cyclical compliance with the Requirements of Participation. To achieve this, the facility must implement policies and procedures for continuous monitoring to sustain compliance.

## Survey and Enforcement

In each state, the designated State Survey Agency is responsible for inspecting nursing facilities and making recommendations to the CMS to determine the provider's eligibility to participate in the Medicare and Medicaid programs. Two types of surveys are currently in use. Most nursing homes are inspected under the traditional survey. A new survey process called the Quality Indicator Survey (QIS) is being gradually phased in to replace the traditional survey over the next few years. The new survey is based on larger patient samples using computer automation, and it rates the facility to be surveyed on a comprehensive set of Quality of Care Indicators (QCIs).

### Types of Survey

The State Operations Manual provides for four types of surveys: standard, abbreviated standard, extended, and post-survey revisit.

### Standard Survey

A standard survey is the most common type of survey. This periodic, unannounced survey is conducted for the purpose of certification renewal and is generally conducted within 9 to 15 months of a previous survey. Timing of the survey is not confined to weekdays and normal business hours; surveys may also be conducted in the evening (after 6 p.m.), early in the morning (before 8 a.m.), or on weekends.

### Abbreviated Standard Survey

An abbreviated standard survey is a standard survey of shorter duration and of a limited scope. This survey focuses on particular tasks that relate, for instance, to complaints received or to a change of ownership, administrator, or director of nursing. During the survey, however, a determination can be made to investigate any other area of concern.

## Extended Survey

An extended survey, in which the scope and duration of a standard survey is expanded, may become necessary when indications are present that quality of care may be substandard. An extended survey requires a more detailed investigation of problems and a closer review of the facility's policies and procedures. A partial extended survey may follow an abbreviated survey on the grounds of substandard quality of care.

## Post-Survey Revisit

A post-survey revisit involves a follow-up survey to confirm that the facility is in compliance and has the ability to remain in compliance. The follow-up survey reevaluates the specific care and services that were cited as noncompliant during the original standard, abbreviated, or extended survey. The nature of noncompliance dictates the scope of the revisit.

## Survey Process and Protocols

Regulations governing survey and enforcement procedures are published in the Code of Federal Regulations, Title 42, Part 488. The State Operations Manual contains a detailed description of the survey protocols and procedures. This section provides a brief overview of the survey process. A standard survey consists of seven successive tasks:

- Offsite preparation.
- Entrance conference.
- Initial tour.
- Resident sample selection.
- Information gathering.
- Determination of compliance.
- Exit conference.

## Task 1: Offsite Preparation

Offsite preparation before the actual visit to the facility includes preselection of residents and potential areas of concern at the targeted facility. During the actual visit, surveyors will initially focus on determining whether the previously identified concerns indeed exist.

Offsite preparation is based primarily on reports generated by the state's database. Each facility is required by law to use a patient assessment instrument called the minimum data set (MDS), discussed in Chapter 7. Each facility is required to electronically transmit the MDS information to the state in which the facility is licensed. The MDS information is used by the state to compile three main facility-specific reports that are available to the surveyors:

1. Facility Characteristics Report, which provides demographic information about the patient population in the facility. It includes information on gender, age, payment source, diagnostic characteristics, type of assessment, stability of conditions, and discharge potential.

2. Facility Quality Measure/Indicator (QM/QI) Report, which ranks the facility on quality indicators that apply to both chronic care (long-stay) and

post-acute care (short-stay) patients in the facility. The percentile ranking of the facility indicates how it compares with other facilities in the state.

3. Resident Level QM/QI Report, which provides resident-specific information. The report indicates whether a given resident has a particular condition, such as pressure ulcers or behavioral problems, or whether a given resident is at a high or low risk of developing a condition.

Other sources of information include (1) areas of noncompliance on the previous survey, (2) any patterns of noncompliance based on the past four surveys (***OSCAR*** Report 3, where states are required to maintain comprehensive information about past and current surveys and complaint investigations in CMS's OSCAR database; see Chapter 14 for more details), (3) findings from complaints that were investigated and complaints that have not been investigated, and (4) any areas of concern reported by the State Ombudsman Office (see Chapter 4 about the role of the ombudsman). Information about any other potential areas of concern, such as events reported in the news media, may also be included.

## Task 2: Entrance Conference

The survey team coordinator has an on-site meeting with the administrator (or other person in charge of the facility in the administrator's absence) to provide introductions, explain the purpose of the visit, and obtain some basic information that would facilitate the survey. For example, surveyors will need copies of the actual work schedules for licensed and registered nursing staff, a copy of the written information that is provided to

patients regarding their rights, and copies of admission contracts for all patients. The administrator is given copies of the QM/QI and other reports used in the off-site preparation. Signs are posted in the facility to notify the residents, employees, and the general public that a survey is in progress and that the surveyors are available to meet with any concerned individual.

## Task 3: Initial Tour

In an average-size nursing home of approximately 100 beds, the tour may take about two hours. Members of the survey team may go around independently, with or without members of the facility's staff accompanying them. The surveyors talk to residents, employees, and visitors in the facility; visit some patient rooms and key departments, such as the kitchen; and make general observations. The purpose is to make a general assessment in conjunction with the information compiled during off-site preparation. Information is gathered about concerns identified in Task 1 and any new concerns observed during the tour are added. During the tour, the main areas of focus are quality of care, quality of life, the emotional and behavioral conduct of patients and the reactions and interventions by staff, and any environmental and safety issues.

## Task 4: Resident Sample Selection

Information gathered during off-site preparation and the tour is used to develop a resident sample for detailed investigation of patient care. A "case mix stratified" sampling method is used. It is designed to include patients who require heavy care as well as those who require light care and patients who have sufficient memory and comprehension to be interviewed as well as those who cannot be interviewed. To the extent possible, the sample should include patients who may be particularly vulnerable, such as those who have indwelling catheters, are tube fed, are mentally impaired, or have speech or hearing disorders. Patients who have sustained a weight loss, those at risk of dehydration, those with pressure ulcers, or those with other associated risk factors are also included in the sample.

## Task 5: Information Gathering

Most of the surveyors' time in the facility is spent on the investigative phase of the survey process. Some main areas of investigation include patient care, medication errors, food preparation and dining services, residents' quality of life, facility environment and safety, procedures for protecting residents against abuse and neglect, and an evaluation of the facility's quality improvement program.

The process includes direct observations; interviews with the facility's residents, staff, and visitors; and a review of records. Close observations are made of meal preparation; dining services; medication pass; care being given; staff interactions with patients; infection control practices; and the condition of the environment such as cleanliness, sanitation, presence of any pests, safety hazards, functioning of equipment, and the proper and safe storage of drugs and biological and housekeeping chemicals and equipment. Record review particularly includes a review of patient assessments, plans of care, and outcomes of clinical interventions. The main purpose of record review is to obtain information necessary to validate or clarify information obtained through observation and interviews. Formal structured interviews are conducted for quality of life assessment.

Even though Task 5 is investigative in nature, the State Operations Manual recommends that dialogue between the surveyors and facility staff members be ongoing. The objective is to prevent any surprises for the staff on the surveyors' conclusions at the end of the survey.

## Task 6: Determination of Compliance

The surveyors determine the facility's compliance with each of the standards associated with the Requirements for Participation. A *deficiency* is cited for each of the standards not met. The survey team must evaluate the evidence documented during the survey to determine whether a deficiency exists. Any negative patient outcomes resulting from a failure to meet a requirement must also be documented.

Deficiencies are characterized as resident centered or facility centered. Resident-centered requirements must be met for each resident, and a violation affecting any single resident is cited as a deficiency. Facility-centered violations refer to the operational systems such as staffing, food preparation, and infection control. Deficiencies are also evaluated in terms of their severity and scope. *Severity* is determined by the extent of actual or potential harm and negative health outcomes as a result of not meeting a standard. *Scope* describes the number of patients that are potentially or actually affected as a result of not meeting a standard. Severity is rated according to four levels and scope is categorized in three types.

### Severity Levels

*Level 1.* A deficiency that has the potential for causing no more than a minor negative impact on the resident(s).

*Level 2.* Noncompliance that results in no more than minimal physical, mental, and/or psychosocial discomfort to the resident and/or has the potential (not yet realized) to compromise the resident's ability to maintain or reach his or her highest practicable physical, mental and/or psychosocial well-being.

*Level 3.* Noncompliance that results in a negative outcome that has compromised the resident's ability to maintain or reach his or her highest practicable physical, mental, and/or psychosocial well-being.

*Level 4.* There is immediate jeopardy that warrants an immediate corrective action. ***Immediate jeopardy*** means that the noncompliance with a standard has caused or is likely to cause serious injury, harm, impairment, or death to a resident receiving care in the facility.

## Scope Levels

1. *Isolated.* Scope is isolated when one or a very limited number of residents are affected and/or one or a very limited number of staff are involved, and/or the situation has occurred only occasionally or in a very limited number of locations.

2. *Pattern.* Scope is a pattern when more than a very limited number of residents are affected, and/or more than a very limited number of staff are involved, and/or the situation has occurred in several locations, and/or the same resident(s) have been affected by repeated occurrences of the same deficient practice. The effect of the deficient practice is not found to be pervasive throughout the facility.

3. *Widespread.* Scope is widespread when the problems causing the deficiencies are pervasive in the facility and/or represent systemic failure that has affected or has the potential to affect a large number or all of the facility's residents. Widespread scope refers to the entire facility population, not a subset of residents or one unit of a facility. In addition, widespread scope may be identified if a systemic failure in the facility (e.g., failure to maintain food at safe temperatures) would be likely to affect a large number of residents and is, therefore, pervasive in the facility.

## Severity/Scope Grid

On the basis of both its severity and scope, each deficiency is assigned to one of 12 categories using a grid (Figure 6–1). The categories determine how serious a deficiency is. A *category A* deficiency is the least serious and is isolated in scope, whereas a *category L* deficiency is the most serious and has been evaluated to be a widespread problem that presents immediate jeopardy. The 12 categories have been summarized into four levels that reflect the seriousness of each deficiency:

*Level 1.* A deficiency categorized as A, B, or C has the potential for causing no more than a minor negative impact on the resident(s). If only Level 1 deficiencies are present, the facility is deemed to be in substantial compliance. Categories D through L indicate that the facility is not in substantial compliance.

*Level 2.* A deficiency categorized as D, E, or F has caused no actual harm, but has the

**Figure 6–1** Severity/Scope Grid for Rating Nursing Home Deficiencies

| | Isolated | Pattern | Widespread |
|---|---|---|---|
| **Immediate Jeopardy** to Resident Health or Safety | J | K | L |
| **Actual Harm** That Is Not Immediate Jeopardy | G | H | I |
| No Actual Harm with **Potential for More than Minimal Harm** That Is Not Immediate Jeopardy | D | E | F |
| No Actual Harm with **Potential for Minimal Harm** | A | B | C |

Severity (vertical axis) — Scope (horizontal axis)

*Source:* Centers of Medicare and Medicaid Services.

potential to cause more than minimal harm and may compromise residents' ability to maintain or reach their highest practicable physical, mental, or psychosocial well-being.

*Level 3.* A deficiency categorized as G, H, or I has resulted in a negative outcome, but it does not present an immediate jeopardy.

*Level 4.* A deficiency categorized as J, K, or L presents an immediate jeopardy. Unless immediate corrective action is taken, the facility's noncompliance is likely to cause serious injury, harm, impairment, or death to a resident or residents.

Substandard quality of care is indicated for categories J, K, L, H, I, and F when one or more of the following Requirements of Participation are involved: resident behavior and facility practices, quality of life, and quality of care (see Exhibit 6–1).

## Task 7: Exit Conference

In the exit conference, the surveyors meet face to face with facility officials to present their findings. The administrator may request a copy of the patient sample, provide additional information that may have been overlooked, or ask for further clarifications. Information provided during the exit conference enables the nursing home staff to start remedial action and address the most critical areas of deficiency.

## Plan of Correction

A few days after the exit conference, the facility receives a Statement of Deficiency (Form CMS-2567; see Exhibit 6–2). It is a federal document that records the deficiencies cited as a result of the survey. This form is then used by the facility to record its *plan of correction (POC)*, which constitutes the

**Exhibit 6–1**  Requirements of Participation for SNF, NF, and Dual Certification

1. **Resident rights.** These rights provide for a physician of one's choice to be fully informed of one's medical condition and treatments, to refuse treatment, to formulate advance directives, and to authorize the facility to manage personal funds and require accounting for the funds, the right to personal privacy and confidentiality, and the right to voice grievances without fear of retaliation. In addition, residents cannot be prevented, coerced, or discriminated against in the course of exercising their rights as citizens of the facility or citizens of the United States.

2. **Admission, transfer, and discharge rights.** These rights provide residents certain safeguards against transfer or discharge from a facility and allow one to return to the same facility after brief periods of hospitalization or therapeutic leave. It also requires equal access and delivery of services regardless of the source of payment.

3. **Resident behavior and facility practices.** It limits the facility's use of physical and chemical restraints and prohibits mistreatment, neglect, or abuse of residents.

4. **Quality of life.** The facility must promote each resident's individuality, dignity, and respect. Exercise of choice and self-determination must be allowed. Residents have the right to interact with the community. Residents can organize resident and family groups for mutual support and planned activities, or to air grievances. The facility must make reasonable accommodation for individual preferences, such as meals and roommates. The facility must provide an ongoing program of activities and medically related social services. The standard also requires a clean, safe, comfortable, and homelike environment that will promote maintenance or enhancement of the quality of life of each resident.

5. **Resident assessment.** Within fourteen days of admission and at least annually thereafter the facility must undertake a comprehensive assessment of each patient's functional capacity and medical needs. The assessment must be reviewed at least quarterly. Based on the need assessment, the facility must develop a comprehensive plan of care for each resident and provide the services necessary to provide that care.

6. **Quality of care.** Each resident must receive and the facility must provide the necessary care and services to attain or maintain the highest practicable physical, mental, and psychosocial well-being in accordance with the comprehensive assessment and plan of care. The facility must provide appropriate treatments to maintain or improve a resident's functioning and range of motion, unless it is unavoidable. The facility must ensure that residents receive proper treatment and assistive devices to maintain vision and hearing abilities. Other patient care requirements include adopting measures to prevent pressure sores, providing appropriate treatment for pressure sores, ensuring adequate nutrition and hydration, providing special treatments as necessary, limiting use of antipsychotic drugs, and confining medication errors rates to less than 5%. The standards also address appropriate use of urinary catheters and nasogastric tubes.

7. **Nursing services.** The facility must have sufficient nursing staff, including licensed nurses, to provide necessary care on a 24-hour basis.

8. **Dietary services.** The facility must provide a nourishing, palatable, and well-balanced diet that meets the daily nutritional and special dietary needs of each resident.

9. **Physician services.** A physician must approve each admission, and each resident must remain under the care of a physician. Unless otherwise prohibited, the physician may delegate tasks to a physician assistant, nurse practitioner, or clinical nurse specialist.

*(continues)*

**Exhibit 6–1** Requirements of Participation for SNF, NF, and Dual Certification (Continued)

10. **Specialized rehabilitative services.** The facility must provide specialized rehabilitative therapies by qualified personnel under written orders of a physician.

11. **Dental services.** The facility must assist residents in obtaining routine and 24-hour emergency dental services.

12. **Pharmacy services.** The facility must provide pharmaceutical services with consultation from a licensed pharmacist. If state law permits it, unlicensed personnel may administer drugs, but only under the general supervision of a licensed nurse. The standard also requires monthly review of drug regimen for each resident and appropriate labeling and storage of drugs.

13. **Infection control.** The facility must have an infection control program and maintain records of incidents and corrective actions.

14. **Physical environment.** The facility must comply with the *Life Safety Code* of the National Fire Protection Association. The facility should provide for emergency electrical power in case of power failure. The building must have adequate space and equipment for dining, health services, and recreation. Resident rooms must meet certain requirements as to size and furnishings.

15. **Administration.** The facility must operate in compliance with all applicable federal, state, and local regulations and must be licensed by the state. The governing body has legal responsibility for the management and operation of the facility. The governing body must appoint a licensed nursing home administrator to manage the facility. Nurse aides working at the facility must receive required training, a competency evaluation, periodic performance review, and needed in-service education. The facility must also designate a physician to serve as medical director. The facility must provide or obtain needed laboratory, radiology, and other diagnostic services. The facility must maintain clinical records on each resident, have detailed written plans and procedures to meet all potential emergencies and disasters, have a written transfer agreement with a hospital that participates in the Medicare and Medicaid programs, and maintain a quality assessment and assurance committee.

facility's written plan for corrective action to achieve sustained compliance with the cited standards in response to deficiencies. The POC must be submitted to the state within 10 days of receiving form CMS-2567. For a POC to be acceptable, it must address five elements for each deficiency cited:

1. Details on how the facility will correct the deficiency as it relates to the patients found to have been affected by the deficient practice.

2. How the facility will act to protect residents in similar situations.

3. The measures the facility will take or the systems it will alter to ensure that the problem does not recur.

4. How the facility plans to monitor its performance to make sure that solutions are sustained. A plan should be developed, implemented, evaluated for its effectiveness, and integrated into the quality improvement program.

Exhibit 6–2 The *Statement Of Deficiencies and Plan of Correction* (CMS-2567)

DEPARTMENT OF HEALTH AND HUMAN SERVICES
CENTERS FOR MEDICARE & MEDICAID SERVICES

FORM APPROVED
OMB NO. 0938-0391

**STATEMENT OF DEFICIENCIES
AND PLAN OF CORRECTION**

| | (X1) PROVIDER/SUPPLIER/CLIA IDENTIFICATION NUMBER: | (X2) MULTIPLE CONSTRUCTION A. BUILDING _____ B. WING _____ | (X3) DATE SURVEY COMPLETED |
|---|---|---|---|

NAME OF FACILITY      STREET ADDRESS, CITY, STATE, ZIP CODE

| (X4) ID PREFIX TAG | SUMMARY STATEMENT OF DEFICIENCIES (EACH DEFICIENCY SHOULD BE PRECEDED BY FULL REGULATORY OR LSC IDENTIFYING INFORMATION) | ID PREFIX TAG | PLAN OF CORRECTION (EACH CORRECTIVE ACTION SHOULD BE CROSS-REFERRED TO THE APPROPRIATE DEFICIENCY) | (X5) COMPLETION DATE |
|---|---|---|---|---|

Any deficiency statement ending with an asterisk (*) denotes a deficiency which the institution may be excused from correcting providing it is determined that other safeguards provide sufficient protection to the patients. (*See reverse for further instructions.*) Except for nursing homes, the findings stated above are disclosable 90 days following the date of survey whether or not a plan of correction is provided. For nursing homes, the above findings and plans of correction are disclosable 14 days following the date these documents are made available to the facility. If deficiencies are cited, an approved plan of correction is requisite to continued program participation.

LABORATORY DIRECTOR'S OR PROVIDER/SUPPLIER REPRESENTATIVE'S SIGNATURE     TITLE       (X6) DATE

FORM CMS-2567 (02/99) Previous Versions Obsolete   EF 11/2004       If continuation sheet Page ____ of ____

(*continues*)

**Exhibit 6–2** The Statement Of Deficiencies and Plan of Correction (CMS-2567) (Continued)

## INSTRUCTIONS FOR COMPLETION OF THE STATEMENT OF DEFICIENCIES AND PLAN OF CORRECTION (CMS-2567)

I. **PURPOSE**

This document contains a listing of deficiencies cited by the surveying State Agency (SA) or Regional Office (RO) as requiring correction. The Summary Statement of Deficiencies is based on the surveyors' professional knowledge and interpretation of Medicare and/or Medicaid or Clinical Laboratory Improvement Amendments requirements.

II. **FORM COMPLETION**

**Name and Address of Facility** – Indicate the name and address of the facility identified on the official certification record. When surveying multiple sites under one identification number, identify the site where a deficiency exists in the text of the deficiency under the Summary Statement of Deficiencies column.

**Prefix Identification Tag** – Each cited deficiency and corrective action should be preceded by the prefix identification tag (as shown to the left of the regulation in the State Operations Manual or survey report form). For example, a deficiency in Patient Test Management (493.1107) would be preceded by the appropriate D-Tag in the 3000 series. A deficiency cited in the Life Safety Code provision 2-1 (construction) would be preceded by K8. Place this appropriate identification tag in the column labeled ID Prefix Tag.

III. **Summary Statement of Deficiencies** – Each cited deficiency should be followed by full identifying information, e.g., 493.1107(a). Each Life Safety Code deficiency should be followed by the referenced citation from the Life Safety Code and the provision number shown on the survey report form.

IV. **Plan of Correction** – In the column Plan of Correction, the statements should reflect the facility's plan for corrective action and the anticipated time of correction (an explicit date must be shown). If the action has been completed when the form is returned, the plan should indicate the date completed. The date indicated for completion of the corrective action must be appropriate to the level of the deficiency(ies).

V. **Waivers** – Waivers of other than Life Safety Code deficiencies in hospitals are by regulations specifically restricted to the RN waiver as provided in section 1861(e)(5) of the Social Security Act. The long term care regulations provide for waiver of the regulations for nursing, patient room size and number of beds per room. The regulations provide for variance of the number of beds per room for intermediate care facilities for the mentally retarded. Any other deficiency must be covered by an acceptable plan of correction. The waiver principle cannot be invoked in any other area than specified by regulation.

VI. **Waiver Asterisk(*)** – The footnote pertaining to the marking by asterisk of recommended waivers presumes an understanding that the use of waivers is specifically restricted to the regulatory items. In any event, when the asterisk is used after a deficiency statement, the CMS Regional Office should indicate in the right hand column opposite the deficiency whether or not the recommended waiver has been accepted.

VII. **Signature** – This form should be signed and dated by the provider or supplier representative or the laboratory director. The original, with the facility's proposed corrective action, must be returned to the appropriate surveying agency (SA or RO) within 10 days of receipt. Please maintain a copy for your records.

According to the Paperwork Reduction Act of 1995, no persons are required to a collection of information unless it displays a valid OMB control number. The valid OMB control number for this information is 0938-0391. The time required to complete this information collection is estimated to average 15 minutes per response, including the time to review instructions, search existing data resources, gather the data needed, and complete and review the information collection. If you have any comments concerning the accuracy of the time estimate(s) or suggestions for improving this form, please write to: CMS, Attn: PRA Reports Clearance Officer, 7500 Security Boulevard, Baltimore, Maryland 21244-1850.

*Source:* Department Of Health And Human Services Form Approved Centers For Medicare & Medicaid Services.

5. Dates when corrective action will be completed.

The POC serves as the facility's allegation of compliance. The facility is notified whether or not the POC has been accepted. However, acceptance of the POC by the State Survey Agency does not mean that the facility is in substantial compliance until it is determined through a post-survey revisit that the deficiencies no longer exist.

Federal regulations require each state to establish an informal dispute resolution process to allow facilities to contest deficiencies within 10 days of receiving CMS-2567. The 10-day period allowed for an informal dispute resolution cannot be used to delay filing the POC and to take corrective action.

## Enforcement and Remedies

The enforcement response by the state and federal authorities is based on the seriousness of deficiencies. There are three remedy categories (Exhibit 6–3). In Category 1 for example, the state may impose a ***directed plan of correction*** if state regulators do not believe that the facility can formulate and implement an effective POC on its own. For example, the state may require the facility to retain a nurse consultant. Other remedies that the state can impose include denial of payment for services (Category 2), civil monetary penalties or fines (Categories 2 and 3), temporary management appointed by the state (Category 3), or termination from the Medicare and Medicaid programs (Category

**Exhibit 6–3** Remedy Categories

| Category 1 | Category 2 | Category 3 |
|---|---|---|
| Directed Plan of Correction State Monitor; and/or Directed In-Service Training | Denial of Payment for New Admissions Denial of Payment for All Individuals imposed by CMS; and/or Civil money penalties: $50–$3,000/day $1,000–$10,000/instance | Temporary management Termination **Optional:** Civil money penalties $3,050–$10,000/day $1,000–$10,000/instance |

**Denial of payment for new admissions** must be imposed when a facility is not in substantial compliance within 3 months after being found out of compliance.

**Denial of payment and State monitoring** must be imposed when a facility has been found to have provided substandard quality of care on three consecutive standard surveys.

**NOTE:** Termination may be imposed by the State or CMS at any time.

*Source:* Centers of Medicare and Medicaid Services.

3). The nursing home has the right to appeal the enforcement action.

## Life Safety Code

Modern health care facilities are designed and built to exacting building codes that are primarily concerned with people's life and safety. As discussed in the previous section, the CMS has developed the Requirements of Participation, but it has not developed its own fire safety standards. Instead, the CMS has adopted standards developed by the National Fire Protection Association (NFPA) and has incorporated them by reference into the Requirements of Participation.

The NFPA is an international private non-profit organization and the world's leading advocate of fire prevention and public safety. Its primary mission is to reduce the worldwide burden of fire and other hazards. Among the many codes and standards developed by the NFPA, the one that applies to nursing facilities is NFPA 101®, *Life Safety Code®* (LSC). The LSC establishes minimum requirements for new and existing buildings to protect their occupants from fire, smoke, and toxic fumes. It covers construction, protection, and operational features. The LSC is not applicable where CMS finds that a state has in effect a fire and safety code imposed by state law that adequately protects patients in health care facilities. The LSC applies to all facilities referred in the code as "health care occupancy," which is defined as any inpatient facility that provides medical services or delivers care simultaneously to 4 or more patients where such patients are incapable of self-preservation because of age, physical or

mental disability, or because of security measures not under the occupants' control (NFPA, 2009). The LSC is a complex document that also incorporates by reference a number of other NFPA codes. Hence, expert consultation is almost always necessary especially when an organization is planning to undertake new construction, expansion of existing facilities, and major renovations. Exhibit 6–4 provides an overview of the code.

One lingering issue with the enforcement of LSC is waivers granted to older facilities. The law provides for waivers that may be granted to exempt older facilities from having to comply with current LSC standards in areas where full compliance would present unreasonable hardship. For example, older nursing homes are exempt from having automatic fire sprinklers because of the costs of retrofitting these facilities with sprinkler systems. A waiver is granted to accommodate the undue hardship provided the health and safety of the residents would not be at risk. In 2003, however, 31 residents died in nursing home fires in Hartford, Connecticut, and Nashville, Tennessee. Federal fire safety standards did not require either nursing home to have automatic sprinklers even though they have proven to be very effective in reducing the number of multiple deaths from fires. Actually, there has never been a multiple-death fire in a fully sprinklered nursing home (General Accountability Office, 2004).

The survey and enforcement process described in the previous section includes verification of compliance with the LSC. Deficiencies are cited on form CMS-2567, the same form used for other types of deficiencies. Most states use fire safety specialists within the State Survey Agency to conduct fire safety inspections. Several states, however, contract with their state fire marshal's offices to conduct the inspections. Hence, the

---

*Life Safety Code®* and 101® are registered trademarks of the National Fire Protection Association, Quincy, MA.

**Exhibit 6–4** NFPA *101, Life Safety Code*

Note: Main requirements as found in the 2009 edition of the LSC are summarized here for illustrative purposes following 10 general principles of fire protection. Sections of the LSC, and any other NFPA codes, are given in parentheses.

1. **Fire-resistive construction.** There are two major groups based on the construction materials: noncombustible construction (Types I and II) and combustible construction (Types III, IV, and V). Type I buildings are noncombustible, made of concrete and steel, and provide the highest degree of fire resistance. Type II buildings are also of noncombustible construction; however, the level of fire resistance is usually less than that required for Type I structures. All new construction is required to be fully sprinklered (18.1.6.1).

   Corridor walls are required to be continuous from the floor to the floor or roof deck above. These walls must rise through suspended ceilings and any other types of spaces (19.3.6.2.1) and must have a minimum of ½-hour fire resistance rating (19.3.6.2.2). With the exception of doors protecting vertical openings, exits, or hazardous areas, doors protecting corridor openings must be 1¾ in. thick of solid-bonded core wood construction and must be able to resist the passage of fire for at least 20 minutes (19.3.6.3.1). Clearance between the bottom of the door and floor covering is to be no more than 1 in. (19.3.6.3.4). The doors must be capable of fully closing on their own when a force of 5 lbf (pound-force: a unit of force) is applied at the latch edge of the door (19.3.6.3.5). These requirements do not apply to doors for toilet rooms, bathrooms, shower rooms, sink closets, and similar auxiliary spaces that do not contain flammable or combustible materials. Fireplaces are not permitted in patient rooms. They can be located in areas that are separated from patient sleeping rooms by construction that has at least a 1-hour fire-resistance rating and must have an approved enclosure that can withstand a temperature of 650° F (19.5.2.3).

2. **Subdivision of spaces.**

   *Areas of refuge*

   Large spaces must be compartmentalized to provide fire and ***smoke compartments*** inside a building. Every storey with more than 30 patients must have at least two smoke compartments. In addition, the size of a smoke compartment must not exceed 22,500 sq. ft. and the travel distance to the smoke compartment must not be greater than 200 ft. Required smoke barriers must have a minimum of ½-hour fire-resistance rating (19.3.7). In newer buildings, smoke barriers must have a 1-hour fire-resistance rating. An ***area of refuge*** is a zone of safety within a building that is protected from the effects of fire and smoke, and provides direct access to an exit. It permits a delay in egress so that people can safely wait in the area of refuge until professional help arrives.

   *Fire barriers*

   Fire barriers are used to provide enclosure, subdivision, or protection by using building materials that have fire-resistance ratings. The ratings must be determined by a nationally recognized testing agency in accordance with NFPA standards (8.3.3.2). All fire-rated products, such as doors and windows, must bear an approved label, which must be maintained in a legible condition (8.3.3.2.3). Fire doors are required to be self-closing or automatic-closing.

3. **Protection of vertical openings.** Vertical openings are open shafts through the floors of a building, such as stairways, elevator shafts, and laundry chutes, or they may be openings through a roof. Doors in stair enclosures must be self-closing and must normally be kept in the closed position (19.3.1.7).

*(continues)*

**Exhibit 6–4** NFPA *101, Life Safety Code* (Continued)

4. **Provision of adequate means of egress.** Means of egress refers to a continuous and unobstructed way of travel that enables a person to exit a building. At least two separate exits must be accessible from every part of every story of a building (19.2.4.2). As a general rule, door openings in means of egress must be at least 32 inches in clear width (7.2.1.2.3.2). They must be 41½ inches in new construction for means of egress from patient rooms (18.2.3.6). Dead-end corridors must not exceed 30 ft (18.2.5.2), and common path of travel to a means of egress shall not exceed 100 ft (18.2.5.3) in new construction. If locks are used, they must provide egress without having to use a key, a tool, special knowledge, or effort for opening the door (7.2.1.5). For stairs that are a component of the means of egress, the new code requires a width of 36 in., provided the total number of occupants (occupant load) served by the stairs is less than 50. Risers should be between 4 and 7 in. and tread depth should be 11 in. (7.2.2.2.1.2). Dimensions for existing stairs: width to be 36 in.; risers to be 8 in. or less; tread depth to be at least 9 in. Stairs and ramps must have handrails on both sides (7.2.2.4.1.1) and must continue for the full length of each flight of stairs (7.2.2.4.2).

5. **Provision of exit marking, exit illumination, and emergency power.** Exists must be clearly visible. If not, the route to every exit must be clearly marked. On signs reading EXIT, the letters must be at least 6 in. high and ¾ in. wide. Exits should also be illuminated. In addition, each exit door must have tactile signage that must comply with ICC/ANSI A117.1, American National Standard for Accessible and Usable Buildings and Facilities (7.10.1.3).

*Emergency power supply*

The facility must either have a Type 60, Class 2, Level 2 emergency power supply system or an approved emergency generator that has a fuel supply to operate for 2 hours. The room where the generator is located must be separated from the rest of the building by fire barriers having a minimum 1-hour fire-resistance rating (7.2.3.12). The equipment must be tested twice a year by approved personnel and a log of the results must be maintained (7.2.3.13). The emergency generator must kick on within 10 seconds of a power failure (7.9.1.3) and it must illuminate all means of egress. Emergency illumination must be provided for a minimum of 1½ hours (7.9.2.1).

6. **Limits on the use of interior finish materials.** Interior wall and ceiling finishes are classified into three categories according to their capacity to spread fire and produce smoke (10.2.3.4):

Class A: Flame spread index, 0–25; smoke developed index, 0–450

Class B: Flame spread index, 26–75; smoke developed index, 0–450

Class C: Flame spread index, 76–200; smoke developed index, 0–450

Chapter 10 of the NFPA *101, Life Safety Code* (2009 edition) provides details on when certain materials such as textile, vinyl, plastic, and paper may or may not be used.

Interior floor finishes are classified into two categories that indicate the flammability of the materials. These materials are classified according to their critical radiant flux rating that is determined by a test called the flooring radiant panel test:

Class I: critical radiant flux rating of at least 0.45 W/cm$^2$ (watts per square centimeter).

Class II: critical radiant flux rating of between 0.22 W/cm$^2$ and 0.44 W/cm$^2$.

*(continues)*

**Exhibit 6–4** NFPA *101, Life Safety Code* (Continued)

Draperies, curtains, and other similar loosely hanging furnishings and decorations must be made of flame-resistant materials and shall have a permanently affixed label bearing the identification of size and material type as required by NFPA 701 (10.3.1). Upholstered furniture and mattresses must be resistant to a cigarette ignition (smoldering). Generally, a Class I rating on the materials, in accordance with NFPA 260, is permitted.

7. **Fire alerting facilities.** The building must be adequately protected with fire alarms and smoke alarms. Even when a facility has automatic fire detection systems to initiate the fire alarm system, no less than one manual fire alarm box must be provided (9.6.2.6).

8. **Control of smoke movement.** Dividing a building into compartments helps limit the spread of fire and restrict the movement of smoke. Walls and partitions serve as smoke barriers when all openings between floors and ceilings through which smoke can travel are appropriately sealed with smoke-resistant materials to create smoke compartmentation.

9. **Protection of hazardous areas.** Some of the main hazardous areas in health care facilities are boiler rooms; fuel-fired heater rooms; central laundries; repair shops; paint shops; soiled linen rooms; trash collection rooms; and laboratories employing flammable, combustible, or hazardous materials (19.3.2.1.5). Hazardous areas must be protected with either an automatic extinguishing system or a fire barrier having a 1-hour fire resistance rating (19.3.2.1). Protection or separation is not required in areas where domestic cooking equipment is used for food warming or limited cooking (19.3.2.5.2). Commercial cooking equipment that produces grease-laden vapors must be protected by fire-extinguishing equipment (10.1.1, NFPA 96). An automatic fire-extinguishing system should be installed as primary protection and portable fire extinguishers should be provided as secondary backup (10.2.1, NFPA 96).

10. **Operational features.**

    *Fire safety plan and fire drills*

    The administration must develop a plan for the protection of all persons in the event of fire. The plan must include evacuation to areas of refuge within the building and evacuation from the building when necessary. Written copies of the plan must be made available to all supervisory personnel. Periodic instruction and review of duties must be provided to all employees. Fire drills must be conducted at least quarterly on all shifts. The drills must include the transmission of a fire alarm signal and simulation of emergency fire conditions, except that coded announcements instead of audible alarms are permissible when drills are conducted between 9:00 p.m. and 6:00 a.m. Employees must also receive instruction in life safety procedures and devices (19.7.1). Fire safety steps are covered in greater detail in Chapter 13.

    *Smoking*

    "No smoking" signs must be posted and smoking prohibited in enclosed spaces where flammable liquids, combustible gases, or oxygen are used or stored. Patients classified as "not responsible" must not be allowed to smoke except when the patient is under direct supervision by a staff member. Noncombustible ashtrays and metal containers with self-closing covers into which ashtrays can be emptied must be available in all areas where smoking is permitted (19.7.4).

LSC portion of a standard survey may or may not be conducted concurrently with the quality of care review, particularly in states that contract with the state's fire marshal.

A facility has three options to address LSC deficiencies (Figure 6–2): (1) Submit a plan of correction, as discussed earlier. (2) Petition for a waiver. If a waiver is granted, it may be temporary or permanent. (3) Undergo a Fire Safety Evaluation System (FSES) assessment. FSES was developed by the Department of Commerce's National Institute of Standards and Technology to provide a means for providers who participate in the Medicare and Medicaid programs to meet the fire safety objectives of the standards without necessarily being in full compliance with every standard. FSES uses a grading system to compare the overall level of fire safety in a specific facility to a hypothetical facility that exactly matches each requirement of the fire safety standards. Once a facility has been certified using FSES, it can continue to be certified on that basis in subsequent years provided there are no significant changes

that might alter the FSES score (General Accountability Office, 2004).

## General Accessibility Standards

Accessibility for disabled people is required under the Americans with Disabilities Act (ADA) of 1990. The legislation is a general civil rights law designed to protect the rights of handicapped people in all aspects of their lives, including employment, recreation, and their use of buildings and facilities. The ADA also covers access to transportation and communication. Nursing home buildings and facilities must be accessible by individuals with disabilities. Under the law, a ***disability*** can be a physical or mental impairment that substantially limits one or more major life activities.

Title III of the ADA prohibits discrimination on the basis of disability in "places of public accommodation" (i.e., businesses that serve the public) and "commercial facilities"

**Figure 6–2** How Nursing Homes May Address Fire Safety Deficiencies

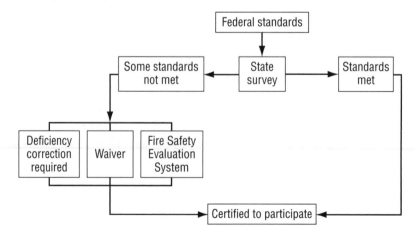

*Source:* General Accountability Office. 2004. *Nursing Home Fire Safety: Recent Fires Highlight Weaknesses in Federal Standards and Oversight.* Washington, DC: General Accountability Office.

(i.e., other businesses). Although the law does not specifically mention nursing facilities, health care establishments fall within the category of public accommodation. The law requires that certain adaptations, whenever necessary be made to provide access by the disabled to such public accommodations. For example, there should be no architectural barriers that might prevent access to the building from sidewalks and parking areas. Adequate parking spaces must be reserved for the handicapped. Access ramps must be installed. At least one accessible entrance to the building must be protected from the weather by canopy or roof overhang. Such entrances are also required to incorporate a passenger loading zone.

Inside the building, barriers to accessibility should also be removed. Examples of things a facility can do to make its services accessible include positioning telephones, water coolers, and vending machines so that they are easy to reach and use by people in wheelchairs; installing elevator control buttons with raised markings; using flashing fire alarm lights; installing raised toilet seats and grab bars in the bathrooms, and allowing enough room to maneuver a wheelchair; and avoiding high-pile carpeting that makes steering a wheelchair difficult. All building features and equipment must be maintained in operable working condition except for temporary interruptions in services or access due to maintenance or repairs.

At least 50% of the patient rooms and toilets in long-term care facilities must be designed and constructed to be accessible. In addition, all public use and common use areas must be accessible and usable by the disabled. In facilities or units of a facility where treatments and rehabilitation of conditions that affect mobility are rendered, all patient rooms and toilets must be accessible.

The ADA also requires facilities to provide auxiliary aids for effective communication. Such aids include interpreters, note takers, telecommunication and sound amplifying devices suited for the deaf, audio recordings, videotext displays, and large-print books and publications. However, the facility is not required to provide personal devices and services such as eyeglasses and hearing aids. Any segregation of patients within the facility should be based on clinical factors, not on a person's disability, because segregation based solely on disability is discriminatory. Another law, the Fair Housing Amendments Act of 1988, prohibits disability-based discrimination in public and private living quarters.

# OSHA and Workplace Safety

The Occupational Safety and Health Administration (OSHA) was created under the Occupational Safety and Health Act of 1970. OSHA's primary mission is to ensure the safety and health of America's employees by setting and enforcing standards and encouraging continual improvement in workplace safety and health.

According to the U.S. Bureau of Labor Statistics, of the 22 main occupational categories, nurse aides, orderlies, and attendants had the highest incidence rate (number of injuries per 10,000 full-time workers) of 465.3 per 10,000 workers in 2007. Of the various types of injuries, musculoskeletal disorders were the most common (252 cases per 10,000 workers among nurse aides, orderlies, and attendants; Bureau of Labor Statistics, 2008). Often referred to as ergonomic injuries, *musculoskeletal disorders (MSDs)* are injuries or illnesses affecting the connective tissues of the body such as muscles, nerves, tendons, joints, cartilage, or spinal discs. MSDs include conditions such as low back pain, sciatica, rotator cuff injuries, epicondylitis, and carpal tunnel syndrome. Injuries or disorders caused by slips, trips, falls, motor vehicle accidents, or similar incidents are not MSDs.

Nursing homes are legally required to comply with OSHA standards. However, OSHA also provides education and consultation, particularly to small and medium-size employers such as nursing homes. For example, OSHA has developed guidelines to help reduce MSDs. These Guidelines for Nursing Homes: Ergonomics for the Prevention of Musculoskeletal Disorders (see "For Further Learning") are advisory in nature and informational in content. OSHA's educational and consultation services are available free of charge and are independent of the agency's regulatory role.

## OSHA Standards and Enforcement

Under the Occupational Safety and Health Act of 1970, states can establish OSHA-approved workplace safety and health standards that are comparable to federal standards. OSHA approves and monitors state plans and provides up to 50% of an approved plan's operating budget. A state must conduct inspections to enforce its standards. As of December 2007, 26 states and jurisdictions were operating OSHA-approved state plans, 4 of which—Connecticut, New Jersey, New York, and the Virgin Islands—covered only public employees.

In general, OSHA standards require employers to maintain conditions that protect employees on the job; comply with general industry standards and standards applicable to their establishments; and ensure that employees use personal protective equipment when required. The general industry standards (29 CFR 1910), which are exhaustive, and the most frequently cited violations in nursing homes can be accessed at the OSHA website (see "For Further Learning"). Nursing Home eTool is another Web-based tool developed by OSHA that provides standards and recommendations to assist employers and employees identify and control hazards. Topics covered under Nursing Home eTool include bloodborne pathogens, ergonomics, dietary, laundry, maintenance, the nurse's station, pharmacy, tuberculosis, housekeeping, whirlpool/shower, and workplace violence (see "For Further Learning").

Businesses can be cited and fined if they do not comply with OSHA standards. When standards are violated, OSHA assesses penalties and seeks abatement of any hazards. In extreme cases, the matter may be referred to the Department of Justice for criminal investigation. The agency focuses its inspections on the most hazardous workplaces. Federal OSHA unprogrammed inspections are conducted in response to alleged hazardous conditions and include imminent dangers, fatalities/catastrophes, complaints, and referrals. Programmed inspections are selected according to national scheduling plans for safety and health. When employers are found to be in violation of OSHA standards, they are issued citations. Many of these violations result in penalties. OSHA penalties can reach up to $70,000 depending on the type of violation and how likely it is that the violation would result in serious harm to employees. There are five types of penalties that OSHA can impose:

*Willful.* The employer intentionally and knowingly commits a violation. Willful violations may have penalties as high as

$70,000. A willful citation does not require a death, but the U.S. Department of Justice may bring a criminal action against an employer whose willful violation of a standard results in death.

*Repeated.* OSHA finds a substantially similar violation during a reinspection within a three-year timeframe. Repeat violations may have penalties as high as $70,000.

*Serious.* Death or serious physical harm could result and the employer knew or could have known of the hazard. Serious violations may have penalties up to $7,000.

*Other-than-Serious.* Directly related to job safety and health, but will not cause death or serious physical harm. Other-than-serious violations often carry no penalties, but may result in penalties of up to $7,000.

*Failure to Abate.* An additional penalty of up to $7,000 per day for failure to correct a previously cited violation by the assigned abatement date.

## OSHA Recordkeeping Requirements

OSHA rules require employers to maintain records on all recordable work-related injuries and illnesses. The records must be kept on file for five years following the year to which they pertain. Completing these records does not mean that the employer or worker was at fault or that an OSHA standard was violated. An injury or illness is considered work related if an event or exposure in the work environment caused or contributed to the condition or significantly aggravated a preexisting condition. An injury or illness is recordable if it involves any of the following:

- Death.
- Loss of consciousness.
- Days away from work.

- Restricted work activity or job transfer.
- Medical treatment beyond first aid.
- A significant injury or illness diagnosed by a physician or other licensed health care professional.
- Cancer, chronic irreversible disease, a fractured or cracked bone, or a punctured eardrum.
- Any needlestick injury or cut from a sharp object that is contaminated with another person's blood or other potentially infectious material.
- Any case requiring an employee to be medically removed under the requirements of an OSHA health standard (e.g., in case of chemical poisoning).
- Tuberculosis infection as evidenced by a positive skin test or diagnosis by a physician or other licensed health care professional after exposure to a known case of active tuberculosis.

Three different reports must be filled out and maintained:

1. *Injury and Illness Incident Report (Form 301).* This is the first report to fill out. It must be completed within seven calendar days after a recordable work-related injury or illness occurs.

2. *Log of Work-Related Injuries and Illnesses (Form 300).* It is used to classify work-related injuries and illnesses and to note the extent and severity of each case. Each log entry must also include specific details about what happened and how it happened. The log requires each case to be classified into one of six categories: injury, skin disorders, respiratory conditions, poisoning, hearing loss, and all other illnesses. The log requires the

employee's name and job title. However, certain types of injuries or illnesses are regarded as privacy concern cases. For such cases, "privacy case" must be entered in the space normally used for the employee's name and job title. The nursing home must maintain a separate confidential list of the case numbers and employee names for the privacy concern cases. Privacy concern cases include the following:

- An injury or illness to an intimate body part or to the reproductive system.

- An injury or illness resulting from a sexual assault.

- A mental illness.

- A case of HIV infection, hepatitis, or tuberculosis.

- A needlestick injury or cut from a sharp object that is contaminated with blood or other potentially infectious material.

- Other illnesses, if the employee independently and voluntarily requests that his or her name not be entered on the log.

3. *Summary of Work-Related Injuries and Illnesses (Form 300A).* This form is completed at the end of the calendar year. It shows the totals for the year in each category of injury and illness. No later than February 1 of the following year, the Summary (not the Log) must be posted in a visible location where the employees can see it and become aware of the injuries and illnesses occurring in their workplace. The Summary must remain posted until April 30.

---

## For Further Thought

1. What attitudes do you think nursing home administrators ought to have toward regulations that are often regarded as onerous?

2. As a nursing facility administrator what would you do to ensure that your organization is in compliance with the various regulatory standards?

---

## For Further Learning

Accessibility standards under the Americans with Disabilities Act of 1990

   http://www.ada.gov/reg3a.html#Anchor-59404

*NFPA 101, Life Safety Code*

The complete text of the LSC can be read online. Sign in as "all other visitors."

   http://www.nfpa.org/freecodes/free_access_document.asp?id=10109

OSHA—Forms for recording work-related injuries and illnesses

http://www.osha.gov/recordkeeping/new-osha300form1-1-04.pdf

OSHA—Guidelines for Nursing Homes: Ergonomics for the Prevention of Musculoskeletal Disorders

http://www.osha.gov/ergonomics/guidelines/nursinghome/final_nh_guidelines.pdf

OSHA—Most frequently cited standards in nursing homes and personal care facilities

http://www.osha.gov/SLTC/nursinghome/standards.html

OSHA—Nursing Home eTool

http://www.osha.gov/SLTC/etools/nursinghome/index.html

OSHA—General industry standards (29 CFR 1910)

http://www.osha.gov/pls/oshaweb/owastand.display_standard_group?p_toc_level=1&p_part_number=1910

Overview of the QIS (Quality Indicator Survey) Process and Demonstration

http://www.cms.hhs.gov/SurveyCertificationGenInfo/downloads/SCLetter06-02att.pdf

Requirements of Participation

http://www.access.gpo.gov/nara/cfr/waisidx_05/42cfr483_05.html

State Operations Manual. Appendix P: Survey Protocol for Long Term Care Facilities—Part I

http://www.cms.hhs.gov/manuals/Downloads/som107ap_p_ltcf.pdf

State Operations Manual. Appendix PP: Guidance to Surveyors for Long-Term Care Facilities

http://www.cms.hhs.gov/manuals/Downloads/som107ap_pp_guidelines_ltcf.pdf

---

## REFERENCES

Bureau of Labor Statistics. 2008. *News: Nonfatal Occupational Injuries and Illnesses Requiring Days Away from Work, 2007*. Retrieved December 2008 from http://www.bls.gov/news.release/pdf/osh2.pdf.

General Accountability Office. 2004. *Nursing Home Fire Safety: Recent Fires Highlight Weaknesses in Federal Standards and Oversight*. Washington, DC: General Accountability Office.

NFPA. 2009. *NFPA 101, Life Safety Code*. 2009 edition. Quincy, MA: National Fire Protection Association.

# Chapter 7

---

# Financing and Reimbursement

## What You Will Learn

- Financing is the mechanism by which nursing home clients pay for the services. Payers determine the method and amount of reimbursement, except for private-pay rates that are established by the facility.

- Private financing includes out-of-pocket payment for services and coverage under private long-term care insurance. Several factors should be taken into account in establishing private-pay rates.

- Medicare is a federal program that is uniform across the United States. It covers three categories of people. Services for eligible people in a Medicare-certified facility are covered under Part A. However, Medicare is not a comprehensive long-term care program.

- Some long-term care services can be covered under Medicare Part B, which essentially covers outpatient services. Part C does not generally apply to nursing homes. Private-pay and dually covered patients can receive prescription drug benefits under Part D.

- Medicare reimburses certified nursing homes according to a case-mix-based prospective payment system. Assessment plays a critical role in case-mix-based reimbursement.

- Medicaid covers comprehensive long-term care services, but it is a welfare program for the indigent. Those who have assets must spend down to the state-established threshold levels to qualify. Unlike Medicare, the program varies from state to state.

- The PACE program aims to provide long-term care in community settings to those who risk being placed in a nursing home. Money is pooled from Medicare, Medicaid, and private sources to provide a capitated rate to the PACE organization.

- Managed care financing is based on capitation. Managed care organizations are active players in the Medicaid and Medicare programs as well as in the private market.

- Different types of partnership arrangements are possible between nursing homes and hospitals. Contracts with the Veterans Health Administration (VHA) are also common.

- The HIPAA legislation expanded the government's power to prosecute fraud as a criminal offense. Other fraud and abuse provisions in the law prohibit upcoding and kickbacks for patient referrals. The False Claims Act includes the *qui tam* provision that encourages whistleblowers to confront fraud and abuse through the legal system.

# Financing and Its Importance

Financing and reimbursement are viewed as the backbone of long-term care (LTC) services because they provide the financial resources necessary for sustaining internal facility operations. For the most part, health care financing is governed by external factors, notably politics, social changes, the economy, competition, and changes in the broader health care delivery system.

Much of the information covered in this chapter is of value to more than just nursing home corporations and administrators. Social workers and patient accounts managers should also have a clear understanding of financing so they can furnish advice and assistance to current and prospective patients, families and guardians, and the community. *Financing* is the means by which patients receiving services in nursing facilities pay for those services. Institutional LTC is expensive. In 2008, the national average cost of skilled nursing care for someone paying out of his or her personal funds was $191 per day for a semi-private room and $212 per day for a private room. Costs in some states are much higher. For example, semi-private costs aver-

aged $566 in Alaska and $335 in Connecticut (MetLife, 2008). Few patients or their families can afford such costs if they pay with their own funds. Although individual LTC insurance has grown, it is not widely popular, and only a small fraction of national nursing home expenditures are paid for by private insurance. Public financing, mainly Medicaid and Medicare, remains the predominant source of financing nursing home care. Sources of financing for nursing home care are illustrated in Figure 7–1.

Often the critical issue for nursing facility operators is how much the various publicly financed programs would pay—that is, how much reimbursement they can expect for services delivered to patients receiving public benefits. *Reimbursement* covers two aspects of financing: (1) the method used by a payer to determine the amount of payment and (2) the amount that is actually paid to a facility on behalf of a patient.

Trends in nursing home financing show that people's ability to pay for LTC from private sources has declined, although some stability can be observed since 2004. In 1990, private sources of payment financed almost 50% of nursing home care nationwide. By

**Figure 7-1** Sources of Nursing Home Payments, 2006 (All nonhospital based facilities)

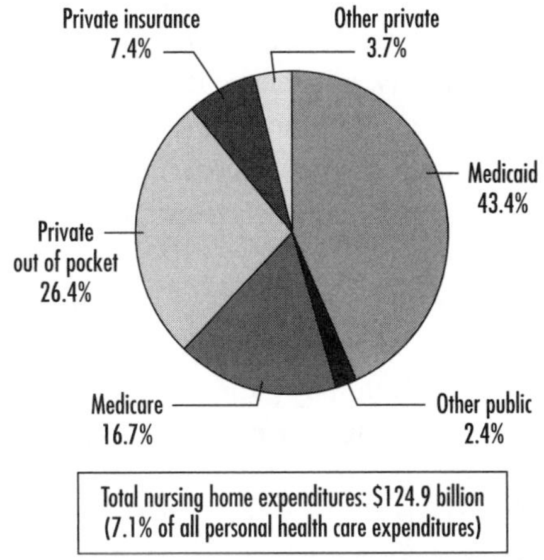

Private insurance 7.4%
Other private 3.7%
Medicaid 43.4%
Private out of pocket 26.4%
Medicare 16.7%
Other public 2.4%

Total nursing home expenditures: $124.9 billion (7.1% of all personal health care expenditures)

*Source:* Data from U.S. Department of Health and Human Services. *Health, United States, 2008.* (p. 417). Hyattsville, MD: U.S. Department of Health and Human Services.

2000, the proportion of total private payments declined to 43%. Between 2004 and 2006, private payments have ranged between 37 and 38%. Consequently, the cost burden of public programs has increased from 51% in 1990 to 62.5% in 2006 (DHHS, 2008, p. 417). To restrain escalating expenditures, both state and federal governments have been trying to place some limitation on the amount of reimbursement to providers. Also, fraud and abuse by providers have come under increased government scrutiny and have resulted in numerous criminal as well as civil prosecutions.

The Centers for Medicare and Medicaid Services (CMS) establishes Medicare reimbursement rates, whereas each state sets its own rates for Medicaid payment. The actual rate-setting mechanisms are quite complex. Nursing home administrators can obtain details of the Medicaid rate-setting methodology from their own state agencies.

# Private Financing

Of the two main types of private financing, direct out-of-pocket payment is the most common. The other type, presently much smaller in size, is private LTC insurance. For example, in 2006, private insurance paid for 7.4% of nursing home expenditures; out-of-pocket payments amounted to 26.4% (see Figure 7–1)

## Out-of-Pocket Financing

Out-of-pocket financing may come from cash savings, stocks, bonds, or annuities. For some people, such resources may provide adequate income to pay for nursing home care. In most instances, however, assets may have to be sold to generate cash.

A home is often the largest asset that most people have. Reverse mortgaging is a new creative way to tap into the built-up equity in a home without having to sell the property. But the owner has to continue to live in the home, which makes this option unavailable for nursing home care, although it can be used for in-home medical and assistive services. It can also be used to purchase private LTC insurance. A ***reverse mortgage*** is a type of loan against the equity in a home. It is available to people 62 and older who own their home and have few or no mortgage payments left. By using this method, an individual can choose to receive either a one-time loan against the equity or monthly cash payments. Even though it is a loan, the borrower does not have to repay the loan as long as he or she lives in the home. The lending institution retains a financial interest in the home. The borrowed amount is paid back when the home is sold.

Long-term care facilities are free to establish their own private-pay rates or prices. For noncertified beds (see Chapter 5), a facility may label its services as "intermediate care," "personal care," or "residential care." No clear-cut definitions exist for these terms, and a facility can establish its own criteria for determining its different levels of services and how much it will charge for those services. The terms all signify a level of care that is clinically much less complex than what is provided in SNF and NF certified facilities (see Chapter 5 on the types of certifications). For such custodial levels of care, nursing facilities may establish private-pay per-diem (daily) rates that are lower than Medicare or Medicaid rates. Private pay rates can be lower as long as the services are provided in noncertified beds. On the other hand, when private-pay patients are placed in a section of the facility that is certified as SNF or NF, administrators must be careful when setting private-pay rates. They risk having the Medicare and Medicaid rates reduced if the all-inclusive private-pay rate happens to be lower than what the public programs are paying. Generally, private-pay rates are the highest, and admission of private-pay patients often helps subsidize services provided to Medicaid patients because of low reimbursement.

Even though private-pay rates may be established at any level, they are governed by market forces and competition. Additional factors such as amenities that a facility offers should also be considered and compared with those of its competitors while setting private-pay rates. Patients and their families who have sufficient private funds available are often willing to pay extra for a better living environment. A facility with a reputation for providing high-quality care can also charge its private-pay clients a premium.

As discussed in Chapter 5, federal certification enables a facility to serve Medicare or Medicaid clients. Although certified beds can also be used for private-pay patients, these patients cannot be provided better quantity or quality of services for clinical needs that are similar to those of patients on public assistance. For example, certified beds occupied by private-pay patients cannot have extra staffing or extra amenities such as a more exclusive menu because these extra services would be construed as discrimination against patients on public assistance if they do not get these extra services. For these reasons, many facilities have a separate noncertified section to care for private-pay patients because the facility can then deliver extras and charge for them.

Private-pay rates may be set as all-inclusive (or bundled) rates, although this option is not the general practice. A *bundled rate* (also called package price) is one set price that includes all services that a patient may require. Generally, the rates are unbundled, meaning that each particular level of care has a basic room-and-board rate, which includes nursing care, meals, social services, activities, housekeeping, and maintenance services. Charges are added for ancillaries such as pharmaceuticals; supplies such as catheters, dressings, and incontinence pads; and services such as oxygen therapy or rehabilitation therapy. The basic rates and the charges for ancillary products and services are spelled out in a contract between the facility and the patient.

## Private Insurance

General health insurance plans sponsored by employers may have limited coverage for LTC services. Some retirees may also have similar limited coverage available under their company's health insurance plan for retirees. In most instances, however, people have to buy their own LTC policies sold by various private insurance companies. Some insurers may allow the use of life insurance death benefits in an existing insurance policy to cover the cost of long-term care. However, this option will reduce the dollar amount of the death benefit that the beneficiary will receive.

Long-term care insurance is available in a wide range of choices for services covered and prices. In addition to nursing home care, insurance also generally covers community-based services such as home health care or adult day care. Insurance policies (or plans) also vary in terms of the dollar amount of benefits to be paid on a daily basis. Depending on the plan, there may or may not be a maximum limit on the benefits. To be eligible for benefits, the insured person must meet the criteria for disability specified in the plan. Such criteria may include cognitive dysfunction or inability to perform certain activities of daily living (ADLs). Other criteria may be more loosely stated, such as medical necessity. In almost all instances, medical need for LTC must be certified by a physician.

When admitting patients with private insurance coverage, the facility's business office manager should carefully review the coverage, such as the type of care covered by the insurance plan. Some plans pay for only the skilled level of nursing home care, others include both skilled care and assisted living, and others are more comprehensive in coverage. Most plans have restrictions on the length of coverage, amount the plan will pay each day, coverage for ancillaries such as supplies and therapies, and elimination period. Comprehensive policies, however, are growing at a faster rate than other types of LTC plans.

# Medicare

Medicare—also called Title 18 of the Social Security Act—is a federal program that is uniform across the United States. It finances medical care for three categories of people: (1) persons who are age 65 and over, (2) disabled individuals who are entitled to Social Security benefits, and (3) people who have end-stage renal disease. The program is operated under the administrative oversight of the Centers for Medicare and Medicaid Services. Medicare is not a comprehensive program. Actually, the benefits for LTC are very limited. Medicare consists of four separate programs called Part A, Part B, Part C, and Part D.

## Part A of Medicare

Part A—also called Hospital Insurance (HI)—provides for care in a facility certified as SNF for a period not to exceed 100 days. Medicare does not pay for services provided in facilities that are not certified as SNFs.

Medicare does not meet the needs of people who require LTC for a long period of time. It is also not a comprehensive LTC program because it does not pay for care in an assisted living facility or in the various community-based programs, with the exception of home health care under certain conditions. A patient may be covered for less than 100 days in a SNF. In fact, in 2005, the average days of care in a SNF amounted to only 26 days per admission, which is up from 23 days in 1998 (CMS, 2007). Apart from being short-term, the Medicare benefit for SNF is a post-acute program. Before it will pay for services in a SNF, Medicare requires hospitalization for at least three consecutive nights. The patient must be in need of skilled nursing care as certified by a physician and be admitted to a SNF within 30 days after discharge from the hospital.

The maximum of 100 days of care is allowed within each benefit period. A ***benefit*** *period* begins when a patient is hospitalized for a particular spell of illness and ends when the beneficiary has not received care in a hospital or SNF for 60 consecutive days for that particular spell of illness. Four key criteria determine a benefit period:

- A spell of illness or principal condition for which a patient is hospitalized. Different spells of illness can trigger new benefit periods.
- Hospitalization, treatment in a SNF, or both. If a spell of illness for which a patient is hospitalized subsequently requires skilled nursing care in a SNF, the benefit period continues.
- A benefit period associated with a given spell of illness ends when the patient remains out of the hospital or SNF for 60 consecutive days.
- Readmission to a hospital or SNF within the 60 days is considered the same benefit period.

If the patient goes into the hospital after one benefit period has ended, a new benefit period begins. The number of benefit periods a patient can have is unlimited. Part A also covers hospital inpatient services, home health services for intermittent or part-time skilled nursing care, and hospice care in a Medicare-certified hospice.

At the time of admission, the facility's business office manager should determine eligibility for Part A coverage by finding out whether the patient is enrolled in Part A, whether he or she had a hospital stay of at least three consecutive days, whether the patient is being admitted within 30 days of discharge from the hospital, and the number of SNF days that may already have been used up in the benefit period. Details on admis-

sion and billing procedures are published in the Medicare Skilled Nursing Facility Manual (see "For Further Learning").

## Part A Deductibles and Copayments

A *deductible* is the amount the patient must first pay when a benefit period begins. Medicare starts paying only after the patient has paid the deductible ($1,068 per benefit period in 2009). In almost all instances, however, the deductible requirement is met during the three-day hospitalization before a patient comes to the SNF.

A *copayment* is the amount an insured patient must pay out of pocket each time a particular type of service is used. Medicare fully pays for just the first 20 days of SNF care in a benefit period. From days 21 through 100, the patient must pay a copayment ($133.50 per day in 2009). Medicare pays nothing after 100 days, even if the patient's condition may justify the need for ongoing services in a nursing facility. The copayments as well as payment for services that may be needed beyond the 100 days must be paid either privately or by Medicaid, provided the patient meets the eligibility criteria for Medicaid coverage (discussed later). It is illegal for nursing facilities to attempt to recover any payments that exceed the applicable deductible and copayments for services covered under the public programs.

## Part A Services: Skilled Nursing Care

The definition of skilled nursing care, as it applies to SNFs under the Medicare program, includes subacute care services. Hence, the same rules govern skilled nursing care and subacute care. According to Medicare law, skilled nursing care may include skilled nursing or skilled rehabilitation services. It has specific characteristics, summarized here:

- The services must be ordered by a physician.
- The care furnished must be for treating conditions for which the patient was hospitalized, or for conditions that arose while the patient was receiving care in a SNF.
- Skilled nursing services must be needed and must be provided seven days a week, except for skilled rehabilitation, which must be needed and provided five days a week.
- The services must require the skills of, and must be furnished directly by or under the supervision of, registered nurses (RNs), licensed practical (or vocational) nurses (LPNs or LVNs), physical therapists, occupational therapists, or speech pathologists.

"Under the supervision of" means that some of the actual hands-on care can be provided by paraprofessionals, such as certified nursing assistants, physical therapy assistants, and occupational therapy assistants. Skilled services are inherently complex and are required for medical conditions that can be treated safely and effectively only by the personnel just mentioned.

Examples of complex nursing services include intravenous or intramuscular injections, enteral feeding (delivery of liquid feedings through a tube), nasopharyngeal aspiration (suctioning through the nose and pharynx), tracheostomy (direct opening into the windpipe for breathing), insertion and irrigation of urinary catheters, dressings for the treatment of infections, treatment of pressure ulcers or widespread skin disorders, heat

treatments, start of oxygen therapy, and rehabilitation nursing. Examples of skilled rehabilitation include assessment of rehabilitation needs and restorative potential (probability of functional improvement), therapeutic exercises or activities, gait training, range-of-motion exercises, maintenance therapy that requires the skills of a professional therapist, ultrasound treatment, short-wave treatment, application of hot packs, infrared treatments, paraffin baths, whirlpool treatments, services needed for the restoration of speech or hearing, and therapy for swallowing disorders. The skilled care criteria do not require that a potential for restoration be present. Even if recovery or improvement is not possible, preventing further deterioration is a sufficient justification for providing skilled care. If a SNF contracts with a rehabilitation company to provide therapeutic services to its patients, that service company cannot bill Medicare directly for Part A services. The facility is responsible for paying that company.

A patient who requires only custodial care—such as assistance with ADLs—does not qualify for Part A coverage. Additional examples of custodial care include administration of routine oral medications, eye drops, or ointments; general maintenance of colostomy (attachment of colon to a stoma) and ileostomy (attachment of the small intestine to a stoma); routine maintenance of bladder catheters; dressings for noninfected conditions; care of minor skin problems; care for routine incontinence; periodic turning and positioning; and other routine and basic nursing services.

## Other Part A Services

According to Title 42 of the Code of Federal Regulations (Part 409, Subpart C), post-hospital services provided in a SNF include certain incidental services that are part of a person's nursing home stay:

- Bed and board (i.e., lodging and meals) in connection with the furnishing of nursing care. Medicare pays for semi-private accommodations. However, Medicare will pay for a private room if the patient's condition requires clinical isolation or if the SNF does not have semi-private accommodations available.

- Medical social services, which include services such as assessment and treatment of social and emotional issues, adjustment to the facility, and discharge planning.

- Prescription drugs, biologicals (medical preparations—serums, vaccines, etc.—made from living organisms), supplies, appliances, and equipment. Medicare pays for these items during the inpatient stay. To facilitate a patient's discharge from the facility, Medicare pays for only a limited supply of the drugs and equipment that the patient must continue to use after leaving the facility.

Part A benefits in a nursing home do not cover services that only a hospital can provide. Also, Medicare does not pay for services of a private-duty nurse or attendant.

## Part B of Medicare

Part B of Medicare—also called Supplementary Medical Insurance (SMI)—covers outpatient services. In general, these services include physician services, X-rays, laboratory tests, other diagnostic tests, ambulance services, and outpatient rehabilitation therapies. These services are generally delivered by providers other than SNFs, and the providers bill Medicare directly for the services.

From an eligibility standpoint, there is a major difference between Part A and Part B. Medicare Part A is a true entitlement program. People who qualify for one of the three categories mentioned earlier are eligible for benefits without having to pay any premiums, because all working Americans pay a Medicare payroll tax that funds Part A. Medicare Part B, on the other hand, requires voluntary enrollment and payment of a monthly premium. Effective 2007, the premium became income based. The standard premium in 2009 was $96.40 per month. For those earning more than $85,000 and filing individual tax returns (or earning more than $170,000 and filing joint tax returns), 2009 premiums range between $134.90 and $308.30, depending on income. Because Part B premiums are heavily subsidized by general taxes, 95% of the Medicare beneficiaries have chosen to purchase Part B coverage. At the price the elderly pay to purchase Part B coverage, they will not be able to buy a similar plan in the private insurance market. For those who also qualify for Medicaid, the state pays the Part B premiums.

Part B benefits are based on an annual basis, not on a benefit period basis. Hence, annual deductibles and copayments apply. The annual deductible for 2009 was $135. Copayments are paid according to a coinsurance of 80:20, meaning that after the deductible has been paid, Medicare pays 80% of the costs and the beneficiary pays the remaining 20%.

## Part B Services

Although Part B does not include SNF services, it is essential for nursing home administrators and business office personnel to understand Part B benefits. Certain services are paid under Part B while the patient is receiving SNF services under Part A. An example is physician services that are billed under Part B by the patient's attending physician. Similarly, diagnostic services and outpatient mental health care are covered under Part B. Other services, such as therapies, can be covered under Part B even after a patient's Part A benefits expire, and the patient may continue to stay in the nursing home as a private payer or as a Medicaid beneficiary. Certain preventive health screenings and immunizations, authorized under the Balanced Budget Act of 1997, are also included in Part B. Exhibit 7–1 summarizes Part B benefits.

## Part C of Medicare

Part C is also called Medicare Advantage. In reality, Part C is not a special program that offers specifically defined medical services. It gives an option to the beneficiaries to enroll in managed care health plans. The beneficiaries, however, do have the choice to remain in the original Medicare fee-for-service program. Because skilled care services are covered under Part A, Part C does not generally apply to nursing homes.

## Part D of Medicare

Part D, the prescription drug program, was added to the existing Medicare program under the Medicare Prescription Drug, Improvement, and Modernization Act (MMA) of 2003 and was fully implemented in January 2006. The program is available to anyone, regardless of income, who has coverage under Part A or Part B. Like Part B, the program is voluntary because it requires payment of a monthly premium, which varies from plan to plan. For 2008, the average was estimated to be $25 per month for a basic plan. More generous plans can cost more than $100 per month.

Prescription drugs under Part D can be obtained through two types of private plans approved by Medicare: (1) stand-alone prescription drug plans (PDPs) that offer only drug coverage are available to those who want to stay in the original Medicare fee-for-service program; (2) Medicare Advantage prescription drug plans (MA-PDs) are available to those who want to obtain all health care services through managed care organizations participating in Part C. Because nursing home patients are generally not covered under Part C, their coverage is mainly through PDPs. The PDPs have contracts with long-term care pharmacies that provide drugs to nursing homes (see Chapter 3).

For Medicare beneficiaries receiving services in a SNF under Part A, Part D does not apply because prescription drugs are included in the reimbursement that nursing homes receive. Part D affects dually covered beneficiaries who have both Medicare and Medicaid. These beneficiaries must enroll in a PDP. Similarly, private-pay patients can receive the prescription drug benefit if they are enrolled in a PDP. Selection of a PDP, however, is not an easy task for nursing home residents, many of whom have cognitive impairments. Even for cognitively intact residents, assessing and comparing different plans is a difficult task. Because of variations in PDP plans, it is conceivable that some patients would be enrolled in plans that are less able to meet their medication needs. Such issues have sparked concerns about quality-of-care problems resulting from potential gaps or restrictions in PDP drug coverages and the increased complexity

**Exhibit 7–1**  Benefits Under Medicare Part B

---

**Medically Necessary Services**
- Physicians' services
- Outpatient medical and surgical services and supplies
- Diagnostic tests
- Outpatient therapy*
- Outpatient mental health services
- Some preventive health care services
- Other medical services

**Preventive Services**
- Bone mass measurement
- Colorectal cancer screening
- Diabetes services and some supplies
- Glaucoma screening
- Mammogram screening
- Pap test/pelvic exam/clinical breast exam
- Prostate cancer screening
- Vaccinations such as flu and pneumonia shots

**Other Part B Services**
- Clinical laboratory services, such as blood test and urinalysis
- Home health care: Part-time skilled care and home health aide services
- Durable Medical Equipment (DME) when supplied by a home health agency (HHA) while delivering Medicare-covered home health care
- Outpatient hospital services
- Blood when needed as an outpatient
- Ambulance service

*As of September 1, 2003, Medicare placed limits on how much it would cover for outpatient physical (PT), occupational (OT), and speech (SLP) therapy. For 2009, the limits are $1,840 per calendar year for PT and SLP combined and $1,840 per calendar year for OT. After the patient has paid the $135 yearly Medicare Part B deductible, Medicare pays 80% of the cost up to the maximum limits.

for nursing homes to work across multiple plans (Stevenson et al., 2007).

# Medicare Prospective Payment System

Section 4432(a) of the Balanced Budget Act of 1997 required Medicare to develop a prospective payment system (PPS) to reimburse SNFs. When it was implemented in 1998, the PPS replaced the retrospective cost-based reimbursement system. The new method provides for a per-diem rate based on a facility's case mix. The rate is all-inclusive, which means that it is a bundled rate that includes payment for all SNF services that a Medicare recipient is eligible to receive under the program.

The former retrospective, cost-based system reimbursed, with some limitations, the actual costs for routine services, ancillary service costs, and cost of capital. These same costs are now consolidated in the PPS rate.

The reimbursement setting methodology is summarized here:

- A base payment rate (base amount of reimbursement) is determined by the mean costs of various SNFs in a base year. The base rates are computed separately for urban and rural facilities.
- The base rate is adjusted annually for inflation according to a market-basket index, an index of input prices for SNFs. The base rate is also adjusted by the hospital inpatient wage index to account for geographic variation in wages. The unadjusted base rates were established in 1998, and they are proposed to be updated in 2009.
- A case-mix adjustor is assigned to each resident of a facility. The adjustment reflects the estimated resource costs of caring for that resident.

## Case-Mix-Based Reimbursement

The aggregate level of clinical severity (acuity level) of patients in a facility is referred to as its *case mix*. The case mix varies from facility to facility. The level of case mix rises as the number of seriously ill patients increases. Patients who are more seriously ill require more intensive use of resources and incur greater cost to the facility. Therefore, a higher case mix calls for greater reimbursement.

A case-mix-adjusted rate of reimbursement is based on the intensity of care needed by patients in a SNF. It is based on the premise that a nursing home should be paid in accordance with the use of resources necessary for delivering care to its patients. For example, some residents require total assistance with their ADLs and have complex nursing care needs. Other residents may require less assistance with ADLs but may require skilled rehabilitation.

## Patient Assessment and Reimbursement

Patient assessment plays a critical role in prospective reimbursement because it is used to determine the case mix. A trained registered nurse in the facility oversees the assessment process for which a standardized Resident Assessment Instrument (RAI), called the minimum data set (MDS 3.0 is scheduled to be launched in 2009), must be used to conduct a comprehensive assessment of each patient's needs. The MDS contains extensive information on the resident's nursing care needs, ADL impairments, cognitive status, behavioral problems, and medical diagnoses (See Appendix 7–I).

A SNF must complete an initial assessment on a patient within 14 days of admission. Subsequent assessments must be completed by the 14th day and again by the 30th day. For patients staying longer than 30 days for Part A services, assessments must also be done by the 60th and 90th days, as the case may be. MDS information is electronically transmitted to the state, and the state transmits it to the CMS.

The facility's case mix is derived from a patient classification system, called resource utilization groups (RUG III version 5.20 is currently in use. RUG IV is under study). ***Resource utilization groups (RUGs)*** provide a classification system that is designed to differentiate Medicare patients by their levels of resource use. The MDS information provides the input for classifying each patient in one of the 53 RUG classes, which are mutually exclusive; a resident can be classified in only one class, and the patient is assigned a code for that class. When classified, the patient goes into the highest group for which he or she is eligible, based on the MDS assessment (Baker, 2000). The original 44-group RUG was updated to the 53-group system and made effective in 2006. The additional 9 groups identify high-cost patients who receive both rehabilitation therapy and extensive care services.

The methodology for determining RUG categories is complex. Various commercial software packages are available to accurately determine RUG scores, assign patients to RUG categories, and transmit the data to the state. The CMS also has developed RAVEN, a computerized data-entry system for LTC facilities that offers users the ability to collect and transmit MDS assessments and calculate RUG scores.

Figure 7–2 gives an overview of the RUG classification system. Residents in the Re-

habilitation + Extensive Services categories (9 RUGs) have the highest level of combined nursing and rehabilitation need. Hence, they also are reimbursed at the highest rate. Residents in the Rehabilitation categories (14 RUGs) have the next highest level of need, followed by the remaining 6 categories: Extensive Services (3 RUGs), Special Care (3 RUGs), Clinically Complex (6 RUGs), Impaired Cognition (4 RUGs), Behavior Only (4 RUGs), and Reduced Physical Function (10 RUGs).

The new MDS 3.0 version is designed to incorporate advances in assessment measures, increase the clinical relevance of items, improve the accuracy and validity of the tool, and increase input from residents by introducing more resident interview items. Providers, consumers, and other technical experts in nursing home care requested that MDS 3.0 revisions focus on improving the tool's clinical utility, clarity, and accuracy. The CMS also wanted to shorten the tool while maintaining the ability to use MDS data for quality indicators, quality measures, and reimbursement.

# Medicaid

Medicaid—also called Title 19 of the Social Security Act—is a jointly funded federal–state health insurance program. Medicaid is a welfare program for the indigent. People with very low incomes and those with little or no assets generally qualify. The eligibility criteria are set by the different states, so they vary from state to state. However, states are also required to follow federal guidelines. Under the guidelines, Medicaid must cover people receiving Supplemental Security Income (SSI). It includes many of the elderly, the blind, and the disabled.

**Figure 7-2** RUG-53 Classification System

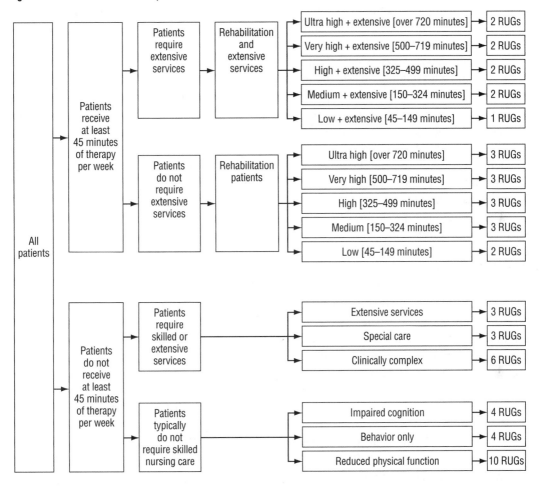

*Source:* Figure adapted from Government Accountability Office. 2002. *Skilled nursing facilities: Providers have responded to Medicare payments systems by changing practices*, no. GAO-02-841. Washington, DC: GAO.

States have the option to include people regarded as "medically needy" and many states have opted to do so. This option allows states to extend Medicaid eligibility to individuals who may have too much income to qualify otherwise. People who have excess income or assets to qualify outright for Medicaid must ***spend down*** to Medicaid eligibility thresholds by incurring medical or remedial care expenses to offset their ex-

cess income, thereby reducing it to a level below the maximum allowed by that state's Medicaid plan. The resource limits for spend down, meaning the amount of funds a person may keep in order to apply for Medicaid, generally vary between $2,000 and $3,000. This provision is particularly significant for nursing facilities because it allows the middle-class elderly to qualify for Medicaid once they have exhausted their personal assets. An estimated one-fourth of the patients who are initially admitted to a nursing facility on a private-pay basis eventually switch over to the Medicaid program after their personal assets have been exhausted. If individuals who qualify for Medicaid receive income from any sources, they are required to apply most of that income toward nursing home expenses; Medicaid will then pay the rest. Under federal law, it is a felony to shelter or distribute personal assets with the intention of making oneself eligible for Medicaid coverage.

The spend-down provision of Medicaid was modified under the Medicare Catastrophic Coverage Act (MCCA) of 1988. Although much of the MCCA was repealed, the portions affecting Medicaid remain in effect. The law protects the assets of an institutionalized person's spouse if the spouse must remain at home. The law was designed to prevent the impoverishment of the spouse remaining in the community. When one spouse enters a nursing home, there is a maximum amount of resources that the spouse at home is allowed to keep. This maximum amount, which varies from one state to another, is called Community Spouse Resource Allowance (CSRA). The community spouse is also allowed to keep a portion of the monthly income, an amount referred to as Community Spouse Monthly Income Allowance (MIA), which guarantees the spouse at home a basic monthly allowance for living expenses. Medicaid eligibility rules are complex. Specific details can be obtained from a local social/human services office.

Unlike Medicare, Medicaid is a comprehensive health care program. Medicaid has no limit on the number of days a person may stay in a nursing facility. Hence, Medicaid pays the largest share of national expenditures for nursing home services (see Figure 7–1). Many states also periodically (generally once a year) pay for eyeglasses, hearing aids, dental care, and other needed services. Also, as discussed in Chapters 2 and 3, states have been expanding coverage of community-based LTC services under the home and community-based services (HCBS) waiver program. The waiver program allows those who may currently be in nursing homes or qualify for care in a nursing home to live in the community and received community-based LTC services.

Determination of reimbursement rates for nursing facilities is left up to each state. States employ diverse methods and policies to determine the per-diem rates, and the amount of the per-diem reimbursement varies greatly from one state to another. Many states have adopted the case-mix method or a modified method similar to the Medicare prospective payment system discussed earlier.

# Program of All-Inclusive Care for the Elderly

The Program of All-Inclusive Care for the Elderly (PACE) was authorized under the Balanced Budget Act of 1997, but it is not available in all states. Where available, the program can be used by both Medicare and Medicaid beneficiaries. The main aim of the program is to provide LTC services in community settings to people who otherwise risk being placed in nursing homes. To achieve this, PACE employs four major strategies (Eleazer & Fretwell, 1999):

• It exclusively targets the frail older adult.
• It offers the full spectrum of acute care and long-term care services.

- Care is integrated by an interdisciplinary team of service providers.
- Financing is integrated through Medicare, Medicaid, and private funds into a single capitation rate.

To qualify for the program, an individual must be at least 55 years old, must be frail enough to meet the state's criteria for nursing home admission, and must be able to safely live in a community setting. The interdisciplinary team of professionals includes primary care physicians, nurses, rehabilitation therapists, social workers, personal care attendants, and dietitians. The team determines which services will best meet the enrollee's needs; it ensures the delivery of services in accordance with a plan of care; and it coordinates the needed services. Services are available 24 hours a day, 7 days a week. The PACE service package must include all Medicare and Medicaid services provided by the state. In addition, the PACE organization provides any service determined necessary by the interdisciplinary team. Basic services—such as primary care, social services, rehabilitation therapies, personal care and supportive services, nutritional counseling, recreational therapy, and meals services—are generally provided in an adult day care center setting. Other needed services are obtained through referral. These services include home health care, services from medical specialists, laboratory and other diagnostic services, hospitalization, and nursing home care. The number of nursing home placements is rising in PACE as the population is aging.

PACE organizations are paid a fixed monthly payment per enrollee. The reimbursement amount remains fixed during the contract year regardless of the services an enrollee may need.

# Managed Care and Health System Partnerships

The growing health care burden for an aging population will, by necessity, make public financing more stringent. It means that nursing home administrators will have to find innovative ways to increase revenues from private sources, something that will increasingly involve other organizations for financing and delivery of care.

## Managed Care Financing

Managed care was introduced in Chapter 3. All managed care organizations (MCOs) are private organizations, but they can contract with Medicare or Medicaid to deliver health care to beneficiaries covered by these public programs. The key to understanding the general concept of managed care is the delivery of services on a prepayment basis, which means that an MCO must provide all needed services to enrolled beneficiaries in exchange for a fixed monthly payment agreed to in advance. The fixed monthly payment that covers all services is called *capitation*. The nursing facility must manage the cost of providing the services within the capitation amount received. If the cost of services exceeds the capitated reimbursement, the nursing facility will lose money. Capitation is designed to control inappropriate use of services and to control the escalating costs of health care delivery.

In determining the capitation rates, a method called "risk adjustment" is used to account for variations in beneficiary health status. *Risk adjustment* accounts for the expected consumption of health care resources in accordance with the patients' health status.

For example, the MDS-based RUG system (discussed earlier) is a risk-adjustment method used for setting payment levels.

Under HCBS waivers, states can deliver community-based LTC services to Medicaid beneficiaries by contracting with MCOs. The Medicare program offers limited access to a social managed care plan, which provides the full range of Medicare benefits plus additional services, including care coordination; prescription drugs; short-term nursing home care; and a full range of home and community-based services such as homemaker, personal care services, adult day care, respite care, and medical transportation. Other services that may be provided include eyeglasses, hearing aids, and dental benefits. Currently, only four social managed care plans exist. They are located in Portland, Oregon; Long Beach, California; Brooklyn, New York; and Las Vegas, Nevada.

Apart from the managed care programs that deliver services to Medicare and Medicaid beneficiaries, MCOs also contract with nursing homes to deliver services to their enrollees. MCOs generally negotiate per-diem rates with nursing facilities. A nursing facility could have contracts with several different MCOs to provide services to clients covered under private or public financial arrangements. Refinements in basic per-diem reimbursement are likely to be made as administrators become savvy in associating costs with case-mix variations.

Nursing facility administrators are faced with both an opportunity and a challenge to meet higher demands for subacute care. They must also develop contracting and negotiating skills to deal with MCOs, skills in costing and pricing skilled care and subacute services, and skills to manage clinical services that have become increasingly complex. On the other hand, many hospitals have developed

transitional care (or extended care) units that deliver post-acute services after a patient is discharged from acute care. This puts hospitals in the driver's seat to steer patients away from nursing homes when these patients require post-acute care in a skilled nursing facility. That means stiffer competition for freestanding community nursing facilities. On the other hand, not all hospitals have post-acute care units. In either case, a nursing facility can establish partnerships with area hospitals to at least serve the overflow of patients that may require post-acute care. An MCO may also partner with a hospital-based health system and one or two nursing facilities. Getting a piece of the action unquestionably presents difficult challenges for nursing home administrators. The task can be daunting without administrative leadership that is firmly based on the open-system model discussed in Chapter 4.

## Hospital and Health System Partnerships

Partnership between a hospital and nursing home can be attractive to MCOs because MCOs look for organizations that can offer a full range of services, along with high quality and low cost. Beck (1996) proposed four different partnership options that nursing home administrators can explore:

1. One relatively low-risk form of partnership with a hospital is in the form of a sponsorship agreement. Under this arrangement, a hospital "sponsors" skilled nursing care for a specific patient or patients, essentially acting as a third-party payer for the patient at a predetermined rate. The hospital benefits by discharging a patient who no longer needs to be hospitalized and for whom the hospital will have to ab-

sorb the costs under PPS and capitation payment methods. The nursing facility can benefit from a relatively high payment from the hospital.

2. A second form of partnership is a bed-reserve agreement. Under this plan, a hospital pays a fixed amount for each bed that it reserves in a SNF for use by its patients. Unlike sponsorship, bed-reserve agreements may not be patient specific. In fact, payment must be made even if the reserved beds are not used. In this case, it is important to check with the state's Medicaid program that such an arrangement would be acceptable.

3. Nursing facilities and hospitals can initiate a shared service arrangement. Such an arrangement is desirable when either a hospital needs LTC expertise to establish a subacute program or a SNF needs specific expertise to upgrade its level of care. Monetary arrangements between the providers are determined by the services provided.

4. A hospital that seeks to establish a skilled nursing unit for subacute care can contract with a nursing home to manage that unit. Frequently, the nursing facility is paid a management fee, which is usually a percentage of the profits generated from the operation. The hospital holds the license, and the nursing facility handles day-to-day operations. The nursing home can admit the overflow of patients to its own facility.

Summa Health System, an integrated health system in northeastern Ohio, is an example of the type of partnerships that can be formed among various organizations. In this case, Summa and skilled nursing providers in northeastern Ohio have come together to be part of a systemwide Care Coordination Network that is designed to meet the complex, post-discharge needs of older adult patients. Summa has partnered with 28 SNFs that have been designated as preferred providers. To provide a seamless transfer of patients, the network developed a communication program and defined methods of transfer. Each facility works closely with Summa to set clinical guidelines and works to improve the outcomes of patients who are transferred from Summa (McCarthy & Beck, 2007).

## Veterans Health Administration Contracts

The VHA is responsible for providing nursing home care to any veteran in need of such care. The care may be provided directly in VHA's own facilities, or the veterans needing care may be placed in community nursing homes. For instance, in 2005, VHA nursing homes served 18,000 veterans, but the VHA also outsourced more than 4,400 veterans to community nursing homes (General Accounting Office, 2006). To participate in the program, a nursing facility must enter into a contractual arrangement with the VHA. Roughly one in five nursing homes has a contract with the VHA. The contract is generally for a one-year term and is renewable. Reimbursement is contractually established between the facility and the VHA.

## Fraud and Abuse

Fraud and abuse by providers who participate in the Medicare and Medicaid programs have been a growing concern in recent years. Because fraud and abuse siphon off resources that could otherwise be used for providing legitimate services to needy people, the government has been cracking down on providers who abuse the system. Both criminal and civil laws can be enforced.

## Federal Fraud and Abuse Law

The federal fraud and abuse law is a criminal statute. The legislation has evolved over time in the form of amendments to the Social Security Act. Most recently, the statute was expanded in the form of the Health Insurance Portability and Accountability Act (HIPAA) of 1996. The HIPAA legislation created the Health Care Fraud and Abuse Control Program, which gave the government expanded powers to investigate and prosecute fraud in the delivery of health care services.

Various provisions to curtail fraud and abuse have also been passed down through amendments to the Social Security Act. Here are the main provisions of the fraud and abuse statutes as they apply to nursing homes:

1. It is a felony to make false statements or claims regarding services provided to Medicare or Medicaid patients. Violations are punishable with fines up to $25,000 or imprisonment of up to five years. Examples of violations include false billings or attempts to obtain payments for services not provided. *Upcoding*, that is, billing for services that procure a higher reimbursement than the services actually provided and that should have been billed at a lower rate of reimbursement, is also a felony. For example, manipulating the MDS to increase the case mix would be considered upcoding.

2. It is a felony to induce referrals of Medicare or Medicaid patients by offering or receiving any kind of remuneration, kickback, or bribe, regardless of whether they are in cash or kind. Same penalties as in item 1 apply. This category would include gifts to physicians or other referral agents. Anti-kickback provisions may also apply to situations in which the nursing home refers services to external providers (such as pharmacies, laboratories, and medical equipment suppliers) in exchange for services received. For example, a nursing facility may ask a clinical laboratory for free services such as chart review or infection control. These are services that nursing homes are required to provide, and they are included in the reimbursements nursing homes receive from Medicare and Medicaid. The clinical laboratory is in a position to financially benefit from referral of clinical tests and other laboratory work from the facility. Under these circumstances, free services to the nursing home may be construed as inducement for referrals to the laboratory. Either offering or receiving any kind of remuneration to induce referrals violates the anti-kickback statute.

3. Under HIPAA, any felony conviction for fraud, theft, embezzlement, or other financial misconduct by a health care provider must also result in the provider's expulsion from Medicare and Medicaid programs.

## False Claims Act

The civil False Claims Act (FCA) was originally enacted in 1863 during the Civil War as a measure against fraud by companies furnishing supplies to the Union Army. The law was amended in 1986, under the Reagan presidency, to curtail widespread reports of fraud in the defense industry. In the health care industry, the law relates primarily to the making of false or fraudulent claims for payment from public payers such as Medicare and Medicaid. For example, it makes it illegal to provide and bill for services that are medically unnecessary, to provide and bill for services that are not covered under a federal program, or to try to claim payment for unbundled services by submitting separate bills when in fact the services should be bundled. Damages under the False Claims Act are severe. For all claims made after September 29, 1999, an entity that violates the act must repay three times the amount of damages suffered by the government plus a mandatory civil penalty of at least $5,500 and no more than $11,000 per claim.

Apart from penalizing facilities for filing fraudulent claims, the FCA has also been used to punish facilities that fail to provide adequate care. For example, in 1996, the U.S. Attorney's Office for the Eastern District of Pennsylvania filed a civil complaint against the owner and former administrator of a nursing facility in Philadelphia. The government contended that the defendants had violated the FCA when they submitted claims for payment, despite the fact that the residents did not receive adequate care, because three residents in the facility had suffered from malnutrition and inadequate wound care. The case was settled for a $600,000 fine and consent by the facility to implement quality standards. Failure to hire adequate staff to provide sufficient care may be regarded as deliberate intent to render substandard services and can fall under the provisions of the FCA.

A unique feature of the FCA that has been widely credited for its success is the *qui tam* (informer or whistleblower) provision. Any individual who has knowledge that a person or an entity is submitting false claims or otherwise defrauding the federal government can bring a lawsuit on behalf of the government and can share in the damages recovered as a result of the lawsuit. The person who brings the case is referred to as a ***qui tam relator*** or whistleblower, who is often an employee or a former employee of a company. But a competitor, a subcontractor, a patient, or a family member can also be a relator if they have evidence of fraud against the government. As long as the information is not publicly disclosed and the government has not already sued the individual or company for the fraud, the relator may bring a *qui tam* lawsuit. Depending on various factors, the relators are entitled to between 15 and 30% of whatever amount the government recovers as a result of their *qui tam* lawsuits (Phillips & Cohen, 2003). A *qui tam* suit initially remains under seal, which allows the Department of Justice to review the case and decide whether to join the legal action.

The law provides certain protections to the relators. For example, the law prohibits an employer from harassing or retaliating against a relator. If retaliation occurs, the relator can recover damages including reinstatement, double the amount of back pay, and legal costs.

## For Further Thought

1. Suppose you have just been appointed the administrator of a chain-affiliated 110-bed facility in which all the beds are dually certified. Your superior, who is a corporate official, comments on the low percentage of private-pay patients in the facility even though the overall occupancy rate has been 98%. In your discussions, the supervisor suggests that whenever a bed is vacant you should wait for a private-pay patient to occupy it and that you should advise Medicaid and Medicare clients that no beds are available. How will you address this issue with your superior?

2. Mabel Brown resides in an assisted living facility and is admitted to a hospital following a stroke. After a hospital stay of eight days, Ms. Brown returned to her apartment at the assisted living center, but she needs assistance with personal care and some speech therapy. Will Medicare pay for the personal care services and speech therapy? Explain.

3. Hilda Smith, who had osteoporosis, sustained a hip fracture because of a fall in her home. After 5 nights in an acute care hospital, she is admitted to a SNF where she spends 16 days for rehabilitation, nursing care, and assistance with ADLs. The patient is then discharged to her own home where a physical therapist from a home health agency comes in to train her to use a walker and build strength. After being at home for 25 days, Mrs. Smith develops deep venous thrombosis (blood clot in a vein) in her thigh and is admitted to the hospital, from where she is transferred to a SNF after spending 2 nights in the hospital. Assuming that Mrs. Smith meets Medicare criteria for the services described here, how many days of SNF care is Mrs. Smith entitled to during her most recent stay (assume that she qualifies for the full 100 days)? How much in deductibles and copayments does Mrs. Smith have to pay (use 2009 figures given in the text)?

## For Further Learning

Information on the release of MDS 3.0 and the final report on its development are available at the CMS website.

http://www.cms.hhs.gov/NursingHomeQualityInits/25_NHQIMDS30.asp

## REFERENCES

Baker, J.J. 2000. *Prospective Payment for Long-Term Care: 2000–2001.* Gaithersburg, MD: Aspen Publishers.

Beck, D.C. 1996. Partnerships may tame subacute rivalry. *Contemporary Longterm Care* 19, no. 7: 72.

CMS. 2007. Retrieved December 2008 from Centers for Medicare and Medicaid Services, http://www.cms.hhs.gov/MedicareMedicaidStatSupp/downloads/Table6.8.pdf

DHHS. 2008. *Health, United States, 2008*. Hyattsville, MD: National Center for Health Statistics, Department of Health and Human Services.

Eleazer, P., & M. Fretwell. 1999. The PACE model (Program for All Inclusive Care of the Elderly): A review. In P.R. Katz et al. (eds.). *Emerging Systems in Long-Term Care*, vol. 4 (pp. 88–117). New York: Springer Publishing.

General Accounting Office. 2006. *VA Long Term Care: Trends and Planning Challenges in Providing Nursing Home Care to Veterans*. Washington, DC: General Accounting Office.

McCarthy, D., & Beck, C. 2007. Summa Health System's Care Coordination Network. Retrieved December 2008 from http://www.commonwealthfund.org/innovations/innovations_show.htm? doc_id=520262MetLife. 2008. *The MetLife Market Survey of Nursing Home and Assisted Living Costs, October 2008*. New York: Metropolitan Life Insurance Company.

Phillips & Cohen: Attorneys at Law. 2003. *The False Claims Act: How It Works*. http://www.whistle-blowers.com/html/frm/howks_f.htm

Stevenson, D.G., et al. 2007. *Medicare Part D, Nursing Homes, and Long-Term Care Pharmacies*. Washington, DC: MedPAC.

**Appendix 7-1** MINIMUM DATA SET (MDS) 3.0

# MINIMUM DATA SET (MDS) 3.0
## DRAFT

| Section A | Identification Information |
|---|---|

**A0100. Facility Provider Numbers**

A.    National Provider Identifier (NPI):

B.    CMS Certification Number (CCN):

C.    State Provider Number:

**A0200. Type of Provider**

Enter [ ] Code

Type of provider
1.   **Nursing home (SNF/NF)**
2.   **Swing Bed**

**A0300. Type of Assessment/Tracking**

Enter [ ] Code

A.    **Federal OBRA Reason for Assessment/Tracking**
01.  **Admission assessment** (required by day 14)
02.  **Quarterly review assessment**
03.  **Annual assessment**
04.  **Significant change in status assessment**
05.  **Significant correction to prior full assessment**
06.  **Significant correction to prior quarterly assessment**
10.  **Discharge transaction-return not anticipated**
11.  **Discharge transaction-return anticipated**
20.  **Entry transaction**
99.  **Not OBRA required assessment/tracking**

Enter [ ] Code

B.    **PPS Assessments**
**PPS Scheduled Assessments for a Medicare Part A Stay**
01.  **5-day scheduled assessment**
02.  **14-day scheduled assessment**
03.  **30-day scheduled assessment**
04.  **60-day scheduled assessment**
05.  **90-day scheduled assessment**
06.  **Readmission/return assessment**
**PPS Unscheduled Assessments for a Medicare Part A Stay**
07.  **Unscheduled assessment used for PPS** (OMRA, significant change, or significant correction assessment)
08.  **Swing Bed clinical change assessment**
09.  **End of Medicare coverage assessment – EMCA**
**Not PPS Assessment**
99.  **Not PPS assessment**

Enter [ ] Code

C.    **PPS Other Medicare Required Assessment – OMRA**
0.   **No**
1.   **Yes**

Enter [ ] Code

D.    **State Required Assessment**
0.   **No**
1.   **Yes**

Enter [ ] Code

E.    **Is this assessment the first assessment (OBRA or PPS) since the most recent admission?**
0.   **No**
1.   **Yes**

*(continues)*

## Appendix 7-1 MINIMUM DATA SET (MDS) 3.0 (Continued)

# Section A    Identification Information

### A0400. Submission Requirement

| Enter [ ] Code | 1. **Federal required submission** |
|---|---|
| | 2. **State but not federal required submission** |
| | 3. **Neither federal or state required submission** (e.g. HMO, other insurance, etc.) |

### A0500. Legal Name of Resident

A. **First Name:**

[                    ]

B. **Middle Initial:**

[  ]

C. **Last Name:**

[                                ]

D. **Suffix:**

[     ]

### A0600. Social Security and Medicare Numbers

A. **Social Security Number:**

[      ] - [   ] - [      ]

B. **Medicare number** (or comparable railroad insurance number):

[               ]

### A0700. Medicaid Number — Enter "+" if pending, "N" if not a Medicaid recipient

[                        ]

### A0800. Gender

| Enter [ ] Code | 1. **Male** |
|---|---|
| | 2. **Female** |

### A0900. Birth Date

[    ] - [    ] - [      ]

month    day    year

### A1000. Race/Ethnicity — Complete only for first assessment (OBRA or PPS) since the most recent admission (A0300E = 1)

↓ Check all that apply

| [ ] | A. | **American Indian or Alaska Native** |
|---|---|---|
| [ ] | B. | **Asian** |
| [ ] | C. | **Black or African American** |
| [ ] | D. | **Hispanic or Latino** |
| [ ] | E. | **Native Hawaiian or Other Pacific Islander** |
| [ ] | F. | **White** |
| [ ] | Z. | **Unable to determine or unknown** |

### A1100. Language

| Enter [ ] Code | A. | **Does the resident need or want an interpreter to communicate with a doctor or health care staff?** |
|---|---|---|
| | | 0. **No** |
| | | 1. **Yes** → Specify in A1100B, Preferred Language |
| | | 9. **Unable to determine** |
| | B. | **Preferred Language** |

[                    ]

*(continues)*

**Appendix 7-1** MINIMUM DATA SET (MDS) 3.0 (Continued)

## Section A  Identification Information

**A1200. Marital Status**

Enter Code ☐
1. **Never married**
2. **Married**
3. **Widowed**
4. **Separated**
5. **Divorced**

**A1300. Optional Resident Items**

A.  **Medical Record Number:**

B.  **Room number:**

C.  **Name by which resident prefers to be addressed:**

D.  **Lifetime occupation(s)** – put "/" between two occupations:

**A1500. Preadmission Screening and Resident Review (PASRR)**

Has the resident been evaluated by Level II PASRR and determined to have a **serious mental illness and/or mental retardation or a related condition?**

Enter Code ☐
0.  **No**
1.  **Yes**
9.  **Not a Medicaid certified unit**

**A1550. Conditions Related to MR/DD Status**

↓ Check all conditions that are related to MR/DD status that were manifested before age 22, and are likely to continue indefinitely

**MR/DD with organic condition**
☐ A.  **Down's syndrome**
☐ B.  **Autism**
☐ C.  **Epilepsy**
☐ D.  **Other organic condition related to MR/DD**

**MR/DD without organic condition**
☐ E  **MR/DD with no organic condition**

**No MR/DD**
☐ Z.  **Not applicable**

**A1600. Entry Date** (date of this admission/reentry into the facility)

month — day — year

**A1700. Type of Entry**

Enter Code ☐
1.  **Admission**
2.  **Reentry**

**A1800. Entered From**

Enter Code ☐☐
01.  **Community** (private home/apt., board/care, assisted living, group home)
02.  **Another nursing home or swing bed**
03.  **Acute hospital**
04.  **Psychiatric hospital**
05.  **Inpatient rehabilitation facility**
06.  **MR/DD facility**
07.  **Hospice**
99.  **Other**

MDS 3.0 Item Set Draft-Version 0.5

3

*(continues)*

Appendix 7-1  MINIMUM DATA SET (MDS) 3.0 (Continued)

## Section A   Identification Information

### A2000. Discharge Date

[  ][  ] - [  ][  ] - [  ][  ][  ][  ]
month   day   year

### A2100. Discharge Status

Enter [ ] Code

01. **Community** (private home/apt., board/care, assisted living, group home)
02. **Another nursing home or swing bed**
03. **Acute hospital**
04. **Psychiatric hospital**
05. **Inpatient rehabilitation facility**
06. **MR/DD facility**
07. **Hospice**
08. **Deceased**
99. **Other**

### A2200. Previous Assessment Reference Date for Significant Correction — Complete only for significant correction to prior full assessment and significant correction to prior quarterly assessment (A0300A = 05 or 06)

[  ][  ] - [  ][  ] - [  ][  ][  ][  ]
month   day   year

### A2300. Assessment Reference Date

Observation end date:

[  ][  ] - [  ][  ] - [  ][  ][  ][  ]
month   day   year

### A2400. Medicare Stay

Enter [ ] Code

A.  **Has the resident had a Medicare-covered stay since the most recent entry?**
   0.  **No** → Skip to B0100, Comatose
   1.  **Yes** → Continue to A2400B, Start date of most recent Medicare stay

B.  **Start date of most recent Medicare stay:**

[  ][  ] - [  ][  ] - [  ][  ][  ][  ]
month   day   year

C.  **End date of most recent Medicare stay** — Enter 99-99-9999 if stay is ongoing:

[  ][  ] - [  ][  ] - [  ][  ][  ][  ]
month   day   year

**Appendix 7-1** MINIMUM DATA SET (MDS) 3.0 (Continued)

**Look back period for all items is 7 days unless another time frame is indicated.**

## Section B    Hearing, Speech, and Vision

| | |
|---|---|
| **B0100. Comatose** | |
| Enter<br>☐<br>Code | **Persistent vegetative state/no discernible consciousness**<br>  0.  **No** → Continue to B0200, Hearing<br>  1.  **Yes** → Skip to G0100, Activities of Daily Living (ADL) Assistance |
| **B0200. Hearing** | |
| Enter<br>☐<br>Code | **Ability to hear** (with hearing aid or hearing appliances if normally used)<br>  0.  **Adequate** – no difficulty in normal conversation, social interaction, listening to TV<br>  1.  **Minimal difficulty** – difficulty in some environments (e.g. when person speaks softly or setting is noisy)<br>  2.  **Moderate difficulty** – speaker has to increase volume and speak distinctly<br>  3.  **Highly impaired** – absence of useful hearing |
| **B0300. Hearing Aid** | |
| Enter<br>☐<br>Code | **Hearing aid or other hearing appliance used**<br>  0.  **No**<br>  1.  **Yes** |
| **B0600. Speech Clarity** | |
| Enter<br>☐<br>Code | **Select best description of speech pattern**<br>  0.  **Clear speech** – distinct intelligible words<br>  1.  **Unclear speech** – slurred or mumbled words<br>  2.  **No speech** – absence of spoken words |
| **B0700. Makes Self Understood** | |
| Enter<br>☐<br>Code | **Ability to express ideas and wants**, consider both verbal and nonverbal expression<br>  0.  **Understood**<br>  1.  **Usually understood** – difficulty communicating some words or finishing thoughts **but** is able if prompted or given time<br>  2.  **Sometimes understood** – ability is limited to making concrete requests<br>  3.  **Rarely/never understood** |
| **B0800. Ability To Understand Others** | |
| Enter<br>☐<br>Code | **Understanding verbal content, however able** (with hearing aid or device if used)<br>  0.  **Understands** – clear comprehension<br>  1.  **Usually understands** – misses some part/intent of message **but** comprehends most conversation<br>  2.  **Sometimes understands** – responds adequately to simple, direct communication only<br>  3.  **Rarely/never understands** |
| **B1000. Vision** | |
| Enter<br>☐<br>Code | **Ability to see in adequate light** (with glasses or other visual appliances)<br>  0.  **Adequate** – sees fine detail, including regular print in newspapers/books<br>  1.  **Impaired** – sees large print, but not regular print in newspapers/books<br>  2.  **Moderately impaired** – limited vision; not able to see newspaper headlines but can identify objects<br>  3.  **Highly impaired** – object identification in question, but eyes appear to follow objects<br>  4.  **Severely impaired** – no vision or sees only light, colors or shapes; eyes do not appear to follow objects |
| **B1200. Corrective Lenses** | |
| Enter<br>☐<br>Code | **Corrective lenses (contacts, glasses, or magnifying glass) used**<br>  0.  **No**<br>  1.  **Yes** |

MDS 3.0 Item Set Draft-Version 0.5

5

*(continues)*

**Appendix 7-1**  MINIMUM DATA SET (MDS) 3.0 (Continued)

## Section C   Cognitive Patterns

**C0100. Should Brief Interview for Mental Status (C0200-C0500) be Conducted?** – Attempt to conduct interview with all residents

Enter
☐
Code

  0.  **No** (resident is rarely/never understood) → skip to C0600, Should the Staff Assessment for Mental Status be Conducted?

  1.  **Yes** → Continue to C0200, Repetition of Three Words

**Brief Interview for Mental Status (BIMS)**

Conduct interview on day before, day of, or day after Assessment Reference Date (A2300)

**C0200. Repetition of Three Words**

Ask resident: *"I am going to say three words for you to remember. Please repeat the words after I have said all three. The words are: sock, blue, and bed. Now tell me the three words."*

Enter
☐
Code

**Number of words repeated after first attempt**

  0.  **None**

  1.  **One**

  2.  **Two**

  3.  **Three**

After the resident's first attempt, repeat the words using cues (*"sock, something to wear; blue, a color; bed, a piece of furniture"*). You may repeat the words up to two more times.

**C0300. Temporal Orientation** (orientation to year, month, and day)

Ask resident: *"Please tell me what year it is right now."*

Enter
☐
Code

**A.**  **Able to report correct year**

  0.  **Missed by >5 years or no answer**

  1.  **Missed by 2–5 years**

  2.  **Missed by 1 year**

  3.  **Correct**

Ask resident: *"What month are we in right now?"*

Enter
☐
Code

**B.**  **Able to report correct month**

  0.  **Missed by >1 month** or no answer

  1.  **Missed by 6 days to 1 month**

  2.  **Accurate within 5 days**

Ask resident: *"What day of the week is today?"*

Enter
☐
Code

**C.**  **Able to report correct day of the week**

  0.  **Incorrect or no answer**

  1.  **Correct**

**C0400. Recall**

Ask resident: *"Let's go back to an earlier question. What were those three words that I asked you to repeat?"*

If unable to remember a word, give cue (something to wear; a color; a piece of furniture) for that word.

Enter
☐
Code

**A.**  **Able to recall "sock"**

  0.  **No** – could not recall

  1.  **Yes, after cueing** ("something to wear")

  2.  **Yes, no cue required**

Enter
☐
Code

**B.**  **Able to recall "blue"**

  0.  **No** – could not recall

  1.  **Yes, after cueing** ("a color")

  2.  **Yes, no cue required**

Enter
☐
Code

**C.**  **Able to recall "bed"**

  0.  **No** – could not recall

  1.  **Yes, after cueing** ("a piece of furniture")

  2.  **Yes, no cue required**

**C0500. Summary Score**

☐☐
Enter Score

**Add scores** for questions C0200–C0400 and fill in total score (00–15)

**Enter 99 if unable to complete one or more questions of the interview**

*(continues)*

**Appendix 7-1** MINIMUM DATA SET (MDS) 3.0 (Continued)

## Section C    Cognitive Patterns

| | |
|---|---|
| **C0600. Should the Staff Assessment for Mental Status (C0700-C1000) be Conducted?** | |
| Enter ☐ Code | 0.  **No** (resident was able to complete interview) → Skip to C1100, Procedural Memory<br>1.  **Yes** (resident was unable to complete interview) → Continue to C0700, Short-term Memory OK |

**Staff Assessment for Mental Status**

Do not conduct if Brief Interview for Mental Status (C0200–C0500) was completed

| | |
|---|---|
| **C0700. Short-term Memory OK** | |
| Enter ☐ Code | Seems or appears to recall after 5 minutes.<br>0.  **Memory OK**<br>1.  **Memory problem** |
| **C0800. Long-term Memory OK** | |
| Enter ☐ Code | Seems or appears to recall long past.<br>0.  **Memory OK**<br>1.  **Memory problem** |

**C0900. Memory/Recall Ability**

↓ Check all that the resident was normally able to recall

| | | |
|---|---|---|
| ☐ | A. | Current season |
| ☐ | B. | Location of own room |
| ☐ | C. | Staff names and faces |
| ☐ | D | That he or she is in a nursing home |
| ☐ | Z. | None of the above were recalled |

| | |
|---|---|
| **C1000. Cognitive Skills for Daily Decision Making** | |
| Enter ☐ Code | Made decisions regarding tasks of daily life.<br>0.  **Independent** – decisions consistent/reasonable<br>1.  **Modified independence** – some difficulty in new situations only<br>2.  **Moderately impaired** – decisions poor; cues/supervision required<br>3.  **Severely impaired** – never/rarely made decisions |

| | |
|---|---|
| **C1100. Procedural Memory** | |
| Enter ☐ Code | **Procedural Memory OK** – Can perform all or almost all steps in a multitask sequence without cues.  Code for recall of what was learned or known.<br>0.  **Yes**, Memory OK<br>1.  **Memory problem** |

**Delirium**

**C1300. Signs and Symptoms of Delirium (from CAM©)**

Code **after completing** Brief Interview for Mental Status or Staff Assessment and reviewing medical record

| Coding: | ↓ Enter Codes in Boxes | |
|---|---|---|
| 0.  **Behavior not present**<br>1.  **Behavior continuously present, does not fluctuate**<br>2.  **Behavior present, fluctuates** (comes and goes, changes in severity) | ☐ A. | **Inattention** – Did the resident have difficulty focusing attention (easily distracted, out of touch or difficulty following what was said)? |
| | ☐ B. | **Disorganized thinking** – Was the resident's thinking disorganized or incoherent (rambling or irrelevant conversation, unclear or illogical flow of ideas, or unpredictable switching from subject to subject)? |
| | ☐ C. | **Altered level of consciousness** – Did the resident have altered level of consciousness? (e.g., **vigilant** – startled easily to any sound or touch; **lethargic** – repeatedly dozed off when being asked questions, but responded to voice or touch; **stuporous** – very difficult to arouse and keep aroused for the interview; **comatose** – could not be aroused) |
| | ☐ D. | **Psychomotor retardation** – Did the resident have an unusually decreased level of activity such as sluggishness, staring into space, staying in one position, moving very slowly? |

*(continues)*

**Appendix 7-1** MINIMUM DATA SET (MDS) 3.0 (Continued)

## Section C — Cognitive Patterns

**C1600. Acute Onset Mental Status Change**

| Enter Code ☐ | **Is there evidence of an acute change in mental status** from the resident's baseline? |
| --- | --- |
| | 0. **No** |
| | 1. **Yes** |

## Section D — Mood

**D0100. Should Resident Mood Interview be Conducted?** – Attempt to conduct interview with all residents

| Enter Code ☐ | 0. **No** (resident is rarely/never understood) → Skip to D0400, Should the Staff Assessment of Mood be Conducted? |
| --- | --- |
| | 1. **Yes** → Continue to D0200, Resident Mood Interview (PHQ-9©) |

**D0200. Resident Mood Interview (PHQ-9©)**

Conduct interview on day before, day of, or day after Assessment Reference Date (A2300)

Say to resident: "*Over the last 2 weeks, have you been bothered by any of the following problems?*"

If symptom is present, enter 1 (yes) in column 1, Symptom Presence.
If yes in column 1, then ask the resident: "*about **how often** have you been bothered by this?*"
Read and show the resident a card with the symptom frequency choices. Indicate response in column 2, Symptom Frequency.

**Symptom Presence**
0. **No** (Leave column 2 blank)
1. **Yes** (Proceed to column 2)
9. **No Response** (Leave column 2 blank)

**Symptom Frequency**
0. **1 Day** (Rarely)
1. **2–6 Days** (Several days)
2. **7–11 Days** (Half or more of the days)
3. **12–14 Days** (Nearly every day)

| | | 1. Symptom Presence | 2. Symptom Frequency |
| --- | --- | --- | --- |
| | | ↓ Enter Scores in Boxes ↓ | |
| A. | *Little interest or pleasure in doing things* | ☐ | ☐ |
| B. | *Feeling down, depressed, or hopeless* | ☐ | ☐ |
| C. | *Trouble falling or staying asleep, or sleeping too much* | ☐ | ☐ |
| D. | *Feeling tired or having little energy* | ☐ | ☐ |
| E. | *Poor appetite or overeating* | ☐ | ☐ |
| F | *Feeling bad about yourself – or that you are a failure or have let yourself or your family down* | ☐ | ☐ |
| G. | *Trouble concentrating on things, such as reading the newspaper or watching television* | ☐ | ☐ |
| H. | *Moving or speaking so slowly that other people could have noticed. Or the opposite – being so fidgety or restless that you have been moving around a lot more than usual* | ☐ | ☐ |
| I. | *Thoughts that you would be better off dead, or of hurting yourself in some way* | ☐ | ☐ |

**D0300. Total Severity Score**

| Enter Score ☐ | **Add scores for all selected frequency responses in Column 2**, Symptom Frequency. Total score may be between 00 and 27. Enter 99 if unable to complete interview (i.e., Symptom Frequency not present for 3 or more items). If Symptom Frequency is not present for 1 or 2 items, the total score is adjusted. |
| --- | --- |

**D0350. Follow-Up to D0200I** – Complete only if D0200I1 = 1 indicating possibility of resident self harm

| Enter Code ☐ | **Was responsible staff or provider informed that there is a potential for resident self harm?** |
| --- | --- |
| | 0. **No** |
| | 1. **Yes** |

(*continues*)

**Appendix 7-1** MINIMUM DATA SET (MDS) 3.0 (Continued)

## Section D    Mood

**D0400. Should the Staff Assessment of Mood be Conducted?**

Enter [ ] Code

0. **No** (because Resident Mood Interview was completed) → Skip to E0100, Psychosis
1. **Yes** (because 3 or more items in Resident Mood Interview not completed) → Continue to D0500, Staff Assessment of Mood

**D0500. Staff Assessment of Resident Mood (PHQ-9-OV©)**

Do not conduct if Resident Mood Interview (D0200-D0300) was completed

Say to staff: *"Over the last 2 weeks, did the resident have any of the following problems or behaviors?"*

If symptom is present, enter 1 (yes) in column 1, Symptom Presence.
If yes in column 1, then move to column 2, Symptom Frequency, and indicate symptom frequency.

| Symptom Presence | Symptom Frequency | | |
|---|---|---|---|
| 0. **No** (Leave column 2 blank) | 0. **1 Day** (Rarely) | **1.** Symptom Presence | **2.** Symptom Frequency |
| 1. **Yes** (Proceed to column 2) | 1. **2–6 Days** (Several days) | | |
| | 2. **7–11 Days** (Half or more of the days) | | |
| | 3. **12–14 Days** (Nearly every day) | ↓ Enter Scores in Boxes ↓ | |

| | | 1. Symptom Presence | 2. Symptom Frequency |
|---|---|---|---|
| A. | Little interest or pleasure in doing things | [ ] | [ ] |
| B. | Feeling or appearing down, depressed, or hopeless | [ ] | [ ] |
| C. | Trouble falling or staying asleep, or sleeping too much | [ ] | [ ] |
| D. | Feeling tired or having little energy | [ ] | [ ] |
| E. | Poor appetite or overeating | [ ] | [ ] |
| F | Indicating that s/he feels bad about self, is a failure, or has let self or family down | [ ] | [ ] |
| G. | Trouble concentrating on things, such as reading the newspaper or watching television | [ ] | [ ] |
| H. | Moving or speaking so slowly that other people have noticed.  Or the opposite – being so fidgety or restless that s/he has been moving around a lot more than usual | [ ] | [ ] |
| I. | States that life isn't worth living, wishes for death, or attempts to harm self. | [ ] | [ ] |
| J. | Being short-tempered, easily annoyed. | [ ] | [ ] |

**D0600. Total Severity Score**

[ ][ ] Enter Score

Add scores for all selected frequency responses in **Column 2**, Symptom Frequency.  Total score may be between 00 and 30.  Enter 99 if unable to complete staff assessment (i.e., Symptom Frequency not present for 3 or more items).  If Symptom Frequency is not present for 1 or 2 items, the total score is adjusted.

**D0650. Follow-Up to D0600I** – Complete only if D0500I1 = 1 indicating possibility of resident self harm

Enter [ ] Code

Was responsible staff or provider informed that there is a potential for resident self harm?
0. **No**
1. **Yes**

*(continues)*

**Appendix 7-1** MINIMUM DATA SET (MDS) 3.0 (Continued)

## Section E    Behavior

**E0100. Psychosis**

↓ Check all that apply

| | |
|---|---|
| ☐ | A. **Hallucinations** (perceptual experiences in the absence of real external sensory stimuli) |
| ☐ | B. **Illusions** (misperceptions in the presence of real external sensory stimuli) |
| ☐ | C. **Delusions** (misconceptions or beliefs that are firmly held, contrary to reality) |
| ☐ | Z. **None of the above** |

### Behavioral Symptoms

**E0200. Behavioral Symptom – Presence & Frequency**

Note presence of symptoms and their frequency

| Coding: | ↓ Enter Codes in Boxes |
|---|---|
| 0. **Behavior not exhibited** in the last 7 days | ☐ A. **Physical behavioral symptoms directed toward others** (e.g., hitting, kicking, pushing, scratching, grabbing, abusing others sexually) |
| 1. **Behavior of this type occurred 1 to 3 days** of the last 7 days | ☐ B. **Verbal behavioral symptoms directed toward others** (e.g., threatening others, screaming at others, cursing at others) |
| 2. **Behavior of this type occurred 4 to 6 days,** but less than daily<br><br>3. **Behavior of this type occurred daily** | ☐ C. **Other behavioral symptoms not directed toward others** (e.g., physical symptoms such as hitting or scratching self, pacing, rummaging, public sexual acts, disrobing in public, throwing or smearing food or bodily wastes, or verbal/vocal symptoms like screaming, disruptive sounds) |

**E0300. Overall Presence of Behavioral Symptoms**

| Enter ☐ Code | Were any behavioral symptoms in questions E0200 coded 1, 2 or 3?<br>    0. **No** → Skip to E0800, Rejection of Care<br>    1. **Yes** → Considering all of E0200, Behavioral Symptoms, answer E0500 and E0600 below |
|---|---|

**E0500. Impact on Resident**

Did any of the identified symptom(s):

| Enter ☐ Code | A. **Put the resident at significant risk for physical illness or injury?**<br>    0. **No**<br>    1. **Yes** |
|---|---|
| Enter ☐ Code | B. **Significantly interfere with the resident's care?**<br>    0. **No**<br>    1. **Yes** |
| Enter ☐ Code | C. **Significantly interfere with the resident's participation in activities or social interactions?**<br>    0. **No**<br>    1. **Yes** |

**E0600. Impact on Others**

Did any of the identified symptom(s):

| Enter ☐ Code | A. **Put others at significant risk for physical injury?**<br>    0. **No**<br>    1. **Yes** |
|---|---|
| Enter ☐ Code | B. **Significantly intrude on the privacy or activity of others?**<br>    0. **No**<br>    1. **Yes** |
| Enter ☐ Code | C. **Significantly disrupt care or living environment?**<br>    0. **No**<br>    1. **Yes** |

**Appendix 7-1** MINIMUM DATA SET (MDS) 3.0 (Continued)

## Section E | Behavior

| | |
|---|---|
| **E0800. Rejection of Care – Presence & Frequency** | |
| Enter<br>☐<br>Code | **Did the resident reject evaluation or care** (e.g., bloodwork, taking medications, ADL assistance) **that is necessary to achieve the resident's goals for health and well-being?** Do not include behaviors that have already been addressed (e.g., by discussion or care planning with the resident or family), and/or determined to be consistent with resident values, preferences, or goals.<br><br>0. **Behavior not exhibited**<br>1. **Behavior of this type occurred 1 to 3 days**<br>2. **Behavior of this type occurred 4 to 6 days,** but less than daily<br>3. **Behavior of this type occurred daily** |
| **E0900. Wandering – Presence & Frequency** | |
| Enter<br>☐<br>Code | **Has the resident wandered?**<br><br>0. **Behavior not exhibited** → Skip to E1100, Change in Behavioral or Other Symptoms<br>1. **Behavior of this type occurred 1 to 3 days**<br>2. **Behavior of this type occurred 4 to 6 days,** but less than daily<br>3. **Behavior of this type occurred daily** |
| **E1000. Wandering – Impact** | |
| Enter<br>☐<br>Code | **A.** **Does the wandering place the resident at significant risk of getting to a potentially dangerous place** (e.g., stairs, outside of the facility)?<br><br>0. **No**<br>1. **Yes** |
| Enter<br>☐<br>Code | **B.** **Does the wandering significantly intrude on the privacy or activities of others?**<br><br>0. **No**<br>1. **Yes** |
| **E1100. Change in Behavioral or Other Symptoms** – Consider all of the symptoms assessed in items E0100 through E1000. | |
| Enter<br>☐<br>Code | How does resident's current behavior status, care rejection, or wandering **compare to prior assessment (OBRA or PPS)?**<br><br>0. **Same**<br>1. **Improved**<br>2. **Worse**<br>9. **N/A** because no prior MDS assessment |

*(continues)*

Appendix 7-1  MINIMUM DATA SET (MDS) 3.0 (Continued)

## Section F — Preferences for Customary Routine and Activities

**F0300. Should Interview for Daily and Activity Preferences be Conducted?** – Attempt to interview all residents able to communicate. If resident is unable to complete, attempt to complete interview with family member or significant other.

Enter Code | 0. **No** (resident is rarely/never understood **and** family not available) → Skip to F0700, Should the Staff Assessment of Daily and Activity Preferences be Conducted?
1. **Yes** → Continue to F0400, Interview for Daily Preferences

**F0400. Interview for Daily Preferences**

Conduct interview on day before, day of or day after Assessment Reference Date (A2300)

Show resident the response options and say: "*While you are in this facility…*"

↓ **Enter Codes in Boxes**

Coding:
1. **Very important**
2. **Somewhat important**
3. **Not very important**
4. **Not important at all**
5. **Important, but can't do or no choice**
9. **No response or nonresponsive**

A.  how important is it to you to **choose what clothes to wear?**

B.  how important is it to you to **take care of your personal belongings or things?**

C.  how important is it to you to **choose between a tub bath, shower, bed bath, or sponge bath?**

D.  how important is it to you to **have snacks available between meals?**

E.  how important is it to you to **choose your own bedtime?**

F.  how important is it to you to **have your family or a close friend involved in discussions about your care?**

G.  how important is it to you to **be able to use the phone in private?**

H.  how important is it to you to **have a place to lock your things to keep them safe?**

**F0500. Interview for Activity Preferences**

Conduct interview on day before, day of or day after Assessment Reference Date (A2300)

Show resident the response options and say: "*While you are in this facility…*"

↓ **Enter Codes in Boxes**

Coding:
1. **Very important**
2. **Somewhat important**
3. **Not very important**
4. **Not important at all**
5. **Important, but can't do or no choice**
9. **No response or nonresponsive**

A.  how important is it to you to have **books, newspapers, and magazines to read?**

B.  how important is it to you to **listen to music you like?**

C.  how important is it to you to **be around animals such as pets?**

D.  how important is it to you to **keep up with the news?**

E.  how important is it to you to **do things with groups of people?**

F.  how important is it to you to **do your favorite activities?**

G.  how important is it to you to **go outside to get fresh air when the weather is good?**

H.  how important is it to you to **participate in religious services or practices?**

**F0600. Daily and Activity Preferences Primary Respondent**

Enter Code | Indicate primary respondent for Daily and Activity Preferences (F0400 and F0500).
1. **Resident**
2. **Family or significant other** (close friend or other representative)
9. **Interview could not be completed** by resident or family/significant other ("No Response" to 3 or more items)

**End of Daily and Activity Preferences Interview**

**Appendix 7-1**  MINIMUM DATA SET (MDS) 3.0 (Continued)

| Section F | Preferences for Customary Routine and Activities |
|---|---|

**F0700.  Should the Staff Assessment of Daily and Activity Preferences be Conducted?**

Enter [ ] Code

0.  **No** (because Interview for Daily and Activity Preferences (F0400 and F0500) was completed by resident or family/significant other) → Skip to G0100, Activities of Daily Living (ADL) Assistance

1.  **Yes** (because 3 or more items in Interview for Daily and Activity Preferences (F0400 and F0500) were not completed by resident or family/significant other) → Continue to F0800, Staff Assessment of Daily and Activity Preferences

**F0800.  Staff Assessment of Daily and Activity Preferences**

Do not conduct if Interview for Daily and Activity Preferences (F0400 – F0500) was completed

**Resident Prefers:**

↓ Check all that apply

| | | |
|---|---|---|
| ☐ | A. | Choosing clothes to wear |
| ☐ | B. | Caring for personal belongings |
| ☐ | C. | Receiving tub bath |
| ☐ | D. | Receiving shower |
| ☐ | E. | Receiving bed bath |
| ☐ | F. | Receiving sponge bath |
| ☐ | G. | Snacks between meals |
| ☐ | H. | Staying up past 8:00 p.m. |
| ☐ | I. | Family or significant other involvement in care discussions |
| ☐ | J. | Use of phone in private |
| ☐ | K. | Place to lock personal belongings |
| ☐ | L. | Reading books, newspapers, or magazines |
| ☐ | M. | Listening to music |
| ☐ | N. | Being around animals such as pets |
| ☐ | O. | Keeping up with the news |
| ☐ | P. | Doing things with groups of people |
| ☐ | Q. | Participating in favorite activities |
| ☐ | R. | Spending time away from the nursing home |
| ☐ | S. | Spending time outdoors |
| ☐ | T. | Participating in religious activities or practices |
| ☐ | Z. | None of the above |

*(continues)*

**Appendix 7-1** MINIMUM DATA SET (MDS) 3.0 (Continued)

## Section G Functional Status

### G0100. Activities of Daily Living (ADL) Assistance

Code for most dependent episode

**Coding:**

0. **Independent** – resident completes activity with no help or oversight
1. **Set up assistance**
2. **Supervision** – oversight, encouragement, or cueing provided throughout the activity
3. **Limited assistance** – guided maneuvering of limbs or other nonweight-bearing assistance provided at least once
4. **Extensive assistance, 1 person assist** – resident performed part of the activity while one staff member provided weight-bearing support or completed part of the activity at least once
5. **Extensive assistance, 2 + person assist** – resident performed part of the activity while two or more staff members provided weight-bearing support or completed part of the activity at least once
6. **Total dependence, 1 person assist** – full staff performance of activity (requiring only 1 person assistance) at least once. The resident must be unable or unwilling to perform any part of the activity.
7. **Total dependence, 2 + person assist** – full staff performance of activity (requiring 2 or more person assistance) at least once. The resident must be unable or unwilling to perform any part of the activity.
8. **Activity did not occur** during entire period

↓ **Enter Codes in Boxes**

| | |
|---|---|
| A. | **Bed mobility** – moving to and from lying position, turning side to side and positioning body while in bed |
| B. | **Transfer** – moving between surfaces including to or from: bed, chair, wheelchair, standing position (**excludes** to/from bath/toilet) |
| C. | **Toilet transfer** – how resident gets to and moves on and off toilet or commode |
| D. | **Toileting** – using the toilet room (or commode, bedpan, urinal); cleaning self after toileting or incontinent episode(s), changing pad, managing ostomy or catheter, adjusting clothes (**excludes** toilet transfer) |
| E. | **Walk in room** – walking between locations in his/her room |
| F. | **Walk in facility** – walking in corridor or other places in facility |
| G. | **Locomotion** – moving about facility, with wheelchair if used |
| H. | **Dressing upper body** – dressing and undressing above the waist, includes prostheses, orthotics, fasteners, pullovers |
| I. | **Dressing lower body** – dressing and undressing from the waist down, includes prostheses, orthotics, fasteners, pullovers |
| J. | **Eating** – includes eating, drinking (regardless of skill) or intake of nourishment by other means (e.g., tube feeding, total parenteral nutrition, IV fluids for hydration) |
| K. | **Grooming/personal hygiene** – includes combing hair, brushing teeth, shaving, applying makeup, washing/drying face and hands (**excludes** bath and shower) |
| L. | **Bathing** – how resident takes full-body bath/shower, sponge bath and transfers in/out of tub/shower (**excludes** washing of back and hair) |

### G0300. Balance During Transitions and Walking

After observing the resident, **code the following walking and transition items for most dependent**

**Coding:**

0. **Steady at all times**
1. **Not steady, but able to stabilize without human assistance**
2. **Not steady, only able to stabilize with human assistance**
8. **Activity did not occur**

↓ **Enter Codes in Boxes**

| | |
|---|---|
| A. | **Moving from seated to standing position** |
| B. | **Walking** (with assistive device if used) |
| C. | **Turning around and facing the opposite direction while walking** |
| D. | **Moving on and off toilet** |
| E. | **Surface-to-surface transfer** (transfer between bed and chair or wheelchair) |

### G0400. Functional Limitation in Range of Motion

Code for limitation that interfered with daily functions or placed resident at risk of injury.

**Coding:**

0. **No impairment**
1. **Impairment on one side**
2. **Impairment on both sides**

↓ **Enter Codes in Boxes**

| | |
|---|---|
| A. | **Upper extremity** (shoulder, elbow, wrist, hand) |
| B. | **Lower extremity** (hip, knee, ankle, foot) |

14

*(continues)*

**Appendix 7-1** MINIMUM DATA SET (MDS) 3.0 (Continued)

## Section G    Functional Status

| **G0600. Mobility Devices** | | |
|---|---|---|
| ↓ Check all that were normally used | | |
| ☐ | A. | Cane/crutch |
| ☐ | B. | Walker |
| ☐ | C. | Wheelchair (manual or electric) |
| ☐ | D. | Lower extremity limb prosthesis |
| ☐ | Z. | **None of the above** were used |

**G0800. Bedfast**

| Enter ☐ Code | Has the resident been in bed or in recliner in room for more than 22 hours on at least 4 of the past 7 days?<br>0.  **No**<br>1.  **Yes** |
|---|---|

**G0900. Functional Rehabilitation Potential** – Complete only for the first assessment (OBRA or PPS) since the most recent admission (A0300E = 1)

| Enter ☐ Code | A. | Resident believes he or she is capable of **increased independence** in at least some ADLs.<br>0.  **No**<br>1.  **Yes**<br>9.  **Unable to determine** |
|---|---|---|
| Enter ☐ Code | B. | Direct care staff believe resident is capable of **increased independence** in at least some ADLs.<br>0.  **No**<br>1.  **Yes** |

*(continues)*

Appendix 7-1  MINIMUM DATA SET (MDS) 3.0 (Continued)

## Section H   Bladder and Bowel

### H0100. Appliances

↓ Check all that apply

| | | |
|---|---|---|
| ☐ | A. | Indwelling bladder catheter |
| ☐ | B | External (condom) catheter |
| ☐ | C. | Ostomy (including suprapubic catheter, ileostomy, and colostomy) |
| ☐ | D. | Intermittent catheterization |
| ☐ | Z. | None of the above |

### H0200. Urinary Toileting Program

**Enter** ☐ **Code**  A.  **Has a trial of a toileting program** (e.g. scheduled toileting, prompted voiding, or bladder training) **been attempted** on admission/reentry or since urinary incontinence was noted in this facility?
- 0. **No** → Skip to H0300, Urinary Continence
- 1. **Yes** → Continue to H0200B, Response
- 9. **Unable to determine** → Skip to H0200C, Current toileting program or trial

**Enter** ☐ **Code**  B.  **Response** – What was the resident's response to the trial program?
- 0. **No improvement**
- 1. **Decreased wetness**
- 2. **Completely dry** (continent)
- 9. **Unable to determine or trial in progress**

**Enter** ☐ **Code**  C.  **Current toileting program or trial** – Is a toileting program (e.g. scheduled toileting, prompted voiding, or bladder training) currently being used to manage the resident's urinary continence?
- 0. **No**
- 1. **Yes**

### H0300. Urinary Continence

**Enter** ☐ **Code**  Urinary continence – Select the one category that best describes the resident
- 0. **Always continent**
- 1. **Occasionally incontinent** (less than 7 episodes of incontinence)
- 2. **Frequently incontinent** (greater than or equal to 7 with at least one episode of continent voiding)
- 3. **Always incontinent** (no episodes of continent voiding)
- 9. **Not rated**, resident had a catheter (indwelling, condom), urinary ostomy, or no urine output for entire 7 days

### H0400. Bowel Continence

**Enter** ☐ **Code**  Bowel continence – Select the one category that best describes the resident
- 0. **Always continent**
- 1. **Occasionally incontinent** (one episode of bowel incontinence)
- 2. **Frequently incontinent** (2 or more episodes of bowel incontinence, but at least one continent bowel movement)
- 3. **Always incontinent** (no episodes of continent bowel movements)
- 9. **Not rated,** resident had an ostomy or did not have a bowel movement for the entire 7 days

### H0500. Bowel Toileting Program

**Enter** ☐ **Code**  Is a toileting program currently being used to manage the resident's bowel continence?
- 0. **No**
- 1. **Yes**

### H0600. Bowel Patterns

**Enter** ☐ **Code**  Constipation present?
- 0. **No**
- 1. **Yes**

*(continues)*

**Appendix 7-1** MINIMUM DATA SET (MDS) 3.0 (Continued)

## Section I — Active Disease Diagnosis

**Active Diseases in the last 30 days** – Check all that apply

**Cancer**

| | | |
|---|---|---|
| ☐ | I0100. | **Cancer** (with or without metastasis) |

**Heart/Circulation**

| | | |
|---|---|---|
| ☐ | I0200. | **Anemia** (includes aplastic, iron deficiency pernicious, and sickle cell) |
| ☐ | I0300. | **Atrial Fibrillation and Other Dysrhythmias** (includes bradycardias, tachycardias) |
| ☐ | I0400. | **Coronary Artery Disease (CAD)** (includes angina, myocardial infarction, atherosclerotic heart disease (ASHD)) |
| ☐ | I0500. | **Deep Venous Thrombosis (DVT)/Pulmonary Embolus (PE) or Pulmonary Thrombo-Embolism (PTE)** |
| ☐ | I0600. | **Heart Failure** (includes congestive heart failure (CHF), pulmonary edema) |
| ☐ | I0700. | **Hypertension** |
| ☐ | I0800. | **Hypotension** |
| ☐ | I0900. | **Peripheral Vascular Disease/Peripheral Arterial Disease** |

**Gastrointestinal**

| | | |
|---|---|---|
| ☐ | I1100. | **Cirrhosis** |
| ☐ | I1200. | **Gastroesophageal Reflux Disease (GERD)/Ulcer** (includes esophageal, gastric, and peptic ulcers) |
| ☐ | I1300. | **Ulcerative Colitis/Crohn's Disease/Inflammatory Bowel Disease** |

**Genitourinary**

| | | |
|---|---|---|
| ☐ | I1400. | **Benign Prostatic Hyperplasia (BPH)** |
| ☐ | I1500. | **Renal Insufficiency or Renal Failure/End-Stage Renal Disease (ESRD)** |

**Infections**

| | | |
|---|---|---|
| ☐ | I1600. | **Human Immunodeficiency Virus (HIV) Infection** (includes Acquired Immunodeficiency Syndrome (AIDS)) |
| ☐ | I1700. | **Methicillin Resistant Staphylococcus Aureus (MRSA), Vancomycin-Resistant Enterococci (VRE), Clostridium Difficile infection/colonization** |
| ☐ | I2000. | **Pneumonia** |
| ☐ | I2100. | **Septicemia** |
| ☐ | I2200. | **Tuberculosis** |
| ☐ | I2300. | **Urinary Tract Infection (UTI)** |
| ☐ | I2400. | **Viral Hepatitis** (includes Hepatitis A, B, C, D, & E) |

**Metabolic**

| | | |
|---|---|---|
| ☐ | I2900. | **Diabetes Mellitus (DM)** (includes diabetic retinopathy, nephropathy, and neuropathy) |
| ☐ | I3100. | **Hyponatremia** |
| ☐ | I3200. | **Hyperkalemia** |
| ☐ | I3300. | **Hyperlipidemia** (includes hypercholesterolemia) |
| ☐ | I3400. | **Thyroid Disorder** (includes hypothyroidism, hyperthyroidism, and Hashimoto's thyroiditis) |

**Musculoskeletal**

| | | |
|---|---|---|
| ☐ | I3700. | **Arthritis** (Degenerative Joint Disease (DJD), Osteoarthritis, and Rheumatoid Arthritis (RA)) |
| ☐ | I3800. | **Osteoporosis** |
| ☐ | I3900. | **Hip Fracture** (includes any hip fracture that has a relationship to current status, treatments, monitoring. Includes subcapital fractures, fractures of the trochanter and femoral neck) (last 60 days) |
| ☐ | I4000. | **Other Fracture** |

**Neurological**

| | | |
|---|---|---|
| ☐ | I4200. | **Alzheimer's Disease** |
| ☐ | I4300. | **Aphasia** |
| ☐ | I4400. | **Cerebral Palsy** |
| ☐ | I4500. | **Cerebrovascular Accident (CVA)/Transient Ischemic Attack (TIA)/Stroke** |
| ☐ | I4800. | **Dementia** (Non-Alzheimer's dementia, including vascular or multi-infarct dementia, mixed dementia, frontotemporal dementia (e.g., Pick's disease), and dementia related to stroke, Parkinson's, Huntington's, Pick's, or Creutzfeldt-Jakob diseases) |
| ☐ | I4900. | **Hemiplegia/Hemiparesis** |
| ☐ | I5000. | **Paraplegia** |
| ☐ | I5100. | **Quadriplegia** |
| ☐ | I5200. | **Multiple Sclerosis** |
| ☐ | I5300. | **Parkinson's Disease** |
| ☐ | I5400. | **Seizure Disorder** |
| ☐ | I5500. | **Traumatic Brain Injury** |

MDS 3.0 Item Set Draft-Version 0.5

17

*(continues)*

Appendix 7-1  MINIMUM DATA SET (MDS) 3.0 (Continued)

## Section I    Active Disease Diagnosis

**Nutritional**

☐ I5600.  **Malnutrition** (protein or calorie) or at risk for malnutrition

**Psychiatric/Mood Disorder**

☐ I5700  **Anxiety Disorder**
☐ I5800.  **Depression** (other than Bipolar)
☐ I5900.  **Manic Depression** (Bipolar Disease)
☐ I6000.  **Schizophrenia**
☐ I6100.  **Post Traumatic Stress Disorder (PTSD)**

**Pulmonary**

☐ I6200.  **Asthma/Chronic Obstructive Pulmonary Disease (COPD) or Chronic Lung Disease** (includes chronic bronchitis and restrictive lung diseases such as asbestosis)

**Vision**

☐ I6500.  **Cataracts, Glaucoma, or Macular Degeneration**

**None of Above**

☐ I7900.  **None of the above active diagnoses** within the last 30 days

**Other**

☐ I8000.  **Additional Diagnoses**
Enter diagnosis on line and ICD code in boxes.  Include the decimal for the code in the appropriate box.

A. _____

B. _____

C. _____

D. _____

E. _____

F. _____

G. _____

H. _____

I. _____

J. _____

**Appendix 7-1** MINIMUM DATA SET (MDS) 3.0 (Continued)

## Section J    Health Conditions

**J0100. Pain Management** – Complete for all residents, regardless of current pain level

At any time in the last 7 days, has the resident:

| Enter [ ] Code | A. | **Been on a scheduled pain medication regimen?**<br>0. **No**<br>1. **Yes** |
|---|---|---|
| Enter [ ] Code | B. | **Received PRN pain medications?**<br>0. **No**<br>1. **Yes** |
| Enter [ ] Code | C. | **Received nonmedication intervention for pain?**<br>0. **No**<br>1. **Yes** |

**J0200. Should Pain Assessment Interview be Conducted?** – Attempt to conduct interview with all residents.
Conduct interview on day before, day of, or day after Assessment Reference Date (A2300).
If resident is comatose, skip to J1100, Shortness of Breath (Dyspnea).

Enter [ ] Code

  0. **No** (resident is rarely/never understood) → Skip to J0800, Indicators of Pain
  1. **Yes** → Continue to J0300, Pain Presence

### Pain Assessment Interview

**J0300. Pain Presence**

Enter [ ] Code

Ask resident: *"Have you had pain or hurting at any time in the last 7 days?"*
  0. **No** → Skip to J0800, Indicators of Pain
  1. **Yes** → Continue to J0400, Pain Frequency
  9. **Unable to answer** → Skip to J0800, Indicators of Pain

**J0400. Pain Frequency**

Enter [ ] Code

Ask resident: *"How much of the time have you experienced pain or hurting over the last 7 days?"*
  1. **Almost constantly**
  2. **Frequently**
  3. **Occasionally**
  4. **Rarely**
  9. **Unable to answer**

**J0500. Pain Effect on Function**

| Enter [ ] Code | A. | Ask resident: *"Over the past 7 days, has pain made it hard for you to sleep at night?"*<br>0. **No**<br>1. **Yes**<br>9. **Unable to answer** |
|---|---|---|
| Enter [ ] Code | B. | Ask resident: *"Over the past 7 days, have you limited your day-to-day activities because of pain?"*<br>0. **No**<br>1. **Yes**<br>9. **Unable to answer** |

**J0600. Pain Intensity** – Administer one of the following pain intensity questions (A or B)

| Enter [ ] Rating | A. | **Numeric Rating Scale (00–10)**<br>Ask resident: *"Please rate your worst pain over the last 7 days on a zero to ten scale, with zero being no pain and ten as the worst pain you can imagine."* (Show resident 0–10 pain scale.)<br>**Enter two-digit response. Enter 99 if unable to answer.** |
|---|---|---|
| Enter [ ] Code | B. | **Verbal Descriptor Scale**<br>Ask resident: *"Please rate the intensity of your worst pain over the last 7 days."* (Show resident verbal scale.)<br>1. **Mild**<br>2. **Moderate**<br>3. **Severe**<br>4. **Very severe, horrible**<br>9. **Unable to answer** |

**End of Pain Assessment Interview**

(continues)

Appendix 7-1 MINIMUM DATA SET (MDS) 3.0 (Continued)

## Section J | Health Conditions

### Staff Assessment for Pain

**J0800. Indicators of Pain or possible pain**

↓ Check all that apply

| | A. | Nonverbal sounds (crying, whining, gasping, moaning, or groaning) |
| | B. | Vocal complaints of pain (that hurts, ouch, stop) |
| | C. | Facial expressions (grimaces, winces, wrinkled forehead, furrowed brow, clenched teeth or jaw) |
| | D. | Protective body movements or postures (bracing, guarding, rubbing or massaging a body part/area, clutching or holding a body part during movement) |
| | Z. | None of these signs observed or documented |

**J0900. Pain Control**

| | Adequacy of current therapeutic regimen to control pain (from resident's point of view) |
| Enter | 0. No issue of pain |
| | 1. Pain intensity acceptable to resident, no treatment regimen or change in regimen required |
| | 2. Controlled adequately by therapeutic regimen |
| Code | 3. Controlled when therapeutic regimen followed, but not always followed as ordered |
| | 4. Therapeutic regimen followed, but pain control not adequate |
| | 5. No therapeutic regimen being followed for pain; pain not adequately controlled |

### Other Health Conditions

**J1100. Shortness of Breath (dyspnea)**

↓ Check all that apply:

| | A. | Shortness of breath or trouble breathing with exertion (e.g., walking, bathing, transferring) |
| | B. | Shortness of breath or trouble breathing when sitting at rest |
| | C. | Shortness of breath or trouble breathing when lying flat |
| | Z. | None of the above |

**J1300. Current Tobacco Use**

| Enter | Tobacco use |
| | 0. No |
| Code | 1. Yes |

**J1400. Prognosis**

| Enter | Does the resident have a condition or chronic disease that may result in a **life expectancy of less than 6 months**? (Requires physician documentation. If not documented, discuss with physician and request supporting documentation.) |
| | 0. No |
| Code | 1. Yes |

**J1500. Problem Conditions**

↓ Check all that apply:

| | A. | Fever |
| | B. | Vomiting |
| | D. | Dehydrated; output exceeds input |
| | H. | Internal bleeding |
| | Z. | None of the above |

Appendix 7-1 MINIMUM DATA SET (MDS) 3.0 (Continued)

## Section J | Health Conditions

**J1700. Fall History on Admission** – If this is not the first assessment (OBRA or PPS) since the most recent admission (A0300E = 0) → Skip to J1800, Any Falls Since Last Assessment

| Enter Code | A. | Did the resident fall one or more times in the **last month** prior to admission? |
|---|---|---|
| | | 0. **No** |
| | | 1. **Yes** |
| | | 9. **Unable to determine** |

| Enter Code | B. | Did the resident fall one or more times in the **last 1–6 months** prior to admission? |
|---|---|---|
| | | 0. **No** |
| | | 1. **Yes** |
| | | 9. **Unable to determine** |

| Enter Code | C. | Did the resident have any **fracture related to a fall in the 6 months** prior to admission? |
|---|---|---|
| | | 0. **No** |
| | | 1. **Yes** |
| | | 9. **Unable to determine** |

**J1800. Any Falls Since Admission or Prior Assessment (OBRA or PPS), Whichever is More Recent**

| Enter Code | Has the resident **had any falls since admission or the prior assessment** (OBRA or PPS), whichever is more recent? This applies to all falls, whether within the facility or during a temporary absence from the facility. |
|---|---|
| | 0. **No** → Skip to K0100, Swallowing Disorder |
| | 1. **Yes** → Continue to J1900, Number of Falls Since Admission or Prior Assessment (OBRA or PPS), Whichever is More Recent |

**J1900. Number of Falls Since Admission or Prior Assessment (OBRA or PPS), Whichever is More Recent**

↓ Enter Codes in Boxes

| Coding: | | |
|---|---|---|
| 0. **None** | A. | **No injury** – no evidence of any injury is noted on physical assessment by the nurse or primary care clinician; no complaints of pain or injury by the resident; no change in the resident's behavior is noted after the fall |
| 1. **One** | B. | **Injury (except major)** – skin tears, abrasions, lacerations, superficial bruises, hematomas and sprains; or any fall-related injury that causes the resident to complain of pain |
| 2. **Two or more** | C. | **Major injury** – bone fractures, joint dislocations, closed head injuries with altered consciousness, subdural hematoma |

## Section K | Swallowing/Nutritional Status

**K0100. Swallowing Disorder**

Signs and symptoms of possible swallowing disorder

↓ Check all that apply:

| ☐ | A. | Loss of liquids/solids from mouth when eating or drinking |
| ☐ | B. | Holding food in mouth/cheeks or residual food in mouth after meals |
| ☐ | C. | Coughing or choking during meals or when swallowing medications |
| ☐ | D. | Complaints of difficulty or pain with swallowing |
| ☐ | Z. | None of the above |

**K0200. Height and Weight**

| inches | A. **Height** (in inches). Record most recent height measure since admission. |
|---|---|
| pounds | B. **Weight** (in pounds). Base weight on most recent measure in last 30 days; measure weight consistently, according to standard facility practice (e.g., in a.m. after voiding, before meal, with shoes off, etc.) |
| | C. **Body Mass Index (BMI)**<br>(BMI = K0200B * 703 / K0200A$^2$) |

**K0300. Weight Loss**

| Enter | Loss of 5% or more in the last month or loss of 10% or more in last 6 months. |

*(continues)*

Appendix 7-1  MINIMUM DATA SET (MDS) 3.0 (Continued)

## Section K   Swallowing/Nutritional Status

| | |
|---|---|
| **Code** | 0. **No** or unknown<br>1. **Yes, on** physician-prescribed weight-loss regimen<br>2. **Yes, not on** physician-prescribed weight-loss regimen |

**K0500. Nutritional Approaches**

↓ Check all that apply:

| | | |
|---|---|---|
| ☐ | A. | **Parenteral/IV feeding** |
| ☐ | B. | **Feeding tube** – nasogastric or abdominal (PEG) |
| ☐ | C. | **Mechanically altered diet** – require change in texture of food or liquids (e.g., pureed food, thickened liquids) |
| ☐ | D. | **Therapeutic diet** (e.g., low salt, diabetic, low cholesterol) |
| ☐ | Z. | **None of the above** |

**K0700. Percent Intake by Artificial Route** – Complete K0700 only if K0500A or K0500B is checked

| | | |
|---|---|---|
| Enter<br>☐<br>Code | A. | **Proportion of total calories the resident received through parenteral or tube feedings**<br>1. **25% or less**<br>2. **26–50%**<br>3. **51% or more** |
| Enter<br>☐<br>Code | B. | **Average fluid intake per day by parenteral or tube feedings**<br>1. **500 cc/day or less**<br>2. **501 cc/day or more** |

## Section L   Oral/Dental Status

**L0100. Able to Perform Dental Exam**

| | |
|---|---|
| Enter<br>☐<br>Code | 0. **No** → Skip to M0100, Determination of Pressure Ulcer Risk<br>1. **Yes** |

**L0200. Dental**

↓ Check all that apply:

| | | |
|---|---|---|
| ☐ | A. | **Broken or loosely fitting full or partial denture** (chipped, cracked, uncleanable, or loose) |
| ☐ | B. | **No natural teeth or tooth fragment(s)** (edentulous) |
| ☐ | C. | **Abnormal mouth tissue** (ulcers, masses, oral lesions, including under denture or partial if one is worn) |
| ☐ | D. | **Obvious or likely cavity or broken natural teeth** |
| ☐ | E. | **Inflamed or bleeding gums or loose natural teeth** |
| ☐ | F. | **Mouth or facial pain, discomfort or difficulty with chewing** |
| ☐ | Z. | **None of the above were present** |

*(continues)*

**Appendix 7-1** MINIMUM DATA SET (MDS) 3.0 (Continued)

## Section M | Skin Conditions

| For all items involving a count of the number of ulcers, if more than 9, enter 9 |
|---|

**M0100. Determination of Pressure Ulcer Risk**

↓ Check all that apply

| | A. | **Resident has a stage 1 or greater, a scar over bony prominence, or a nonremovable dressing, device** |
|---|---|---|
| | B. | **Formal assessment** (e.g., Braden, Norton, or other) |
| | C. | **Clinical judgment** |
| | Z. | **None of the above** |

**M0150. Risk of Pressure Ulcers**

| Enter ☐ Code | **Is this resident at risk of developing pressure ulcers?** <br> 0. **No** <br> 1. **Yes** |
|---|---|

**M0200. Presence of Pressure Ulcer**

| | A. | **Date of most recent routine** (e.g., weekly) **pressure ulcer assessment:** <br><br> ☐☐–☐☐–☐☐☐☐ <br> month    day        year |
|---|---|---|
| Enter ☐ Number | B. | **Number of Stage 1 pressure ulcers** <br> **Stage 1:** Intact skin with nonblanchable redness of a localized area usually over a bony prominence. Darkly pigmented skin may not have a visible blanching; in dark skin tones only it may appear with persistent blue or purple hues |
| Enter ☐ Code | C. | **Does this resident have one or more unhealed pressure ulcer(s) at Stage 2 or higher, or one or more likely pressure ulcers that are unstageable at this time?** <br> 0. **No** → Skip to M0900, Healed Pressure Ulcers <br> 1. **Yes** |

**M0400. Current Number of Unhealed** (nonepithelialized) **Pressure Ulcers at Each Stage**

| | A. | **Stage 2:** Partial thickness loss of dermis presenting as a shallow open ulcer with a red or pink wound bed, without slough. May also present as an intact or open/ruptured serum-filled blister |
|---|---|---|
| Enter ☐ Number | | 1. **Number of pressure ulcers at Stage 2** → If 0, skip to M0400B, Stage 3 |
| Enter ☐ Number | | 2. **Number of these that were present upon admission/reentry** – enter how many were noted within 48 hours of admission/reentry and not acquired in the facility |
| | B. | **Stage 3:** Full thickness tissue loss. Subcutaneous fat may be visible but bone, tendon, or muscle is not exposed. Slough may be present but does not obscure the depth of tissue loss. May includes undermining and tunneling |
| Enter ☐ Number | | 1. **Number of pressure ulcers at Stage 3** → If 0, skip to M0400C, Stage 4 |
| Enter ☐ Number | | 2. **Number of these that were present upon admission/reentry** – enter how many were noted within 48 hours of admission/reentry and not acquired in the facility |
| | | 3. **Date of onset of Stage 3 pressure ulcers in this facility's care** – Enter 99-99-9999 if unknown <br> A. **Oldest or only:** <br><br> ☐☐–☐☐–☐☐☐☐ <br> month    day        year |
| M0400 Continued on next page | | B. **Newest:** <br><br> ☐☐–☐☐–☐☐☐☐ <br> month    day        year |

(continues)

Appendix 7-1  MINIMUM DATA SET (MDS) 3.0 (Continued)

## Section M    Skin Conditions

---

**M0400. Current Number of Unhealed Pressure Ulcers at Each Stage** – Continued

**C.** **Stage 4:** Full thickness tissue loss with exposed bone, tendon or muscle.  Slough or eschar may be present on some parts of the wound bed.  Often includes undermining and tunneling

Enter [ ] Number
1. **Number of pressure ulcers at Stage 4** → If 0, skip to M0400D, Unstageable: Known or likely but not stageable due to nonremovable dressing

Enter [ ] Number
2. **Number of these that were present upon admission/reentry** – enter how many were noted within 48 hours of admission/reentry and not acquired in the facility

3. **Date of onset of Stage 4 pressure ulcers in this facility's care** – Enter 99-99-9999 if unknown
   A. **Oldest or only:**

   [ ][ ] - [ ][ ] - [ ][ ][ ][ ]
   month    day      year

   B. **Newest:**

   [ ][ ] - [ ][ ] - [ ][ ][ ][ ]
   month    day      year

**D.** **Unstageable:** Known or likely but not stageable due to nonremovable dressing

Enter [ ] Number
1. **Number of pressure ulcers unstageable due to nonremovable dressing** → If 0, skip to M0400E, Unstageable: Known or likely but not stageable due to coverage of wound bed by slough and/or eschar

Enter [ ] Number
2. **Number of these that were present upon admission/reentry** – enter how many were noted within 48 hours of admission/reentry and not acquired in the facility

**E** **Unstageable:**  Known or likely but not stageable due to coverage of wound bed by slough and/or eschar

Enter [ ] Number
1. **Number of pressure ulcers unstageable due to coverage of wound bed by slough and/or eschar** → If 0, skip to M0400F, Unstageable: Suspected deep tissue injury in evolution

Enter [ ] Number
2. **Number of these that were present upon admission/reentry** – enter how many were noted within 48 hours of admission/reentry and not acquired in the facility

3. **Date of onset of these unstageable pressure ulcers in this facility's care** – Enter 99-99-9999 if unknown
   A. **Oldest or only:**

   [ ][ ] - [ ][ ] - [ ][ ][ ][ ]
   month    day      year

   B. **Newest:**

   [ ][ ] - [ ][ ] - [ ][ ][ ][ ]
   month    day      year

**F** **Unstageable:**  Suspected deep tissue injury in evolution.

Enter [ ] Number
1. **Number of pressure ulcers unstageable with suspected deep tissue injury in evolution** → If 0, skip to M0500, Number of Unhealed Stage 2 Pressure Ulcers Known to be Present for More Than One Month

Enter [ ] Number
2. **Number of these that were present upon admission/reentry** – enter how many were noted within 48 hours of admission and not acquired in the facility

---

**M0500. Number of Unhealed Stage 2 Pressure Ulcers Known to be Present for More Than One Month**

Enter [ ] Number
If the resident has one or more unhealed Stage 2 pressure ulcers, record the number present today that were first observed more than one month ago.

---

**Appendix 7-1** MINIMUM DATA SET (MDS) 3.0 (Continued)

## Section M   Skin Conditions

**M0600. Dimensions of Unhealed Stage 3 or 4 Pressure Ulcers or Eschar**

Complete only if M0400B1, M0400C1, or M0400E1 is greater than 0

If the patient has one or more unhealed (nonepithelialized) Stage 3 or 4 pressure ulcers or an eschar, identify the pressure ulcers with the longest dimension and record in centimeters:

| | |
|---|---|
| ☐☐.☐ cm | **A. Pressure Ulcer Length:** Longest length in any direction |
| ☐☐.☐ cm | **B. Pressure Ulcer Width:** Width of the same pressure ulcer, greatest width measured at right angles to length |
| ☐☐ – ☐☐ – ☐☐☐☐<br>month    day       year | **C. Date Measured** |

**M0700. Tissue Type for Most Advanced Stage**

| Enter<br><br>Code | Select the best description of the most severe type of tissue present in the ulcer bed of the **largest pressure ulcer at the most advanced stage**<br>1.  **Epithelial Tissue** – new skin growing in superficial ulcer.  It can be light pink and shiny, even in persons with darkly pigmented skin.<br>2.  **Granulation Tissue** – pink or red tissue with shiny, moist, granular appearance<br>3.  **Slough** – yellow or white tissue that adheres to the ulcer bed in strings or thick clumps, or is mucinous<br>4.  **Necrotic Tissue (Eschar)** – black, brown, or tan tissue that adheres firmly to the wound bed or ulcer edges, may be softer or harder than surrounding skin. |
|---|---|

**M0800. Worsening in Pressure Ulcer Status Since Prior Assessment (OBRA or PPS)**

If this is the first assessment (OBRA or PPS) since the most recent admission (A0300E = 1) → Skip to M1020, Other Ulcers, Wounds, and Skin Problems

Indicate the number of current pressure ulcers that were **not present or were at a lesser stage** on prior assessment (OBRA or PPS). If no current pressure ulcer at a given stage, enter 0.

↓ **Enter number of pressure ulcers in boxes**

| | |
|---|---|
| ☐ | A.    Stage 2 |
| ☐ | B.    Stage 3 |
| ☐ | C.    Stage 4 |

**M0900. Healed Pressure Ulcers**

If this is the first assessment (OBRA or PPS) since the most recent admission (A0300E = 1) → Skip to M1020, Other Ulcers, Wounds, and Skin Problems

| Enter<br><br>Code | A.    Were pressure ulcers present on the prior assessment (OBRA or PPS)?<br>    0.   **No** → Skip to M1020, Other Ulcers, Wounds and Skin Problems<br>    1.   **Yes** → Continue to M0900B, Stage 2 |
|---|---|

Indicate the number of pressure ulcers that were noted on the prior assessment (OBRA or PPS) that have completely closed (resurfaced with epithelium).  If no healed pressure ulcer at a given stage since the prior assessment (OBRA or PPS), enter 0.

↓ **Enter number of pressure ulcers in boxes**

| | |
|---|---|
| ☐ | B.    Stage 2 |
| ☐ | C.    Stage 3 |
| ☐ | D.    Stage 4 |

**M1020. Other Ulcers, Wounds, and Skin Problems**

↓ **Check all that apply**

| | | |
|---|---|---|
| ☐ | A. | **Venous or arterial ulcers** |
| ☐ | B. | **Diabetic foot ulcer(s)** |
| ☐ | C. | **Other foot or lower extremity open lesion(s) or infection (cellulitis)** |
| ☐ | D. | **Wound infection other than on foot or lower extremity** |
| ☐ | E. | **Surgical wound(s)** |
| ☐ | F. | **Open lesion(s) other than ulcers, rashes, cuts** (e.g., cancer lesion) |
| ☐ | G. | **Burn(s)** (second or third degree) |
| ☐ | Z. | **None of the above** were present |

(continues)

Appendix 7-1  MINIMUM DATA SET (MDS) 3.0 (Continued)

## Section M   Skin Conditions

**M1100. Number of Venous and Arterial Ulcers** – Complete only if M1020A is checked

| Enter [ ] Number | Enter the total number of **venous and arterial ulcers present** |
|---|---|

**M1200. Skin and Ulcer Treatments**

↓ Check all that apply

| [ ] | A. | **Pressure reducing device for chair** |
|---|---|---|
| [ ] | B. | **Pressure reducing device for bed** |
| [ ] | C. | **Turning/repositioning** |
| [ ] | D | **Nutrition or hydration intervention** to manage skin problems |
| [ ] | E. | **Ulcer care** |
| [ ] | F. | **Surgical wound care** |
| [ ] | G. | **Application of dressings** (with or without topical medications) other than to feet |
| [ ] | H. | **Applications of ointments/medications** other than to feet |
| [ ] | I. | **Application of dressings to feet** (with or without topical medications) |
| [ ] | Z. | **None of the above** were provided |

## Section N   Medications

**N0300. Injections**

| [ ] Days | Record the **number of days that injectable medications were received** during the last 7 days or since admission/reentry if less than 7 days. |
|---|---|

**N0400. Medications Received**

↓ Check all medications the resident received at any time during the last 7 days or since admission/reentry if less than 7 days:

| [ ] | A. | **Antipsychotic** |
|---|---|---|
| [ ] | B. | **Antianxiety** |
| [ ] | C. | **Antidepressant** |
| [ ] | D. | **Hypnotic** |
| [ ] | E. | **Anticoagulant** (warfarin, heparin, or low-molecular weight heparin) |
| [ ] | Z. | **None of the above** were received |

26

*(continues)*

Appendix 7-1  MINIMUM DATA SET (MDS) 3.0 (Continued)

## Section O    Special Treatments and Procedures

### O0100. Special Treatments and Programs

Indicate whether and when each of the following procedures was performed during the last 14 days.

| Procedure performed *while NOT a resident* of this facility and within the *last 14 days*. Only code column 1 if resident was admitted IN THE LAST 14 DAYS. If resident was admitted 14 or more days ago, leave column 1 blank.<br>0.  **No**<br>1.  **Yes** | Procedure performed *while a resident* of this facility and within the *last 14 days*.<br>**Code for all residents.**<br>0.  **No**<br>1.  **Yes** | 1.<br>**While NOT a Resident** | 2.<br>**While a Resident** |
|---|---|---|---|
| | | ↓ Enter Codes in Boxes ↓ | |
| **Cancer Treatments** | | | |
| A.  **Chemotherapy** | | ☐ | ☐ |
| B.  **Radiation** | | ☐ | ☐ |
| **Respiratory Treatments** | | | |
| C.  **Oxygen Therapy** | | ☐ | ☐ |
| D.  **Suctioning** | | ☐ | ☐ |
| E.  **Tracheostomy care** | | ☐ | ☐ |
| F.  **Ventilator or respirator** | | ☐ | ☐ |
| G  **BIPAP/CPAP machine** | | ☐ | ☐ |
| **Other** | | | |
| H.  **IV medications** | | ☐ | ☐ |
| I.   **Transfusions** | | ☐ | ☐ |
| J.  **Dialysis** | | ☐ | ☐ |
| K.  **Hospice care** | | ☐ | ☐ |
| L.  **Respite care** | | ☐ | ☐ |
| M.  **Isolation or quarantine for active infectious disease** (does not include standard body/fluid precautions) | | ☐ | ☐ |

### O0200. Influenza Vaccine

Enter ☐ Code

**A.**  Did the **resident receive the Influenza Vaccine in this facility** for this year's Influenza season (October 1 through March 31)?
  0.  **No** → Continue to O0200B, If Influenza Vaccine not received, state reason
  1.  **Yes** → Skip to O0300, Pneumococcal Vaccine
  9.  **Does not apply because assessment is between July 1 and Sept 30** → Skip to O0300, Pneumococcal Vaccine

Enter ☐ Code

**B.**  If Influenza Vaccine not received, state reason:
  1.  **Not in facility** during this year's flu season
  2.  **Received outside of this facility**
  3.  **Not eligible** – medical contraindication
  4.  **Offered and declined**
  5.  **Not offered**
  6.  **Inability to obtain vaccine**
  9.  **None of the above**

*(continues)*

Appendix 7-1  MINIMUM DATA SET (MDS) 3.0 (Continued)

## Section O — Special Treatments and Procedures

### O0300. Pneumococcal Vaccine

**Enter Code** [ ]  **A. Is the resident's Pneumococcal Vaccination up to date?**
  0. **No** → Continue to O0300B, If Pneumococcal Vaccine not received, state reason
  1. **Yes** → Skip to O0400, Therapies

**Enter Code** [ ]  **B. If Pneumococcal Vaccine not received, state reason:**
  1. **Not eligible** – medical contraindication
  2. **Offered and declined**
  3. **Not offered**

### O0400. Therapies

Record the **total number of minutes** each of the following therapies was administered in the last 7 days in Column 1, Minutes.
Record the **number of days** each therapy was administered, for at least 15 minutes a day in the last 7 days, in Column 2, Days.
Record the **dates** the most recent therapy regimen (since the last assessment) started and ended in Columns 3, Therapy Start Date, and 4, Therapy End Date.

| | 1. Minutes (if minutes = 0000, leave columns 2, 3 and 4 blank) | 2. Days | 3. Therapy Start Date (most recent regimen since last assessment) mm/dd/yyyy | 4. Therapy End Date (enter 99/99/9999 if therapy is ongoing) mm/dd/yyyy |
|---|---|---|---|---|
| A. Speech/language pathology and audiology services | | | __/__/__ | __/__/__ |
| B. Occupational Therapy | | | __/__/__ | __/__/__ |
| C. Physical Therapy | | | __/__/__ | __/__/__ |
| D. Respiratory Therapy | | | __/__/__ | __/__/__ |
| E. Psychological Therapy (by any licensed mental health professional) | | | __/__/__ | __/__/__ |
| F. Recreational Therapy (includes recreational and music therapy) | | | __/__/__ | __/__/__ |

### O0500. Nursing Rehabilitation/Restorative Care

Record the **number of days** each of the following rehabilitative or restorative techniques was administered (for at least 15 minutes a day) in the last 7 calendar days (enter 0 if none or less than 15 minutes daily).

| Number of Days | Technique |
|---|---|
| [ ] | A. **Range of motion (passive)** |
| [ ] | B. **Range of motion (active)** |
| [ ] | C. **Splint or brace assistance** |

| Number of Days | Training and skill practice in: |
|---|---|
| [ ] | D. **Bed mobility** |
| [ ] | E. **Transfer** |
| [ ] | F. **Walking** |
| [ ] | G. **Dressing or grooming** |
| [ ] | H. **Eating or swallowing** |
| [ ] | I. **Amputation/prostheses care** |
| [ ] | J. **Communication** |

MDS 3.0 Item Set Draft-Version 0.5

28

*(continues)*

**Appendix 7-1** MINIMUM DATA SET (MDS) 3.0 (Continued)

| Section O | Special Treatments and Procedures |
|---|---|

**O0600. Physician Examinations**

| | Over the last 14 days, **on how many days did the physician (or authorized assistant or practitioner) examine the resident?** |
|---|---|

Days

**O0700. Physician Orders**

| | Over the last 14 days, **on how many days did the physician (or authorized assistant or practitioner) change the resident's orders?** |
|---|---|

Days

| Section P | Restraints |
|---|---|

**P0100. Physical Restraints**

Physical restraints are any manual method, physical or mechanical device, material or equipment attached or adjacent to the resident's body that the individual cannot remove easily, which restricts freedom of movement or normal access to one's body.

↓ Enter Codes in Boxes

| | Used in Bed |
|---|---|
| | A. **Bed rail** (any type; e.g., full, half, one side) |
| | B. **Trunk restraint** |
| | C. **Limb restraint** |
| | D. **Other** |

**Coding:**
0. **Not used**
1. **Used less than daily**
2. **Used daily**

| | Used in Chair or Out of Bed |
|---|---|
| | E. **Trunk restraint** |
| | F. **Limb restraint** |
| | G. **Chair prevents rising** |
| | H. **Other** |

(*continues*)

Appendix 7-1 MINIMUM DATA SET (MDS) 3.0 (Continued)

| **Section Q** | **Participation in Assessment and Goal Setting** |
|---|---|

**Q0100. Participation in Assessment**

Enter
☐
Code

**A. Resident participated in assessment**
    0. **No**
    1. **Yes**

Enter
☐
Code

**B. Family or significant other participated in assessment**
    0. **No**
    1. **Yes**
    9. **No family or significant other**

**Q0200. Return to Community**

Ask resident (or family or significant other if resident unable to respond): "*Do you want to talk to someone about the possibility of returning to the community?*"

Enter
☐
Code

    0. **No**
    1. **Yes**
    9. **Unknown or uncertain**

**Q0300. Resident's Overall Goals** – Complete only for the first assessment (OBRA or PPS) since the most recent admission (A0300E = 1)

Enter
☐
Code

**A. Select one for resident's goals established during assessment process.**
    1. **Post-acute care** – expects to return to live in community
    2. **Post-acute care** – expects to have continued NH needs
    3. **Respite stay** – expects to return home
    4. **Other reason for admit** – expects to return to live in community
    5. **Long-term care** for medical, functional, and/or cognitive impairments
    6. **End-of-life care** (includes palliative care and hospice)
    9. **Unknown or uncertain**

Enter
☐
Code

**B. Indicate information source for this item**
    1. **Resident**
    2. If not resident, then **family or significant other**
    3. **Not resident, family or significant other**

| **Section T** | **Therapy Supplement for Medicare PPS** |
|---|---|

**T0100. Ordered Therapies** – Complete only if this is a Medicare PPS 5-day scheduled assessment (A0300B = 01) or Medicare PPS readmission/return assessment (A0300B = 06)

Enter
☐
Code

**A.** Has the physician ordered any of the following therapies to begin in first 14 days of stay: physical therapy, occupational therapy, or speech/language pathology service?
    0. **No** → Skip to Section Z, Assessment Administration
    1. **Yes**

Enter
☐
Code

**B.** Were therapy evaluations completed?
    0. **No** → Skip to Section Z, Assessment Administration
    1. **Yes**

Enter Number
☐☐
of days

**C.** Through day 15, provide an estimate of the number of days when at least 1 therapy service can be expected to have been delivered

Enter Number
☐☐☐☐
of minutes

**D.** Through day 15, provide an estimate of the number of therapy minutes (across the therapies) that can be expected to be delivered

(*continues*)

**Appendix 7-1** MINIMUM DATA SET (MDS) 3.0 (Continued)

## Section Z — Assessment Administration

**Z0100   Medicare Part A Billing**

A. Medicare Part A HIPPS code for billing:

(RUG group followed by assessment type indicator)

B. RUG version code:

**Z0200. State Medicaid Billing (If required by the state)**

A. RUG Case Mix group:

B. RUG version code:

**Z0300. Insurance Billing**

A. RUG Case Mix group:

B. RUG version code:

**Z0400. Signature of Persons Completing the Assessment**

I certify that the accompanying information accurately reflects resident assessment information for this resident and that I collected or coordinated collection of this information on the dates specified. To the best of my knowledge, this information was collected in accordance with applicable Medicare and Medicaid requirements. I understand that this information is used as a basis for ensuring that residents receive appropriate and quality care, and as a basis for payment from federal funds. I further understand that payment of such federal funds and continued participation in the government-funded health care programs is conditioned on the accuracy and truthfulness of this information, and that I may be personally subject to or may subject my organization to substantial criminal, civil, and/or administrative penalties for submitting false information. I also certify that I am authorized to submit this information by this facility on its behalf.

| Signature | Title | Sections | Date |
|-----------|-------|----------|------|
| A. | | | |
| B. | | | |
| C. | | | |
| D. | | | |
| E. | | | |
| F. | | | |
| G. | | | |
| H. | | | |
| I. | | | |
| J. | | | |
| K. | | | |
| L. | | | |

**Z0500. Signature of RN Assessment Coordinator Verifying Assessment Completion**

A. Signature

B. Date RN Assessment Coordinator signed assessment as complete:

month     day     year

Note: CMS made this draft available at the time the book manuscript was being prepared. The final MDS 3.0 may reflect some changes.

Chapter 8

---

# Internal Environment and Culture Change

## What You Will Learn

- Building codes, construction, and layout for a young and growing nursing home industry in the 1960s were adapted from hospitals. Competition during the 1980s prompted nursing homes to emphasize residential and aesthetic features. Contemporary models focus on person-centered care.

- The philosophy of long-term care greatly diverges from the sick-role model that governs hospital care. The long-term care model of person-centered care must integrate three major components: socioresidential, clinical, and overarching human factors.

- Nursing homes encounter four main challenges to a full integration of the three main components. The challenges include need for clinical care, economic constraints, patient-related constraints, and regulations.

- The clinical organization of a nursing home includes nursing units, and adequately staffed and well-equipped nursing stations.

- The socio-residential environment should emphasize both personal and public domains. These domains emphasize security of person and property, safety against potential hazards, wayfinding, autonomy and self-determination, personal privacy, compatible relationships, the dining experience, and opportunities for socializing.

- Modern architectural designs, such as cluster design and nested single rooms, emphasize many of the socio-residential factors.

- Aesthetics are an important element of homelike environments that also promote a sense of well-being. Choice of lighting, colors, and furnishings require special considerations in creating therapeutic environments for nursing home residents.

- Enriched environments are physically and psychologically support-ive environments. They incorporate the theories of biophilia and thriving. Creating an enriched environment first requires a philoso-phy of person-centered care in which clinical care, socio-residential elements, and human factors are integrated. The environment then incorporates elements that provide a moderate degree of positive stimulation and also opportunities for silent contemplation and in-ner reflection.

- A growing movement has been advocating culture change in nurs-ing homes. Culture change requires person-centered care, enriched environments, and staff empowerment based on adoption of new mindsets of managing people.

- The Eden Alternative and the Green House Project are two contem-porary models of culture change.

- Environments for dementia patients are based on the modern con-cepts of creating enriched environments.

The internal environment and organization of nursing homes have traditionally evolved as both a direct and indirect result of health pol-icy. It is only recently that enriched environ-ments and innovative designs have started to emerge through the influence of consumer ad-vocacy and market forces.

## Evolution of Nursing Home Internal Environments

The poorhouses (discussed in Chapter 2) were the common ancestors of both hospitals and nursing homes. In the late 1800s and early 1900s, hospitals became separate insti-tutions mainly because medical discoveries—such as anesthesia, antiseptic surgery, and X-ray imaging—required an institutional setting where physicians could administer medical and surgical treatments and where

physicians could be trained. It was not until 1935, when the Old Age Assistance (OAA) program was created, that a private nursing home industry emerged. The OAA enabled many elderly to pay for services in homes for the aged and boarding homes. The new law had purposely prohibited payments to any-one living in poorhouses. Poorhouses closed down in large numbers, and private old age homes were in high demand. Private opera-tors acquired various types of buildings—old schools, hotels, and dormitories—and con-verted them into old-age homes. At this time, building standards and oversight for care de-livery were practically nonexistent. The old age homes provided basic nursing care and supervision, much as today's personal care homes do, and the very sick stayed in hospi-tals. Policies during the 1950s expanded the OAA program, and additional funding was made available for care in nursing homes. Legislation in 1958 and 1959 authorized the

Small Business Administration and the Federal Housing Administration to aid the construction of for-profit nursing homes, and there was a nursing home construction boom. The industry experienced explosive growth after the creation of Medicare and Medicaid in 1965.

By this time, hospitals were well established as institutions where the healing arts were practiced. For a young and growing nursing home industry, hospital layout and clinical arrangements became the obvious model. Building codes for nursing home construction were also adapted from hospitals. The result was hospital-like nursing homes characterized by long corridors, shared occupancy, and large cafeteria-style dining rooms. Licensing and certification rules further reinforced the hospital design because the nursing home was viewed as a place where convalescent treatment would continue following discharge from hospitals, as laid out in Medicare rules. Thus, by default, hospital design was adapted for nursing home construction. Clinical organization in nursing homes also followed the hospital-based medical model, with central nursing stations, buzzers, and call signals; noisy shower and bathing areas; lack of privacy; scheduled routines; and hallways cluttered with medication carts, soiled linen hampers, food carts, housekeeping carts, and similar items.

During the 1980s, construction of new nursing facilities and renovation of existing ones began emphasizing residential and aesthetic features. These changes were triggered mainly by market competition, which created the need to attract new patients to keep the beds filled. Competition also prompted efforts by nursing facilities to cater to the private-pay clientele. Competition came from newer nursing homes that adopted contemporary designs, the emergence of modern assisted living facilities, and expansion of substitute services such as home health care. Many private-pay patients have found the residential and social lifestyles in assisted living facilities to be much more appealing than skilled nursing facilities. In response, most nursing facilities operating today have taken at least some steps toward creating homelike and social environments that are more aesthetically pleasing than those found in older facilities.

New choices and alternatives to traditional nursing home care are molding people's expectations about long-term care (LTC). In response to the changing expectations, current trends suggest a gradual transformation from traditional hospital-inspired facilities to contemporary architectural features with a more residential look and feel. Other contemporary models are focusing on ***person-centered care***, a philosophy that integrates physical layout and design with empowerment of the residents, families, and staff. A cultural and social change is under way, with clients demanding that nursing home environments be made more appealing and less institutionalized. A gradual move away from the medical model and toward a more holistic socio-residential model that allows individuals to pursue their own lifestyles—rather than be governed by established routines and schedules—is where we are today in nursing home evolution.

## Philosophy of Care Delivery

Traditionally, both the physical architecture and the philosophy of care delivery in nursing homes was influenced by hospitals. In a hospital, the ***sick-role model*** proposed by Parsons (1972) governs patients' social relationships. The patient is expected to relinquish individual control to medical personnel and comply with their directives. The sick role promotes an institutional orientation to patient care, which is manifested in four ways: (1) rigid daily routines; (2) social distance between staff members and the patient; (3) care practices that lend to depersonalization, such as loss of privacy; and (4) "blocking routines" that require patients to do certain things at pre-arranged times, mainly for the convenience of staff (Kruzich & Berg, 1985).

Unlike acute care hospitals, however, a nursing facility is both a clinical and a social establishment. It took some time for nursing home professionals and regulators to fully grasp this. Unlike hospitals, patients stay in nursing homes for extended periods of time. For some, the stay is permanent and, in a sense, the nursing home becomes their home. Although patients are admitted to skilled nursing facilities primarily to receive therapeutic interventions, these services must be delivered according to a philosophy that emphasizes personal preferences, independence, dignity, and self-esteem as overarching factors in the living environment and the delivery of care. Today, quality of life has become just as important as quality of care.

Creation of an environment of person-centered care (also called client-centered care) in modern nursing facilities is guided by three main factors (Figure 8–1):

- The socio-residential component creates the physical environment in which the resident receives room-and-board services and considers the nursing facility as his or her home. Amenities in the environment include personal and social spaces, aesthetic décor and designs, and various conveniences such as a barber/beauty salon. Accommodations must pro-

vide privacy, even though the most common type of living arrangement in nursing homes is a semi-private room. The environment must promote individual pursuits and leisure on the one hand and social interaction and engagement on the other. Meals must meet the nutritional and therapeutic needs, but must also be palatable and attractively served. Internal spaces must facilitate private visits with family and other visitors from the community. Social spaces must allow for a communal environment in which people can engage in meaningful social relationships.

- The elements of clinical care (listed in Figure 8–1) are highly individualized. They must be delivered by qualified professionals and paraprofessionals in accordance with accepted standards of clinical care.

- The overarching human factors—personal preferences, independence, dignity, and self-esteem—must blend into every aspect of the patient's life and the delivery of services. Such integration is not naturally achieved and requires staff training. Traditional nursing home care has been based on an expert approach to meeting the physical and medical needs of patients (Collopy, 1995). Well-meaning staff members are often ill-prepared to reconcile their technical training and priorities with the fact that residents are entitled to make their own choices. As a result, caregivers may experience difficulty relating to residents because of this conflict (Chapman et al., 2003).

When human factors are integrated into the other two components, it creates an

Figure 8-1 Main Components of Client-centered Care

| Overarching Human Factors | | |
| --- | --- | --- |
| Personal preferences<br>Independence<br>Dignity<br>Self-esteem | | |
| Socio-Residential Component | | Clinical Component |
| Room and Board | Amenities | Clinical Care |
| Accommodation<br>• Privacy<br>• Safety<br>• Cleanliness<br>• Comfort<br><br>Meals<br>• Nutrition<br>• Choice<br>• Adequacy<br>• Attractiveness<br>• Palatability | Private rooms<br>Personal space<br>Social space<br>Dining rooms<br>Layout<br>Décor and aesthetics<br>Barber/beauty salon<br>Gift shop<br>Library<br>Chapel | Medical oversight<br>Nursing care<br>Rehabilitation<br>Social services<br>Dietary services<br>Recreational activities<br>End-of-life care |

environment in which a person's physical, mental, social, and spiritual needs are met. Unlike the sick-role model, the person-centered model is characterized by shared control between the patient and the facility personnel. It promotes individual autonomy and decision making, even when a resident's decision-making capacity is limited. It embraces the idea that a LTC facility is not merely a clinical setting; it is also a place that many people call home.

## Challenges to a Full Integration

Integration of the three components will continue to be a challenge for nursing home professionals, and there are four main reasons: primacy of clinical care, economic necessity, patient-related constraints, and regulatory burden. In spite of these constraints, nursing home professionals must strive to achieve a balance among the three factors just discussed.

## Primacy of Clinical Care

The primary reason for admitting patients to a nursing facility is to meet their clinical needs. The fundamental purpose of a nursing home is defeated if it does not provide clinical care in accordance with accepted standards that require current medical and nursing knowledge and use of technology. As explained in Chapter 5, this is also a nursing facility's primary legal and moral duty. Hence, the sick-role model can be compromised but cannot be entirely dispensed with. For example, giving medications and other treatments in a patient population of any size requires certain routines based on medical directives. Medical examinations result in some loss of personal control by the patient. Necessary staff assistance with daily living activities does create some dependency.

## Economic Constraints

Nursing facilities exist because of economic necessity. If it were feasible, almost every nursing home patient would choose to be cared for in a private residence by a private-duty nurse. The reality, however, is that unless an individual is very wealthy, neither the individual patient nor the society can afford to incur the expense that private-duty care would entail. Expensive as it is, delivery of care in a nursing facility is highly cost effective compared with private-duty nursing. From this perspective, the residential nature of a nursing facility should not be construed to mean that it is a private residence. It must, by necessity, provide services to a relatively large number of patients 24/7. In spite of suggestions to downplay or to criticize the institutional nature of nursing facilities, the fact remains that nursing facilities must function as efficient organizations.

## Patient-Related Constraints

Nursing homes face constraints related to patient characteristics. Examples include behavioral problems, such as frequent combativeness or screaming episodes that can disrupt the environment. By its very nature, any group living arrangement, whether large or small, creates an environment in which small-scale conflicts of everyday life are likely to occur. First, respecting autonomy can be "vexatious because the conditions that bring elders into long-term care—confusion, dementia, wandering, and a host of chronic conditions associated with being old—are such that the very capacity for choice and rational decision making is seriously compromised, if not absent" (Agich, 1995, p. 113). In a relation of dependency, it may be quite natural for a caregiver to simply take over the care-delivery process. Yet, an effort must be made to return to the elder patient some of the responsibilities for his or her own health care in a caring and respectful way.

## Regulatory Burden

Nursing home regulation and enforcement were discussed in Chapter 6. The nursing home industry particularly views the regulatory process to be onerous, adversarial, and punitive. As a result, the culture of nursing home administration has suffered from paranoia of the regulatory system. Inadequate financing under Medicaid, the largest payer for nursing home care, is also seen as a major constraint to procure needed resources. Collopy (1995, p. 149) argued that the nursing home industry is often slow to respond and is largely reactive in the way that it invokes moral values, mainly to protect itself against possible regulatory sanction. Such a highly risk-averse stance mutes the providers' own moral agency, so regulators and advocates for the elderly have seized the ethics agenda and have taken the initiative to prescribe minute regulatory details. Such a state of affairs will change only when the industry's leadership asserts the values that are most desired by its clients. The culture change, discussed later in this chapter, is an effort in this direction initiated by the industry's leadership, not by any regulatory requirements.

## Need for Balance

A perfect integration of clinical, socio-residential, and human factors is almost impossible. Nevertheless, nursing home staff must strive for a balance in person-centered caregiving. There is, however, no standard rule that can be followed to help people adapt to change in their lives. People try to adapt in their own unique ways through various interpretive efforts. The nursing facility, however, can provide physical surroundings and a basic sense of personal space to help the process of adjustment. Familiarity and closeness in the caregiver–patient relationship that is built on the foundation of respect for the patient can also help patients maintain their sense of identity despite the ravages of impairment (Agich, 1995). In a nursing facility, each resident's desires, interests, and actions can directly affect the interests and legitimate expectations of other residents (Arras, 1995). For example, patients who wander into others' rooms, rummage through others' belongings, dip their hands into other diners' plates, make yelling noises, or display combativeness disrupt the quality of life of other residents. To deal with such conflicts in an institutional setting, the facility must achieve an appropriate balance among the needs of these groups. Arras (1995) suggested that a model other than the one in which the patient's best

interest becomes the overriding goal is necessary. This alternative model is based on the notions of fairness, accommodation, compromise, and negotiation. Again, each situation is going to be different, but in a social environment, no one patient's interests are legitimately outweighed by the competing interests of other patients. Also, modern architectural features and adoption of cultural change can facilitate the creation of a balanced environment.

## Clinical Organization

The vast majority of nursing homes use a traditional clinical set-up, which is described in this section. Many newer facilities that are being built use innovative design concepts to downplay the clinical organization.

## Nursing Units

A nursing unit or wing is a section of a facility that consists of a certain number of patient rooms served by a nursing station. Depending on its size, a facility may have clinically distinct nursing units, each providing a somewhat distinct level of care, such as rehabilitation, dementia care, or specialized care. Distinct nursing units can also be designated according to the type of certification (see Figure 5–4 in Chapter 5). To achieve staff efficiency, most clinical units are self-contained, having their own bathing rooms, dining or feeding rooms and lounges for patients and visitors. An adequate number of clean linen closets should be located in the hallways of each nursing unit. An enclosed area or a hallway nook for depositing soiled linens is located in the unit, with marked containers to ease sorting and to separate lightly soiled linens from those that are heavily soiled. When utility closets are easily accessible to staff, hallways are kept free of clutter, and odors are kept to a minimum. An enclosed soiled utility area, rather than a nook in the hallway, is ideal because it can be equipped with a rinse tub to eliminate heavy wastes. Modern ventilation and waste-elimination systems are designed to keep odors to a minimum. Also, staff members should be trained in sanitation and odor control methods. Chemical deodorizers should not be used to mask odors.

A facility of 80 or more beds is likely to have more than one nursing unit. To the extent that it can do so, a facility should segregate patients on the basis of clinical criteria. Distinctly separate specialized care units are often provided for subacute care or Alzheimer's care. Such specialized units allow the facility to match staff skills to special patient needs. Rehabilitation aides (paraprofessionals who follow up on rehabilitation therapies), for instance, are most appropriately stationed in the SNF unit where most of the Medicare patients are located. A separate nursing unit, however, is not generally feasible for every type of specialization. Several clinically complex services such as ventilator care, head trauma care, care for spinal injuries, and treatment for pressure ulcers and wounds can be located on one unit that is served by the same nursing station. Also, neatly categorizing patients in terms of their needs for care is not always practical. Comorbidities often present a challenge to LTC clinicians about where a patient with given health conditions can be best accommodated. On the other hand, facilities must give due consideration to each patient's clinical needs as well as the patient's quality of life. For instance, every effort should be made to segregate patients with cognitive impairments or behavioral problems from those who do not have such disorders.

Some facilities focus on private-pay clients by furnishing a separate noncertified unit where the living environment is enhanced and amenities are upgraded. This type of segregation in a noncertified section allows a facility to provide upscale services to private-pay clients without discriminating against those on public assistance. It also shelters the noncertified section from certification surveys.

## Nursing Station

The hub of clinical care is an appropriately located, adequately staffed, and well-furnished nursing station. This station can be regarded as a service center from where all nursing care is delivered to a certain number of patients, generally on an entire nursing unit.

## Location of Nursing Stations

A nursing station should be centrally located to enable the nursing staff to observe and supervise a certain number of patient rooms and to respond effectively to patient needs. A facility may have more than one station, depending on its size, acuity level of patients, and complexity of care. On the other hand, having too many stations would be inefficient because each station must be individually staffed. As a general rule, a separate nursing station serves each clinical unit or wing in a facility. The maximum distance allowed from a nursing station to the farthest patient room is generally specified in state licensure regulations.

Other areas of a clinical unit that may be adjacent to the nursing station include rooms for bathing and showering, special dining areas to accommodate patients who need assistance with eating, and patient lounges, including any lounges designated for smokers.

Of course, not all patient dining rooms and lounges need to be in the vicinity of a nursing station—only those where supervision from staff is necessary.

## Staffing of Nursing Stations

Staffing is one of the most important issues in nursing homes. State licensure regulations often specify minimum staff-to-patient ratios, and facility administrators may tend to believe that those minimum standards represent adequate staffing levels. State standards set a minimum requirement (which is, at best, arbitrary) because it does not take into account the level of patients' clinical acuity. Clinical load rather than state regulations should govern staff-to-patient ratios, and higher ratios are needed in specialized and heavy-care units. Determination of staffing levels is addressed in Chapter 16.

## Nursing Station Furnishings

The layout and furnishing of a nursing station should enhance staff effectiveness. The station itself is an enclosed area, with a counter behind which nurses and other staff members perform administrative tasks. No one but authorized staff members should have access to the area behind the counter. Among other things, a nursing station's furnishings must include three important components: a patient call signal system, medical records, and a pharmaceuticals room.

### Patient Call Signals

A call system is a critical component of a nursing unit. The system connects devices at all patient bedsides and in toilets to the nursing station. It should also connect the station to the bathing-and-shower rooms, dining areas, and lounges located on a given nursing unit. The system enables the patients themselves and staff members working with patients to summon help when needed. Ideally, the system should have audio-visual as well as voice capabilities. A patient uses a sensory device—such as a call button—that sets off the audio-visual signal at the nursing station. This audio-visual signal consists of a light and a sound to alert the staff that a patient is calling for assistance and also to identify the patient who needs help. A voice or "talk-back" feature is useful when the staff member attending to a patient needs to communicate with staff members located at the station; this device saves time that otherwise will be spent walking back and forth from the nursing station. For communication among staff members, modern wireless communication devices such as portable pagers are increasingly being used. They reduce the need for frequent paging over the intercom, which makes the environment noisy and stressful.

### Medical Records

Located at the nursing station, there must be a separate medical chart for every patient on the unit. The medical records must be readily accessible to all authorized staff members. Confidentiality, however, must be maintained at all times. Medical records are increasingly being automated by using computer-based information systems. Automation can greatly facilitate the tasks of keeping records up to date and retrieving them quickly. Privacy practices must comply with HIPAA standards (see Chapter 5).

### Pharmaceuticals Room

The pharmaceuticals room, or medication room, as it is commonly called, should be quickly accessible from the nursing station.

This room is locked to safeguard all medications. The pharmaceuticals room is also commonly used to store nursing treatment supplies and a first-aid box. The room is furnished with a refrigerator for storing medications that require refrigeration. Additional details on the management of pharmaceuticals and safeguarding of controlled substances are found in Chapter 10.

# Socio-Residential Environment

Although a nursing facility is considered a patient's home, it is also a community. The social and residential elements are closely intertwined, and the environment itself should promote the healing of the body, mind, and spirit. A healing environment relieves the clinical infrastructure of pressures that might otherwise be imposed on it from social conflict or individual ill-adjustment. As mentioned earlier, segregating patients with severe dementia and those with behavioral problems from other patients is particularly important. A disruptive environment creates commotion and confusion. It is mentally and emotionally upsetting for those who prefer quietude and wish to engage in productive social, mental, and spiritual pursuits. The facility's set-up should also make it easier for patients to explore their compatibilities with others and engage in social interactions in accordance with personal preferences. The socio-residential environment should emphasize both personal and public domains.

## Personal Domain

At a personal level, the main concerns people have are security, safety, wayfinding, autonomy, and privacy. In coping with change, opportunities for introspection, a sense of personal space, and the support of others may be more important for the patient than the ability to socialize with others.

## Security

Security is a basic human need. It entails physical safety and psychological peace of mind. It includes a variety of conditions that contribute to freedom from risk, danger, anxiety, or doubt (Schwarz, 1996). A nursing facility is responsible for its patients' personal security and the safekeeping of their belongings and private funds if the latter are deposited in a patient's trust account that the facility manages. Security considerations often vary from one patient to another. A patient may have a tendency to wander out unnoticed and compromise his or her safety. But if this same person can wander out into a protective environment, such as a fenced-in walkway, it can have a therapeutic effect. Another may insist on wearing expensive jewelry that someone could remove or that could get lost. Another may hallucinate and imagine that someone is assaulting her.

Not all nursing homes are located in safe neighborhoods. The administrator must evaluate external security concerns, which include protecting residents and their property from intruders. To the extent that patients can feel safe and secure, they can choose to spend time indoors and outdoors.

## Safety

In building design, safety requirements are primarily governed by federal, state, and local codes and regulations. Among these, the *Life Safety Code* provides the most comprehensive set of rules (see Chapter 6). Other considerations are also important in creating a safe environment:

- The elderly are particularly vulnerable to falls. Great caution and vigilance needs to be exercised around wet floors, power cords, fallen objects, and throw rugs.

- Potential hazards should be eliminated or closely monitored. Access to products such as drugs, lotions, and ointments on medication and treatment carts should be adequately supervised. Patients could also gain access to other unattended toxic substances, such as cleaning chemicals left unattended on housekeeping carts, or sharp objects, such as certain maintenance tools.

- Access to areas such as the kitchen, mechanical rooms, and laundry are generally prohibited. However, kitchen and laundry areas can provide stimulating and meaningful engagement for some patients, including those with mild to moderate dementia. With some supervision, cooking or laundry activities can add to patients' quality of life, particularly when smaller household-style kitchens are included in the facility's design.

- All major safety concerns should be incorporated into the patient's plan of care, and they ought to be addressed by a multi-disciplinary team of professionals because the patient may require therapeutic intervention from trained staff. For example, a person's medications may need to be reviewed or behavior modification may be necessary.

## Wayfinding

*Wayfinding* refers to features that can help people find their way through a large institution with relative ease. Residents in nursing homes are often susceptible to disorientation because of a decline of various senses. Sameness and repetition—similar layouts, regular pattern of doors, and similar furniture throughout a facility—are the common sources of disorientation (Drew, 1992). Orientation involves much more than use of signs. In addition to clear and readable signage, wayfinding can be facilitated by using a variety of means such as employing different color schemes and patterns in different sections of the facility; color-coded handrails; varying furniture styles; varying layout and arrangement; use of pictures, tapestry, hanging quilts, and window displays; and placement of public accessories such as telephones and water coolers in planned locations. On the other hand, doors leading to utility rooms and areas not meant for residents should be painted to blend with the adjacent walls.

## Autonomy

*Autonomy* can be defined as "a cluster of notions including self-determination, freedom, independence, and liberty of choice and action. In its most general terms, autonomy signifies control of decision making and other activity by the individual. It refers to human agency free of outside intervention and interference" (Collopy, 1988). In any type of health care delivery, the patient assumes a dependent role in relation to the provider of care, as observed by Talcott Parsons (1972) in the sick-role model; the patient must concede some degree of autonomy. This dependence, however, does not mean that the patient should be made to give up all choice and decision making. To the contrary, because health care by its very nature creates dependency, providers have an obligation to ensure the maximum preservation of patient autonomy.

On the other hand, a patient's autonomy cannot be taken to an extent that it infringes on the rights of others.

Autonomy for patients also requires that they be allowed to personalize their living quarters with familiar things, and such personal items as radios, small television sets, family pictures, mementos, artifacts, plants, music, personal furniture, bed accessories, etc. Emotions and memories from past experiences and events often stimulate conversation and social interaction. Although space is almost always limited, a display shelf in each room can help people personalize their space by displaying memorabilia and other items. Certain personal belongings may also pose safety concerns. For instance, too many electrical gadgets may overload the circuits and create a fire hazard. Long extension cords and floor rugs pose a tripping hazard.

Autonomy also means that a patient must be able to make informed choices. Although the nursing facility must encourage informed choice, it also has the responsibility to do what is in the patient's best interest. Occasionally, conflicts may arise between a patient's autonomy and the facility's duty toward the patient. Such conflicts should be resolved by taking into consideration legal requirements, regulatory constraints, and ethics. Such situations are often not clear-cut. For instance, should a nursing facility use funds out of a patient's trust account to purchase new glasses or new hearing aids after the patient has already broken or lost two or three of them? Such decisions can be best addressed in a multi-disciplinary forum—such as an ethics committee—in which decision makers take into account the patient's wishes and past practices if the patient is unable to participate in decision making. But, if the patient can participate, his or her wishes must be carried out.

## Privacy

Almost all individuals require some privacy in terms of space, time, and person.

### Privacy of Space

In a health care facility, privacy of space is first determined by the type of accommodation: private or shared. Many facilities maintain a small number of private rooms for single accommodation. As a general rule, however, occupying a private room is considered a luxury for which someone has to pay more. Unless a medically determined need exists for private accommodation, public as well as private insurers do not cover it. So, in most instances, a patient must spend out-of-pocket funds if a private room is desired. Hence, for most patients, shared accommodation is the norm, which in most facilities constitutes double occupancy (rather than triple or quadruple accommodation). In these circumstances, privacy rests on how much physical space each individual has, including closet and storage space. Privacy also entails the need for intimacy (Westin, 1967). *Intimacy* refers to a person's privacy during visits with family, friends, and legal or spiritual counselors. Residents can also express their sexuality in a private environment if their intimacy is assured. Because privacy is generally compromised in a multiple-occupancy setting, the facility should provide secluded areas that may be used for intimate dining experiences with family and friends, for private visits, or for sexual intimacy.

### Privacy of Time

Privacy of time is often compromised by clinical routines that are established for the sake of staff efficiency. However, such routines tend to make patients' lives regimented. In most nursing homes, wake-up and morning hygiene chores must be completed before breakfast. Because assigning staff members to every resident at the same time is not possible, certain residents must wake up before others, and there may be little provision for patients to sleep in late. Meal hours are also generally fixed. Bathing and shower routines are scheduled ahead of time. Yet, within the parameters of such scheduled routines, patients' individual preferences should be accommodated whenever possible. Privacy of time also includes the need for personal reclusion, that is, have time for oneself and be free from unwanted intrusion, to be alone for quiet reflection. For this purpose, quiet and secluded spaces such as small libraries and chapels are highly desirable.

### Privacy of Person

A disregard of privacy of person is dehumanizing. Privacy of person can be equated with dignity. A basic rule for facilities to follow is to treat every person with dignity, regardless of whether he or she can perceive indignities (Kane, 2001). Knocking at the door before entering a patient's room, closing the door for a patient while that patient is using the toilet, drawing privacy curtains during treatment, providing appropriate personal covering for a trip to the common bathing-and-shower area, providing proper grooming during a trip to the therapy room or dining room, and giving lap robes to female patients in wheelchairs are examples of how personal privacy is respected to preserve individual dignity.

## Public Domain

Loneliness and isolation are common concerns among the elderly. Unless a person chooses to remain alone, opportunities must be provided for wholesome social interaction. The range of opportunities depends on how well a nursing facility functions as a social community. The three most important experiences from this perspective are compatibility, the dining experience, and socializing.

## Compatibility

Social interactions in the public domain are primarily driven by compatibility because compatible relationships are something people naturally seek. The issue of compatibility first arises when a new patient is admitted to the facility and has to share a room with another patient who is a complete stranger. Gender compatibility has been a long-established practice. Room sharing by two individuals of the opposite sex is permitted only in case of legitimate couples. Apart from such obvious types of compatibility, the main consideration in assigning a room to two people is how well the two individuals are likely to get along and engage in a meaningful social rapport. Compatibility is also an important consideration in other situations requiring social groupings, such as dining at the same table or participating in social and recreational events.

Relationship building and bonding can be facilitated in several ways. Some nursing home residents assist other residents with simple tasks, such as escorting a friend to the dining room or assisting someone in a wheelchair. People who have disabilities of their own can find meaning in being helpful to others; it builds their own self-esteem. Nursing home residents can also develop appropriate relationships with volunteers and staff members.

## Dining

Dining goes beyond mere physical sustenance and good nutrition. It can provide opportunities for people to interact with others in a social setting. Seating arrangements should be such that they create opportunities for those who can socially interact. Of course, a patient's clinical condition will determine to what extent interaction is possible. For patients who require feeding assistance or who may have other special needs, dining may become a clinical event, but staff interaction can still help make it a social event. To the extent possible, clinical dining areas for those who cannot eat on their own should be separated from social dining areas so that those who are able to dine in a social setting can enjoy the dining experience without interruption or distraction.

The dining environment should be relaxed. Comfortable chairs, tablecloths or placemats, cloth napkins, table centerpieces, and soft music contribute to a relaxed and enjoyable experience. A facility should also have some special tables to accommodate wheelchairs, but ambulatory and wheelchair patients should be allowed to sit and dine together.

## Socializing

Socializing often depends on an individual's capacity to interact with others. Well-planned facilities offer varied spaces where people can spend time in the company of others. The facility must schedule programs that offer numerous daily opportunities for patients to socialize according to their personal interests. Social events also enable patients with dementia and other limitations to receive sensory stimulation by just being present. Events should be held in both interior and exterior spaces.

Interior spaces include lounges, dining areas, craft and game rooms, and chapels. Some modern facilities also have spaces such as mini-malls, ice cream parlors, and barber and beauty shops where residents can enjoy some of the social activities they once pursued. Interior spaces should be comfortable and pleasing, with appropriate furniture, lighting, fixtures, and décor that allow people to associate with one another in pleasant surroundings.

Exterior spaces include courtyards, patios, balconies, terraces, vegetable and flower patches, gazebos, and the spaces around bird feeders and fountains. The building's design should permit all residents easy access to the exterior. The outdoor spaces should have appropriate seating arrangements so that the patients can spend time relaxing, socializing, and simply enjoying the surroundings.

## Modern Architectural Designs

The average size of a nursing facility has increased by 44% from 75 beds in 1973 to 108 beds in 2006 (National Center for Health Statistics, 2007). Although the larger size creates operational efficiencies, it detracts from a residential environment. In response, some innovative architectural plans have emerged. Modern architectural designs try to incorporate a balance between the clinical and socio-residential factors. A homelike environment is achieved by a facility's structural design, furnishings, décor, and a proper emphasis on the socio-residential elements discussed earlier. Increasingly, in new constructions, private rather than shared rooms are in vogue, to give patients more personal space. In addition, current architectural designs no longer feature the traditional long corridors that are lined with rooms on both sides, which often get cluttered with all kinds of barrels and carts and create an institutional look and feel. High-pitched roofs, varied plan configurations, and the connection of indoor to outdoor spaces can make a building seem more like a condominium than a nursing home (Nursing home architecture, 1997). The medical character of the facility can be further deemphasized by eliminating the traditional nursing station and creating more shared spaces for social contact (Cohen & Day, 1993). In large institutions, some smaller self-contained units can be created, each with its own household-style kitchen and a common room that can serve as a multi-purpose room for dining, activities, and socializing.

## Cluster Design

The cluster design is gradually replacing the traditional corridor design in modern nursing home architecture. The design places decentralized self-contained clusters within the larger clinical units, creating relatively small residential groupings. Even though a nursing station is present, the design helps deemphasize it. The cluster concept is sometimes called "neighborhood living," and the clusters may be called "household clusters." Each cluster functions as a residential unit or neighborhood, with its own living room and a room for various activities and for dining, surrounded by resident rooms (Dunkelman, 1992). Seating configurations are designed to create intimate social spaces. The design allows for plenty of windows for natural lighting and a panoramic view of the exterior. Clusters also tend to offer better flexibility in segregating residents than traditional layouts do. For instance, patients requiring heavy care could be accommodated in the same cluster.

Clusters are typically designed for between 8 and 12 residents, and three or more clusters are grouped together for staffing efficiency (Browning, 2003). As an example,

Figure 8–2 illustrates three 9-bed clusters, totaling 27 beds. High construction costs for clusters present a major challenge to facilities, although better functional efficiencies are often gained. By decentralizing staff and services and giving associates quick access to utilities, a cluster layout can make associates more productive and the delivery of care can be improved. Small nurse aide stations—generally no more than a desk and chair—enable the staff to be in close proximity to residents, allowing for prompt attention to their needs. In Figure 8–2, each of the three clusters has its own nurse aide station. The self-contained clusters also have their own bathing rooms, linen closets, and soiled utility closets. Associates can function more efficiently because this arrangement shortens walking distances and saves time. Services are brought to each cluster instead of transporting residents to the nursing station, dining room, or therapy room (Dunkelman, 1992). A group of permanent caregivers assigned to each cluster can also provide opportunities for interaction and bonding between caregivers and residents.

## Nested Single-Room Design

To counter the high construction costs of private rooms, the architectural firm of Engelbrecht & Griffin (now named EGA, PC) pioneered the design of nested single rooms. Cost is conserved by efficient use of space. Although nested rooms are much smaller than regular rooms, they are self-contained bedrooms with their own private half-bathrooms that have a toilet and a sink (Figure 8–3). Nested single rooms offer privacy, and when they are placed in a cluster setting, they can also provide opportunities for socializing through "neighborhood living" arrangements (Figure 8–4). Easy access to common lounge

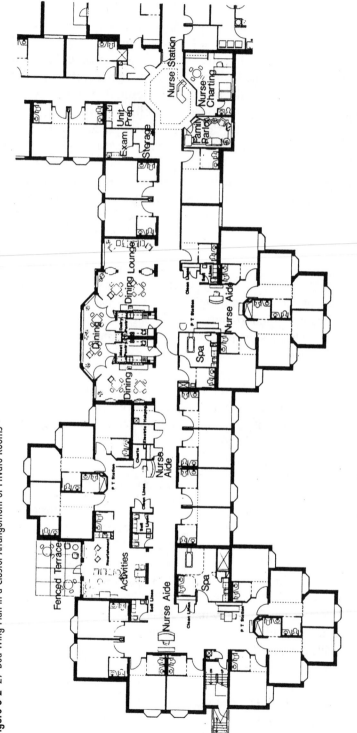

**Figure 8-2** 27 Bed Wing Plan in a Cluster Arrangement of Private Rooms

*Source:* PDT Architects/Planners, Cincinnati, Ohio. Designed by Mark B. Browning, AIA, for Cedar Village, Mason, Ohio. Reprinted with permission from Mark B. Browning.

**Figure 8-3** Overhead One-Point Interior Perspective of Nested Rooms

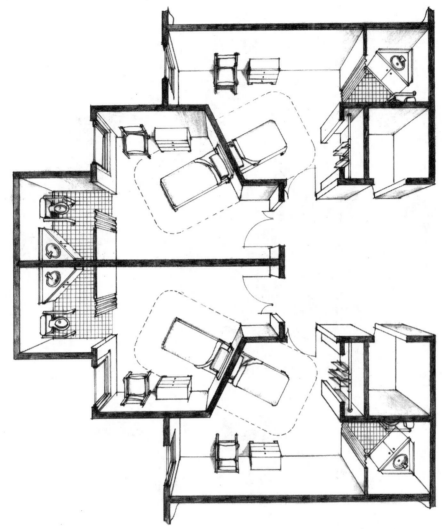

*Source:* EGA, P.C. "Designs for Living."

**Figure 8-4** Partial Floor Plan of Cluster Scheme

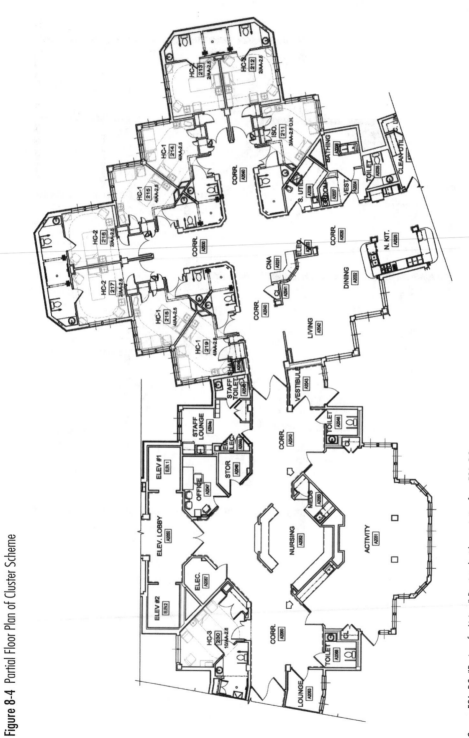

*Source:* EGA, P.C. "Designs for Living." Reprinted with permission from EGA, P.C.

areas in the vicinity of the rooms encourages residents to get out of their rooms to meet and converse with familiar neighbors and provides a comfortable setting for visiting with family and friends.

# Aesthetics

Aesthetics are necessary to promote a sense of well-being. Light and color, for example, influence patients' sleep, wakefulness, emotions, and health. Use of lighting, color, and furnishings create an environment that is both aesthetically appealing and comfortable. The physical environment can also affect social behavior and certain clinical outcomes.

## Lighting

Vision impairment increases with age and it diminishes people's quality of life. Compared with community-dwelling elders, nursing home residents suffer from far greater visual impairment (West et al., 2003). Inadequate lighting affects sleep and depression and can cause falls that can otherwise be prevented. Lighting issues in LTC facilities should be addressed by (1) raising light levels substantially, (2) balancing natural light and electric light to achieve even light levels, and (3) eliminating direct as well as reflected glare (Brawley & Noell-Waggoner, Undated).

Natural sunlight is known to have positive effects on overall health. Facility design should incorporate as much natural lighting as possible, while also incorporating artificial light. Patios and porches enable residents to enjoy fresh air as well as direct sunlight. Windows, skylights, atriums, and greenhouse windows can be used to bring some of the natural daylight indoors. Low windows in patient rooms, lounges, and corridors allow residents to see the exterior grounds from their beds and wheelchairs. Window treatments should be used to regulate sunlight and minimize glare. Horizontal mini-blinds are generally preferable to vertical blinds, but light-filtering pleated shades are considered even better. Valances can be added to create a homelike look.

Lighting needs of the elderly are quite different from those of younger people. As their sight and visual acuity decline, the elderly require higher levels of illumination, but glare must be minimized. Glare can lead to agitation, confusion, anger, and falls. Most glare can be controlled either by shielding the light source from direct view or balancing the light in the room. A facility can ensure proper lighting for patients and also enhance the homelike feel by using chandeliers, wall sconces, recessed lighting, table lamps, floor lamps, and other light fixtures. In resident rooms, night lights are essential. Along with clear pathways to the toilet, night lights can facilitate safe trips to the bathroom and help prevent falls (Brawley, 1997).

## Color

Colors used in health care settings have changed dramatically in recent years. Traditional colors such as white, bold yellow, beige, and green are no longer considered appropriate. More pleasing and stimulating colors have now become popular. Such colors include soft apricot, peach, salmon, coral, soft yellow-orange, and a variety of earth-colored tones. Patterns and colors in wall coverings and decorative borders can liven up some otherwise unexciting areas. Bedrooms, bathrooms, dining rooms, living rooms, and alcoves are all appropriate places where wall coverings can enhance residential quality. Coated wall coverings can be used in areas such as hallways, where soiling is a serious problem. Handrails are necessary in hallways and other areas, but with a natural wood finish, they help maintain the residential look.

Colors are also used to promote safety. Aging reduces a person's ability to distinguish colors. To compensate for this reduced visual function, high-contrast colors should be used. For example, the color of grab bars in the toilet should contrast sharply with the color of the wall, to ensure maximum visibility. Countertop colors should stand out strongly from those of floors. For many nursing home residents, being able to use the toilet may depend on being able to locate it. In a totally white bathroom, some patients will find it difficult to distinguish the toilet from the floor or the adjacent wall. Colored toilet seats create visible contrasts against the surroundings and can facilitate locating the toilet. Conversely, a colored wall can provide visual contrast against a white toilet.

## Furnishings

Carpeting adds warmth and softens sounds. It also provides cushioning against falls and can prevent serious fractures of the hip or wrist. Today's high-performance carpets, which are resistant to stains and odors, are also cost effective. New carpets are treated with a vinyl moisture barrier and an antimicrobial coating (Yarme & Yarme, 2001). Proper installation and regular maintenance can make carpeting last for several years. Of course, carpeting is not appropriate for all areas in the building. Slip-resistant tile is by far the most widely used flooring material. Resilient flooring with low sheen can be used in certain high-use areas without creating an institutional appearance. For example, these hard-surface floorings also come in beautiful wood-grain patterns that add a homelike

touch. Also available are new soft-surface floorings that are made of easy-to-maintain sheet vinyl material with a dense, soft, carpet-like surface and a cushioned backing. These materials have been tested to ensure that they reduce injuries from falls (Yarme & Yarme, 2001). Highly polished and buffed surfaces are not recommended for the elderly because they produce glare, appear wet or slick, and can be a source of anxiety and confusion.

A variety of furniture is now available that is specifically designed for LTC facilities. Lounge chairs, sofas, and rocking chairs can add charm and variety as well as comfort. Use of upholstered furniture has actually become quite common. Some manufacturers are producing foam cushions that are soft enough to be comfortable and yet firm enough for residents to rise easily from chairs and sofas (Child, 1999). Brawley (1997) commented on several enhancements in high-tech finishing of upholstery fabrics. These include soil- and stain-resistant finishes, lamination with vinyl, fluid barriers, and antimicrobial finishes. For nursing home use, these fabrics must also be flame-retardant. "Super fabrics," such as Crypton, have built-in stain and moisture resistance and have been tested for fire and microbial resistance. These new fabrics have replaced vinyl coverings for chairs and sofas, and a range of colors, textures, and patterns are now available to enhance the residential environment in nursing facilities.

## Enriched Environments

The environment is viewed as a "silent partner" in caregiving because it is a contributing factor to the healing process (Noell, 1995). *Enriched environments* (or enhanced environments) are physically and psychologically supportive environments that promote positive feelings, harmony, and thriving and reduce boredom and stress.

## Theoretical Foundations

Creation of enriched environments finds support in two complementary theories: biophilia framework and theory of thriving.

### Biophilia Framework

E.O. Wilson, a biologist, coined the term ***biophilia*** for the human propensity to affiliate with other life forms. In short, it describes the human tendency to pay attention to, affiliate with, and respond positively to nature (Wilson, 1984). People not only have an inborn biophiliac tendency to relate to animals and to natural settings, but people's relationship with nature is essential to their thriving. Plants, animals, water, and soil are the most common elements of the natural environment (Wohlwill, 1983). Based on an integrative review of the literature, Jones and Haight (2002) reported consistent findings that interactions with the natural environment, which can be experienced both indoors and outdoors, produce beneficial effects in human beings, such as positive mood and mental restoration. A recent study of hospitalized patients recovering from an appendectomy showed that patients with plants in their rooms had a significantly lower need for pain medication, had lower blood pressure and heart rates, and had less anxiety and fatigue than their counterparts in the control group with no plants in their rooms (Park & Mattson, 2008).

### Theory of Thriving

***Thriving*** means living life to the full. It is also a growth process that occurs as a result of humans interacting in a symbiotic relationship with their environments to enhance their physical, mental, social, and spiritual well-being. According to Haight et al. (2002), the integrative model of thriving includes three elements (1) the person; (2) the human environment comprising family, friends, caregivers, and others; and (3) the nonhuman environment comprising the physical and ecological surroundings of the person. Thriving occurs when the relationship among the three entities is mutually engaging, supportive, and harmonious. Conversely, a failure to thrive occurs when discordance exists among the person, the human environment, and the nonhuman environment. When thriving occurs, certain critical attributes are noticeable in the person: social connectedness, finding meaning in life, adaptation, and positive cognitive/affective function.

## Principles of Enrichment

Enriched environments are created by incorporating three main principles:

- All three elements of person-centered care (clinical care, socioresidential elements of the physical environment, and overarching human factors) must be integrated, as discussed earlier. In a person-centered environment, care delivery is congruent with the values, needs, and preferences of care recipients (Eales et al., 2001). Health care professionals empower residents to assert their rights and preferences. This empowerment is achieved through a bonding between residents and caregivers who place supreme value on listening to the individual's preferences while offering professional advice and instruction on the risks and benefits of the choices the resident wants to make. The resident's autonomy and the freedom to take some risks are respected.

- The environment provides a moderate degree of positive stimulation and distraction. Prolonged exposure to low levels of environmental stimulation can lead to boredom, negative feelings, and depression. In the absence of positive distractions, patients begin to focus on their own problems and end up increasing their level of stress. Positive distractions elicit good feelings, hold attention, and generate interest. Happy faces, laughter, people passing by, pets, fish in aquariums, birds, flowers, trees, plants, water, pleasant aromas, and soothing music can all be positive distractions. Negative distractions, on the other hand, are stressors. They simply assert their unwanted presence because it is difficult to ignore them. Visual stimulation from pictures, artwork, and television watching can be positive for patients, but abstract art and uncontrolled loud noise from television are negative distractions.

- Thriving is not entirely a function of external stimulus. Thriving also requires solitude, reflection, introspection, spiritual contemplation, study, and a sense of one's individuality and self-worth. Contemplation and inner reflection often occur in a passive relationship with serene natural surroundings. On the other hand, thriving also requires active engagement in meaningful social relationships, caring for live plants or animals, lending a helping hand to a fellow patient, playing with children, or working on hobbies such as gardening or woodworking. In its ultimate sense, thriving is achieved when a person feels a deep sense of belonging to and connection with the physical environment comprised of people and things, and also feels closeness to a Supreme Being in accordance with one's own belief system.

# Culture Change

The ideas presented in this chapter are at the heart of what has been loosely referred to as "culture change." The change is from the traditional nursing home environments and care processes driven by the sick-role model to the ones that promote client-centered care in enriched environments. Hence, *culture change* is the integration of the three elements of person-centered care along with enriching the environments in which people live. In addition, culture change requires empowerment of associates. Empowerment requires a change in management philosophy and practice. As a guiding principle, administrators and department managers start treating their associates as they would want the associates to treat the elders. There is no room for any practices that devalue workers, most of whom are women who typically earn just a little above the federal minimum wage. Empowerment also requires a decentralized management approach in which decision making is taken back to the elders and to the families and caregivers, and these stakeholders are given a voice in the elders' daily routine and life. For example, in the archetypal nursing home culture, the resident must comply with schedules and routines preset by the organization. Through culture change, residents and staff design schedules that reflect the residents' personal needs and desires. For instance, within reason, residents can decide whether they prefer a shower or a bath in the morning or in the evening (Andreoli et al., 2007). Culture change requires a new mindset on the part of management and associates.

The *Pioneer Network* played a critical role in advocating culture change in nursing homes. It began as a grassroots movement of caregivers, consumer advocates, and others who were concerned about the quality of life in even some of the finest conventional nursing homes. Beginning in 1997, nursing home professionals and advocates, referred to as "pioneers," began informal meetings to define common areas of endeavor and opportunities for bringing about a cultural change in nursing facilities. A few nursing home professionals, who had already experimented with some innovative approaches, were invited to share their experiences with various stakeholders, including regulators, nursing home administrators, directors of nursing, and social workers. Subsequently, regular meetings of these pioneers led to the formation in 2000 of a formal organization, named the Pioneer Network, an organization that had the aim of providing leadership to the grassroots movement. Since then, it has evolved into a growing national movement. The Network has continued to make some impact in the areas of education, in sharing information and ideas to form coalitions, and in advocacy to influence public policy.

The Centers for Medicare and Medicaid Services (CMS) has endorsed the principles of culture change. From 2004 to 2006, CMS sponsored a project in 21 states to teach nursing home operators the principles and practices of culture change. In 2006, the CMS funded and co-developed the Artifacts of Culture Change, a tool to help nursing homes measure concrete changes realized as a result of implementing the culture change philosophy (Appendix 8–I). Culture change is also referenced in consumer guidelines issued by the CMS in choosing a nursing home.

There is no single model of culture change because of several variables involved. For example, leadership, ownership, and case-mix factors vary from facility to facility (Wiener et al., 2007). According to a 2007 national survey of nursing homes, 43% of the facilities were operating according to the traditional model, 31% had adopted the changes, and 25% were striving to adopt culture change. In general, nursing homes have been most successful in increasing resident autonomy and, to a certain extent, empowering caregivers. But, very few facilities have changed their physical environment to support culture change. For example, very few nursing homes have renovated their traditional facilities into "neighborhoods" or "households" with their own kitchens, dining areas, and living areas (Doty et al., 2008). The high cost of constructional modifications is one reason. Also, many of the older buildings present daunting challenges because of their layout and lack of available space that must be devoted to providing essential services such as nursing care and rehabilitation.

Doty et al. (2008) demonstrated that a greater degree of adoption of culture change results in greater benefits in terms of staff retention, higher occupancy rates, better competitive position, and improved operational costs. As these benefits become more widely known, a greater degree of adoption is likely to occur. It is also surmised that, compared with previous generations, baby boomers on the verge of retirement will be more inclined to search for LTC options that promote comfort and quality of life in an environment comparable to their own homes (Ragsdale & McDougall, 2008).

# Contemporary Models of Culture Change

## The Eden Alternative

Of all the various movements advocating enriched environments in LTC facilities, the Eden Alternative is perhaps the best known. In the early 1990s, Dr. William Thomas, while working as a physician in nursing homes, undertook a pilot project sponsored by the state of New York. Working with the staff in an 80-bed nursing home, which served mostly patients with dementia, Thomas developed some new ideas and a set of principles for creating a garden-like environment. As an advocate for change, Thomas explained:

> I want an alternative to the institution. The best alternative I can think of is a garden. I believe when we make a place that's worthy of our elders, we make a place that enriches all of our lives—caregivers, family members, and elders alike. So the Eden Alternative provides a reinterpretation of the environment elders live in, going from an institution to a garden . . . There are kids running around and playing. There are dogs and cats and birds, and there are gardens and plants. I want people to think that this can't be a nursing home. Which it isn't—it's an alternative to a nursing home . . . The future of caregiving belongs to people and organizations who can dream new dreams about how to care for our elders (McLeod, 2002, pp. 14–15).

The *Eden Alternative*, a trademark of its founding organization, entails viewing the surroundings in facilities as habitats for human beings rather than as facilities for the frail and elderly, as well as applying the lessons of nature in creating vibrant and vigorous settings. It is based on the belief that the companionship of pets, the opportunity to give meaningful care to other living crea-tures, and the spontaneity that marks an enlivened environment have therapeutic values (Eden Alternative, 2002). One of the main objectives of Eden Alternative is to banish from the lives of nursing home residents the loneliness, helplessness, and boredom that Thomas has called "the three plagues of nursing homes" (Bruck, 1997). To counteract these ills, residents need companionship, variety, and a chance to feel needed (Stermer, 1998).

According to the 10 principles on which the Eden Alternative is founded (Exhibit 8–1) the antidote to loneliness is meaningful contact with plants, animals, and children, as well as easy access to human and animal companionship; the remedy for helplessness is giving as well as receiving care; and the cure for boredom is unexpected and unpredictable interactions and happenings in surroundings that deliver variety and spontaneity (Eden Annual, 2003). Among methods to build relationships between staff members and residents, alternative means of healing such as massage therapy and aromatherapy are suggested, based on the belief that a back-rub or foot-rub may eliminate the need for sleep-inducing medications, and the belief that the smell of lavender or peppermint can have a calming effect.

*Edenizing* is the expression used for achieving culture change by implementing the Eden principles. For a long time, many nursing homes have, at least to some extent, involved their residents in nature-oriented activities such as pet therapy, gardening, and nature walks. Programs in collaboration with local schools and day care centers have also been developed to promote intergenerational companionship. Edenizing more fully incorporates the concepts of biophilia. It promotes surroundings rich in plants, animals, and children. Involving the residents in the care

**Exhibit 8-1** The Eden Alternative Principles

1. The three plagues of loneliness, helplessness and boredom account for the bulk of suffering among our Elders.

2. An Elder-centered community commits to creating a Human Habitat where life revolves around close and continuing contact with plants, animals and children. It is these relationships that provide the young and old alike with a pathway to a life worth living.

3. Loving companionship is the antidote to loneliness. Elders deserve easy access to human and animal companionship.

4. An Elder-centered community creates opportunity to give as well as receive care. This is the antidote to helplessness.

5. An Elder-centered community imbues daily life with variety and spontaneity by creating an environment in which unexpected and unpredictable interactions and happenings can take place. This is the antidote to boredom.

6. Meaningless activity corrodes the human spirit. The opportunity to do things that we find meaningful is essential to human health.

7. Medical treatment should be the servant of genuine human caring, never its master.

8. An Elder-centered community honors its Elders by de-emphasizing top-down bureaucratic authority, seeking instead to place the maximum possible decision-making authority into the hands of the Elders or into the hands of those closest to them.

9. Creating an Elder-centered community is a never-ending process. Human growth must never be separated from human life.

10. Wise leadership is the lifeblood of any struggle against the three plagues. For it, there can be no substitute.

*Source:* Eden Alternative. Retrieved April 2009 from http://www.edenalt.org/about/our-10-principles.html. Used with permission of Eden Alternative®.

of plants and animals, and in interaction with children such as playing with them, helping them color, or reading them stories, enriches everyone's lives. A facility can have an on-site child day care center, providing opportunities to integrate child care with the care of the elderly. Children playing with toys in the facility's living room, or playing outdoors on a swing and slide set add to variety and spontaneity. But edenizing goes beyond these steps. It also incorporates other aspects of culture change, such as resident and caregiver empowerment.

Actions by a few states, such as North Carolina and South Carolina, to establish coalitions promoting the Eden Alternative have legitimized the concept by establishing partnerships with the respective state's regulatory and public health agencies. Voluntary regional coordinators have also been appointed in various locations across the country, under the auspices of the Eden organization, to promote education about the Eden Alternative and to create a registry program to recognize organizations that make a commitment to change. On the other hand, widespread adoption of the Eden principles by individual nursing homes has failed to materialize; only 300 to 400 facilities (2% or less) nationwide have edenized to date.

Published literature on the actual outcomes of edenizing is scant, but one unpublished study of five nursing homes in Texas concluded that adopting the Eden Alternative had decreased behavioral incidents by 60%, formation of pressure sores by 57%, prevalence of bed confinement by 25%, and use of restraints by 18%. Positive outcomes were also reported on increased occupancy (11%), reduced employee absenteeism (48%), and decreased worker injuries (11%) (Cerquone, 2001). A more recent study reported lower levels of boredom and helplessness, but not loneliness (Bergman-Evans, 2004). Some individual nursing homes have also reported decreases in staff turnover as a result of edenizing. On the other hand, a peer-reviewed published study that compared an edenized facility with a control (nonedenized) facility, using indicators of residents' well-being measured at baseline and a year later, reported that the Eden site had significantly greater proportions of residents who had fallen, residents who were experiencing nutritional problems, and those who required hypnotic drug prescriptions. However, because of a number of uncontrolled variables in the study, the authors concluded that quantitative measures suggested no major effects of the Eden intervention, but anecdotal qualitative information indicated that an extended period of implementation of edenizing may yield positive changes (Coleman et al., 2002). In short, at this time, scientific evidence in favor of the Eden Alternative remains inconclusive.

Edenizing may pose some risks in the form of allergies, injuries, and illnesses. **Zoonosis** is the transmittal of infections from vertebrate animals to humans. Examples of zoonotic diseases include dermatophytosis, psittacosis, bartonellosis, toxocariasis, pasturellosis, Q fever, and leptospirosis (Guay, 2001). However, potential problems can be managed with appropriate veterinary care and infection-control practices.

Proponents of the Eden Alternative explain that their approach is not a quick fix for serious problems. Not every facility should embark on making such changes. Acceptance of the Eden Alternative by staff members and their training are necessary prerequisites because, right off the bat, questions come up about the staff's extra responsibilities of caring for the pets and cleaning up after them. Particularly in unionized facilities where union–management contracts prescribe tasks and duties of staff members, edenizing can be challenging. Costs of training and implementation may be another deterrent: in 2000, the costs to implement the Eden Alternative were estimated to be $30,000 over two years (Reese, 2000). Also, the quality of life in long-term care facilities can be improved in ways other than edenizing.

Changing an organization's culture takes time, effort, and leadership skills. Implementing the Eden principles can take an estimated three to five years (Hannan & Schaeffer, 2003).

## The Green House Project

The founder of the Eden Alternative had envisioned edenizing as a never-ending process. But, perhaps because of the inherent difficulties in initiating and maintaining the necessary changes in large institutional settings, the Eden model has not been widely adopted (Rabig, 2003). An outgrowth of the Eden Alternative, and also a brainchild of Dr. Thomas, the Green House Project takes edenizing a step further by revolutionizing the way in which nursing home services are organized and delivered in small-scale settings.

In the New York State pilot project described earlier, Thomas experimented with restructuring the caregiving staff into permanent care teams designed to serve a particular "neighborhood" of elders according to those elders' special needs. The teams—consisting of nurses, social workers, housekeepers, dietary employees, and members of the activities staff—tried to adapt the traditional large-scale caregiving approach for smaller groups of residents. Each team participated in extensive training in communication and problem solving, and some teams eventually became responsible for scheduling their own hours of work (Hannan & Schaeffer, 2003). In the Green House model, these organizational ideas are applied to physically distinct small-neighborhood architectural units. Also, unlike edenizing a large institutional structure, the Green House model relies more on natural outdoor activities, such as watching and feeding birds and squirrels, and less on indoor pets because the small design of the buildings allows ready access to the outdoors (Rabig, 2003).

The term ***Green House*** stands for architectural renderings of small freestanding cottages, each designed to house just 7 to 10 residents who live together in a homelike setting (Figure 8–5). The freestanding cottages are spread across a campus (Figure 8–6). The first Green House project in Tupelo, Mississippi, opened its doors in June 2003.

Each Green House has self-contained private rooms that include a commode, a sink, and a shower. To accommodate even the frailest elders, rooms are equipped with ceiling lifts for transferring. The lift operates on a ceiling track that runs from the bed to the bathroom sink and commode. In some instances, these lifts can be operated independently by the residents. Residents can bring their own furniture and they can choose their room's décor. The residential units are connected by short hallways to a central hearth room, open kitchen, and dining area. Other amenities include a spa room, laundry room, alcove, and storage space. The small size eliminates the need for nursing stations and

medication carts. The nurse-call system is wireless, using silent pagers that can be activated from pendants worn by the residents (Rabig & Thomas, 2003). In all aspects, the Green Houses fully comply with *Life Safety Code* and other building and safety standards described in Chapter 6.

Each Green House is staffed by cross-trained nursing assistants, who do cooking and cleaning in addition to delivering personal care. The Green Houses are supported by the traditional organization of a skilled nursing facility in which functions such as professional nursing, rehabilitation therapies, medical records, accounting, billing, purchasing, and plant maintenance are located (Rabig & Thomas, 2003). The cross-trained, self-managed worker teams create a decentralized organizational structure that eliminates the typical supervisor–subordinate relationships. Interdisciplinary clinical support teams that include physicians, nurses, therapists, social workers, dieticians, and others located in the support organization carry out individualized clinical assessment and care planning and visit the elders to meet their treatment needs. Clinical practice guidelines based on medical research and standards, as well as emergency protocols, are developed for use by caregivers (Rabig & Thomas, 2003).

The Green House Project proposes other cultural changes, such as referring to the cross-trained workers as "elder assistants" instead of "nursing assistants" or "nurse aides" and referring to patients as "elders" instead of "residents," who are "welcomed into" rather than "admitted to" the Green Houses. Physicians, nurses, and other clinical professionals who visit the patients are expected to assume a "visitor's role" and behave as guests, giving the elders the maximum control possible over clinical information

**Figure 8-5** 10-Bed Skilled Nursing Green House (Methodist Senior Services, Tupelo, Mississippi)

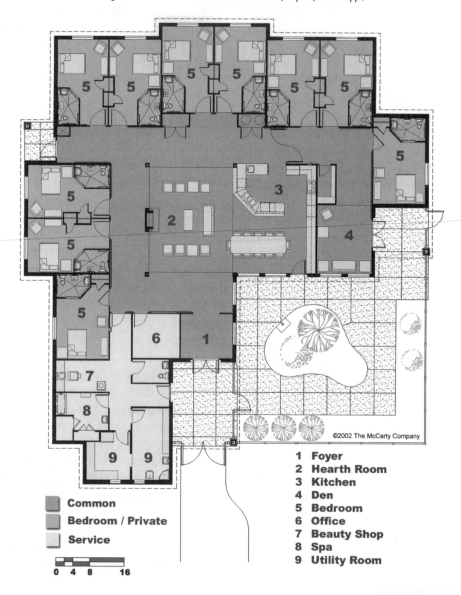

1 Foyer
2 Hearth Room
3 Kitchen
4 Den
5 Bedroom
6 Office
7 Beauty Shop
8 Spa
9 Utility Room

Common
Bedroom / Private
Service

0   4   8      16

©2002 The McCarty Company

*Source:* The McCarthy Company, Tupelo, Mississippi. Reprinted with permission from The McCarty Company (courtesy of Stephen Ladd).

and decisions. Individual choices and preferences are preserved by allowing the elders the maximum possible latitude in establishing their own daily routines for sleep, rest, meals, personal care, and activities. Elders are also encouraged to participate in meal preparation, gardening, cleaning, and laundry work. Weekly joint meetings or "house discussions" between elder assistants and elders provide feedback on quality of care, identify unmet

**Figure 8-6** Overhead Perspective of Green Houses (small residential structures spread across a campus)

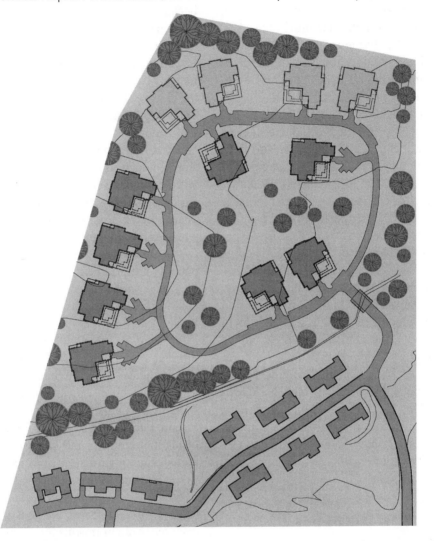

*Source:* The McCarty Company. Schematic Site Plan: Greenhouse Project, Methodist Senior Services, Tupelo, Mississippi. Reprinted with permission from the McCarty Company (courtesy of Stephen Ladd).

needs or concerns, and give input for household decisions (Rabig & Thomas, 2003).

The Green House philosophy requires close relationships between staff members and elders based on the concept of *intentional community*, the intrinsic need shared by elders and caregivers to "come together" to form a bond and "live together" for a common purpose. For example, the concept is applied when assistants and elders sit around a large common dining table and together enjoy a family-style meal. The assistant may help feed the patient sitting in the next chair. Even tube-fed patients may be brought to the dining table for sensory stimulation from the music, the chatter, and the aroma. The term *convivium* (from Latin, meaning "feast" or, more broadly, "living together") is used in Green Houses to describe the experience of a pleasurable dining experience in an enriched environment (Rabig, 2003).

To date, a number of positive outcomes have been observed: high satisfaction levels among residents, family members, and staff; few regulatory complaints; no unexpected weight loss and almost no nutritional supplement use; less decline in ADLs; staff turnover of less than 10%; no transfer-related back injuries to elders or staff; less prevalence of depression; and less use of anti-psychotic drugs (Robert Wood Johnson Foundation, 2005).

The Robert Wood Johnson Foundation has awarded a $10 million five-year grant to NCB Development Corp. to establish more Green Houses around the country. NCB's staff provides technical assistance and predevelopment loans to support long-term care organizations that want to establish a Green House. The objective is to establish at least one Green House in every state within the next 5 years (Robert Wood Johnson Foundation, 2005).

## Environment for Patients With Dementia

For people with dementia, small groupings of residents in a setting that resembles a home—and not a large institution—provide a more effective therapeutic setting. The smaller scale of the living quarters reduces stress that such patients may experience from the overwhelming effect of being placed in complex, unfamiliar surroundings. This is because a link to the person's past home environments becomes essential for exercising his or her remaining capabilities. In dementia patients, long-term memory generally remains relatively intact until the later stages of the disease (Cohen & Day, 1993).

In a pilot study, Brush et al. (2002) found that improved lighting and table-setting contrast had a positive effect on food consumption and functional abilities of patients with dementia. Generally, a moderate level of stimulation from the environment is best. When the environment provides too many stressors and fewer opportunities to relax, dysfunctional behaviors are observed among patients with dementia (Rader, 1991). Unpleasant sounds, intense lighting, and bold colors produce a high level of stimulation that causes stress. For patients with Alzheimer's, sharp color contrasts and patterns can be disturbing. Pastel colors tend to work best for these patients (Kretschmann, 1995).

Patient safety is an important factor. Electronic guards to prevent wandering are essential. Protected pathways for wandering, residential kitchens and laundries, and contained outdoor gardens are particularly helpful in caring for patients with dementia (Regnier, 1998). Nature-related activities are often an essential but unused therapeutic resource in environments for people with dementia (Day & Cohen, 2000). Connection to nature extends to people's interaction with animals. There is some evidence that meaningful decreases in agitated behaviors and improvements in social interactions of dementia patients can occur as a result of pet therapy (Richeson, 2003).

## For Further Thought

1. As a nursing home administrator who has just been appointed to manage a skilled nursing facility that was built in the 1970s, how would you go about delivering person-centered care?

2. Many nursing homes have limited financial resources. What can they do to enrich their environments?

3. The presence of dogs and cats does not appeal to everyone because of allergies or other health-related factors. As a nursing home administrator, how would you address such concerns?

## For Further Learning

Eden Alternative: Official website

www.edenalt.com

The Green House Project. Access through the NCB Capital website

http://www.ncbcapitalimpact.org

The Pioneer Network: Official website

http://www.pioneernetwork.net

## REFERENCES

Agich, G.J. 1995. Actual autonomy and long-term care decision making. In L.B. McCullough and N.L. Wilson (eds.). *Long-Term Care Decisions: Ethical and Conceptual Dimensions* (pp. 113–136). Baltimore: Johns Hopkins University Press.

Andreoli, N.A., et al. 2007. Serving culture change at mealtimes. *Nursing Homes: Long Term Care Management* 56, no. 9: 48–50.

Arras, J.D. 1995. Conflicting interests in long-term care decision making: Acknowledging, dissolving, and resolving conflicts. In L.B. McCullough and N.L. Wilson (eds.). *Long-Term Care Decisions: Ethical and Conceptual Dimensions* (pp. 197–217). Baltimore: Johns Hopkins University Press.

Bergman-Evans, B. 2004. Beyond the basics: Effects of the Eden Alternative Model on quality of life issues. *Journal of Gerontological Nursing* 30, no. 6: 27–34.

Brawley, E.C. 1997. *Designing for Alzheimer's Disease: Strategies for Creating Better Care Environments.* New York: John Wiley & Sons.

Brawley, E., & Noell-Waggoner, E. Undated. Lighting: Partner in Quality Care Environments. Retrieved April 2009 from http://www.pioneernetwork.net/Data/Documents/BrawleyNoell-WagonerLightingPaper.pdf.

Browning, M.B. 2003. Letter to the author dated August 18, 2003, on cluster design plan.

Bruck, L. 1997. Welcome to Eden. *Nursing Homes Long Term Care Management* 46, no. 1: 28–33.

Brush, J.A., et al. 2002. Using the environment to improve intake for people with dementia. *Alzheimer's Care Quarterly* 3, no. 4: 330–338.

Cerquone, J. 2001. Administrating Eden. *Balance* 5, no. 6: 4–6.

Chapman, S.A., et al. 2003. Client-centered, community-based care for frail seniors. *Health and Social Care in the Community* 11, no. 3: 253–261.

Child, M. 1999. Comfort is the key. *Nursing Homes Long Term Care Management* 48, no. 9: 61–62.

Cohen, U., & Day, K. 1993. *Contemporary Environments for People with Dementia*. Baltimore: Johns Hopkins University Press.

Coleman, M.T., et al. 2002. The Eden Alternative: Findings after 1 year of implementation. *Journal of Gerontology* 57A, no. 7: M422–M427.

Collopy, B.J. 1988. Autonomy in long-term care: some crucial distinctions. *The Gerontologist* 28, suppl.: 10–17.

Collopy, B.J. 1995. Safety and independence: Rethinking some basic concepts in long-term care. In L.B. McCullough and N.L. Wilson (eds.). *Long-term care decisions: Ethical and conceptual dimensions* (pp. 137–152). Baltimore: Johns Hopkins University Press.

Day, K., & Cohen, U. 2000. The role of culture in designing environments for people with dementia: A study of Russian Jewish immigrants. *Environment and Behavior* 32, no. 3: 361–399.

Doty, M.M., et al. 2008. *Culture Change in Nursing Homes: How Far Have We Come?* New York: The Commonwealth Fund.

Drew, S.G. 1992. Designing for special needs of the elderly. In A. Bush-Brown and D. Davis (eds.). *Hospitable Design for Healthcare and Senior Communities*. New York: Van Nostrand Reinhold.

Dunkelman, D.M. 1992. Individualized cluster. In A. Bush-Brown and D. Davis (eds.). *Hospitable Design for Healthcare and Senior Communities*. New York: Van Nostrand Reinhold.

Eales, J., et al. 2001. Seniors' experiences of client-centered residential care. *Aging and Society* 21: 279–296.

Eden Alternative, The. 2002. What is Eden? http://www.edenalt.com/about.htm.

Eden Annual 2003. 2003. *Come Grow with Us*. In J. Thomas (ed.). Norwich, NY: Chenango Union Printing.

Guay, D. 2001. Pet-assisted therapy in the nursing home setting: Potential for zoonosis. *American Journal of Infection Control* 29, no. 3: 178–186.

Haight, B.K., et al. 2002. Thriving: A life span theory. *Journal of Gerontological Nursing* 28, no. 3: 15–22.

Hannan, M., & Schaeffer, K. 2003. The Eden Alternative: More than just fuzzy props and potted plants. http://www.edenmidwest.com/about_eden.html.

Jones, M.M., & Haight, B.K. 2002. Environmental transformations: An integrative review. *Journal of Gerontological Nursing* 28, no. 3: 23–27.

Kane, R.A. 2001. Long-term care and a good quality of life: Bringing them closer together. *The Gerontologist* 41, no. 3: 293–304.

Kretschmann, A. 1995. Design touches to make the SCU a "home." *Nursing Homes Long Term Care Management* 44, no. 6: 31–34.

Kruzich, J.M. & Berg. W. 1985. Predictors of self-sufficiency for the mentally ill in long term care. *Community Mental Health Journal* 21, no. 3: 198–207.

McLeod, B.W. 2002. *And Thou Shalt Honor: A Caregiver's Companion.* Emmaus, PA: Rodale Press. www.rodalestore.com.

National Center for Health Statistics. 2007. *Health, United States 2007.* Hyattsville, MD: Department of Health and Human Services.

Noell, E. 1995. Design in nursing homes: Environment as a silent partner in caregiving. *Generations* 19, no. 4: 14–19.

Nursing home architecture. 1997. *Contemporary Long-term Care* 20, no. 8: 43–44.

Park, S. & Mattson, R.H. 2008. Effects of flowering and foliage plants in hospital rooms on patients recovering from abdominal surgery. *HortTechnology* 18: 549–745.

Parsons, T. 1972. Definitions of health and illness in the light of American values and social structure. In E.G. Jaco (ed). *Patients, Physicians and Illness: A Sourcebook in Behavioral Science and Health,* 2nd ed. New York: Free Press.

Rabig, J. 2003. Personal conversation, September 25, 2003.

Rabig, J., & Thomas, W. 2003. The Green House project: An alternative model of elder care. Unpublished manuscript.

Rader, J. 1991. Modifying the environment to decrease use of restraints. *Journal of Gerontological Nursing* 17, no. 2: 9–13.

Ragsdale, V., & McDougall, G.J. 2008. The changing face of long-term care: Looking at the past decade. *Issues in Mental Health Nursing* 29, no. 9: 992–1001.

Reese, D. 2000. Alternative lifestyle. *Contemporary Long-term Care* 23, no. 7: 38–42.

Regnier, V. 1998. Look homeward. *Contemporary Long-term Care* 21, no. 3: 92–94.

Richeson, N.E. 2003. Effects of animal-assisted therapy on agitated behaviors and social interactions of older adults with dementia. *American Journal of Alzheimer's Disease & Other Dementias* 18, no. 6: 353–358.

Robert Wood Johnson Foundation. 2005. Developing small community homes as alternatives to nursing homes. Retrieved January 2009 from http://www.rwjf.org/newsroom/newsreleases detail.jsp?productid=21757.

Schwarz, B. 1996. *Nursing Home Design: Consequences of Employing the Medical Model.* New York: Garland Publishing.

Stermer, M. 1998. Notes from an Eden alternative pioneer. *Nursing Homes Long Term Care Management* 47, no. 11: 35–36.

West, S.K., et al. 2003. A randomized trial of visual impairment interventions for nursing home residents: Study design, baseline characteristics and visual loss. *Ophthalmic Epidemiology* 10, no. 3: 193–209.

Westin, A. 1967. *Privacy and Freedom.* New York: Atheneum Press.

Wiener, J.M., et al. 2007. *Nursing Home Quality: Twenty Years After the Omnibus Budget Reconciliation Act of 1987.* Menlo Park, CA: Henry J. Kaiser Family Foundation.

Wilson, E.O. 1984. *Biophilia: The Human Bond with Other Species*. Cambridge, MA: Harvard University Press.

Wohlwill, J.F. 1983. The concept of nature: a psychologist's view. In I. Altman and J.F. Wohlwill (eds.). *Behavior and the Natural Environment* (pp. 5–37). New York: Plenum Press.

Yarme, J., & Yarme, H. 2001. Flooring and safety. *Nursing Homes Long Term Care Management* 50, no. 10: 82–83.

**Appendix 8-1** Artifacts of Culture Change

| | |
|---|---|
| Home Name _____ Date _____ | |
| City _____ State _____ Current number of residents _____ | |
| Ownership: _____ For Profit _____ Non-Profit _____ Government | |

**Care Practice Artifacts**

| | |
|---|---|
| 1. Percentage of residents who offered any of the following styles of dining:<br>• restaurant style where staff take resident orders;<br>• buffet style where residents help themselves or tell staff what they want;<br>• family style where food is served in bowls on dining tables where residents help themselves or staff assist them:<br>• open dining where meal is available for at least 2 hour time period and residents can come when they choose; and<br>• 24 hour dining where residents can order food from the kitchen 24 hours a day. | _____ 100 – 81%  (5 points)<br>_____ 80 – 61%  (4 points)<br>_____ 60 – 41%  (3 points)<br>_____ 40 – 21%  (2 points)<br>_____ 20 – 1%  (1 point)<br>_____ 0  (0 points) |
| 2. Snacks/drinks available at all times to all residents at no additional cost, i.e., in a stocked pantry, refrigerator, or snack bar. | _____ All residents (5 points)<br>_____ Some (3 points)<br>_____ None (0 points) |
| 3. Baked goods are baked on resident living areas. | _____ All days of the week (5 point)<br>_____ 2–5 days/week (3 points)<br>_____ < 2 days/week (0 points) |
| 4. Home celebrates residents' individual birthdays rather than, or in addition to, celebrating resident birthdays in a group each month. | _____ Yes (5 points)<br>_____ No (0 points) |
| 5. Home offers aromatherapy to residents by staff or volunteers. | _____ Yes (5 points)<br>_____ No (0 points) |
| 6. Home offers massage to residents by staff or volunteers. | _____ Yes (5 points)<br>_____ No (0 points) |

*(continues)*

**Appendix 8-1** Artifacts of Culture Change (Continued)

| | |
|---|---|
| 7. **Home has dog(s) and/or cat(s).** | _____ At least one dog or one cat lives on premises (5 points)<br>_____ The only animals in the building are when staff bring them during work hours (3 points)<br>_____ The only animals in the building are those brought in for special activities or by families (1 point)<br>_____ None (0 points) |
| 8. **Home permits residents to bring own dog and/or cat to live with them in the home.** | _____ Yes (5 points)<br>_____ No (0 points) |
| 9. **Waking times/bedtimes chose by residents.** | _____ All residents (5 points)<br>_____ Some (3 points)<br>_____ None (0 points) |
| 10. ***Bathing without a Battle* techniques are used with residents.** | _____ All residents (5 points)<br>_____ Some (3 points)<br>_____ None (0 points) |
| 11. **Residents can get a bath/shower as often as they would like.** | _____ Yes (5 points)<br>_____ No (0 points) |
| 12. **Home arranges for someone to be with a dying resident at all times (unless they prefer to be alone)—family, friends, volunteers, or staff.** | _____ Yes (5 points)<br>_____ No (0 points) |
| 13. **Memorials/remembrances are held for individual residents upon death.** | _____ Yes (5 points)<br>_____ No (0 points) |
| 14. **"I" format care plans, in the voice of the resident and in the first person, are used.** | _____ All care plans (5 points)<br>_____ Some (3 points)<br>_____ None (0 points) |
| **Care Practice Artifacts Subtotal:** Out of a total 70 points, you scored _____. | |

*(continues)*

Appendix 8-1 Artifacts of Culture Change (Continued)

| **Environmental Artifacts** | |
|---|---|
| **15. Percent of residents who live in households that are self-contained with full kitchen, living room, and dining room.** | _____ 100 – 81% (100 points)<br>_____ 80 – 61%  (80 points)<br>_____ 60 – 41%  (60 points)<br>_____ 40 – 21%  (40 points)<br>_____ 20 – 1%   (20 point)<br>_____ 0        (0 points) |
| **16. Percent of residents in private rooms.** | _____ 100 – 81% (50 points)<br>_____ 80 – 61%  (40 points)<br>_____ 60 – 41%  (30 points)<br>_____ 40 – 21%  (20 points)<br>_____ 20 – 1%   (10 point)<br>_____ 0        (0 points) |
| **17. Percent of residents in privacy enhanced shared rooms where residents can access their own space without trespassing through the other resident's space.** This does not include the traditional privacy curtain. | _____ 100 – 81% (25 points)<br>_____ 80 – 61%  (20 points)<br>_____ 60 – 41%  (15 points)<br>_____ 40 – 21%  (10 points)<br>_____ 20 – 1%   (5 point)<br>_____ 0        (0 points) |
| **18. No traditional nurses' stations or traditional nurses' stations have been removed.** | _____ No traditional nurses stations (25 points)<br>_____ Some traditional nurses' stations have been removed (15 points)<br>_____ Traditional nurses' stations remain in place (0 points) |
| **19. Percent of residents who have a direct window view not past another resident's bed.** | _____ 100 – 51% (5 points)<br>_____ 50 – 0% (0 points) |
| **20. Resident bathroom mirrors are wheelchair accessible and/or adjustable in order to be visible to a seated or standing resident.** | _____ All resident bathroom mirrors (5 points)<br>_____ Some (3 points)<br>_____ None (0 points) |

*(continues)*

Appendix 8-1 Artifacts of Culture Change (Continued)

| | |
|---|---|
| **21. Sinks in resident bathrooms are wheelchair accessible with clearance below sink for wheelchair.** | _____ All resident bathroom sinks (5 points) <br> _____ Some (3 points) <br> _____ None (0 points) |
| **22. Sinks used by residents have adaptive/easy-to-use lever or paddle handles.** | _____ All sinks (5 points) <br> _____ Some (3 points) <br> _____ None (0 points) |
| **23. Adaptive handles, enhanced for easy use, for doors used by residents (rooms, bathrooms, and public areas).** | _____ All resident-used doors (5 points) <br> _____ Some (3 points) <br> _____ None (0 points) |
| **24. Closets have movable rods that can be set to different heights.** | _____ All closets (5 points) <br> _____ Some (3 points) <br> _____ None (0 points) |
| **25. Home has no rule prohibiting, and residents are welcome, to decorate their rooms any way they wish including using nails, tape, screws, etc.** | _____ Yes (5 points) <br> _____ No (0 points) |
| **26. Home makes available extra lighting source in resident room if requested by resident such as floor lamps and reading lamps.** | _____ Yes (5 points) <br> _____ No (0 points) |
| **27. Heat/air conditioning controls can be adjusted in resident rooms.** | _____ All resident rooms (5 points) <br> _____ Some (3 points) <br> _____ None (0 points) |
| **28. Home providers or invites residents to have their own refrigerators.** | _____ Yes (5 points) <br> _____ No (0 points) |
| **29. Chairs and sofas in public areas have seat heights that vary to comfortably accommodate people of different heights.** | _____ Chair seat heights vary by 3" or more (5 points) <br> _____ Chair seat heights vary by 1–3" (3 points) <br> _____ Chair seat heights do not vary in height (0 points) |
| **30. Gliders that lock into place when person rises are available inside the home and/or outside.** | _____ Yes (5 points) <br> _____ No (0 points) |

*(continues)*

**Appendix 8-1** Artifacts of Culture Change (Continued)

| | |
|---|---|
| 31. Home has store/gift shop/cart available where residents and visitors can purchase gifts, toiletries, snacks, etc. | _____ Yes (5 points)<br>_____ No (0 points) |
| 32. Residents have regular access to computer/Internet and adaptations are available for independent computer use such as large keyboard or touch screen. | _____ Both Internet access and adaptations (10 points)<br>_____ Access without adaptations (5 points)<br>_____ Neither (0 points) |
| 33. Workout room available to residents. | _____ Yes (5 points)<br>_____ No (0 points) |
| 34. Bathing rooms have functional and properly installed heat lamps, radiant heat panels, or equivalent. | _____ All bathing rooms (5 points)<br>_____ Some (3 points)<br>_____ None (0 points) |
| 35. Home warms towels for resident bathing. | _____ Yes (5 points)<br>_____ No (0 points) |
| 36. **Protected outdoor garden/patio accessible for independent use by residents.** Residents can go in and out independently, including those who use wheelchairs, e.g., residents do not need assistance from staff to open doors or overcome obstacles in traveling to patio. | _____ Yes (5 points)<br>_____ No (0 points) |
| 37. Home has outdoor raised gardens available for resident use. | _____ Yes (5 points)<br>_____ No (0 points) |
| 38. Home has an outdoor walking/wheeling path that is not a city sidewalk or path. | _____ Yes (5 points)<br>_____ No (0 points) |
| 39. Pager/radio/telephone call system is used where resident calls register on staff's pagers/radios/telephones and staff can use it to communicate with fellow staff. | _____ Yes (5 points)<br>_____ No (0 points) |
| 40. Overhead paging system has been turned off or is only used in case of emergency. | _____ Yes (5 points)<br>_____ No (0 points) |
| 41. Personal clothing is laundered on resident household/ neighborhood/unit instead of in an general all-home laundry, and residents/families have access to washer and dryer for own use. | _____ Available to all residents (5 points)<br>_____ Some (3 points)<br>_____ None (0 points) |
| **Environmental Artifacts:** Out of a total 320 points, you scored _____. | |

(continues)

**Appendix 8-1** Artifacts of Culture Change (Continued)

| Family and Community Artifacts | |
|---|---|
| **42. Regularly scheduled intergenerational program in which children customarily interact with residents at least once a week.** | _____ Yes (5 points)<br>_____ No (0 points) |
| **43. Home makes space available for community groups to meet in home with residents welcome to attend.** | _____ Yes (5 points)<br>_____ No (0 points) |
| **44. Private guestroom available for visitors at no, or minimal, cost for overnight stays.** | _____ Yes (5 points)<br>_____ No (0 points) |
| **45. Home has café/restaurant/tavern/canteen available to residents, families, and visitors at which residents and family can purchase food and drinks daily.** | _____ Yes (5 points)<br>_____ No (0 points) |
| **46. Home has special dining room available for family use/ gatherings, which excludes regular dining areas.** | _____ Yes (5 points)<br>_____ No (0 points) |
| **47. Kitchenette or kitchen area with at least a refrigerator and stove is available to families, residents, and staff where cooking and baking are welcomed.** | _____ Yes (5 points)<br>_____ No (0 points) |
| **Family and Community Artifacts Subtotal:** Out of a 30 possible points, you scored _____. | |
| **Leadership Artifacts** | |
| **48. CNAs attend resident care conferences.** | _____ All care conferences<br>(5 points)<br>_____ Some (3 points)<br>_____ None (0 points) |
| **49. Residents or family members serve on home quality assessment and assurance (QAA) (QI, CQI, QA) committee.** | _____ Yes (5 points)<br>_____ No (0 points) |
| **50. Residents have an assigned staff member who serves as "buddy," case coordinator, Guardian Angel, etc. to check with the resident regularly and follow up on any concerns.** This is in addition to any assigned social service staff. | _____ All New residents (5 points)<br>_____ Some (3 points)<br>_____ None (0 points) |
| **51. Learning circles or equivalent are used regularly in staff and resident meetings in order to give each person the opportunity to share their opinion/ideas.** | _____ Yes (5 points)<br>_____ No (0 points) |
| **52. Community Meetings are held on a regular basis bringing staff, residents, and families together as a community.** | _____ Yes (5 points)<br>_____ No (0 points) |
| **Leadership Artifacts Subtotal:** Out of a total 25 points, you scored _____. | |

*(continues)*

**Appendix 8-1** Artifacts of Culture Change (Continued)

| Workplace Practice Artifacts | |
|---|---|
| **53. RNs consistently work with the residents of the same neighborhood/household/unit (with no rotation).** | _____ All RNs (5 points)<br>_____ Some (3 points)<br>_____ None (0 points) |
| **54. LPNs consistently work with the residents of the same neighborhood/household/unit (with no rotations).** | _____ All LPNs (5 points)<br>_____ Some (3 points)<br>_____ None (0 points) |
| **55. CNAs consistently work with the residents of the same neighborhood/household/unit (with no rotation).** | _____ All CNAs (5 points)<br>_____ Some (3 points)<br>_____ None (0 points) |
| **56. Self-scheduling of work shifts.** CNAs develop their own schedule and fill in for absent CNAs. CNAs indepedently handle the task of scheduling, trading shifts/days, and covering for each other instead of a staffing coordinator. | _____ All CNAs (5 points)<br>_____ Some (3 points)<br>_____ None (0 points) |
| **57. Home pays expenses for nonmanagerial staff to attend outside conferences/workshops, e.g., CNAs, direct care nurses.** Check yes if at least one nonmanagerial staff member attended an outside conference/workshop paid by home in past year. | _____ Yes (5 points)<br>_____ No (0 points) |
| **58. Staff is not required to wear uniforms or "scrubs."** | _____ Yes (5 points)<br>_____ No (0 points) |
| **59. Percent of other staff cross-trained and certified as CNAs in addition to CNAs in the nursing department.** | _____ 100 – 81% (5 points)<br>_____ 80 – 61% (4 points)<br>_____ 60 – 41% (3 points)<br>_____ 40 – 21% (2 points)<br>_____ 20 – 1% (1 point)<br>_____ 0 (0 points) |
| **60. Activities, informal or formal, are led by staff in other departments such as nursing and housekeeping or any departments.** | _____ Yes (5 points)<br>_____ No (0 points) |
| **61. Awards given to staff to recognize commitment to person-directed care, e.g., Culture Change award, Champion of Change award.** This does not include Employee of the Month. | _____ Yes (5 points)<br>_____ No (0 points) |
| **62. Career ladder positions for CNAs, e.g., CNA II, CNA III, team leader, etc.** There is a career ladder for CNAs to hold a position higher than base level. | _____ Yes (5 points)<br>_____ No (0 points) |

*(continues)*

**Appendix 8-1** Artifacts of Culture Change (Continued)

| | |
|---|---|
| **63. Job development program, e.g., CNA to LPN to RN to NP.** | _____ Yes (5 points)<br>_____ No (0 points) |
| **64. Day care onsite available to staff.** | _____ Yes (5 points)<br>_____ No (0 points) |
| **65. Home has on staff a paid volunteer coordinator in addition to activity director.** | _____ Full time (30 hours/week or more) (5 points)<br>_____ Part time (15–30 hours/week) (3 points)<br>_____ No paid volunteer coordinator (0 pointss) |
| **66. Employee evaluations include observable measures of employee support of individual resident choices, control and preferred routines in all aspects of daily living.** | _____ All employee evaluations (5 points)<br>_____ Some (3 points)<br>_____ None (0 points) |
| **Workplace Practice Artifacts Subtotal:** Out of a total 70 points, you scored _____. | |
| **Outcomes** | |
| **67. Average longevity of CNAs.**<br>Add length of employment in years of permanent CNAs and divide by number of staff. | _____ Your CNA average longevity<br>Above 5 years (5 points)<br>3–5 years (3 points)<br>Below 3 years (0 points) |
| **68. Average longevity of LPNs (in any position).**<br>Add length of employment in years of permanent staff LPNs and divide by number of staff. | _____ Your LPN average longevity<br>Above 5 years (5 points)<br>3–5 years (3 points)<br>Below 3 years (0 points) |
| **69. Average longevity of RN/GNs (in any position).**<br>Add length of employment in years of all permanent RN/GNs and divide by number of staff. | _____ Your RN/GN average longevity<br>Above 5 years (5 points)<br>3–5 years (3 points)<br>Below 3 years (0 points) |
| **70. Longevity of the Director of Nursing (in any position).** | _____ Longevity as DON<br>_____ Longevity at home<br>Above 5 years (5 points)<br>3–5 years (3 points)<br>Below 3 years (0 points) |

(continues)

**Appendix 8-1** Artifacts of Culture Change (Continued)

| | |
|---|---|
| **71. Longevity of the Administrator (in any position).** | _____ Longevity as NHA<br>_____ Longevity at home<br>Above 5 years (5 points)<br>3–5 years (3 points)<br>Below 3 years (0 points) |
| **72. Turnover rate for CNAs.** | Number of CNAs who left, voluntary or involuntary, in previous 12 months divided by number of total CNAs employed = turnover rate<br>Your home's figure _____<br>0 percent (5 points)<br>20 – 39% (4 points)<br>40 – 59% (3 points)<br>60 – 79% (2 points)<br>80 – 99% (1 points)<br>100% and above (0 points) |
| **73. Turnover rate for LPNs.** | Number of LPNs who left, voluntary or involuntary, in previous 12 months divided by number of total LPNs employed = turnover rate<br>Your home's figure _____<br>0 – 12% (5 points)<br>13 – 25% (4 points)<br>26 – 38% (3 points)<br>39 – 51% (2 points)<br>52 – 65% (1 points)<br>66% and above (0 points) |
| **74. Turnover rate for RNs.** | Number of RNs who left, voluntary or involuntary, in previous 12 months divided by number of total RNs employed = turnover rate<br>Your home's figure _____<br>0 – 12% (5 points)<br>13 – 25% (4 points)<br>26 – 38% (3 points)<br>39 – 51% (2 points)<br>52 – 65% (1 points)<br>66% and above (0 points) |

*(continues)*

**Appendix 8-1** Artifacts of Culture Change (Continued)

| | |
|---|---|
| **75. Turnover rate for DONs.** | _____ Number of DONs in the last 12 months<br>1 (5 points)<br>2 (3 points)<br>3 (0 points) |
| **76. Turnover rate for Administrators.** | _____ Number of NHAs in the last 12 months<br>1 (5 points)<br>2 (3 points)<br>3 (0 points) |
| **77. Percent of CNA shifts covered by agency staff over the last month.** | Total number of CNA shifts in a 24 hour period (all shifts no regardless of hours in a shift)<br><br>_____ Multiplied by number of days in last the last full month<br><br>_____ Of this number, number of shifts covered by an agency CNA<br><br>_____ Your percentage (agency shifts/total number X days × 100)<br>0% (5 points)<br>1 – 5% (3 points)<br>Over 5% (0 points) |
| **79. Current occupancy rate.** | _____ Your home figure<br>Above 86%                    (5 points)<br>At average 83 – 85%      (3 points)<br>Below 83%                   (0 points)<br>(Using the national 2004 average of 84.2% form CMS) |
| **Outcomes Subtotal:** Out of a total 65 points, you scored _____. | |

(continues)

**Appendix 8-1** Artifacts of Culture Change (Continued)

| Artifacts | Potental Points | Your Subtotal Scores |
|---|---|---|
| Care Practices | 70 | |
| Environment | 320 | |
| Family and Community | 30 | |
| Leadership | 25 | |
| Workplace Practice | 70 | |
| Outcomes | 65 | |
| **Artifacts of Culture Change** | **580** | **Grand Total** |

*Source:* Developed by Centers for Medicare and Medicare Services and Edu-Catering, LLP. For more information contact Karen Schoeneman at karen.schoeneman@cms.hhs.gov or Carmen S. Bowman at carmen@edu-catering.com.

# PART III

# Organization and Delivery of Services

This section makes a transition from studying the external and internal environments to understanding the facility's clinical and administrative organization and processes that are essential for patient care delivery. The six chapters in this section cover the main service departments found in a mid-sized facility of 100 to 120 beds. Each chapter discusses staffing and how the processes of administration and delivery of services are carried out.

- Chapter 9 covers the purpose of social services; skills, roles, and competencies necessary for social workers; an understanding of the aging process; diversity and cultural competence; and the admission and discharge processes. The chapter also includes sections on resident council, family management, and dealing with death and terminal illness.

- Chapter 10 explains how patients receive medical care, nursing care, pharmacy services, and rehabilitation. The critical functions of assessment and care planning are explained. The roles and functions of the medical director and the director of nursing are discussed. The chapter also outlines the main features

of an effective infection control program. Special areas of nursing care management include falls and fall prevention, pressure ulcers, physical restraints, urinary incontinence, and mental and cognitive disorders (depression, delirium, and dementia). The section on pharmacy services includes controlled substances and psychotropic drugs. The chapter concludes with a discussion of restorative and rehabilitation therapies.

- Chapter 11 covers recreational activities that must be individualized and designed to achieve several key goals. Sensory stimulation, reality orientation, reminiscence, validation therapy, and multisensory stimulation are explained. A special section deals with activities for patients with dementia. The main factors in the recruitment and retention of volunteers are also outlined.

- Chapter 12 includes staffing and consultation in the dietary department, menu planning and meal plans, nutritional adequacy, inventory and cost control, food production and food service options, therapeutic diets and intensive nutrition techniques, and food safety.

- Chapter 13 explains the various plant and environmental services such as maintenance, housekeeping, laundry, security, fire and disaster planning, evacuation, waste management, and environmental safety.

- Chapter 14 covers the main business office functions that include compliance with the Fair Labor Standards Act for payroll and compensation, accounts payable, the imprest system of petty cash, accounts receivable and collections, and regulations governing patient trust accounts. Medical records, their contents, and purpose are discussed. The chapter also covers the benefits of information systems and integrated networks and various factors to consider before investing in commercial information systems.

The organizational chart of a typical skilled nursing facility includes the preceding functional departments as illustrated in Figure III–1. In mid-sized facilities, each of these services is managed by a mid-level manager who reports directly to the administrator. Some of these managers are actually working supervisors. For example, depending on a facility's size, a housekeeping supervisor may clean some rooms or polish floors but also supervise a crew of housekeepers.

The various support services are adjuncts to the central nursing care process and must interface with clinical care using a multidisciplinary approach. Building a multidisciplinary team requires the administrator's involvement, and the administrator must develop an organizational culture of interdepartmental communication and cooperation to address patient needs in a holistic system of care.

In an integrated multidisciplinary approach to patient care, professionals who provide medical, nursing, social services, recreational activities, and dietary services share their observations, discuss clinical goals, and develop interventions in which a variety of services interface. Professionals in each discipline are aware of what others are doing to address the multifaceted needs of each patient. Developing an individual plan of care for each patient is a multidisciplinary effort. The overarching goal is to address all aspects of a patient's needs without duplicating or disregarding any patient needs. Often, problems and issues are addressed in committees, with service providers from all pertinent disciplines interacting and providing their professional inputs.

By nature, a nursing facility is a lean organization with a relatively flat hierarchy. The layers of management found in many other types of organizations are mostly absent from the organizational structure of a typical nursing facility. A flat structure implies that the nursing home administrator (NHA) has a broader span of administrative responsibilities when compared with other types of organizations with a tall hierarchical structure. The day-to-day management of the organization requires the NHA to be closely involved in internal operational details. Hence, the NHA must acquire a certain level of expertise in the various departmental functions and processes. Materials covered in this section are intended to help administrators understand the purpose and function of each department. This knowledge will improve the administrator's own effectiveness in managing the facility and should be useful in hiring qualified supervisors when vacancies occur.

**Figure III-1** Organizational Chart of a Typical Skilled Nursing Facility

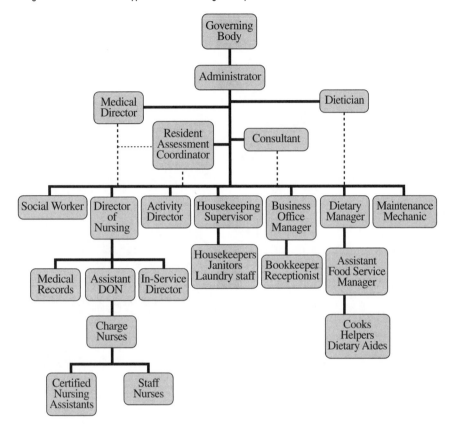

# Chapter 9

## Social Services, Admission, and Discharge

### What You Will Learn

- From the standpoint of patient care, social services focus on helping individuals cope and adapt in an environment that is complex for most people and in which social conflict often occurs. Planning and coordinating admission and discharge are also essential components of social services.

- Size of the facility and scope of responsibility are two main factors on which staffing is based. In addition to a bachelor's degree, social workers must possess knowledge of gerontology.

- Stereotyping the elderly is a gross error because people age differently. A person's background and social history often render useful information in helping the individual get the most out of life.

- Understanding of the activity theory, continuity theory, and labeling theory can help prevent stereotyping and ageism. Some common stereotypes are about inactivity, lack of desire to remain attractive, lack of sexual desire, inability to learn, dependency, and family detachment.

- Delivering long-term care to a culturally diverse population will be a growing challenge. Health care organizations will have to acquire cultural competence and train their associates in dealing with their ethnocentric biases. Cultural accommodation should be based on individual preferences, not on general information about a culture or religion.

- Certain skills are essential to effectively perform social service roles and tasks. They include skills of engagement, assessment, communication, conflict resolution, interviewing, and documentation.

- Social workers perform a variety of different tasks that are too numerous to enumerate, but social service functions can be best understood through six different roles: informational, case manager, coordination, enabler, intervention, and advocacy.

- Admission and discharge functions include preadmission inquiry, admission and orientation, and discharge planning. The Preadmission Screening and Resident Review is an important consideration in nursing home placement.

- The resident council provides the residents a means of empowerment through involvement in decision making about their quality of life. Family management is a proactive approach to minimize dissatisfaction and conflict by addressing family members' emotions about placing someone in a nursing home.

- Death is a reality in health care facilities. Nursing home staff have to address certain legal, emotional, and supportive elements of death and dying.

# Overview of Social Services

The nature of social work in a long-term care facility brings the social worker into extensive contact with current and potential clients. The practice of social work requires sensitivity to people's needs and an understanding of the problems and issues that people may face when they have to live within social systems that can be large and complex. Because many complex social issues cannot be resolved in the best interest of everyone, the focus of social services is on the coping and adaptive capacities of individuals (Dubois & Miley, 1999, p. 44). In some instances, it may be possible to modify certain aspects of a patient's immediate environment to facilitate coping and adaptation. For example, ongoing personality clashes between two individuals—two residents, a resident and a family member, a family member and an as-

sociate, or a resident and an associate—would require some sort of physical separation between the two. In other instances, conflicts must be resolved between what a patient or family wants and what the social environment can offer. Social services are an essential component of long-term care from preadmission planning through a patient's stay in the nursing facility to the time of discharge. The social worker performs key planning and coordinating functions through these stages of change in a person's life.

# Social Services Department

## Staffing

In an average-sized facility of 100 to 120 beds, the social services department typically consists of one full-time social worker, who holds the position of department head and reports to the nursing home administrator. Larger facilities generally have a director of social services, who is in charge of one or more assistant social workers in the department. A facility of 120 beds or more may also have an additional position of director of admissions, admissions coordinator, or director of admissions and marketing, who may report to the administrator or to the director of social services.

Federal regulations mandate a full-time social worker for facilities that have more than 120 beds. Facilities with 120 or fewer beds must still provide social services, even though a full-time social worker is not required by regulations. Apart from these minimum requirements, however, staffing considerations should be based on the overall scope of responsibilities assigned to the social services department. In very small facilities, which range between 40 and 60 beds, one full-time person may be given the responsibilities of both social work and activities. Supplemental part-time staff may be scheduled as needed. In facilities that have between 60 and 100 beds, a full-time social worker may be assigned additional responsibilities such as marketing and public relations. Larger facilities may need additional positions in social services, admissions, or marketing.

## Qualifications

Qualifications of social workers are specified by state nursing home licensure regulations. Depending on what a state requires, social workers may or may not have to be licensed professionals. Typically, a bachelor's degree in social work (BSW) is the minimum academic preparation necessary. In addition to the bachelor's degree, individuals who have less than a specified amount of experience—typically one year—must receive regular consultation from someone who holds a master's degree in social work (MSW). Not all states require education in the social work field. Some states allow facilities to have the position of *social work designee*, a position filled by someone who has a related degree but not a BSW, in which case consultation from someone with an MSW is required. Professionals with an academic degree in social work, however, are generally better prepared for the various roles and responsibilities of a social worker.

In addition to academic qualifications, social workers in a geriatric setting must have an understanding of the physical and psychosocial changes that accompany the aging process. They must understand the unique needs of the elderly and demonstrate a desire to work with the problems and issues confronting clients who need to be admitted to a nursing facility.

The client population in nursing homes will continue to become increasingly diverse in race and ethnicity. This is particularly true in geographic areas where there are sizable numbers of ethnic groups. Working with these clients requires knowledge and understanding of cultural differences.

Social workers should also possess certain personality traits such as trustworthiness, compassion, patience, thoughtfulness, and ability to listen. They must have professional maturity and objectivity in addressing a diversity of issues. They must be knowledgeable of community resources, and they need to establish linkages with various external agencies in order to obtain needed services for patients and their families. Finally, trustworthiness is a necessary trait.

# Knowledge of Aging and the Elderly

An understanding of aging and the special needs of the aged is essential for anyone working in a long-term care setting. Caregivers' attitudes regarding older people can influence how the elderly are treated. The social worker is often called upon to assist other staff members in the facility with resident-related issues that may arise because of a lack of understanding of the aging process. Social workers also generally provide staff training on issues pertaining to *gerontology*—an area of knowledge that deals with the understanding of the aging process, the changes accompanying aging, and the special problems associated with aging.

## Understanding Aging

In our society, people are generally considered elderly or a "senior" when they are in their mid-60s. At this age, people frequently take formal retirement from work, become eligible for Social Security and Medicare, and start paying more attention to some of the symptoms that naturally accompany advancing age. However, age itself merely provides a chronological context. In fact, different people age differently. Attitudes toward one's own aging, and behaviors associated with the issues of aging, differ from person to person. From this perspective, the elderly are a very heterogeneous group.

Categorizing every elderly person according to a stereotype is a gross error. The need to avoid stereotyping is one reason that assessments, plans of care, and interventions require careful individualized attention. Attitudes and behaviors also differ among diverse cultural and ethnic groups. Family support, values and expectations, level of trust, and re-

action to nursing home placement may be associated with a resident's cultural orientation.

Aging is loosely regarded as the culmination of a life cycle that started at birth. Although aging may be the final stage of life, this stage can last a long time, and, as further changes occur, sub-stages within this stage manifest themselves. Hence, a person's background and social history—upbringing, education, hobbies and interests, marriage, divorce, death of spouse, children, siblings, major illnesses, occupation, economic achievement, dysfunctions, and recent occurrences—provide meaningful information that should be used for planning strategies to help the individual cope, adapt to new circumstances, and get the best out of life despite current illness and declining physical functioning. Life changes and stressful life encounters affect the psychological well-being of the elderly. Factors associated with background and life changes can differ substantially according to one's culture and ethnicity.

## Theories of Aging

During the past 40 years or so, a number of theories have been proposed in an effort to understand behaviors associated with aging. Each theory has its limitations, and even together all the theories do not account for every possible situation. Of the several theories, three are considered most useful for their application in nursing home settings:

- Activity theory.
- Continuity theory.
- Labeling theory.

### Activity Theory

According to this theory, people in their old age seek to remain active. This theory counters the "rocking chair" stereotype, according to which the elderly are often visualized as sitting passively in a rocking chair and dozing off because of inactivity. Satisfaction in old age depends on a person's ability to substitute new roles and activities for those that the individual pursued during pre-retirement years. A career postal worker, for example, may enjoy distributing mail to other nursing home residents. Many elderly women still enjoy baking, cooking, knitting, and other activities that should be incorporated into the facility's recreational planning. Most elderly can maintain or improve their self-esteem when they feel they are engaged in doing something useful. Although many residents find independence and life satisfaction by volunteering to do activities they had once enjoyed, it is also important to realize that not everyone wants to remain active and that the notion of what constitutes satisfying activity can differ significantly from one person to another. In fact, among nursing home residents, disengagement from activities is more common because these elderly have both age- and health-related issues.

## Continuity Theory

The major assumption of this theory is that the experiences of one's earlier years prepare an individual to adapt to and cope with the demands of aging, which may help explain why some people adapt to new situations better than others. Current behaviors of elderly individuals can be best understood by examining their behaviors in earlier stages of life, such as past habits, goals, preferences, hobbies, and leisure pursuits. Understanding the patient's past can enable facility personnel to assist the individual in adjusting to the new environment. This understanding can also help facility personnel think about ways in

which routines can be made more flexible to accommodate certain past practices, which would help the person better adapt to a new setting.

## Labeling Theory

This theory helps one understand how a person's self-concept is molded by the labels others use for that person. It strikes at the negative stereotypes of the elderly because the elderly may believe these stereotypes are true, and they may assimilate those stereotypes into their behavior. For example, the belief that once people become old, they become dependent may actually promote dependency in elders (Harrigan & Farmer, 1992).

## Inaccurate Views of Aging

Myths and distorted views about aging encourage stereotyping, which results in treating the elderly in ways that are detrimental to their self-esteem, independence, and psychosocial as well as physical health. Prejudicial treatment of the elderly based on stereotypes is called *ageism*. Ignorance is the main cause of ageism, which creates barriers for adequate delivery of health care and social services to the elderly.

Certain changes—such as sensory decline in vision, hearing, tactile feeling, smelling, and tasting—occur naturally as a person ages. Sleep disorders may also become more common. But getting old does not necessarily mean becoming ill and disabled. Many biological and psychological changes that are commonly associated with aging actually start occurring at a much younger age. These changes do not take place uniformly in all people. Earlier life choices and unforeseen accidents have an effect on health in later years. Hence, chronological age is a poor indicator of health and vigor (Harrigan & Farmer, 1992). Although some elders succumb to illness and disability and require assistance, most continue to live healthy and fulfilling lives. However, the risk of functional impairment increases with age as chronic conditions and comorbidities set in. But in spite of the heightened risk, only a small percentage of the elderly will require institutional care over a long period. Roughly 80% of the elderly over the age of 65 have at least one chronic condition, but more than 80% of the noninstitutionalized elderly independently manage their activities of daily living (ADLs) (Newman & Newman, 1987).

Old age does not necessarily mean that people lose the desire to remain physically attractive. Economic and physical constraints may interfere with one's ability to maintain proper grooming. Assuming that inactivity results from old age is also wrong. Because of sleep disorders, some elderly individuals may compensate for lack of sleep at night by taking naps during day, or they may fall asleep while sitting because of boredom and inactivity. Presuming that physical exertion is harmful for older people is also inaccurate. Within the parameters of physical limitations, most elderly people can engage in various types of physical activities under proper medical supervision. Although sexual functioning declines naturally, particularly in males, most elders retain the desire to express their sexuality.

Dementia and confusion do not naturally accompany aging. Even though only 5% of the elderly population has dementia that is severe enough to substantially hamper their independent functioning, many such patients require care in nursing facilities. Prevalence of dementia in nursing homes is estimated to be between 42 and 78% of the patient population (Weintraub et al., 2000). Estimates of new admissions with dementia may be as high as 67% (German et al., 1992).

Another area in which the elderly are quite heterogeneous is whether they are set in their ways or whether they can learn new things. Many older adults can successfully adapt to changes and learn new skills, such as those demanded by new hobbies, crafts, or using the computer. Older people generally also have their long-term memory quite intact.

It is erroneous to think that the elderly like being dependent on others. To the contrary, older adults like to have control over their life decisions, and to the extent they can, they wish to take care of their own needs. Independence is closely related to self-esteem. A high level of dependency causes many patients in nursing facilities to have low self-esteem. The concept of interdependence may provide a more appropriate way for addressing the needs of the elderly (Harrigan & Farmer, 1992). **_Interdependence_** can be defined as a state of living together (symbiosis) in a mutually beneficial relationship. In most cases, people are in nursing homes because of impairments, and to that extent, their dependent position cannot be helped. However, while being dependent in some ways, residents may be able to make a contribution to the community in other ways. A sense of being useful, competent, and needed must be preserved as much as possible. Interdependence often develops mutual bonds with other residents and pets in the nursing home.

Contrary to popular opinion, the elderly in America are not alienated, ignored, or abandoned by their families. Adult children and their elderly parents generally prefer to live separately—in many other countries, a lack of resources and housing often make it necessary for older parents to live with their grown-up children and grandchildren. At the same time, most long-term care and assistance with ADLs are provided to elders by family members on an informal basis. The family continues to play a vital role in delaying or preventing institutionalization of elders. Community-based services, when available, are used to supplement family care as necessary. As a general rule, only when community-based care cannot adequately address an elder's needs is the elder admitted to a nursing facility. On the other hand, intergenerational conflicts in families do arise. Abuse and neglect, including verbal abuse and psychological mistreatment, exist at all socioeconomic levels of society and in all racial and ethnic groups (Harrigan & Farmer, 1992).

# Diversity and Cultural Competence

In the United States, by 2020, the proportion of ethnic minorities is projected to reach 23% among the 65 and older population group. This is a substantial increase from 13% in 1990 (Pandya, 2005). There is some evidence that nursing home utilization rates among Hispanics, Asians, and Native Americans are much lower than those for whites and African Americans (Himes et al., 1996). The extent of informal caregiving by family members is the highest among Asians, followed by Hispanics, African Americans, and whites. These differences correlate with the extent to which the belief that children are expected to take care of the parents in their old age is prevalent among these ethnic groups (AARP, 2001). However, factors other than culture—such as socio-economic status, family size, and language barriers—may also play a role in molding such expectations. On the other hand, cultural variations exist even among some whites. Hence, delivering long-term care

to a diverse population will be a growing challenge.

***Cultural competence*** is the term used for an organization's ability to deliver health care services in accordance with the cultural needs and preferences of the clients. The idea of cultural competence evolved from research that has consistently demonstrated racial and ethnic disparities in health care delivery. In nursing homes, for example, a greater proportion of African American residents was found to be associated with poorer quality (Singh, 1997). Cultural competence initiatives later evolved into eliminating cultural and linguistic barriers that can interfere with the effective delivery of health care. These initiatives are based on the assumption that removal of any type of barrier between patients and caregivers can enhance quality of care. In addition to language barriers, beliefs and values based on a person's religion and other sociocultural elements define people's preferences and taboos.

Cultural competence begins with respect for the individual. It requires engagement skills that help caregivers understand the differences in another person's beliefs and values and how those differences can be accommodated. It requires that caregivers honestly assess their personal biases and try to understand cultural differences with a nonjudgmental attitude. Cultural stereotyping can be just as detrimental as ageism. Another type of bias is ***ethnocentrism***—a belief that one's way of life and view of the world are inherently superior to those of others and that those views are desirable for others to acquire. It involves judging another's culture as inferior to one's own (Barger, 2004). According to Barger, "Addressing ethnocentrism is not a matter of trying *not* to be ethnocentric. This is an impossible task, since we will never experience every life situation of everyone around the world. We will always have our assumptions about life based on our existing limited experience. So a much more productive approach is to catch ourselves when we are being ethnocentric and to control for this bias as we seek to develop better understandings." Associates working with ethnically diverse populations should be trained in dealing with their ethnocentric biases.

## Cultural Accommodations

Certain types of accommodations are relatively simple to make. These include choice of apparel, preference for male or female attendants, dietary restrictions from a cultural standpoint, and ability to follow certain religious practices. Other restrictions, particularly those that may have implications for a person's health and well-being or that may be disruptive to other residents, require a more careful approach. In some situations, it would be wise to obtain legal counsel because they may have implications for a person's civil rights under Title VI of the Civil Rights Act of 1964 (see Chapter 5). There are other issues that a social worker may be called upon to address. For example, conflicts based on ethnic diversity can arise between residents or between residents and visitors.

Soliciting information from someone of a different ethnic origin requires tact. For instance, an outright inquiry about a person's religion is generally not appropriate. It may also be inappropriate to ask someone, "Do you understand English?" Many immigrants from other countries speak and understand English quite well and may perceive such a question as an insult. Instead, it would be appropriate to pose exploratory questions, such as, "Do you have any particular needs that we should be aware of? We want you to feel very comfortable in our facility."

Learning about cultural beliefs and customs is important to gain an understanding about other cultures. But, caution must be exercised in how such learning is applied: there are many subcultures that often differentiate among people from the same general background. For example, not everyone from Vietnam is a Buddhist, not everyone from the Middle East is a Muslim or a Jew, and not everyone from India is a Hindu. Hence, broad assumptions should not be made. Also, people from the same ethnic or religious background often have individual differences; some are orthodox, others are liberal, most are likely to be somewhere in between. Many westernized Hindus eat beef, many unorthodox Muslims use alcohol, and many nonobservant Jews consume pork products. Hence, it is critical to ascertain individual needs and preferences.

It is almost impossible to furnish accurate details on all different cultures and subcultures found in the United States today. However, some main cultural differences in the areas of religious observances, dietary restrictions, and health care preferences are summarized here:

• *Observances.* Catholics and most Christian denominations observe Sunday as a day of religious observance. Orthodox Jews and Seventh-day Adventists (members of a Christian denomination) observe Saturday as a holy day. More specifically, they observe the Sabbath from sundown on Friday evening to sundown on Saturday evening. Muslims observe Friday as a day for prayers. Christmas, on December 25, is the most widely celebrated Christian holiday; however, some Christians regard the holiday as anti-Christian and pagan. On the other hand, social celebrations associated with

Christmas are not offensive to most people. Hanukkah is the most widely celebrated Jewish holiday, which also falls in December, but the actual dates vary according to the Hebrew calendar. Other major Jewish observances are the Passover, which occurs in the Spring, and Yom Kippur (day of atonement), considered as the holiest of all Jewish observances, comes in the Fall. Most observant Jews fast during Yom Kippur. Ramadan, the month of fasting, is observed by devout Muslims during the daylight hours. Catholics and some other Christians observe the season of Lent, which begins with Ash Wednesday and culminates with Easter Sunday. Catholics particularly refrain from eating meat (a practice called "abstinence") on Fridays during Lent. Other devout Catholics observe abstinence on all Fridays of the year. By many Christians, Good Friday and Easter are considered more important than Christmas in remembrance of the death and resurrection of Jesus Christ. Many Christians, such as the Amish and the Mennonites, observe Thanksgiving and New Year's Day as religious holidays. Many Christians say a short prayer before a meal; many Jews pray both before and after a meal.

- *Dietary restrictions.* Most Christians do not have any faith-based dietary restrictions, but many do. Among Seventh-day Adventists, for example, about half are strict vegetarians. Those who consume meat, poultry, and fish confine themselves to foods considered biblically clean, which are listed in Leviticus, Chapter 11, of the Bible. Some of the unclean meats include pork, rabbit, frog, squid, shellfish, and fish that do not have scales. Most Seventh-day Adventists do not

drink caffeinated beverages. They also shun tobacco in all its forms and the use of any kind of alcohol, and consider such practices to be offensive. The Mormon church also prohibits use of tobacco, alcohol, and caffeinated beverages. For Jehovah's Witnesses, tobacco and alcohol are forbidden. They also do not eat certain meats such as sausages because they may contain blood. Jewish dietary practices are also based on Leviticus, except that meat and milk may not be served together. To be considered kosher, animals and poultry must be slaughtered in accordance with Jewish law. A similar practice of ritual killing is followed by Muslims for meat or poultry to be considered *halal*. Muslims also do not eat pork. Many Buddhists and Hindus are vegetarians. Those who eat meat generally prefer chicken or fish over beef, or they may shun beef and veal altogether.

- *Health care preferences.* Nontraditional or alternative medical treatments, such as use of herbs, acupuncture, and rites and rituals are historically embedded in many cultures. People from these cultures accept Western medicine, but may also insist on using alternative remedies. Patients have the legal right to follow or not to follow treatments prescribed by a physician. For example, Jehovah's Witnesses refuse blood transfusion on religious grounds. In other cultures, immunization such as flu shots is refused. Treatment such as artificial prolongation of life may be refused by some. Religion may also govern certain ritualistic practices that can vary considerably among cultures. For example, various forms of prayers, singing of hymns, sacraments for the sick, anointing with oil, and so forth, may be practiced according to different belief systems.

Making cultural accommodations does not require a faith-based organization to compromise its religious philosophies and values. Many nursing homes in the United States are operated by various Christian denominations and Jewish congregations. They accept patients regardless of their religious affiliations but do not compromise their own principles. A nursing home run by the Catholic church, for example, will hold regular mass services; but attendance will be optional. A Jewish nursing home will serve only kosher meals. A Seventh-day Adventist nursing facility will not serve pork or other meats considered biblically unclean but may allow family members to bring in such products for individual consumption.

## Skills and Competencies

As discussed later in this chapter, social workers serve in a variety of roles. To carry out these roles effectively, social workers must learn and develop skills in at least six main areas:

- Engagement skills.
- Assessment skills.
- Communication skills.
- Conflict resolution skills.
- Interviewing skills.
- Documentation skills.

### Engagement Skills

This skill is basic to all social work practice because it entails recognizing client needs,

demonstrating sensitivity and concern, and being committed to addressing client needs. Effective engagement with the elderly client is built on respect. Engagement requires building rapport with patients and their families.

Young adults may tend to treat older adults as children, a process called ***infantilization***. It is not uncommon for nursing home staff members to address patients by their first names, which may be taken as demeaning, even though the patient is not likely to openly protest about it. Similarly, addressing patients as "cutie," "sweetie," "baby," or "honey" is regarded as condescending. Patients are already dependent upon the caregivers; infantilization further strips away the patients' self-respect and dignity.

Deficiencies in human relations skills can severely hamper a social worker's effectiveness. Skilled social workers can play an especially important role in training other staff members in effective ways to interact with the elderly, and social workers can periodically reinforce the need for appropriate staff-resident relations. Caregiving relationships are often characterized by ***intimacy***, meaning closeness or proximity of the caregiver to the dependent elder; intimacy goes beyond mere familiarity (Agich, 1995). Without conscious thought, intimacy can lead to infantilization and reinforce a resident's sense of dependency, which is the antithesis of autonomy.

### Assessment Skills

Assessment is akin to an exploratory study that forms the basis for decision making and action (Coulshed, 1991, p. 25). It is a systematic investigation of all basic and special needs of the individual, including the patient's own perspective as well as that of his or her family or surrogates. Special attention is paid to the person's biophysical functioning in relation to psychological and social processes, such as the patient's attitudes about being in the nursing facility, economic needs, family support, and race or cultural issues. An initial assessment is generally quite comprehensive, but because needs change over time, assessment should be an ongoing process. The information gathered from the assessment is used to determine how the facility's resources and services will be deployed to best address the needs of the patient as well as the needs of family or surrogates. Such a plan of action takes into account any limitations in resources the nursing facility may have. When a facility is unable to furnish the resources necessary to address all the identified needs of a patient, services from outside the facility must be utilized or the patient should be moved to a more appropriate setting.

## Communication Skills

Communicating with the elderly requires special skills apart from speaking, listening, writing, and presentation skills. Particular attention must be paid to language use with older adults. Use of technical jargon is commonplace among nursing home associates, but such jargon should be avoided when communicating with clients and their families. For example, associates should use the term "food service" instead of "dietary;" "recreation" instead of "activities;" and "safety device" instead of "restraint." Kropf and Hutchison (1992) make several practical suggestions to improve communication. Simple and straightforward language is the most effective method of verbal communication. A handshake or touch adds warmth to the communication process. Sitting in close proximity to an older client aids understanding of what is being said and is also taken as a sign of acceptance. Active listening, repeating, and feedback are essential techniques for communicating with the elderly to ensure understanding. Because hearing impairment is a common problem among nursing home clients, use of clear diction and a slow pace of talking are important. Another good strategy is to use the patients' names frequently, so they know that they are being addressed.

## Conflict Resolution Skills

Conflict occurs in various types of human interactions. It occurs when one party perceives that its interests are blocked by another (Allen et al., 2007). Conflicts can be attributed to several sources, such as disagreement or differences in values, attitudes, needs, and expectations. Conflict can also arise from miscommunication (Conerly & Tripathi, 2004). The results can be residents who withdraw and get depressed, residents who lash out at other residents or staff, or irate family members. Social workers are commonly asked to intervene in such situations, but they may themselves experience resistance when, for example, the social worker decides to do what is best for the resident but the resident insists on having his or her own way.

A four-dimensional conflict-resolution model can be used to address various types of conflicts. According to this model, the social worker should evaluate four main factors (Allen et al., 2007): (1) needs of the resident; (2) evidence of how urgent the resident's need is; (3) legal and ethical implications; and (4) likelihood of resistance from some entity—such as associates, management, or family—to what the social worker may propose. A simultaneous review of these four factors can lead to one of five possible resolutions according to the Thomas-Kilmann Conflict Model:

*Avoiding.* The social worker would work on improving the situation through education, subtle suggestions, or better relationships (Allen et al., 2007), but the conflict is not dealt with directly. For example, a family member may insist that caregivers help the patient dress even though the patient may be able to dress herself given adequate time. This family member may require some education about why it is important for the resident to do such tasks independently to the extent possible. Avoiding can also be accomplished by separating two individuals who cannot get along. For example, two roommates may be assigned to different rooms. In most other instances, however, avoiding is not a good strategy. When left unresolved, the underlying issue may fester and create an explosive situation later on. For example, avoiding a family member who routinely complains about the services is likely to make this person more irritable as time goes on.

*Compromising.* This involves bargaining (each party gives up something to get something) and taking a middle ground. This approach is used when the four factors play a moderate role. Allen et al. (2007) provide example of a situation in which a resident insists on smoking as a social release, even though there are contraindications on medical grounds and the facility has a nonsmoking environment. Through compromise, the resident may be allowed to smoke occasionally outside the facility in the presence of a staff member.

*Accommodating.* Here, the social worker can help the resident best by smoothing relationships, repairing trust, and reopening lines of communication (Nelson, 2000). It requires low assertiveness. This strategy is valuable when it is important to appease the other party because the facility is wrong on the issue and the issue may not be very important. As an example, a resident's night gown did not get returned from the laundry and could not be located despite a thorough search. The social worker may ask the administrator to authorize the small amount of money it would cost to replace the gown.

*Collaborating (or problem solving).* This approach requires a careful definition of the problem, alternative solutions, evaluation of costs and effectiveness of each solution, and choosing a solution that best accommodates the needs of those involved. It is based on the input from several interested parties. This approach is useful when resident needs are high and low resistance from associates or management is expected (Allen et al., 2007). For example, a resident with severe dementia may have chronic shortage of appropriate clothes to wear and the associates may be constantly running out of clothes to dress this person appropriately. A meeting with the family may involve the social worker and one or two caregivers to discuss alternatives. If the family is not interested, the social worker and other associates may discuss alternatives such as using the resident's personal funds to buy new clothing, asking a faith-based organization to donate clothing, or purchasing used clothing.

*Forcing (or confronting).* When faced with a high degree of resistance, forcing may become necessary when the resident's needs present urgency and high legal or ethical stakes are involved. Examples include flagrant violation of patient rights, negligence, or abuse. Confrontation would require that the social worker present clear and convincing evidence of the resident's compelling need (Allen et al., 2007).

## Interviewing Skills

Interviewing is commonly used for gathering facts about individual situations. As an interactive tool that is generally used when dealing with specific issues, interviewing involves communicating in a more focused way than usual. Effective interviewing generally requires some prior preparation, such as gathering background or other preliminary information that is used as the basis for further probing to obtain more pertinent and detailed information. When preparing for the interview, the social worker needs to think through what specific questions to ask.

The actual interview requires a private and quiet place and adequate uninterrupted time. Effective interviewing employs the skills of engagement and communication just described. But it goes beyond a mere use of those skills. An interview should get to the main point of the issue and begin with a summary of the issue and the purpose of the interview. It is important to pose questions that get to facts and feelings. Questions posed accusingly or in a suspicious manner are likely to generate negative reactions. During the interview, particular attention must be paid to special cues that may require further probing. For example, the individual may try to dodge an issue or may be hesitant to respond to a question. A victim of abuse may be reluctant to discuss it because of embarrassment or for fear of retaliation. The interview should conclude with a summary that puts the total interview in perspective for the client, who should then be asked if any information has been misrepresented or omitted (Kropf & Hutchison, 1992). The social worker should also explain what follow-up will take place.

## Documentation Skills

Documentation often requires the use of prescribed forms and formats, but much of this work is now computerized. Documentation must be timely, accurate, complete, and descriptive—but concise. In this manner, social service documentation should provide a complete record of the patient's initial history, assessment, care planning, progress (or lack thereof), interventions, and discharge. A number of documents are also completed upon a patient's admission to the facility, as discussed later in this chapter.

# Social Service Roles

Social workers perform a variety of different tasks that are too numerous to describe. Most situations that require social work intervention cannot be foreseen and must be dealt with as they arise. The roles discussed in this section paint a general portrait of what a social worker employed in a nursing facility does. These roles also highlight the importance of the social worker's position in a nursing facility. The various roles and functions can be classified into six main categories:

- Informational role.
- Case manager role.
- Coordination role.
- Enabler role.
- Intervention role.
- Advocacy role.

## Informational Role

The social worker is generally the main source of information on several fronts: on the facility and its services, on eligibility for public financing and the services covered under programs such as Medicare and Medicaid, on resources and services available in the community and their suitability for a particular client, and on various issues related to long-term care. A social worker must acquire comprehensive knowledge in all these areas.

People who inquire about nursing home placement for a family member or acquaintance are often the primary recipients of information about the facility. But professionals in other health care and social service agencies also need to be educated about nursing home services. One skilled nursing facility can differ substantially from another on the basis of the level of specialization, philosophy of care, socio-residential environment, and so forth. Such differentiating factors should be used in marketing the facility to potential sources of patient referrals.

## Case Manager Role

Case management was discussed in Chapters 1 and 3. The nursing home social worker performs a similar role for the residents in the facility. Basically, case management is the process of matching client needs with available services that are likely to best address those needs. Case management encompasses assessment, planning, follow-up, and reevaluation.

As a case manager, the social worker generally coordinates external resources to meet the total care needs of each patient. When a resident is admitted to a nursing facility, the facility takes on the responsibility of providing or procuring all appropriate services that the patient may need—a concept called "total care" (see Chapter 1). Services not provided by the facility are obtained from external sources. For example, a resident may require eyeglasses or dental care or may need a psychiatric evaluation. A referral for such services may require obtaining orders from a physician, involving family or other responsible party, follow-up on financing, making an appointment with an appropriate professional, arranging transportation, and follow-up to ensure that the patient has actually received the service.

## Coordination Role

The social worker's coordination role goes beyond case management. Each admission and discharge requires careful coordination with both key staff members within the facility and with relevant parties outside the facility. The social worker is generally the facilitator of the resident council within the facility or a family support group sponsored by the facility. The social worker is also generally called upon to assist the facility administrator in sharing the facility's expertise with the community through well-coordinated programs on geriatric issues and financing for long-term care. An illustrative list of such outreach programs is included in Chapter 4.

## Enabler Role

Although it is also referred to as the counseling role, giving advice and expressing personal opinions to patients or families are seldom appropriate in nursing home social work. The nature of social work counseling is primarily based on helping patients help themselves. Hence, this role is more appropriately called the "enabler role" (Kropf &

Hutchison, 1992), in which the social worker functions as a facilitator.

New residents require adjustment to the new surroundings and the unfamiliar routines of the facility. The process and time required for adjustment varies from one patient to another. Social workers help residents adjust by frequently visiting them and by encouraging them to express their fears, anxieties, and feelings. The social worker can facilitate social adjustment by assessing compatibilities and introducing residents to others to encourage social bonding (Patchner & Patchner, 1991).

The resident's family also requires adjustment. Family members often carry feelings of guilt from putting a relative in a nursing home. There may be conflict among family members over the decision. The social worker can help family members explore their own feelings, clarify areas of disagreement, and confront the realities of the situation.

## Intervention Role

The social worker is called upon to address a variety of problems that a nursing home patient may face. It often requires good communication and conflict resolution skills, as discussed earlier. In most instances, the patient has a conflict or lacks the ability to cope with his or her environment. Examples of this type of conflict include a patient repeatedly losing her eyeglasses or not having enough clothes to wear. The conflict may involve other people, such as an associate or family. For instance, the family may find it too expensive to replace lost items and may not favor purchasing new eyeglasses or hearing aids. The family may blame the facility for losing items of clothing and decline to replace them, with the result that the patient has insufficient or inappropriate items to wear. There may be conflict between two residents who may or may not be sharing a room or a dining table. Certain problems may call for the use of external resources, requiring the social worker to function as a case manager. Other types of conflict arise from psychosocial problems or dementia and may require therapeutic intervention in the form of reality orientation, validation therapy, or sensory stimulation (Patchner & Patchner, 1991). Activity personnel can assist with these therapies.

## Advocacy Role

As an advocate, the social worker looks out for the best interests of the patient. It is the social worker's responsibility to inform patients of their rights (see Chapter 5). The social worker also monitors the enforcement of patient rights in the facility and educates the staff on the meaning and importance of patient rights. Many patients cannot express their desires and cannot determine on their own what is best for them. In the advocacy role, the social worker does not try to guess the patient's wishes or try to determine what is best for the patient. Rather, the social worker is responsible for bringing such issues to the attention of the administration and any other parties whose involvement may be necessary for decision making and initiating action. For instance, a resident may have already lost two hearing aids and may be unable to express whether he or she needs a new one. The family may resist investing money in another hearing device. This patient needs someone to stand up as an advocate on his or her behalf.

Effectively managed nursing homes have ethics committees to address such issues. The social worker brings issues to the attention of the committee for decision and resolution. An ***ethics committee*** is a multidisciplinary forum that may include the administrator, a nurse, a physician, social worker, activity director, and others as necessary. Depending on the issue, the committee may also include a member of the clergy, an ethicist, a legal representative, a dietician, or a therapist. Generally, family members are also invited to attend and to provide their input. The committee's purpose is to discuss situations and resolve issues in view of what is best for the patient. A multidisciplinary forum allows for different insights and viewpoints. It relieves the social worker of the responsibility for making complex decisions independently. When the consequences of a decision turn out to be negative, blame cannot be assigned to one person. Finally, the decision of a committee is more likely to be accepted by individuals, such as family or staff members, whose action or support is necessary for carrying out that decision.

# Admission and Discharge

## Preadmission Inquiry

The social worker is generally the one to first meet a prospective client, unless the facility has a separate director of admissions, who would then be the one to take most inquiries. A prospective client or a referral agency may call the facility and make arrangements for a family to visit the facility. In other instances, an inquirer may walk in unannounced. The facility must be prepared at all times to handle either situation promptly and professionally, because in today's competitive environment, an inquiry delayed is an admission lost.

Handling an inquiry is akin to making a sale, but using a social service approach. This approach requires the intake worker, who may be the social worker or the admissions coordinator, to function as an information

disseminator and case manager. The focus is not simply on finding new patients for admission to the facility but also on determining whether the nursing home is appropriately suited to meet the patient's needs. The preadmission inquiry process needs to be well organized.

## PASRR Compliance

*PASRR* stands for Preadmission Screening and Resident Review (formerly, PASARR—Preadmission Screening and Annual Resident Review. The requirement for an annual review was dropped in 1997.). One of the provisions of the Nursing Home Reform Act (OBRA-87) was to eliminate inappropriate placement of people with mental illness, mental retardation, and developmental disabilities in Medicaid-certified nursing homes, that is, nursing homes with NF certification (see Chapter 5). The law required the states to establish procedures to screen Medicaid-eligible patients before admission to a nursing home. These screening procedures vary from state to state. In some states, the nursing home may have the responsibility to do the PASRR. A review is also required when there is a significant change in the patient's condition. Nursing facilities should not admit anyone who has not been through the PASRR. Only when a patient is admitted for less than 30 days based on a physician's certification is the PASRR not required.

There are two levels of PASRR screenings. Level I screening is required before admission. A person with mental illness, mental retardation, or developmental disability may be admitted as long as he or she also requires nursing home care; that is, the patient's needs cannot be adequately met by community-based services. Level II screening provides for a more detailed assessment and serves as the basis for determining whether the nursing home setting is appropriate for individuals who have a serious mental illness, mental retardation, or related condition; whether their rehabilitative needs can be met in the nursing home setting; and, if so, what specialized rehabilitation services related to their mental illness or mental retardation are necessary.

Once the resident is admitted, the nursing facility is obligated to provide the necessary care and services the resident requires to attain or maintain the highest practicable physical, mental, and psychosocial well-being. For example, the facility may have to obtain specialized mental health services while the patient is a resident at the facility.

## Written Procedure

The facility should have a written procedure for handling inquiries. The procedure should include a list, in descending order of preference, of backup personnel in case the primary intake worker is not available. For instance, the list of personnel could start with the director of admissions and include the social worker, a second social worker (if the facility has one), the administrator (or an administrative staff member such as an assistant administrator, if the facility has one), the director of nursing, and the activity director.

The point here is that the facility should always have someone to provide complete information, regardless of whether the inquiry is initiated over the phone or in person. The procedure should include the main steps in handling inquiries, in which all personnel assigned to this task must be properly trained. The list of staff members should be available to the receptionist, so each inquiry can be appropriately directed, based on who is available at the time. The facility should also have a plan for handling inquiries after regular business

hours and on weekends. For example, many well-run nursing facilities designate a weekend manager. This role is carried out by the primary and secondary intake professionals mentioned earlier, who cover the role of weekend manager in rotation. An evening charge nurse or nurse supervisor should be trained to handle the occasional inquiry that may come in after regular business hours.

## Initial Interview

The facility should provide an office or other private area for the interview. This setting should be comfortable, inviting, and cheerfully decorated, but not to the point of being distracting. Handling an inquiry is an art, which is perfected with time and practice. An inquiry form in a checklist format can greatly facilitate the interview. Even if the intake process is computerized, making computer entries during the interview should be avoided because it depersonalizes the process.

The objective of the interview is to obtain essential information about the patient, starting with his or her name, age, gender, current location such as hospital or home, name of referring agency (if any), attending physician, when accommodation may be needed, diagnosis, ADL status, hobbies and interests, any special needs, and so forth. The inquiry form should also have space for the inquirer's name, relationship, phone number, and address. Even though all pertinent information is obtained at this time to make a judgment about the patient's needs, this is not a formal assessment, nor should an attempt be made at this juncture to make one.

Once the basic information has been obtained, the interview moves on to a discussion of the facility's services that can best meet the patient's needs, according to the best clinical judgment that can be made, given the information provided. If necessary, the intake worker—that is, the person handling the interview—can call the referral agency to seek further clarification. The intake worker should also call in the director of nursing, a specialized nurse, a therapist, or the dietician to provide additional expertise if specific issues arise during the interview. The facility should evaluate the case objectively. Admitting a patient and then not providing adequate services because the facility is not equipped to handle the care that the patient's condition demands would be a mistake. On the other hand, if a community-based long-term care program or a residential institution is determined to be more suitable for a prospective client, the intake worker should make appropriate referrals. Establishing exchange partnerships with external agencies can result in two-way referrals, creating a win–win situation for both parties.

## Facility Tour

Prospective clients seldom decline to tour the facility, but it can happen if the initial interview turns them off. This phase of the inquiry process consists of a guided tour, during which the inquiring party is accompanied by the intake worker. Well-managed facilities have written procedures for giving an effective guided tour. The written tour plan is also used for training staff members who may be called upon to conduct facility tours in the absence of the primary intake personnel.

The tour should highlight the various elements of the internal environment and caregiving philosophies from the standpoint of person-centered care (see Figure 8–1 in Chapter 8). Some of the main areas of the facility to include in the tour are dining rooms, lounges, social and private spaces, amenities, and the activity room and calendar. Facilities must have a large, wall-size calendar of activities and events. In addition, safety features and practices, comfort factors, privacy aspects of care, and enrichment of the environment and culture change (see Chapter 8) should be emphasized in the conversation while touring the facility. The visitor must be able to observe and feel the caregiving environment to the fullest extent possible without compromising the privacy of patients receiving care. For example, activity sessions and certain therapies, such as gait training, can be observed without compromising privacy. It is inappropriate to take visitors into occupied patient rooms unless permission to see their rooms has been obtained in advance. Some facilities set apart one or two furnished model rooms for visitors to see and to get some ideas about how a room may be personalized by bringing items such as small television sets, memorabilia, plants, personal furniture, and bed accessories. Visitors should not be taken inside the kitchen because it violates sanitation regulations.

## Concluding Interview

The conclusion of a tour always brings the inquirer back to the place where the initial interview was conducted. The intake worker now continues to judge the client's reactions and provides an opportunity for questions and answers. At this point, financing should be discussed. If appropriate, the patient accounts manager may join the conversation to answer questions about financing. For instance, the patient may be eligible for Medicare, Medicaid, or both. An application may have to be made for Medicaid coverage. If the patient would come in under Medicare, an approximate length of stay and out-of-pocket costs should be discussed. Private-pay rates should be furnished if that is appropriate. If the patient has private insurance or coverage under a managed care plan, all necessary information on the coverage should be obtained. Bed availability, wait-list status, or a tentative date of admission can also be discussed at this time.

## Information Packet

Before the prospective client leaves, he or she must receive an information packet, and the intake worker should briefly go over some of the materials contained in the packet. The information packet should be professionally designed and should contain all relevant information that may be needed for making a decision about placing someone in the facility. If the client has no further questions, the interview is concluded. The client should be courteously escorted to the main lobby and given a personal send-off.

## Follow-up

When different personnel are involved in handling separate inquiries, all inquiries should be channeled to the person who has the primary responsibility for inquiry intake, such as the director of social services or the director of admissions. This individual should follow up on all inquiries, and the final disposition should be noted. If a prospective patient was considered an appropriate client for the facility but was not admitted, an attempt should be made to find out the reason the facility was not selected. Inquiry dispositions should be periodically reviewed with the administrator. Over time, this information can be useful in identifying weak spots and taking appropriate measures to improve operational policies, procedures, and services.

## Admission and Orientation

Nursing home admission trauma is common and affects most patients. But the social worker can take steps to minimize a patient's fear and anxiety. One source of anxiety for the patient, and of guilt for the family, is stereotyped and unpleasant images of nursing homes. Despite efforts made by industry leaders to change the gloomy portrayal of nursing homes, the effect of these images has not been overcome. Lingering negative perceptions require the industry to do more to change people's perceptions. The adoption of culture change and incorporating the concepts of enriched environments discussed in Chapter 8 are likely to overcome the negative perceptions over time.

## Planning and Preparation

Once a family has decided to admit a family member to the facility, the social worker should make a personal visit, if possible, to meet the new patient at his or her current residence. The purpose of such a visit is to attempt to allay unfounded fears that the new patient may have. A sizable number of patients are admitted to nursing facilities on a short-term basis for rehabilitation and convalescence. If that is the case, the fact that it will be a short-term stay must be emphasized to the patient, who otherwise may be thinking that admission to the facility may be his or her final living arrangement before death. If a long stay is contemplated, the social worker should emphasize the social and vibrant living environment of the facility and describe how the patient may become an active participant in that environment. Autonomy, privacy, and other features discussed in Chapter 8 should be highlighted. This is also an appropriate time for the social worker to discuss with the family which personal belongings may or may not be brought to the facility.

Any special instructions from the family should be passed on to the staff members who will be involved in the patient's care. Having a meeting with the associates on the nursing unit where the patient will be admitted is a good practice. Associates can be better prepared if they know in advance the patient's requirements, such as assistance with specific ADLs, incontinence, patient's preferences, or other special needs.

Before admission, the patient's room must be given special attention to ensure that everything is in order. Paying attention to minute details is critical. For example, a corner of the room may need additional cleaning, a wall may need some touch-up paint, or a leaky faucet in the bathroom may need fixing. On the day of admission, a flower arrangement in the room is always a welcoming sign.

## Admission Records

An important part of the admission process is ensuring that all pertinent medical records have been forwarded to the facility at the time of admission. If the patient is coming from the hospital or another nursing facility, the transfer of medical records is arranged with that institution. If the patient is coming from home or a residential facility, medical records must be obtained from the admitting physician's office. Records must include current physician's orders certifying the need for admission to the facility and orders for medications, nursing treatments, rehabilitation therapies, therapeutic diets, etc.

By the day of admission, the social worker should also complete the admission paperwork. The resident or the responsible party should sign an admission agreement, which is a contract between the facility and the patient (or his or her representative). Another important document contains the rights and responsibilities of patients. The patient or the representative must sign this document to acknowledge that they have received it. Other documents should also be completed as required by regulations and facility policies. Generally, facilities have packets of admission forms prepared in advance to ensure that all paperwork gets completed. A monetary deposit may also be required. Besides the admission packet, the social worker completes a social history of the patient. The social history and assessment are incorporated into the patient's individualized plan of care.

## Orientation

The purpose of orientation is to help new residents adjust to the facility and its routines. On the first day, the new resident should be introduced to a handful of key staff members, such as the unit's charge nurse, one or two nursing assistants, the activity director, and the dietician or food service director. The administrator may also stop by for a welcoming handshake. If the admission takes place close to meal time, the family or friends who are accompanying the patient should be invited to dine with the patient in a private area. The patient may, however, express a preference to dine alone in the room or go to the dining room. In any event, the patient's wishes should be respected. Every effort should be made to make the dining experience as pleasant as possible. During the first week, the social worker should contact the patient and staff regularly to find out how the patient is adjusting to his or her new surroundings. Communication with the family should also be maintained to ensure satisfaction with the services or to simply stay in touch. Such on-going contact can prevent conflicts down the road because it enables the facility to address minor issues as they arise. It also projects a caring attitude and allays family's anxiety.

An integral part of orientation is educating new residents about their rights and the decisions and choices they can make. Patients should be encouraged to participate in decision making so that they do not fall into a pattern of "learned helplessness" because of their dependent position. Staff interactions should be supportive. Within their limitations, patients should be allowed to do for themselves as much as possible.

## Discharge Planning

***Discharge planning*** is a process, not an event. The process includes decisions about when a patient may need to be discharged

from the facility and what may be needed to make a smooth transition from one level of care to another or from the facility to living independently. Discharge planning is more appropriately described as continuity-of-care planning (O'Hare, 1988). According to the continuity-of-care model (Figure 9–1), discharge planning begins when a patient is admitted to the nursing facility. Upon admission, assessment and care planning are approached with discharge outcomes in mind. Discharge planning takes a multidisciplinary approach. Associates from various disciplines, such as medical, nursing, dietary, rehabilitation, and social work, provide their input into the clinical and psychosocial progress made by the patient, their reevaluation of the patient's current status, and the patient's prognosis for discharge from the facility. Thus, discharge planning becomes a continuous process as illustrated in Figure 9–1. The family should also be involved in

**Figure 9-1** Continuity of Care Model

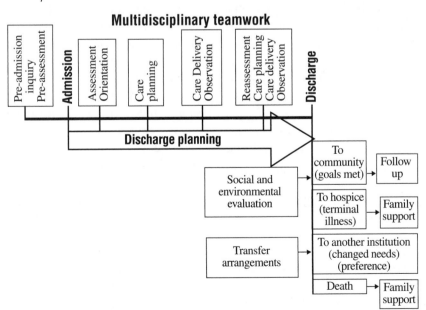

discharge decisions. The social worker is primarily responsible for coordinating the process.

Financial considerations, such as coverage under Medicare, are an important consideration in discharge planning. As discussed in Chapter 7, Medicare does not cover long-term stay in a skilled nursing facility. Length of stay depends on the patient's diagnosis, assessment, and rehabilitation potential. If additional length of stay in the facility is necessary after Medicare benefits have been exhausted, the patient must pay privately or, if he or she is eligible, apply for Medicaid. Otherwise, the multidisciplinary team must prepare for the patient's discharge from the facility. Facilities that are certified to serve Medicare and Medicaid patients are required to comply with certain discharge planning standards:

- The facility must provide sufficient preparation and orientation to residents to ensure safe and orderly transfer or discharge from the facility.

- Medical records should contain a final discharge summary that addresses the resident's post-discharge needs.

- Facilities are to develop a post-discharge plan of care, developed with the participation of the resident and his or her family, that will assist the resident in adjusting to his or her new living environment. This plan should include the assessment of continuing care needs and a plan to ensure that the individual's needs will be met after discharge from the facility into the community.

Ensuring continuity of care after discharge is a primary consideration in the facility's decision about where the patient will be discharged to and what ongoing services the patient may still need. If a patient will go back to his or her home, the social worker will do a social evaluation to determine whether adequate support services will be available to the patient. The facility may refer the patient to a home health agency, in which case the follow-up tasks are turned over to that agency. The key to successful discharge planning is to make arrangements so that all available resources are used to provide all the appropriate services that a patient needs after discharge. Follow-up is often essential to ensure that the arranged services are being delivered (Patchner & Patchner, 1991).

# Resident Council

A *resident council* is an independent semi-formal body made up of all residents who are able to participate. The purpose of this forum is to empower the residents so they can have a say in the facility's operations. An active resident council in the nursing facility helps promote resident autonomy and gives the residents a sense of control. This council is also a means of promoting self-esteem among residents who are able to participate in decision making concerning their own quality of life in the nursing home.

The social worker generally has the responsibility to assist the residents in organizing a council and to facilitate their regular meetings. For example, the social worker can assist the residents in electing council officers such as a president, a secretary, and a liaison for special events. Space should be designated where regular meetings can be held in privacy. Existence of the council should be publicized, and all residents who are able to participate should be encouraged to do so. Individual involvement, however, is totally voluntary. In some facilities, primary responsibility for the resident council is delegated to the activity director.

Because the resident council is a self-governing forum, the administrator and other associates attend the meetings only when invited. However, the administrator or other associates may ask the president for time when they can address the council on important issues and policies and provide follow-up reports on any previous concerns expressed or recommendations made by the council.

# Family Management

*Family management* is a proactive approach to minimize dissatisfaction and conflict by addressing family members' emotions about placing someone in a nursing home. Once a patient has been placed in a nursing facility, the patient's family becomes a secondary client. Treating the patient's family as a client and addressing their emotional needs is important for the overall well-being of the patient, who is the primary client. Maintaining the patient's family ties becomes an important task of social work. The first step in this process is for the facility's administration to promote a policy of unrestricted visiting hours for family members.

Families often do not anticipate and prepare for placing a loved one in a nursing facility. In many instances, admission to a nursing home is preceded by a family crisis such as the death of the patient's spouse or that of some other informal caregiver, sudden hospitalization for some unforeseen complication, an accident such as a fall that results in a hip fracture, or the relocation of adult children who may have been providing informal care. Such events can trigger rapid deterioration of a patient's physical health, mental health, or both. In such situations,

families may show signs of desperation, frustration, anger, guilt, or conflict. Also, some families have had a history of internal dissension and resentment. Such dysfunctional family relationships can greatly complicate the staff's ability to adequately deal with the patient's needs, because family members may perpetuate disagreements and interference with the facility's practices.

Greene (1982) advocated actively engaging the family in the preadmission inquiry process. Asking questions about the circumstances leading to the institutionalization, about family support and caring arrangements before admission, and about problems and stresses faced by the family and their methods of coping with them can provide valuable insights into family dynamics. Involvement of all key family members in this exploratory process may help the family better cope with the "crisis of institutionalization" because they may have never discussed such issues, and such a discussion may help them to clarify what they want. The social worker's role in this process is to show acceptance and empathy and to provide a supportive outlet for family members to express their true feelings but also face the realities of institutionalization.

During and after admission, reemphasizing the family's responsibility to stay involved is important provided, of course, that the relationship between the patient and the family has been positive. If a family is no longer involved in the patient's life, the patient may feel rejected by his or her family. Most families, fortunately, continue to visit, phone, write, and care for the patient following institutionalization.

The social worker's task becomes daunting indeed when bitterness and resentment have been, or remain present between the patient and family members. Trying appropriate interventions and setting reasonable goals and expectations become necessary to attempt mending dysfunctional family relationships, but only if these measures are in accord with the family's own wishes and their willingness to mend broken relationships (Greene, 1982). Otherwise, facility staff may have to accept the fact that tenuous family relationships exist and that staff members should be prepared for occasional tensions between the staff and family. On such occasions, it is critical for the facility's associates to remain politely and pleasantly communicative with the family members.

The social worker can also assist families with making their visits with the patient more meaningful and enjoyable, especially when the patient is disoriented, confused, or bedridden. To keep the family involved, the facility can find ways to establish exchange relationships with family members. For instance, family members can become volunteers or informally adopt some patient who does not have a family. The nursing home can also help families by scheduling support group meetings and educational seminars. Programs and classes about visiting skills, processes of aging, institutionalization procedures, nursing home financing, facility policies, the relative merits of assistance and independence, roles and functions of different departments in the facility, volunteering opportunities, relationships with caregivers, and other topics can be very informative and productive. Such educational programs can also provide an opportunity for families to meet key facility associates, some of whom they would otherwise never get to meet. These events help families better understand the challenges faced by the facility, and they also help family members form more realistic expectations of what the facility can and cannot

do. Family forums can also carry out an important advocacy role for the facility by expressing common concerns of the facility and family members. Although family members, on an individual basis, should be encouraged to express their dissatisfactions and complaints, educational seminars help focus on more productive issues. When creatively managed, these seminars can prevent family group sessions from turning into gripe sessions.

## Death and Terminal Illness

Death is a reality in health care facilities. Many long-term care patients spend their final days in a nursing facility and die there. Although the association of nursing homes with death is an unfortunate stereotype, how a nursing home addresses end-of-life issues and how it provides appropriate services for dying patients and their families is an important concern. Many patients will experience a natural death and pass away without any forewarning. Others may be terminally ill and may have, according to medical opinion, only a few months to live. Hospice care is an appropriate end-of-life service for many patients. However, the decision on whether to accept this alternative is left up to patients and their families. The social worker is generally responsible for counseling the patient and family members about the hospice alternative. The patient must also give written consent that any attempts to cure terminal illness or active interventions to save life will not be pursued, if that is what the patient wants.

Traditionally, death has been determined with the complete cessation of respiration and heartbeat. Brain death is the latest criterion for determining death (Knox, 1989). A physician also needs to pronounce or certify that a person has expired; hence, the patient's attending physician should be notified immediately. In some states, a registered nurse can make the pronouncement of death. It is also more appropriate for a nurse than a social worker to break the news to the family. Unless the family is present in the nursing home at the time of death, a simple but professional approach over the telephone would be, "It is with deep regret that I must inform you that (the patient's name) just passed away. I would like to extend my deepest sympathy to you and your family" (Geary, 1982). Depending on state laws, the death may also have to be reported to the police and coroner or medical examiner. At the time of admission, many nursing homes obtain information about funeral arrangements in case of death. If such information exists in the patient's medical record, the funeral home should be contacted to arrange for the removal of the body.

People may perceive death in a nursing home to be a normative event, meaning it is normal for old people to die. Such an overgeneralization, however, can become a stereotype. Even for the geriatric patient, death is an individual event. Geriatric patients have the same tensions, fears, and despair as any other age group facing death. Also, the family's reactions to death are not homogeneous (Kosberg, 1977).

Social workers, nurses, and even physicians are not always prepared to cope with death and dying. Yet, the social worker must be prepared to lend support to family members who have lost a loved one and also to caregivers who often feel the loss of a patient they have been intimately involved in caring for. Social workers can help terminally ill patients and their families by simply being present and using kind words. Many scholars have documented the need to help patients and families overcome the feelings of isolation and abandonment (Parry, 1989). Terminally ill patients generally go through the stages of denial and isolation as initial defense mechanisms; anger and resentment because of frustration and helplessness; depression emanating from feelings of guilt, failure, and despair; and, finally, acceptance of one's fate and gradual detachment from the surroundings, including close loved ones. Family members also go through similar stages (Kübler-Ross, 1997). Throughout this process, feelings of fear and anxiety may be expressed. Family members, on the other hand, may carry feelings of guilt. Stress and contention among family members may be observed. Social workers and other associates can do very little to help people overcome these emotions. But, they can be supportive and understanding throughout the process.

## For Further Thought

1. How can the three basic theories of aging discussed in this chapter be applied to promote individual autonomy of a patient residing in a nursing facility?

2. Describe some ways in which a nursing facility can promote interdependence to help residents feel useful and maintain their self-esteem.

## For Further Learning

The American Hospice Foundation supports programs that serve the needs of terminally ill and grieving individuals of all ages.

www.americanhospice.org

The National Association of Social Workers is the largest organization of professional social workers in the world, dedicated to improving the professional growth and development of its members, to creating and maintaining professional standards, and to advancing sound social policies.

www.naswdc.org

The National Council on Aging (NCOA) is a private, nonprofit organization that provides information, training, technical assistance, advocacy, and leadership in all aspects of aging services and issues. NCOA publications are available on topics such as lifelong learning, senior center services, adult day care, long-term care, financial issues, senior housing, rural issues, intergenerational programs, and volunteers in aging.

www.ncoa.org

## REFERENCES

AARP. 2001. In the middle: A report on multicultural boomers coping with family and aging issues. Washington, DC: AARP.

Agich, G.J. 1995. Actual autonomy and long-term care decision making. In L.B. McCullough and N.L. Wilson (eds.). *Long-Term Care Decisions: Ethical and Conceptual Dimensions* (pp. 113–136). Baltimore: Johns Hopkins University Press.

Allen, P.D., et al. 2007. Navigating conflict: A model for nursing home social workers. *Health & Social Work* 32, no. 3: 231–234.

Barger, K. 2004. Ethnocentrism. Retrieved January 2009 from http://www.iupui.edu/~anthkb/ethnocen.htm.

Conerly, K., & Tripathi, A. 2004. What is your conflict style? *Journal of Quality & Participation* 27, no. 2: 16–20.

Coulshed, V. 1991. *Social Work Practice: An Introduction*. London: MacMillan.

Dubois, B., & Miley, K.K. 1999. *Social Work: An Empowering Profession*. 3rd ed. Boston: Allyn and Bacon.

Geary, D.P. 1982. *How to Deliver Death News*. San Francisco: Compass Publishing Company.

German, P.S., et al. 1992. The role of mental morbidity in the nursing home experience. *The Gerontologist* 32, no. 2: 152–158.

Greene, R.R. 1982. Families and the nursing home social worker. *Social Work in Health Care* 7, no. 3: 57–67.

Harrigan, M.P., & Farmer, R.L. 1992. The myths and facts of aging. In R.L. Schneider and N.P. Kropf (eds.). *Gerontological Social Work: Knowledge, Service Settings, and Special Populations*. Chicago: Nelson-Hall Publishers.

Himes, C.L., et al. 1996. Living arrangements of minority elders. *Journal of Gerontology* 51B, no. 1: S42–S48.

Knox, J. 1989. *Death and Dying*. New York: Chelsea House Publishers.

Kosberg, J.I. 1977. Social work with geriatric patients and their families: Past neglect and present responsibilities. In E.R. Prichard et al. (eds.). *Social Work with the Dying Patient and the Family* (pp. 155–168). New York: Columbia University Press.

Kropf, N.P., & Hutchison, E.D. 1992. Effective practice with elderly clients. In R.L. Schneider and N.P. Kropf (eds.). *Gerontological Social Work: Knowledge, Service Settings, and Special Populations*. Chicago: Nelson-Hall Publishers.

Kübler-Ross, E. 1997. *On Death and Dying*. New York: Simon & Schuster.

Nelson, H.W. 2000. Injustice and conflict in nursing homes: Toward advocacy and exchange. *Journal of Aging Studies* 14, no. 1: 39–61.

Newman, B.M., & Newman, P.A. 1987. *Development Through Life: A Psychosocial Approach*. Chicago: Dorsey Press.

O'Hare, P.A. 1988. An overview of discharge planning. In P.A. O'Hare and M.A. Terry (eds.). *Discharge Planning: Strategies for Assuring Continuity of Care*. Rockville, MD: Aspen Publishers.

Pandya, S. 2005. Racial and ethnic differences among older adults in long-term care service use. AARP Public Policy Institute. Retrieved January 2009 from http://www.aarp.org/research/longtermcare/trends/fs119_ltc.html.

Parry, J.K. 1989. *Social Work Theory and Practice with the Terminally Ill*. New York: Haworth Press.

Patchner, M.A., & Patchner, L.S. 1991. Social work practice in nursing homes. In M.J. Holosko and M.D. Feit (eds.). *Social Work Practice with the Elderly*. Toronto: Canadian Scholars' Press.

Singh, D.A. 1997. *Nursing Home Administrators: Their Influence on Quality of Care*. New York: Garland Publishing.

Weintraub, D., et al. 2000. Racial differences in the prevalence of dementia among patients admitted to nursing homes. *Psychiatric Services* 51, no. 10: 1259–1264.

# Chapter 10

# Medical Care, Nursing, and Rehabilitation

## What You Will Learn

- Medical services for long-term care patients differ quite substantially from hospital care. The actual treatments are rendered by nurses in accordance with the attending physician's orders.

- Good patient care in nursing facilities is the product of teamwork in which a multidisciplinary team of professionals is responsible for patient assessment, care planning, and delivery of clinical services.

- A licensed physician must be appointed as the medical director, who should help implement best practice standards of care, offer medical advice and training, and represent the facility to the medical community.

- The director of nursing is responsible for ensuring that there is adequate staff, that the staff's skills remain current, that any patient care issues are promptly addressed, that patient care policies are updated as necessary, and that the nursing department functions smoothly. The nursing department hierarchy includes charge nurses. Larger facilities have an assistant director of nursing and/or nursing supervisors. Certified nursing assistants provide most of the hands-on nursing care to residents.

- Assessment is essential for evaluating the patient's strengths and needs for care. A plan of care for each resident is developed by a multidisciplinary team to specify goals and interventions.

- An effective infection control program focuses on prevention. It requires policies, screening of residents and associates, aseptic and antiseptic practices, standard and transmission-based precautions, surveillance for early detection, education, and prompt control when outbreaks occur.

- Falls can be caused by environmental hazards, physical effects of aging, and certain medical conditions and side effects of drugs. Numerous steps can be taken to prevent falls.

- Pressure ulcers can be traced to a number of causes. Preventive measures and early treatment are essential.

- In most instances, use of restraints does not promote safety. Their use is illegal, except when they are temporarily used according to a physician's orders.

- Many causes of urinary incontinence are reversible and transient. Toileting programs and other therapies should begin after the underlying causes have been treated. Catheters are indicated only when other measures have failed.

- Depression, delirium, and dementia can be difficult to diagnose. These problems are common in nursing homes, and they pose special challenges. Recognition of symptoms and caregiving strategies can help nursing home associates deal with them.

- Pharmacy services and pharmacy consultation are required by regulations. Facilities must have policies and procedures to safeguard controlled substances and to maintain an emergency kit. Psychotropic drugs present special challenges.

- Rehabilitation therapies can be restorative, maintenance, and adaptive.

The need for medical care, nursing services, and rehabilitation therapies is the main reason that patients are admitted to nursing homes, particularly when these services cannot be obtained adequately in community-based settings. Hence, these services form the core of services delivered in a long-term care facility. The other services interface with this clinical core.

# Medical Care

## Attending Physicians

Each patient's individual care is under the general direction of an attending physician, who is a general internist or family practitioner. The patient has the right to receive care from his or her own physician. Often, the patient has been under the care of a community-based physician for some time and, after being admitted to a nursing facility, may have the same physician follow up with medical care in the facility. Many physicians, however, avoid nursing home practice. In that case, the patient is given the option of selecting a physician from among those who make regular nursing home visits. Time constraints, rigid regulatory requirements, negative perceptions of nursing homes, litigation, and inadequate reimbursement for their services are some of the main reasons many physicians do not participate in nursing home care.

The medical services for long-term care patients differ quite substantially from hospital care, which focuses on acute episodes, medical procedures, and surgical interventions. Medical care in a nursing facility is more akin to primary care office-based practice, except that the physician must make regular visits to the nursing facility instead of the patient going to the physician's clinic. Typically, physician visits are infrequent, generally occurring every 30 days or longer, because most chronic conditions do not require frequent medical evaluation and treatment. Attending physicians diagnose medical problems and prescribe treatment and medications, but the actual treatments are rendered by nurses in accordance with the attending physician's orders. Nurses routinely monitor the patient's condition. Any substantial changes, nonresponse to treatments, or other negative observations are immediately relayed to the attending physician who then decides on the course of action to pursue. If a patient's condition changes for worse or some complication develops, most physicians require that the patient be transferred to a hospital.

Both physicians and nurses feel the need for shared communication to facilitate treatment decisions. Physicians must typically rely on nurses' skills. Nurses often express pride in their ability to judge clinical situations, report them to physicians by telephone, and get orders they need to give good care (Hanson et al., 2002).

Good patient care in nursing facilities is the product of teamwork in which a multidisciplinary—also referred to as "interdisciplinary"—team of professionals is responsible for patient assessment, care planning, and delivery of clinical services. The attending physician should be a member of this team. Medical oversight by the physician is critical, but it must incorporate the input from other disciplines such as nursing, rehabilitation, social work, dietetics, recreational therapy, and pharmacy. Another important aspect of medical care in nursing facilities is involvement of the patient and family in the plan of treatment.

The attending physician also makes referrals when specialized services are needed. The referral may be for transfer to a hospital for acute episodes that the nursing facility is not equipped to handle. Other types of common referrals are to medical specialists such as cardiologists, nephrologists, and orthopedists. Nursing facilities generally provide the more common types of specialty services through contracts with independent practitioners such as podiatrists, dermatologists, and ophthalmologists who may do routine screenings and evaluations in addition to receiving sporadic referrals.

## Medical Director

Nursing home regulations require the appointment of a licensed physician to function as the medical director. In all but a handful of large nursing homes, the administrator contracts with a community physician to fill the position on a part-time basis. In an average-sized facility, the medical director can be expected to spend 2 to 4 hours per week (Krein, 2003).

The medical director reports to the administrator but has an advisory relationship with the rest of the organization (see Figure III–1 in the Part III opening text). Through regular communications with the medical director, the administrator can keep abreast of major patient care issues in the facility. On the other hand, by regularly communicating with the administrator, the medical director can remain in touch with administrative policies and management issues that may have a bearing on patient care services.

In spite of the social and professional stigma that is sometimes associated with working in nursing homes, physicians report that caring for nursing home residents is gratifying and meaningful work. In a qualitative study conducted by medical students, physicians working in nursing homes reported that relationships with residents, families, and staff members; interesting and meaningful patient care; and autonomy were the most positive aspects of their role. Less desirable aspects included staff turnover, difficult expectations, and administrative issues (Bern-Klug et al., 2003). This type of information about what physicians value about their work in nursing facilities can help administrators structure more desirable roles and attract more physicians to meet the growing demand in nursing homes.

## Personal Traits and Qualifications

The medical director should be a team player with good interpersonal and conflict-resolution skills that will enable him or her to work effectively with the multidisciplinary team. He or she should have a flexible nature and be a good listener, with tolerance for addressing regulatory issues (Krein, 2003).

The medical director may have either the MD or the DO degree (see Chapter 3 for differences and similarities between them). Ideally, the medical director should be a geriatrician, but physicians who have this kind of specialization are rare. The next best choice is to have someone who has substantial experience in geriatric medicine or someone who has an interest in the field and is committed to acquiring the necessary knowledge and skills through continuing education. *Geriatrics* is a specialized area of medicine that deals with the special health problems faced by the elderly. Knowledge of geriatrics is essential for effectively treating a wide array of medical conditions in a diverse elderly population residing in nursing homes.

An important aspect of geriatric medicine focuses on managing chronic health problems and comorbidities that require simultaneous interventions. Comorbidities present special medical challenges in long-term care. For example, when congestive heart failure and chronic obstructive pulmonary disease are both present in the same patient, the treatment for one condition worsens the other (Peck, 2001). Adverse drug interactions can occur, presenting serious consequences. It is also important to distinguish between changes that normally accompany aging and symptoms of illness that are treatable. Treatable medical conditions such as joint pain are sometimes trivialized as normal age-related problems. Similarly, delirium and dementia (discussed later) are not necessarily natural symptoms of old age but may be manifestations of hypothyroidism, multiple emboli, fluid and electrolyte imbalance, or drug toxicity (Levenson, 1985). Numerous other symptoms common in the elderly are frequently misdiagnosed and incorrectly treated. Other factors should also be taken into account. The elderly may show different responses to prescription drugs than younger people. Because the elderly may have reduced tolerance to some drugs, inadvertent overdose may be more likely in elderly patients than in younger ones. Hence, a judicious medical approach becomes necessary. Otherwise, *iatrogenic* problems, that is, complications caused by medical treatment, are the likely results. Hydration and nutrition are of special concern when caring for the elderly patient. Multivitamins or special food supplements may have to be prescribed, particularly when regular food intake is inadequate. Certain organ functions may have declined, leading to impaired metabolism. Loss of skin turgor can lead to skin breakdown and development of pressure ulcers, which are often, although not always, preventable. Depression or other psychological disorders may accompany physical conditions. Dementia, delirium, and depression present symptoms that are quite similar, but each requires a different medical approach. Geriatric medicine also includes palliative care during terminal illness.

The American Medical Directors Association (AMDA) has developed the Curriculum on Geriatric Clinical Practice in Long-Term Care to train attending physicians in both administrative and clinical management. AMDA also offers certification as a Certified Medical Director based on demonstrated competence in clinical medicine and medical direction/administrative medicine in long-term care. A number of residency programs in internal medicine and family practice also provide additional training in geriatric medicine. The American Board of Internal Medicine and the American Board of Family Practice confer a Certificate of Added Qualification in Geriatric Medicine on physicians who complete this training and pass the examination. However, only a few physicians hold such certification.

## Functions

The medical director functions as a key consultant to the nursing facility on almost all aspects of patient care. Not uncommonly, the medical director is also the attending physician for most patients in a facility. As an attending physician, the medical director is in a position to obtain first-hand knowledge of the adequacy and appropriateness of clinical care provided to the patients and to become involved in consultations to improve quality of care for all residents.

In light of anti-kickback legislation (see Chapter 7), the medical director should be paid fair compensation for his or her administrative responsibilities. The medical director's involvement as an attending physician must be a completely separate practice as far as reimbursement and compensation are concerned.

The main functions of the medical director can be classified into four essential roles:

- Oversight.
- Advisory.
- Teaching.
- Representative.

### Oversight Role

The medical director must help implement evidence-based best practice standards. As the chief medical officer for the facility, the medical director helps ensure that clinical services meet or exceed established standards and also helps identify potential risks. Standards of care are defined in written policies and procedures. Some examples of clinical practices in which policies and procedures are necessary include infection control practices, minimizing the use of indwelling urinary catheters, catheterization procedures, obtaining urine and stool specimens, isolation practices, handling contaminated linen, preventing and treating pressure ulcers, disease-specific precautions (e.g., HIV and hepatitis), immunizations for residents and staff members, minimizing use of restraints, preventing falls, and investigating accidents or incidents. The medical director should also assist the facility with the oversight of infection control, vaccination programs, efforts to reduce the risk of falls and use of restraints, adequacy of nutrition, hydration and skin integrity programs, and quality improvement analysis and processes (Krein, 2003).

Regular rounds, observations, and attentiveness to any patient care concerns expressed by patients, associates, and family members are generally the means of monitoring the adequacy of clinical care. Any breakdowns in the facility's skill capacity must be addressed with the administrator. Such breakdowns generally occur when the facility experiences turnover of key staff, or when it adds a new service.

## Advisory Role

The medical director's advisory role directly stems from his or her effectiveness in carrying out the oversight role. Admission policies should be periodically reviewed to ensure that the facility has adequate skill capacity to deliver services to the types of patients being admitted. Similarly, other policies and procedures should be periodically reviewed to ensure that they remain current. The medical director also functions as an advisor to the various committees such as the infection control committee, quality improvement committee, utilization review committee, medical records committee, pharmaceutical review committee, safety committee, and ethics committee. Most of these committees meet once a quarter, and, for the sake of efficiency, meetings of the various committees are often combined.

## Teaching Role

The medical director plays an active role in staff training and can be very influential in establishing a professional and caring culture in the organization (Krein, 2003). This role is mostly carried out informally during routine interactions with caregivers or while making bedside rounds with nurses. Occasionally, the medical director may also be invited to make presentations in formal training sessions. Communicating with families and educating them about issues that are commonly misunderstood and the medical director's participation in family seminars can help establish better relationships among the patients, families, and associates.

## Representative Role

The medical director is the facility's representative to the medical community. During interactions with colleagues, he or she should function as the facility's advocate and as an expert on medical care issues in long-term care in general. Nursing facilities often have to address regulatory noncompliance issues related to the required frequency of visits and documentation with attending physicians. Even though noninterference with the practice of medicine is a well-recognized professional code of conduct, and although physicians have, as a result, developed a high degree of autonomy, a medical director's collegial influence can go a long way in helping the facility gain compliance from attending physicians. On the other hand, the medical director does have a responsibility to oversee that the delivery of medical care by other physicians is adequate and appropriate. In consultation with the administrator, he or she may have to take steps if attending physicians do not comply with basic standards of medical practice. One remedy is to advise and assist the patient in choosing another physician. Nursing facilities also feel the frustration when medical information does not follow a patient at the time he or she moves from a hospital to the nursing home. The medical director should meet with the appropriate hospital personnel and establish mutually agreed-upon transfer criteria and information-sharing protocols (Krein, 2003).

# Nursing Services

Nursing is the largest department, employing about 70% of the nursing home associates. Nursing services are also the central hub, and the nursing staff generally has the most interaction with residents and their families. But nursing's central role should not be interpreted as dominant over other services. The best patient care can be delivered only when each discipline—including nursing—recognizes the interdependency between the various departments and services. Organization of the nursing department is depicted in Figure III–1, but variations do exist.

## Nursing Administration

The nursing department is headed by a director of nursing (DON). The DON is generally supported by an assistant director of nursing (ADON), who may be responsible for staffing and also function as the in-service director (director of training) in average-size nursing homes. In larger facilities, an alternative to the ADON is to have a nursing supervisor on each shift—three supervisors covering the three shifts—in which case, a separate in-service director's position would be necessary. If the facility operates a nursing assistant (nurse aide) training program, the in-service director must be a registered nurse (RN). Because resident assessment has become a critical driver of the Medicare prospective payment system (discussed in Chapter 7), most average-size facilities also have a RN in

the position of resident assessment coordinator. This position, as well as the in-service director, may report to either the DON or the administrator.

## Director of Nursing

The DON has a position of substantial responsibility. In most facilities, the position is second only to that of the administrator. Actually, the DON is often in charge of the facility during the administrator's absence. In large nursing homes where an assistant administrator may be employed, there is sometimes a direct chain of command between the administrator and the DON, whereas the assistant administrator may have direct responsibility for the remaining departments. Effectively managed nursing facilities have a triad relationship among the administrator, the medical director, and the DON, and this triad is involved in making many top-level evaluations and decisions regarding the facility's operation.

## Skills, Qualifications, and Functions

The DON must be an RN, and the position requires a composite of clinical and management skills. However, DONs who have formal training in both nursing and management are rare. Most acquire management skills through experience, although management skill development through continuing education, seminars, or college-level courses is highly recommended. On the clinical side, some DONs possess a bachelor's degree in nursing, but many have nursing preparation through a two-year associate's degree or an RN diploma. A small number have master's degrees. Some have completed certification requirements in gerontology, but many have not. Regardless of their level of clinical preparation, however, DONs—like other high-level clinical personnel—must be knowledgeable in gerontology and geriatric care.

The DON is not a direct caregiver but mainly performs administrative and supervisory functions, which at times can be quite challenging. The main responsibilities of this position can be summarized under five main categories:

- Staffing.
- Training.
- Patient care.
- Policy.
- Administration.

## Staffing

The DON is responsible for ensuring that the nursing units are adequately staffed and that the nursing personnel are adequately trained. Staffing can pose some daunting challenges, because depending on labor-market conditions, nurses may be in short supply. Recruiting and retaining qualified staff members is often difficult, and a typical facility experiences high turnover and absenteeism among certified nursing assistants (CNAs). Staff shortages coupled with the need to have adequate staff coverage 24 hours a day, 7 days a week present special challenges in staffing and scheduling. Large facilities often designate a full-time person to the tasks of recruiting and scheduling CNAs.

## Training

The DON must ensure adequate levels of skill competency among the nursing staff. Needs for individual as well as group training should be evaluated periodically. Many fa-

cilities also operate CNA training programs. Regulations require that these programs be under the DON's general supervision. The DON, however, is not permitted to do the actual training, which should be delegated to a qualified nurse instructor. To provide well-rounded instruction, professionals from other disciplines such as the medical director, physical and occupational therapists, dietician, pharmacist, social worker, activities director, fire and safety expert, and nursing home administrator should also be included. The law prohibits states from approving nurse aide training programs at facilities found to have substandard quality of care or that have been subject to certain enforcement actions such as civil monetary penalties.

## Patient Care

The DON oversees timely execution of patient assessments, development of an individualized plan of care for each patient, and the delivery of nursing care. The nursing staff looks to the DON for leadership and expertise when care-related problems arise. The DON also plays a vital coordinating role with attending physicians by facilitating timely visits and ensuring that they receive the necessary nursing support.

## Policy

The DON is an active participant in the various patient care committees, such as the infection control committee, quality improvement committee, utilization review committee, medical records committee, pharmaceutical review committee, safety committee, and ethics committee. The DON's input into the policy and decision-making process is often indispensable. The DON generally provides information and data for evaluation and deliberation by the various committees. At a minimum, policies and procedures for nursing services must be established to comply with the state licensure regulations and Medicaid and Medicare certification requirements. However, this area of responsibility must extend beyond the minimum requirements with the objective of continuous improvement in the quality of patient care. The facility's nursing care policies, procedures, and practice guidelines constitute the standards of patient care delivery. They are compiled into a nursing policies and procedures manual, which is used as a reference and training resource for new associates. This manual becomes a living document that is updated as policies and practices are revised.

### Administration

The DON is responsible for the effective management of the nursing department. The DON is also involved in a variety of administrative tasks that free up the caregivers so that they can devote their time and energy to delivering patient care. Although, as a matter of routine, the DON is in the facility during regular business hours, some variation from routine is necessary so that the DON has some ongoing contact with the staff, patients, and families during evenings, nights, and weekends. Many families can visit the facility only during evenings or weekends. Therefore, charge nurses on the evening and weekend shifts should be trained to address family concerns. A communication system should be implemented so that family complaints and concerns regarding patient care are related to the DON. On the other hand, periodic availability of the DON during nonroutine hours can lend support to the nursing staff, and contact with families can help resolve issues before they turn into bigger problems. Having a large staff, and a preponderance of licensed practical (vocational) nurses (LPNs/LVNs) in relation to RNs, the DON is frequently involved in ongoing training and consultation and in handling staff-related issues that include disciplinary action for nonperformance of duties.

## Nursing Organization

A nursing facility's physical structure, constituting nursing units and nursing stations, and the criteria for staffing were discussed in Chapter 8. The nursing units form the basis for establishing the organizational structure of the department, with each nursing unit headed by a charge nurse. Nursing home regulations require a charge nurse, who can be an RN or an LPN/LVN, on each tour of duty. Regulations also require the facility to employ an RN for eight consecutive hours per day, seven days per week. The DON is prohibited from serving as a charge nurse unless the facility has an average daily occupancy of 60 or fewer residents (Gittler, 2008).

Charge nurses report to the nursing supervisors, the ADON, or the DON, depending on how the nursing department is organized. In most facilities of moderate size, charge nurses report directly to the DON. Charge nurses are responsible for assessing patient needs and planning care, supervising associates on the unit, communicating with physicians and family members regarding patient care issues, and supervising patient care delivery.

Qualifications of the two main categories of nurses employed in long-term care facilities were discussed in Chapter 3. The number of nurses on each nursing unit, skill mix of nurses (ratio of RNs to LPNs/LVNs), and the ratio of CNAs to patients on each shift are dictated by the number of patients and the level of clinical care required by the patients. Most RNs working in long-term care are graduates of hospital-based diploma programs or two-year associate's degree (ADN) programs. RNs are generally responsible for patient assessment, care planning, and quality assessment. LPNs render treatments and administer medications. Several states allow the routine administration of medications by specially trained medication aides (or medication technicians) under the general supervision of licensed nurses. Use of qualified medication aides or technicians can relieve nurses, enabling them to devote their time to other nursing care and monitoring functions.

CNAs provide most of the hands-on nursing care to residents. To deliver effective care, CNAs must possess basic nursing skills that include taking vital signs such as temperature, pulse rate, and blood pressure; measuring height and weight; recognizing abnormal changes in body functions such as urine output and bowel function; reporting changes in patient's condition to the charge nurse; and documenting observations. CNAs assist patients with their ADLs and personal care such as bathing, dressing, grooming, oral hygiene, eating assistance, hydration, transferring, positioning, turning, toileting assistance, cleaning up and drying after incontinence, and changing bed linens. CNAs also provide maintenance rehabilitation such as range of motion exercises, bowel and bladder training, and use of assistive devices to promote independence. Some facilities have specially trained rehabilitation aides to carry out maintenance rehabilitation functions. CNAs are also required to meet the residents' mental health and social needs by responding to changes in behavior, providing family support, and caring for residents with dementia or other special needs such as physical hand-

icaps. The nature of these tasks requires CNAs to have appropriate training in how to communicate with residents and visiting family members. In addition, CNAs must be trained in infection control practices; they must be prepared to use fire and safety procedures in case of an emergency; and they must understand how to preserve and promote the patients' rights to privacy, confidentiality, autonomy, dignity, and freedom from abuse and neglect.

# Patient Assessment and Care Planning

Since 1998, a facility participating in the Medicare and Medicaid programs is required to conduct a comprehensive resident assessment for each individual patient. The primary tool used in patient assessment is the Minimum Data Set (MDS) [see Appendix 7–I in Chapter 7]. Assessment can be regarded as the first step in patient care planning and the delivery of patient care. *Assessment* is defined as the process through which health care professionals attempt to reliably characterize the patient's physical health, functional abilities, cognitive functioning, psychological state, social well-being, and past and current use of formal services (Kane 1995). Patient assessment serves two major purposes:

1. The process helps the facility staff learn about the resident's strengths, problems, and needs. These strengths and needs are subsequently addressed in the individualized plan of care for the resident.

2. It enables the staff to track important changes in the patient's overall status and to revise care plans accordingly.

Comprehensive patient assessment requires a multidisciplinary approach. Although the nursing department often coordinates and oversees the process, input from other disciplines such as social services, activities, dietary, and rehabilitation are also necessary. Included in the formal assessment are history and physical information obtained from the admitting physician. The patient's and family's involvement in the assessment and care planning process have become increasingly more important because they can furnish nonmedical information vital to holistic care. Perhaps the most significant advance in MDS 3.0 is the use of direct interview items to consistently elicit the resident's input. This is because often the most accurate way to assess many topics is to ask the resident directly. Studies have shown that for areas such as cognition, mood, preferences, and pain, staff or family impressions often fail to capture the resident's real condition or preferences (Saliba & Buchanan, 2008).

At the time the manuscript for this second edition was prepared, it was unclear whether the Resident Assessment Protocols (RAPs) would be retained when MDS 3.0 is implemented sometime in 2009. RAPs were discussed in the first edition of this book. Subsequently, clinicians informed the Centers for Medicare and Medicaid Services (CMS) that the use of RAPs had been confusing and replete with problems and that it did not promote multidisciplinary care planning. A survey conducted by the American Health Care Association and a RAP workshop meeting conducted by the Agency for Healthcare Research and Quality confirmed that the RAPs in their current form were not being used, except for paper compliance, and were not helpful to the majority of nursing home interdisciplinary teams.

## Plan of Care

Nursing facilities are mandated by regulations to prepare a comprehensive plan of care (or care plan) for each resident within seven days of completing the assessment. A *plan of care* is a written plan developed through team participation of various professional disciplines to clearly outline how each identified need of a given patient will be addressed and what specific goals will be accomplished. It is like a blueprint that guides the staff in providing routine interventions necessary for accomplishing clinical goals for a specific patient. Examples of intervention include nursing treatments, medications, special diets, rehabilitation therapies, social interventions, and participation in recreational activities. A professional staff member such as an RN or social worker is assigned the responsibility of scheduling care plan meetings and inviting representatives from the various disciplines to participate and share their input.

The plan of care is based on the patient's limitations, strengths, and needs ascertained by the assessment process. It specifies approaches for addressing the problems and needs, it stipulates what action various disciplines will take, and it establishes goals against which progress will be evaluated. A care plan is comprehensive. It must address the multiple issues faced by elderly patients. Because physical, psychosocial, emotional, and spiritual issues must be addressed in a holistic manner, care planning requires a multidisciplinary approach.

As the plan of care is carried out, each member of the multidisciplinary team adds progress notes to the patient's medical record. Progress made, or lack thereof, in achieving the established goals is evaluated over time and is carefully documented. The progress evaluations provide further guidance in establishing new goals and in deciding which interventions should be discontinued, modified, or added. Care plans are generally reviewed and revised every 60 to 90 days, or when a major change has occurred in the patient's condition.

# Infection Control

Infections are a common problem in health care settings. The elderly in particular are predisposed to various types of infections because of weakened immune systems. In addition, cognitive impairments among many nursing home residents may compromise their basic sanitary habits such as hand-washing and personal hygiene, passing disease-causing bacteria to other people. Also, residents live in close proximity to others, come in contact with staff and visitors, and are served food and beverages from a common source. Such an environment facilitates both the introduction and subsequent transmission of certain infectious agents in a vulnerable population (Strausbaugh et al., 2003).

In nursing homes, most infections affect the urinary tract, respiratory tract, skin and soft tissues, or gastrointestinal tract (Ouslander et al., 1997). Complications resulting from infections constitute the main reason for transferring patients from a long-term care facility to an acute care hospital. Hence, preventing and containing infections should be a primary concern. Because overuse of antibiotics in recent years has rendered certain bacterial and viral strains resistant to drugs, treating some infections is presenting major medical challenges. Multi-drug resistant organisms (MDROs) are becoming common in nursing facilities. These microbes include methicillin-resistant *Staphylococcus aureus* (MRSA) and vancomycin-resistant enterococci (VRE), as well as strains of Streptococcus pneumoniae, Pseudomonas spp., Neisseria gonorrhea, Salmonella spp., and others (Sharbaugh, 2003). Of these, MRSA and VRE are the most common. MRSA causes "staph" infections that are resistant to treatment with common antibiotics such as methicillin, penicillin, oxacillin, and amoxicillin. MRSA can cause serious and potentially life-threatening infections, such as bloodstream infections and pneumonia. VRE are bacteria that live in the intestines and in the female genital tract and become resistant to the antibiotic vancomycin. These bacteria can cause infections of the urinary tract, the bloodstream, or wounds. The main mode of transmission to other patients for both MRSA and VRE is through unwashed hands. Hence, hand hygiene is the primary preventive vehicle.

State and federal regulations require nursing facilities to implement infection control programs. *Infection control* is a comprehensive program to prevent the transmission of infections protecting the residents, the staff, and visitors from contracting infections while in the facility. An effective infection control program focuses on prevention.

Generally, the task of surveillance and monitoring of infections is assigned to a registered nurse, such as the ADON. This individual is often called the *infection control practitioner (ICP)*. But infection control is not merely a nursing responsibility. An effective program requires the involvement of all departments. In the following sections, the main features of an effective infection control program are described:

- Policies and procedures.
- Screening.

- Infection control practices.
- Surveillance.
- Education.
- Control of infectious outbreaks.

## Policies and Procedures

The facility should develop and update infection control policies and procedures in consultation with the infection control committee. The policies should cover areas such as admission and transfer of residents, employee health, immunizations, guidelines for visitors, housekeeping practices, laundry procedures, food preparation, food poisoning, procedures for cleaning and sterilizing equipment, isolation procedures, waste disposal, removal of biohazardous waste, pest control, detection and control of infection outbreaks, and staff education. Nursing practices such as caring for wounds, inserting catheters, and collecting urine specimens require sterile techniques, which should be outlined in written procedures.

## Screening

The patient's history and physical at the time of admission should be carefully reviewed for the presence of any infections or contagious disease. Associates who show symptoms of transmissible infections, such as influenza or staphylococcus infection, should not come to work until they are declared safe to return.

New tuberculosis (TB) cases, caused by bacteria called *mycobacterium tuberculosis*, occur more frequently among the elderly than among younger age groups, except those infected with the human immunodeficiency virus (HIV). A survey of 15,379 reported cases in 29 states indicated that the incidence

(i.e., new cases) of TB among nursing home residents was 39.2 cases per 100,000 population compared with 21.5 cases per 100,000 population among elderly persons living in the community. In other words, living in a nursing home approximately doubles a patient's risk of developing TB. Also, the TB case rate for nursing home employees was three times higher than the rate expected for other employed adults of similar age, race, and gender (CDC, 1990).

All patients admitted to nursing homes must be screened for TB in accordance with state health department guidelines. All associates must have an initial physical examination at the time of employment and subsequent annual physicals to screen for any infectious diseases. Screening for TB is done by using a tuberculin skin test such as the Mantoux test, which uses TB antigens (TB protein) called purified protein derivative (PPD). In case of a positive test, further testing such as a chest X-ray is necessary.

## Infection Control Practices

*Asepsis*, the absence of harmful microorganisms called *pathogens*, requires practicing clean procedures. The primary goal of asepsis is to prevent cross-contamination, that is, transferring pathogens from soiled surfaces to clean ones. Frequently washing hands with soap and clean water is among the most important aseptic practices but is often neglected. Hand hygiene should also incorporate hand *antisepsis*: removing or destroying microorganisms. Hand antisepsis can be achieved by using an alcohol-based hand rub, which is waterless and therefore does not require a sink and paper towels. The microbe-killing action of an alcohol-based hand rub is twice as fast as that of traditional hand-washing. Alcohol rubs have also been proven to be gentler on the hands than soap and water because they contain emollients or moisturizers, which help the skin retain more of its natural water content, which soap and water often strip away (Hand hygiene, 2001).

Other aseptic practices include washing food and utensils in the kitchen before cooking, cleaning food preparation surfaces, separating and properly handling clean and soiled linens, and removing trash with specific techniques. Infection control training and practices are particularly important for nursing staff members, who are frequently exposed to soil and body wastes. They also provide patient care and then touch clean surfaces. Without frequent hand-washing in between clean and soiled contact, they can spread disease-causing pathogens. The environment should also be protected while transporting trash or soiled linens. All trash must be properly bagged and placed in sealed containers. Similarly, soiled linens should be placed in sealed containers when they are transported through the facility.

Isolation precautions constitute another important aspect of infection control. Two types of isolation precautions are used (Grubbs & Blasband, 2000):

- Standard precautions.
- Transmission-based precautions.

*Standard precautions (SPs)*, previously called universal precautions, are used when caring for all residents, regardless of whether or not they have an infectious disease. SPs are designed to protect caregivers from infection through exposure to blood, body fluids, and body substances. It is assumed that all body fluids are potentially infectious. The precautions include wearing gloves during patient care, wearing gowns when the caregiver's clothing may come in contact with body fluids, and wearing masks and protective eye wear when body fluids may splash. SPs also include preventing injuries and infections from sharps, such as needles and blades, which must be disposed of in appropriately marked sharps containers.

*Transmission-based precautions* are required during care for residents who may have a communicable disease. Transmission-based precautions are used in addition to standard precautions. The facility must establish procedures for visitors to report to the nursing station before visiting patients for whom transmission-based precautions are indicated.

## Surveillance

Surveillance for *nosocomial* infections—infections caused by the process of health care delivery—has been clearly established as a key element of all infection control programs (Stevenson, 1999). *Surveillance* refers to identifying and reporting all cases of infection in the facility and identifying all infected residents and staff (CDC, 1990). The purpose is early detection that would allow for timely interventions to check the spread of infections. Surveillance may give early warning about the outbreak of an epidemic. A strong surveillance program requires all nursing staff members to be vigilant and report all cases of infection.

## Education

Ongoing education of staff and visitors about infection control is a critical preventive measure. All staff members in the facility should participate in infection control training. These educational programs should be repeated often, particularly given the high staff turnover common in nursing homes.

## Control of Infectious Outbreaks

An *epidemic* is defined as the excessive prevalence of a negative health condition in the facility. Epidemic outbreaks are noted by clustered cases of symptoms such as diarrhea, urinary tract infections, influenza, or scabies (Garibaldi et al., 1981). Influenza outbreaks, for example, can lead to substantial morbidity and mortality among the elderly when preventive measures are not rapidly deployed. Influenza outbreaks can be prevented by annual flu shots for residents and associates.

Prompt control of any outbreaks is essential. The medical director should work closely with the nursing staff in identifying the pathogen, preventing its spread, treating the affected patients and staff members, and, if necessary, reporting and coordinating recommended measures with the appropriate public health agency.

Access to a laboratory must be available to perform rapid antigen testing, and influenza antiviral medication must be available to control outbreaks. The DON-administrator-medical director triad should work together to isolate and address any outbreaks as swiftly as possible. The local health department is also typically involved in assisting the facility with a systematic approach to controlling infectious outbreaks.

## Special Areas of Nursing Care Management

Nursing care deals with numerous health conditions found in a diverse elderly population. Some of these conditions require special attention from caregivers and nursing managers. The topics discussed in this section also have a great deal of relevance for improving the quality of patient care.

## Falls and Fall Prevention

Injuries sustained from falls, and subsequent decline in the ability to carry out daily activities, are one reason nursing home placement becomes necessary in the first place. In nursing homes, approximately 50% of the residents fall each year (Yarme and Yarme, 2001), and an estimated 10% of falls result in serious injury (Tinetti, 2003). Fall-related injuries result in substantial legal liability for the nursing facility, as well as pain, suffering, loss of function, and death among residents. Carroll et al. (2008) estimated the cost of falls to be about $6,300 per resident per year in long-term care facilities. About 60% of this amount was attributed to hospitalization costs. Among the elderly who are admitted to hospitals after falling, only about half remain alive a year later. Recovery from fall-related injuries is slow in older persons, which in turn increases the risk of subsequent falls (Rubenstein, 2006). Psychological factors such as anxiety and depression may follow.

From an evaluation of 12 studies that carefully investigated and assigned a "most likely" cause for the falls among the elderly (Rubenstein, 2006), it was concluded that roughly one-third of the falls can be attributed to environmental factors such as poor lighting, wet floors, loose objects, incorrect bed height, and improperly fitted or maintained wheelchairs. According to Rubenstein, many falls attributed to environment-related accidents really stem from the interaction between identifiable environmental hazards and increased individual susceptibility from the effects of age and disease. The second most common cause was related to gait problems, balance disorders, and weakness. This was followed by dizziness, which is a very common symptom among the elderly. Other specific causes of falls include disorders of the central nervous system, cognitive deficits, poor vision, drug side effects, anemia, unstable joints, and severe osteoporosis. The growing use of antidepressants in nursing homes also increases the risk of falls (Messinger-Rapport et al., 2007).

A fall prevention program begins with evaluating potential risks for falling. At a very basic level, a person with a history of falls is likely to fall again, but other risk factors may be discovered in a person who has never fallen before. These risk factors include muscle weakness, poor balance, gait deficit, visual deficit, limited mobility, cognitive impairment, impaired functional status, and postural hypotension (Rubenstein, 2006).

Nursing interventions—such as working with new residents until they become properly oriented to where the bed is in relation to the chair and the bathroom, teaching residents how to safely navigate from the bed to the bathroom and back, strength training to improve gait and balance, and monitoring and supervision by the nursing staff—can all play a role in preventing falls. In collaboration with the nursing staff, the physical therapist should evaluate whether assistive devices are needed for safe ambulation. Staff members should monitor the patient's ability to use them properly during ambulation and transfer, and provide training as necessary. One study reported that almost half of the falls in nursing homes occur on the 3 p.m. to 11 p.m. shift. Adding one staff member on this shift, repositioning room furniture, and adding a physical activity program on that shift curtailed the total number of falls by 38% and the total number

of fractures by 50% (Hofmann et al., 2003). In some cases, it may be necessary to reduce or withdraw certain drugs that are potentially related to falls through their sedating, hypotensive, or cognitive effects (Lipsitz et al., 1997).

Safety of the environment is one of the key elements in fall prevention. Nursing facilities, as a rule, already have railings in hallways, grab bars in bathrooms, and other required safety adaptations. However, a program should be in place to routinely check these devices for proper maintenance and repairs. Janitorial procedures should be evaluated for resident safety during cleaning and mopping floors and during carpet vacuuming or floor buffing, when long electric cords running through hallways can become a tripping hazard. Patient incontinence can leave urine puddles, which may not be easy for other patients to detect. The nursing staff should be trained to observe such hazardous conditions and promptly clean up the affected areas.

In patient rooms, a clearly visible passage should be maintained from the bed and chair to the bathroom. Bed height should be adjusted, or protective floor pads used, for those who may roll over and fall during sleep. For high-risk patients, it may be necessary to put the mattress on the floor. High-risk patients may also be fitted with hip pads to prevent hip fractures from falls. An alarm system can also be installed to alert staff when a high-risk patient tries to get out of bed.

## Pressure Ulcers

A ***pressure ulcer***, also called a pressure sore or decubitus ulcer, is a localized area of soft-tissue injury resulting from compression between a bony prominence and an external surface (Smith, 1996). Pressure on the skin is normal when a person is sitting or lying down.

With aging, however, the skin tissue develops reduced tolerance for pressure. Limited ability to change position while in bed or a wheelchair that causes prolonged pressure against bony prominences, friction against wrinkled bed sheets or objects such as casts and braces, exposure to moisture from urine or feces, and poor nutrition (especially low calorie and protein intake) can all play a part in forming pressure ulcers. Neurological and cardiovascular disease can predispose the elderly to sores (Bennett, 1992).

Once formed, pressure ulcers are slow to heal. They are also susceptible to infections, a vulnerability that can lead to further complications such as permanent disability and even death (Bliss, 1992). Therefore, prevention and early treatment are essential features of pressure ulcer management. Pressure ulcer prevention begins with proper nutrition and hydration. Basic care routines such as proper bed-making, positioning the patient properly while sitting or lying down, use of pads and pillows to relieve pressure, repositioning at least once every two hours, keeping the patient clean and dry, and skin care are important in preventing pressure ulcers. At least once a day, skin should be systematically inspected in patients at risk. The skin should be cleansed at regular intervals and whenever it is soiled. Hot water and drying soaps should be avoided for skin care. Areas of redness over bony prominences should not be massaged or rubbed. To treat dry, flaky, scaly skin, optimum environmental humidity should be maintained and moisturizers used. Mobility through rehabilitation should be encouraged (Bergstrom, 1997). Various types of pressure-relieving devices are also available and should be used as necessary.

Pressure ulcers are categorized into four stages according to the depth of tissue destruction (Exhibit 10–1). Once developed, there can be rapid deterioration. Stage I is the beginning stage with a notable discoloration of the skin. This stage is actually not a true ulcer, because the skin is intact. However, a stage I pressure area increases the risk of additional ulcers by tenfold (Allman, 1999), and stage I can be difficult to recognize in persons with dark skin (Dharmarajan & Ahmed, 2003). At stage IV, the most advanced stage, muscle or bone become exposed. Treatment is to be directed by the attending physician. Depending on their stage, treatment may include bed rest in a special pressure-relieving bed, use of anti-inflammatory drugs, antibiotics, special dressings called

**Exhibit 10–1**  Pressure Ulcer Stages

| | |
|---|---|
| Stage 1 | A persistent area of skin redness (without a break in the skin) that does not disappear when pressure is relieved. |
| Stage 2 | A partial thickness loss of skin layers that presents clinically as an abrasion, blister, or shallow crater. |
| Stage 3 | A full thickness of skin is lost, exposing the subcutaneous tissues — presents as a deep crater with or without undermining adjacent tissue. |
| Stage 4 | A full thickness of skin and subcutaneous tissue is lost, exposing muscle or bone. |

*Source:* MDS 2.0, Centers for Medicare and Medicaid Services.

occlusive dressings that keep tissue hydrated, whirlpool treatment, removal of dead tissue by surgical debridement, and skin grafting.

## Use and Misuse of Physical Restraints

A *restraint* is a device that is used to restrict a person's freedom of movement (Grubbs & Blasband, 2000). Examples of physical restraints include waist belts or chest jackets to prevent people from getting out of a chair or bed, geri-chairs with secured tray tables, bed siderails, roller bars for wheelchairs, mitts, and wrist ties. In the past, these restraints were in common use because of the widespread belief that restraining was necessary to keep patients from falling or otherwise hurting themselves. However, studies found that their value in promoting patient safety was, at best, marginal. Contrary to what was earlier believed, restraint use often caused injuries and resulted in negative physical and psychological outcomes. For example, between 1985 and 1995, 649 adverse events associated with bed siderails in hospitals and nursing homes were reported to the Food and Drug Administration (FDA), which regulates hospital beds as medical devices. One study based on the FDA database reported that during this period, there were 111 cases of entrapment in which the patient was found caught, trapped, entangled, or strangled by the rail while in bed. Of these cases, 65% resulted in death and 23% resulted in injuries (Todd & Ruhl, 1997). In 1995, because of increasing numbers of death and injury reports, the FDA issued a safety alert on hazards associated with bed siderails.

Formerly, restraints were also widely used to control behavioral disorders such as agitation and aggression. *Agitation* is defined as verbal, vocal, and motor activities that are repetitive and outside of socially acceptable norms (Cohen-Mansfield & Billig, 1986). Often, restraint use resulted in increased anger and further agitation because of frustration with restricted freedom. The use of various types of restraints was estimated to cause approximately 1 in every 1,000 deaths in nursing homes. When restraints are removed, quality of life and functional status improve; there does not appear to be an increase in serious falls, and serious injuries even decline (Palmer et al., 1999).

In contemporary nursing practice, use of restraints is seldom considered appropriate. When considered medically necessary, restraints should only be used temporarily and under physician's orders and close supervision by the nursing staff. Otherwise, their use is illegal (see Chapter 5). Use of restraints should be considered only when alternative means to ensure safety have failed because patients have the right to receive care in an environment that is the least restrictive. When patients manifest agitation or aggression, nursing professionals must first evaluate the underlying causes. For example, agitation may stem from depression or some other psychiatric disorder, in which case therapy should be directed toward the underlying disorder (Ouslander et al., 1997).

## Urinary Incontinence and Catheters

It is estimated that more than half of all nursing home residents are unable to control urination (Resnick & Baumann, 1997). The starting point for addressing this problem is to maintain a bladder record over a period of 5 to 7 days to determine the type and frequency of incontinence. A clinical evaluation and treatment of reversible causes is the next step. Reversible or transient causes include urinary tract infection, urinary retention, delirium, restricted mobility, atrophic vaginitis, urethritis, fecal impaction, and pharmaceuticals. Other serious conditions—such as bladder cancer, prostate cancer in men, stones or other types of blockage—may also lead to incontinence. Once the underlying reversible causes have been treated, therapeutic programs should be instituted as the next step. Developing toileting schedules has been a common approach. Some residents may require staff assistance for toileting every two hours; others can do quite well on a schedule of every three or four hours (Helping residents stay dry, 2003). The schedule is based on the voiding patterns observed. Staff support with transfer and ambulation should be provided as necessary, and the resident should have easy access to the toilet or a portable commode. Low-intensity exercise programs to strengthen the pelvic muscles can be combined with the toileting program.

Use of a catheter would be indicated only when other measures have failed to control incontinence. Condom catheters are used in men who have difficulty retaining urine. An ***indwelling catheter***, that is, a catheter that remains in the bladder to drain urine into a bag, is used in both men and women when medically indicated and approved by the attending physician. Some of the highest infection rates among nursing home residents are attributed to indwelling catheters. Hence, their use should be minimized.

## Mental and Cognitive Disorders

### Depression

Traditional nursing home environments tend to promote dependency and negative affect, which increase the risk of depression (Meeks et al., 2006). However, biological, psychological, and social factors also contribute to the cause of depression. Among patients with dementia, 25 to 35% may experience depression (Aalten et al., 2005). Depression is associated with higher morbidity, greater mortality, and poor quality of life. Although nurses and CNAs do not formally diagnose depression, they play a key role in observing the mental, emotional, and behavioral state of patients. However, depression in the elderly is difficult to recognize. Still, nurses and CNAs may be able to recognize between 56 and 78% of patients with depression (Brühl et al, 2007). Common depressive symptoms include the following:

- Loss of interest in things that otherwise bring enjoyment.
- Feelings of worthlessness.
- Diminished ability to make decisions.
- Fatigue.
- Underactivity (psychomotor retardation) and, sometimes, overactivity (psychomotor agitation).
- Loss of appetite.
- Sleeping too much.
- Insomnia.
- Recurrent thoughts of death or suicide.

Depending on the number of symptoms and their duration, depression can be mild or severe. Both biological (such as drugs, light therapy, and exercise) and psychological treatments are available to treat depression (Thakur & Blazer, 2007).

### Delirium

***Delirium*** is an acute organic brain disorder. It is a state of acute mental confusion that often manifests itself in the form of disorientation, incoherent speech, and physical agitation due to distress. Memory impairment and hallucinations may also be present. Delirium is often caused by acute illness or toxicity. It may be precipitated by immobility, use of physical restraints, use of bladder catheters, psychotropic medications (discussed later), malnutrition, or dehydration. A good sensory environment, appropriate lighting levels, mobility and activities, reality orientation, and one-on-one care can help alleviate or prevent delirium (George et al., 2006). The condition is treatable, but a quick medical diagnosis is critical because the underlying causes can lead to a fatal outcome. Without proper diagnosis, delirium can be mistaken for dementia or depression. For example, delirium is thought to occur four to five times more often in a person with dementia (Fick & Mion, 2007). Such comorbid conditions can leave delirium unrecognized. A delirious patient must show all of the following signs (American Psychiatric Association, 1994):

- A lack of awareness of one's environment and a reduced ability to focus, sustain, or shift attention.

- A change in cognition such as memory deficit, disorientation, or language disturbance.

- Development of the disturbance over a few hours or days and tendency of the disturbance to fluctuate during the course of the day.

- Existence of evidence that the disturbance is caused by a direct physiological consequence of a general medical condition, substance intoxication, or substance withdrawal.

Management of delirium requires treatment of the underlying cause. Low doses of a psychotropic medication may be prescribed.

## Dementia

*Dementia* is a generic term for progressive mental dysfunction that results in complex cognitive decline. *Alzheimer's disease* is the most common type of dementia. Alzheimer's is a progressive degenerative disease of the brain, producing memory loss, confusion, irritability, and severe functional decline. The disease becomes progressively worse and eventually results in death.

Dementia affects the majority of residents in nursing homes and assisted living facilities. Diagnosing dementia is challenging, particularly in its early stage. Depression and delirium must first be ruled out. Dementia can be classified into mild, moderate, severe, and very severe stages (Sloane et al., 2001):

- *Mild dementia.* Unreliable memory for recent events. Difficulty managing various instrumental activities of daily living (IADLs). May need supervision for dressing and bathing. Difficulty in carrying out a conversation.

- *Moderate dementia.* Very poor memory for recent events. Easily confused or upset by changes in routine, new places, or unfamiliar people. Needs 24-hour supervision and assistance with bathing, dressing, and grooming. Displays confusion, repetitive questioning, disorientation, mood swings, delusions, and wandering.

- *Severe dementia.* Poor memory for both recent and past events. Recognizes only persons seen very regularly. Difficulty following daily schedules. May develop gait instability and sustain falls. Resists caregiving, may have delusions, and may display physical abusiveness, such as hitting and biting, and other socially inappropriate behaviors, such as saying inappropriate things and disrobing in public.

- *Very severe dementia.* Little awareness of surroundings. Speaks in a few words or unintelligible sounds. Rarely recognizes individuals, even close family members. Needs almost total assistance with ADLs. May be able to shuffle short distances with assistance or is nonambulatory. Incontinence of bowel and bladder. Resists caregiving and has screaming episodes.

Unlike depression and delirium, dementia is irreversible. Because of the issues mentioned, caregiving becomes challenging, and the burden of caregiving increases as the disease progresses. Patients with Alzheimer's disease may live for 8 to 10 years after the disease is first diagnosed and often progress to the very severe stage.

Emotional behavior of caregivers can be sensed by even patients suffering from severe dementia. For example, negative behaviors by CNAs may contribute to increased behavioral problems and agitation in dementia patients. Person-centered communication strategies can help calm down the patient. Hobson (2008) recommended the following:

- Communication with body language becomes more common in patients with advanced dementia. Hence, watch for body language.
- The caregiver should introduce him- or herself. Communicate in short and simple sentences. Complex information can lead to frustration. Allow plenty of time for the person to respond.
- Try to ask questions that require a "yes" or "no" answer.

- During caregiving, try to explain what will be done. Explain each step of a process.
- What works with one patient may not work with another because people with dementia are not all alike. Getting to know the person is important.
- When offering things, try to limit the choice to two items.

Planning and delivering care to patients with early dementia is likely to be quite different from those in the final stages of dementia. For example, patients with advanced dementia are prescribed a larger number of medications from numerous medication classes, and prescribing patterns change over time (Blass et al., 2008). It is suggested that for the management of advanced dementia in its terminal stage, palliative care may be the most appropriate strategy and should include appropriate emphasis on quality of life, dignity, and comfort (Volicer, 2007).

# Pharmacy Services

A nursing facility is required by regulations to provide pharmaceutical services and to have consultation from a licensed pharmacist. As discussed in Chapter 3, long-term care pharmacies specialize in meeting the special needs of nursing homes.

The facility should have a written agreement with the pharmacist, who should also be an active member of the multidisciplinary team. The pharmacist assists the facility in developing policies and procedures for the dispensing, storage, administration, review, discontinuation, and disposal of drugs. Pharmacy standards require a monthly review of the drug regimen for each resident and appropriate labeling and storage of drugs. Drug interactions and unexpected response to a given medication are special concerns in the medical care of the elderly. Hence, prescribing drugs requires careful monitoring in conjunction with changes in the patient's condition, results of laboratory tests, and use of any over-the-counter (nonprescribed) medications. State laws govern how medications are dispensed and labeled. Drugs should be stored in locked cabinets to which only authorized personnel should have access. Certain medications require proper refrigeration.

A system that allows separate storage of medications for each patient should be used. The unit-dose medication distribution system has become the industry standard. In a unit-dose system, medications are prepackaged and labeled in unit-of-use form and are ready to be given to the patient. This eliminates the need for a nurse to take out the medication from a bottle and prepare medicine cups for each patient. Internet-based drug ordering systems are also becoming common. These systems save time, reduce medication errors, and minimize drug waste.

## Controlled Substances

Specific policies and procedures govern the safeguarding and authorized use of controlled substances, which must be stored in a double-locked cabinet. Proper recordkeeping and verification are necessary to prevent unauthorized use. A system must be in place to adequately account for all used and unused medications for each patient. The prescription, dispensing, and use of *controlled substances*—narcotics, stimulants, depressants, hallucinogens, anabolic steroids, and chemicals—are governed by the Controlled Substances Act (CSA), Title II of the Comprehensive Drug Abuse Prevention and Control Act of 1970. Except as provided under the law, possession or use of controlled substances is illegal. Controlled substances are listed in Schedules I through V of the CSA:

*Schedule I.* These substances are illegal because they have no currently accepted medical use in the United States. Examples include heroin, LSD, and marijuana.

*Schedule II.* These substances have a currently accepted medical use in the United States and generally have severe restrictions. Examples include morphine, cocaine, and methamphetamine.

*Schedule III.* These substances have a medical use and also have less potential for abuse than substances in Schedules I and II. Examples include anabolic steroids and painkillers containing codeine or hydrocodone.

*Schedule IV.* These substances have less potential for abuse than substances in Schedule III. Examples include Darvon and Valium.

*Schedule V.* These substances have the least potential for abuse. Examples include cough medicines containing codeine.

Schedule II through V substances have a useful and legitimate medical purpose when appropriately prescribed by a physician, but their abuse generally has a substantial and detrimental effect on health and general welfare—hence the need for strict control. A facility must store controlled substances in a double-locked cabinet and implement proper recordkeeping and verification systems. When an order for a controlled substance is discontinued for any reason, federal regulations require the controlled substance to be destroyed and its destruction to be duly witnessed and documented. Individual states may issue their own regulations for safeguarding controlled substances.

## Emergency Kit

Nursing facilities must also maintain an emergency medication kit. The pharmaceutical review committee should determine its contents. In general, the emergency kit contains drugs needed during life-threatening emergencies such as cardiac arrest, severe allergic reaction, or seizures. The drugs in the emergency kit are the responsibility of the pharmacist. They are often limited to a 72-hour supply. The kit is kept sealed (not locked), and records are kept whenever anything is used from the kit.

## Psychotropic Drugs

Psychotropic (or psychoactive) drugs include antipsychotics, antidepressants, anxiolytics (anti-anxiety), sedatives, and hypnotics. In the past, these drugs were overprescribed for nursing home residents. Some of these drugs were prescribed as "chemical restraints" to sedate patients who were considered overly aggressive, disruptive, or assaultive. As a result of nursing home reform efforts, OBRA-87 contains specific rules for the use of psychotropic drugs in nursing facilities with the objective of reducing their use. For example, the legislation prescribes that antipsychotics can be used only when certain specified conditions have been documented. Less severe conditions for which these drugs should not be prescribed are also specified. Other requirements of the law include grad-

ual dose reductions unless such action is clinically contraindicated. Whenever appropriate, behavioral interventions should be tried first, such as modifying the environment and implementing approaches to care delivery that would accommodate the resident's behavior to the largest degree possible. This is a broad requirement, which needs to be carefully evaluated when mental or behavioral problems are observed. For example, depression may be attributed to certain medications the patient may be on, in which case the nursing staff should work with the physician and the pharmacist to review the patient's drug regimen. If the depression is not severe enough, the patient may come out of it in a few days. Instead of rushing to seek pharmacological therapy, the nursing staff should carefully observe the resident's behavior and maintain appropriate documentation. Nonpharmacologic approaches should also be tried in cases of anxiety, which is another common problem in nursing home residents. Interventions such as biofeedback, relaxation techniques, and participation in recreational programs may be useful for some residents (Ouslander et al., 1997). One study of 16 skilled nursing facilities in Wisconsin, involving 1,650 residents, demonstrated a significant overall decrease in the use of antipsychotic drugs. However, the change varied dramatically across facilities, from an 85% reduction to a 19% increase. Greater reductions were found in facilities with a person-centered culture, a less severe case mix, and a higher nurse-to-resident staffing ratio (Svarstad et al., 2001). A recent review of research literature suggests that a combination of pharmaceutical drug regimen review and educational interventions for physicians and nursing staff may also be effective in reducing psychotropic drug use (Nishtala et al., 2008).

# Rehabilitation

In the geriatric context, *rehabilitation* can be defined as the process of delivering the minimal services that maintain the present or highest possible level of function (Osterweil, 1990). Rehabilitation has three main objectives: (1) to restore functional status lost through disease, injury, or surgical intervention; (2) to maintain residual function and prevent further decline; and (3) to help disabled individuals adapt to their functional deficits. Hence, rehabilitation therapies can be restorative, maintenance, and adaptive in design. In many instances, restoring an individual to his or her former functional status may not be possible. In that case, maintaining or maximizing remaining function would be the goal.

For nursing facilities, the overarching standard has been established by OBRA-87 regulations, according to which the facility must provide necessary services and appropriate treatments for residents to maintain or improve their functioning and range of motion.

## Restorative Rehabilitation

The goal of *restorative rehabilitation* is to help regain or improve function. It requires intensive short-term treatments. Restorative therapy is generally provided immediately after the onset of a disability. Examples of cases requiring short-term restorative therapy include orthopedic surgery, stroke, limb amputation, and prolonged illness. Frequently, the expected outcome of intensive short-term rehabilitation is to enable the patient to return to independent living. In other cases, especially when a patient must continue receiving long-term care because of other chronic needs, longer-term maintenance rehabilitation is necessary after short-term restorative care has ceased.

Restorative rehabilitation is based on assessment and care planning by a multidisciplinary team. Rehabilitation professionals are part of the multidisciplinary team. The attending physician must authorize all short-term rehabilitation treatments. Short-term treatments are carried out by professionally trained therapists—mainly, registered physical therapists (PTs), physical therapy assistants (PTAs), registered occupational therapists (OTs), certified occupational therapy assistants (COTAs), and speech/language pathologists (SLPs) [see Chapter 3 for details].

*Physical therapy* treatments are geared toward improving ambulation, range of motion, physical strength, flexibility, coordination, balance, and endurance. PTs also specialize in fitting and training patients to use artificial limbs, canes, and walkers. PTs are also trained to give treatment modalities such as hot packs, cold packs, massage, ultrasound, paraffin bath, electrical stimulation, compression therapy, and hydrotherapy. PTs can assist and train the nursing staff in techniques for preventing falls.

*Occupational therapy* is tailored for the adaptive use of the upper extremities for performing various tasks. OTs can help patients with fine motor skills, adaptive equipment, splints, and other support mechanisms that are tailor-made to facilitate the performance of daily tasks (Ramsdell, 1990). OTs also play a vital role in evaluating the independent living environment when the patient is scheduled for discharge to home.

*Speech/language pathology* encompasses evaluation and treatment of speech, language, and communication disorders. Speech/language pathologists treat several kinds of disorders such as *aphasia*, in which a person's ability to communicate is impaired; *dysarthria*, in which speech is slurred or unintelligible because of muscle weakness; or motor speech disorders such as *apraxia*, in which the tongue, lips, and vocal cords are unable to work together (Reynolds & Slott, 1999). As a result, the person is unable to say what he or she wants to say. *Dysphagia*, or the inability to swallow, is another common problem SLPs are called upon to treat in nursing facilities.

## Maintenance Rehabilitation

*Maintenance rehabilitation* has the goal of preserving the present level of function and preventing secondary complications. Certain capabilities cannot be recovered, but patients should be assisted to adapt to their deficits so that they can do for themselves as much as they possibly can in their daily activities. Maintenance rehabilitation is based on maximizing the use of remaining capacities. Without maintenance therapy, complications such as pressure ulcers, contractures, muscle atrophy, constipation, fecal impaction, and edema can result. Ambulation and range of motion are two common types of exercise programs. These programs often continue restorative treatments initiated by PTs and OTs. The treatment is generally less intense and of longer duration than restorative therapy. Long-term maintenance therapy is carried out by paraprofessionals such as specially trained rehabilitation aides or CNAs.

---

## For Further Thought

1. Discuss the ways in which nursing plays a central role in a nursing facility. How can the centrality of nursing sometime result in conflict with other departments? As an administrator, how would you prevent such conflicts?

2. As a nursing home administrator, you are recruiting a new medical director. What are some of the main elements you should discuss during the interview?

3. What are some of the elements you think ought to be included in a contract between the facility and its medical director?

---

## For Further Learning

The American Geriatrics Society is the premier professional organization of health care providers dedicated to improving the health and well-being of older adults.

www.americangeriatrics.org

American Medical Directors Association is the professional association of medical directors and physicians practicing in the long-term care continuum, dedicated to excellence in patient care by providing education, advocacy, information, and professional development.

http://www.amda.com

National Association of Directors of Nursing Administration in Long Term Care (NADONA-LTC) is a professional organization of directors and assistant directors of nursing in long-term care. It has established standards of practice for directors of nursing and also has a certification program for directors of nursing.

www.nadona.org

National Gerontological Nursing Association (NGNA), an organization of nurses specializing in care of older adults, informs the public on health issues affecting older people, supports education for nurses and other health care practitioners, and provides a forum to discuss topics such as nutrition in long-term care facilities and elder law for nurses. NGNA offers information on gerontological nursing and conducts nursing research related to older people.

www.ngna.org

National Mental Health Association is the country's oldest and largest nonprofit organization addressing all aspects of mental health and mental illness. It allows a search feature.

www.nmha.org

National Rehabilitation Information Center (NARIC), funded by the Department of Education, provides information on rehabilitation of people with physical or mental disabilities. Contact NARIC for database searches on all types of physical and mental disabilities, as well as referrals to local and national facilities and organizations.

www.naric.com

## REFERENCES

Aalten, P., et al. 2005. The course of neuropsychiatric symptoms in dementia. Part I: Findings from the two-year longitudinal Maasbed study. *Psychiatry* 20, no. 6: 523–530.

Allman, R.M. 1999. Pressure ulcer. In W.R. Hazzard et al. (eds.). *Principles of Geriatric Medicine and Gerontology*, 4th ed. (pp. 1577–1583). New York: McGraw-Hill.

American Psychiatric Association. 1994. *Diagnostic and Statistical Manual of Mental Disorders*, 4th ed. Washington, DC: American Psychiatric Association.

Bennett, G.C.J. 1992. Pressure sores—aetiology and prevalence. In J.C. Brocklehurst, R.C. Tallis, and H.M. Fillit (eds.). *Textbook of Geriatric Medicine and Gerontology*, 4th ed. Edinburgh, U.K.: Churchill Livingstone.

Bergstrom, N.I. 1997. Strategies for preventing pressure ulcers. *Clinical Geriatric Medicine* 13, no. 3: 437–454.

Bern-Klug, M., et al. 2003. 'I get to spend time with my patients': Nursing home physicians discuss their role. *Journal of the American Medical Directors Association* 4, no. 3: 145–151.

Blass, D.M., et al. 2008. Medication use in nursing home residents with advanced dementia. *International Journal of Geriatric Psychiatry* 23: 490–496.

Bliss, M.R. 1992. Pressure sore management and prevention. In J.C. Brocklehurst, R.C. Tallis, and H.M. Fillit (eds.). *Textbook of Geriatric Medicine and Gerontology,* 4th ed. Edinburgh, U.K.: Churchill Livingstone.

Brühl, K.G., et al. 2007. Nurses' and nursing assistants' recognition of depression in elderly who depend on long-term care. *Journal of the American Medical Directors Association* 8, no. 7: 441–445.

Carroll, N.V., et al. 2008. Fall-related hospitalization and facility costs among residents of institutions providing long-term care. *Gerontologist* 48, no. 2: 213–222.

CDC. 1990. Prevention and control of tuberculosis in facilities providing long-term care to the elderly recommendations of the Advisory Committee for Elimination of Tuberculosis. Retrieved January 2009 from Centers for Disease Control and Prevention, http://www.cdc.gov/mmwr/preview/mmwrhtml/00001711.htm.

Cohen-Mansfield, J., & Billig, N. 1986. Agitated behaviors in the elderly. I. A conceptual review. *Journal of the American Geriatric Society* 34, no. 10: 711–721.

Dharmarajan, T.S., & Ahmed, S. 2003. The growing problem of pressure ulcers. *Postgraduate Medicine* 113, no. 5: 77–83.

Fick, D., & Mion, L. 2007. Assessing and managing delirium in older adults with dementia. *Annals of Long-Term Care*. Retrieved November 2008 from http://www.annalsoflongtermcare.com/article/7861.

Garibaldi, R.A., et al. 1981. Infections among patients in nursing homes: Policies, prevalence, and problems. *New England Journal of Medicine* 305: 731–735.

George, J., et al. 2006. *The Prevention, Diagnosis and Management of Delirium in Older People: National Guidelines*. London, U.K.: Royal College of Physicians.

Gittler, J. 2008. Governmental efforts to improve quality of care for nursing home residents and to protect them from mistreatment: A survey of federal and state laws. *Research in Gerontological Nursing* 1, no. 4: 264–284.

Grubbs, P., & Blasband, B. 2000. *The Long-Term Care Nursing Assistant*. Upper Saddle River, NJ: Prentice-Hall.

Hand hygiene. 2001. Yale-New Haven Hospital, Quality Improvement Support Services. Retrieved October 2003 from http://info.med.yale.edu/ynhh/infection/precautions/ handhygiene.html.

Hanson, L.C., et al. 2002. As individual as death itself: A focus group study of terminal care in nursing homes. *Journal of Palliative Medicine* 5, no. 1: 117–125.

Helping residents stay dry. An interview with Mary H. Palmer, Ph.D. 2003. *Nursing Homes Long Term Care Management* 52, no. 6: 70–72.

Hobson, P. 2008. Understanding dementia: Developing person-centered communication. *British Journal of Healthcare Assistants* 2, no. 4: 162–164.

Hofmann, M.T., et al. 2003. Decreasing the incidence of falls in the nursing home in a cost-conscious environment: a pilot study. *Journal of the American Medical Directors Association* 4, no. 2: 95–97.

Kane, R.A. 1995. Decision making, care plans, and life plans in long-term care: Can case managers take account of clients' values and preferences? In L.B. McCullough and N.L. Wilson(eds.). *Long-Term Care Decisions: Ethical and Conceptual Dimensions*. Baltimore: Johns Hopkins University Press.

Krein, K. 2003. Choosing a medical director: One size does not fit all. *Nursing Homes Long Term Care Management* 52, no. 4: 15–21.

Levenson, S.A. 1985. The physician. In G.H. Maguire (ed.). *Care of the Elderly: A Health Team Approach*. Boston: Little, Brown and Company.

Lipsitz, L.A., et al. 1997. Falls. In J.N. Morris et al. (eds.). *Quality Care in the Nursing Home* (pp. 258–277). St. Louis, MO: Mosby-Year Book.

Meeks, S., et al. 2006. Activity participation and affect among nursing home residents: Support for a behavioural model of depression. *Aging and Mental Health* 11, no. 6: 751–760.

Messinger-Rapport, B.J., et al. 2007. Intensive session: New approaches to medical issues in long-term care. *Journal of the American Medical Directors Association* 8, no. 7: 421–433.

Nishtala, P.S., et al. 2008. Psychotropic prescribing in long-term care facilities: Impact of medication reviews and educational interventions. *American Journal of Geriatric Psychiatry* 16, no. 8: 621–632.

Osterweil, D. 1990. Geriatric rehabilitation in the long-term care institutional setting. In B. Kemp, K. Brummel-Smith, and J.W. Ramsdell (eds.). *Geriatric Rehabilitation*. Boston: College-Hill Press.

Ouslander, J.G., et al. 1997. *Medical Care in the Nursing Home*, 2nd ed. New York: McGraw-Hill.

Palmer, L., et al. 1999. Reducing inappropriate restraint use in Colorado's long-term care facilities. *Joint Commission Journal on Quality Improvement* 25, no. 2: 78–94.

Peck, R.L. 2001. Perspectives. *Nursing Homes Long Term Care Management* 50, no. 2: 36–38.

Ramsdell, J.W. 1990. A rehabilitation orientation in the workup of general medical problems. In B. Kemp, K. Brummel-Smith, and J.W. Ramsdell (eds.). *Geriatric Rehabilitation*. Boston: College-Hill Press.

Resnick, N., & Baumann, M. 1997. In J.N. Morris et al. (eds.). *Quality Care in the Nursing Home*. (pp. 258–277). St. Louis, MO: Mosby-Year Book.

Reynolds, C., & Slott, S. 1999. Geriatric speech pathologist. In T.L. Kauffman (ed.). *Geriatric Rehabilitation Manual*. New York: Churchill Livingstone.

Rubenstein, L.Z. 2006. Falls in older people: Epidemiology, risk factors and strategies for prevention. *Age and Ageing* 35, suppl. 2: ii37–ii41.

Saliba, D., & Buchanan, J. 2008. *Development and Validation of a Revised Nursing Home Assessment Tool: MDS 3.0*. Baltimore: Centers for Medicare and Medicaid Services.

Sharbaugh, R.J. 2003. When drugs don't kill bugs. *Nursing Homes Long Term Care Management* 52, no. 5: 70–72.

Sloane, P.D., et al. 2001. Care for persons with dementia. In S. Zimmerman et al. (eds.). *Assisted Living: Needs, Practices, and Policies in Residential Care for the Elderly* (pp. 242–270). Baltimore: Johns Hopkins University Press.

Smith, D.M. 1996. Pressure ulcers. In R.W. Besdine and L.Z. Rubenstein (eds.). *Medical Care of the Nursing Home Resident*. Philadelphia: American College of Physicians.

Stevenson, K.B. 1999. Regional data set of infection rates for long-term care facilities: Description of a valuable benchmarking tool. *American Journal of Infection Control* 27, no. 1: 20–26.

Strausbaugh, L.J., et al. 2003. Infectious disease outbreaks in nursing homes: An unappreciated hazard for frail elderly persons. *Clinical Infectious Diseases* 36, no. 7: 870–876.

Svarstad, B.L., et al. 2001. Variations in the treatment culture of nursing homes and responses to regulations to reduce drug use. *Psychiatric Services : A Journal of the American Psychiatric Association* 52, no. 5: 666–672.

Thakur, M., & Blazer, D.G. 2007. Depression in long-term care. *Journal of the American Medical Directors Association* 9, no. 2: 82–87.

Tinetti, M.E. 2003. Preventing falls in elderly persons. *New England Journal of Medicine* 348, no. 1: 42–49.

Todd, J.F., & Ruhl, C.E. 1997. Injury and death associated with hospital bed side-rails: Reports to the US Food and Drug Administration. *American Journal of Public Health* 87, no. 10: 1675–1977.

Volicer, L. 2007. Goals of care in advanced dementia: Quality of life, dignity and comfort. *Journal of Nutrition, Health, and Aging* 11, no. 6: 481.

Yarme, J., & Yarme, H. 2001. Flooring and safety. *Nursing Homes Long Term Care Management* 50, no. 10: 82–83.

# Chapter 11

---

# Recreation and Activities

## What You Will Learn

- Meaningful activities should achieve several goals and promote holistic health. Therapeutic recreation is mostly program oriented.

- Federal and state regulations have not established the qualifications for activity personnel, but those certified by the National Certification Council for Activity Professionals automatically satisfy federal requirements.

- Activity professionals must have skills in assessment, documentation, communication, engagement, planning, and coordinating. They must be innovative and resourceful. A pleasant disposition is also essential.

- Activity programming should take into consideration the age of participants, nature and extent of their disabilities, space availability and timing, supplies and equipment, staffing, and use of community resources.

- Activities must be designed to build strength, stimulate the mind, promote social interaction, express one's individuality, build self-esteem, and provide spiritual fulfillment.

- Activities need to be spaced out during the day. Some evening and weekend activities should also be scheduled. Participation may be active or passive. Interaction with children is enriching.

- Intervention approaches can be designed for sensory and cognitive stimulation. These interventions include sensory stimulation, reality orientation, reminiscence, validation therapy, and multisensory stimulation.

- Both small-group and individually tailored one-to-one activities may be appropriate for patients with dementia.

- Activities must be matched with individual needs and interests, and the resident's risk awareness profile must be taken into account.

- Programs should be planned with certain outcomes in mind. Achievement of expected outcomes should be the focus of program evaluation.
- Recruiting and retaining volunteers is an important responsibility of the activity director.

Activity programming is not simply a matter of putting together some recreational programs to comply with regulatory requirements. Meaningful activities call for a great deal of skill and resourcefulness. Activity programs must strike a balance between quantity and quality. Perhaps the biggest challenge for those who oversee activity programs in a facility is to make sure that the programs meet the needs of individual residents regardless of their physical, mental, social, or emotional status.

## Activities: Their Goals and Purpose

In this chapter, the term *activity* means active or passive involvement of patients in any activities—outside the activities of daily living (ADLs)—that provide meaning and personal enrichment. Meaningful activities must achieve several goals: (1) promote a sense of well-being, (2) build self-esteem, (3) give pleasure, (4) create a sense of personal fulfillment, (5) provide a sense of accomplishment, (6) promote physical and mental fitness, and (7) accomplish social and spiritual fulfillment.

Meaningful activities involve more than just games and outings. "Activities should do more than produce an occasional bright spot of entertainment in an otherwise dull existence; activities must help people learn new information, skills, or behaviors or improve their feelings of self-worth . . ." (Carroll et al., 1978). A well-rounded activity program addresses the physical, mental, social, and spiritual aspects to promote holistic health.

The purposes and roles of activities must be distinguished from the purposes and roles of social work (see Chapter 9) and rehabilitation therapies (see Chapter 10), although the goals pursued by each of these disciplines generally overlap. For instance, maximizing independent functioning, promoting self-esteem, meeting psycho-social needs, and enhancing quality of life are the overarching goals pursued by all three disciplines. Yet, there are two main differences: (1) each is a specialized discipline that addresses patient care issues that other disciplines do not address, and (2) the approach used for achieving the common goals just mentioned is different in each discipline. Therapeutic recreation is the primary approach used in activities, which is quite distinct from the other two disciplines: *social services* focus mainly on coping and social adaptation; *rehabilitation* therapies employ a clinical approach to specific functional deficits, mainly by using established therapeutic modalities. By their nature, social services and rehabilitation are intervention oriented. They deal with problems and issues that are clearly defined. In activities, intervention may be used, but only to a limited degree. Among the three disciplines, recreational activities also allow the greatest degree of latitude for residents to pursue their own interests.

For the most part, activities are program oriented rather than intervention oriented. *Program orientation* means that programs are structured with the needs of various residents taken into consideration, but residents' participation is voluntary. Compared with intervention-oriented therapies, participation in activities allows the resident a much greater degree of voluntary choice, personal control, autonomy, and self-confidence. *Intervention orientation* respects autonomy and choice to a degree, but participation is nonvoluntary unless the patient signs a release refusing treatment.

Activities must offer a wide variety of programs that enable individuals to pursue their personal interests and to develop new interests, with the objective of finding meaning and purpose in life despite chronic illness, frailty, and functional impairment. Social adaptation and maintenance rehabilitation are often the by-products of activities, although they may not be specifically pursued. Activities allow residents freedom of expression, which, from a holistic viewpoint, adds a necessary dimension to nursing home services that no other discipline in the facility can furnish. Achieving self-fulfillment by engaging in meaningful recreational diversions adds necessary balance and a sense of control to the lives of residents in an otherwise restricted environment. Because personal interests can vary substantially across the resident population in a nursing facility, activity programming presents special challenges in creativity and resourcefulness.

# Activity Department
## Staffing

Each state specifies the staffing levels and required qualifications for activity personnel, but clear-cut guidelines are generally lacking. Because of the unique nature of activities, a facility needs a separate activities department headed by an activity director or activity coordinator. The director or coordinator reports to the administrator. In small facilities, one full-time person may be assigned the responsibilities of both social work and activities. However, to the extent possible, the administrator should try to have separate departments for these two services; otherwise, the effectiveness of both services is likely to be compromised. In facilities with more than 50 beds, a full-time activity director is generally needed. Additional personnel are necessary in facilities with more than 100 beds. Part-time activity assistants may be used to fill in as needed.

## Qualifications

The Omnibus Budget Reconciliation Act of 1987 (OBRA-87) mandates that activity programs be directed by qualified professionals. Federal regulations do not specify the qualifications, but activity professionals certified by the National Certification Council for Activity Professionals (NCCAP) automatically satisfy federal requirements. The types of certification offered by the NCCAP were discussed in Chapter 3.

Directors may also meet OBRA-87 requirements by satisfying the licensure or registration requirements specified by their state. Directors who do not meet the qualifications specified by the state are required to have regular consultation from an outside qualified activities consultant. The consultant's role is to train the activity staff, evaluate existing programs, make recommendations for program enhancement, assist in implementing new programs, and ensure that all requirements mandated by federal and state regulations are met (Tedrick & Green, 1995).

## Skills and Competencies

Activity staff members participate in the multidisciplinary team discussed in previous chapters. As such, they contribute to resident assessment, care planning, and documentation in the patient's medical record. Hence, activities programming requires a therapeutic perspective. These requirements of the position must be carefully evaluated when activity professionals are recruited and trained.

Many of the general skills that activities specialists need for effective performance are very similar to those necessary for social workers discussed in Chapter 9. For instance, the skills of engagement, assessment, communication, and documentation are necessary for activity directors. They must also have knowledge of aging and the elderly (see Chapter 9). Indeed, these skills can actually improve the performance of any professional who needs to interact with nursing home patients as a care provider.

The Minimum Data Set (MDS) contains a special section for assessing activity preferences. Assessment yields valuable information on the needs and desires of each resident and forms the basis for planning and developing appropriate programs. Similar to other members of the multidisciplinary team, activity professionals also have responsibilities for care planning and documentation of patients' activity goals and progress.

Activity professionals also need to have special skills of engagement and communication with the residents and family members. For example, during assessment, vital information must be obtained from both the residents and their family members, the latter being the key providers of information in case of residents who are cognitively impaired. Motivating the elderly to participate in activities is one of the special challenges for activity professionals. Because motivation varies from person to person, getting to know each individual resident's needs, interests, and abilities is essential (Hastings, 1981).

Friendliness, cheerfulness, and a pleasant disposition are special personality traits administrators should try to cultivate in activity personnel. Activity professionals must be innovative in designing appropriate programs to meet individual needs, resourceful in engaging family members and volunteers to enhance the activity programming, skilled in planning and coordinating a wide variety of programs, and able to evaluate the effectiveness of the different programs.

## Program Development

Understanding a number of factors clearly is essential for developing effective activity programming. The various factors discussed in this section should be evaluated carefully to generate ideas that can add variety, novelty, appeal, and meaning to resident activities.

### Basic Considerations

Programming requires developing and carrying out a meaningful plan. *Programming* means structured methods of delivering needed services. Planning an effective program requires that the activity professional consider the kind of service to deliver, the manner in which it will be delivered, and its anticipated effect on the residents involved (Lanza, 1997).

Six basic considerations are valuable in developing a well-rounded activity program (Greenblatt, 1988; Lanza, 1997):

1. *Age of participants.* Nursing facilities are likely to have substantial age differences among residents, and individual interests often vary according to a person's age group.

2. *Nature and extent of disabilities.* Disabilities must be assessed because active participation requires a certain level of functioning. Certain activities are suitable for passive participation by those who may be unable to have active involvement. Abilities and skills required for participation may be limited by disorders in any of the three behavioral arenas (Greenblatt, 1988):

   • Sensory motor skills are affected by poor ambulation, strength, range of motion, vision, or hearing.

   • Cognitive functioning is affected by disorders such as inability to recognize, store, or retrieve information; make judgments; or maintain attention span.

   • Affective functioning is impaired by depression, anxiety, anger, agitation, fear, or frustration.

   Activity planning must consider the needs of residents who have functional limitations in any of the three areas. Also, any medical contraindi-

cations must be carefully considered. For example, patients with serious cardiovascular conditions, asthma, or respiratory problems may require medical clearance for participation in certain types of activities. Use of certain medications produce side effects such as dizziness, drowsiness, and sensitivity to sunlight that require necessary precautions, such as assisting residents on certain medications to move slowly or using sunscreen for outdoor activities. Regardless of the type of limitation, therapeutic activities should use patients' unaffected capabilities; otherwise, functional loss in these remaining areas is likely to occur. This additional functional loss, called ***secondary disability***, can be reversed or prevented. For example, an elderly person with the primary condition of hearing loss may tend to isolate himself, which can lead to deterioration of other types of functional capabilities (Greenblatt, 1988).

3. *Space availability and timing.* Availability of space is an important consideration, especially for group programs. Certain individual pursuits such as knitting, crocheting, reading, drawing, painting, or listening to music can be effectively carried out in the patient's own room. However, most facilities have limited space for group activities. An activity room is often provided in medium-size and large facilities. This room is generally equipped for crafts, cooking, and baking and can accommodate small- to medium-size groups. Large facilities may also have a chapel for religious services. Other activities generally

require some ingenuity in adapting existing common spaces. For example, dining rooms, day rooms, lounges, lobby areas, open spaces near nursing stations, and alcoves can, with some improvisation, all be used for different activities, even though they may not be ideal. Use of common areas for activities requires proper planning and coordination to minimize interference with other services that must also be carried out. For instance, activities should not interfere with the use of dining areas for meals. Only a limited number of programs can be effectively conducted at a given time so that space is also available for individual leisure or private visiting. When weather conditions permit it, outdoor spaces such as patios, gazebos, and balconies should be used for certain types of activities. Outdoor gardening, tending to flowers and shrubs, and bird-feeding are therapeutic for many residents.

Activity schedules should take into account possible conflict with meal times and nursing care routines. Structured activities should be scheduled to take place when patients are likely to be inactive and bored. At the same time, residents should be given the choice to engage in individual pursuits. Activities should also be planned for evenings, weekends, and holidays. The length of each program will depend on the physical and mental endurance of participants.

4. *Supplies and equipment.* Reusable supplies and equipment are acquired over time. Simple, inexpensive equipment is generally quite sufficient for most activities. Additional needs can be met by seeking donations or purchasing things in good condition at garage sales. Any remaining needs should be met by allocating adequate financial resources in the annual budget. In most facilities, a multipurpose, folding mobile cart is an important piece of equipment for bringing games, crafts, magazines, books, and other items to residents in their rooms, particularly those who are room-bound. The same cart can be used for serving refreshments and distributing items at parties and other large gatherings (Hastings, 1981). Some equipment commonly used for activity programs includes folding tables and chairs; adjustable over-the-bed tables for use with wheelchairs; movie projectors, slide projectors, and portable screens; compact disk and cassette players; VCR and DVD equipment; movable organs or pianos; cameras; radios; woodworking tools; garden tools; ceramic kilns; cooking utensils; microwave ovens; ice cream makers; popcorn makers; barbecue grills; Christmas ornaments and other festival or seasonal decorations; and a variety of games, puzzles, and large-print books. Use of the computer for information and fun has become increasingly popular.

5. *Staffing.* Creativity and resourcefulness are actually more basic requirements than supplies, equipment, or space (Lanza, 1997). Staffing considerations also should not be ignored. The number of associates, and their qualifications, training, experience, and personality traits, are key factors

in developing and implementing quality programs. Building strong volunteer support is often necessary to supplement staffing in the activity department, because additional hands are often needed for programs such as parties, shows, and outings. Involvement of families can also be successfully pursued, because many of the residents' family members are retired but in good health, and family and friends often would like to stay involved in the lives of their loved ones. The activity director should work closely with the social worker to identify families who are likely to become volunteers at some point.

6. *Community resources.* Maintaining a link with the outside community and building exchange relationships is vital to enhancing the residents' quality of life. Local religious establishments, clerical associations, schools, Boy Scouts, Girl Scouts, nonprofit social service agencies, businesses, libraries, shopping malls, and many other types of organizations and establishments can support the facility's activity programs by offering their resources. Using community resources does not always mean bringing the resources into the facility. Community resources are also used when residents are taken for outings. For example, a trip to the mall may require making advance arrangements to accommodate a relatively large group of residents at the ice-cream parlor, or a group visit to a department store would require some coordinating so that residents could be taken at an appropriate time to look at preselected merchandise display areas.

## Meeting a Variety of Needs

Federal guidelines require that activity programming be multifaceted. Programs must incorporate each individual resident's needs. Programs should also provide "stimulation or solace; promote physical, cognitive and/or emotional health; enhance to the extent practicable each resident's self-respect by providing, for example, activities that allow for self-expression, personal responsibility and choice" (Lanza, 1997). The theories of biophilia and thriving, and creation of enriched environments, presented in Chapter 8, provide the guiding principles for developing programs that incorporate a variety of needs.

Multifaceted programming must cover the main human needs in a holistic context, and every need category is associated with goal achievement:

| Need | Goal Achievement |
| --- | --- |
| Physical | Build strength |
| Cognitive and educational | Stimulate the mind |
| Social | Promote interaction |
| Affective | Express one's individuality |
| Integration or awareness | Build self-esteem |
| Spiritual | Provide spiritual fulfillment |

Physical needs require some activities that provide exercise, movement, and general physical stimulation of the body parts. Programs such as dance therapy, exercise programs, and walking outdoors specifically address physical needs. Exercises and sports programs often require simulation. For example, a balloon volleyball, in which residents toss the balloon among themselves while seated in a circle, can simulate the real game.

Cognitive and educational needs demand programs designed to stimulate the mind and promote learning. Word games, games such as Trivial Pursuit, discussions of current events, and book reviews are activities that fall into this group. Nursing facilities must also provide residents with computers, Internet access, and other self-directed pastimes.

Social needs call for activities that provide opportunities for active and passive interaction and companionship with others. Examples of such programs include parties, functions, room visits, sing-alongs, and birthday parties and other celebrations.

Affective needs require activities that enable residents to express their feelings, emotions, and creativity. Art therapy, music therapy, touch therapy, pet therapy, bird-feeding, entertainment, and other types of programs that provide sensory stimulation and foster reminiscence are some examples. Entertainment programs require resourcefulness and planning. Movies are a common form of entertainment, but a resourceful activity director can arrange for a variety of other things, such as puppet shows, fashion parades, magic shows, live bands, chamber music, plays and skits, and cooking demonstrations. Some residents may be interested in journal-writing to reminisce their past.

Integration or awareness needs call for participation in programs that can help build self-esteem. Examples of such programs include roles in which the resident is needed by others, such as mail delivery, folding linens in the laundry, participation in resident council, acting as surrogate grandparents to children from the local day care center, and telling stories to children.

Spiritual needs are answered, in the lives of many elderly residents, by religious and spiritual pursuits considered important in their lives for achieving personal satisfaction, well-being, and self-realization and as a means of coping with stressful situations. Private devotions, quiet meditation, reading, and congregational religious programs brought in by local churches and synagogues are examples of activities in which many elders like to engage to find personal fulfillment and peace.

## Scheduling

High-quality activity programming calls for a variety of scheduling patterns. As a rule of thumb, scheduling should attempt to mirror the residents' usual patterns of rest and recreation before they were institutionalized. In this regard, Greenblatt (1988) proposes that holidays, to the extent possible, should be celebrated on the days they actually occur. Crafts and hobbies ought to be pursued in late morning before lunch; the elderly often take naps or just rest after lunch. Parties normally take place in late afternoon or early evening. Residents like to have leisure time after dinner, which is generally over by 6:30 p.m. On weekends, family visits are common; hence, fewer activities may be needed. On the other hand, it is also an irony that activity programming is frequently curtailed during periods when the residents have the most leisure time available. This lack of scheduled activity can result in boredom, frustration, agitation, and functional decline. Hence, scheduling of activities poses some challenges, but striving for balance is the key. As a rule of thumb, some morning activities should be offered starting at around 10:00 a.m.; then afternoon activities, starting at around 2:30 p.m.; and evening activities, starting at around

7:00 p.m. Within these guidelines, residents' own preferences for activity times should be accommodated (Lanza, 1997).

## Active and Passive Stimulation

A variety of activities suitable for individual participation, or for participation in small and large groups, must be planned to accommodate each resident's personal preferences. Residents can get active and passive stimulation during individual activities as well as in group activities. Some residents are intimidated by small group settings, in which more active participation is generally required, whereas others may not like being in large groups. Small groups often form spontaneously as friendships between people develop. The activity staff can help such groups find something meaningful to do together. Structured group activities, as opposed to informal group activities, are particularly beneficial for depressed residents (Meeks et al., 2007).

*Passivity* is characterized by a decline in human emotions, withdrawal from interactions with others and surroundings, and a decrease in motor activity (Colling, 1999). Passivity can lead to isolation, and cognitive and functional decline (Kolanowski & Buettner, 2008). Residents who cannot actively participate can simply be passive "bystanders" and receive stimulation from listening and watching other active participants. Other activities based on a resident's life history can be incorporated (Kolanowski & Buettner, 2008). Such activities may include music, massage, and reminiscence (discussed later).

## Intergenerational Appeal

Children's interactions with the elderly are enriching and have universal appeal. Eyes brighten up, smiles begin to form, and muffled laughter is often heard when the elderly are exposed to little children. Children also get a special sense of fulfillment when they can sit in an older person's lap, tell a tale, show the elder their favorite toy, or ask the elder some question. Every nursing home should explore ways to facilitate intergenerational contact. By working with local schools, child day care centers, and parents, many facilities across the country have developed formal programs that allow small children to make regular visits to nursing homes and to participate in activities with the elders.

## Intervention Approaches

In contrast to most other types of activity programming, therapeutic services for cognitive disorders generally require an intervention approach. Using such an approach means that voluntary choice and personal control do not play as much of a role as they do in most program-oriented approaches, because in many instances residents who need therapeutic services are unable to express their wishes. However, the patients' past practices and habits are taken into account to develop appropriate interventions. This section categorizes activities that are specifically designed for sensory and cognitive stimulation. A variety of programs are appropriate for individual as well as group interaction, including:

- Sensory stimulation.
- Reality orientation.
- Reminiscence.
- Validation therapy.
- Multisensory stimulation.

## Sensory Stimulation

*Sensory stimulation* incorporates therapies that stimulate the senses in patients with dementia or in those in comatose or vegetative states. It can benefit residents who have cognitive, visual, or hearing impairments, or those who are bedridden and are likely to undergo sensory deprivation over time. Sensory deprivation speeds up degenerative changes in mind and body and accelerates the loss of functional cells in the central nervous system. This loss can lead to secondary physical and psychological abnormalities (Oster, 1976). A patient's perception and alertness can be improved by eliciting responses to stimuli in the five sensory areas: vision, hearing, smell, taste, and touch. Use of objects with bright colors, lighted objects, music therapy, aroma therapy, and pet therapy are means of providing sensory stimulation.

## Reality Orientation

*Reality orientation* is a form of therapy for demented, confused, or disoriented individuals and consists of reiteration of the person's identity, orientation to time and place, and reinforcement of consistency in daily routine. Repeated attempts are made to draw the person into conversation, using simple questions, pictures, or whatever may spark their interest. Simple, straightforward, factual information on a regular basis can help residents with substantial cognitive disabilities or those experiencing delirium remain oriented and communicative. Facts such as the resident's name, the name of the facility where the patient is residing, the day, the date, and the season are presented to the resident one at a time, and the resident is encouraged to verbalize the information. Use of calendars, clocks, pictures, and information boards are used as aids (Buettner & Martin, 1995; Lanza, 1997).

## Reminiscence

*Reminiscence*—remembering, and in some way reliving, past experiences—is important for emotional well-being. Engaging in certain activities can help bring back "the good old days" and pleasant events that a person experienced in the past. Such activities for residents include singing or listening to old-time favorite songs, seeing clips of old TV shows, watching old movies, going through photo albums, or discussing memorabilia from a certain era.

## Validation Therapy

In *validation therapy*, a person's belief that he or she is actually living in the past is accepted and validated by the staff members working with the patient. Many elderly, especially before death, want to return to the past to wrap up loose ends. Demented patients often "live in the past." The theory behind this therapeutic approach is that validation or acceptance of the values and beliefs of a person, even if they have no basis in reality, helps the individual come to grips with the past. The therapy involves listening with empathy. In the absence of such therapy, the person is likely to withdraw. Hence, if a 70-year-old man says that he is a senior in high school, and has to go to school so he can run the 100-yard dash, a validation therapist accepts it as real.

## Multisensory Stimulation

*Multisensory stimulation* (MSS), also known as multisensory behavior therapy (MSBT), is commonly known as *Snoezelen* in European countries, and it is becoming increasingly popular in the United States. Snoezelen® is now a registered trademark of ROMPA Ltd, England, a developer and marketer of sensory products. The objective of MSS is to stimulate all of the primary senses—touch, hearing, sight, smell, and taste—through a combined effect of textured objects, soft music, colored lighting, aromas, and favorite foods. Sensory experiences are manipulated, intensified, or reduced in relation to the needs and desires of the individual (Botts et al., 2008). MSS procedures have not been standardized, but according to Baker and colleagues (2001), three main characteristics differentiate MSS from other therapies:

- Visual, auditory, tactile, olfactory, and gustatory stimulation is offered to patients, often in a specially designed room—sometimes called a Snoezelen room or multisensory environment (MSE)—using a variety of lights, soft music, aromas, and tactile objects.

- Associates work one-on-one with patients, adopting a nondirective, enabling approach in which they follow the patients' lead. Patients are encouraged to engage with sensory stimuli of their choice.

- Stimuli used are nonsequential and unpatterned, experienced moment-by-moment without relying on short-term memory to link them to previous events. They present few specific attentional or intellectual demands on the patient with dementia.

MSS therapy has been used with autistic children, people who have developmental disabilities, and older people with dementia. In controlled clinical studies, MSS has been shown to promote positive emotions and relaxation, but it does not appear to reduce aggressive and adaptive behaviors (Chan et al., 2005). MSS also does not appear to have positive effects on mood and cognition in dementia patients (Baker et al., 2003). There is some evidence, however, that MSS may reduce apathy and agitation and improve activities in patients who have moderate to severe dementia (Chung et al., 2002; Staal et al., 2007).

## Activities for Dementia Patients

Patients with dementia present special challenges. Wandering, soliloquizing, repetitious yelling, and other types of agitation, crying, or staring are some of the commonly observed behaviors in patients with dementia. Generally, these residents possess a lot of nervous energy that must be channeled into more constructive outlets. Otherwise, a noisy and chaotic environment can provoke a sense of bewilderment and anxiety in such patients, which, in turn, reinforces disruptive patterns of behavior, such as combativeness and other aggressive manifestations.

Passive behaviors are also among the most common behavioral symptoms of dementia patients. It should be recognized that as cognitive and physical abilities change, individuals with dementia may not be able to engage in activities they once found enjoyable. Some activities may lead to extreme frustration because of a mismatch with the individual's current skill level (Kolanowski & Buettner, 2008). People in mid- to late-stage dementia may not be able to tolerate the stimulation of group activity; one-to-one activities may be more appropriate (Haitsma & Ruckdeschel, 2001).

Under a grant from the New York State Department of Health, one facility discovered that a small-group program may best address the needs of dementia patients. This model proposes a staff-to-resident ratio of 1:8, particularly when patients with mid-stage dementia are involved (Hutson & Hewner, 2001). Focusing on the residents' cognitive and affective needs is critical. The small-group program requires cross-trained staff teams consisting of social workers, activity assistants, and certified nursing assistants. One associate works with a small group of 6 to 10 residents at a time, and practitioners of the three disciplines rotate among the small groups. Group composition is roughly homogeneous; for example, wanderers are in one group and patients displaying disruptive behaviors are in another group (Hutson & Hewner, 2001).

The day often begins for women with grooming and makeup that involves personal touch. Men are in a separate group, in which staff members engage them to talk about the news or sports. These activities allow residents to reminisce and do something with which they are familiar. Staff members take the time to listen, and they provide physical contact, such as hugs and holding hands. They use gentle touches as aids to communication and as reassurances that someone is present and listening. Wandering residents are taken for walks, both indoors and outdoors, and they are asked to hold hands with one another to feel connected and safe (Hutson & Hewner, 2001).

Cognitive function and behavior can be improved with reminiscence therapy (Nawate, et al., 2008). Dementia patients can also be involved in constructive activities, such as folding towels and other simple "household" chores. Cognitive activities, such as matching painted rocks with colors painted inside

an egg carton, can also be employed. Other activities meet the residents' affective needs. For example, soothing music often elevates mood and counters social withdrawal and depression (Humphrey, 2000). Music has been consistently demonstrated to have a positive impact when it is individualized. For example, with individuals for whom English is not the first language, music played in the language of origin is more effective than music played in English (Runci et al., 1999). Technology-based therapies, in the form of audio tapes, DVDs, and technology-assisted sensory stimulation machines that emit water sounds, are also available. Use of bright lights in the care environment may reduce agitation for persons with disturbed sleep-wake cycles (Lyketos et al., 1999).

## Program Planning and Implementation

The number and types of activity programs are limited only by the resources that a facility is able to provide and by the knowledge, creativity, and resourcefulness of its activity staff. However, the activity director should work within these constraints and plan programs that provide the greatest variety of activities in accordance with the interests of most residents, yet no one's needs should be left out. In essence, the special challenge for activity professionals is to create maximum recreational opportunities for each resident and appropriate interventions for those who lack the ability to choose. Implementation requires three stages:

- Identifying suitable programs by evaluating the numerous factors discussed in the various sections on program development.

- Planning programs by selecting and scheduling specific activities.
- Conducting each activity in accordance with the plan.

## Identifying Suitable Programs

Identification of appropriate programs begins with resident assessment. The next step after resident assessment requires compiling information on individual interests and needs and putting them into a composite profile. An interest checklist (Lanza, 1997) can be developed to facilitate this task. Such a checklist can be easily created using a standard spreadsheet program such as Excel, in which a horizontal row can be assigned to each resident and the vertical columns can be marked with various interests such as art, baking, dancing, fishing, reading, etc. Columns can also be used for the degree of social activity preferred. The computer spreadsheet enables the activity director to produce useful summaries of the data. The summaries can be very effective in planning the range of programs without leaving out any resident. This information can be easily updated on a regular basis as the facility's population changes over time. Lanza (1997) recommends developing a *risk awareness profile*, which can also be maintained on a computer spreadsheet. Risk awareness profiles are based on residents' functional limitations as well as cautionary information about things such as allergies or other health conditions or treatments that may require associates to observe certain precautions, as in case of drug side effects.

## Planning Programs

The step just described is likely to identify a large number of programs suitable for the fa-

cility's residents. However, specific programs should be selected on the basis of various considerations such as space, equipment, staffing, and availability of community resources. Activities that would meet the common needs of most residents become the core activity programs. Additional activities should be planned to accommodate the special needs and interests of the remaining residents. A policies and procedures manual for activities should include a variety of choices to suit various resident needs and interests. Much like a recipe book, the procedures section of the manual should list the "ingredients" for various activities, such as the name and description of each activity, the resources the activity requires, the amount of time it takes, the functions of the associates involved in carrying it out, and the type of resident for whom the activity is appropriate.

Activity calendars provide the most effective means for planning. A master calendar is prepared to earmark the main activities for an entire year. This calendar helps the activity staff plan and prepare for major events, special celebrations, and seasonal festivities well in advance. The master calendar is also used to identify programs of wide appeal that would be offered on a regular basis and programs for which some lead-time is necessary.

A tentative weekly calendar of activities, showing the time and place for each activity, should be circulated among department heads, key nursing staff, and the administrator a couple of weeks in advance. This review helps address any potential conflicts and allows for sufficient time to finalize the weekly calendar. The final weekly calendar should be sent to all key departments and personnel a few days in advance, but it should not be posted until Monday morning; otherwise, it is likely to be mistaken for the current week's calendar by residents and families.

A large, wall-size activity calendar should be prominently displayed at one or more designated locations within the facility. An activity calendar with well-planned programs listed on it is also an asset in marketing the facility to prospective clients during the facility tour. During the preadmission inquiry process, a stop at the posted activity calendar and some comments by the tour-giver on the variety and substance of the activities must be part of the facility tour.

No clear guidelines exist regarding the number of programs that should be offered. The key is to find the right balance between quantity and quality. A full schedule with a number of large group activities may not be effective in meeting the needs of some patients. The greatest benefit to residents may come from having fewer activities but activities that are of high quality and truly meet residents' needs (Carroll et al., 1978). At the other extreme, a schedule with very few activities is also undesirable because it would lack variety and would leave residents with large blocks of time with not much to do.

In planning time for activities, Carroll and colleagues (1978) suggested that each full-time associate should spend approximately 25 hours per week actually conducting activities and devote the remainder to planning, documentation, and attending meetings. Twenty-five hours of programming per full-time associate allows for 12 or 13 separate group activities per week. Synergies can be added by using volunteers to complement staffing, which is often short-handed. Realistic amounts of time should be allowed to set up the activity location, to prepare materials and equipment, to transport nonambulatory residents to and from the activity location, and to return the area to its original set-up.

Nursing staff members generally help with transporting or assisting the residents to the activity area. Cooperation from nurses is also needed for dressing residents appropriately, helping residents use the toilet before activities, and dispensing medications and treatments in a way that will not interfere with the resident's ability to participate in activity programs. Hence, nursing schedules are often an important consideration in activity planning. The dietary staff may be involved when refreshments are a part of the activity. Housekeeping and maintenance staff members are needed for special set-ups that require moving and arranging furniture and cleaning up after activities (Carroll et al., 1978).

## Conducting Activities

The actual implementation of an activity is greatly facilitated by how well a program is planned. Execution of most routine programs simply requires bringing together the planned resources. But for larger programs such as parties, functions, and outings, efforts and resources must be coordinated, and follow-up is necessary, to make sure that everything proceeds smoothly. Each program should be carried out in accordance with the plan, while allowing for any unforeseen circumstances that may occur. Whenever possible, if a planned program must be canceled, an appropriate substitute activity should be provided in accordance with a contingency plan. Hence, some backup programs that can be carried out on short notice are necessary.

## Program Evaluation

*Program evaluation* is the process of systematically appraising a program to determine whether expected results are being achieved. Evaluating activity programming is a necessary prerequisite for improving the quality of a program. New and improved programs can be created only if the effectiveness of current programs can be objectively evaluated. When the evaluation validates the effectiveness of programs that associates have helped create, their morale is improved. On the other hand, evaluation should not be used to criticize or penalize activity personnel.

For effective evaluation, program goals and expected results must be established at the planning stage: programs should be planned with certain outcomes in mind. Determining whether the expected outcomes are achieved is the focus of program evaluation. The primary focus should be to determine whether residents' needs are being met. When desired outcomes are not achieved, program directors must try to discover the reasons these goals were not reached. An outside activity consultant may be employed to either do the program evaluation or to train the activity staff on how to do the evaluation.

The process of program evaluation involves continuous and systematic collection of relevant data. Because resource inputs such as staff time for activities are generally fixed, data collection pertains mainly to the outcomes. To collect outcome data, two main records should be kept. First, an accurate attendance record should be maintained for each activity. A computer spreadsheet can greatly facilitate this type of recordkeeping. The data should reflect each resident's participation by the specific program he or she attends and by how many times the resident attended each program. These attendance data would yield two critical pieces of information: which programs are the most popular and the level of participation for each resident.

The second type of record involves qualitative information on the goals and progress of the program in relation to the goals planned for each resident in the care plan. This information is directly related to the assessment, care planning, and progress of the resident and can greatly facilitate documentation in each patient's medical record. When these two types of records are analyzed for each patient, it will be clear how well the activity programming is addressing each patient's individual needs and what changes may be necessary when certain needs are not met.

## Volunteer Support

The activity director is generally responsible for developing and coordinating the facility's volunteer program. With proper training and supervision, volunteers from the local community can provide valuable assistance in a number of nontechnical areas in which staff resources are often scarce. Hence, volunteer support is a critical adjunct to staff efforts to augment services and to improve the quality of life for the residents. Because most volunteers have regular and frequent contact with the facility, they establish an important link between the facility and the local community.

Volunteer roles are not just confined to helping with activity programs. Depending on personal interests, volunteers may complement the efforts of the staff by passing meal trays during lunch or dinner, pouring water, sweeping up the dining room after dinner, maintaining wheelchairs in working order, and other such tasks. Volunteers may also assist with shopping and other chores for patients, or provide transportation for outings.

Some key factors in recruiting and retaining volunteers are listed here:

- A facility that has successfully established exchange relationships with the community is likely to have an easier time finding people interested in volunteering than facilities that have not formed such exchanges. Recruitment efforts must be ongoing.

- People most likely to volunteer are retirees, homemakers without small children to take care of, and young adults in school. Various avenues can be pursued for recruiting interested people from these three groups. As mentioned earlier, some family members are also potential recruits for volunteering. Involvement by family members in activities can be a successful avenue for a facility to build positive relationships with families.

- A facility's advertising budget is generally small, and advertising may not be a very effective avenue for recruiting volunteers. Methods such as contacting potential volunteers directly, visiting local schools and discussing after-school opportunities, using current volunteers to recruit others, offering incentives, or sponsoring a volunteer recruitment day in collaboration with other service agencies are some of the more effective means.

- Volunteers' availability, skills, and interests should be matched with the needs of the residents. The facility may state what its most critical needs are, but it should not pressure any volunteer into filling a certain role. The desired areas of service should be chosen by the volunteers.

- Volunteers must be carefully selected using a formal process that should include filling out an application, screening, interviewing, and reference checks. Orientation and training must follow.

- Maintain a log book for recording the time each volunteer spends in the facility.

- Praise and recognition are paramount. Apart from providing the opportunity for personal gratification that the volunteer derives from helping others, recognizing the volunteer's work is the only way that the facility compensates volunteers for their efforts. Effectively managed facilities have an annual dinner and award ceremony exclusively for volunteers. Letting volunteers have meals at the facility at subsidized prices or for free, depending on the tasks they perform while they are in the facility, is also a good policy.

## For Further Thought

1. As a nursing home administrator, how would you determine whether or not you have an effectively run activity program in your facility?

2. What types of policies are appropriate for residents' participation in religious activities in nursing homes that are affiliated with religious organizations? What type of policies for religious activities are appropriate for residents in nursing homes that do not have such religious affiliations?

## For Further Learning

The National Association of Activity Professionals is the only national group that represents activity professionals in geriatric settings exclusively.

www.thenaap.com

The National Certification Council for Activity Professionals is one of the certifying bodies recognized by federal law and is the only national organization that exclusively certifies activity professionals who work with the elderly.

www.nccap.org

## REFERENCES

Baker, R., et al. 2001. A randomized controlled trial of the effects of multi-sensory stimulation (MSS) for people with dementia. *British Journal of Clinical Psychology* 40, no. 1: 81–96.

Baker, R., et al. 2003. Effects of multi-sensory stimulation for people with dementia. *Journal of Advanced Nursing* 43, no. 5: 465–477.

Botts, B.H., et al. 2008. Snoezelen, emperical review of product representation. *Focus on Autism and Other Developmental Disabilities* 23, no. 3: 138–147.

Buettner, L., & Martin, S.L. 1995. *Therapeutic Recreation in the Nursing Home.* State College, PA: Venture Publishing.

Carroll, K., et al. 1978. *Therapeutic Activities Programming with the Elderly.* Minneapolis: Ebenezer Center for Aging and Human Development.

Chan, S., et al. 2005. The clinical effectiveness of multisensory therapy on clients with developmental disability. *Research in Developmental Disabilities* 26, no. 2: 131–142.

Chung, J.C., et al. 2002. Snoezelen for dementia. *Chochrane Database of Systematic Reviews* [electronic resource] 2002, no. 4: pp. CD003152.

Colling, K.B. 1999. Passive behaviors in dementia: Clinical application of the Need-Driven Dementia Compromised Behavior Model. *Journal of Gerontological Nursing* 25, no. 9: 27–32.

Greenblatt, F.S. 1988. *Therapeutic Recreation for Long-Term Care Facilities.* New York: Human Sciences Press.

Haitsma, K.V., & Ruckdeschel, K. 2001. Special care for dementia in nursing homes: Overview of innovations in programs and activities. *Alzheimer's Care Quarterly* 2, no. 3: 49–56.

Hastings, L.E. 1981. *Complete Handbook of Activities and Recreational Programs for Nursing Homes.* Englewood Cliffs, NJ: Prentice-Hall.

Humphrey, M.A. 2000. Alzheimer's disease meets the 'Mozart effect.' *Nursing Homes Long Term Care Management* 49, no. 6: 50–51.

Hutson, J.A., & Hewner, S.J. 2001. Activities 'plus' improve Alzheimer's care. *Nursing Homes Long Term Care Management* 50, no. 6: 52–55.

Kolanowski, A., & Buettner, L. 2008. Prescribing activities that engage passive residents. *Journal of Gerontological Nursing* 34, no. 1: 13–18.

Lanza, S.E. 1997. *Essentials for the Activity Professional in Long-Term Care*. Albany, NY: Delmar Publishers.

Lyketos, C., et al. 1999. A randomized control trial of bright light therapy for agitated behaviors in dementia patients residing in long-term care. *International Journal of Geriatric Psychiatry* 14, no.7: 520–525.

Meeks, S., et al. 2007. Activity participation and affect among nursing home residents: Support for a behavioural model of depression. *Aging and Mental Health* 11, no. 6: 751–760.

Nawate, Y., et al. 2008. Efficacy of group reminiscence therapy for elderly dementia patients residing at home: A preliminary report. *Physical and Occupation Therapy Geriatrics* 26, no. 3: 57–68.

Oster, C. 1976. Sensory deprivation in geriatric patients. *Journal of the American Geriatrics Society* 24, no. 10: 461–464.

Runci, S., et al. 1999. Empirical test of language-relevant interventions for dementia. *International Psychogeriatrics* 11, no. 3: 301–311.

Staal, J.A., et al. 2007. The effects of Snoezelen (multi-sensory behavior therapy) and psychiatric care on agitation, apathy, and activities of daily living in dementia patients on a short term geriatric psychiatric inpatient unit. *International Journal of Psychiatry in Medicine* 37, no. 4: 357–370.

Tedrick, T., & Green, E.R. 1995. *Activity Experiences and Programming within Long-Term Care*. State College, PA: Venture Publishing.

# Chapter 12

## Dietary Services

### What You Will Learn

- Food services are guided by three main principles: individual nutritional needs, sensory gratification, and social interaction.

- The food service director is mainly responsible for food purchase, food preparation, food service, and dietetics under consultation from a registered dietitian. Traditional facilities have cooks, helpers, and dietary aides to staff the kitchen.

- Menu planning requires consideration of meal plans, menu choice, and menu cycle.

- Several factors should be considered when selecting menu items. Menus must be nutritionally balanced, include dishes that are palatable, and be within budgetary cost allowances. Standardized recipes and portions are designed to yield consistent quality and cost.

- Selection of vendors should be based on reliability, quality, and cost. Ordering schedules vary by the type of food product. Dietary supplies and emergency supplies should be on hand.

- Blind receiving is a more reliable method than invoice receiving for order delivery. Food storage temperatures must be monitored.

- Ordering cycles and state regulations determine the number of days worth of food supplies that must be on hand. Adequate inventory control is based on perpetual and physical inventory systems. The physical inventory is also used to determine food cost.

- Food production requires planning and contingency arrangements. Each of the main production methods has its advantages and disadvantages.

- Therapeutic diets can range from simple to complex. Nourishments served in between meals are beneficial for some residents. Issues related to food intake should be addressed.

- Various conditions may necessitate the use of enteral or parenteral feeding methods to maintain adequate nutritional intake.

- Centralized food service is more traditional than decentralized service. Each has its advantages and disadvantages that must be evaluated before making a switch from one type of service to another. Maintaining foods at their right serving temperatures is a main challenge in food service.
- Food poisoning is almost entirely preventable by practicing good sanitation and good food handling techniques.

# Food Service Principles

The dietary operation in a nursing facility comprises clinical food services whose main objective is to meet the nutritional needs of each patient. In many nursing facilities, the dietary department is also responsible for preparing meals for the staff, visitors, and volunteers. In most cases, preparing food separately for residents, staff members, and guests is impractical. Hence, the basic menu should be designed to meet the needs of all these groups. The dietary department is generally also responsible for making refreshments or special preparations for certain activities such as parties and functions. Some large facilities may also have contracts to prepare meals for the local Meals On Wheels program. Food services may also be contracted from outside vendors. However, most facilities operate their own kitchens to serve the particular needs of their residents. In newer facilities in particular, smaller household-style kitchens and dining services are catching on as part of the culture change movement (see Chapter 8).

Food has universal appeal as a necessity for physical sustenance, as a means of sensory gratification, and as an agent for creating social interaction. These three major aspects of food provide the basic principles that guide food preparation and service in nursing facilities. For patients who have special dietary needs, food intake must also serve a therapeutic purpose. Loss of appetite, inability to feed oneself, problems with chewing, swallowing difficulties, and inadequate nutrition are some common problems among nursing home residents. Other dietetic needs are related to diseases such as diabetes, heart conditions, or liver disease. To meet these special dietetic needs and to address these common problems, dietary services in nursing facilities have to combine the functions of food service and dietetics.

# Dietary Department

## Supervision

After nursing services, dietary is the second largest department in a nursing facility. The department is managed by a full-time food service director, also known as dietary manager, who reports to the administrator. The dietary manager has both management and clinical responsibilities. This individual is responsible for staffing functions that include hiring, training, and scheduling; purchasing food and supplies; inventory management; and managing the food preparation and food service within the departmental budget. The dietary manager supervises all aspects of dietary operations such as food storage, food production and preparation of therapeutic diets, meal service, dish washing, and sanitation. Clinical responsibilities of this position include nutritional screening, assessment, care planning, diet planning, and documenting progress notes under the consultation from a clinical dietitian.

Large facilities require one or more assistant food service managers. Dietary managers and assistants should supervise the preparation and service of all meals and share clinical responsibilities. Supervision should also be provided on weekends and holidays, particularly when special meals are planned and when the facility is likely to have more than the usual number of visitors, some of whom may have a meal with the residents they may be visiting.

State regulations specify the qualifications required for the position of dietary manager. A registered dietitian (RD) fulfills the requirements for this position in all states. RDs are difficult to recruit in nursing facilities, although some facilities may be able to recruit a part-time dietitian. Only some very large facilities may be able to afford a full-time RD. The two most common choices for filling the dietary manager's position are a registered dietetic technician (DTR), who holds an associate's degree in general dietetics from a program approved by the American Dietetic Association (ADA), or a Certified Dietary Manager (CDM), who has completed the requirements for certification by the Dietary Managers Association (DMA).

A DTR often works in partnership with a registered dietitian to screen, evaluate, and educate patients. In addition to a two-year associate's degree from an ADA-approved dietetics program located in an accredited college or university, DTRs also must have had supervised practical experience in dietary services, and they must pass a national examination and take continuing education courses throughout their careers. Both RDs and DTRs are certified by the Commission on Dietetic Registration (CDR), the credentialing agency for the ADA.

## Food Service Assistants

The dietary department has three main categories of food service workers who perform a number of functions in the main kitchen under the general direction of the dietary manager, and assistant food service manager, if the facility has the latter position. They include cooks, cook's helpers, and dietary aides (see Figure III–1). Cooks and their helpers are responsible for food preparation according to preplanned menus and standard recipes. Cooks prepare the main dishes (also known as entrées) and are responsible for portion control. Cook's helpers may assist with the preparation of main dishes, but their main job is to prepare side dishes, such as potatoes, pasta, vegetables, and salads. Dietary aides are responsible for portioning out food at the tray line, clean-up, and dishwashing. Cross-training these employees is often necessary, especially to allow cook's helpers and dietary aides to perform more skilled functions when they must fill in for cooks and helpers because of sickness and other instances when cooks and helpers need time off.

During meal service, as a general rule, certified nursing assistants (CNAs), preferably with additional help from volunteers, pick up meal trays at the end of the kitchen tray line and serve patients in the dining room. Trays are also served from carts transported to any auxiliary dining rooms located in other sections of the facility. CNAs are also responsible for collecting trays and dishes after each meal and for bringing them to the dishwashing area.

Dietary aides operate the dishwasher and clean cooking utensils. Some large facilities have a position of night cleaner who comes in after the kitchen has been closed to thoroughly clean floors; equipment; and other cooking, service, and storage areas.

## Dietary Consultation

Therapeutic functions, which include menu planning based on nutritional guidelines, are under the direction of an RD. When a nursing home does not have an RD on its staff, regulations require the services of a dietary consultant who works under contract. Multifacility chains are likely to have one or more clinical RDs in a corporate-level position to provide consultation to the facilities operated by the chain. The extent and frequency of consultation is specified by nursing home regulations in each state.

The consultant RD must have active involvement in planning menus, developing recipes, ensuring the nutritional adequacy of food served, and assessing nutrition-related resident problems, such as weight loss or feeding issues. The consultant dietitian must also review dietary assessment and care plans, determine equipment needs, review dietary policies and procedures, and make recommendations for sanitary and safe food preparation and storage practices.

After each consultation, the RD must furnish the dietary manager with a written report, and the administrator should receive a copy of this report. The administrator should also have periodic face-to-face meetings with the dietitian to remain involved with any issues or concerns. The consultant dietitian should also meet with charge nurses to address specific patient problems and consult regularly with the director of nursing. Diet and nutritional issues should also be discussed with the patient's attending physician.

## Dietary Screening

Nutritional status of the patient is a critical aspect of holistic care, and determining a patient's nutritional needs begins with nutritional screening. The purpose of **nutritional screening** is to identify patients who may be at risk for nutritional problems. Examples of at-risk patients include those who sustain weight loss, those on therapeutic diets, and those who either cannot take food by mouth or have difficulty eating. Nutritional screening relies on the physician's diet orders and on a comprehensive screening by the dietitian.

## Menu Planning

The menu is central to food service operations because it determines how the resources of the department will be used. Hence, menu planning is a major function carried out with the assistance of the clinical dietitian.

In multifacility chains, menu planning is generally centralized at the corporate office. Standardized menus and recipes are developed for use by affiliated facilities. In this situation, corporations must allow their individual facilities some flexibility for variation to accommodate local tastes. Too rigid a system is likely to result in patient dissatisfaction. In nonchain independent facilities, the consulting dietitian helps the dietary manager develop appropriate menus for the facility.

Three considerations are fundamental to menu planning. First, menu planning requires a policy on the **meal plan**, that is, the number of meals to be served per day. The daily nutrient intake should be distributed in a balanced fashion over the number of meals served (Mahaffey et al., 1981). The second factor is choice. A facility may or may not offer a choice of entrées. Accordingly, the facility will have selective or nonselective menus. A third planning consideration is the menu cycle or rotation.

## Meal Plans

### Conventional Three-Meal Plan

Nursing facilities typically follow a three-meal plan consisting of breakfast, lunch, and dinner (also known as supper). Federal and state regulations specify the maximum time lapse between dinner served at night and breakfast the following morning. A maximum time lapse of 14 hours is the common standard. Regulations also generally require that residents be offered a light bedtime snack, such as crackers, cheese, cookies, ice cream, milk, fruit, or juice. Typically, under the three-meal plan, breakfast is served between 7:30 and 8:30 a.m., lunch at 11:00 to 12:30 p.m., and dinner at 5:30 to 6:30 p.m.

### Modified Five-Meal Plan

In recent years, a modified meal plan with five daily meals has come into vogue, and this plan has received enthusiastic acceptance from both residents and caregivers. The modified plan gives residents flexibility with their daily lives. The extended meal service hours give residents greater access to meals with less disruption of their preferred daily routines. In contrast, under the conventional meal plan, residents need to be up, toileted, and dressed for the scheduled breakfast service. The mornings become the busiest and the most rushed time for the nursing staff, and many patients resist having to get up early in the morning and to be hurried through daily hygiene chores.

Under the modified five-meal plan, a continental breakfast consisting of items such as rolls, muffins, yogurt, custard, juice, and coffee is served at 7:30 a.m. Residents can sleep in if they do not wish to be up that early. By the time a more substantial brunch is served, from around 10:30 to 11:30 a.m., almost all residents are up and around. The other three meals include a lunchtime snack consisting of beverages and high-calorie items served from 1:30 to 2:00 p.m., a regular dinner at around 6:00 p.m., and a late evening snack before bedtime.

Choice of multiple small meals during the day can lead to greater client satisfaction as well as greater nutritional intake. In a study evaluating family members' preferences for a range of treatment alternatives designed to improve nursing home residents' oral food and fluid intake, three nutritional interventions were rated as the most desirable: improving food quality, providing feeding assistance, and making multiple small meals and snacks available throughout the day (Simmons et al., 2003).

## Menu Choice

A *nonselective menu* does not regularly offer a choice of entrées to all residents. It is the most common type in nursing homes. One main dish is specified for each of the three meals. The main dish on the menu is served unless it conflicts with the resident's preferences as noted in the resident's records. Regulations require that an alternate food item of equal nutritional value be made available to accommodate individual preferences.

Upscale facilities, with a high proportion of private-pay residents, typically offer a *selective menu* that offers a choice between two entrées from which each resident can make a selection. A full selective menu also generally offers two choices of vegetables and desserts. Offering a selective menu can lower plate waste (food left unconsumed), increase personal satisfaction, and still be accommodated within the food budget. To accomplish this goal, Puckett and Miller (1988) proposed pairing an expensive entrée with an inexpensive one to offset costs. However, a selective menu is likely to require some additional staff time and is more expensive to produce than a nonselective menu.

Another alternative to a selective menu is a buffet offering a variety of food choices. A buffet can also be used as an alternative to a five-meal plan, straddling the hours of the brunch and light lunch services, and offering greater mealtime flexibility to residents.

## Menu Cycle

Dietary policies and procedures should specify the length of time for menu rotation. A set of menus is developed to cover a predefined period, generally three or four weeks, during which the main items on the menus are not repeated. At the end of this period, the same daily menus are repeated in the same order. Different cycle menus can be created to go with changing seasons. For example, hot soups are more popular in winter, whereas cold cuts and salads go well in summer. Cycle menus do not have to be rigid. There should be flexibility to include festive menus for holidays and other social occasions. Special ethnic themes, such as Chinese, Italian, or Hawaiian, can also be incorporated to

break the monotony of regular meal service, especially when special menus are coordinated with social activities promoting some ethnic theme. An outdoor barbecue in summer or a picnic in early fall also add variety to the menu and provide a nonroutine social setting.

## Menu Development

Once the meal plan, menu choice, and menu cycle have been established, the clinical dietitian and the dietary manager should work together in selecting appropriate main and side dishes for each meal. Several factors should be considered when selecting menu items:

- General food preferences.
- Variety of foods.
- Adherence to Dietary Reference Intakes.
- Appearance and palatability.
- Cost.
- Facility resources and capabilities.
- Emergency menus.

Food preferences are based on cultural, geographic, and religious traditions. Items selected for the menu should appeal to as many residents as possible, but there is a growing demand to accommodate individual culture-based diet preferences such as vegetarian and kosher diets.

Unless a resident has special nutritional requirements, a balanced combination of foods can meet the nutritional needs of most people. The U.S. Department of Health and Human Services (DHHS) and the U.S. Department of Agriculture (USDA) jointly publish dietary guidelines to promote nutritional adequacy. The following key recommendations are made in the 2005 *Dietary Guidelines for Americans* (DHHS/USDA, 2005):

- Consume a sufficient amount of fruits and vegetables while staying within energy needs. Two cups of fruit and 2½ cups of vegetables per day are recommended for a reference 2,000-calorie intake, with higher or lower amounts depending on the calorie level.

- Choose a variety of fruits and vegetables each day. In particular, select from all five vegetable subgroups (dark green, orange, legumes, starchy vegetables, and other vegetables) several times a week.

- Consume three or more ounce-equivalents of whole grain products per day, with the rest of the recommended grains coming from enriched or other grain products such as pasta. In general, at least half the grains should come from whole grains.

- Consume three cups per day of fat-free or low-fat milk or equivalent milk products.

- Consume less than 10 percent of calories from saturated fatty acids and less than 300 mg/day of cholesterol, and keep transfatty acid consumption as low as possible.

- For vegetarians, give special attention to their intakes of protein, iron, and vitamin B12, as well as calcium and vitamin D if avoiding milk products. Legumes, nuts, and soy products must be included in meals as appropriate meat substitutes to furnish adequate proteins for vegetarians.

- Older adults should also consume extra vitamin D from vitamin D–fortified foods and/or supplements.

- A substantial proportion of individuals over age 50 have reduced ability to absorb naturally occurring vitamin B12, but they can absorb the crystalline form. They should take foods fortified with vitamin B12 such as fortified cereals or take the crystalline form of vitamin B12 supplements.

- Dietary potassium can lower blood pressure and blunt the effects of salt on blood pressure in some individuals.

- Dietary fiber is important for laxation (bowel movement). Constipation may affect up to 20 percent of people over 65 years of age, so older adults should consume foods rich in dietary fiber. Hydration is also important for laxation.

Before the menus are finalized, their nutrient content must be evaluated to comply with the Dietary Reference Intakes (DRIs). The DRI consist of two sets of values, called Recommended Dietary Allowances (RDAs) and Adequate Intake (AI). Both these sets of values establish levels of calories and nutrients such as proteins, vitamins, and minerals. DRIs establish not only recommended daily intakes necessary to help maintain health, but also tolerable upper intake limits to help avoid any potential harm from excessive intake. AI suggests nutritional adequacy when not enough scientific evidence exists to establish an RDA. The DRIs have been compiled by the Food and Nutrition Board of the Institute of Medicine at the National Academy of Sciences (DRIs for older adults can be accessed over the Web; see For Further Learning at the end of this chapter).

Pleasing combinations of dishes should be included on the menu by varying color, flavor, texture, shape, consistency, and method of preparation (Graves & Stewart, 1985). Food served to the residents must be both palatable and attractive.

One of the most challenging aspects of menu planning is to keep the cost of food to a minimum without compromising quality. The dietary department is generally allowed a per-patient-day (PPD) cost for the raw food budget. The daily raw food budget will be a dollar amount calculated as follows:

*Daily raw food budget = PPD cost ×*
*Census (or, Number of patients)*

To stay within the budgeted allowance, the daily food cost allowance should first be allocated to each meal and food category. Then the cost of each item on the menu should be calculated (Sullivan & Atlas, 1998). Lunch is generally the most expensive of the three meals, followed by dinner and then breakfast. The cost of bedtime snacks must also come out of the food budget.

Preparation methods, time required for food preparation, skills of the kitchen staff, storage space, serving temperatures, and type of kitchen equipment are things to consider when planning a menu. In other words, facility resources and capabilities must be taken into account.

In addition to the menus included in the regular menu cycle, the facility's dietary policies and procedures should specify menus for emergency situations such as when the facility has a prolonged power failure or when the dietary department may have to be operated on a skeletal crew because of emergencies such as snowstorms, floods, or other natural events that prevent most of the scheduled staff from getting to work. Under these conditions, preparing the regular menu would be impractical. Emergency menus require the use of canned, preserved, packaged, and precooked food items. The facility must also make prior arrangements for procuring bottled water in case of an emergency.

## Standardized Recipes and Portions

The menu functions as the "road map" for dietary operations, and standard recipes provide the "directions" on the road map. A standard recipe is a blueprint for food preparation and is essential for controlling food costs. Recipes are designed and tested so that a consistent product with known quality, quantity, and taste will be produced. Standard recipes will also yield consistent costs, predictable labor hours, and nutritional value (Ninemeier, 1985). Each recipe must provide details on the specific raw ingredients and their quantity, method of preparing, utensils and equipment needed, method and temperature for cooking, amount of time needed for preparation and cooking, total yield, number of portions, size of each portion, temperature for serving, and any other pertinent information. Recipes based on 100 portions can be easily adapted to serve any number of people. Recipes are commonly printed on plastic-coated recipe cards so that they can be easily filed and retrieved when needed.

## Purchasing Food and Supplies

### Vendor Arrangements

The facility should make arrangements with reputable food vendors to procure dry goods, frozen foods, fresh produce, and dairy products. Several vendors should be asked for competitive bidding based on written specifications. Reliability, regular delivery schedule, consistent quality, and price are important considerations when selecting the vendors. Depending on the location of their facilities, multifacility chains often have a great deal of purchasing power to select the vendors that their affiliated facilities are required to use. Independent facilities and small chains can explore the possibilities of participating in cooperative or group-purchasing arrangements that can give even small facilities some buying power. Food vendors have different grades of products to meet the needs of a variety of customers. For instance, quality can vary according to brand, grade, size, thickness, weight, or count. Because of these variations, a facility ought to have written specifications for the food it buys as part of its contracts with vendors. Prices are also negotiated in advance but are subject to change with sufficient advance notice by the vendor.

## Food Ordering

The planned menu and recipes provide the basis for food purchasing. However, careful planning is necessary to ensure that the needed food items will be available in time for food production. Size of the order is governed by the patient census, anticipated number of guest meals, and meals for volunteers and staff. In essence, the number of portions to be served must be carefully forecasted, and the time lapse between food preparation and delivery must be taken into account. The frequency of delivery depends on the vendor's delivery schedule, the type of food item delivered, and the facility's storage capacity. Puckett and Miller (1988) suggested the following steps for economical food delivery:

- Frozen food: weekly or semi-monthly.
- Chilled meat, fish, and poultry: twice a week.
- Fresh produce: once or twice a week.
- Canned goods and staples: weekly, semi-monthly, or monthly.
- Fresh dairy items, breads, and baked goods: daily or every other day.
- Butter, eggs, and cheese: weekly.

## Dietary Supplies

Supplies used in the dietary department can be classified into three main categories: supplies used in the kitchen for food production, such as aluminum foils, plastic wraps, and storage bags; supplies used for serving meals; and chemicals and supplies for dishwashing and cleaning. Service supplies can be categorized as reusable or disposable. Such supplies include trays, dinnerware, tableware, hollowware, glassware, and disposable paper, plastic, and styrofoam products.

Reusable supplies come in a variety of materials, such as rubber, plastic, fiberglass, and other materials, such as vitrified china, which is designed for both durability and attractiveness. Stainless steel cutlery resists tarnish, is durable, and is easy to clean. Some disposables are used on a regular basis when needed, but they should mostly be kept on hand for emergency use. An adequate amount of disposable plates, cups, and cutlery should be kept in stock to be used when a power outage occurs or when the dishwashing equipment is out of order. Regular use of disposables in the long run is quite expensive, yet it comes across as "cheap" to residents and visitors and diminishes the aesthetic appeal of the dining experience. Tablecloths, cloth napkins, and table centerpieces used at least for the main meal add to the quality of the dining experience.

## Food Storage and Inventory
### Receiving

The dietary department should have effective control procedures to ensure that the food and supplies delivered by vendors match the quality and quantity of items ordered. Dietary policies should assign the job of receiving to authorized personnel, and receiving responsibilities and procedures should be clearly described. Two receiving methods are commonly used (Puckett & Miller, 1988): invoice receiving and blind receiving.

## Invoice Receiving

Invoice receiving is a method in which the items delivered are checked against the original order. The focus is on finding any discrepancies between what was ordered and what is received. Shortages, substitutions, deviations from quality specifications, and any rejections should be carefully noted by the receiver.

## Blind Receiving

Blind receiving is a method in which the original order shows the specific items but not the quantities. The quantities of the items received are recorded by the person checking the order. This method is more reliable than invoice receiving because the receiver may fail to do accurate comparisons when using the invoice receiving method. In either case, the facility should use its own ordering record rather than the supplier's delivery invoice to ensure that all items received are exactly as they were ordered.

## Storage

The facility should have adequate, secure, and sanitary space for storage of various food items at their proper temperatures. Three types of food storage space are necessary: dry storage, refrigeration, and freeze storage.

The dry storeroom must be clean, cool, and dry. It should also have adequate ventilation and lighting. The recommended temperature range for dry food storage is between 50° F and 70° F (10° C to 21° C) (Puckett & Miller, 1988). All food must be on shelves or kept above the floor on dollies or pallets, which should be 6 to 12 inches above the floor, depending on state regulations. Off-the-floor storage makes it possible to keep the entire floor area clean. Chemicals and cleaning supplies should be stored in a separate area away from food and other dietary supplies.

Refrigerator temperatures should be maintained at 40° F (4° C) or lower. To prevent cross-contamination, raw meat should be separated from other foods and should be stored on the bottom shelves so meat juices do not drip on other foods.

Frozen foods should be kept at 0° F (–18° C) or below. Refrigerators and freezers should be equipped with functioning thermometers. A temperature log should be maintained to record regular temperature readings for refrigerators and freezers. Any malfunctions should be reported to the maintenance department for prompt rectification.

## Inventory Control

Determining how large a food inventory should be on hand at any given time depends on two main factors: immediate needs and contingency needs. Adequate quantities of food supplies required for the menus must be available when needed. A sufficient stock of food must be on hand at all times to prepare meals for the next four to seven days, depending on the ordering cycle.

In accordance with the policy on emergency menus, adequate nonperishable food items must be held in stock to last for three to four days. State regulations may also specify how many days worth of food inventory and nonperishable emergency food supplies must be maintained.

Two methods of keeping track of inventory are used conjointly for adequate control: the perpetual inventory system and the physical inventory system.

## Perpetual Inventory System

A perpetual inventory system is used to maintain a continuous record of the quantity on hand for each item. A separate inventory card is maintained for each item. The card has three or four columns for recording purchases, amounts used, and amount remaining on hand:

> *Amount on hand = Amount on hand shown on the previous line + Purchases – Amount withdrawn*

This system provides a running balance of quantities remaining on shelves at any given time.

## Physical Inventory System

In the physical inventory system, each item in storage is actually counted. Physical inventory gives an accurate count of what is on hand. The quantities on hand should tally with the amounts on hand shown on the inventory card. Discrepancies may suggest either pilferage or errors in recording data (Sullivan & Atlas, 1998). This inventory is generally taken once a month.

Many operations do not use the perpetual inventory system because it is time consuming. Quantities must be recorded each time items are added or withdrawn. This process can be facilitated by using commercial software programs for inventory management.

Rotating the inventory is important to prevent spoilage. The first-in first-out system, abbreviated as FIFO, requires that all products be dated when received. Secondly, newly received products should be stored at the back of the shelves; products already on the shelf should be moved to the front. When products are needed for food preparation, they should be picked from the front. This system ensures that older products are used first.

---

# Food Cost

All facilities should at least take a monthly physical inventory to accurately determine the food cost, which is calculated as follows:

(a) *Cost of physical inventory at the end of the previous month*

+

(b) *Cost of all food invoices (food purchased) during the current month*

–

(c) *Cost of physical inventory at the end of the month*

=

(d) *Gross food cost for the month [(a) + (b) – (c)]*

–

(e) *Cost of meals served to nonpatients:*

$$\frac{(d)}{\textit{Total number of meals served}} \times \textit{Number of nonpatient meals served}$$

=

(f) *Net patient food cost for the month [(d) – (e)]*

(g) *Food cost per patient day (PPD):*

$$\frac{(f)}{\textit{Number of patient days for the month}}$$

Note: Patient days = Cumulative census for the month

A high food cost does not necessarily indicate that the food being served is of high quality. The dietary manager must always be conscious of food waste and the potential for pilferage. Periodic monitoring of receiving procedures and regular checks of receiving and storage areas can reveal problems that may otherwise go unnoticed. Food in poor condition may have to be discarded, but the department must have a strict policy that no food is to be discarded without specific approval from the dietary manager. Ordering foods not called for by the menus, ordering in excessive quantities, and overproduction are other factors that often lead to waste and higher food cost than what is necessary. Theft and pilferage may be occurring that may go unobserved. The dietary manager should do occasional spot checks to reconcile invoiced and received items.

The administrator should be aware that even though the food service director and his or her assistants have the responsibility for controlling dietary products, the supervisors may themselves be involved in theft. This consideration does not automatically imply guilt, but it should increase awareness of the possibility of theft by supervisors, especially when the actual food cost exceeds the menu cost. Pre-costing menus establishes the expected food cost. When the actual food cost substantially exceeds or routinely exceeds the expected cost, the administrator should first look into the methods being used for inventorying food and calculating the food cost before investigating probable breaches of security.

# Food Production

## Production Planning

Menu planning, standard recipes, food purchasing, storage, and inventory management are the essential prerequisites for food production in a facility. But food production itself requires planning ahead. For instance, frozen meats must be thawed in the refrigerator three to four days in advance so that they are available for cooking on the day they are on the menu. Some food items require full or partial cooking on the day before the menu is to be served. However, in spite of the best planning efforts, some deviation from the menu may sometimes become necessary. For example, an item needed for the menu might not be received on time, or the quantity of raw ingredients might not be sufficient. In such cases, occasional substitutions become necessary and the facility must make contingency plans, because the need for substitutions generally crops up at the last moment. Menu substitutions should match the nutritive value of the food item replaced, and all substitutions should be properly documented.

## Production Methods

Three basic types of food preparation methods are commonly used in health care institutions (Puckett & Miller, 1988). Each method has its advantages and disadvantages, which should be carefully evaluated during menu planning. The food service objectives of each nursing facility will determine the right blend of these methods:

- Cook-and-serve.
- Cook-and-chill or -freeze.
- Assemble-and-serve.

## Cook-and-Serve Method

The cook-and-serve method is the traditional approach to food production, in which most menu items are prepared primarily from raw ingredients on the day they are to be served. After cooking, the food is kept hot or cold until serving time. Cook-and-serve requires a relatively large inventory and more labor than the other two methods. Another disadvantage is the limited time the staff generally has to get the food ready for serving. Greater control over quality is one of the main advantages. Food cooked from scratch has the "home-cooked" appeal. Use of seasonal fresh produce makes food even more appealing. Home-style cooking can be marketed to prospective clients as an added value. Some facilities prepare fresh bakery items, such as breads and pies, on a daily basis. The pleasant aroma of freshly baked goods permeating throughout the facility appeals to most people, and it adds to the homelike atmosphere. This aroma can be easily achieved by using premixed products, which are widely available in dry or frozen form.

## Cook-and-Chill or -Freeze Method

Chilling or freezing after cooking requires two stages of heating: initial cooking and reheating before serving. The cooking stage can be done up to six weeks in advance for cook-and-chill items, and earlier for cook-and-freeze items.

In the cook-and-chill method, the food is first completely cooked. It is then rapidly chilled to between 32° F (0° C) and 40° F (4° C), using an ice bath or blast chiller. Typically, complete chilling is accomplished in 90 minutes to two hours, using special cook-chill equipment. It is critical to maintain the specified temperature range during storage until the food is ready to be served, when it is reheated to a temperature of 165° F (74° C).

The cook-and-chill and cook-and-freeze methods are similar in all respects except that the latter involves freezing the food to 0° F (—8° C) or below, instead of chilling. Cook-and-freeze requires a fast-freezing unit, which increases the cost of the equipment. Quick-

freeze also requires additional packaging, which adds to the cost. One major advantage of cook-and-freeze items is that they can be kept on hand for contingency use or be used during a subsequent menu cycle.

Incorporating these methods is also helpful when selective menus are offered. Menus can be planned in such a way that low labor productivity (slack time) on certain days can be used to prepare additional items to be served on a later day. Another major advantage is that chilled or frozen foods are less perishable and retain nutrients longer than foods cooked and held at serving temperatures for relatively long periods in the cook-and-serve systems. The freezing process does not destroy nutrients. One major drawback is that not all chilled and frozen foods can be successfully prepared without extensively modifying the ingredients or recipes. Certain foods lose their flavor or texture after freezing. Such foods include vegetables such as cabbage, cucumbers, lettuce, and radishes; foods with eggs or milk; and mayonnaise, gelatin, and salad dressings. Staff must be skilled in exercising strict temperature controls for precooking, quick chilling or freezing, and reheating in order to prevent bacterial growth. Limited refrigeration and freezer space presents additional obstacles.

Frozen food should never be thawed at room temperature because it promotes the growth of illness-causing bacteria. Frozen foods must be thawed in the refrigerator, in the microwave, or in clean cold water that is frequently changed.

## Assemble-and-Serve Method

This method is also called the "convenience system" because only minimal food preparation is necessary. The foods are commercially prepared and packaged. Depending on how they will be used on the menu, a variety of prepared products can be purchased in fresh, frozen, canned, or dehydrated forms. Menu variety is often greater in assemble-and-serve systems than in most cook-and-serve systems. But inconsistent quality and greater upfront expense are the main drawbacks. Despite its advantages, the higher cost of assemble-and-serve products cannot be justified unless it reduces labor costs.

## Therapeutic Diets and Nourishments

A regular well-balanced diet is the most appropriate diet for most elderly patients. Certain medical conditions, however, necessitate diet modification or supplementation. Nutritional needs can also be altered by disease, stress, and drugs. The need for modified diets or food supplements should be evaluated by the dietitian, nurses, and the patient's attending physician.

### Modified Diets

Therapeutic diets are commonly referred to as modified diets because, in most instances, only minor modifications of the regular menus are necessary. For instance, a mechanical soft diet is produced by simply grounding or chopping the food so it requires minimum chewing. For a puréed diet, the regular food is pulverized to a puréed consistency, using a food processor. These are the simplest types of therapeutic diets.

Restricted diets are also relatively simple modifications of regular menu items, and these diets generally require restricting or eliminating certain condiments. For example, in a sodium-restricted diet, salt and processed foods that may have a high salt content are restricted. In a bland diet, irritants such as

caffeine and spices are left out. A low-cholesterol diet requires restricting foods rich in saturated fats.

More complex diets than those just described call for substituting certain items on the regular menu and may need nutrients to be balanced. Examples include low-fiber and high-fiber diets in which appropriate foods must be added or eliminated from the diet. A diabetic diet requires a careful balance of carbohydrates, proteins, and fats, and sugar substitutes are used in place of natural sugars. High-carbohydrate and high-protein diets also must be carefully balanced. Clear-liquid and full-liquid diets are based on a judicious selection of appropriate liquids such as clear broths and gelatin-based products. Certain food allergies or food intolerances also call for appropriate substitutions.

Commercially prepared oral supplements are used for patients who may not be eating enough to get balanced nutrition. Oral supplements have been formulated to meet almost any type of special nutritional requirement. Examples include nutritionally complete puddings, calorically dense supplements, or protein supplements (Gerwick, 1992).

Maintaining nutritional content and ensuring the patient's acceptance of the diet are the biggest challenges in preparing special diets. It can be argued that overly rigid enforcement of a dietary regimen may not be in a patient's best interest if the patient will not consume the food and will remain unhappy. Imposing severe restrictions may lead to stress, anger, anxiety, or depression (Robinson & Leif, 2001). Such issues should be resolved by the multidisciplinary team, in consultation with the patient's attending physician. In recommending therapeutic diets, the potential benefits must be evaluated against the possible detriments to optimal food intake and the disruption in the resident's quality of life (Gerwick, 1992). The patient is responsible for following the recommended nutrition care plan, but also has the right to refuse medical treatment, including a therapeutic diet. But if the resident refuses to follow the nutrition care plan, he or she bears the responsibility for any adverse consequences. However, such incidents must be addressed in care-plan meetings and carefully documented in the patient's medical record. The documentation should specify what efforts the staff may have made to try and persuade the patient to follow the dietary regimen.

## Nourishments and Food Intake

Nourishments consist of light foods that are served in between the main meals, generally two to three hours after a regular meal. A nourishing snack must be offered to all patients before bedtime, although many patients do not desire it. During the day, however, most patients do not require additional snacks if they have adequate food intake. Snacks may actually diminish a person's appetite for consuming the regular meals. Yet some patients may not be consuming the regular meals properly. Depression, certain medications, and difficulty in chewing or swallowing may curtail a person's appetite.

Food intake problems are also related to a decline in self-feeding skills or improper positioning while eating. Such problems should be evaluated by an occupational therapist (OT), who may recommend proper positioning or adaptive tableware to improve a patient's self-feeding skills. Problems related to swallowing should be addressed by a speech/language pathologist.

Food intake and plate waste must be documented for each patient. The multidisciplinary team should also evaluate any food acceptance problems. Refusal of food should be addressed with the resident. Simply reevaluating a patient's likes and dislikes and providing appropriate substitutes may solve food acceptance problems. Only when regular food intake becomes a chronic issue, particularly when adverse health problems such as weight loss are observed, should the need for supplemental nourishments be addressed with the dietitian and with the patient's attending physician. Widespread plate waste among residents often indicates poor choice of foods for the resident population or preparation methods that most people do not like. In such cases, menus must be revised. Such issues can be best addressed through the resident council and call for prompt action before the meals become a pervasive cause for discontentment.

## Intensive Nutrition

Intensive nutrition support, commonly called tube feeding, may be necessary for patients who are unable to maintain adequate food intake with either a regular or a modified diet. Conditions that may require tube feeding include protein-energy malnutrition, liver or kidney failure, coma, or dysphagia because of stroke, brain tumor, or head injury. Patients who are receiving radiation therapy or chemotherapy treatments for cancer may also be candidates for tube feedings (Edgren, 2003). Although the care and monitoring of feeding tubes is a nursing responsibility and not something overseen by the dietary staff, intensive nutrition is discussed here because it is an integral part of meeting patients' total nutritional needs.

Enteral and parenteral nutrition are two types of intensive feeding methods, and which one is used depends on the patient's condition.

The dietitian, nurses, and the attending physician determine what the patient's medical needs are, and they also determine the appropriate method of nutrient delivery.

The cost of commercially prepared enteral and parenteral formulas is generally not regarded as a food expense. This cost is best classified as a separate line item on the budget, either under the nursing department or under the dietary department. To correctly calculate the regular food cost, the number of patient days incurred by patients receiving intensive nutrition should be subtracted from the total number of patient days.

## Enteral Feeding

*Enteral feeding* is a method of delivering liquid food directly into the stomach. Enteral feeding is a safe method of providing nutrients to patients who have a normally functioning gastrointestinal system, but who cannot eat normally. Depending on the patient's medical needs, tube feeding may be necessary for only a short time, or permanently.

Enteral feeding may be used as the sole source of nutrition or as a supplement to inadequate oral intake. Commercially prepared liquid formulas are used according to the patient's nutritional needs, and either a small bedside pump controls the amount of liquid to be delivered or the feeding is allowed to drip naturally into the tube. In other instances, puréed or liquefied foods may be used, requiring special preparation by the dietary department.

There are two common methods of enteral feeding: a *nasogastric (NG) tube* passes through the nasal openings, down the esophagus, and into the stomach; a *gastrostomy (G) tube* passes through a surgical opening in the abdomen and into the stomach.

Other less common tube-feeding methods include those that use nasoduodenal, esophagostomy, and jejunostomy tubes. A *nasoduodenal tube* passes through the patient's nose and goes down into the duodenum, the first part of the small intestine, thus bypassing the stomach. This method is particularly indicated for patients who have an abnormally functioning pylorus (the opening between the stomach and the duodenum); problems with aspirating stomach contents into the lung (which can cause lung damage or pneumonia); or delayed gastric emptying. An *esophagostomy tube* is a small tube that enters a surgical incision on the side of the neck and is generally removed after each feeding. The tube allows food to enter the esophagus, bypassing the mouth, and then flow down into the stomach. Esophagostomy tubes are particularly indicated for patients who cannot swallow. A *jejunostomy (J) tube* is a surgically placed tube that enters the small intestine from an opening in the belly. This feeding method may be indicated for those who have impaired digestion, may aspirate food into their lungs, or have pancreatic disease.

## Parenteral Feeding

*Parenteral nutrition* is a method of delivering balanced nutrition directly into the bloodstream, a method used when the gastrointestinal tract is not functioning properly. A special liquid formulation, called total parenteral nutrition (TPN), is infused into the bloodstream by inserting a catheter in a central or peripheral vein (Robinson & Leif, 2001). The process must be carefully monitored by licensed nurses. Parenteral nutrition may be necessary in cases of severe malnutrition or when a patient is unable to use the gastrointestinal tract.

# Food Service

## Centralized and Decentralized Systems

Tray service is the most common method of serving food to residents in nursing facilities. Most facilities use the system called centralized meal service in which all trays are assembled at the kitchen service line. At meal time, the food service station is staffed by several kitchen workers in order to minimize the serving time.

Another system that may be appropriate for some facilities is decentralized meal service, in which food produced in the main kitchen is transported in bulk to various smaller dining locations where the food is portioned and served. For example, the cluster architectural design with decentralized dining rooms (see Chapter 8) requires this type of food service. The service can be modified if the serving location has an auxiliary kitchen, which can be furnished with salad, beverages, and bread. In this case, the main dish and vegetables are prepared in the facility's central kitchen, and food is transported in bulk to individual dining areas. The food is kept hot on steam tables from where it is dished out on plates and served family style, eliminating tray service (Noell, 1995). Even when tray service is used, some facilities have improvised family-style dining by taking the plates off the trays while serving. Thus, instead of putting a tray in front of the resident, food and beverages are placed before the resident in individual plates and glasses.

Positive nutritional and clinical outcomes can result by changing from a centralized food-delivery system to a decentralized system. Portioning food in the residents' dining room (as opposed to the kitchen) simulates a homelike atmosphere and thereby encourages increased food consumption, which can contribute to residents' improved nutritional status. Studies have reported a significant increase in the average food consumption of residents after a bulk food portioning system (portioning of food in the dining room) is introduced. Family-style meals stimulate daily energy intake and protect nursing home residents against malnourishment (Shatenstein & Ferland, 2000; Nijs et al., 2006). However, before implementing a decentralized bulk food service, managers should take into consideration concerns of employees who may experience frustration because of increased demands on their time, as one Canadian study pointed out (Shatenstein et al., 2001).

Noell (1995) reported that serving meals in "neighborhood" family-style settings also resulted in cost savings by reducing waste and by curtailing the need to provide nutritional supplements because of low food intake. Hence, evaluating the cost-benefit aspects of these alternative service methods is necessary. For example, cost savings from reductions in the use of nutritional supplements or an increased facility census because of better perceived value by prospective clients may compensate for increased spending on family-style table service.

## Food Service Station

In traditional tray service, the food service station is a food holding and food assembly area. As each tray is assembled, a nonpowered conveyor system moves the trays on rollers from the serving area to a platform where they are picked up by the serving staff.

In efficient kitchen design, the food service station is located between the food production and tray pickup areas. Cooked food is transferred from the cooking area to the service station where all foods are maintained at appropriate temperatures and assembled for service to patients. Any cold food is put on the plate first, and then the plate is moved to the hot section where hot food is dished out from a steam table. Infrared lamps are also used to keep certain foods hot. Holding wells in the steam table are replenished as needed. The recommended holding and serving temperatures are ≤40° F (5° C) for cold foods, and ≥140° F (60° C) for hot items. Clean thermometers must be available at the serving station to periodically monitor food temperatures during meal service. The holding equipment is not meant for reheating food, only to maintain food at the right serving temperature.

All food service staff must be trained in portion control. Standardized recipes establish the size of portion to be served for each food item. Measuring scoops, ladles, serving spoons, food-weighing scales, and other serving equipment are essential for portioning food. Some food items are prepared in predetermined portions, which makes service both quicker and easier.

## Accuracy

Individual trays are assembled using a diet card or diet ticket. Diet tickets are now generated by computerized systems, whereas diet cards are used in the manual system. A separate diet card is maintained for each patient, and it is updated to reflect any changes in diet or food preferences. To minimize diet errors, a trained individual must work at the end of the tray line as a checker. The checker is responsible for ensuring that the food items on the patient tray are what should be on the tray in accordance with the diet orders, individual preferences, and any contraindications noted on the patient's diet card.

## Food Transportation Systems

In larger facilities, if centralized tray service is used, food often must be transported from the kitchen to auxiliary dining rooms located away from the main kitchen and dining areas. In this case, food is dished out in the main kitchen where the diet cards are maintained. The trays are loaded onto enclosed carts, which are transported to auxiliary dining areas. The challenge is to maintain foods at their right serving temperatures. To facilitate this goal, a variety of food transportation systems are available. Heated pellets have been in use for a long time. A pellet is a metal plate that requires heating in a pellet dispenser before the food plate is placed on the heated pellet. The pellet system requires removing the hot pellet before serving the tray to prevent burns to residents. To overcome these drawbacks, insulated trays with hot and cold compartments can be used. With either the pellet system or the insulated tray system, basic transportation carts are used. These carts do not have heat or refrigeration capabilities.

Carts with temperature controls are equipped with heat and refrigeration mechanisms. Specially designed split trays can slide into a cart that has hot and cold sections. In this system, half the tray is held in a heated compartment and the other half in a refrigerated compartment. All hot foods are placed on one side of the tray, and cold foods are placed on the other side of the tray. A major drawback of all food transportation carts is the difficulty of maneuvering them because of their heavy weight (Greathouse & Gregoire, 1997).

Finally, specialized trays can be used with rethermalization carts. The trays have special cut-out areas for entrée, soup, and vegetable dishes so that, when the trays are loaded onto the rethermalization carts, the dishes make contact with the conduction heat element in the cart (Greathouse & Gregoire, 1997).

When properly used, all of these systems can work quite satisfactorily. But each system has its own advantages and disadvantages, which must be carefully evaluated by the administrator and the dietary manager when deciding on which system to use.

## The Dining Experience

Dining plays a critical role in a resident's quality of life because most residents look forward to mealtime. A satisfying experience can also improve clinical outcomes through better nutrient intake. Jackson (2003) pointed out that dietitians and food service managers who routinely circulate in dining rooms during mealtime can gather a wealth of information by simply observing and talking to residents. Such observation can reveal, among other things, which menu items are well accepted, whether the food presentation is attractive, whether personal food preferences are respected, whether diet orders are being followed, and whether portion control standards are adhered to. Routine observation of dining rooms may also bring other problems to light that may require a change in care plans. Similarly, the nursing staff should ensure that patients are properly positioned while eating. Inappropriately positioned patients can aspirate, experience difficulty eating, or get tired and frustrated (Jackson, 2003).

## Food Safety and Sanitation

Promoting food safety and preventing food-borne illnesses are of critical importance in nursing facilities. Compared with the general population, residents in nursing homes are likely to be more susceptible to illness and may exhibit more severe adverse outcomes when they are ill. An outbreak of disease can place severe burdens on the nursing home staff and result in much adverse publicity in the community. Yet, food poisoning is almost entirely preventable by practicing good sanitation and good food handling techniques.

All staff members involved with the handling, cooking, and service of food must receive training in food sanitation and safety. Hygienic practices, such as hand-washing, cleaning and sanitizing equipment and food preparation surfaces, and washing fresh produce and all types of meats before use must be enforced by management. All staff members must wear appropriate head covering. The dietary department must also have written policies on food safety, and the staff must be trained on the proper storage and use of cleaning chemicals.

Food-borne illnesses can result when food is contaminated by bacteria, viruses, parasites, or chemicals. Bacterial infection is the most common cause of food-borne illness because bacteria can easily grow and produce toxins in foods. Almost half of all bacterial outbreaks (incidents involving two or more single cases) are the result of cross-contamination (Cody, 1997). Common examples of cross-contamination sources include using the same knife or cutting surface to prepare raw and cooked foods, using a contaminated sink for thawing frozen food, and unsanitary food handling. Flies, cockroaches, and rodents can transmit pathogens (disease-causing organisms) to food. Therefore, pest control by a reputable firm is an essential part of food sanitation.

The most common illness-causing bacteria include *Salmonella*, *Clostridium botulinum*, and *Escherichia coli*. They can be destroyed by heat. Hence, internal temperatures in meats should be monitored using a probe thermometer during cooking. Beef, veal, and lamb should be cooked to an internal temperature of 145° F (63° C); pork and ground meats to 160° F (71° C); and poultry to 165° F (74° C) (USDA, 2006). *Staphylococcus aureus* is another organism that can be destroyed by heating, but the toxins that are produced in food are relatively heat stable. Therefore, practice of food hygiene by all associates is essential.

Maintaining proper food holding temperatures is critical because bacteria thrive best at temperatures between 40° F (5° C) and 140° F (60° C), the range regarded as the ***temperature danger zone***. In the temperature danger zone, bacteria can double in number in as little as 20 minutes (USDA, 2006). In general, food should not be held at room temperature for longer than two hours. Simply reheating food that has been left out for that long may not destroy pathogens if they are present (Cody, 1997).

Another frequent cause of temperature-related food-borne disease is improper cooling when cooked food requires storage. Leftover foods must be quick cooled and refrigerated within two hours. Refrigerators should be maintained at a temperature no higher than 40° F (5° C). Before serving, foods should be reheated to an internal temperature of 165° F (74° C) (USDA, 2006).

Proper dishwashing procedures for cleaning and sanitizing tableware and kitchenware are also critical. A three-compartment sink for washing, rinsing, and sanitizing is recommended for hand-washing utensils and equipment. Sanitizing can be achieved by immersion in hot water at 170° F (77° C) or by using chlorine or iodine at recommended strengths. The recommended temperatures for mechanical dishwashing are 140° F (60° C) for wash, 160° F (71° C) for rinse, and 180° F (82° C) for final rinse and sanitizing (Sullivan & Atlas, 1998). Dishes and utensils should be left on racks to air-dry. Wiping with cloths can result in cross-contamination.

## For Further Thought

1. What can the administrator of a nursing facility do to minimize pilferage of assets such as supplies and food?

2. Discuss some factors that should be evaluated to determine the costs and benefits of providing family-style meal service in a nursing facility.

3. Discuss some ways in which the administrator can have continuous involvement in striving toward the goal of 100% client satisfaction with the food the facility serves.

## For Further Learning

*Dietary Guidelines for Americans*, 2005. Jointly published by the U.S. Department of Health and Human Services and the U.S. Department of Agriculture.

http://www.health.gov/dietaryguidelines/dga2005/document/pdf/DGA2005.pdf

Dietary Reference Intakes for Older Adults

http://nutritionandaging.fiu.edu/DRI_and_DGs/DRI%20Table%203%20pages%209-13-2004.pdf

---

# REFERENCES

Cody, M.M. 1997. Current issues in food safety. In R. Jackson, (ed.), *Nutrition and Food Services for Integrated Health Care: A Handbook for Leaders*. Gaithersburg, MD: Aspen Publishers.

DHHS/USDA. 2005. *Dietary Guidelines for Americans*, 2005. 6th ed., Washington, DC: U.S. Government Printing Office, U.S. Department of Health and Human Services/U.S. Department of Agriculture.

Edgren, A.R. 2003. Tube feedings. *Gale Encyclopedia of Medicine*. LookSmart, Ltd. http://www.findarticles.com/cf_dls/g2601/0014/2601001406/p1/article.jhtml.

Gerwick, C.L. 1992. *Nutrition Care in Nursing Facilities*, 2nd ed. Chicago: The American Dietetic Association.

Graves, N., & Stewart, S. 1985. Patient/client services: Provide food services. In J.D. Ninemeier (ed.), *Managing Food-Service Operations: A Systems Approach for Healthcare and Institutions*. West Lafayette, IN: Purdue Research Foundation.

Greathouse, K.R., & Gregoire, M.B. 1997. Options in meal assembly, delivery, and service. In R, Jackson (ed.), *Nutrition and Food Services for Integrated Health Care: A Handbook for Leaders*. Gaithersburg, MD: Aspen Publishers.

Jackson, R. 2003. The dining experience: Making it pleasurable for long-term care residents. *Health Care Food and Nutrition Focus* 20, no. 1: 1–4.

Mahaffey, M.J., et al. 1981. *Food Service Manual for Health Care Institutions*. Chicago: American Hospital Association.

Nijs, K.A.N.D., et al. 2006. Effect of family-style meals on energy intake and risk of malnutrition in Dutch nursing home residents: A randomized control trial. *Journal of Gerontology: Medical Sciences* 61A, no. 9: 935–942.

Ninemeier, J.D. 1985. *Managing Food-Service Operations: A Systems Approach for Healthcare and Institutions*. West Lafayette, IN: Purdue Research Foundation.

Noell, E. 1995. Design in nursing homes: Environment as a silent partner in caregiving. *Generations* 19, no. 4: 14–19.

Puckett, R.P., & Miller, B.B. 1988. *Food Service Manual for Health Care Institutions*. Chicago: American Hospital Publishing.

Robinson, G.E., & Leif, B.J. 2001. *Nutrition Management and Restorative Dining for Older Adults*. Chicago: American Dietetic Association.

Shatenstein, B., et al. 2001. Employee reactions to the introduction of a bulk food distribution system in a nursing home. *Canadian Journal of Dietetic Practice and Research* 62, no. 1: 18–25.

Shatenstein, B., & Ferland, G. 2000. Absence of nutritional or clinical consequences of decentralized bulk food portioning in elderly nursing home residents with dementia in Montreal. *Journal of the American Dietetic Association* 100, no. 11: 1354–1360.

Simmons, S.F., et al. 2003. Family members' preferences for nutrition interventions to improve nursing home residents' oral food and fluid intake. *Journal of the American Geriatrics Society* 51, no. 1: 69–74.

Sullivan, C.F., & Atlas, C. 1998. *Health Care Food Service Systems Management.* Gaithersburg, MD: Aspen Publishers.

USDA. 2006. *Safe Food Handling: How Temperatures Affect Food.* U.S. Department of Agriculture. Retrieved January 2009 from http://www.fsis.usda.gov/Fact_Sheets/How_Temperatures_ Affect_Food/index.asp.

# Chapter 13

# Plant and Environmental Services

## What You Will Learn

- Plant and environmental services include maintenance, housekeeping, laundry, and safety.

- Maintenance operations must plan for urgent service calls, routine repairs and preventive maintenance must be carried out, and routine and open-call contracts should be established. Job-unit contracts are occasionally needed.

- Housekeeping practices require daily routine cleaning, weekly heavy-duty attention, and periodic reconditioning. Certain sanitizing and infection control practices specifically apply to housekeeping.

- Laundry operations require microbicidal washing, standard precautions, and prevention of cross-contamination. To ensure an adequate linen supply, the administrator should institute par levels and inventory control systems.

- A security audit should be part of the physical security operation. Procedural security systems are implemented to control supplies, capital assets, and access to various areas of the building.

- All associates must be trained in fire protection steps represented by the acronym RACE. The facility must have designated areas of refuge during a fire or disaster emergency. Updated plans must outline all procedures, including partial and total evacuation. Simulation drills must be used for training.

- Most waste generated in nursing facilities is similar to domestic garbage. However, handling and disposal of hazardous waste require special precautions.

- Environmental safety practices must be followed to prevent accidents.

# Functions and Objectives

The main functions of plant and environmental services in a nursing facility are to maintain the physical plant, support the clinical and socio-residential structures, and promote a safe environment in the nursing facility. Adequate fire and disaster plans and preparations must be in place before any calamities occur.

Plant and environmental services are organized with two main objectives in mind: (1) maintaining and protecting the structures so they continue to function in the most effective and efficient manner while providing a clean, comfortable, and safe environment and (2) protecting people who live and work in these structures against the threat of bodily harm. Plant and environmental services should help optimize clinical care as well as the residents' quality of life.

Complete environmental support is necessary, not only for patients but for associates and visitors as well. Griffith (1995) suggested that the environmental support system provides all the services of a hotel, but with narrower tolerances. Compared with hotels, environmental services in health care facilities require narrower tolerances for temperature and humidity controls, air quality, cleanliness, waste removal, and environmental safety. Environmental services should also support the aesthetic appeal of the facility's exterior.

Environmental services can be classified into housekeeping, maintenance, laundry, security, and safety functions. The main environmental functions include cleaning all spaces; removing waste; controlling pests; performing general maintenance and repairs on the building and all of its components; ensuring an adequate supply of clean linens;

enhancing the external appearance of grounds and building; having adequate security so that patients, visitors, and associates feel safe in and around the building; preventing property loss and pilferage; protecting against potential fires and disasters; and preventing accidents.

# Organization of Environmental Services

The organization of environmental services departments varies according to the size of the facility and the skill levels of the supervisory personnel working in the environmental services departments. Some large nursing homes have a position of *facilities manager* responsible for all plant and environmental services. Most facilities have separate supervisors managing each main function.

## Maintenance Department

In most facilities, maintenance is a separate department, even though it may be staffed by just one or two people. An average-size facility of 100 beds needs one full-time person responsible for all maintenance and repairs. A half-time person may be added for each additional 50 to 60 beds. Staffing for maintenance will vary according to how much of the routine work, such as groundskeeping, is contracted out. For the winter season, snow removal is generally contracted out, especially if the facility has large parking areas and walkways. Many facilities add temporary staff during summer to do their own groundskeeping, whereas others outsource this service. Large facilities may find it cost effective to have a painter on staff. As a rule of thumb, every patient room and private bathroom should be completely repainted once every two to three years. Some areas of the building may require more frequent painting than others. Touch-up painting to keep walls free of scuff marks is an ongoing function.

In a typical nursing home, the maintenance department is headed by a maintenance mechanic (usually called "maintenance man"), although the position is formally referred to as *maintenance supervisor*, This individual must be multitalented and need not have special skills in any particular craft. This individual should be able to handle simple plumbing, heating, ventilation, air conditioning, and electrical problems. Apart from handling routine repair jobs, the maintenance supervisor is responsible for an ongoing preventive maintenance program in the facility. Other than minor troubleshooting and repairs, mechanical system breakdowns are restored by calling outside service contractors (Magee, 1988). By working alongside these external tradesmen, the maintenance supervisor can develop substantial skills in handling more than just basic problems.

## Housekeeping and Laundry Departments

Housekeeping and laundry departments are generally headed by one supervisor. In facilities that operate their own laundries, housekeeping and laundry are considered two separate departments, even though they may have a common supervisor. Depending on the size and layout of the facility, the person heading housekeeping and laundry operations may be a working supervisor; he or she may take on routine cleaning assignments for certain sections of the building or may perform specific tasks such as floor polishing. A position strictly confined to supervisory duties may be necessary only when the number of beds exceeds 150, provided that the facility operates its own in-house laundry. The other option for management is to have separate working supervisors for housekeeping and laundry.

The facility should determine the number of housekeepers needed according to the square footage, the layout of the facility, and the number of resident rooms. Adequate weekend coverage is also essential, and a skeleton crew should cover the evenings to finish cleanup chores after dinner and attend to any other sanitation needs in the facility. Most facilities also require janitorial staff for routine floor and carpet maintenance and for handling other heavy work such as window-washing and moving furniture.

The laundry requires personnel in two categories: sorting and washing soiled laundry and drying and folding clean laundry. Separating these two functions is essential to prevent cross-contamination.

The maintenance supervisor and the supervisor of housekeeping and laundry departments report to the administrator (see Figure III–1) and are considered heads of departments. In large facilities, these supervisors may report to the assistant administrator if such a position exists.

## Security and Safety Functions

In many locations, security has become a growing concern for facilities. Except for some very large retirement living and nursing care complexes, a typical nursing facility does not have a security department. In fact, most facilities do not employ any security personnel. Nevertheless, the security function is essential. In the absence of a designated person being in charge of security, the responsibility for security falls on the administrator's shoulders.

*Safety* specifically means fire and disaster preparation and accident prevention. Some aspects of safety and physical security (discussed later) can be delegated to the maintenance supervisor. Accident prevention, on the other hand, requires leadership from the administrator but is the responsibility of everyone working in the facility.

# Maintenance Operation

The main operations in the maintenance department can be classified into four areas: urgent service calls, routine repairs, preventive maintenance, and contract work.

## Urgent Service Calls

Because emergencies arise without warning, an unexpected breakdown of critical mechanical systems, components, or equipment can severely disrupt vital services, compromise patient safety, or result in loss of property. For example, a breakdown of the heating system in the middle of winter will severely disrupt patient care and threaten the safety of patients. Failure of the food storage freezer can result in the loss of hundreds or even thousands of dollars worth of food. Such breakdowns or a failure of the facility's emergency systems, such as fire alarms, fire suppression system, or emergency power generator, must be attended to immediately.

Along with the administrator, the director of nursing (DON) and the maintenance supervisor are on call 24 hours a day, 7 days a week. If by chance the maintenance supervisor is not available during an emergency, the administrator should be notified so that an outside firm can be called to deal with the situation. Similar authority should be given to the DON and also to the dietary manager in case urgent attention is needed for any dietary equipment.

## Routine Repairs

Routine repair work is organized by instituting a system in which all routine requests for repairs are submitted on a work order. Each department and each nursing station keeps a box where their work orders are placed. The orders are picked up daily by the maintenance supervisor, who makes a round of the building to observe anything that may require prompt attention. The work orders are prioritized to plan the day's work. Other routine tasks such as lawn care should be included in a weekly schedule. Local trips to purchase needed supplies and parts should also be planned to minimize the number of trips away from the facility. With proper planning, no more than one trip should be necessary each week.

A work order system generally works well for reporting problems that hinder staff members' ability to do their jobs, or to address complaints from residents and family members. However, this system misses many other problems that go unreported. To address unreported concerns, the facility needs a preventive maintenance program.

## Preventive Maintenance

Preventive maintenance is the term used for routine inspections and performance of certain tasks that are planned in advance and are carried out to prevent unexpected equipment failures (Niebel, 1985). Over the long run, a good preventive maintenance program is cost effective because it prevents costly breakdowns, delays the need to replace equipment that may otherwise wear out prematurely, and minimizes disruption of vital services. Appropriate training is needed to set up and manage a well-designed preventive maintenance program. All equipment must be periodically checked for smooth operation. Equipment coils and motors require periodic cleaning. In accordance with the manufacturer's recommendations, equipment may also require periodic lubrication, filter changes, or inspection and replacement of components that show signs of wear and tear. If the maintenance supervisor does not possess the necessary training and skills to perform this maintenance, the administrator may outsource preventive maintenance work to a private independent firm. At the very least, however, the facility must have a basic preventive maintenance program that includes three main preventive functions:

- Routine checks.
- Revolving inspections.
- Ongoing upkeep.

## Routine Checks

Routine checks are necessary to ensure that all emergency systems are operating. A written or electronic log of these tests must be maintained. Emergency systems include the fire alarms, automatic fire doors, smoke detectors, and emergency power generators. The *Life Safety Code* requires testing the fire alarm system quarterly, but many facilities do this check more frequently.

## Revolving Inspections

A plan must be instituted by the facility to ensure that every day, in accordance with a rotating schedule, a different specified section of the building interior and exterior is closely inspected. The goal should be to conduct a revolving inspection so that all patient rooms, bathrooms, utility rooms, kitchen, laundry, mechanical rooms, and all other areas receive

a close inspection once every four to six weeks. The administrator can monitor this schedule by requiring that the maintenance department keep a written or electronic log and provide a report to the administrator as inspections are completed in each area of the building. Such inspections often reveal irregularities that do not get reported through the routine work order system. Repair problems that frequently go unreported include leaky faucets; leaks at the bottom of toilet bowls; windows that do not close or lock; doors that do not completely shut; missing ceiling tiles; ventilation or exhaust problems in bathrooms, kitchen, laundry, or utility areas; scuffed walls in need of painting or repair to the wall covering; and curtains and window coverings in disrepair. The administrator should do periodic spot checks to see whether a revolving inspection program is being followed.

During the detailed inspections, the maintenance supervisor should look for safety problems such as missing fire extinguishers, torn or buckled carpeting, nonfunctional patient call systems, missing floor tiles, and burned-out light bulbs. Sanitation problems may be noticed near the garbage dumpster, which can attract vermin and other scavengers. Broken screens or missing exterior screen doors may allow flies to enter food preparation areas. Signs of pest activity, such as droppings, may be noticed in the kitchen, food storage areas, or patient rooms. Outside the building, lights may be missing, the parking lot may be in need of cleaning, cracks in pavement may require sealing, or shrubs may require trimming.

## Ongoing Upkeep

Ongoing maintenance of a facility's internal and external appearance is also an important part of preventive maintenance. Damage to walls caused by wheelchairs and other equipment is a common occurrence. However, effectively managed facilities set themselves apart from others by instituting a daily touch-up painting program. When undertaken on a daily basis, touch-up painting only requires a fraction of the time it would take to paint large sections of the building that have been left unattended. Wall coverings should be cleaned and repaired periodically and replaced when they are heavily worn or faded. The parking lot also needs daily attention to pick up loose trash and cigarette butts. Effectively managed facilities maintain attractive lawns, have some basic landscaping, and plant seasonal flowers to present an inviting appearance.

## Contract Work

The need for contracting is unavoidable, but the maintenance supervisor should oversee the work of outside contractors to ensure that the agreed-upon work is completed satisfactorily. Professional completion of work includes any cleanup and removal of debris after a job is finished.

Some contracts for services that are performed on a regular basis, called *routine contracts*, are generally executed annually. Routine contracts include agreements covering pest control, waste removal, snow removal, lawn care, annual inspection of emergency equipment, inspection and maintenance of elevators, and expert preventive maintenance. Routine contracting is undertaken by the administrator, in consultation with the maintenance supervisor. As a matter of policy, no contract should exceed one year. This limit allows the administrator to review each year the quality of services performed and to compare the prices of a con-

tractor's competitors before renewing an existing contract or going with a new one.

Nonroutine contracts include open-call contracts and job-unit contracts. *Open-call contracts* are established with preferred contractors to provide services on an as-needed basis. Contracts for heating and cooling, plumbing, and electrical work are the most common types of open-call contracts. This type of contracting eliminates the time and administrative effort required in setting up a separate contract each time the need for services arises (Heintzelman, 1987). By making a commitment to use the same contractor on an open-call basis, the facility can often negotiate discounted service fees.

A second type of nonroutine arrangement is a *job-unit contract*, which is established each time a need arises for infrequent major jobs (Heintzelman, 1987). The contract automatically terminates when the specified work has been completed and paid for. Job-unit contracting is appropriate for jobs that are occasionally needed, are planned ahead of time, and generally involve substantial capital outlays. Examples include renovation projects, roof repair or replacement, installation of major equipment, and major landscaping.

## Housekeeping Operations

The housekeeping department is responsible for maintaining a sanitary, pleasant, and safe environment in the facility. The department must develop policies and procedures for cleaning, sanitizing, infection control, and safety. Unlike hotels and motels, the housekeeping staff in nursing facilities must not handle either clean or soiled linens. The tasks of bed-making, replacing clean linens in patient rooms, and removing soiled linens are assigned to nursing assistants.

## Cleaning, Reconditioning, and Floor Care

Housekeeping jobs can be classified as daily cleaning, weekly cleaning, reconditioning, and floor care. *Daily cleaning* consists of routine procedures for cleaning, sweeping, mopping, and vacuuming all patient care and public areas in the facility. *Weekly cleaning* tasks include dusting furniture and fixtures, cleaning baseboards, paying attention to floor edges and corners, polishing bathroom fixtures, cleaning draperies and cubicle curtains, and other heavy-duty tasks. The housekeeping supervisor should develop a rotating schedule so that all areas of the building receive weekly heavy-duty cleaning. To accomplish this goal, certain sections of the building are included in the daily cleaning schedules to receive the weekly heavy-duty attention. On weekends, many facilities have reduced staffing to perform the daily tasks; in that case, weekly tasks are covered using a five-day rotating schedule.

*Reconditioning* involves thorough cleaning of certain areas, particularly patient rooms. Reconditioning is always performed after a patient has been discharged and involves tasks such as cleaning and sanitizing the bed and mattress. All patient rooms should receive reconditioning attention on a rotating basis every five to six weeks. *Floor care* is generally assigned to custodians, who are responsible for stripping, waxing, and polishing floors and for shampooing carpets.

## Sanitizing

The term *sanitizing* describes a process that results in a reduction of microbes to relatively safe levels on an inanimate object (Belkin, 2003). Sanitizing requires the appropriate use of disinfectants approved by the U.S. Environmental Protection Agency (EPA), which oversees the registration of antimicrobial products. A list of registered antimicrobials is available at the EPA's website (see For Further Learning). The listed categories include sterilants, tuberculocides, anti-HIV products, anti-HBV (hepatitis B virus) products, anti-HCV (hepatitis C virus) products, and products that are effective against methicillin-resistant *Staphylococcus aureus* (MRSA). A fresh solution of diluted household bleach (1 part bleach to 10 parts water) made up every 24 hours is also considered appropriate to disinfect environmental surfaces and decontaminate sites. Contact time for bleach solution is generally considered to be the time it takes the product to air-dry. Rinsing is necessary after sanitizing with 1:10 bleach solution.

The housekeeping supervisor should periodically determine whether the housekeeping procedures are effective on a microbiological level. Such an evaluation is done by taking periodic cultures from various surfaces for bacterial colony counts.

## Infection Control

The housekeeping staff plays a vital role in controlling infections in the facility by following sanitary practices that can prevent the spread of microorganisms. Disease-causing pathogens can spread through dust particles, air particles, and surface contact. Properly cleaning and sanitizing floors and other surfaces is a means of infection control. But housekeeping practices employed while performing daily tasks are equally important. For instance, a housekeeper who gives a quick shake to a dust rag after using it to dust furniture is spreading germs through the air. Hence, plain dry sweeping, for example, has no place in health care housekeeping practices because it can disseminate microorganisms in the air; chemically treated disposable dust cloths should be used for preliminary cleaning before wet mopping. Vacuum cleaners used for carpeted areas should have effective microbial filters to avoid disseminating bacteria from the vacuum exhaust. Wet-mopping should employ a double-bucket technique, with one bucket for cleaning with a disinfectant solution and the other for rinsing the mop (Vesley & Greene, 1973). Frequently changing the mop water is also necessary for minimizing the spread of microorganisms along the floors. Hand-washing is critical when contact is made with clean surfaces after touching soiled objects or surfaces.

## Laundry Operations

The nursing home laundry department is responsible for the processing, distribution, and storage of washable linens, garments, and other such items (Goldberg & Buttaro, 1990). The basic laundry tasks include sorting, washing, drying, folding, storing, and delivering. Soiled linens are brought to the laundry by nursing assistants, or bags of soiled laundry are conveyed to the laundry down a laundry chute in multistory buildings. Clean linen is delivered to the patient care areas by the laundry staff. Clean linens must be transported through the facility using covered carts to prevent cross-contamination. Nursing home laundries generally do not do ironing and mending. Widespread use of no-iron linens has eliminated the need for ironing. An alternative to operating an on-site laundry is to have a contract with a commercial laundry service. For small facilities in particular, it may not be cost effective to operate an on-site laundry.

## Microbicidal Washing

The microbicidal (killing of microbes) action of the normal laundering process is affected by several physical and chemical factors. Soaps or detergents loosen soil and also have some microbicidal properties. Hot water provides an effective means of destroying microorganisms. A temperature of at least 160° F (71° C) for a minimum of 25 minutes is commonly recommended for hot-water washing of laundry. Chlorine bleach in the wash provides an extra margin of safety (Office of Health and Safety, 2002). The last action performed during the washing process is to add a mild acid to neutralize any alkalinity in the water supply, soap, or detergent. Detergents that can reduce microbial contamination at lower water temperatures are also available. Instead of the microbicidal action of hot water, low-temperature laundry cycles rely heavily on the presence of bleach to reduce levels of microbial contamination.

## Standard Precautions

Nursing facilities must follow standard precautions (discussed in Chapter 10) when handling all soiled laundry. Standard precautions constitute a system of barrier precautions to be used by all personnel when handling items that may contain blood, body fluids, secretions, and excretions, regardless of the patient's diagnosis. Laundry workers should use gloves, gowns, and masks when sorting and washing linens. Laundry should be handled as little as possible and with minimal agitation. To avoid punctures from improperly discarded syringes, personnel should hold laundry bags and linens away from the body and avoid squeezing when transporting them. Using normal washing cycles in accordance with the laundry detergent manufacturer's recommendations should be quite sufficient for thorough washing. However, patient linens should be washed separately from kitchen laundry and patients' personal clothing.

As mentioned earlier, soiled-laundry sorting and clean-linen processing must be separated. A separate room, equipped with negative-pressure ventilation, is best for the sorting process. The negative pressure allows air to move from a clean to a soiled area, and not vice versa, and is designed to prevent movement of airborne particles from the soiled area to the clean linen processing area (Vesley, 1973).

## Linen Inventory

A system of linen inventory is essential for control purposes. This system requires a secured linen storage room to which only authorized personnel have access. The main institutional linens include bed sheets, bath towels, hand towels, and wash cloths. After washing, drying, and folding, all institutional linens are stored in the linen room. Patients' personal clothes are delivered to their individual rooms. The nursing facility must have enough quantities of linens so that after washing all linens get a chance to "rest" for at least 24 hours before being put into service again. Adequate linen quantities are also necessary to meet all patient care needs over the weekend when the laundry operation is generally shut down. Goldberg and Buttaro (1990) proposed a stratified inventory system that assumes that for every piece of linen in use, four others are being processed or are in storage. Under such a system, the linen inventory should consist of the number of items used daily multiplied by five. The resulting number is called the ***par level***. It

refers to the minimum number of units of an item the facility should maintain in the inventory, including items in circulation and storage.

A certain amount of linen loss is to be expected. Such losses can result from wear and tear as well as pilferage. An inventory control system is used to find out the extent of loss and to determine the quantities of linen that should be purchased to replenish the stock to par levels. A running linen inventory record includes the following entries:

> *Initial inventory (quantity on hand at the beginning of the period after the last physical inventory was taken)*
> *+ Purchases*
> *− Discards (frayed or heavily stained linens taken out of circulation)*
> *= Closing inventory*

The facility should take a physical inventory of linens once every three or four months to compare the actual linen count to the closing inventory. The difference shows how much linen is being lost that must be replenished to maintain the par levels. See Chapter 18 and Exhibit 18–7 for more information on inventory control.

## Security Operations

Rowland and Rowland (1984) pointed to two basic facets of security: physical and procedural.

### Physical Security

*Physical security* encompasses three main areas: (1) protecting people against bodily harm by intruders from the outside, (2) protecting residents from wandering out and getting injured, and (3) protecting the property of both residents and the facility against theft. Physical security generally requires integrating a variety of protective measures, including control of the facility's parameter, intrusion alarms, lock-up procedures, and electronic surveillance. Installing and maintaining security systems and hiring security personnel can be quite expensive. However, some minimal equipment installed in strategic locations may be necessary. Undertaking risk assessment and cost-benefit evaluation are essential before a large investment is committed for security. Potential costs to the facility include restitution to the party harmed, legal action against the facility, and loss to the facility's image if a resident or associate is harmed and the injury is attributed to lax security. The probability of such losses should be taken into account in doing a cost-benefit evaluation.

The administrator should work with the local law enforcement agencies to evaluate security needs. Following their recommendations, the administrator can then work with two or three reputable security firms to obtain recommendations and bids for appropriate security technology. At a minimum, the facility must ensure that all parking areas and the building's exterior are adequately lit. The administrator should also arrange with local law enforcement to have the facility on routine police patrol. A high-visibility patrol is one of the best deterrents against crime (Sells, 2000).

All facilities must have policies specifying who is responsible for locking up designated entrances after specified hours in the evening and for locking up the remaining entrances for the night. Self-locking timer devices can be installed to minimize human error. Security policies may also specify that after certain hours no employee can go outside the building unaccompanied.

Many facilities provide employee lockers for safeguarding personal effects such as purses and cash. Most facilities also have resident policies that discourage keeping valuables, such as expensive jewelry, or more than minimal amounts of cash on one's person or in the room.

A variety of monitoring systems are available to prevent unnoticed wandering by residents who may be particularly vulnerable because of dementia or confusion. In many locations, local or state codes allow installation of a delayed opening system on fire exit doors. With these devices the doors will not open for a set time, usually 15 seconds, when someone tries to open a fire exit door. During the delay period an alarm sounds to alert the staff on duty (Sells, 2000). This short delay, along with the sound of the alarm, may be sufficient to dissuade a patient who may be attempting to exit unnoticed.

## Security Audit

Periodically, the administrator should undertake a *security audit*. In this audit, all physical security measures and potential lapses should be closely examined. A comprehensive audit must be undertaken any time a significant security incident occurs or a problem that could have resulted in an incident is reported. A security audit would be undertaken in addition to a thorough investigation and documentation of any actual incidents. The purpose of an audit is to prevent recurrence of an incident or prevent the occurrence of a nonrelated incident. All security audits and corrective actions resulting from such audits should be documented.

## Procedural Security

*Procedural security* involves control systems to prevent internal theft and pilferage of supplies and materials. Three different systems are needed to protect the facility's assets:

- A system for ordering, receiving, storing, and controlling the inventory for all supplies and materials.
- A tagging and inventory system for all movable capital assets.
- A key control system that restricts access to various storage and office areas.

### Supplies and Materials

In addition to the control systems for food and dietary supplies discussed in Chapter 12, the facility must have a central system for ordering, receiving, storing, and controlling the inventory for all supplies and materials. Other than food, supplies and materials that may be vulnerable to theft include linens, cleaning chemicals, maintenance tools and equipment, and medical supplies. Large facilities may have a central storeroom with a stock clerk responsible for all items other than food. In most facilities, however, each department head has the responsibility for ordering and maintaining supplies used by the department. In this case, each department manager must exercise adequate controls over the supplies and materials by using inventory systems to minimize theft.

### Movable Capital Assets

A tagging and inventory system is used to identify and control all movable capital assets, such as television sets, cameras, computers, office equipment, and medical equipment.

Permanent, nondetachable metal tags with the facility's name and a tag number should be affixed to all movable assets. A record, which can be easily computerized, should identify each item, its tag number, location, date of acquisition, and cost. This record should also bear the date of retirement after an item has been retired from service. An annual or biannual inventory should verify that each item still in service is actually present in the facility.

### Access Control

Access to various parts of the building is controlled by establishing a centralized system to regulate distribution of keys to authorized personnel only. This function is best controlled by the administrator or assistant administrator. Working with a master locksmith, the facility should plan and implement a hierarchical system of grand master keys, master keys, submaster keys, and individual keys. The system allows authorized personnel to have access to more than one locked areas, using no more than two keys. For instance, the administrator and the assistant administrator can have access to all secured areas using the grand master key. A submaster key may allow the DON to have access to all secured areas except food storage and maintenance areas.

Records must be kept to account for every key issued. Keys must be retrieved and accounted for as personnel leave their positions. Appropriately maintained key inventory records can help track missing keys. When keys are missing, a decision can be made whether to rekey or change the locks in certain areas of the building. Establishing a key control system initially requires rekeying all locks in the building, something that can be quite expensive. First, a cost-benefit evaluation of a key control system should be done. Second, if a decision is made to implement the key control system, the system must be maintained. A facility can quickly lose most of the benefits of such a system and its investment in it if the system is allowed to break down. "Do not duplicate" should be engraved on all keys as a deterrent against unauthorized duplication. It is not known to what extent nursing homes may be using electronic key or pass systems. At any rate, installation and maintenance of such systems would be quite expensive.

# Fire and Disaster Planning

All facilities must have written fire safety, disaster, and evacuation plans. These plans must outline duties and responsibilities of various staff members and the steps to be taken during emergencies such as a tornado, hurricane, earthquake, flood, or snow blizzard. These plans are best developed and rehearsed in conjunction with the local fire department and other civil defense agencies. The plans must address the individual characteristics of the particular facility and take into account the availability of local resources and the response time of emergency services to deal with events in which the safety of residents is paramount. All supervisory personnel must have copies of the emergency plan, and all associates must be periodically trained and kept informed with respect to their duties under the plan. A copy of the plan must also be available at the main business office.

## Fire Safety Plan and Steps

The *Life Safety Code* requires a written fire safety plan to include the following: use of

alarms, transmission of alarms to fire department, emergency phone call to fire department, response to alarms, isolation of fire, evacuation of immediate area, evacuation of smoke compartment (defined in Chapter 6), preparation of floors and building for evacuation, and extinguishment of fire.

All associates must receive training in basic sequential fire-protection steps represented by the acronym RACE (Kavaler & Spiegel, 1997):

R—Rescue and remove anyone in immediate danger.

A—Activate the nearest fire alarm.

C—Confine and contain the fire and smoke by closing all doors and windows.

E—Extinguish the fire with portable extinguishers, wet sheets, and blankets.

The most critical step in fire protection is to activate the fire alarm. This step is vital because the fire department must be notified immediately when fire is suspected. The *Life Safety Code* requires that the fire alarm system be connected to an outside agency, such as a fire security company, that will transmit the alarm to the nearest fire department. Pulling the fire alarm is the quickest way to summon the fire brigade to the facility. When the alarm box is activated, a fire alarm goes off within the facility, and all fire doors close automatically.

The facility's fire safety protocols should also include a pre-established code phrase, such as "Doctor Red" or "Code 99." The code is used to alert all associates in case of a fire during fire drills conducted between 9:00 p.m. and 6:00 a.m. or during a malfunction of the building fire alarm system. The code phrase is generally announced over the intercom system.

The real danger from a fire is usually not the flames, but smoke that can travel quickly to areas far from the fire. Smoke inhalation is the major cause of death during a fire. Hence, closing doors and windows and using wet towels to cover any open spaces between the doors and the floor must be given top priority after patients in immediate danger have been evacuated and the fire alarm has been activated. The associates should start closing doors and windows throughout the facility as soon as the alarm is sounded. In all emergency situations, the staff must remain calm and reassure patients and visitors that appropriate procedures are being followed.

Fire safety procedures should clearly designate the person who takes charge when a fire or suspected fire is discovered. Generally, the administrator, the DON (in the administrator's absence), or a charge nurse (on the night shift) will ascertain whether smoke or fire is present anywhere in the facility. Once the presence of fire is confirmed, a phone call should also be made to the local fire department to confirm that there is a fire. An associate should be posted at the front entrance of the facility to direct the fire department personnel to the location of the fire in the building, while the person in charge of fire safety directs associates to secure all patients and follow the RACE steps.

On the other hand, when no smoke or fire is detected, notice of a false alarm should be relayed by telephone to confirm that there is no fire, because an alarm would have been previously relayed if a fire alarm had been activated. In most instances, however, the fire brigade is already on its way by the time the person in charge of fire safety has confirmed the state of "all clear." In this case, the individual should meet the fire brigade at the front entrance and explain the situation. Some fire personnel may still want to go through the building and ensure complete safety before leaving the premises.

## Emergency Evacuation

*Evacuation* is the removal of patients and vital equipment from an unsafe area to a safe area during a fire or other emergency situation (Tweedy, 1997). It does not necessarily refer to evacuation of the building.

Evacuation plans should cover both partial and total evacuation of patients. When a fire alarm is activated, automatic closure of fire doors segregates the point of origin of the fire from other areas on the same floor. Because fire doors provide a barrier against smoke and flames, a safety zone is created beyond the fire doors away from the point of origin of the fire (Figure 13–1). Such a space becomes an area of refuge, which the *Life Safety Code* defines as either (1) "a story in a building where the building is protected throughout by an approved, supervised automatic sprinkler system and has not less than two accessible rooms or spaces separated from each other by smoke-resisting partitions," or (2) "a space located in a path of travel leading to a public way that is protected from the effects of fire, either by means of separation from other spaces in the same building or by virtue of location, thereby permitting a delay in egress travel from any level." In simple terms, an *area of refuge* is a zone of safety within a building that is protected from the effects of fire and smoke, and provides direct access to an exit.

A partial evacuation consists of moving patients from the area of fire to a neighboring area of refuge. Total evacuation consists of removing patients and vital equipment from an entire wing or floor or evacuating the entire building. Bed-bound patients should be removed on stretchers because rolling beds

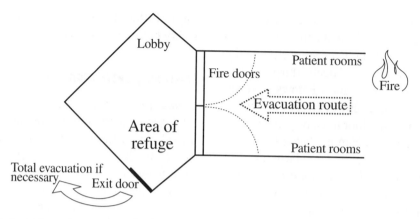

**Figure 13–1** Partial Evacuation to an Area of Refuge or Total Evacuation during a Fire Emergency.

into the hallways can quickly clog vital evacuation routes. Nonambulatory patients who are not bed bound can be rolled out in wheelchairs. Ambulatory patients should be led as a group, holding each other's hands. An associate should lead such a human chain, with another associate following the chain. After patients have been moved to an area of refuge, they must remain under staff supervision.

For the purpose of total evacuation, the facility must make prior arrangements for temporary shelter for residents in a local school, hospital, or Red Cross center. Evacuation plans should include transfer of patients; protecting and transferring medical records; continuing critical medical care services; and maintaining vital functions such as providing food, water, and clean linens.

## Simulation Drills

The facility must conduct regular fire drills on all shifts. The *Life Safety Code* requires that the facility conduct an unannounced fire drill on each shift once a quarter. Because of staff turnover, however, more frequent fire drills are recommended. The facility's associ-

ates are not expected to function as firefighters, but they must know how to operate a portable fire extinguisher. The staff members' main role is to contain any immediate danger and minimize the spread of fire till the fire brigade gets to the scene, at which point the firefighters will take over. A disaster simulation drill is necessary once a year to rehearse the response of the associates and the response of the local civil defense teams. All fire drills and disaster simulation drills must be documented, and training should follow to address areas of weak response. Simulation drills are also used to educate associates about the importance of remaining calm and thinking clearly during unexpected emergencies.

## Waste Management

### General Waste

As much as 90% or more of the waste produced by nursing care facilities is regarded as "nonrisk" general waste, which is comparable to domestic garbage and can be safely disposed of by contracting with a reputable waste removal company. A dumpster of sufficient size is essential, however, so that trash does not overflow at any time. The dumpster must be a covered container, and it must remain covered after each use. No loose trash should be thrown into the container; all garbage and waste must be appropriately bagged. The ground around the dumpster should be kept clean at all times. This function is generally the responsibility of the maintenance department.

## Hazardous Waste

The facility must have policies and procedures in effect for the safe handling, removal, and disposal of all wastes regarded as hazardous. The most common types of hazardous waste can be classified as infectious wastes, pathological wastes, and sharps. *Infectious waste* can pose health risks from communicable infectious agents. Such waste can come from patients who have been isolated for infections, dressings from infected wounds, human excreta, or laboratory cultures. *Pathological waste* is human waste that may contain human tissue, blood, or body fluids. It includes stoma bags, incontinence pads, and protective gloves and masks used by associates. *Sharps* can be any objects that can cut or puncture, such as needles, blades, broken glass, and nails.

Hazardous waste must not be deposited in the regular dumpster used for general waste. Safe handling requires caution to avoid injury from sharps and to prevent cross-contamination from infectious and pathological waste. Special puncture-proof containers are used for all sharps. Infectious and pathological waste is bagged in clearly marked or color-coded heavy-duty plastic bags that are also leak proof. The plastic bags are placed in rigid leak-proof containers, never on the floor. Unlike most hospitals, nursing facilities generally do not have on-site disposal or incineration facilities because of the costs involved. Contracts must therefore be established with qualified waste carriers for the regular removal and disposal of all hazardous wastes. Any storage of waste before collection for off-site disposal should be in a secure location designated for the purpose (Prüss et al., 1999).

## Environmental Safety

Safety is one of the primary elements to be incorporated in the various environmental policies and procedures discussed in this chapter. Personnel working in a facility's environmental services departments need specific training in safe work habits and in monitoring the environment for safety. For instance, monitoring hot water in patient rooms and bathrooms is a critical aspect of safety that prevents scalding. As a general rule, hot water temperature in these areas should not exceed 110° F (43° C). Hot water supply to patient areas and public areas is equipped with thermostatically controlled mixing valves to keep the water temperature from rising above the specified limits. The maintenance supervisor must pay particular attention to this area and record daily temperature readings to ensure safety. On the other hand, adequate supply of water that is hot enough for washing and sanitizing in the kitchen and laundry is equally important. Because the hot water temperatures required for patient care areas and for sanitizing functions differ substantially, a common practice is to have separate hot water systems and booster heaters that are locally mounted on sanitizing equipment to achieve the desired results.

Maintenance and housekeeping personnel must pay close attention to their equipment. If equipment is left unattended, it presents a hazard. Floor cleaning and polishing chemicals should be nonskid. Safety signs must be used while mopping floors. Mopping the hallways lengthwise, doing one half of the hallway at a time, leaves the other half for safe passage.

Furniture and equipment must be kept away from traffic paths and exits. Various electrical gadgets are operated with long cords, which should be kept along the baseboards and not cross the hallway. Heavy housekeeping trucks, food transportation carts, and linen carts can cause serious injury. They often block the operator's view and require caution, especially when turning blind corners. Strategically placed mirrors can help associates using these carts to see people around the corner and use caution to prevent injuries.

## For Further Thought

1. What would be some of the important clauses to include in (a) routine contracts, (b) open-call contracts, and (c) job-unit contracts?

2. What may be some of the reasons for not allowing the housekeeping staff in nursing facilities to handle either clean or soiled linens, unlike hotel and motel operations?

3. Discuss how certain environmental standards in the facility can be effectively used to convey value to potential clients.

## For Further Learning

U.S. Environmental Protection Agency: Provides information on registered antimicrobial products. http://www.epa.gov/oppad001/chemregindex.htm

## REFERENCES

Belkin, N.L. 2003. Disinfecting versus sanitizing. *Health Facilities Management* 16, no. 11: 34–36.

Goldberg, A.J., & Buttaro, R.A. 1990. *Hospital Departmental Profiles*, 3rd ed. Chicago: American Hospital Publishing.

Griffith, J.R. 1995. *The Well-Managed Health Care Organization*, 3rd ed. Ann Arbor, MI: AUPHA Press/Health Administration Press.

Heintzelman, J.E. 1987. *The Complete Handbook of Maintenance Management*. Englewood Cliffs, NJ: Prentice-Hall.

Kavaler, F., & Spiegel, A.D. 1997. Assuring safety and security in health care institutions. In F. Kavaler and A.D. Speigel (eds.), *Risk Management in Health Care Institutions: A Strategic Approach*. Boston: Jones and Bartlett Publishers.

Magee, G.H. 1988. *Facilities Maintenance Management*. Kingston, MA: R.S. Means Company.

Niebel, B.W. 1985. *Engineering Maintenance Management*. New York: Marcel Dekker Publisher.

Office of Health and Safety, Centers for Disease Control and Prevention. 2002. *Guidelines for Laundry in Health Care Facilities*. http://www.cdc.gov/ od/ohs/biosfty/laundry.htm

Prüss, A., Giroult, E., & Rushbrook, P. 1999. *Safe Management of Wastes from Health-Care Activities*. Geneva: World Health Organization.

Rowland, H.S., & Rowland, B.L. 1984. *Hospital Management: A Guide to Departments*. Rockville, MD: Aspen Systems Corporation.

Sells, D.H. 2000. *Security in the Healthcare Environment*. Gaithersburg, MD: Aspen Publishers.

Tweedy, J.T. 1997. *Healthcare Hazard Control and Safety Management*. Boca Raton, FL: Lewis Publishers.

Vesley, D. 1973. Selected topics in environmental health. In R.G. Bond, G.S. Michaelsen, and R.L. DeRoos (eds.), *Environmental Health and Safety in Health-Care Facilities*. New York: Macmillan Publishing.

Vesley, D., & Greene, V.W. 1973. Sterilization, disinfection, and cleaning techniques. In R.G. Bond, G.S. Michaelsen, and R.L. Deroos (eds.), *Environmental Health and Safety in Health-Care Facilities*. New York: Macmillan Publishing.

# Chapter 14

# Administrative and Information Systems

## What You Will Learn

- Facilities must be staffed to perform basic bookkeeping and reception functions. Protocols should be established for reception of visitors and incoming telephone calls.

- Payroll and compensation practices are governed by the federal Fair Labor Standards Act. The act specifies exempt and nonexempt worker categories, minimum wage, and overtime pay. Other compensation matters are governed by the facility's own policies.

- The facility is responsible for FICA and FUTA withholdings and court-ordered wage garnishments.

- The facility's bookkeeping staff also generally handle accounts payable, petty cash, billings and collections for patient services delivered, the patient trust fund, and cash receipts and deposits. Management of the patient trust fund must comply with federal and state regulations.

- Regulations require nursing homes to maintain medical records on each patient. The records include the patient's identifying information, but the bulk of it contains clinical information.

- Medical records enable caregivers to coordinate services, and the records provide evidence of actual care rendered. Medical records can also be used for legal purposes.

- Information systems have numerous applications. Mainly because of cost constraints, adoption of integrated networks has been slow.

- The CMS collects national data on nursing homes through its OSCAR system. On the basis of these data, the CMS provides information for consumers through the Nursing Home Compare Program.

> • Before purchasing a commercial information system, the administrator should evaluate current capabilities and carefully consider the objectives to be achieved. Desired capabilities, support, and training are other factors that should be weighed in addition to costs.

Administrative and information systems support the management and clinical functions in the facility. In a hospital, these support functions are generally segregated into several departments. In nursing facilities, however, the functions are generally consolidated in one department.

## The Business Office and Its Functions

The business office generally combines reception, secretarial, clerical, and bookkeeping functions. These four functions form the business office core, which closely interfaces with the work of the administrator. The medical records office is typically a separate administrative function under the supervision of the director of nursing (see Figure III–1).

Visitors, patients, family members, and associates have frequent contact with the business office. Most facilities have a front desk staffed by a receptionist and an adjoining office occupied by bookkeeping and other clerical staff. The receptionist also performs some secretarial and clerical duties.

The number of bookkeepers needed by the facility depends on two factors: the size of the facility and the business and accounting functions performed at the facility. Multifacility chain operations centralize most accounting and finance functions at their corporate offices, but the corporate office relies on the facility's business office for vital inputs needed to prepare financial and management reports. Stand-alone facilities often contract with an accounting firm to carry out most accounting and finance functions. Again, bookkeeping staff at the facility performs basic routine functions and prepares inputs for accountants.

The business office is supervised by a business office manager who is a department head reporting to the administrator. This individual also handles the facility's bookkeeping. Even though the business office is open five days a week during regular business hours, facilities with 100 to 120 beds or more should have a receptionist for evenings and weekends. In smaller operations, telephone answering duties are taken over by a designated nursing station when the business office is closed.

Regulations do not mandate specific qualifications for the employees who staff the business office. Finding qualified people who possess the necessary combination of receptionist, secretarial, and clerical skills is not always easy. Nevertheless, every effort should be made to staff the front office with personnel who can display a pleasant demeanor in person as well as on the telephone and also have the mental capacity to carry out clerical and secretarial duties in an atmosphere in which frequent interruptions and distractions are common.

Bookkeepers must be skilled in basic accounting functions. However, bookkeepers also have regular interactions with patients and families, so they must also have good communication skills to interact with clients. The bookkeepers also generally relieve the receptionist for lunch and break time, sickness, and vacations. Cross-training may also enable a facility to use other personnel, such as the medical records clerk, to cover the reception desk for brief durations.

## Reception

To most first-time visitors, the front office provides a window into the facility. With their first contact, many people form lasting opinions about the rest of the operation and its services. A smile, a warm greeting, an offer of assistance, and an eagerness to meet people's needs create a positive impression. A warm human touch can have a soothing effect in calming down people's anxiety, anger, frustration, and other negative emotions.

Effectively managed facilities have written protocols for interacting with visitors and assisting telephone callers. Some administrators may regard it as petty, but standardized procedures are vital for consistent quality and for staff training. Adhering to well-formulated protocols helps the facility project a professional image.

Every visitor to the facility must be made to feel welcome. The receptionist must interrupt whatever he or she is doing and attend to the visitor. Once greeted, the visitors should be asked how they could be assisted. Knowledge of the facility, the location of resident rooms, the key functions of the different departments, the names of residents, and knowledge of some of the residents' routines and habits can all play an essential role in directing visitors appropriately. The receptionist's length of employment and experience with the facility can pay rich dividends here. The front office must maintain an updated roster of residents, along with their room numbers.

Effectively managed facilities maintain a notification system for the receptionist to know when certain key personnel are out of the facility or in meetings. A small board with the names of all key personnel can be easily updated to avoid embarrassing moments when a visitor may be kept waiting for someone who is eventually found to be unavailable.

As stated in Chapter 9, the facility must have a written plan for handling inquiries for potential admissions. The receptionist is not responsible for providing detailed information about the facility and its services. But the facility must have protocols in place, so the receptionist knows who is available at any given time to attend to a walk-in or telephone inquiry.

The receptionist should also know when resident activities are taking place in the facility and which residents may be away from the facility for an outing or a shopping trip. Some acquaintance with residents is also important. Just imagine how awkward it could be when a church pastor comes to visit a particular resident, but, because the receptionist does not know who that resident is, the pastor is directed to the resident's room while the resident is sitting right there in the front lobby.

Having a written protocol for answering the telephone is another hallmark of an effectively managed facility. A telephone call must be answered within the first three to four rings. When more calls than one come in at the same time, keeping the caller on hold for several minutes after saying "Can you hold, please?" or "one moment, please," is inappropriate. The bookkeeper(s), and other personnel if necessary, should assist the receptionist when the switchboard gets busy. Once the call is picked up, the recommended protocol is an appropriate greeting followed by the name of the facility, followed by "how may I help you." The call should then be directed promptly to the appropriate individual. Depending on the facility's protocols, the call may be directed to another individual (in case of an inquiry or other important matter), the person may be paged, or a message may be taken. In many facilities, key associates now have portable pagers to minimize use of the intercom system.

## Secretarial and Clerical

Depending on the facility's size, the receptionist may be assigned additional duties, such as clerical work, minor bookkeeping tasks, filing, faxing, handling mail, and photocopying. Use of computers has eliminated the need to use typewriters for correspondence, which allows the administrator and department heads to type their own letters using a word-processing program. At the administrator's discretion, the receptionist may be responsible for handling the patient trust fund, or this task may be assigned to the bookkeeper. Clerical functions that are often assigned to the receptionist include processing employee time cards for payroll and processing vendor invoices for accounts payable. As stated earlier, size of the facility is a key factor that determines the extent to which clerical functions can be handled effectively by the receptionist.

## Accounting and Bookkeeping

The main accounting and bookkeeping functions include payroll, accounts payable, the petty cash fund, billing for patient services, accounts receivable, the patient trust fund, and cash deposits. Trained bookkeepers may also be able to perform more advanced accounting functions, such as posting to the general ledger, doing payroll accounting and processing payroll checks for employees, processing payable checks for vendors, and completing quarterly tax forms. In this case, preparation of financial statements (income statement, balance sheet, cash flow statement, and certain managerial reports) will be contracted out to an accounting firm. For nursing homes affiliated with a hospital or multifacility corporation, these functions are generally centralized at the corporate office, and the costs are passed on to the facility in the form of management fees. Nevertheless, for chain-affiliated facilities, centralized accounting functions are more cost-effective than outsourcing them to an accounting firm.

## Payroll and Compensation

Payroll accounting comprises three main activities: determining gross wages, deducting payroll withholdings, and calculating payroll-based contributions made by the employer on behalf of the employee. The actual pay employees receive is gross wages minus the withholdings. Employer contributions are regarded as benefits. An example of these contributions is one-half of the Social Security and Medicare taxes paid by the employer on behalf of each employee. Some employers also make contributions to the employees' retirement saving accounts.

Employees are paid on the basis of their rates of pay and the hours they work. The Fair Labor Standards Act (FLSA) requires employers to maintain accurate payroll records that include certain identifying information about each employee, along with data about the hours worked and wages earned. The administrator should authorize the initial rate of pay when an employee is first put on the payroll. For later changes in the established rate of pay, controls must be instituted for proper authorizations that would prevent any irregularities. The number of hours worked must be calculated strictly in accordance with established payroll policy.

This section is intended to provide only an overview of the main FLSA requirements. The law can be complex when dealing with certain specific situations, in which case legal counsel would be necessary. The Wage and Hour Division of the U.S. Department of Labor is responsible for administering and enforcing federal labor laws.

## Exempt and Nonexempt Employees

Under FLSA, all employees must be classified as either exempt or nonexempt. ***Nonexempt employees*** are paid an hourly rate, which must at least equal the minimum wage established under law. Nonexempt employees are also entitled to overtime pay (discussed later). Most employees in a nursing facility are nonexempt and are paid an hourly wage. These employees are issued time cards for each pay period and are required to punch a time clock that records the times when an employee came in to work (clocked-in) and when the employee left work (clocked-out).

***Exempt employees*** are most often salaried and are exempt from the overtime provisions of the law. However, just being salaried or having a certain job title does not determine exempt status. Two main criteria that determine exempt status are the employee's compensation and specific job duties. Both criteria must be met.

## Criterion 1: Compensation

To qualify for exemption, employees must be paid no less than $455 per week on a salary basis. As a general rule, the full salary must be paid regardless of the number of days or hours worked during a given week. Exempt employees do not need to be paid for any workweek in which they perform no work.

## Criterion 2: Job Duties

The emphasis is on the primary duties that constitute the nature of an exempt employee's job even though a person may perform some nonexempt duties. FLSA regulations define three main "white-collar" categories. These categories, however, cannot be used arbitrarily with the intent of classifying certain employees as exempt:

- *Executive:* The duties are primarily managerial in nature; the person supervises and directs the work of two or more full-time employees; and the person makes at least substantive recommendations on personnel decisions such as hiring, firing, or advancement of other employees. Under these guidelines, the facility's administrator, assistant administrator, director of nursing, food service director, and perhaps the facilities manager in charge of all plant and environmental services would be exempt, provided they also meet the compensation test. Other department head positions in nursing homes are unlikely to be classified as exempt.

- *Administrative:* The employee's primary duty must be the performance of office or nonmanual work directly related to the management or general business operations of the employer or the employer's customers. In addition, the employee's primary duties must include the exercise of discretion and independent judgment with respect to matters of significance. It means that the employee has the authority to make an independent choice, free from immediate direction or supervision

(Neumeister & Fuller, n.d.). Except in very large facilities, it is unlikely that any nursing home employee would fall into this category.

- *Professional:* The employee's primary duty must be the performance of work requiring advanced knowledge, defined as work that is predominantly intellectual in character and that includes work requiring the consistent exercise of discretion and judgment. The advanced knowledge must be in a field of science or learning. The advanced knowledge must be customarily acquired by a prolonged course of specialized intellectual instruction. Only physicians and nurse practitioners are likely to qualify as exempt under this category.

FLSA has a special category of "highly compensated employees," referring to those earning $100,000 or more and at least $455 per week on a salaried basis. These employees are exempt as long as they customarily and regularly perform at least one of the duties of an exempt executive, administrative, or professional employee.

There are other exemptions that generally do not apply to health care facilities. On the other hand, nothing in the FLSA law prevents an employer from paying a worker at or above the minimum wage or overtime pay even if the worker is not, by law, subject to the minimum wage or overtime pay requirements.

## Minimum Wage

On July 24, 2008, the federal minimum wage was increased to $6.55 per hour. This was the second of the three scheduled increases. The next increase to $7.25 per hour took effect on July 24, 2009. Future minimum wage increases are not automatic. Congress must pass a bill and the president must sign it into law before the minimum wage can go up. Many states also have minimum wage laws. In those states, the employee is entitled to the higher of the state or federal minimum wage.

## Overtime Compensation

A workweek, which can begin on any day of the week, is seven consecutive 24-hour periods or 168 consecutive hours. Federal law mandates that nonexempt workers be paid overtime for any hours worked in excess of 40 hours in a work week. Although the 40-hour week is generally the standard for determining overtime, FLSA permits employers to enter into an agreement with a certain category of employees, such as nurses, whereby a work period of 14 consecutive days (instead of seven) may be established. Commonly known as the 8-80 rule, this alternative requires paying overtime for any hours in excess of eight hours in any one day or for any hours in excess of 80 hours during the 14-day work period (Pozgar, 1992).

Overtime must be paid at the rate of time-and-a-half the regular rate of pay. Even when overtime is not authorized, if an employee has incurred it, it must be paid. Nonexempt employees cannot be given compensatory time off in lieu of overtime. Such a practice is illegal for private-sector employers. It is not illegal, however, in the case of exempt employees.

The law does not require employers to pay more than an employee's established rate of pay for working the evening shift, night shift, or weekends. However, to ensure adequate staffing, many facilities have established extra pay as an incentive for late shifts, weekends, and holidays.

## Limits to FLSA's Jurisdiction

There are a number of employment practices that FLSA does not regulate. For example, the FLSA law does not regulate:

1. Vacation, holiday, severance, or sick pay.
2. Meal or rest periods, holidays off, or vacations.
3. Premium pay for weekend or holiday work.
4. Pay raises or fringe benefits.
5. A discharge notice, reason for discharge, or immediate payment of final wages to terminated employees.

These compensation matters are governed mainly by the facility's own policies and practices. State laws, however, generally specify the requirement that workers be given time off for meals and rest. A half-hour unpaid meal break is common on a standard shift of between six to eight hours. There are instances, however, when meal time can become compensable. Such matters of dispute are governed by laws other than FLSA. To avoid paying employees for meal time, the employees must be fully relieved of all duties and be free to leave their work stations, or the facility, during their meal breaks. It is particularly important to monitor meal breaks in facilities experiencing staff shortages and in facilities where well-meaning employees may have a tendency to "grab a quick bite" at the work station itself in order to minimize interruptions in patient care. If this is the case, the law would probably require that the employee be compensated for meal time. Similarly, meal breaks may be compensable if the employer requires that employees be available to respond to patient

care needs when called. An example would be requiring employees not to leave the facility or wear pagers while on meal breaks. In *Hoffman v. St. Joseph's Hospital*, the court held that respiratory therapists should be compensated for their 30-minute meal break because hospital policy required the employees to wear pagers during their meal breaks and they were subject to discipline if they failed to respond to pages.

Facility policy should also specify the amount of time allowed as incidental time for preparatory and concluding activities. For instance, at the change of shift, workers may have to clean equipment, wash their hands, etc. Also, many workers need to clock-in or clock-out at the same time, but generally some waiting time is involved, because they cannot all use the time clock simultaneously. This waiting time could be considered incidental, time which is not compensable under law. Determining where to begin and where to end the compensable time for a worker's shift can be difficult. As a rule of thumb, the facility must compensate nonexempt employees for all work and work-related activities required by the facility. Compensable work also includes orientation, training, and in-service education that an employee may be required to have.

## Payroll Withholdings

Employers are legally required to withhold taxes from their employees' pay and to deposit the withheld amounts with the appropriate tax agencies (Jacksack, 1998). Taxes normally withheld from employee paychecks include federal, state, and local income taxes. Employers who fail to withhold and deposit taxes in a timely manner are subject to severe penalties and interest charges (Seawell, 1992). Under the Federal Insurance Contributions

Act (FICA), employers must also withhold half of the Social Security and Medicare taxes from the employees' paychecks. The other half of these FICA taxes is to be paid by the employer. Also, under federal law, employers must pay unemployment taxes on behalf of the employees under the Federal Unemployment Tax Act (FUTA). In most states, the employer must also pay a state unemployment tax. These taxes are based on taxable wages paid to employees. In some states, employers are required to pay a disability insurance tax for workers' compensation. Most states, however, allow the employer to cover workers' compensation through private insurance purchased from a commercial insurance company (Seawell, 1992).

The employer may also be required to withhold union dues for employees who belong to a trade union. Wage garnishment is another type of compulsory withholding. A *wage garnishment* is any legal or equitable procedure through which some portion of an employee's earnings must be withheld by an employer to pay a debt incurred by the employee. Most garnishments are made by court order with which employers must comply. Other types of legal or equitable procedures include levies by the Internal Revenue Service (IRS) or a state tax-collection agency for unpaid taxes and federal agency administrative garnishments for nontax debts owed to the federal government.

There may be other withholdings that are voluntary, and these usually require the employee's written consent. Voluntary withholdings include the employee's portion of health insurance and life insurance premiums; employee's contribution into a retirement plan; dental plan premiums; and premiums for other types of insurance, such as accident and disability.

# Other Bookkeeping Tasks

Most of the bookkeeping tasks are carried out according to general business practices. Management of the patient trust fund, particularly for Medicare and Medicaid patients, must comply with federal and state regulations.

## Accounts Payable

*Accounts payable* is the accounting term for money owed to vendors from whom goods, supplies, and services have been purchased on credit. With the exception of minor and nonroutine purchases, most goods and services are purchased on a noncash basis. An invoice showing the amount due generally accompanies the goods at the time they are delivered to the facility. Other vendors deliver the products and then separately mail the invoice. Service vendors also provide their services and issue an invoice later.

A common practice among most vendors is to extend credit for 30 days. Utility companies for telephone, gas, electricity, water, and sewer may allow less than 30 days for full payment of the amounts due. Payments are generally made by check and are recorded in the general ledger, which is maintained on a computer-based accounting system. As each invoice is paid, it is indelibly stamped or perforated "PAID" to prevent double payment (Seawell, 1992). All invoices must be authorized by the appropriate department heads before they are paid. Department heads must carefully check to ensure that the items on the invoice were actually received and note any discrepancies.

## Petty Cash Fund

As a general rule, all purchases must be paid for by check through the accounts payable system. In some situations, however, payment by check is impractical. To pay for certain cash purchases and other small incidental expenses, a facility must maintain a petty cash fund. The facility should establish a policy on the imprest amount, and on the maximum amount per disbursement that the business office can incur without requiring authorization from the administrator. The ***imprest amount*** is a fixed amount, such as $400 or $500, which is maintained by periodically replenishing the petty cash that has been used. Petty cash is maintained in a locked box or drawer.

Each disbursement from the petty cash fund requires completion of a petty cash voucher, to which any supporting documentation, such as a sales receipt from a store, is attached. The voucher is signed by the person receiving the money. Under the imprest system, the cash and the amounts shown on the vouchers must always add up to the imprest amount. This system allows the administrator to periodically check the petty cash fund. When the amount of cash drops below a predetermined level, the vouchers are removed and totaled. Cash equaling this total is added to the petty cash fund. At that point, the petty cash fund should equal the imprest amount. Inconsequential shortages may occur because of errors, but substantial or frequent shortages may indicate mishandling of funds.

## Billing, Accounts Receivable, and Collection

Just as the nursing facility receives products and services from outside vendors and does not pay cash for them right away, similarly it provides services to patients but does not get paid for those services immediately. The facility, however, has the legal right to receive money at a future date. The amounts that remain to be collected by the facility for services already rendered are called ***accounts receivable***.

The facility must bill the respective payers such as Medicare, Medicaid, private insurance companies, or individual private parties responsible for paying. Bills are prepared and sent to the payers once a month. Medicaid and Medicare bills, called ***claims***, are submitted electronically to the fiscal intermediaries contracted by Medicaid and Medicare to pay claims from providers.

The billing system should be set up so each patient is accurately classified according to pay type. It is particularly important to keep track of changes in pay status, when a patient's payment status switches from one pay type to another, such as from Medicare to Medicaid, or from Medicare to private pay. The billing system must also separate the co-payment and any other amounts that must be collected from the patient.

The basis for daily charges is the midnight census report, which is prepared each night by the charge nurse on duty and verified by the director of nursing. The ***midnight census report*** verifies the presence of each patient in the facility during the night. On a daily basis, the bookkeeper should match patients in the billing system against the midnight census report. The report must be reconciled daily because, from time to time, a facility may have patients on ***bed-hold***, which happens when patients are temporarily away (to a hospital, or with family), but their beds are being held for them and must be paid for.

The daily charge, or the *per-diem rate*, covers room, board, nursing care, and other routine services. Depending on the payer, other services may or may not be covered by the per-diem rate. Any services or supplies not covered by the per-diem rate must be billed separately. All services and supplies must be itemized and billed when a patient is private pay. To accomplish this task, nursing must have a system to identify and charge for all supplies used by each individual patient. Recording these ancillary charges requires cooperation from the nursing staff, who must be adequately trained on how the system works. The business office must also receive charge tickets from independent contractors, such as barbers and beauticians, who provide personal services to patients.

On a daily basis, the various patient charges as well as all payments received are posted to each patient's ledger account. These ledger accounts are used to prepare a monthly accounts receivable *aging report*, which is a managerial report, not a financial statement. Also known as an *aging schedule*, this report provides a detailed account-by-account analysis of outstanding balances on unpaid patient accounts. It also shows account balances according to the number of days a given balance has been outstanding (Seawell, 1992). For instance, each account shows the receivable balance under columns for 0–30 days, which is considered "current;" 31–90 days past due; 91–120 days past due; and over 120 days past due, as shown in Exhibit 18–8. The older an unpaid account gets, the less likely it is to be collected.

Third-party claims are often rejected because of billing errors. The only way such accounts can be collected is by rectifying the errors and resubmitting corrected claims. To collect past-due balances owed by private individuals, the facility must have collection policies and procedures.

The following guidelines can be used by facilities to formulate their own collection policies: accounts receivable are considered current during the first 30 days. However, even before an account balance gets to be 30 days old, a telephone call should be made to the party responsible for paying the private portion of the bill. The objective of this call is to remind the individual that the payment is due and to tell the payer what is the exact amount of the balance due. The caller should also ask when payment might be expected and try to reach an agreement with the payer on a payment date that is no later than one week after the phone call. A week later, a second call should be made if payment has still not been received. The caller should now try to find out whether there is a reason why payment was not made and whether there is some problem with the bill and the amount due. Again, the caller should try to obtain some form of a promise to pay (Frew & Frew, 1982). A friendly tone must be maintained by the facility's representative during these telephone conversations. The administrator should institute a mechanism that enables the staff to conduct timely follow-ups and maintain documentation on each conversation. Detailed notes are helpful for any subsequent follow-up. Generally, when an account is in arrears for 45 days or more, a letter should be mailed to the party responsible for paying the bill. The letter should contain a polite request for payment in a manner that is firm but does not present an ultimatum (Frew & Frew, 1982). Any subsequent letters should still be polite but should contain a stronger tone, including a warning that use of a collection agency may be required if the balance is not paid by a given date. By the 90th day of being past due, an account should be turned over to a collection agency.

## Patient Trust Fund

Residents of a nursing home may ask the facility to manage their personal funds. When asked to do so, the nursing home is obligated to establish a patient trust fund. The facility should also inform residents and their families that they have the option to use the patient trust fund. Nursing home regulations, however, allow residents to retain the right to manage their own financial affairs. Residents who choose to manage their own money cannot be required by the nursing facility to deposit funds in the patient trust account managed by the facility. The facility is not allowed to charge Medicare and Medicaid patients any fee for managing the trust fund.

Most state laws have established limits on the maximum amount a facility is required to manage for each resident. Under Michigan law, for example, a nursing home must hold and manage up to $5,000 for each resident. A facility cannot refuse to handle funds of less than $5,000, although it may refuse to handle funds that exceed that amount.

Medicare and Medicaid certification regulations mandate that nursing homes deposit into an interest-bearing account all individual patient funds exceeding $50. Up to $50 per resident may be held in a non-interest-bearing account or petty cash fund held at the facility. Depending on state law, the requirements may vary for noncertified facilities that admit only private-pay patients.

Patient funds are in a demand trust with the facility, which means that the funds are available to the patient upon request (Abramovice, 1988). In addition, the money can only be spent by the facility with specific permission from the patient or from someone authorized by the patient. To manage the patient trust fund, the facility should:

- Open an interest-bearing account; this account must be separate from the facility's own bank account.

- Maintain a petty cash system that is separate from the facility's own petty cash fund. Patients must have access to their funds during normal office hours.

- Implement a cash receipt or cash ledger system to record each transaction. The records should include the patient's name, account number, amount of cash withdrawn or deposited, and the purpose for which funds were withdrawn (such as cash, telephone bill, purchase of clothing, etc.). The signature of the patient or the patient's authorized representative should be required for each transaction, unless there is an invoice bearing the patient's name to support the disbursement of funds.

- As a safeguard against misuse of funds, balances must be reconciled each month by someone other than the person responsible for maintaining the fund.

- Regulations require the facility to provide the patient or the authorized person a statement at least once every quarter. The quarterly statement should include, at a minimum, the balance at the beginning of the period, current balance, amount of interest earned, total deposits and withdrawals, and detailed information on each transaction.

- The full balance of funds belonging to a patient must be returned promptly after a patient has been discharged from the facility. After a patient's death, a written statement must be sent to the administrator of the resident's estate.

- The facility must notify Medicare and Medicaid residents when the funds attain a level within $200 of the resource limit for Supplemental Security Income (SSI) or Medicaid. Such residents must be informed that if they go over the SSI or Medicaid resource limits, they may lose eligibility for the SSI and Medicaid programs.

- The facility is required by law to purchase a surety bond or provide evidence of self-insurance, such as facility funds that are irrevocably set aside for repaying the residents in case of loss.

## Cash Receipts and Deposits

Control of cash receipts is a critical function. All cash and checks must be recorded on a cash receipt voucher that shows the exact amount received. Actual cash received must be kept separate from any other cash funds such as the petty cash fund or the patient trust fund. No cash disbursement should ever be made out of cash receipts (Seawell, 1992). Cash and checks must be deposited into the facility's bank account daily. The bank deposit slip should be reconciled against the cash receipt vouchers, which are then used for posting credits to the respective patients' ledger accounts. The ledger account for each patient shows the debits or amounts initially owed, credits or amounts paid, and the accounts receivable due.

## Medical Records

### Staffing

Depending on the size of the facility, medical record services are staffed by a full- or part-time individual. Credentials of registered health information administrator (RHIA) or technician (RHIT), conferred by the Ameri-can Health Information Management Association (AHIMA), is a necessary qualification for hospital medical records personnel. Certification is based on academic qualifications and an examination. Only large nursing homes may be able to employ someone credentialed as RHIA or RHIT. Most facilities designate a clerical person with some relevant experience or training to handle medical records and contract with a duly certified medical records consultant, who provides routine oversight.

### Functions

The medical records clerk must ensure that medical records are completed within a reasonable time. When a resident is first admitted, a new chart for that resident is opened by the medical records clerk. In case of a re-admission, the previously closed record is reactivated. Open records are maintained at the nursing station responsible for the care of the patient. The medical records clerk is responsible for ensuring that the records are maintained in an organized manner in accordance with current laws and accepted professional standards. Quality is ensured by auditing records according to an audit schedule. Upon discharge, the patient's clinical record is closed and moved to the medical records office. Before the closed records are filed away, they are reviewed for completeness and compliance with regulations and the facility's policies.

Standardized methods exist for systematizing, indexing, and filing medical records. The medical records clerk is responsible for the safekeeping, confidentiality, and retrieval of stored records. Paper medical records on patients who have been in the facility for a long time can become quite bulky. Such records can be thinned in accordance with the facility's policies and regulatory provisions.

However, clinical medical records in nursing homes are increasingly being computerized, although the progress is slow.

## Medical Record Content

A nursing facility is required by law to maintain individual medical records on each patient. The record contains all significant information on the care of the patient from admission to final discharge. Thus, it becomes a permanent and comprehensive historical record of the patient's medical condition, the course of treatment and specific services delivered during the patient's stay in the facility, and the clinical outcomes. The facility's medical records should contain only original notes and reports. Records sent from another facility are retained in a file but are not considered a legal part of the medical record (Burger et al., 1986). However, when a patient is transferred from the hospital to a skilled nursing facility, a summary of the acute care stay should be part of the nursing home records. The instructions and orders for skilled care must also be entered into the medical record as the patient's care continues (Kiger, 2003). Timeliness, objectivity, accuracy, and brevity without the sacrifice of essential facts are the hallmarks of effective medical recording (Bruce, 1988).

The medical record includes a patient's identifying information as well as the patient's clinical information. The patient's identifying information includes name, address, gender, date of birth, Social Security number, Medicare and/or Medicaid claim number, marital status, name and contact information on next of kin, race and ethnicity, and religious preference. Clinical information includes records of medical and social history, physical examinations, principal diagnoses, results of the initial assessment and any subsequent reassessments,

informed consent and advance directives (see Chapter 5), plan of care, treatments prescribed, diet plan, therapeutic procedures carried out, and medications administered. Also included in the clinical information are records of laboratory test results, clinical observations, response to treatment, any change in condition and action taken, any incidents or accidents, any treatment errors and action taken, any adverse reaction to medications, any use of restraints and psychotropic drugs, and discharge summary. All physicians' orders must be signed and dated by the attending physician.

Typically, medical records are arranged in chronological sequence and divided into sections by the source of documentation. Thus, typical sections include those for physicians' notes, clinical laboratory, social services, nurses' notes, and dietary records. Another method uses an integrated format in which physicians and other health care professionals enter all progress notes in chronological order on one form, rather than in separate sections. This format promotes interdisciplinary collaboration because each discipline can easily see documentation furnished by others (Kiger, 2003).

State laws dictate the length of time for which medical records must be stored. The length of time for retaining medical records should also take into consideration the ***statute of limitations***, a period prescribed by law within which a legal action can be taken, which varies from one state to another (Bruce, 1988).

## Purpose of Medical Records

Maintaining complete medical records is critical from several different perspectives:

- Coordinating interdisciplinary care.
- Ensuring continuity of care.

- Documenting compliance and medical necessity.
- Providing data to improve care.
- Recording services rendered.

The primary purpose of medical records is to assist caregivers in coordinating services provided to a patient. Individual medical records provide all relevant information on each patient in one place to a diverse group of caregivers. These records help the interdisciplinary caregivers coordinate their efforts.

From the patient's standpoint, the medical record ensures continuity of care because it provides vital information needed by all caregivers. Each caregiver can also see what staff members from the other disciplines may be doing to address patient needs.

Medical records provide documentary evidence of actual care rendered. Regulators and third-party payers rely on the medical records as a basis for determining compliance with requirements. The documentation also forms the basis for payment for services delivered and for evaluating whether the services provided were clinically necessary. Medical records provide vital information for improving quality and for research.

Attorneys pursuing malpractice cases rely on the medical records to determine whether there were any lapses in care. As part of a facility's defense during litigation proceedings, timely, complete, and accurate medical records are essential to demonstrate that all reasonable and necessary care was provided. It is important for nursing home administrators to become familiar with the system of medical records used in their facilities. Administrators should review these records as part of their investigation when allegations of lapses in care are made by family members, regulators, or others. Common

abbreviations used in patient documentation are listed in Appendix 14–I.

The facility retains ownership of the medical record, but the information contained in it belongs to the patient. Privacy of patient information contained in the medical records is a legal requirement under the Health Insurance Portability and Accountability Act (HIPAA) of 1996 (see Chapter 5).

## Information Systems

As in other health care settings, nursing homes are moving toward electronic systems for administrative and clinical records and various types of management applications. *Information systems* are computer-based applications used for transforming raw data into information that can be used in a variety of ways to improve operational efficiencies and the quality of services. Currently, the most common application of information systems in nursing homes is for patient assessment, Minimum Data Set (MDS) reporting, and billing. Most nursing homes are also using information systems to manage admissions, transfers, and discharges (Resnick et al., 2008). In future, however, information systems will play an increasingly important role in effective management.

Data themselves do not constitute information. Discrete data become information only when the data have been accurately recorded, organized, processed, interpreted, and used. Large quantities of data can be processed by computer software programs to produce summaries and reports that can help employees do their jobs more effectively and to help managers make decisions for improving the operations. Examples include information on patient case mix, effectiveness of clinical interventions, costs for taking care of different categories of patients, budgetary variances, and marketing. Meaningful information can facilitate instituting managerial controls, making timely decisions, making quality assessments, and delivering improved patient care. For example, summaries of accounts payable help management identify unauthorized payments to vendors. Other reports help management to study labor-hour use and overtime in order to control labor costs; to monitor aging of accounts receivables to identify and collect past due accounts; and to control costs using budget variances. Illustrations of these reports are included in Chapter 18.

Sophisticated software programs can provide information such as the cost of producing a particular type of service. Such information is necessary for contract negotiations with managed care or VA entities and can also be used for evaluating payoffs from interventions such as new quality initiatives. The efficiency of self-managed work teams (discussed in Chapter 16) can be greatly enhanced by integrated networks because work teams assume a variety of decision-making and problem-solving responsibilities that are left to management in traditional work settings. Such systems need careful designing because both information shortfalls (too little information) and information overload (excessive information) can reduce the users' effectiveness. The quality of information systems has a direct effect on processes and procedures—and on the use of resources (Yeatts & Hyten, 1998).

Since the 1990s, information system applications have been expanded into clinical areas such as patient assessment, care planning, progress notes, and quality improvement. Related applications include other internal functions such as staff scheduling, menu planning

and food ordering, inventory management, activity planning, and preventive maintenance scheduling. Information systems can also be used to manage the facility's marketing program and to keep track of inquiries, follow-up, and admissions generated from inquiries. Finally, electronic communications by e-mail and messaging have become commonplace because of their superior efficiency.

## Integrated Networks

Griffith (1995) suggested that not every computer application is part of an information system. An application becomes part of an information system when the information is integrated to provide immediate electronic access. Integrated information systems go a step beyond the functions described in the previous section. These systems are designed to integrate multiple functions and provide multiple users access to the same information. Several examples can be given to illustrate how integrated information systems can support more efficient management planning and decision making:

- *Staffing:* Integrated systems can enable the facility to incorporate absenteeism and turnover patterns into staff scheduling to minimize understaffing. Staff turnover patterns can be projected to determine future hiring and training needs. Clinical information can be incorporated to determine the appropriate staffing levels and skill mix needed in accordance with the overall patient acuity levels represented by the facility's case mix.

- *Capital budgeting:* Preventive maintenance and repair history can be used for forecasting future capital needs for equipment replacement. Such information can help the administrator decide at what point it makes better financial sense to replace equipment than to repair it.

- *Quality improvement:* Data pertaining to a variety of clinical outcomes—such as infections, falls, and medication errors—can be analyzed to better understand their causes and to propose actions for minimizing negative outcomes. Standardized clinical practice guidelines can be integrated with assessment and care plans to improve care delivery. Clinical practice guidelines are protocols based on research and expert opinion for patient care delivery in specifically identified areas needing clinical intervention, such as falls reduction, pain management, prevention of pressure ulcers, and incontinence care. Use of these guidelines is an important step toward ensuring high-quality nursing home care.

- *Operational budgeting:* Historical data on census patterns, associated revenues, and costs can be automatically retrieved to project future budget needs.

- *Marketing:* Data on inquiries, follow-up, and admissions can be analyzed to determine the type of patients the facility is admitting in terms of pay types and acuity levels. The system can also help identify the major sources of referral and determine why certain patients may have selected other facilities.

## National Data

Comparison of a facility's operations with state and national benchmarks will become increasingly common. To some extent, national databases compiled by the Centers for Medicare and Medicaid Services (CMS) are already being used by consumers, consumer advocates, providers, and researchers. Integrated care will be the next step. Centralized data from the MDS, for example, may help one day to coordinate long-term care services along the continuum of care that would include home care, custodial care, skilled nursing care, and mental health services.

The On-line Survey Certification and Reporting (OSCAR) system is a national database of certification deficiencies and other information collected during facility surveys. Every institutional health care provider in the United States that is certified to provide services under Medicare or Medicaid is listed in OSCAR. The most extensive data in OSCAR are on nursing homes. One important use of this database is in providing benchmarks on survey deficiencies. For example, CMS now makes available on its website detailed information on survey results and staffing for every certified nursing home in the United States. The program, called Nursing Home Compare, reports the date of inspection, the standard that was not met, when the deficiency was corrected, level of harm ranging from least to most, and how many residents were affected.

Nursing Home Compare was launched primarily to help consumers compare and select a nursing home on the basis of some measure of quality. The system rates each nursing home from a low of one star to a high of five stars based on three critical areas: health inspection results, quality measures, and staffing levels. It also provides an overall rating. The health inspection rating contains information from the last three years of on-site inspections (discussed in Chapter 6). The quality measure rating has information on 10 different physical and clinical measures, such as the prevalence of pressure sores or changes in resident mobility. The staffing rating is based on the average hours of care provided to each resident each day by the nursing staff.

It takes into account the differences in the acuity levels of residents because residents with higher acuity levels require more hours of care.

## Security Issues

Integrated information networks are fast becoming indispensable, but safeguarding of sensitive information presents challenges. Administrators must grapple with the critical question of who should have access to what information on the network. For instance, the facility's financial information should not be accessible to everyone who uses a computer terminal in the facility. The system must also have adequate safeguards to prevent tampering with existing data. Some high-profile cases of break-ins by external hackers into computer systems of major U.S. corporations and the government further highlight the need for adequate security measures. Other security issues pertain to the physical security of the equipment. For instance, having backup records, in case a system is destroyed in a disaster or is vandalized, is essential.

## System Development

Most nursing facilities do not have the resources to employ personnel skilled in information technology, often because the facilities are not large enough. In most cases, facilities must rely solely on outside vendors to meet the needs of their information systems. Numerous vendors specialize in hardware, software, and set-up of *local area networks* (LANs) within the facility. A LAN links a group of computers to a central server so the LAN users can access the same information. Because a turnkey system can be quite expensive, a decision to upgrade existing systems should not be undertaken without careful study and planning. The administrator must first define the objectives of the system in terms of what the system should be able to accomplish. These objectives must specify the level of integration a proposed information system must achieve. Current capabilities should then be evaluated in conjunction with these desired objectives. In some cases, certain upgrades may enable the facility to reach its objectives. In other instances, replacing the existing system may be the best alternative.

Several reputable vendors should be invited to evaluate the current systems and desired objectives and to submit detailed written proposals along with costs. The facility may not be able to purchase a fully integrated system immediately. In that situation, feasibility of future upgrades should be discussed. In any case, making a firm commitment is not advisable without a test run to ensure that the system would indeed accomplish what the facility desires. Finding out what kind of ongoing support and training the vendor provides, and how often the vendor upgrades products to meet changing needs and improve informational efficiency, are also critical. Another important consideration is the system's compatibility with Medicare and Medicaid billing and with clinical data requirements. For instance, the system should enable electronic billings as well as electronic transmission of patient assessment information. Finally, the system must comply with all applicable laws and regulations.

## For Further Thought

1. Why is it important that the petty cash and patient trust fund be reconciled each month and that the reconciliation be done by someone other than the person responsible for maintaining the funds?

2. Develop some policies pertaining to meal breaks and incidental preparatory and concluding activities to provide clear guidance on compensable and noncompensable time.

## For Further Learning

Nursing Home Compare is accessible through the main Medicare website.

http://www.medicare.gov

The U.S. Department of Labor website provides comprehensive information on the various aspects of the Fair Labor Standards Act and other payroll and workplace issues such as unemployment compensation. It also provides links to other department agencies such as OSHA.

http://www.dol.gov/

## REFERENCES

Abramovice, B. 1988. *Long Term Care Administration*. New York: The Haworth Press.

Bruce, J.A.C. 1988. *Privacy and Confidentiality of Health Care Information*, 2nd ed. Chicago: American Hospital Publishing.

Burger, S.G., et al. 1986. *A Guide to Management and Supervision in Nursing Homes*. Springfield, IL: Charles C. Thomas Publisher.

Frew, M.A., & Frew, D.R. 1982. *Medical Office Administrative Procedures*. Philadelphia: F.A. Davis Company.

Griffith, J.R. 1995. *The Well-Managed Health Care Organization*, 3rd ed. Ann Arbor, MI: UPHA Press/Health Administration Press.

Jacksack, S.M. 1998. *Start, Run, and Grow a Successful Small Business*. Riverwoods, IL: CCH Inc.

Kiger, L.S. 2003. Content and structure of the medical record. In M.A. Skurka (ed.), *Health Information Management: Principles and Organizations for Health Information Services*, 5th ed. (pp. 19–44). San Francisco: Jossey-Bass/John Wiley & Sons.

Neumeister, J.R., & Fuller, A.D. n.d. *Revisions to the Fair Labor Standards Act*. Retrieved February 2009 from http://www.thompsonhine.com/news/nl/le_august04.pdf.

Pozgar, G.D. 1992. *Long-Term Care and the Law: A Legal Guide for Health Care Professionals*. Gaithersburg, MD: Aspen Publishers.

Resnick, H.E., et al. 2008. Use of electronic information systems in nursing homes: United States, 2004. *Journal of the American Medical Informatics Association* (Web publication). Retrieved February 2009 from http://www.jamia.org/cgi/reprint/M2955v1.

Seawell, L.V. 1992. *Introduction to Hospital Accounting*, 3rd ed. Dubuque, IA: Kendall/Hunt Publishing.

Yeatts, D.E., & Hyten, C. 1998. *High-Performing Self-Managed Work Teams*. Thousand Oaks, CA: Sage Publications.

**Appendix 14-1**  Common Abbreviations Used in Patient Documentation

| | | | |
|---|---|---|---|
| act | before meals | DOB | date of birth |
| ad lib. | as desired | Dx | diagnosis |
| AMA | against medical advice | ELOS | estimated length of stay |
| A&O | alert and oriented | end | endurance |
| aq | water | ESRD | end stage renal disease |
| ASS: | assessment | et | and |
| ATC | around the clock | ETOH | alcohol |
| B | both | EXP | expired |
| B&B | bowel and bladder | FAM | family |
| b.i.d. | twice daily | F.B. | foreign body |
| bin | twice a night | FBS | fasting blood sugar |
| b.i.w. | twice a week | Fe | iron |
| BKA | below knee amputation | flds | fluids |
| BM | bowel movement | Fx | fracture |
| BP | blood pressure | gt. | drop |
| BR | bed rest | gtt. | drops |
| B.R. | bathroom | HBP | high blood pressure |
| b.t. | bedtime | HL | hearing loss |
| BTW M | between meals | H&P | history and physical |
| BUE | both upper extremities | hr | hour |
| CBR | complete bed rest | h.s. | at bedtime |
| CHO | carbohydrate | Hx | history |
| chr | chronic | I&O | intake and output |
| c/o | complains of | IV | intravenous |
| COPD | chronic obstructive pulmonary disease | K | potassium |
| ct. | count | LBP | lower back pain |
| CV | cardiovascular | lf | left |
| CVA | cardiovascular accident | lg | large |
| CXR | chest x-ray | MB | mix well |
| d/c | discharged | MI | myocardial infarction |
| d.c. | discontinued | M/S | mental status |
| decub | decubitus | NA | not applicable |
| def | deformity | N/A | no authorization |
| D.F.A. | difficulty falling asleep | Na | sodium |
| Diab | diabetic | NGT | nasogastric tube |

**Appendix 14-1**  Common Abbreviations Used in Patient Documentation (Continued)

| | | | |
|---|---|---|---|
| NKA | no known allergies | qw | once a week |
| noct | at night | ROM | range of motion |
| NPO | nothing by mouth | Rx | prescription, treatment |
| NSC | no significant change | SHx | social history |
| OBS | organic brain syndrome | si/sx | signs/symptoms |
| o.d. | once a day | S/O | standing order |
| om | every morning | SOS | only if necessary |
| on | every night | ss | one-half |
| OOB | out of bed | Stat | at once |
| os | mouth | T | temperature |
| P | after | TB | tuberculosis |
| pc | after meals | TF | tube feeding |
| PN | pneumonia | Tid | three times daily |
| po | by mouth | Tin | three times a night |
| p.p. | after meals | Tiw | three times a week |
| p.r.n. | whenever necessary | T/O | telephone order |
| pt | patient | T&P | turn and position |
| PTA | prior to admission | TPN | total parental nutrition |
| pvt. | private | TPP | temperature, pulse, and respiration |
| q | every or each | ung | ointment |
| qam | every morning | URI | upper respiratory infection |
| qd | every day | UTI | urinary tract infection |
| qh | every hour | VS | vital signs |
| qhs | every bedtime | w/ | with |
| ql | as much as desired | W/C | wheelchair |
| qn | every night | w/o | without |
| qod | every other day | X3 | oriented to time, person, and place |
| q/s | every shift | | |

*Source:* Excerpted from Miller, R.M., and M.E. Groher. 1990. *Medical speech pathology.* Rockville, MD: Aspen Publishers, Inc. Used with the authors' permission.

# PART IV

# Governance and Management

Effectively managing a nursing facility is a complex undertaking because it involves a wide spectrum of responsibilities and actions that require careful balancing in accordance with the varied organizational needs. Leadership and management skills must be constantly developed and refined in conjunction with frequent self-evaluation. But, in spite of an ongoing commitment toward self-improvement, the nursing home administrator will no doubt encounter new and unforeseen challenges. The various skills and tools discussed in this part provide a basic foundation for effective management, but they must be practiced along with common sense and personal judgment. Taking risks based on well-informed decisions is part of the process in executive development. Successful executives also recognize their own weaknesses but are resourceful in finding help and using strengths that others, both within or outside the organization, may possess. Above all, successful executives keep their organization's vision, mission, values, and major goals in clear sight and focus on actions that are consistent with the objectives outlined in them.

By effectively managing available resources, the administrator's main objective should be to create maximum value for the patients, the associates, the corporation, and the community. In a nutshell, creating value is the main purpose for which managers are hired. This value creation builds internal organizational strengths needed for accomplishing the organization's strategic objectives, especially when changes in the external environment pose new challenges.

With few exceptions, most facilities do not have separate positions of human resource manager, financial officer, marketing director, and quality control manager. Thus, a typical nursing home administrator wears several different hats. Governing boards and corporate officers exercise varying degrees of control over the facility and allow varying degrees of autonomy to the administrator. But, regardless of the extent of autonomy, a typical nursing facility administrator is expected to take personal responsibility for the management roles described in the five chapters contained in this section:

- Chapter 15 begins with a description of governance, the governing board's composition and its main functions, and the seven principles of corporate compliance. The chapter describes the three main expectations from an effective nursing home administrator and how these expectations can be met through effective leadership and management. The chapter concludes with an explanation of the various tools necessary for effective management.

- Chapter 16 emphasizes that human resource management in long-term care facilities requires special skills in creative recruitment, determination of staffing levels and skill mix, management of absenteeism and turnover, and empowerment of front-line associates such as certified nursing assistants. The chapter includes issues pertaining to unionization, and it concludes with an overview of workers' rights and antidiscrimination laws.

- Chapter 17 explains that value creation is at the heart of marketing. Also, marketing is not just externally focused activities; a client-focused attitude must permeate the entire organization. Typical marketing topics such as segmentation, market targeting, positioning, differentiation, personal selling, and public rela-

tions are applied to long-term care marketing.

- Chapter 18 presents an understanding of financial statements. Using a number of exhibits, the chapter also discusses several financial management tools such as variance analysis, inventory management, midnight census report, and aging schedule. The chapter concludes with the techniques of budgeting revenues, expenses, and margins.

- Chapter 19 clarifies the common misconceptions related to quality and productivity. It explains the different facets of quality and emphasizes that quality improvement must go beyond regulatory compliance by implementing the concepts of continuous quality improvement and adoption of evidence-based best practices. The Donabedian model of quality and Deming's principles are described. The chapter concludes with an overview of the Wellspring model that is being used in four different states.

# Chapter 15

# Effective Governance, Leadership, and Management

## What You Will Learn

- The governing board's composition and focus should reflect the nursing home's mission. The board mainly provides direction and oversight. The administrator manages the facility on a day-to-day basis.

- Corporate compliance begins with the development of policies, standards, and procedures; it requires training, lines of communication, internal review, and enforcement.

- Depending on the decision-making authority delegated to the administrator, he or she may be employed in the role of a CEO, COO, or administrative officer.

- The effective administrator manages the facility by maintaining a balance among the business aspect, work and workers, and the facility's obligations to the community and society.

- Leadership is people focused. It can be understood through differences between the Theory X and Theory Y approaches, the balance between task orientation and relationship orientation, and use of different styles to fit a given situation. Leadership should be directed toward building commitment among the associates.

- Management is about getting things accomplished on a daily basis. The nursing home administrator functions in a variety of management roles identified by Henry Mintzberg.

- Like almost all other managers, the nursing home administrator performs the basic functions of planning, organizing, leading, and controlling.

- The purpose of a vision is to clarify what an organization should become. The mission guides its main objectives and defines what stakeholders can expect. Values provide an ethical framework of conduct for the administrator and associates.

- A facility's goals, rules, policies, and procedures help facilitate decision making. Complex decisions involve an interplay of facts, opinions, judgments, dissenting views, and consensus. Rational decisions involve a process, but intuition can also play a role.

- Meetings should be planned in accordance with their main purpose, such as information sharing or problem solving. By providing pertinent information on a docket, time can be saved. A different approach is needed when meeting with external stakeholders.

- Depending on its nature and extent, conflict can be either healthy or dysfunctional. Various conflict management techniques can be employed, depending on the situation.

- The boss-subordinate relationship is based on mutual dependence. Understanding the boss's personality, behaviors, and expectations is a key step in avoiding friction. Information sharing may help when counter-dependent or over-dependent behaviors occur.

- Besides risks affecting patients and patient care, a risk management program should include potential risks to associates, contracted staff, visitors, and facility assets.

## Governance and Corporate Compliance

Governance and its role from an open-systems perspective were introduced in Chapter 4. In short, *governance* refers to stewardship of an organization's resources—that is, how the organization's material, financial, and human resources are used to produce outcomes that benefit the organization's stakeholders. A nursing home's main stakeholders are its clients, the community at large, the associates employed by the organization, regulators, and third-party payers. The governing body, or board, bears ultimate authority and accountability for the organization's affairs. Hence, the board has the responsibility to provide direction to the nursing home administrator (NHA) and exercise oversight regarding how the nursing home is run.

## The Board's Composition

Health care organizations generally have *self-perpetuating boards*, in which the board itself selects new members to succeed the ones who will no longer serve. Selection of board members should be guided by the ownership structure (discussed in Chapter 5) and by the organization's mission. For example, the board of a publicly owned facility will include people who can best represent the organization's charity mission. The board may include one or two city or county administrative and health officials, a representative of the local social services department, one or two community physicians who mainly serve Medicare and Medicaid clients, a public health nurse, and an official from the local hospital.

In privately owned corporations, both for-profit and nonprofit, the board generally includes some corporate officers, such as the corporation's president or chief executive officer (CEO), the vice president of operations, the vice president of human resources, and the chief financial officer (CFO). In these organizations, it is often a mistake to not include representatives from the community and some local business leaders. Also, regardless of the type of ownership, the NHA should be a member of the board.

Board members should be carefully selected from among respected leaders in the community on the basis of their qualifications and character. The skills and social standing of potential board members should be carefully reviewed to help select people who can assist the NHA in establishing positive exchange relationships; provide technical expertise in health care, finance, law, or public relations to the extent possible; represent the community and clients; and bring their own individual perspectives to the operation of the facility.

## The Board's Functions

In the public sector, the board will focus particularly on the facility's charity mission, while also ensuring that the facility remains financially viable. In the nonprofit sector, the special focus should be on meeting the health care needs of the community, which should include a charity function to justify the corporation's tax-exempt status. In the for-profit sector, maximizing profits and creating value for the owners or shareholders are the main goals. But the facility must also establish meaningful exchange relationships with the community and provide services of a quality that is acceptable to the community. In addition, long-term care facilities operated by various religious organizations, which are private, nonprofit entities, may adhere to certain religious tenets, spiritual values, and moral commitments upheld by the sponsoring organizations.

In effectively managed organizations, a close relationship based on trust, mutual commitment, communication, and professionalism exists between the board and the administrator. The NHA reports to the board and looks to it for general direction. The main responsibilities of the board are summarized as follows:

- Appoint a qualified administrator to manage the facility. Clarify performance expectations.
- Periodically review the administrator's performance, determine compensation, and make decisions about the administrator's continuing employment.
- Establish or review the mission and vision for the facility, and assist the administrator in establishing a strategic plan that is periodically updated. Establish or approve major goals and objectives for the organization.
- Establish broad policies that provide adequate guidelines to the administrator in making decisions pertaining to finance, budgets, quality of patient care, building and equipment, staffing, employee relations, legal and ethical conduct, and the facility's relationship to its external environment (see Chapter 4).

- Establish policies to protect patient rights (discussed in Chapter 5).

- Provide needed support to the administrator by procuring technical expertise when necessary and by committing adequate resources so that the facility can be effectively managed and an acceptable level of patient care can be delivered.

- Oversee the facility's operations and outputs. Because of its legal accountability, the board must ensure the facility's compliance with quality standards, financial goals, and legal and ethical expectations.

Although the board has the primary responsibility for the functions just outlined, the NHA should be actively involved in developing policies, mission and vision, and strategic direction for the facility. The board must exercise due vigilance, but without undue interference. It should not step over the NHA's authority to make operational decisions, yet it must maintain adequate control.

## Role of the Nursing Home Administrator

The nursing home administrator's position is part of the governance structure. As such, the NHA must have a close working relationship with the board. The NHA must keep the board updated and informed on substantive operational matters, such as quality issues, deficiencies cited on survey inspections (see Chapter 6), any legal issues, any negative publicity, budgetary compliance, need for resources, and staff-related issues.

The NHA functions as the CEO for a nursing facility and reports to the board. The NHA acts as the agent of the board and is responsible for the day-to-day management of the nursing facility.

In managing the facility, the NHA must provide leadership and direction to the department managers. The NHA also has the primary operational responsibility for human resource management, marketing and public relations, budgetary compliance and financial management, and quality and productivity management.

The NHA must adhere to certain policy guidelines in managing the facility. The nursing home's operational policies are largely derived from various laws and regulations. Incorporating laws and regulations into the organization's policies is a major step toward ensuring compliance. In each department, policies and procedures must be revised as new regulations come out and as more effective procedures to deliver services become known. Other operational policies describe the organization's procedures for how certain things must be done. These policies often reflect corporate philosophy and values.

## Corporate Compliance

Accountability to the various stakeholders is the essence of *corporate compliance*. Compliance with the various laws and regulations is a very basic expectation. Governance efforts, however, must go beyond the legal and regulatory realm to incorporate standards of ethics and to "do what is right." The organization's officers must govern with integrity. They must be vigilant, and they must voluntarily take corrective steps before issues turn into major legal and ethical dilemmas.

All activities reflected in ethical and professional behavior should be clarified and written down so that misunderstandings as to what constitutes appropriate behavior can be avoided. An effective corporate compliance program must satisfy seven conditions (Boyle et al., 2001; Willging, 2009):

1. Compliance standards and procedures to be followed by the employees and agents must be developed. While legal compliance is critical, of equal importance are dealings with clients and associates. For example, standards should emphasize the importance of forthright advertising and full disclosure, the requirement for honest assessments of patient conditions and needs, and the imperative of treating both residents and associates with dignity and respect.

2. A high-level corporate officer must be assigned to administer and oversee the program. In smaller companies, this will probably be someone who assumes that responsibility in addition to other duties. The corporate compliance officer must have direct access to the CEO.

3. Effective lines of communication must be established and assured. There can be no barriers that might interfere with the flow of information—in either direction. Communication must be both encouraged and effective. Managers must be open and honest in conveying requirements and expectations to associates. Associates must feel comfortable in both questioning and informing management.

4. All associates must be trained so they become familiar with the standards. It is critical that the associates understand not only the standards but also the procedures to follow when violations of the standards are observed.

5. An internal review and audit protocol must be implemented. Establishing standards of behavior, communication, and training are not sufficient to ensure that the system is working. Verification procedures are a must. Such procedures should spot check not just the adherence to standards of conduct but also associates' belief that standards are being adhered to. It is also important to verify whether the associates feel that violations of acceptable behavior can be reported without fear of retribution. For example, a hotline or toll-free phone number can be instituted to facilitate confidential reporting of violations.

6. Protocols must be established to investigate all allegations of violations. If a violation is found, disciplinary action must be taken. Depending on the perceived severity of the apparent violation, engaging outside legal counsel may be necessary. Especially when violations of federal or state law are the issue, or severe disciplinary measures are contemplated, it would be imprudent to wait too long to engage counsel.

7. After a violation is detected, all reasonable steps to respond to and prevent further violations must be instituted.

## The Executive Roles

There are three distinct executive roles that characterize the position of a nursing home administrator:

- The chief executive officer (CEO) role.
- The chief operating officer (COO) role.
- The administrative officer role.

Although the position encompasses all three roles, which one is predominant depends on the degree of decision-making autonomy given to the NHA by the governing board. The degree of autonomy determines how much authority the NHA will have in the formulation of long-range strategies, major planning decisions, facility policy, and budgets (Figure 15–1). When the administrator is given relatively little autonomy, the governing board exercises a high degree of control over major decisions and the facility's future direction. Low autonomy also suggests that the administrative focus will be primarily on internal operations, and the facility would function mainly as a closed system as opposed to an open system (described in Chapter 4).

Sometimes, a facility's ownership or affiliation may determine how much autonomy the administrator will be given. An owner/administrator who owns the nursing home and also manages it generally functions like the CEO of a small company. In other situations, the owner(s) may have little involvement in the facility's operations and may delegate complete decision-making authority to a CEO administrator appointed to manage the facility. In multifacility corporations, the governing board is mainly composed of corporate officers who generally retain executive authority. But if the corporate officers delegate sufficient responsibility and authority to the administrator, that administrator is likely to adopt the role of a COO. Nearly all nursing facility administrators function in this capacity.

## The Roles of CEO and COO

The main difference between the CEO and the COO roles lies in strategy formulation, which is characterized primarily by having the authority to make long-range decisions and to commit resources over a relatively long period in response to major demands from the ex-

**Figure 15–1** The Three Executive Roles

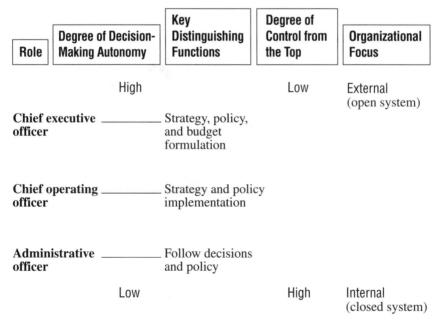

ternal environment (see Chapter 4). In contrast to the CEO role, the COO's role emphasizes strategy implementation, which is to carry out decisions and commitments made by corporate officers. In this sense, the COO role has an internal (implementation) focus, whereas the CEO role has mainly an external (formulation) focus (Griffith & White, 2002).

Even when the nursing facility administrator is employed in the COO role, effective organizations invite the administrator to participate in discussions and to help formulate strategy. The administrator is often more knowledgeable than corporate officers about trends and changes occurring in the local community. Corporate officers, on the other hand, are likely to be more knowledgeable about shifts taking place at the state and national levels. Hence, a strategy-making partnership between the administrator and corporate officers is likely to result in effective long-range decisions about the future direction of a nursing facility. Other key areas of decision making that distinguish between the roles of CEO and COO are the responsibilities these administrators have in formulating broad administrative policies and in planning annual budgets. The two roles differ according to the degree of involvement the administrator has in formulating the facility's operational policies and establishing its annual budget.

## The Administrative Officer Role

A third type of role that could predominate in the administrator's position is akin to that of an administrative officer. Of the three different role types described here, the administrative officer role gives the least decision-making authority to the administrator who, for the most part, is expected to carry out the decisions, policies, or specific directives handed down by the corporate officers. The administrator's position is highly structured, and the corporate officers exercise tighter controls over the facility's operations than they do over facilities with administrators who perform the roles of CEO or COO. Administrators employed in the administrative officer role generally have lower qualifications and are paid less than those employed in the other two roles.

## The Effective Administrator

Effective NHAs come in all shapes and sizes; the only thing they may have in common is the ability to get things done (Drucker, 1985). Regardless of the executive role assigned by the governing board, the administrator should function as the general manager of a nursing facility. Without effective management, a nursing facility can quickly fall into chaos. Applying the manager's tasks described by Drucker (1974) to the NHA position, the administrator must find the right balance among three management domains:

- Managing the business aspect.
- Managing work and workers.
- Managing the facility in community and society.

A balance among the three is necessary because "a decision or action that satisfies a need in one of these functions by weakening performance in another weakens the whole enterprise" (Drucker 1974, p. 398). Thus, effective management becomes a skillful juggling act; it requires expertise in various management disciplines and employs the open-system approach. Figure 15–2 provides a full model of effective nursing home management.

**Figure 15–2** A Model for Effective Nursing Home Management

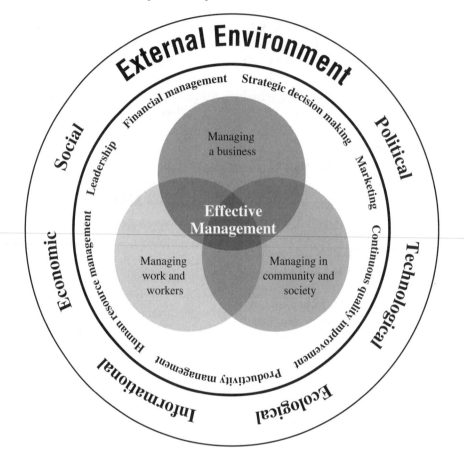

## Managing the Business Aspect

Here, the term *business* is used in the sense of economic performance (Drucker, 1974), which is not confined to for-profit operations only. The essence of business management lies in using resources in a manner that adds value (i.e., worth as perceived by the facility's key stakeholders). By adding value, an organization produces a far greater good for the consumers of services, for the associates, and for society at large than what is inherently contained in the resources themselves. In this broad sense, the term *business* also ap-

plies to nonprofit and public (government-owned) entities. The added value that society expects from a nursing facility is affordable patient care that meetsw certain generally agreed-upon standards of quality. Even though what is "affordable" and what constitutes "agreed-upon standards of quality" are not clearly defined, taken together these terms mean that a nursing facility must satisfy the patients, their families, and the payers. Because the payers include those who pay the facility directly on a private-pay basis or those who pay premiums to purchase private long-term care insurance, as well as government payers—mainly Medicare and Medicaid—who pay indirectly out of taxes levied on citizens, society as a whole has expectations that nursing facilities achieve the twin goals of affordability and quality. These expectations from both the consumer and the larger society hold true regardless of whether a facility's ownership structure is for-profit, nonprofit, or public.

## Managing Work and Workers

One of the essential functions of management is to make work productive (Drucker, 1974). Here the term *productivity* is equivalent to value creation. Productivity incorporates quality as a major output that results from the use of resources over which management has control. ***Productivity*** maximizes quality for each unit of resources used in delivering health care. Thus, effective management aims to deliver quality at an affordable cost.

To make work productive, managers must first understand what work needs to be done and how to organize it. The entire Part III of this book was devoted to understanding and organizing various tasks necessary for effective patient care delivery. All the six main services covered in Part III are organized to either provide direct hands-on patient care or provide essential support services, without which quality cannot be achieved and maintained. For services to be delivered effectively, organizing work and workers into functional departments and positions (as illustrated in Figure III–1) is the first step. As discussed in previous chapters, a nursing home's size is an important factor when considering how the various functions should be organized.

A second and often a more difficult task in achieving productivity is building a cooperative spirit among the workers through leadership and motivation. This second task is difficult because every worker in the organization "is a unique individual, and treatment that will work effectively with one may prove disastrous when meted out to another" (McCarthy 1978, p. 37). The challenge for the effective NHA lies in creating a workplace environment in which each person contributes his or her best efforts toward goals that are important to management. The effective NHA understands that if work and workers are mismanaged, organizational performance will suffer no matter how good the NHA may be in managing the business side of the operation (Drucker, 1974). To increase productivity, an organization must create value for its associates. Because associates constitute a major resource input, the rewards they receive in the form of wages, benefits, personal satisfaction, self-esteem, and individual development must at least be commensurate with what they bring to the organization.

Kelley (1998) offered some practical advice on how to create environments in which exemplary associates are likely to flourish:

- Remove roadblocks to productivity by shielding associates from excessive bureaucratic demands that may interfere with getting real work done. Workers must fill out papers and reports and attend meetings, but such demands can be overdone.

- Associates should be left alone to do their jobs and should be kept free of constant interruptions from administration. Facility administrators can "keep their fingers on the pulse" but also promote self-management because most workers want to manage themselves.

- Participative management is fine, but most workers want to be involved only in decisions that affect them. Above all, exemplary workers are not interested in knowing the trivia about their boss's jobs or their personal lives.

- Although associates want to manage themselves, the NHA must make sure that the various departments' efforts come together. An important aspect of administrative responsibility is to fill any chasms between departments and to promote interdependencies that will enhance the value of the services delivered.

- People are interested in knowing what outcomes their efforts have produced. Similarly, the value added by the synergistic use of interdependencies should be disclosed to associates to promote ongoing cooperation between departments.

## Managing the Facility in Community and Society

In Drucker's words, "None of our institutions exists by itself and is an end in itself. Every one is an organ of society and exists for the sake of society . . . Institutions must be part of the community . . . Mismanaging social impacts eventually will destroy society's support for the enterprise and with it the enterprise as well" (Drucker 1974, pp. 41–43). From this perspective, the effective administrator must frequently evaluate whether the facility is making positive strides in connecting with the community and whether it is adequately discharging its responsibility toward society.

# Leadership

## The Meaning and Purpose of Leadership

*Leadership* can be defined as influencing people to act for certain goals that represent the values and motivations—wants, needs, aspirations, and expectations—of both leaders and followers (Burns, 1998). Although it can have many different meanings, Northouse (2001, p. 3) concluded that four main components are central to leadership:

- Leadership is a process that requires continuity. It is also interactive and involves give-and-take between the leader and followers.

- Leadership affects the followers. The essence of leadership is to influence others.

- Leadership occurs within a group or "people" context. Leadership finds its meaning in relation to other people because the need for leadership dissipates when there are no people to be led. Leaders use their influence to direct people toward a common purpose.

- Leadership involves goal attainment. Leaders direct their energies toward individuals who are trying to achieve something together.

The following words on leadership have been ascribed to the Chinese philosopher Lao Tse, who lived in the 5th century B.C.:

> A leader is best when people barely know that he exists,
> Not so good when people obey and acclaim him,
> Worst when they despise him.
> Fail to honor people, they fail to honor you.
> But, of a good leader, who talks little,
> When his work is done, his aim fulfilled,
> They will say, "We did it ourselves."

The entire process of leadership is people focused. Hence,

the signs of outstanding leadership appear primarily among the followers. Are the followers reaching their potential? Are they learning? Are they devoted to serving? Do they achieve the desired results? (DePree 1998, p. 130)

## Leadership Attitudes and Styles

In management theory, much has been written about leadership styles that explain how leaders think and act when managing workers. Leaders' behaviors emanate from their general attitudes and assumptions about workers. Leaders' personal styles are also oriented in varying degrees toward relationships and tasks. Finally, leadership is situational.

### Two-Model Theory

To explain management behavior, Douglas McGregor (1906–1964) proposed two models known as Theory X and Theory Y, which present two contrasting assumptions leaders make about workers. According to Theory X, leaders assume that:

- Workers are lazy.
- They dislike work and responsibility.
- They will avoid work if not closely supervised.
- They are indifferent to organizational needs and goals.

Traditional leadership was based on Theory X and thus focused on monitoring and controlling people in the organization in an effort to make them obey management's orders or face negative consequences. Theory X assumptions lead to task-oriented behaviors on the part of leaders, as opposed to relationship-oriented behaviors; such leaders will have a tendency to adopt a directive style (Figure 15–3). Directive leadership can be characterized as take-charge, one-directional, and single-handed decision making by the leader. Directive leadership involves giving orders, establishing goals and methods of evaluation, setting time lines, defining roles, and establishing methods and processes for achieving the organization's goals (Northouse, 2001, p. 57).

In what McGregor called Theory Y, leaders have the opposite attitudes toward workers:

- Workers want to take responsibility.
- They like challenging work.
- They desire opportunities for personal development.
- They want to help achieve organizational goals.

Leaders who espouse a Theory Y perspective are likely to adopt relationship-oriented behaviors and will be inclined to use a participative or a delegative style of leadership (Figure 15–3). This relationship orientation results in supportive behaviors in which open communications, listening,

**Figure 15–3** Relationship between Leadership Attitudes, Behaviors and Styles

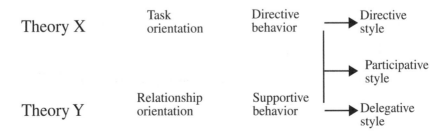

praising, asking for input, and giving feedback are important (Northouse 2001, p. 58). The main characteristic of the participative style is involving other people in decision making and giving their ideas due consideration. The leader may present ideas and invite feedback from workers or solicit new ideas from them. In the delegative style, leaders derive considerable satisfaction from giving decision-making responsibilities to their associates (Brody, 2000).

## Two-Dimensional Model

In the mid-20th century, several independent research studies resulted in two-dimensional models of leadership comprising *task orientation* (also called production orientation, or initiating structure) on one end of a continuum and *relationship orientation* (also called person orientation, or consideration) at the other end. The main contribution of the two-dimensional theory has been in highlighting that leadership is not necessarily a dichotomous phenomenon (as suggested by Theory X and Theory Y) and that leaders could be oriented toward both tasks and people. Accordingly, Blake and Mouton (1964) proposed a managerial grid in which each leader could be rated on both task orientation and person orientation and be classified into one of five leadership styles (Figure 15–4):

1. *Impoverished management.* Characterized by low task orientation and low person orientation, these leaders remain hands-off and aloof.

**Figure 15–4** Blake and Mouton's Managerial Grid and Leadership Styles

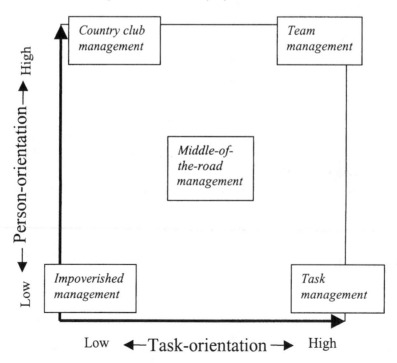

2. *Task management.* These leaders are highly task oriented. They are mainly concerned with getting work done and have minimal concern for people.

3. *Country-club management.* These leaders rate very high on person orientation. They are concerned mainly with creating a pleasant and harmonious working environment and have little concern for accomplishing tasks.

4. *Team management.* These leaders value their workers and solicit their participation in setting goals, making decisions, and accomplishing tasks.

5. *Middle-of-the-road management.* These leaders seek the middle ground and try to balance productivity with worker satisfaction.

## Situational Leadership

Contemporary management theories recognize that leadership styles must fit the situation. Different situations demand different styles, and to be effective, leaders must change their styles according to the situation. Conceptually, this situational approach is similar to Blake and Mouton's managerial grid model. Instead of using task orientation and person orientation, the two dimensions in the *situational model* are directive and supportive behaviors. The situational model, however, goes beyond Blake and Mouton's by suggesting that a leader should apply an appropriate measure of both directive and supportive behaviors as dictated by the competence and commitment of each worker or group. Situational leadership thus matches the style to the development level of subordinates (Figure 15–5):

• *Directing style,* characterized by high directive–low supportive behavior, is appropriate when the development level of a subordinate or group is low. The leader focuses on giving specific instructions and engages in close supervision.

• *Coaching style,* characterized by high directive–high supportive behavior, is useful when the development level of a subordinate or group is moderate to low. The style requires focusing on goals while soliciting input from the subordinate and giving encouragement.

• *Supporting style,* characterized by low directive–high supportive behavior, is useful when the development level of a subordinate or group is moderate to high. In this approach, the leader uses supportive behaviors that bring out the employee's skills. The subordinate is given flexibility in routine decisions, and the leader is available for consultation as needed. Listening, praising, asking for input, and giving feedback are commonly employed.

• *Delegating style* is characterized by low directive–low supportive behavior. The delegating leader lessens his or her involvement in planning, control, and goal clarification. Once agreement is reached on what must be done, the subordinate or group takes responsibility for getting the job done. (Northouse 2001, pp. 57, 58)

## Implications of Leadership Theories

Today, success in achieving high performance depends on building a deep sense of commitment among associates, not obedience extracted by threats. A basic premise of leadership is the belief that most people want to achieve success in their own careers: they want to accomplish something in their current positions and demonstrate their competence

**Figure 15–5** Situational Leaderhips Model

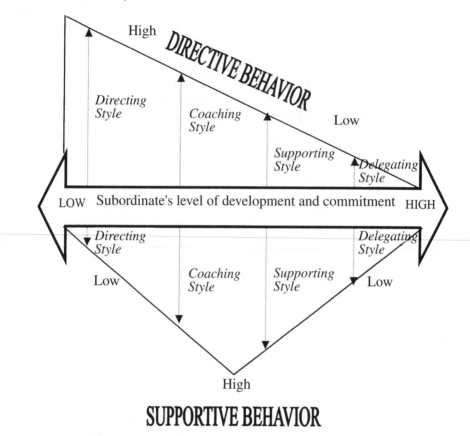

by doing their jobs well. People want to be respected for what they know and what they can do. They expect management's support and training for things they do not know or cannot do so they can grow and develop into better workers. They want to be rewarded for their demonstrated competence and accomplishments. An effective leader taps into people's aspirations by aligning clearly defined facility objectives with the followers' areas of responsibility. Leaders must direct but also engage their followers. Leaders must serve as role models and mentors, not martinets. "Leaders must try to make their fellow constituents aware that they are all stakeholders in a con-

joint activity that cannot succeed without their involvement and commitment" (Gini, 1998).

Building commitment requires a management philosophy in which associates are considered key stakeholders along with customers, exchange partners, the public, and the regulators. As stakeholders, associates also share in the rewards reaped from the organization's success. In the commitment-based approach, each organizational unit in the facility functions as a team that is held accountable for performance. Continuous improvement is emphasized, in accordance with the expectations of clients and society. Compensation policies are based on group achievement. Some of the main obstacles to the commitment approach are the slow change in management philosophies and practices, uncertainty, and fear of exposure to possibilities for failure (Walton, 1992).

# Management

There is no universally accepted definition of management. In a very simplistic sense, ***management*** is what managers do to maintain an organization and to move it forward. Management is about getting things accomplished on a daily basis. Management is the "glue" that holds an organization together; it is the "oil" that keeps the organization functioning as smoothly as possible to fulfill the main purpose for which the organization exists. Management requires the efficient use of resources to accomplish organizational objectives. It requires the NHA to manage the business aspects of the nursing home operation, to manage work and workers to get the job done, and to manage the facility as a member of the community and society. Hence, management is essential work without which an organization will slowly disintegrate into chaos. Effective management is mainly about managing stability and making the organization as effective as possible in doing what it is designed to do. In a nutshell, it is about finding what works and doing it well. Consistently pursuing this objective institutionalizes excellence and places the organization in an enviable position to respond to well-studied change whenever change is necessary to enhance value for the stakeholders.

Describing what managers do can be complex. However, management theorists have tried to simplify the understanding of management by describing management roles and functions.

## Management Roles

During the course of a day, the NHA will function in a variety of roles. For example, the NHA's day may begin by walking over to the dining area for a cup of coffee. On her way back to the office, the maintenance man stops and informs her that he would have to leave at noon to take his sick child to the doctor. The NHA responds, "Certainly . . . and, oh, by the way, Sam, make sure Mr. Hollinger's wheelchair gets fixed before you leave. I don't want to hear from his daughter again." Next, she stops to chat with the director of nursing (DON) about the salary she would be willing to offer to hire the night charge nurse they had both interviewed two days earlier. As soon as she sits down in her office and takes a sip of coffee, the social worker comes in and asks whether the facility will cover the cost of a lost hearing aid for a patient because Medicaid will not pay for it. Then, the receptionist comes in and hands her two messages about phone calls that came in earlier, one from the vice president of operations at the corporate office and the other from a family member. The NHA spends the next 20 minutes returning the two phone calls. The vice president of operations wanted to know why the accounts receivable had escalated during the previous month. A patient's daughter wanted to report that the nurse was very rude to her the previous evening when she asked the nurse about why the leaky faucet in the patient's room was still not fixed. The NHA spends the next 45 minutes in a department head meeting. She announces that the state had accepted the plan of correction submitted in response to the last inspection. To thank the department heads, she would like to arrange a luncheon at a nice restaurant. Going forward, the facility should implement some changes to ensure future compliance.

After the meeting, she receives a phone call from the local chapter of the American Red Cross inquiring whether the facility would participate again in the annual health fair. At 3:00 p.m., the NHA informs the receptionist to hold all phone calls and to not disturb her unless there is some urgent matter because she needs to set aside some undisturbed time to work on the budget for next year. Before going home at 6:00 p.m., the NHA tours the nursing areas and dining room and talks with a few patients. As she drives back home, she makes a mental note about setting up a luncheon meeting with the state representative for her area to discuss budget cuts proposed by the state's governor that may affect Medicaid reimbursement.

On the basis of his observation of managers on the job, Henry Mintzberg identified 10 different but highly interrelated roles:

1. The *figurehead* role is symbolic and ceremonial. At the annual picnic, the NHA may grill hamburgers for the associates. Later, he or she may give out service awards.

2. Role of the *leader* is associated with staffing, motivation, training, performance evaluation, and disciplining.

3. The *liaison* role deals with relationship building, mainly outside the organization. For example, the NHA builds relationships with the local fire department and the local hospital and is involved in professional associations. The relationships pay off in terms of expertise and support that external agencies can provide.

4. In the *monitor* role, the NHA keeps him- or herself informed of changes occurring in the external environment. This information could be of strategic importance. For example, remaining current on legal and regulatory changes, learning about what the competition is doing, and understanding social and cultural changes taking place in the industry can have implications for the nursing facility's long-term success.

5. As a *disseminator*, the NHA provides information to others. In this role, the NHA keeps the board informed on important matters, discusses issues with the department heads, and highlights the facility's services and undertakings to educate the local community.

6. In his or her *spokesperson* role, the NHA represents the organization to outsiders. For example, the NHA may discuss plans for future services with the chamber of commerce. The NHA may be invited to discuss the nursing home's rehabilitation program with the physicians at the local hospital.

7. In the *entrepreneur* role, the NHA initiates plans to bring about certain desirable changes. For example, the NHA may plan to convert some of the existing beds for specialized care.

8. As a *disturbance handler*, the NHA solves problems and addresses areas that require corrective action. Certain problems arise unexpectedly. For example, the DON resigns abruptly. Other problems may be chronic in nature and call for long-term solutions. For example, absenteeism and turnover are chronic problems in many nursing homes.

9. As a *resource allocator*, the NHA must decide how to distribute limited resources. Here are some examples: Should the facility hire a janitor or a

certified nursing assistant (CNA)? Should it create the position of a medication aide? Should it spend money on computerizing the medical records system, or should that money be spent on a new bathing system?

10. In the *negotiator* role, managers bargain to gain certain advantages. Numerous bargaining situations arise almost daily. For example, the NHA may approve a new bathing system provided overtime in the nursing department is cut in half. The NHA may approve a dollar per hour extra pay when nurses and CNAs come in to work at short notice on their days off to alleviate short staffing.

## Management Functions

Like almost all other managers, the NHA performs certain basic functions. These functions can be classified as planning, organizing, leading, and controlling.

## Planning

*Planning* includes defining or clarifying the organization's purpose, establishing objectives, and planning a course of action to achieve those objectives. Planning is forward looking. It requires deciding in advance what to do, how to do it, when to do it, and who is to do it. It makes it possible for things to occur which would not otherwise happen (Koontz & O'Donnell, 1972). An important aspect of planning is to establish standards so that the function of control can be effectively carried out.

Plans can be routine, periodic, or strategic. While driving to work, NHAs routinely think about certain things they plan to address that day. They plan agendas for the regular department head meetings. The annual budget is an example of periodic planning. Strategic plans are long-range plans. Various short-range plans are needed to accomplish long-range plans. For example, major renovations of the facility would require short-range plans about hiring a decorator, engaging a contractor, making alternative arrangements for the continuity of services, etc.

## Organizing

*Organizing* includes determination of what tasks are to be done, who is to do them, how the tasks are to be grouped, who reports to whom, and where decisions are to be made (Robbins, 2000). Part III of this book covered the organizational aspects of a nursing home. Even after an organization has been functioning for a while, the organizing function becomes necessary. For example, a decision to operate a laundry in-house instead of relying on contracted services calls for organizing. It requires decisions such as how many associates need to be hired, what functions will each perform, who will manage them, and so forth. In other areas of nursing home operation, new technology may eliminate certain positions or may alter their job content.

There are certain well-established principles of organization that NHAs should pay attention to:

- *Departmentation* and *division of work* lead to specialization and better performance. This may be true for large traditional nursing home organizations. In smaller organizations, in particular, work has become overly specialized and compartmented, with resultant loss of both motivation and a sense of accomplishment. This latter observation by Koontz and O'Donnell (1972) is particularly applicable to the work of CNAs and other operatives such as housekeepers. Cross-trained self-managed work teams (see Chapter 16) appear to be the antidote to this problem, as has been demonstrated in the Green House model of culture change (see Chapter 8).

- *Line and staff relationships* clarify who reports to whom and who in the organization have formal supervisor–subordination relationships. In Figure III–1, the solid lines indicate *line relationships*, showing the chain of command. Dotted lines indicate *staff* or *advisory relationships.* The medical director, for example, formally reports to the administrator. There is staff relationship between the DON and the medical director. In other words, the medical director is not the DON's boss, the administrator is. Conflicts often arise when line and staff relationships are confused. An organizational chart should include every position in the facility to show where employees can go when they need answers. Within the formal structure, members are granted authority over certain functions, held accountable for certain results, and given incentives for achieving those results (Griffith & White, 2002).

- The principle called *unity of command* means that a subordinate should report to only one supervisor. Otherwise, the subordinate may be subjected to conflicting demands and priorities. On the other hand, unity of command is not absolute. A subordinate may have encountered problems with his or her superior. Efforts should first be made to resolve issues directly with the superior. However, associates need appropriate mechanism to have their grievances addressed at a higher level. For example, associates should be able to bypass the chain of command to address problems related to harassment by a superior, favoritism, unethical conduct, corporate compliance issues, and other situations in which a superior may be misusing his or her authority.

- *Delegation of authority* is another organizational principle. *Authority* refers to the right of making decisions without having to obtain approval from a higher-up (Ivancevich et al., 1980). Worker empowerment is characterized by a greater degree of delegation than traditional management, particularly for decisions regarding patient care.

## Leading

Leadership (discussed earlier) and management are closely intertwined, but the two are not the same. Leadership is an essential tool for effective management. Through leadership, managers influence, inspire, and motivate associates to deliver the various services according to established organizational policies and standards. Management, however, goes beyond being a leader. Management requires skills in planning, organizing, and controlling.

## Controlling

To ensure that things are going as they should, the NHA must monitor the organization's performance against goals and standards. The process of monitoring, evaluating, and correcting constitutes the **controlling** function (Robbins, 2000). It is about controlling the structures and processes, not about controlling or manipulating people.

The functions of planning, organizing, and controlling are closely intertwined. Planning determines what results will be achieved, organizing specifies how those results will be achieved, and controlling determines whether the results are achieved (Ivancevich et al., 1980). In nursing home administration, the control function is perhaps best illustrated by compliance with the Requirements of Participation (discussed in Chapter 6). The NHA must ensure that those standards are understood. Staffing, equipment, policies, and procedures must be in place to accomplish them. Training must be provided as needed. Associates must be motivated through leadership to "buy into" compliance with the standards. Internal review and monitoring systems must be established to evaluate compliance. Finally, reasons for noncompliance must be investigated, and corrective steps must be taken to ensure future compliance.

# Tools for Effective Management

In this section, some of the main tools of effective management are discussed. These tools provide the necessary means for planning, for converting plans into actions, and for day-to-day administration of the facility.

## Vision and Mission

How does the administrator, and for that matter the other members of the organization, know that a certain course is indeed the right direction for a nursing facility? Leadership itself must be channeled toward achieving certain purposes, which should be clearly defined in formal statements. Operating an organization without a clearly defined vision and mission is like navigating in the open seas without a compass.

The *vision* is a compelling picture of how an organization will look and function when its main objectives are achieved (Ciampa & Watkins, 1999). The purpose of a vision is to clarify what an organization should become. The vision grows out of and improves upon the present (Robbins, 2000). It provides long-range direction to the organization. For example, a nursing home's vision may be to incorporate evidence-based practices into a changing cultural environment. Organizational vision often starts with the administrator, but it remains fluid and dynamic. Interactions with the facility's associates, families, corporate officers, and external stakeholders bring in additional inputs for refining and clarifying the vision.

The vision and mission comprise an organization's guiding philosophy (Collins & Porras, 1998). Although much has been written about vision and mission, a lack of clarity still persists about what they are. In terms of focus, a vision is about the organization, whereas a mission is about key stakeholders, particularly the customers and the community.

An organization's *mission* defines its basic purpose and enunciates why the organization exists. A nursing home's mission statement should incorporate its distinct competencies, its clients' needs, and its relationship to the community. Exhibit 15–1 provides an example of a mission statement. The mission is derived from and is closely connected to the vision. However, the mission emphasizes the benefits that would accrue to patients and their families, the associates, and the community as the organization goes about the business of achieving its vision.

Accomplishing the vision and mission is not just a leadership activity. Organizational purposes and direction must be widely shared within the organization. A turning point occurs when the associates begin to share the vision of what can be accomplished and to

**Exhibit 15–1** Example of a Mission Statement

We pledge uncompromising dedication to excellence in helping older adults grow in spirit, live with a sense of fulfillment, experience dignity, and meet the challenges of their changing lives.

We aspire to be consistent in our quality of care, distinctive in our approach, and outstanding in performance and to provide leadership in the field of service to older adults.

We welcome others who will join us in pursuit of our mission.

put their energies behind it (Ross et al., 2002, p. 49).

## Values

The way in which the members of a facility collectively think about what they do—and how they relate to patients, families, and coworkers—is based on certain beliefs and assumptions. Individuals have personal beliefs and values, which guide their thinking and behaviors in various social settings, including work. Such individual beliefs and values are likely to permeate the workplace in a sort of conflicting network unless the NHA clearly defines and communicates the core values on which the facility will base all its decisions, judgments, and actions.

*Values* constitute principles and ideologies "held sacred" by an organization. Organizational values underscore the moral principles by which the organization will be governed as it goes about the business of realizing its vision and mission. Once the values have been defined and communicated, they are viewed by the stakeholders as standards that define the attitudes and philosophies according to which the members of the organization can be expected to behave. When values are clearly defined, communicated, and integrated into decision making and actions, over time they become the main driving force of an organization's culture.

Administrators and corporate officers should develop a set of values that are relevant to the institutional delivery of long-term care. These values should be communicated to all members of the organization and, more importantly, should be espoused in routine conduct and decisions. As examples, some of the relevant core values are:

- *Respect:* How administration and associates are expected to treat coworkers, clients, and other stakeholders.
- *Honesty:* How administration and associates will conduct their affairs so that their ethics are beyond reproach.
- *Openness (or transparency):* What information the stakeholders can expect facility administration to share with them.
- *Fairness:* How administration and associates will conduct their affairs to promote equality and justice.
- *Quality:* How quality is defined and how it will be incorporated into the services provided.
- *Economic gain:* Articulation of why profits are important and how the rewards of success will be shared with relevant stakeholders.

Organizational values also play a vital role in hiring key associates. Besides considering a potential jobseeker's qualifications and other desired characteristics, the job-seeker's values should match those of the facility. Dissonance occurs when employees' values are incompatible with those of the organization, and this mismatch creates cultural discord. A discord in values can eventually lead to dissatisfaction and turnover, which in turn create organizational instability (Singh & Schwab, 1998).

There can be substantial difference in core values among facilities operated under for-profit, nonprofit, and public ownerships. Recent business literature affirms that matching of values is a critical factor in achieving organizational success. For example, studies by Fernández and Hogan (2002) concluded that "the most effective CEOs were those whose values were most like those of the firm, rather than those who had the greatest knowledge of the firm's industry" (p. 26). The lesson here is that governing boards must take into account a candidate's core values when hiring NHAs. Similarly, candidates seeking NHA positions should try to discover the organization's values by asking appropriate questions during the job interview and should evaluate the organization's values against their own values to see whether a good match exists.

## Managerial Decision Making

Decisions are made by people at all levels in an organization, and decisions made at lower ranks are not necessarily less important than those made by the NHA. Decisions made at lower levels can have a major effect on whether a facility meets its objectives in delivering the desired quality of patient care. The main differences between decisions made by lower-level employees and those made by the NHA are in the quantity and complexity of decisions, in their strategic or

tactical significance, and in the processes used for making them. One of the administrator's major responsibilities is to make decisions that are in the best interest of the facility and its main stakeholders. These decisions often require the context of the "big picture," which keeps in view the entire facility, its relationships between departments, its relationship between the facility and the corporation, and its relationship between the facility and its stakeholders. Decisions at lower levels are routine and are guided by established goals, rules, policies, and procedures that facilitate decision making. When the goals, rules, policies, and procedures are aligned with the facility's vision and mission and encompass its organizational values, the facility has taken the first major step toward achieving desired decision making by associates at lower ranks in the facility. Desired decisions are those that contribute to accomplishing the facility's goals, vision, and mission. The second major step is for the NHA to provide leadership. The third step is monitoring compliance with the goals, rules, policies, and procedures.

***Decision making*** is commonly defined as choosing from among different alternatives. Problem solving also requires decision making, although not all decisions involve problem solving. The alternatives a decision maker considers must be relevant to actions needed to accomplish certain desired objectives. Deciding on what objectives ought to be achieved by the facility is a primary managerial responsibility. Next, the administrator "makes the objectives effective by communicating them to the people whose performance is needed to attain them" (Drucker 1974, p. 400). The processes followed by executives for setting objectives, for exploring different alternatives to achieve the objectives, and for selecting from among stated alternatives often involve a rather complex interplay of facts, opinions, judgments, and dissenting views, as well as consensus. These factors are carefully weighed by the NHA to arrive at a decision. In some cases, it may be important to seek consensus. In other instances, the NHA would encourage people's input but make the final decision. Regardless of how the final decision is made, suggestions about possible alternatives as well as information and opinions provided by participants are valuable. An explanation of how and why a particular decision was made may help people understand that their thoughts and views were valued.

The NHA should always be aware that the decision-making process may be tainted with personal biases. Personal biases are not always easy to acknowledge. People's opinions and judgments incorporate biases that may emanate from their own value systems, past experiences, likes and dislikes, and emotions.

Intuition generally plays a role in decision making, because few ideas are subject to factual analysis. Informed opinions and judgments must therefore be taken into account. On the other hand, data-driven decision making can help reevaluate old assumptions or challenge conventional wisdom. Certain decisions require analysis of facts, such as a careful recounting of events as they had occurred, official interpretation of a regulation, information on what competitors are doing, or data on the facility's financial performance. Sometimes, organizations must stray from the norms and look for the "wild card" when making decisions on key issues. The wild card is the instinct for the right time to act—or not to act—in spite of data that indicate the contrary. Taking some risk and acting according to unconventional approaches can stimulate organizational innovation (Ross et al., 2002, p. 235).

The principal criterion for weighing alternatives is the consequences a particular course of action is likely to produce. Another key factor that must be considered while evaluating alternatives is the feasibility of implementation. Sometimes the best alternative has to be rejected because resources needed for its implementation are not available, or it may be too costly to implement, or it may not fit the time schedule for action.

Once a decision has been made, it must be implemented. Finally, its progress and outcomes must be evaluated to determine whether the desired objective is being reached. Figure 15–6 presents a general model for decision making and problem solving. *Rational decision making*, as opposed to intuitive decision making, is a systematic process that begins with carefully evaluating the status of a given situation and articulating what is desired.

Objectives are set in terms of what must be achieved. Generally, all possible alternatives are considered and examined for their feasibility in achieving an objective with present resources at minimal cost. Sometimes, additional resources are necessary for achieving an objective. The chosen alternative is implemented by clarifying what steps will be taken and who will do what, and deciding on how progress will be monitored. Managerial control is necessary to monitor progress, evaluate results against the objective, assess deviations, and take corrective action.

## Effective Meetings

Meetings are an essential tool for management because they promote participation and personal interaction. Open-ended discussion of issues is often richer and more creative than isolated thought and action (Ware, 1992). Meetings can be a valuable tool when

**Figure 15–6** General Model for Rational Decision-Making/Problem-Solving

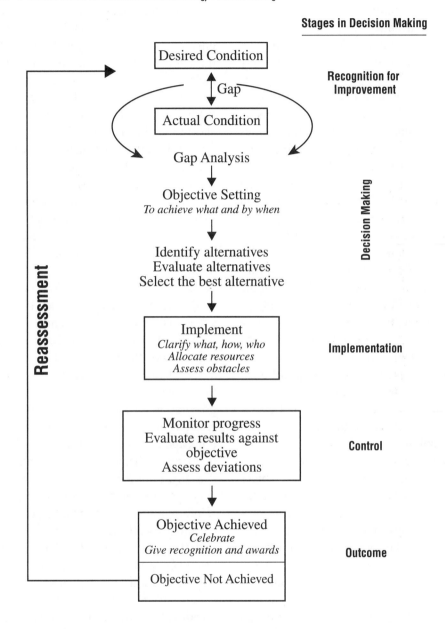

important information must be disseminated to people, particularly when personal interaction such as asking questions by the recipients of information or gauging people's reactions are important to managers. An-

nouncement of some change that may have a significant effect on others is better handled in a meeting than it is through written communication. Sometimes, information is personally conveyed because of its symbolic value, such as achievement of a major goal by the facility. Similarly, a meeting can be an effective avenue for reinforcing the organization's essential values, mission, and broad organizational objectives (Brody 2000, p. 250).

Meetings are also essential when input from others is considered vital for decision making or problem solving. Such meetings may be either for the purpose of information exchange or for actually making a group decision. Problem-solving meetings provide an opportunity to combine the knowledge and skills of several people at once, and participants are selected on the basis of their potential for contributions (Brody, 2000). Generally, information exchange and problem solving should not be combined in the same meeting (Ware, 1992). Other meetings may be routine. In such meetings, "keeping in touch" on a regular basis is valued by the participants. Department head meetings generally fall in this latter category, although they are also used for keeping members abreast of any changes, discussion of operational issues, information exchange, and problem solving.

Whenever people get together as a group, some socializing and casual exchanges occur naturally. On the other hand, meetings must also accomplish their predefined purpose. This purpose may be clear to the NHA, but it must also be communicated to the participants well before the meeting. Open-ended meetings often have a tendency to drift along almost endlessly without accomplishing much of anything. Even informal meetings can be given a sense of direction by having an *agenda*, which may or may not be formally written. An agenda helps the NHA focus on the meeting's purpose, and it provides a plan that helps sort out relevant and irrelevant topics during the discussions.

Another effective technique is to distribute ahead of time an annotated meeting agenda called a *docket*. A docket differs from an ordinary agenda in that the docket lists not only the items to be discussed but also provides pertinent explanations and details for each item. By saving time, a docket can be effectively used to cover a number of items in a short time (Brody, 2000).

Irrelevant topics may slip in during a meeting. The NHA should patiently listen to see whether the discussion has relevance to the meeting and may even ask about how the topic is related to the main issues under discussion. If the topic is not relevant, the NHA must tactfully steer participants back to the main topic.

Every meeting with a clear purpose behind it needs some preparation. Planning an agenda is the first step. Along with communicating the purpose of the meeting to the participants, the participants should also be asked whether they wish to place anything on the docket. Once the agenda is established, preparation for a meeting requires collecting relevant information. The NHA should also think about how the information will be communicated, whether it will be communicated verbally, on a flip chart or chalkboard, in a handout, or using a PowerPoint presentation. If information from other participants is needed, they should be notified ahead of time and clearly advised as to what exactly they should bring to the meeting. At other times, it may be necessary for all participants to review certain information before they come to the meeting. In that case, the materials should be delivered to participants well before the meeting so they have a chance to prepare.

Before a meeting ends, clarifying what should happen next is important. All items requiring follow-up should be reviewed. If certain individuals have responsibility for following up on something, that responsibility should be clarified along with any time schedules by which certain actions ought to be taken. If a follow-up meeting is necessary, it should be scheduled then and there (Ware, 1992).

The administrator is also likely to be involved in meetings with external stakeholders. In such meetings, the NHA should keep in mind a clear purpose but be willing and open to new ideas and face reality, ask questions, and explain value provided that the facility can deliver value. In seeking to establish new linkages with external stakeholders, the first contact is usually exploratory. The purpose of the first contact is often to exchange information and ideas with the objective of finding some common ground that will provide the basis for establishing a win–win relationship for both the facility and the external stakeholders. On the basis of the initial findings, further exchanges are made if both parties see the potential for engaging in a more formal relationship of mutual benefit.

## Conflict Management

Conflict is unpleasant, but it is an unavoidable aspect of an organization. Conflict is often dysfunctional to the organization, but it can also be functional if it stimulates innovation and adaptability. Conflict can be psychologically healthy for people when it enables them to vent frustrations in a constructive manner. Conflict in society may initiate conditions for social change by challenging the status quo (Hatch, 1997). However, conflict taken to its extreme can result in unwanted hostilities, violence, or other destructive behavior. According to modern organizational theory, too little conflict can lead to unhealthy conformance, poor decision making, and stagnation, whereas too much

conflict can lead to uncooperative behavior, loss of productivity, turf battles, and sabotage.

An understanding of conflict can be used as a managerial tool to assess how strongly certain people may feel about an issue, to discern individual personalities and dispositions, to evaluate relationships among people, and to gauge territorialism and power struggles. Evaluating conflict may lead to reevaluating certain work rules. Such evaluation may justify a change in current rules, or it may reveal the need for further clarification on why the rule is important. Conflict may expose certain problems that may otherwise go unnoticed, such as a chronic shortage of supplies or equipment. An investigation may show that the current supplier frequently backlogs needed items or that the maintenance department is far behind in keeping up with repairs. Evaluating conflict may also help administrators understand their own leadership styles, which may prompt them to change the way they handle their interpersonal relationships.

Conflict resolution and administrative intervention become necessary when conflict may create disorder or pose a threat to the achievement of organizational goals. However, no one best way has been devised to manage interpersonal conflict. The NHA may be involved as an adversary, as would occur when a family member barges into the office very upset about some service-related issue. In other situations, the NHA may act as a third party to mediate differences between two or more individuals, such as when an angry associate comes in all upset about a supervisor "playing favorites." In almost all situations, the NHA must keep strong personal feelings under control and remain objective.

Listening attentively is often the first step in resolving a conflict. The administrator must first understand the nature of the conflict and get perspectives from all sides. Administrators must keep in mind that in many situations people are not expecting immediate action. Further investigation, fact-gathering, and getting the "other side of the story" are often necessary before committing to a decision when mediating conflicts between others. Also, when emotions are high, a "cooling off" period often gives time to reevaluate the situation from a fresh perspective. In other situations, accommodation or capitulation may make sense by giving one side what it wants, particularly when that side is right.

Other strategies for resolution of conflicts include negotiation, keeping the conflict controlled within certain boundaries, and constructive confrontation (Ware & Barnes, 1992):

- Negotiation can be used if a compromise is more desirable than outcomes realized without a compromise. Negotiation can provide a win–win outcome, especially when the pursuit of opposing goals by the two sides would be counterproductive.

- Adversarial relationships may be controlled by separating two individuals, such as assigning the two adversaries to work on different units or on different shifts. If the two must work together because such a separation is not practical, control over their conflict ought to be exercised by adopting clear guidelines of behavior and following through with an impartial attitude.

- Constructive confrontation is a strategy that begins not with a confrontation but with an attempt by each party to explore and understand the other party's feelings and perceptions. As such, constructive confrontation may result in a new defi-

nition of what the problem was initially perceived to be, and it may forge new motives for seeking a common solution.

When the NHA is one of the parties involved in a conflict, he or she can retain control of a confrontational situation by focusing on the problem and issues and not engaging in personal attacks even when the other party may initiate such confrontation. Depending on the nature of the conflict, the NHA may withdraw or remain neutral. Capitulation or "giving in" may also be a good idea if the NHA considers the issue of conflict to be relatively minor or when the other side has more power than the NHA does.

## Relationship with Superiors

Management textbooks almost always ignore the important aspect of "managing the boss." In this context, the term *boss* may mean the governing board, the owner(s), or a corporate official. Administrators who are otherwise very capable of managing subordinates and establishing exchange relationships with the stakeholders often ignore this aspect of management. Administrators can have unrealistic assumptions and expectations about the nature of the boss–subordinate relationship, which can lead to conflict in which both the NHA and the facility may end up losing. Managing the relationship with corporate officers becomes even more critical in large, multifacility corporations in which the administrator is often distanced from the corporate office.

The boss–subordinate relationship is based on mutual dependence. The boss needs the administrator's help and cooperation, and the administrator needs the same from his or her boss. According to suggestions by Gabarro and Kotter (1992), the corporate boss can play a critical role in linking the NHA to the rest of the organization; in making sure the NHA's priorities are consistent with organizational goals; in securing the resources the NHA needs to perform well; and in providing inside information about corporate thinking, culture, and values. Administrators make a mistake when they consider themselves as self-sufficient, no matter how well they may be qualified in terms of education and experience.

The first step in managing the boss–subordinate relationship is to understand the boss's management style, strengths, weaknesses, preferred means of communication, priorities, and need for information about facility operations. The NHA should seek out information about his or her boss's goals, problems, and pressures and pay attention to clues in the boss's behavior. Some bosses prefer to be more closely involved in the facility's operations than others. Such bosses may want the NHA to frequently touch base with them. Others do not want to be closely involved but would like to be kept apprised of important problems or changes. The NHA should also understand his or her own needs, strengths, weaknesses, and personal styles (Gabarro & Kotter, 1992).

The potential for friction often exists. The NHA may make a decision or proceed with some action only to be thwarted by his or her boss. Often, the reality is that bosses have their own pressures and concerns that are sometimes at odds with the wishes of the NHA. Depending on their own personalities and predispositions, some NHAs may become resentful (a counter-dependent behavior) and at some point may even become openly rebellious; others may submissively comply (an over-dependent behavior). In both

instances, the NHA should try to provide more information than the parties in conflict have at the beginning. In some instances, the boss's mind may change. In other situations, a compromise may be reached. At the very least, the NHA may gain insights into the boss's thinking regardless of the outcome.

The second critical step for the NHA in managing the boss–subordinate relationship is to understand mutual expectations. The boss may not always be straightforward in expressing what his expectations are. Questions asked during face-to-face meetings may lend important clues to the NHA about the boss's expectations. The NHA can pose questions such as the following: "Am I providing you all key information you need?" "Do you have any particular comments on this?" "How often should I do this?" "Do I need to check back with you on this?" "How important is this to you?"

Gabarro and Kotter (1992) suggested that managers often underestimate what their bosses need to know. Keeping the boss informed is an important rule to follow. Few things are more disabling to bosses than NHAs on whom they cannot depend or NHAs they cannot trust. Inconsistent behavior and unreliability can erode an NHA's credibility very quickly. Shading the truth a little, or playing down problems and concerns, is a bad idea. Such behavior can at some point create surprise problems, when the boss is likely to ask, "Why did you not tell me about this earlier?"

Finally, the NHA should discuss needs for help, guidance, and support with the boss. There should be open discussions about issues that could potentially turn into major concerns. It is all right for the NHA to acknowledge, "I really don't know how to address this. I need some help."

## Risk Management

The health care delivery environment has been characterized by an upsurge in malpractice lawsuits. Regardless of the outcome, legal action against a facility is costly for the facility when the direct costs of defense and indirect costs from loss of reputation are factored in. Considering such undesirable consequences, risk management has become a critical domain of nursing home administration. *Risk management* means identifying, analyzing, and reducing or preventing risks (Becker, 2001). For an administrator, the primary focus of risk management is on risks affecting patients and patient care, but a risk management program should also include consideration of the risks to associates, contracted staff, visitors, and facility assets.

Written policies, procedures, and practices are the first line of defense against potential risks. Such policies should address informed consent, handling of disruptive patients, patient transfers, restraint use, confidentiality, and other concerns discussed in previous chapters. Evidence-based practices should be formally adopted in the delivery of patient care. Policies must also cover routine practices to be followed in the delivery of services by each department of the facility. Ongoing training of the staff and monitoring the staff's work are necessary for compliance with established policies.

Risk identification involves collecting information about all incidents. An *incident* is any unexpected negative occurrence involving a patient, associate, or visitor. Patient care occurrences and all other events that present potential loss to the facility must be investigated. Meticulously documenting patient care assessments, care plans, and progress notes is also essential. Similarly, adverse clinical outcomes, accidents and incidents, errors in treatment, and complaints from patients or family members must be carefully documented. Documentation should include what was done in each situation. Risk identification also requires looking for early warning signs that may appear in security reports, quality improvement studies, licensure and certification inspections, and client complaints (Kavaler & Spiegel, 1997).

Incidents must be reported to the appropriate supervisors, and the facility must have policies and procedures in place so that anyone can report all incidents, regardless of how small they may be. The associates should receive training on how to document incidents, which may involve patients, coworkers, or visitors. The language used in documentation should be accurate, objective, and factual; it should avoid opinions, confessions, or accusations. Inconsistent explanations or remarks to patients or families by different members of staff should be avoided. One person should be designated to handle questions from patients, family members, associates, and external parties (Becker, 2001). Potential as well as actual lawsuits should be reported to the insurance carrier.

---

## For Further Thought

1. Achieving the right balance among what Drucker described as managing a business, managing work and workers, and managing the facility in community and society will vary from one facility to another. As the NHA of a nursing home, how would you decide which area should be given more emphasis than the others?

2. Which of the five leadership styles proposed by Blake and Mouton is likely to be most effective in nursing home administration?

3. Critically evaluate the mission statement in Exhibit 15–1.

4. You are the administrator of a skilled nursing facility. You open an envelope left in your mailbox and learn that your director of nursing (DON) is resigning, giving you one month's notice. You have tried to persuade the DON to stay, but her decision is final. Employ the decision-making model in Figure 15–6 to address this situation.

## For Further Learning

You can take a 100-question test to understand your leadership potential:

http://www.queendom.com/tests/access_page/index.htm?idRegTest=702

## REFERENCES

Becker, S. 2001. *Health Care Law: A Practical Guide,* 2nd ed. Newark, NJ: Matthew Bender & Company.

Blake, R.S., & Mouton J.S. 1964. *The Managerial Grid.* Houston: Gulf Publishing.

Boyle, P.J., et al. 2001. *Organizational Ethics in Health Care: Principles, Cases, and Practical Solutions.* San Francisco: Jossey-Bass.

Brody, R. 2000. *Effectively Managing Human Service Organizations,* 2nd ed. Thousand Oaks, CA: Sage Publications.

Burns, J.M. 1998. Transactional and transforming leadership. In G.R. Hickman (ed.), *Leading Organizations: Perspectives for a New Era* (pp. 133–134). Thousand Oaks, CA: Sage Publications.

Ciampa, D., & Watkins, M. 1999. *Right from the Start: Taking Charge in a New Leadership Role.* Boston: Harvard Business School Press.

Collins, J.C., & Porras, J.I. 1998. Organizational vision and visionary organizations. In G.R. Hickman (ed.), *Leading Organizations: Perspectives for a New Era* (pp. 234–249). Thousand Oaks, CA: Sage Publications.

DePree, M. 1998. What is leadership? In G.R. Hickman (ed.), *Leading Organizations: Perspectives for a New Era* (pp. 130–132). Thousand Oaks, CA: Sage Publications.

Drucker, P.F. 1974. *Management: Tasks, Responsibilities, Practices.* New York: Harper & Row.

Drucker, P.F. 1985. *The Effective Executive.* New York: Harper & Row.

Fernández, J.E., & Hogan, R.T. 2002. Values-based leadership. *The Journal for Quality and Participation* 25, no. 4: 25–27.

Gabarro, J.J., & Kotter, J.P. 1992. Managing your boss. In *Managing People and Organizations,* readings selected by J.J. Gabarro. Boston: Harvard Business School Publications.

Gini, A. 1998. Moral leadership and business ethics. In G.R. Hickman (ed.), *Leading Organizations: Perspectives for a New Era* (pp. 360–371). Thousand Oaks, CA: Sage Publications.

Griffith, J.R. & White, K.R. 2002. *The Well-Managed Healthcare Organization,* 5th ed. Chicago: AUPHA Press/Health Administration Press.

Hatch, M.J. 1997. *Organization Theory: Modern, Symbolic, and Postmodern Perspectives.* New York: Oxford University Press.

Ivancevich, J.M., et al. 1980. *Managing for Performance.* Dallas, TX: Business Publications.

Kavaler, F., & Spiegel, A.D. 1997. Risk management dynamics. In F. Kavaler and A.D. Spiegel (eds.), *Risk Management in Health Care Institutions: A Strategic Approach.* Sudbury, MA: Jones and Bartlett Publishers.

Kelley, R.E. 1998. Leadership secrets from exemplary followers. In G.R. Hickman (ed.), *Leading Organizations: Perspectives for a New Era* (pp. 193–201). Thousand Oaks, CA: Sage Publications.

Koontz, H., & O'Donnell, C. 1972. *Principles of Management: An Analysis of Managerial Functions,* 5th ed. New York: McGraw-Hill.

McCarthy, J.J. 1978. *Why Managers Fail, and What to Do About It.* New York: McGraw-Hill.

Northouse, P.G. 2001. *Leadership: Theory and Practice,* 2nd ed. Thousand Oaks, CA: Sage Publications.

Robbins, S.P. 2000. *Managing Today,* 2nd ed. Upper Saddle River, NJ: Prentice Hall.

Ross, A., et al. 2002. *Leadership for the Future: Core Competencies in Healthcare.* Chicago: Health Administration Press/Washington, DC: AUPHA Press.

Singh, D.A., & Schwab, R.C. 1998. Retention of administrators in nursing homes: What can management do? *The Gerontologist* 38, no. 3: 362–369.

Walton, R.E. 1992. From control to commitment in the workplace. In *Managing People and Organizations,* readings selected by J.J. Gabarro. Boston: Harvard Business School Publications.

Ware, J. 1992. How to run a meeting. In *Managing People and Organizations,* readings selected by J.J. Gabarro. Boston: Harvard Business School Publications.

Ware, J., & Barnes, L.B. 1992. Managing interpersonal conflict. In *Managing People and Organizations,* readings selected by J.J. Gabarro. Boston: Harvard Business School Publications.

Willging, P. 2009. Unpublished communication. January 5, 2009.

# Chapter 16

# Effective Human Resource and Staff Development

## What You Will Learn

- Human resource policies and practices are essential for tapping into the value inherent in an organization's human resources. The main objective of human resource management is to maintain a desirable and stable workforce.

- Long-term care facilities face five main human resource challenges: regulations, unionization, labor competition, meeting the needs of a predominantly female workforce, and diversity.

- To determine adequate staffing levels in nursing, number of patients, patients' clinical acuity, skill-mix, and distribution of staff hours should be taken into account.

- The long-term care industry faces staff shortages. Hence, creative approaches for recruitment are necessary. Certain categories of staff must be licensed. Certification status of nurse aides must be verified.

- Both absenteeism and turnover should be measured. A multipronged approach is necessary to overcome absenteeism and turnover.

- Staff development should extend beyond providing training and knowledge in job skills. Performance appraisal should focus primarily on staff development. Management by objectives can be a useful tool provided it makes staff development a shared responsibility between supervisors and associates.

- Self-managed work teams can increase job performance, workers' self-esteem, and job satisfaction. They also result in less burnout and turnover.

- Problems related to performance and work-related behaviors should be addressed through counseling and disciplining. Termination is used as a final step in a progressive disciplining approach.

- The National Labor Relations Board has established procedures for workers to unionize. Management should guard against certain well-defined unfair labor practices. Good-faith bargaining, contract administration, and dealing with strikes and picketing are aspects of managing unionized facilities.
- Employment laws give various types of rights to today's workers. Violation of any of these laws amounts to discrimination.

## Human Resources and Their Importance

To function effectively, an organization must rely on three main resources: human, financial, and material. *Human resource* refers to the associates employed by the organization. Organizations function as they do because of the human resource. It is the people in the organization who manage and use the other resources to serve the organization's clients. Hence, a nursing facility's staff is its most important asset. An organization with a superior workforce undeniably gains a competitive advantage in the marketplace, because a superior workforce lends internal strengths to an organization for meeting competitive threats and for exploiting new opportunities presented by changes in the external environment. Therefore, effectively managing human resources is a vital aspect of nursing facility management.

An effective workforce brings value to the organization, and management must determine how the potential of this value is tapped. The primary objective of effective management is to transfer this value to the patients in the form of high-quality care and to the organization in the form of cost-efficiency. Other assets, such as buildings, equipment, and supplies are also essential. But a nursing facility's success in accomplishing its goals depends, to a large extent, on human dynamics. Effective leadership and management, discussed in Chapter 15, are crucial for influencing and shaping human behaviors. But the dynamics are also influenced by the number of associates, their qualifications, the facility's training and development opportunities, fair compensation, grievance practices, performance appraisal, termination practices, and employment policies that govern the exchange relationship between the facility and its associates. Hence, sound human resource policies and practices are critical for achieving organizational goals.

## Human Resource Management

*Human resource management* can be defined as the organizational function of planning for human resource needs, recruitment, selection, compensation, development, evaluation, and handling of grievances and labor relations (Boone & Kurtz, 1984). It is also known by other terms, such as "personnel management" or "employee relations." Large nursing homes generally have a designated position, such as a human resource director, to handle human resource functions, or the responsibility is assigned to the assistant administrator. In most facilities, however, the nursing home administrator (NHA) assumes these responsibilities. In facilities affiliated with a hospital or a multifacility chain, the NHA receives some human resource support from the corporate office. Some human resource responsibilities may be delegated to the nursing department, especially the responsibility for hiring and training licensed nurses and certified nursing assistants (CNAs). Other department heads who supervise employees—such as the food service director, business office manager, and activity director—also have some degree of responsibility in hiring, evaluating, training, and disciplining staff members. The administrator should make sure that these managers are adequately trained in human resource functions.

# Goals, Main Functions, and Challenges
## Human Resource Goals

The primary goal of human resource management is to maintain desired staffing levels by having a well-qualified and stable workforce. Effective leadership as well as sound human resource policies and practices play a key role in achieving this. Griffith (1995) proposed that success in attracting and retaining employees tends to be self-sustaining; organizations with a satisfied and well-qualified staff are able to attract capable and enthusiastic people.

## Human Resource Functions

Building a desirable and stable workforce is achieved by recruiting qualified associates when needed, improving the skills of associates, increasing satisfaction among associates, and retaining associates who perform well.

Accordingly, De Cenzo and Robbins (1996) classify human resource management as four main functions:

- *Staffing:* Recruitment of qualified associates; planning staffing levels in accordance with patient needs; and scheduling to maintain adequate staffing while taking into account associates' needs for time off.
- *Training and development:* Orientation of newly hired associates, ongoing coaching and mentoring by senior associates and supervisors, formal training to maintain and advance skill levels, and developing associates for career advancement.
- *Motivation:* Addressing the issues of job performance, job satisfaction, and labor relations.
- *Maintenance function:* Building employee commitment, reducing absenteeism and turnover, and retaining productive associates.

Effectively managed nursing facilities aim at achieving a high level of motivation and satisfaction among their associates. Many associates in the nursing home come into frequent contact with patients, family members, and visitors, so associates have an unusual degree of influence over these stakeholders. "What they say and do for patients and visitors will have more influence on competitive standing than any media campaign the organization might contemplate" (Griffith 1995, p. 662). No wonder staff satisfaction is an important predictor of customer satisfaction! An effectively managed nursing facility should market itself to its associates almost as much as it markets itself to its clients and the community.

## Human Resource Challenges

Managing human resources is a complex task. First, almost every aspect of human resource management is governed by complex labor laws. The main laws are discussed later in this chapter. Nursing facilities must also comply with regulations mandating minimum levels of staffing and licensing, and, in some cases, certification for staff categories. Experts believe that staffing levels in some facilities are not sufficient to meet the minimum needs of residents for provision of quality of care, quality of life, and rehabilitation (IOM, 2001).

The second human resource challenge faced by long-term care facilities is the unprecedented upsurge in union organizing activity and, sometimes, union militancy. Although unionization in most private-sector industries has steadily declined for several years, the health care sector has been one exception. Nursing homes in particular have become vulnerable to unionization as a larger number of facilities are becoming unionized.

The third challenge comes from labor competition. Nursing facilities employ predominantly unskilled or semi-skilled workers. Most nursing home associates are CNAs, housekeepers, laundry workers, and dietary aides. To recruit these associates, long-term care facilities compete against fast-food restaurants, discount stores, hotels, motels, and hospitals. Local hospitals and other health care organizations also present substantial competition for skilled workers such as nurses, social workers, and therapists. Such skilled workers often prefer to work for hospitals and for other agencies in which pay, benefits, and opportunities for training and career growth are better than in nursing facilities.

The fourth challenge is gender based. Nursing home workers are predominantly female, which requires a particular sensitivity on the part of a facility's administration to the needs of female associates because their needs are often intertwined with those of their families.

The fifth challenge is driven by diversity. In most regions of the country, the workforce is becoming more diverse because of an increasing proportion of minority workers. Diversity presents special challenges because various cultural characteristics—such as language, customs, and beliefs—affect how workers relate to patients, family members, fellow employees, and supervisors.

## Human Resource Planning

Nursing facilities are often plagued with staff shortages. One factor that exacerbates this problem is haphazard planning. In the human resource context, the planning function can be defined as the process of systematically reviewing staffing requirements to ensure that the desired number of associates with the required skills is available when needed (Mondy & Noe, 1993).

### Staffing Levels

Both state and federal regulations are vague about staffing levels in nursing homes. State regulations may specify minimum staff-to-patient ratios, but they do not suggest that the specified minimum levels would result in adequate staffing levels to meet the needs of the patients. Federal regulations simply state that the facility must have sufficient nursing staff to provide necessary care on a 24-hour basis. Hence, NHAs, directors of nursing (DONs), and other department heads often have to struggle with planning strategies that ensure adequate staffing.

Conceptually, staffing levels should take into account four main factors:

- *Volume:* This refers to measures such as number of patients to care for, number of meals to prepare and serve, number of rooms to clean, and pounds of laundry to process.
- *Weighting:* This is a measure of the intensity of resource use. In nursing care, the weighting factor incorporates clinical acuity of patients. For example, for nursing care, patients could be classified into three broad categories to determine resource use: light care, intermediate care, and heavy care. In the dietary department, preparing each meal—breakfast, lunch, and dinner—requires different levels of resource consumption.
- *Skill-mix:* **Skill-mix** is the ratio of particular skill type to the total staff in a unit or department. The ratio of registered nurses (RNs) to the total nursing staff on a nursing care unit is an example of skill-mix. The skill-mix on a nursing care unit increases as the number of RNs or licensed practical nurses/licensed vocational nurses (LPNs/LVNs) increases in relation to the total nursing staff on that unit. Similarly, the ratio of cooks to the total dietary staff is an indicator of skill-mix in the dietary department. Both the volume factor and the weighting factor should be used conjointly to determine the required total staff level and the skill-mix. Finally, the skill-mix should take into account any special training that associates may need to adequately address cognitive and behavioral issues.
- *Distribution:* In the nursing department, staff hours must be balanced among the day, evening, and night shifts. Generally, the day shift needs the heaviest staffing, and the night shift requires the least. But, different nursing units are likely to require different day-to-evening and day-to-night staffing ratios. Even within the same shift, certain time periods have heavier patient loads than others. For instance, the morning wake-up and grooming time, the lunch hour, and evening meal time generally require more staff assistance than at other times. The feasibility of adding staff hours to meet peak patient load demands should be assessed.

The biggest staffing challenge lies in the nursing department. The necessity for adequate staff hours for a given patient volume may be evident. However, skill-mix may be even more important. Research shows that simply adding more staff is not a sufficient means of improving quality of care; improving the skill-mix is necessary (Castle & Engberg, 2008). Secondly, both staff hours and skill-mix should reflect the clinical acuity of patients by incorporating the weighting factor. Some Veterans Administration nursing homes have tried using the Resource Utilization Groups (RUGs) (see Chapter 7) as a proxy for clinical acuity. To date, results have been mixed. A major limitation of RUGs is that they explain only little more than half of the variation in resource use and nursing time (Fries et al., 1994).

Matching staffing to patient needs should be accomplished using a systematic approach in which three separate components of nursing tasks—direct patient care, clinical support, and documentation—should be evaluated. Over time, increasing regulatory mandates have required licensed nurses to spend more and more time on documentation, which can take time away from patient care and support of CNAs.

## Scheduling

Scheduling can be viewed as the final step in human resource planning. Associates in each staff category are assigned to fill the time slots on the various shifts for all seven days of the week. Staffing is governed by four factors:

- Filling all slots in the schedule, which depends on having a sufficient number of full-time and part-time associates on the payroll.
- Scheduled personal time off for holidays and vacations.
- Unscheduled time off, which, to some extent, is beyond management's control. Even when all the slots in the schedule are filled, actual shortages in staffing occur because of absenteeism, which is a substantial problem in many nursing homes. Shortages in staffing also occur when people leave their positions without giving advance notice or when the facility is unable to fill vacant positions. If a facility has serious absenteeism and turnover problems, it should try to schedule extra staff in addition to what a full schedule calls for, because the facility anticipates that some associates on the schedule are not going to show up for work. On occasion, this approach will result in overstaffing, but, more frequently, it will offset shortages arising from severe absenteeism or turnover. From an economic perspective, the additional net costs of overstaffing, if any, should be relatively small, because such scheduling would reduce overtime costs and the use of temporary staffing agencies. The payoffs of extra scheduling are high in terms of consistency, quality of patient care, and staff satisfaction.

- Necessary hours for training and orientation, which should be incorporated in the schedule.

# Staff Recruitment and Compensation

## Creative Recruitment

In many labor markets, the long-term care industry faces staff shortages because the demand for qualified staff members is greater than the supply. Some actions that may help nursing homes overcome such imbalances include creative recruiting, compensation incentives, and training programs (Caruth & Handlogten, 1997). Creativity often involves a more effective use of recruitment resources that already exist. For example, a facility's current associates, local schools and colleges, churches, neighborhood newspapers, and the local employment agency can be effective resources for staff recruitment. Other creative approaches may include a job fair or open house at the facility, where current associates are available to explain various job opportunities.

Nursing assistant certification programs are organized by many facilities to attract candidates who otherwise would be unemployable for lack of marketable skills. Other avenues for training include tuition assistance and continuing education for promising associates and financial assistance and scholarships for students currently enrolled in nursing programs. A facility can also provide opportunities for internships to students in nursing and other disciplines. Interns may be paid a stipend that serves as a token of appreciation for the work interns perform as part of their training. Such direct investments in training, consistently undertaken, can help alleviate future staff shortages by providing a steady stream of qualified workers.

## Compensation

Compensation should match market rates of pay. Paying a high premium over market rates can trigger a bidding war, which can raise hiring salaries to artificially high levels and can send ripple effects throughout the organization or through the local long-term care industry. Hence, during periods of critical shortages, many organizations use sign-on bonuses, because they can be discontinued at any time without creating negative economic effects for the rest of the organization. Other forms of nonmonetary rewards can appeal to many people. Four-day work weeks, flexible working hours, and on-site child care are attractive incentives (Caruth & Handlogten, 1997). Market rates of pay apply mainly to starting wages. Once employees are on the job, additional perks (discussed later in this chapter) can be used to reward them for personal development, job performance, and supplementary responsibilities.

## Staff Licensure, Certification, and Registration

Recruiting RNs, LPNs (or LVNs), and CNAs requires compliance with regulatory mandates. RNs and LPNs must be licensed by the state in which they wish to practice. The nursing facility must verify current licensure status of all its RNs and LPNs and must maintain a copy of the license in each employee's personnel record. Similar documentation must be maintained for all other licensed associates—such as therapists and therapy assistants—regardless of whether these workers are directly employed by the facility or are contracted through an agency.

CNAs must have current certification, which is earned through a state's standardized nurse aide training and competency evaluation program as mandated by the Omnibus Budget Reconciliation Act of 1987 (OBRA-87). The objective of this mandate is to establish minimum qualifications for CNAs and to evaluate whether a person possesses basic competencies to work as a CNA in a long-term care facility. Even though CNAs are not required to have a state license, the effect of this legislation is the same as if there were such a requirement.

CNA training programs are offered by nursing facilities, community colleges, and the American Red Cross. Certification is conferred by the state's nurse aide registry after an applicant passes an examination. A ***nurse aide registry*** is a registration system for CNAs that all 50 states and the District of Columbia maintain. The registries enable facilities to verify the certification status of a nurse aide. The registry also provides information on resident abuse, neglect, or misappropriation of personal property in which an aide may have been involved. Before employing a CNA, a facility is required to contact the registries in all states in which the individual is believed to have worked. Noncertified nurse aides employed in permanent positions have a four-month window during which they must receive the required training and receive certification. Laws in many states also require criminal background checks and drug testing when nursing personnel are hired. Legislative proposals have been made for mandating a national information-sharing registry on all long-term care workers.

# Managing Absenteeism and Turnover

Absenteeism and turnover are twin problems. Lower rates of absenteeism, for instance, are associated with higher seniority on the job (Cohen-Mansfield & Rosenthal, 1989).

Effectively managed facilities measure absenteeism and turnover rates on a regular basis. These measures are useful in projecting future staffing needs. They help management gauge the outcomes of any new programs or policies and also provide an on-going measure of staff satisfaction. Adverse trends, for example, may indicate the presence of underlying problems that need probing and investigation.

## Absenteeism

Some absenteeism occurs because of legitimate reasons such as sickness. Much of it, however, is associated with apathy, low morale, and a low sense of self-worth among the workers.

## Measuring Absenteeism

Maintaining records on individual absenteeism is essential; so is keeping track of absenteeism rates for the purpose of staff planning and scheduling, as discussed earlier. Absenteeism rates are calculated as follows:

$$Absenteeism\ rate\ (\%) = \frac{Number\ of\ workdays\ missed\ per\ time\ period}{Average\ number\ of\ employees \times Number\ of\ workdays\ in\ the\ same\ time\ period} \times 100$$

## Managing Absenteeism

Absenteeism is managed by having written policies, which should include a distinction between what the facility considers an excused absence and an unexcused absence. Policies should also specify what level of absenteeism is considered excessive and the consequences associates will bear when their absenteeism is excessive. Absenteeism should be addressed both individually and for the organization as a whole. At an individual level, a counseling session should be held between the employee and the supervisor to seek out the underlying problems and determine how management may be able to assist the employee to overcome those problems. Additional key areas discussed in the next section can also help minimize absenteeism.

## Turnover and Retention

Most nursing homes have a relatively small core of very stable and dedicated associates. But most facilities are also plagued by enormous rates of turnover, which generally exceed those in other industries. Despite efforts to understand why turnover is so common, and despite efforts to slow down the speed at which the exit door revolves, staff turnover remains one of the most daunting problems for the nursing home industry. No single approach exists for increasing staff retention, and piecemeal efforts to address the issue have produced little success to date. This section provides a comprehensive approach that requires coordinated support from governing boards, administrators, and key department heads to carry out a successful campaign against high turnover of staff.

Turnover and retention are flip sides of the same coin—that is, increased staff retention translates into lower rates of turnover. Research has consistently demonstrated that job commitment and intent to stay are strong predictors of actual future turnover.

## Measuring Turnover and Its Costs

Turnover in a facility can be calculated by using the following formula, which can be applied to a particular position, or to the entire staff:

$$Turnover\ rate\ (\%) = \frac{Number\ of\ separations\ per\ time\ period^*}{Average\ number\ of\ employees\ during\ the\ same\ period} \times 100$$

*\*Any period can be used, but a year is the most common. However, keeping track of turnover for each month or for each quarter can help administrators better understand the trends.*

$$Functional\ turnover\ rate\ (\%) = \frac{Number\ of\ separations\ of\ employees\ who\ would\ not\ be\ rehired}{Average\ number\ of\ employees} \times 100$$

$$Dysfunctional\ turnover\ rate\ (\%) = \frac{Number\ of\ separations\ of\ employees\ who\ would\ be\ rehired}{Average\ number\ of\ employees} \times 100$$

Turnover is expensive. The two major costs directly associated with turnover are replacement costs and training costs for the new worker. A rough estimate of these direct costs is two to three times the monthly salary of the departing employee (Sherman et al., 1998). Additional indirect costs include overtime paid to cover vacant positions, tempo-rary staffing agency fees, management time used to find replacements, low productivity before employees quit, and low morale among associates.

## Managing Turnover

Multiple factors are associated with staff turnover. Hence, there is no single remedy that would promote retention. All of the factors discussed in this section should be evaluated, and a multipronged approach is generally necessary to overcome turnover.

### Leadership Stability

Unfortunately, with few exceptions, turnover permeates the typical facility from top to bottom. At the industry level, turnover among NHAs has been estimated to be at least 40%, with the median length of employment at a facility just over two years (Singh & Schwab, 1998). A study of turnover suggested that there actually may be a bidding war among nursing facilities in an attempt to attract qualified NHAs, as indicated by the relatively large proportion of administrators voluntarily leaving their positions after relatively short tenures (average length, 1.3 years) to pursue opportunities for promotions that offer more responsibility, better pay, and so forth (Singh & Schwab, 2000). This phenomenon implies that administrators who possess the qualifications facilities seek are in short supply. This type of instability at the top keeps the entire organization in a state of flux because leadership and strategic direction are interrupted, associates feel the stress of frequent change of leadership, and many other disruptions occur. Similarly, in the nursing department, it has been demonstrated that turnover among RNs may be linked to turnover among CNAs (Brannon et al., 2002).

Hence, stability of key leadership positions is one goal nursing facilities must address. NHA turnover is a governance issue that the boards must address.

## Selection, Orientation, and Mentoring

From the administrator's standpoint, attention to recruitment practices may be the first step in reducing staff turnover. Many people who apply for jobs in nursing homes do indeed have a desire to help the elderly, but they soon become discouraged and disenchanted. As a result, much of the turnover in health care facilities occurs within the first 90 days of employment. Lescoe-Long (2000) cited two main reasons for this phenomenon:

1. The job turns out to be different from what the employee had expected it to be; perhaps the job was made to appear more glamorous than it truly is.
2. Employees feel abandoned after the first few days of employment, and they lack skills to cope with many of the demands of the new job.

The first of these two reasons points to the need for a more in-depth selection process, in which the facility should try to explore the potential employee's expectations in relation to the realities of what the job entails. The second reason underscores the importance of developing coping skills. Technical training, such as a nurse aide certification program, focuses mainly on how to perform certain job-related functions correctly. Even though such training is essential, it does not prepare workers to handle nonroutine and stressful situations. For example, unexpected verbal or physical abuse from a patient or sudden criticism from a family member can leave the employee bewildered and overwhelmed. A new job that already places heavy emphasis on meeting certain standards of care often becomes frustrating when the employee confronts unexpected situations but does not know how to deal with those situations. It is also demoralizing for associates when they have to face consistent staffing shortages and pick up the slack. Such experiences leave the associates feeling disillusioned, powerless, and incompetent.

To overcome early burnout among new associates, a peer mentoring program can be instituted by identifying, training, and rewarding experienced CNAs who are committed to helping new caregivers "learn the ropes." Besides helping retain new associates, such a program cultivates teamwork and enhances understanding of roles and expectations (Hoffman, 2001). Also called the "buddy system," it makes peer resources available to help new associates fit in and to avoid frustration during the most critical period of employment. The new associate generally starts in such a program by observing and following the "buddy," an experienced CNA. The new associate then starts working independently while still in frequent contact with the buddy, and the new associate receives ongoing support from the buddy.

A buddy's duties should be clearly outlined. These duties can include explaining how to use the organization's systems, such as developmental resources and personnel resources. A variation of the buddy system can be used in the preselection process: a job candidate is given the opportunity to spend time informally with a current employee so that the candidate can find out first-hand what the job actually entails ("Buddy system can lower turnover, raise morale," 2002).

## Positive Supervision

Bishop et al. (2008) demonstrated that an important factor that promoted job commitment was the CNAs' perception that their nurse supervisors were respectful and helpful and provided useful feedback. This type of good basic supervision may even be more important than job enhancement such as worker empowerment.

## Social Support

An atmosphere of social support and a sense of belonging are highly conducive to staff retention. The social approach to staff retention views a nursing facility as a community in itself. The organizational culture promotes the feeling of belonging to a family in which people care for each other. Even though the family touch is likely to diminish in inverse proportion to the facility's size, the administration can place increased emphasis on a more flexible, people-centered, participatory, and nurturing atmosphere for both associates and residents.

The philosophy of social support can be reinforced by policies and practices that promote the workers' ability to meet their social obligations. Examples include flexible scheduling, child care, and access to health care when needed.

## Working Conditions

Work environments must be made safer and both worker and resident friendly by adopting the concepts of enriched environments and culture change discussed in Chapter 8. Evidence also suggests that nursing homes that improve their quality may have a positive impact on job satisfaction of associates, and thereby reduce their turnover rates (Castle et al., 2006). Compliance with the Occupational Safety and Health Administration (OSHA) standards is a regulatory requirement. Nursing homes must go beyond these regulations and invest in labor-saving and

safety technology. A change in management philosophy and practices is also necessary to empower direct caregivers who get to know the residents and their routines better than anyone else. Cross-training and adoption of the self-managed work team approach (discussed later) also bring about a better worker environment and build their self-esteem.

## Training

Research shows that the federal guideline requiring 75 hours of nurse aide training is not sufficient to prepare CNAs to deliver adequate levels of care. Studies have also found that inadequate training is one contributing factor that leads to high turnover of CNAs. Subsequent research based on nurse aide training programs in 10 states has suggested that the length of training should be at least 100 to 120 hours, of which 50 to 60 hours should be devoted to clinical training (Hernández-Medina et al., 2006). In the Green House model (see Chapter 8), for example, CNAs receive 120 hours of additional training after they become certified.

## Career Paths

Opportunities for advancement promote job commitment (Bishop et al., 2008). Administrators should make an effort to learn about each individual's needs and goals. On the basis of the findings, career paths can be created for growth-oriented individuals. Some employees may be recognized for their skills in training others and groomed for becoming peer mentors. Others may be able to provide insights into process improvement, such as safety enhancement, disaster planning, or quality assurance. In nursing facilities, which typically have few opportunities for career growth, employee contribution to self-development and achievement must also be rewarded. Hoffman (2001) observed that increased compensation by itself would not slow turnover but that increased compensation tied to professional development can be very effective in promoting self-worth and thus slowing turnover.

### Administrative Support

Other ways to reduce turnover include supporting the staff with adequate resources. Chronic staff shortages and unreasonably heavy workloads promote the feeling that management does not care, as does a deficient staff skill-mix when it does not take into account the heavier staffing weights called for by higher levels of clinical acuity. Despite what administrators might say about quality standards, associates are quick to perceive inconsistencies when resources are inadequate. Employees do not feel that they ought to be the ones to pay the price for inadequate resources in the form of higher stress and personal dissatisfaction. In multifacility chains, NHAs often assign blame to the corporate office and try to portray the governing body as the villain in the eyes of the staff. In most instances, however, governing bodies remain unconvinced with a mere request for additional resources; they want data and analysis to justify the need for additional resources. The point here is that the ultimate responsibility for resource allocation remains largely with the NHA, but the governing board also must develop a more realistic understanding of the challenges of patient care.

### Pay and Benefits

In research findings, front-line workers such as CNAs almost always state that their ability to care for residents is what is most important to them and that it keeps them coming back day after day. However, this does not imply that pay and benefits are not important (Bishop et al., 2008). In fact, compensation may be a factor CNAs are least satisfied with when compared with other factors such as job content, training, and coworkers (Castle, 2007).

## Staff Development
### Staff Development Goals

*Staff development* typically means training associates to enhance their knowledge and expertise. Enhancing staff knowledge and expertise is without doubt an important goal of staff development because it plays a critical role in building internal organizational strengths that a facility needs in a competitive environment. However, the goals of staff development must be extended beyond improving basic skills needed for the performance of routine functions. The overarching goal of staff development should be to make associates productive citizens of the organization and of society. Approaching staff development from this broad perspective can pay rich dividends in better quality, improved morale, higher commitment, and greater retention.

### Staff Development Content

Training should first and foremost focus on the worker's immediate job. As mentioned earlier, training and job orientation should help the associates improve not only their technical skills but also the coping skills that can help them deal with difficult situations. In the broader context discussed here, training should also assimilate them into the organization's community. Training should enable associates to get a clear understanding of the organization's vision, mission, and values. New associates in particular should receive appropriate training in the facility's rules, policies, and procedures. Training should also include other key areas such as patient relations, family relations, teamwork, stress management, conflict resolution, work safety, and quality management. Finally, training should help people become responsible citizens of society. This last element may not appear at first to be work related, but it is. Associates who act responsibly in their social and home lives are also likely to be responsible and committed at work. Administrators know all too well that associates' personal problems frequently become work problems. Nursing home associates predominantly come from low socioeconomic backgrounds. Many have low self-esteem and lack the skills they need to address social and personal conflicts. For many associates, balancing their home lives with the demands of the job is a daily struggle. Money management, family budgeting, problem solving, child care, nutrition, and wellness are only a few areas in which most associates can benefit from training. Staff development in most nursing home organizations lacks the well-rounded approach it takes to build a stable and productive work environment.

# Performance Appraisal

Instead of being a judgmental and punitive tool, the performance appraisal process should focus primarily on staff development. Achieving this objective requires the participation of both the associate and the supervisor who does the evaluation. If both associates and supervisors understand the fa-

cility's philosophy of staff development and its relationship to performance evaluation, the process will not be as difficult for both parties as it often turns out to be.

Performance appraisal is a part of ***management by objectives (MBO)***. Simply put, MBO is based on a joint agreement between supervisors and associates on what specific and measurable objectives will be accomplished over a given time; at the end of that time period, the supervisors evaluate individual associates according to whether they have accomplished these objectives (Bounds & Woods, 1998).

Most people would readily agree that MBO makes intuitive sense. What is often lacking, however, is the awareness of the linkage between performance and staff development. Because staff development is primarily a management responsibility, performance becomes a shared responsibility of supervisors and their associates. Both must be jointly held accountable for improving performance.

For the MBO approach to work, several prerequisites are necessary:

- All associates in the organization must understand clearly what is expected from them individually, commensurate with their qualifications and level of expertise. It requires abandoning the "one-size-fits-all" approach.

- Objectives must be set, such as how many patients the associate is responsible for and what outcomes of care should be expected. The objectives ought to incorporate an assessment of technical skills and the associate's ability to adapt to the facility's policies, procedures, values, schedules, and routines.

- Individual associate's training needs, as well as needs for further orientation, should be based on assessment. This measure would result in training programs that match individual needs.

- Personal development and performance of associates are periodically assessed as a joint undertaking by associates and supervisors, including peer mentors.
- Rewards are linked to participation in training, evidence of personal development, and objective measures of performance.
- Rewards for peer mentors and supervisors are based on their achievements in staff development.

One problem with MBO is its potential for misuse by management when management's focus is on punishing individual employees instead of on using MBO for development purposes. According to W. Edwards Deming, the esteemed marketing guru, MBO and individual work quotas promote short-cuts in quality because individuals work to meet quotas rather than engage in continuous quality improvement. In the self-managed team approach, discussed in the next section, accountability for task accomplishment and quality rests on teams rather than on individuals. According to Deming's philosophy, performance evaluation and rewards would be implemented at the group rather than at the individual level.

# Self-Managed Work Teams

In *self-managed work teams (SMWTs)*— also called self-directed work teams—a group of associates, the "team," are together responsible for performing a range of tasks that include scheduling, planning, and monitoring the team's performance. The use of SMWTs in traditional nursing homes is rare. However, in the emerging models of care that reflect cultural change, such teams play a pivotal role. The Green House model, for example, relies on cross-trained, self-managed work teams that are responsible for providing all basic and routine services to all elders. The teams are also responsible for the environment in each Green House. In this model, the typical supervisor–subordinate relationships are minimized because the workers make team decisions and the teams manage themselves in carrying out all routine tasks and responsibilities.

All members of SMWTs are CNAs. These CNAs routinely work together to perform all daily tasks, and they routinely depend on each other to get the tasks accomplished and to make management decisions related to their work (Yeatts & Seward, 2000). As shifts change, the teams engage in information sharing and coordination for continuity of care. Team members also decide who would serve which residents and what specific services should be provided to each resident (Yeatts & Seward, 2000). Teams generally hold a scheduled "sit-down" meeting once per week for approximately 30 minutes, and impromptu "stand-up" meetings as needed. The latter are used to address any immediate concerns. The weekly scheduled meetings typically follow a set agenda and mainly include discussion of work procedures and review of patients' condition and needs. Issues to be addressed may be brought up by the team members themselves or by the nurses. The teams provide weekly written notes that include their suggestions and concerns to nursing management. In turn, member of nursing management review the notes and provide written feedback (Yeatts et al., 2004).

The effectiveness of SMWTs depends on how well the program is implemented.

Yeatts and Hyten (1998) recommend paying attention to several general rules that are important for SMWTs to function effectively:

- *Establishing a team charter.* The purpose of the team charter is to clarify the team's overall purpose and to establish some ground rules for making decisions. The rules are established with substantial input from team members as well as management.
- *Goals and priorities.* These are established by team members with support from management. The goals should be clear, challenging, and measurable.
- *Work responsibilities and training.* SMWTs are able to match the team members' talents and preferences to the tasks to be performed. This type of matching results in a more specific allocation of responsibilities for individual team members and allows for accountability. The matching process also helps identify the specific areas in which further training is necessary. For example, the entire team may need training in decision making, or a particular team member may need training in rendering maintenance–rehabilitation therapies.
- *Team leader.* The teams determine who will be the team leader. Team leaders rotate within each group as other team members are given the opportunity to take on the role of a team leader. Some teams may require all members to rotate, whereas others have an election that includes only those who are interested in the position.
- *Work procedures and problems.* Team members identify the most appropriate procedures and find effective solutions to work-related problems. When goals

are based on measurable criteria, performance can be effectively monitored. By monitoring their own performance, SMWTs tend to take ownership of any performance problems and take action to improve performance.

Because SMWTs are given the authority to make all or most decisions related to their work, the process results in an enriched work environment and staff empowerment (Yeatts & Hyten 1998, p. 17). The quality of services is positively affected when team members are able to discuss resident desires and needs among themselves (Yeatts & Seward, 2000). Communication links between employees and supervisors are kept open in a work environment with SMWTs. When mid-level managers, such as unit charge nurses, are receptive to advice and input from CNAs and involve them in care planning and group problem solving, turnover rates are reduced (Banaszak-Holl & Himes, 1996). In more recent research, worker empowerment has been found to increase job performance factors such as effective work procedures, patient care processes, and support for other team members. Among CNAs, SMWTs also produce higher levels of self-esteem, less burnout, and greater satisfaction with their jobs and schedules. These CNAs also had fewer intentions to leave their jobs (Cready et al., 2008).

## Counseling, Disciplining, and Terminating

The three steps discussed in this section are progressive and sequential and are undertaken when problems surface in conjunction with associate performance and work-related behaviors. Subsequent steps in the disciplinary process become unnecessary when performance or behaviors improve. But the probability of salvaging an associate becomes increasingly small as the process continues (Figure 16–1).

## Counseling

*Counseling* entails an informal discussion between the associate and the supervisor when an associate needs to make improvement. Almost all associates at one point or another require some type of counseling. Counseling is a mild form of attention-getter that is devoid of any kind of threat to an individual's sense of job security. Expressions such as, "I have been through this myself," or "It is not uncommon for new associates to face this," or "It generally takes some time to get this right, but let's keep working at it," or "It can be serious, so let's focus on this some more" are commonly used by trained supervisors to address issues realistically and constructively and yet address those issues in a context that puts the associate at ease. Counseling is closely related to coaching, but it focuses on exceptions, that is, on behaviors that fall outside the bounds of acceptable job performance. Even though some "hand-holding" may be involved, the goal of counseling is to help associates "take responsibility for and manage their own decision-making" (Bolton 1997, p. 212). However, at this stage, the manager must identify the need for further development and training and find ways to provide those for the associate. Achieving these goals in a nonthreatening way requires tact and skill on the part of the manager.

## Disciplining

A facility's staff development efforts can be regarded as successful when most associates employ self-discipline by adhering to rules and standards of acceptable behavior. But a few associates will not take on the responsibility of self-discipline. Such associates will require some form of extrinsic disciplinary action (De Cenzo & Robbins, 1996).

*Disciplining* involves a more formal approach to work-related problems than counseling. Management's right to discipline others first assumes that the managers them-

**Figure 16–1** Progressive Corrective Steps and the Probability of Salvage

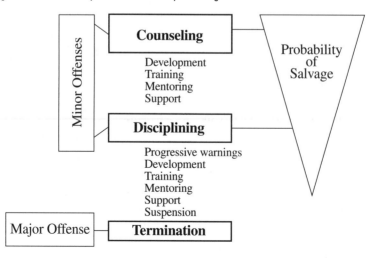

selves have exercised self-discipline and have set the right example for their staff. Starting with the administrator, the department heads and nursing supervisors should set an example before they can expect the associates to engage in positive behaviors. Otherwise, disciplining becomes hypocritical, and associates can see through any double standards.

Common disciplinary problems identified by managers can be classified into four categories (Sherman et al., 1998): (1) attendance and tardiness problems, (2) dishonesty, (3) substandard work performance, and (4) behavioral problems such as violation of rules. Failure to take disciplinary action only compounds a problem that eventually has to be dealt with. By then, inaction will have already done some damage to group morale. Inaction also implies that behaviors and work performance have been acceptable.

Fairness should be the primary guiding principle in any type of disciplinary action. Fairness requires that managers take into consideration some key factors to guide their practices (De Cenzo & Robbins, 1996):

- *Seriousness of the problem.* For example, dishonesty is more serious than occasional tardiness.
- *Duration and frequency.* For example, repeat offenses are more serious than a first occurrence. Discipline should take into account the associate's past work record.
- *Extenuating circumstances.* For example, automobile breakdown on the way to work may be a legitimate excuse for tardiness or absence.
- *Orientation, training, and counseling.* For example, the extent to which an associate may have received assistance in adapting to the organization should be reviewed before that associate is disci-

plined. Disciplining should also be used as an opportunity to assess the need for additional training.

- *Associate's viewpoint.* Before any action is taken, the associate must be given the opportunity to explain his or her position. The associate may not have been aware of the existence of a particular rule. In some situations, an investigation may be necessary to determine whether the associate was at fault. For example, an associate may have failed to give a scheduled shower to a patient because of family's request to wait another day so the patient could have a shower just before her birthday celebration.
- *Fairness.* Fairness demands that all discussions and actions pertaining to disciplining be carried out in private. In effective management practices, humiliating someone in front of other people is never acceptable.

Once disciplinary action has been deemed necessary, the approach to disciplining should be positive. A positive approach requires emphasis on the corrective, rather than punitive, nature of disciplinary action. This emphasis does not mean, however, that punishment can never be a part of disciplinary action. It means that punishment may be employed with the objective of correcting behavior; otherwise, it may lead to adversarial relationships between associates and their supervisors. Sherman et al. (1998) suggested that in positive disciplining, the total responsibility for correcting a problem is placed on the associate. Although the supervisor and the associate engage in joint discussion and problem solving, nothing is imposed by management; all solutions and affirmations are jointly reached.

As a matter of general practice, disciplining should be progressive. Progressive action may be bypassed only for the most serious offenses. Progressive discipline evolves through four main stages:

- *Verbal warning.* Even though the warning itself is verbal, it is documented in the associate's personnel record.
- *Written warning.* The written warning should document the problem, what the associate needs to do to demonstrate that the problem has been corrected, and further disciplinary action that will ensue if the problem remains uncorrected within a specified period. All warnings should be discussed with the associate, and the associate should be asked to sign the disciplinary document.
- *Final written warning or suspension without pay.* At this point, it should be documented that if the problem remains uncorrected for a specified length of time, dismissal will follow.
- *Dismissal.* Termination from employment becomes necessary when agreed-upon results are not demonstrated.

To keep the system fair and balanced, facility administrators should consider instituting an appeals system to resolve any disagreements between associates and supervisors over disciplinary matters. An appeals system that is likely to be most trusted by associates consists of a committee composed of an equal number of worker representatives and management staff. A small committee of no more than four to six members is recommended. The committee renders decisions, either upholding or rescinding a particular disciplinary action, based on reviewing facility policies, examining the evidence, and separately hearing the supervisor and the associate (McCabe, 1988).

## Terminating

*Terminating* employment is generally the final step in progressive discipline when all efforts and opportunities fail to bring about the desired behavior. If progressive discipline is followed, there should be adequate documentation in the associate's personnel record on which the decision to terminate would be based. At times, however, termination becomes necessary for a serious one-time offense such as theft, patient abuse, deliberate destruction of facility property, or using alcohol or illegal drugs on the premises.

Regardless of how serious the offense, terminating an associate on the spot, or proclaiming, "You are fired," is never a good idea. Such an action often raises questions about objectivity and perceived fairness. The associate may disagree with an allegation, and yet management may not want the associate to continue on the job while serious questions remain unanswered, as would be the case when management believes that the associate did abuse a patient. The answer to such a dilemma is found in placing the associate on suspension pending further investigation. The associate is told that he or she is being taken off the schedule and will be notified as soon as an investigation has been completed. If the associate is called back to work, reinstatement is with full back-pay. Once an investigation has been completed and a decision has been made to terminate the associate, a letter notifying the associate of the decision is sent by certified mail. In all disciplinary actions, including termination, the associate should be treated with courtesy.

# Labor Relations and Unionization

The National Labor Relations Act (NLRA) of 1935, also known as the Wagner Act, gave workers the right to organize and join unions without fear of retribution from their employers. The law specifically defined certain conduct as unfair labor practices. The NLRA also required employers to bargain in good faith with a union representing the workers. As part of this law, the National Labor Relations Board (NLRB) was established as an independent federal agency, which has 51 regional, subregional, or resident offices. The NLRB has the authority to conduct union recognition elections and to investigate complaints of unfair labor practices. Since 1974, employees of nonprofit health care institutions, who were previously prevented from joining unions, have been extended the same rights as employees in other private businesses.

## Election for Collective Representation

Unionization is a collective choice of an organization's employees, who have the collective right to join a union, and they also have the collective right not to join a union. If a union is voted in, however, it then has the exclusive right to represent all the employees in a given bargaining unit, which covers categories of employees a union can legitimately represent.

Employees seek union representation mainly because of their ongoing dissatisfaction with employment conditions and their belief that a union would be effective in alleviating at least some of those negative conditions. The main working conditions employees seek to improve include wages, benefits, and perceived unfair treatment

from management. In the final analysis, employees who seek to form a union feel powerless to change things that are important to them. They hope to achieve those results through collective representation. Hence, preventive action through effective leadership and sound human resource practices are the administrator's best defenses against unionization.

Once employees decide to unionize and contact between a small group of employees and union leaders is established, an organizing campaign begins: union leaders hold employee meetings away from the nursing home premises, and informal leaders among the employees try to persuade their coworkers to sign authorization cards. Signing an authorization card is deemed to indicate the employee's willingness to join the union. In reality, however, peer pressure often plays a role. Some employees sign the card just to get a coworker "off their backs." For the NLRB to hold an election, at least 30 percent of the employees in the proposed bargaining unit must sign the authorization cards. As a matter of practice, however, unions seek a much higher number because, to win, the union must get more than 50% of the votes in a secret-ballot election.

Before an election, the NLRB determines the makeup of the *bargaining unit*, which is a distinct group of employees who have common employment interests and who may reasonably be grouped together for the purpose of collective bargaining. An election by secret ballot is conducted by NLRB officials in the presence of representatives from the union as well as the employer. All employees who are included in the bargaining unit have the right to vote. If the union wins by a majority vote, the NLRB will certify the union as the legal bargaining representative for the employees. On the other hand, if the union loses the election, it also loses the right to represent the employees.

## Employee Free Choice Act

In June 2007, the Employee Free Choice Act did not pass in the U.S. Congress. The bill was strongly backed by labor organizers such as the American Federation of Labor–Congress of Industrial Unions (AFL-CIO) and was strongly supported by the Democratic Party. The main purpose of this bill was to set aside the long-existing procedures that culminate in employee vote by secret ballot on whether or not to be represented by a union. Had it been passed, the legislation would have forced employers to recognize a union if the union could collect signed authorization cards from a simple majority (50% + 1) of the employees. Referred to as the card-check process, employees would sign cards in the open rather than indicate their preference privately through secret ballot. Now that the Democratic Party controls the presidency as well as both the houses in Congress, this bill is likely to be resurrected.

## Unfair Labor Practices

Under current regulation, both the employer and the union have the right to present information to employees during a unionization campaign. Management has the right to inform associates, but all information must be factual. Management representatives may also express their opinions but should not engage in deliberate misrepresentation. The facility's administration, for instance, can make appeals in an effort to convince the associates that joining the union would not be in their best interest. Typical appeals include the following (Bounds & Woods, 1998):

- The union can make promises, but it cannot guarantee that it would succeed in delivering on those promises.
- Wages are already good and equal to or better than what the union could negotiate. If the union is voted in, wages and benefits will become negotiable. They may go down, stay the same, or increase.
- Union dues and other costs outweigh the benefits of belonging to a union.
- The union is an outsider, not really attuned to associates' best interests.
- Associates may have to strike even when they do not want to.

In making such appeals, managers must be careful that they do not engage in any *unfair labor practices*. These are actions declared as illegal under the National Labor Relations Act. They can be categorized into four areas:

1. *Promise.* The union can make promises, but management cannot. For example, management cannot promise employees pay increases, better benefits, or other types of rewards in exchange for a "no" vote. The administrator should, however, continue to follow any pre-established wage increase programs.

2. *Threaten.* Management cannot make any type of threats. For example, it is illegal to state that the facility will close down if the union is voted in or that health insurance benefits will have to be curtailed. Intimidating employees with discipline or discharge is also an unfair labor practice. However, supervisors have the right to take any reasonable action to prevent employee solicitation at work stations and dur-

ing work time. Employees, on the other hand, are free to engage in union solicitation in a break room during break or lunch time.

3. *Interrogate.* Supervisors cannot ask employees about how they intend to vote, about their past union affiliation, or about what may have been discussed at the union meetings. On the other hand, if an employee volunteers information to a supervisor, listening is not illegal. It is only illegal for a supervisor to ask.

4. *Spy.* It is illegal for management to spy on union meetings or other activities related to the unionization campaign.

Engaging in unfair labor practices during a unionization campaign carries grave risks for management. The union can petition the NLRB to set aside the election and enforce recognition of the union.

## Collective Bargaining

Once a union has been certified to represent employees, labor laws mandate that both unions and management negotiate in good faith, a process called **collective bargaining**. Bargaining in good faith means that both parties must engage in a genuine process to reach an agreement, even though there is no guarantee that an agreement will be reached. Yet, when an agreement is reached, it must be ratified by a majority vote of the employees in the bargaining unit. The union contract specifies the terms and conditions of employment for the workers who are covered under the contract. Some typical areas covered under a contract include duration of the contract, description of the bargaining unit, wages, benefits, work rules, rights of management, jurisdiction of various jobs, and grievance procedures. Typically, a contract is negotiated for a three-year term. Every contract must be renegotiated at the end of the period it covers.

## Union Contract Administration

Once a union contract has been ratified, the administrator is responsible for ensuring that all supervisors understand its terms. It is important to emphasize the management's rights, which typically include the right to allocate and use resources in a way management sees fit; to give work assignments; to hire, discipline, and terminate employees; and to formulate policies and procedures.

Grievance resolution is an important element of any collective bargaining agreement. "A **grievance** is a formal expression of employee dissatisfaction about some job situation" (Bounds & Woods 1998, p. 413). The union may also protest the way that management has interpreted and enforced certain provisions of the contract. Bringing a complaint to an employee's immediate supervisor is the first step in any grievance procedure. Many grievances can be effectively handled at this level, provided the supervisors are trained in handling grievances.

If the complaint is not resolved, the employee takes the complaint to the union steward. A **union steward** is a unionized employee who works at the facility and officially represents the union to his or her fellow unionized employees at the workplace. Stewards can employ a lot of discretion in handling grievances and can often be more effective than the employee in getting problems resolved by being more objective. If a grievance is not resolved at this level, a representative from the union office meets with the administrator in an effort to reach some compromise. If the issue cannot be resolved in this way, it is submitted to arbitration, a costly process that both parties try to avoid. ***Arbitration*** is a process in which a neutral third party—generally, but not necessarily, a retired judge or attorney who may be recognized by a court jurisdiction or be associated with an arbitration service—hears both sides and renders a decision that is binding on both parties (Bounds & Woods, 1998).

## Strikes and Picketing

Work stoppage as a concerted effort by unionized employees is called a ***strike***. The law requires unions to give a 10-day notice to a nursing facility before calling on the employees to go on a strike. The purpose of this requirement is to allow health care facilities to make plans for continuity of patient care. Striking employees often patrol the perimeter of the facility displaying placards that call attention to the labor dispute they have with management. This concerted action is called ***picketing***.

An ***economic strike*** is the most common type of strike. It occurs when the union and management fail to reach an agreement; that is, an ***impasse*** occurs in the negotiations. Management has the right to hire replacement workers during an economic strike. Striking employees can be replaced either temporarily or permanently. Reinstatement for an employee may occur when a striker makes an offer to return to work with no conditions attached. Reinstatement is not automatic after the strike is over, but preference is given to those who wish to return to work as job vacancies occur.

As a general rule, striking and picketing are not to interfere with the management's right to provide patient care. For instance, picketers may not prevent nonstriking workers and supervisors from entering the facility or obstruct trucks delivering essential supplies and food to the facility. Legal remedies are available for dealing with violent strikes and picketing.

## Employment Laws

The purpose of labor laws is to protect the rights of individuals in an employment relationship, which mainly includes hiring, wages, benefits, promotion, and discharge. Hence, many of the legal requirements discussed here are loosely referred to as *antidiscrimination laws*. These laws are based on the theory that employment practices should be governed by criteria that are job related; management's employment decisions should not be based on personal characteristics that have little to do with an individual's ability to do the job. ***Employment discrimination*** is generally defined as discriminatory action in failing or refusing to hire; in discharging or otherwise discriminating against an individual with respect to terms, conditions, or privileges of employment; or in limiting, segregating, or classifying employees in a way that deprives an individual of employment opportunity, training, advancement, or status.

## Employment-at-Will

Employment laws provide for exceptions to a longstanding legal doctrine called employment-at-will. Historically, the ***employment-at-will*** doctrine has asserted that employment is at the will of both the employer and the employee and that either party may terminate the employment relationship at any time for any reason or for no reason, except when the termination violates a contract or a law.

In recent years, however, there has been a growing trend toward a restricted application of this rule (Pozgar, 1992). Terminating an employee without cause is also limited by various antidiscrimination laws. Although states vary substantially in applying the at-will rule, additional considerations such as an implied covenant of good faith and fair treatment are increasingly entering into court decisions pertaining to the employment-at-will doctrine (Pozgar, 1992).

## Equal Employment Opportunity

Title VII of the Civil Rights Act of 1964 prohibits discrimination on account of race, color, religion, sex, or national origin in any term, condition, or privilege of employment. The Civil Rights Act of 1991 provided for increased financial damages against organizations found guilty of discriminatory practices. The Equal Employment Opportunity Commission (EEOC) has the authority to enforce the various antidiscrimination laws discussed in this section and to conduct investigations when complaints of discrimination are brought before this agency.

## Pregnancy Discrimination

The Pregnancy Discrimination Act of 1978 came about as an amendment to Title VII of the Civil Rights Act of 1964. The law describes pregnancy as a disability and requires that management consider an employee's pregnancy as any other medical condition would be considered. Accordingly, it makes it illegal to deny sick leave or family medical leave for a pregnancy-related condition. The law also prohibits discrimination against pregnant women in hiring, promotion, or termination, provided that they are able to perform the job.

## Age Discrimination

The Age Discrimination in Employment Act (ADEA) was passed in 1967. This act prohibits discrimination in any aspect of employment against persons 40 years and older. The law does not afford protections to people below the age of 40.

## Equal Pay

The Equal Pay Act of 1963 addresses the issue of wage disparities based on gender. Simply stated, the law requires that men and women be given equal pay when both perform equal work in the same establishment. Wages between men and women in the same jobs may differ on the basis of factors such as qualifications, seniority, and job performance, but not on the basis of gender alone. Generally, male and female CNAs or licensed nurses perform similar work and should be paid according to the same wage scale.

## Protecting the Disabled

The Americans with Disabilities Act (ADA) of 1990 protects disabled workers against discrimination. The law does not cover independent contractors providing services to the nursing home or its patients. The law defines a *disabled employee* as one who has a physical or mental impairment that substantially limits one or more major life activities, who has a record of such impairment, or who is regarded as having such impairment. A variety of conditions can be classified as disabilities, including hearing loss, emotional illness, heart disease, cancer, and acquired immune deficiency syndrome (AIDS). The ADA Amendments Act of 2008 requires a broad interpretation of the term *disability* to include impairments that substantially limit a major life activity.

The ADA requires employers to make reasonable accommodation for disabled persons unless such accommodation presents undue hardship. ***Reasonable accommodation*** includes altering facilities and the work environment, job restructuring so that the disabled employee is able to perform the essential functions of the job, and altering or eliminating nonessential aspects of a job. In some situations, it does not matter whether or not the facility's job description calls a function an essential function of the job duties. For example, the job description may state that lifting patients is an essential requirement of an RN's job duties. Under the ADA, however, lifting patients will not be considered an essential function if RNs spend just a few minutes per day repositioning or lifting patients.

Generally, the employee has to request the accommodation unless the disability is obvious. An oral request is considered sufficient. The employer can ask for supporting medical information related to the disability.

## Alcohol or Drug Abuse

The ADA protects current and past alcoholics. For example, ADA requires an employer to accommodate a qualified applicant or employee with past or present substantial limitations relating to alcoholism if this person can competently perform his job and can comply with uniformly applied employer conduct rules that prohibit employees from drinking alcohol at work or being under the influence of alcohol at work. On the other hand, application of the law in the case of misconduct is not clear. For example, is disciplinary action warranted when an alcoholic employee misses work because of a hangover or because of still being drunk from the night before? Circuit courts have not uniformly approached the issue of alcohol-related employee mis-

conduct (Riddle & Bales, 2008). As for testing, an employer may not administer an alcohol test at the time of offering a job. Once employment begins, an alcohol test may be given, but only if the employer has a reasonable belief based on objective evidence that an employee has been drinking on the job or is under the influence of alcohol, may be otherwise unable to perform the essential functions of the job, or may pose a direct threat to safety based on his or her alcoholism.

The law protects past drug abusers, but not those who currently use illegal drugs. Someone who currently engages in the illegal use of drugs is not an individual with a disability. Accordingly, he may be denied employment, disciplined, or fired on the basis of the current illegal use of drugs. The ADA does not prevent employers from testing applicants or employees for current illegal drug use or from making employment decisions based on verifiable results. However, someone who is not currently engaging in the illegal use of drugs but who has a history of past drug addiction is an individual with a disability if the past drug addiction substantially limits a major life activity. If, following a leave of absence for treatment due to drug addiction, an employee is medically cleared for return to work provided she or he continues to attend a support program regularly, the employer may, for a reasonable period of time, require periodic drug testing, verification from the employee that she or he is regularly participating in such a program, or other reasonable assurances that she or he is no longer engaging in the illegal use of drugs.

## Family and Medical Leave

The Family and Medical Leave Act (FMLA) of 1993 allows employees 12 weeks of unpaid leave in a 12-month period for qualified reasons. Qualified reasons include birth of a child, care of a child up to 12 months of age, adoption or foster care for a child, care of a spouse or care of a parent with a serious health condition, or the employee's own serious health condition that prevents the employee from performing the essential functions of the job. To be eligible, the employee must have completed at least one year of employment and worked for the employer for at least 1,250 hours. The law requires that after this unpaid leave, the employee be allowed to return to his or her original position or an equivalent position with the same terms of pay, benefits, and working conditions that the employee had before taking FMLA leave.

## Harassment

In a general sense, harassment at work occurs in the context of what is termed a hostile environment. A *hostile environment* is work environment in which behaviors of managers or coworkers create severe stress that interferes with an individual's ability to perform his or her job. In principle, unlawful harassment was protected under the Civil Rights Act of 1964, although that law specifically focused on discrimination. The Civil Rights Act of 1991 amended Title VII of the Civil Rights Act of 1964 to specifically include unlawful harassment on the basis of sex, religion, national origin, race, and disability (Sherman et al., 1998). It must be emphasized that even though sexual harassment has received a lot of attention, harassment may also take other forms. In determining harassment, it may sometimes be difficult to decide what may or may not be hostile or offensive. Employee complaints may be one clue to whether something is offensive. Note that harassment may not necessarily come from supervisors. An employee may be harassed by coworkers, visitors, salespeople, or clients. Questions that are likely to arise in any litigation over harassment may include whether management knew about the problem (or should have known about it) and if anything was done to stop it.

---

## For Further Thought

1. Many experts believe that implementing SMWTs in nursing homes is not easy. What do you think may be some necessary elements for implementing SMWTs? What main problems might a nursing home administrator encounter when implementing SMWTs?

2. The proposed Employee Free Choice Act attempted to do away with secret ballot union elections. What is your opinion about it? Should such a legislation be passed or not?

---

## For Further Learning

The Equal Employment Opportunity Commission (EEOC)
http://www.eeoc.gov/

The National Human Resources Association (NHRA) is a network of local affiliates focused on advancing the development of human resource professionals.

www.humanresources.org

The National Labor Relations Board (NLRB)

http://www.nlrb.gov/

## REFERENCES

Banaszak-Holl, J., & Himes, M.A. 1996. Factors associated with nursing home staff turnover. *The Gerontologist* 36, no. 4: 512–517.

Bishop, C.E., et al. 2008. Nursing assistants' job commitment: Effect of nursing home organizational factors and impact on resident well-being. *The Gerontologist* 48, special issue 1: 36–45.

Bolton, T. 1997. *Human Resource Management: An Introduction.* Malden, MA: Blackwell Publishers.

Boone, L.E., & Kurtz, D.L. 1984. *Principles of Management,* 2nd ed. New York: Random House.

Bounds, G.M., & Woods, J.A. 1998. *Supervision.* Cincinnati, OH: South-Western College Publishing.

Brannon, D., et al. 2002. An exploration of job, organizational, and environmental factors associated with high and low nursing assistant turnover. *The Gerontologist* 42, no. 2: 159–168.

Buddy system can lower turnover, raise morale. 2002. *Staff Leader: Supervision Strategies* 15, no. 9: 1, 11.

Caruth, D.L., & Handlogten, G.D. 1997. *Staffing the Contemporary Organization: A Guide to Planning, Recruiting, and Selecting for Human Resource Professionals,* 2nd ed. Westport, CT: Quorum Books.

Castle, N.G. 2007. Assessing job satisfaction of nurse aides in nursing homes. *Journal of Gerontological Nursing* 33, no. 5: 41–47.

Castle, N.G., et al. 2006. Determinants of staff job satisfaction of caregivers in two nursing homes in Pennsylvania. *BMC Health Services Research* 6, p. 60.

Castle, N.G., & Engberg, J. 2008. Further examination of the influence of caregiver staffing levels on nursing home quality. *The Gerontologist* 48, no. 4: 464–476.

Cohen-Mansfield, J., & Rosenthal, A.S. 1989. Absenteeism of nursing staff in a nursing home. *International Journal of Nursing Studies* 26, no. 2: 187–194.

Cready, C.M., et al. 2008. CAN empowerment: Effects on job performance and work attitudes. *Journal of Gerontological Nursing* 34, no. 3: 26–35.

De Cenzo, D.A., & Robbins, S.P. 1996. *Human Resource Management,* 5th ed. New York: John Wiley & Sons.

Fries, B.E., et al. 1994. Refining a case-mix measure for nursing homes: Resource utilization groups (RUGs-III). *Medical Care* 32, no. 7: 668–685.

Griffith, J.R. 1995. *The Well-Managed Health Care Organization,* 3rd ed. Ann Arbor, MI: AUPHA Press/Health Administration Press.

Hernández-Medina, E., et al. 2006. *Training Programs for Certified Nursing Assistants.* Washington, DC: AARP Public Policy Institute.

Hoffman, R. 2001. Lessons learned in creating a successful CNA retention program: One organization's solution to the problem of turnover. *Nursing Homes Long Term Care Management* 50, no. 4: 26–29.

IOM. 2001. *Improving the Quality of Long-Term Care,* eds. G.S. Wunderlich and P.O. Kohler. Washington, DC: National Academy Press, Institute of Medicine.

Lescoe-Long, M. 2000. Why they leave. *Nursing Homes Long Term Care Management* 49, no. 10: 70–74.

McCabe, D.M. 1988. *Corporate Nonunion Complaint Procedures and Systems.* New York: Praeger Publishers.

Mondy, R.W., & Noe, R.M. 1993. *Human Resource Management,* 5th ed. Boston: Allyn and Bacon.

Pozgar, G.D. 1992. *Long-Term Care and the Law: A Legal Guide for Health Care Professionals.* Gaithersburg, MD: Aspen Publishers.

Riddle, D., & Bales, R. 2008. Disability claims for alcohol-related misconduct. *St. John's Law Review* 82, no. 2: 699–734.

Sherman, A., et al. 1998. *Managing Human Resources,* 11th ed. Cincinnati, OH: South-Western College Publishing.

Singh, D.A., & Schwab, R.C. 1998. Retention of administrators in nursing homes: What can management do? *The Gerontologist* 38, no. 3: 362–369.

Singh, D.A., & Schwab, R.C. 2000. Predicting turnover and retention in nursing home administrators: Management and policy implications. *The Gerontologist* 40, no. 3: 310–319.

Yeatts, D.E., & Hyten, C. 1998. *High-Performing Self-Managed Work Teams.* Thousand Oaks, CA: Sage Publications.

Yeatts, D.E., & Seward, R.R. 2000. Reducing turnover and improving health care in nursing homes: the potential effects of self-managed work teams. *The Gerontologist* 40, no. 3: 358–363.

Yeatts, D.E., et al. 2004. Self-managed work teams in nursing homes: Implementing and empowering nurse aide teams. *The Gerontologist* 44: 256–261.

# Chapter 17

## Effective Marketing and Public Relations

### What You Will Learn

- Marketing is important for giving a competitive edge to a nursing facility.
- Creation of exchanges based on expected and perceived value is at the heart of marketing.
- Marketing includes certain functional activities. It also incorporates a client-focused attitude that must permeate the entire organization.
- Marketing goals include not only client-oriented exchanges that result in patient admissions to the facility; marketing can also be employed for a variety of other community-based exchange partnerships.
- Depending on the size and nature of the long-term care market, segmentation can help identify the target market from which the nursing facility will draw customers.
- In market targeting, the nursing home administrator decides whether to take a mass-market approach or a segmented approach.
- A statement of position helps management understand how favorably people view the facility in relation to its competitors. Semantic differentiation helps management understand the factors on which people base their perceptions. Repositioning can be undertaken to achieve a desired position.
- The marketing mix provides the tools necessary for positioning a facility in the target market. Product, price, place, and promotion have numerous applications that are specific to long-term care.
- Most nursing facilities can be differentiated in one form or another to create a perception of value. Differentiation is also used for segmentation and niche marketing.

- The preadmission inquiry process is about personal selling but using a social services approach. Associates play a key role in customer relations. An organization's personnel can be regarded as the 5th P of marketing.
- A variety of promotion and public relations tools can be used in nursing home marketing.

## The Importance of Marketing

Marketing has become a central function to distinctively place a facility's offerings before consumers. Marketing is often neglected by nursing home administrators (NHAs), because many NHAs fall victim to what can be called the "word-of-mouth syndrome." Word-of-mouth is actually a powerful communication tool, but without marketing, only a small fraction of its full potential is realized. Through marketing, NHAs can gain clear-cut competitive advantages over those who do not have a marketing function in their organizations.

Because of a fairly widespread misunderstanding of what marketing is, it remains, for many health care facilities, nothing more than a "buzz" word, and some well-intentioned NHAs merely undertake some haphazard steps and call it marketing. This type of random "marketing" efforts are frequently undertaken when new competitors enter the market and an existing nursing facility has an increasing number of empty beds that become more and more difficult to fill. In a state of panic, NHAs may launch an advertising campaign, start renovating the facility, or plan a facility open house. These efforts may produce temporary results, but they often fail to change the long-range outlook.

Marketing is often equated with customer service, advertising, selling, or community relations. These activities are merely some of the action components of marketing, which is much broader in scope. Marketing incorporates a comprehensive strategic conceptualization that calls for developing a plan, carrying out that plan, and taking corrective action as necessary. Marketing must be viewed as an ongoing management strategy, and it must permeate all aspects of a facility's operations. Marketing is not a quick fix for a major census decline. Marketing involves consistent effort.

## Marketing: Its Philosophy and Essence

The American Marketing Association has furnished one of the most widely accepted definitions of marketing: "*Marketing* is the process of planning and executing the conception, pricing, promotion, and distribution of ideas, goods, and services to create exchanges that satisfy individual and organizational goals" (American Marketing Association, 1995). The marketing process—its planning and execution—is undertaken with the goal of creating exchanges between two or more parties in which each party gives something of value to the other party or parties in the exchange. All parties in the exchange perceive benefits from entering into the exchange. It is not a coincidence that marketing is anchored in the open-system philosophy (discussed in Chapter 4).

Although marketing can be applied to any type of exchange, creating an exchange between a business and its customers is often the main focus of marketing. Peter Drucker (1974), a highly regarded management theorist, stated that the purpose of any business is to create customers and that the customers eventually determine what a business is, what it produces, and whether it will prosper. At first thought it may appear as if all customers of nursing home services are looking for the same product, but that is not the case.

## Value Perceptions

Successful marketing strategies are anchored in the basic philosophy of delivering value to the customer. The term *value* signifies the worth that is perceived by each party in an exchange. However, value is individual specific. Each individual tries to determine how his or her needs can be adequately met at the least cost. For example, wide variations exist in how different customers evaluate value when shopping for an automobile. For some consumers, a Mercedes or a Lexus is the best value; for others it may be a Ford Taurus. Some look for value in a brand-new vehicle, whereas others look for the same in a pre-owned car. Similarly, nursing home shoppers determine value by evaluating a number of variables, and not everyone is looking for the same thing. For example, perceived value can vary according to a facility's size, layout, décor, amenities, location, reputation, ownership status (whether the facility is for-profit or nonprofit), and price. Unless the consumer is private pay, price mainly refers to whether the services would be covered under Medicare, Medicaid, or private long-term care insurance.

## Influencing Value Perception

An exchange is likely to occur when the client's expectations and perceptions of value are matched by what the nursing facility has to offer (Figure 17–1). As a first step in marketing, the NHA must understand how value is generally perceived by the community and how the facility and its services may be packaged to project that value. Drucker (1974) stated that the customer, not the business, determines what value is. However, because the perception of value is not something tangible, it can be shaped by information and education. This is where marketing comes in.

Customers do not always know how they should evaluate health care services, and many things are not obvious to people when they first visit a facility. Helping potential clients overcome information barriers adds value. At a very fundamental level, the client should be able to understand how the facility's services would be tailored to address the patient's clinical and social needs, what different options are available to pay for the services, which option might be best, etc. Hence, marketing permeates the entire process after a potential client contacts the facility to inquire about its services.

## Value Creation

Marketing is not just confined to information and influencing people's perception of value. Marketing has much to do with the creation, promotion, and delivery of value demanded by the customer. Following the open-system concept, effective marketers study changes taking place over time in the characteristics, realities, needs, and beliefs of customers. Social and cultural change often redefines expectations and needs. Clients' expectations for long-term care are evolving

**Figure 17–1** Marketing Principles Resulting in Value-based Exchanges

toward more independence, greater control over lifestyle, and living arrangements that are less institutional for the patient. The next generation of well-educated, health-conscious, and financially well-off nursing home consumers will demand emphasis on health promotion, improved amenities and comfort, and having a voice in the facility's operation. Astute NHAs will create value through innovative solutions in nursing home design, furnishing, and service delivery. Successful NHAs of the future will anticipate and respond to change. A facility's complacency in recognizing the forces shaping value creation will risk inviting competitors to enter the market with innovative ideas, and these competitors could snatch away clients. In Drucker's (1974) words, "The aim of marketing is to know and understand the customer so well that the product or service fits him and sells itself" (p. 64). Hence, marketing permeates the very essence of effective management.

## The Marketing Function and Its Goals

Marketing practices embrace two interrelated principles: (1) marketing is a function that incorporates a set of marketing activities, and (2) marketing is an attitude that must permeate the entire organization (Majaro, 1993).

## Functional Activities

As a function, marketing is a continuous management process, which remains dynamic. First and foremost, marketing includes all activities that are necessary for understanding customer wants and needs and for aligning existing services or creating new services to meet those wants and needs. Secondly, marketing activities include effective pricing, communication, and distribution to inform, motivate, and service the markets. Both are "carefully formulated programs, not just random actions" (Kotler & Clarke, 1987, pp. 5–6).

## Organizational Attitudes and Orientation

Marketing is also a client-focused attitude that must permeate the entire organization. Although marketing is much more than making a sale, an old business axiom fittingly illustrates the organization-wide attitude that is necessary for marketing, "The sales department isn't the whole company, but the whole company had better be the sales department" (Czinkota et al., 2000). As discussed in previous chapters, positive leadership and human resource practices are essential for building an organizational culture in which all associates behave according to the values and philosophies desired by the organization's management.

Organizational values provide the underpinnings that define and direct a nursing facility's orientation and thrust. For instance, Majaro (1993) emphasized "customer orientation" as an organizational value above "profit orientation." Customer orientation requires all personnel to focus their activities and behaviors on satisfying the needs and wants of patients, family members, and vis-itors. In essence, customer orientation is a proactive style. Customer orientation is primarily centered on a solution-oriented approach that understands the problems customers now face; it also anticipates new issues and concerns that may emerge. Customer orientation presupposes that a primary focus on profits is unwarranted, because by making customer satisfaction its primary mission, a facility can achieve higher profits than by placing its primary focus on profits. The misplaced emphasis on profits helps explain why many nursing facilities are caught in a downward spiral of losing patients, which inevitably translates into lower profitability.

## Marketing Goals

According to a well-known marketing theorist, Philip Kotler (1991), "Marketing consists of actions undertaken to elicit desired responses to some object from a target audience" (p. 7). The marketing actions referred to in this definition are associated with the functional aspect mentioned earlier, in which the focus of marketing is on carrying out carefully formulated programs. Kotler's definition also highlights the goal, or "end result," that marketing is designed to achieve.

The desired response from a target audience is the consummation of an exchange based on the value expected and perceived by the target audience (Figure 17–1). An exchange results after the nursing facility has successfully communicated value that the client is seeking. Successful communication will lead the client to perceive that the expected value will be realized. The exchange continues, however, only when the delivered value equals the value that was communicated to the client.

As pointed out in Chapter 4, effective administrators manage a full cycle of exchanges in four areas:

- Obtaining critical resources from the external environment.
- Attracting clients whose needs would be met by the facility's services.
- Effective use of resources to adequately meet client needs in terms of quality and satisfaction.
- Returns to the environment in the form of jobs, taxes (by for-profit entities), competition, and community health.

The goal of marketing is to facilitate these exchanges. For example, besides attracting patients, marketing exchanges would also result in successfully recruiting qualified associates; obtaining finances at attractive terms for a new construction project; preserving the facility's licensure, certification, and accreditation status; attaining higher levels of clinical quality, staff satisfaction, and profits; and achieving goodwill in the community. Thus, marketing has much broader goals than simply admitting more patients to the facility. Marketing can also be employed for creating a variety of other community-based exchange partnerships (see Chapter 4).

Most marketing activities are designed to address issues of market competition. Other marketing activities are intended to elicit decisions from family members and other parties to bring patients to a nursing facility. The rest of this chapter focuses on this goal.

# Marketing Strategy

Successful marketing requires a core strategy, which is a comprehensive game plan. Simply put, a marketing strategy outlines where and how the nursing facility will compete in the marketplace (Bovée et al., 1995), which requires spotlighting the target customers. How well the nursing facility will compete depends on how well the facility positions itself in the target market by using an appropriate marketing mix. Figure 17–2 illustrates the steps necessary for developing a marketing strategy.

## Segmentation and the Target Market

The long-term care market is very diverse, because it includes various community-based services and a continuum of institutional settings (see Chapter1). Therefore, identifying and selecting appropriate target markets becomes a necessary strategic step for a facility. To an extent, community-based and institution-based services represent natural segments in the long-term care market, but these broad markets should be further segmented. For example, the skilled nursing facility market can be segmented into Medicaid, Medicare, and private pay. Specialized services, such as Alzheimer's care or intensive rehabilitation, also represent distinct market segments.

## Purpose of Segmentation

Value perceptions vary greatly among those who seek nursing home placement. Hence, in nursing home marketing, a large heterogeneous market should be divided into smaller, more homogeneous segments of customers and potential customers. This process of dividing a large market into smaller segments, each with its distinct characteristics, is called *market segmentation*. The purpose of segmentation is to identify distinct market segments of which one or more will constitute the *target market*, which is that part of the

**Figure 17–2** Steps in Developing a Marketing Strategy

overall market from which the nursing facility will attract customers. One of the main goals of targeting a small number of market segments is to better understand the needs and desires of customers and to better match the facility's package of services to meet those needs. This goal is easier to accomplish in a client group that is more or less homogeneous than it is to achieve in a diverse group. Once the requirements of the target market are clearly defined, the nursing facility gains the advantage of creating or redesigning services most appropriate for those patients. The more

closely a nursing facility can match its services to the value clients are seeking, the more successfully it can market its services and attract patients.

## Segmenting by Demographics, Needs, and Preferences

In spite of their degree of functional impairment, most people do not desire to receive care in a nursing home. People go to nursing homes because they need to, not because they choose to do so. Segmentation is achieved by differentiating the needs and preferences of customers. The nursing home market should be segmented first by demographics, then by clinical needs, and again by client preferences (Exhibit 17–1). For instance, pediatric and geriatric care cannot be mixed unless the facility has distinct areas for such services. Institution-based services have some natural segmentation according to care levels, such as retirement living, assisted living, skilled nursing, and subacute care. Although most nursing homes are confined to delivering skilled nursing care, many have captured other segments of the market by adding assisted living, retirement living, or other services along the continuum of care. Continuing care retirement communities (CCRCs) cover the entire continuum, yet they segment the market on the basis of whether patients have the means to pay an entry fee and whether patients desire to receive continuing care as their health declines. Thus, pay type—whether it is private pay, Medicaid, and Medicare—is another criterion for segmenting the market. Within the private-pay market itself, some subsegments are based on clients' sensitivity to price. Some clients are looking for high-end services and amenities for which they are willing to pay more, whereas other clients are content with more basic services at a cheaper price. The main categories of long-term care clients discussed in Chapter 1—such as older adults, young disabled adults, and people with AIDS—also constitute market segments. Specialized niches for services such as head trauma care, ventilator care, active

**Exhibit 17–1** Market Segments Based on Demographics, Needs, and Preferences

**Demographics**
Pediatrics
Older adults
Young disabled
Women only
Pay source: personal funds, private insurance, Medicare, Medicaid

**Clinical Needs**
Short-term rehabilitation
Skilled nursing care
Independent retirement living
Assisted living
Alzheimer's care
Wound care
Head trauma care
Ventilator care

AIDS care
Adult day care

**Client Preferences**
Facility close to home
Menu selection
High skill mix of staff
High-end private pay
Low-end private pay
Private room
Nonregimented personal routines
Décor and furnishings
Transportation services
Safety
Amenities
Desire for continuing care

rehabilitation, and Alzheimer's care also present an approach to segmenting the market. Clearly, a nursing facility administrator should decide which particular segment(s) of the market the organization can most adequately serve.

## Selecting Market Segments

Choice of market segments should not be driven by what the nursing home thinks it would like to have as its target market. Rather, the facility's choice should be based on a careful evaluation of the needs and desires of the target market and on the extent to which the facility possesses the physical structures, equipment, staff competencies, and other resources to address the needs and desires of potential clients. Apart from a facility's strengths and competencies in providing services, market segments can be identified in areas in which unmet needs exist or in areas in which the competitors may be weak. For example, if the target market is large enough for an upscale facility in which clients would receive pampered treatment, such as private rooms, individual telephones and flat-screen television sets, and restaurant-style table service in a plush dining room, such an operation can fill unmet demand.

To be useful, market segments must be evaluated according to four criteria (Kotler, 2000). Each segment must be:

1. *Measurable.* The size and other characteristics of the segments, such as ability to pay and client preferences, must be measurable. In other words, there must be some way to assess the number of potential clients in the segment.

2. *Sizable.* A segment should be the largest possible homogeneous group worth going after with a tailored marketing program. For example, in a community with a population of 20,000, segmenting the nursing home market will make sense only if there is a sizable number of clients who may need a particular type of service. Otherwise, segmenting the market will not be appropriate because it will simply result in several small segments.

3. *Accessible.* The facility must be able to effectively reach and serve the market. Because accessibility is governed mainly by the facility's location, the facility should evaluate the needs of its surrounding community. It should also assess how far people may be willing to travel to receive certain services not offered by competitors and whether clients will travel to the facility's particular location to get those services. For example, people may travel some distance to get specialized services. On the other hand, clients may not want to travel to a facility located in a working-class neighborhood if they are looking for high-end private-pay services.

4. *Differentiable.* The segments should be differentiable according to client needs and preferences. For example, the Green House concept discussed in Chapter 8 is highly differentiated from traditional nursing homes. But differentiation can be achieved in a number of different ways, as discussed later in this chapter.

## Market Targeting

Market targeting follows segmentation in implementing a marketing strategy. Market segmentation does not imply that the facility must target only one segment. How many segments and which particular segments to target will depend on (1) the segment's overall attractiveness, such as its size, growth potential, and profitability, and (2) the organization's objectives and resources in terms of its mission and competencies (Kotler, 2000). In most instances, a nursing facility can pursue three types of targeting strategies:

- Single-offer, mass-market coverage.
- Single-segment concentration.
- Selective specialization.

## Single-Offer, Mass-Market Coverage

Most nursing homes go for a single-offer, mass-market coverage, in which market segments are ignored. These facilities offer standard skilled nursing care, and they try to attract anyone in order to increase the occupancy. As illustrated in Figure 17–3A, one generic product is designed to suit everyone's needs, and little room is given to accommodating client preferences. Such a strategy may work well in communities where the segments are indistinguishable or the size of different segments is too small to undertake a segmentation approach that would be profitable. In most urban and suburban markets, however, a mass market approach may not produce the results an organization desires.

## Single-Segment Concentration

Single-segment concentration (Figure 17–3B) is a targeting strategy in which the facility produces one specialized offering for a single segment. Examples of this strategy include a specialized rehabilitation facility, a facility specializing in head trauma and ventilator care, or a facility catering to high-end

private-pay clients. Such a strategy can pose high risks, particularly if a facility launches into specialized offerings on the basis of hunches and assumptions rather than on a thorough research of the market. As an alternative, a facility can produce one specialized offering for different segments. For example, the same clinical level of services can be designed to attract private-pay, Medicare, and Medicaid clients.

## Selective Specialization

Depending on a facility's size, layout, location, and resources, a selective specialization approach may be the most desirable. In this strategy, a facility produces specialized offerings tailored to the needs and desires of different market segments (Figure 17–3C). As an example, the same nursing facility can offer high-end décor and amenities for wealthy private-pay clients in one section of the facility, short-stay rehabilitation and post-acute services in a separate Medicare section, and Alzheimer's care in a distinct specialized unit.

## Positioning

Every facility holds a certain position in the marketplace. Potential customers and key stakeholders form mental images and perceptions of the nursing facilities that they are familiar with, have seen advertised, or have heard about in a media report or from friends and neighbors. People use such perceptions to rank a particular facility and its services in relation to the other facilities in the community. People rank a facility in terms of how favorably they view a given facility.

*Positioning* refers to staking out a position in the target market (Bovée et al., 1995). Kotler and Andreasen (1996) define positioning as "the act of designing the organiza-

**Figure 17–3** Marketing Targeting Patterns

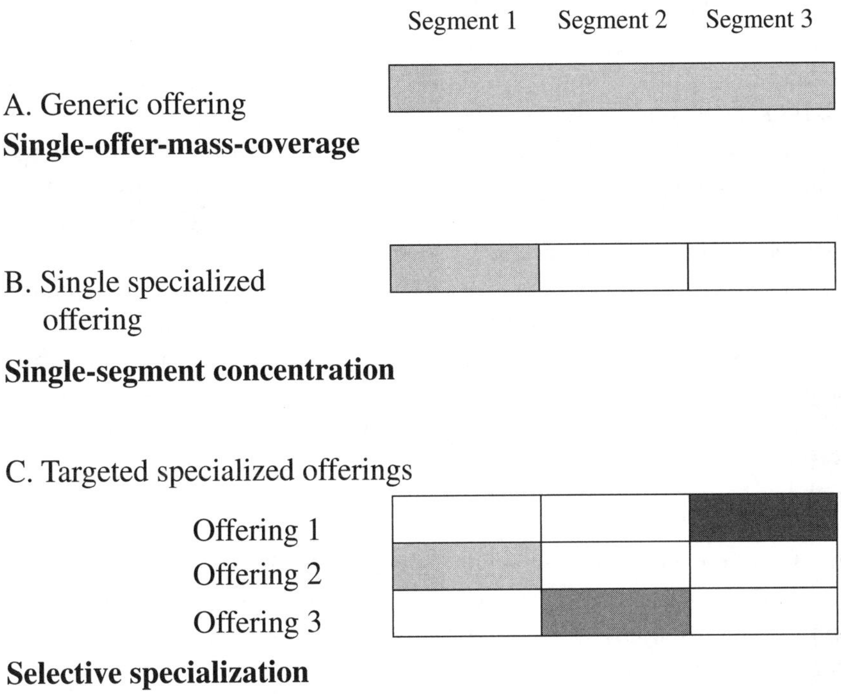

A. Generic offering
**Single-offer-mass-coverage**

B. Single specialized
offering

**Single-segment concentration**

C. Targeted specialized offerings
Offering 1
Offering 2
Offering 3

**Selective specialization**

tion's image and value offer so that the organization's customers understand and appreciate what the organization stands for in relation to its competitors" (p. 191). Positioning starts with a product, such as a nursing home and its services. But positioning is not what is done to the product. Positioning is what a marketer does to the mind of the prospective client. The product is positioned in the mind of the prospective client (Kotler, 2000).

The NHA should find out how the facility is positioned, what people think of it and its services, and what type of reputation the facility has in the community. Two important questions need to be asked:

1. To what extent do people in the target market recognize the facility?

2. How favorably do people feel toward the facility?

Obtaining more detailed information about how people may have arrived at forming a particular image of a nursing facility is often necessary. Such detailed information can be collected using techniques such as *semantic differential* (Kotler & Andreasen, 1996). In this technique, market researchers select a relatively small set of dimensions that are important to people. The dimensions may include items such as quality of care, reputation, friendliness of the staff, comfort, and décor. Potential clients are asked to rate the facility and its competitors on each of these dimensions. The results show a facility's rank on each of the dimensions in relation to its competitors. A facility's position is particularly useful within the context of its target market, because this position shows what potential clients think. Management can then decide whether the facility is appropriately positioned. If the facility is not desirably positioned, semantic differential can help management focus its efforts on improving its areas of weakness.

Market repositioning becomes necessary when a change in the existing position is desired. Before a facility can be effectively positioned, the NHA should put down in writing a "statement of position" and a "positioning statement" (Luther, 2001). The *statement of position* specifies how the facility is currently positioned. The *positioning statement* highlights how the facility should be repositioned. The size of the gap between the current and desired positions will dictate the amount of effort and resources necessary for repositioning the facility. Advertising campaigns, news stories in the local media, open houses and facility tours, exchange relationships with the community, and a marketing mix are some of the means that can be used for achieving the desired position.

## Marketing Mix

The marketing mix provides the tools necessary for positioning a facility in the target market. The four factors of the marketing mix—product, price, place, and promotion (known as the 4 Ps—Figure 17–4)—are well known, but they pose special challenges for implementation in health care marketing. The next section addresses this issue.

## Implementing the Marketing Mix

In health care marketing, the 4 Ps of the marketing mix do not operate in the same manner as they do for a manufactured product that

people can touch, see, try out, and even return if they are not satisfied. The health care product, with the exception of the facilities and amenities, is—for the most part—intangible. The primary clients, the people who make the buying decision and evaluate value, are often not the patients themselves, but their surrogates (such as family members). Services are produced only when customers are there to receive them, and care delivered to the patients goes mostly unobserved by these primary clients. The product's most desired features, such as quality, are not simple to objectively define and evaluate. Pricing is often beyond the facility's control, because the facility relies heavily on third-party reimbursement. Place is generally fixed in terms of where the facility is located, its size, and its layout. Promotion presents challenges, because the product is difficult to showcase.

## Product

The long-term care *product* is a package of some tangible but mostly intangible elements. The socio-residential structures of the internal environment, discussed in Chapter 8, comprise the main tangible component. People can see and feel the living environment. Clients can also taste the food being served; notice the building's cleanliness; smell odors; and, to some extent, observe staff members' attitudes and efficiency. Family members who regularly visit the facility can also observe the patient's personal hygiene and some of the services being provided for the patient. However, a lot more goes unobserved, because clients cannot be in the facility all the time. By extrapolating from what they can observe and feel, clients formulate judgments about the care elements that they do not see.

Bovée and colleagues (1995) described the product component of the marketing mix as a "bundle of value" that meets expectations

**Figure 17–4** The Marketing Mix

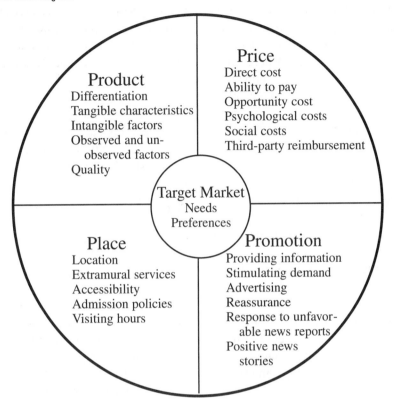

of customers in the target market. The worth of a product is measured in terms of the benefits it delivers. Through the NHA's efforts in leading, coaching, training, and coordinating, the various departments of a facility can work together to deliver what customers want in quality, timeliness of service, and responsiveness to their needs. Differentiating the product, which is discussed later, is another strategy for creating value and positioning the facility in the target market.

## Price

*Price* refers to the cost a consumer bears in exchange for the product or service. Generally, price signifies a direct cost to the customer. In health care, however, third-party financing and reimbursement insulates the customer from the price of services. As pointed out in Chapter 7, the two major payers for nursing home services, Medicaid and Medicare, determine how much they will pay. Therefore, for the most part, the NHA has little control over pricing. Although the consumer bears some out-of-pocket costs to cover deductibles and copayments, these costs are the same regardless of which nursing home the customer chooses. Hence, pricing as a marketing strategy becomes inconsequential in many instances.

Pricing strategies are pertinent in some market segments, such as private pay, and also in managed care and Veterans Administration (VA) contracting (see Chapter 7). Pricing decisions in these market segments are based on such factors as buyers' willingness and ability to pay, the facility's production costs, and market competition. In the private-pay market, high prices are sometimes used to create a top-of-the-line image, whereas low prices can be used to undercut the competition (Bovée et al., 1995). In contracting with managed care and the VA, pricing can be tricky because contracts are generally awarded to the lowest bidder in closed-bid contests. A low cost of production relative to its competitors can enable a facility to offer a price that can win a contract. Sometimes, especially in managed care contracting when open negotiation rather than closed bidding is used, the NHA has more flexibility in pricing.

There are many reasons patients are admitted to facilities in which the building and furnishings may not be upscale, even though these patients are covered under third-party reimbursement, which actually entitles them to go to any certified nursing home of their choice. One common reason for admission to facilities that are not upscale is the unavailability of beds at upscale facilities when the patient needs to be admitted. However, customers also assess three main types of indirect costs that they weigh against the benefits in determining the value of the product they consider purchasing:

1. Family members face the opportunity cost of time required in traveling to the facility for regular visits.

2. Psychological costs are attributed to feelings of anxiety and guilt family members may have.

3. Clients also incur social costs from the embarrassment of placing a loved one in a facility with a poor reputation.

Although travel time is a function of the facility's location in relation to where the family members live, the facility can take steps in helping people overcome their anxiety and guilt through social service counseling, regular communication, and family support groups. The facility should market to the community and to prospective and current clients any such formal programs it may have available. When a facility is spartan in appearance, other features such as friendliness of staff members, security, and other quality of life elements should be emphasized.

## Place

*Place* is where services can be purchased, that is, the facility's physical location (Majaro, 1993). Choosing the site for building a new facility is a strategic decision, but location also deserves close study when acquiring an existing facility to enter a new market. Another situation in which location is a critical factor is when deciding whether to add more beds to an existing building or to open a new facility at a different location. The cost of capital is often the driving consideration in such decisions because expanding an existing facility is cheaper than building a new one. But even in growing markets, facilities can face low census growth after adding new beds when the critical factor of location has not been adequately studied. The trend in recent years has been to locate nursing facilities near growing suburban populations, whereas in the past, facilities were often located close to hospitals to maintain ongoing contact with hospital discharge planners, facilitate transfer of patients, and make it convenient for doctors to visit their patients in the nursing home after they had finished making rounds in the hospital.

Although location is the most obvious factor when one thinks of place, in marketing strategy place also refers to the *channels of distribution*, the mechanisms used for bringing products and customers together to create an exchange. For example, a long-term care facility may offer noninstitutional services, such as home health care, hospice services, and Meals On Wheels; these services are taken to wherever the patients reside, regardless of where the facility itself is located.

Place also refers to physical access. For example, easy accessibility and clearly marked signs on adjacent access roads make it easy to find the facility. An adequate number of parking spaces as close as possible to the facility should be reserved for clients. Well-manicured landscaping, well-maintained lawns, flower beds, and adequate lighting draw attention and create a welcoming appeal. Access also refers to the times when a patient can be admitted to the facility. For example, is the facility ready to admit patients in the evenings and on weekends? What does the facility do when a patient needs to be admitted, but no beds are available? The nursing home should develop relationships with hospitals and other long-term care facilities and have policies that facilitate patient admission at all hours. When a facility is full, it can temporarily place the patient in another facility and work out a smooth transfer when appropriate accommodations become available.

In long-term care, place also includes regular contact between the patient and family. Many facilities have unrestricted visiting hours.

## Promotion

Majaro (1993) defines *promotion* as "the communication system that creates awareness of the product, its features and benefits, and its location of purchase, and also reassures the customer after the purchase has taken place" (p. 22). Promotion can also be defined as a controlled and integrated program that uses communication methods to effectively present an organization and its services to prospective customers and presents need-satisfying attributes to facilitate sales (Engel et al., 1994). Bovée and colleagues (1995) pointed to several objectives to be achieved through promotion:

1. *Providing information.* Information creates awareness, but it also educates and explains how a facility's unique array of services can address problems that potential customers may be facing.

2. *Stimulating demand.* The ultimate goal of all promotion is to influence behavior. Promotion should instill a desire in potential customers to lead them to a purchasing decision when the time comes for placing a patient in a nursing facility.

3. *Differentiating products.* Many nursing homes are alike. A strong promotional program is often what sets these facilities apart. On the other hand, a facility may have differentiated products such as rehabilitation, special dining features, or outdoor events, which can be effectively used for market positioning.

4. *Reminding current customers.* Even existing customers need to be reminded of the facility's benefits in order to prevent them from switching to a different facility. Also, once a patient has been admitted to the facility, family members need reinforcement in thinking that they made the right choice.

5. *Countering competitors.* Without engaging in "name calling" or naming its competitors, a facility can effectively counter promotional campaigns of its competitors.

6. *Responding to negative news.* On occasion, even the best nursing homes are likely to become victims of negative publicity focusing on an unforeseen event—or even something that could have been prevented. In such circumstances, not saying anything can be perceived as admission of guilt and create negative public opinion.

7. *Building image.* Positive news stories of events can be powerful elements in building a facility's image.

Promotion should be driven by the three other Ps discussed in the previous sections. For example, to emphasize its rehabilitation services a facility may provide factual information on how many days an average patient stays in the facility for active rehabilitation before being discharged home. To emphasize value, a facility may highlight how affordable an attractive and comfortable environment can be. Promotion and advertising must clearly emphasize how to get to the facility, as well as how to contact the facility by telephone and by the Internet. Promotional strategy and tools are discussed later in this chapter.

# Competitive Differentiation

Most nursing facilities do not have a sustained marketing program, and those that do often engage in undifferentiated marketing. Also called "mass marketing," ***undifferentiated marketing*** purposefully ignores market segmentation and targets the aggregate market using the same marketing mix for the entire market. Mass marketing takes a generic approach by marketing a uniform package of services to the entire market, using the same product to try and appeal to all prospective clients. Because only one product is promoted, without differentiation, marketing costs are minimized. However, this undifferentiated strategy leaves the facility vulnerable to competitors that can differentiate their products. The stereotypical image of nursing homes is pervasive because most facilities do not differentiate their product offerings from those of their competitors. Marketers refer to this phenomenon as the "me-too" syndrome when nursing facilities operating in the same market provide commonplace services (O'Malley, 2001). In a market in which most other nursing homes are me-too, a facility can gain competitive advantage by distinguishing itself from its competitors. Kotler (1991) asserted that every product and every service, no matter how commonplace, can be differentiated. Innovative architectural designs and methods of service delivery discussed in Chapter 8 are clear examples of how some nursing homes are differentiating their product offering.

## Differentiation Strategy

Differentiation is a competitive strategy in which a facility creates distinctive features that allow customers to distinguish the facility's offer from that of its competitors. Product differentiation can be used effectively for positioning a facility in the target market.

When carefully designed and promoted, distinctive features can create the perception of extra value. For example, two nursing facilities may be similar in their quality of clinical care, but one facility may be able to differentiate itself from the other by offering a selective menu, a restaurant-style dining experience, family-style dining, or a brunch buffet. Other facilities achieve differentiation by offering an array of support services for family members. In fact, by thinking through their marketing mix, administrators can find numerous opportunities for differentiation; most facilities can be differentiated in one form or another. A facility's affiliation with a hospital or other recognized agency, its layout and atmosphere, its variety of quality-of-life features, its recreation and activity programs, its dietary services, its staff skill-mix, and its staffing levels can all be used for differentiation.

In long-term care marketing, differentiated offerings can be used in three ways, depending on what an organization wants to achieve:

1. Creating unique value.
2. Segmenting the market.
3. Niche marketing.

## Creating Unique Value

As already mentioned, distinguishing the facility from other competitors by offering extra value is one use of this strategy, which may be used without segmenting the market. In this case, the facility tries to attract patients by offering extra value that other facilities do not offer. Hence, segmentation is not always necessary, particularly when the market is not large enough for distinctive segments or when the facility's offerings would appeal to all segments.

## Segmenting the Market

Value can also be added by segmenting the market and creating different products and using a different marketing mix for each cho-sen segment. The main advantage of market segmentation is that it enables facility management to focus on the specific needs of one, two, or more selected market segments. Segmentation, by its very nature, requires differentiation and often provides the logical basis on which to create differentiated offerings.

## Niche Marketing

Some long-term care facilities have used the differentiation strategy to concentrate on a single market segment through a high degree of specialization in a particular service. Examples include Alzheimer's care facilities, rehabilitation facilities, and noncertified upscale facilities that cater to wealthy clients. This type of a concentrated marketing strategy is also called *niche marketing* or niche creation.

---

# Personal Selling

Marketing activities have both an external and a personal orientation. Activities discussed so far are directed at the outside market, which, for the most part, is impersonal. *Personal selling*, called "salesmanship" in marketing literature, requires one-on-one contact with clients. The objective of external marketing is to educate the target audience, build awareness, and position the facility so that when potential customers need its services they will right away think of this facility and will know how to reach it. The buying decision, however, is made only after a personal contact.

The main objective of personal selling is to understand individual needs and offer solutions tailored to meet individual needs. In the process, the facility often learns first-hand how its image is perceived by the clients that it comes in contact with. One of the aims in personal selling is to reinforce a positive image; another aim is to change a negative image with information.

The preadmission inquiry process, discussed in Chapter 9, is about personal selling but using a social services approach. For example, one must be forthright if the facility is not equipped to adequately address what the patient needs. Marketing is, by nature, fundamentally focused on satisfying customer needs and desires. A relentless pursuit to fill vacant beds with little regard for the patient's needs and the facility's ability to serve those needs often turns out to be the wrong approach.

Most customers today have several nursing home choices. It is estimated that a customer visits an average of 3.4 facilities and phones 4.2 facilities before choosing a nursing home. Also, a growing trend involves not just the adult children but also the spouse of a potential patient in the selection process (Macknick, 1998). Hence, preadmission inquiry should be a highly professionalized process. The process is also highly individualized and should be adapted to the patient's and the family's specific circumstances. Making people feel at ease and taking the time to listen is an art. Only genuine empathy and mutual trust will make people comfortable enough to disclose some very personal information, because nursing home placement is often accompanied by a sense of guilt. Private issues—such as the patient's incontinence, dementia, or combativeness—are not generally shared with total strangers, nor is information on personal finances. Hence, some "ice-breaking" conversation is necessary before discussing sensitive issues.

McKenna (1991) explains that the deluge of exaggerations and unsubstantiated claims made by various service providers results in confusing people. Customers need reassurance, particularly when they are buying a piece of the future, as they do in purchasing nursing home services. They are looking for an organization that conveys integrity and has credibility before they will entrust a loved one to that organization. Therefore, the facility should adequately train all intake workers and backup personnel.

The facility tour (see Chapter 9) is used primarily to build credibility. This tour should be designed to give a first-hand look into how the facility would meet the multifaceted needs of a patient. With a somewhat informal and personalized approach, the tour should be used to make a connection between the facility and the prospective patient. Key features and services of the facility should be given particular emphasis. For example, a visit to the physical therapy area where other patients are receiving active treatments can be very reassuring. The potential client is often positively impressed when the intake worker introduces the therapist who takes a few minutes to give simple explanations of the therapeutic procedures the prospective patient is likely to receive. Similarly, other key associates, such as the supervising nurse on the nursing unit, should be introduced to the visitors.

The post-tour concluding interview should highlight the main services that would benefit the patient. Explaining how services are customized for the patient is important, as is explaining how various clinical disciplines interface in a multidisciplinary system. The interview must conclude with what is referred to as "closing the sale." Simply put, closing of a sale is an unobtrusive offer to admit the patient. Macknick (1998) pointed out that an offer to admit the patient is extended in only 2% of the cases when prospects come into the facility for a preadmission inquiry. Closing the sale is an art and requires confidence. A simple statement, such as, "We would be delighted to serve Mrs. Kemple's needs through our excellent staff; when can I call you back?" is all that is required, unless the prospective clients clearly are not interested. The next day, a follow-up telephone call is appropriate.

# Customer Relations

Administrators who manage some of the most elegantly furnished and well-decorated facilities sometimes wonder why they lose patients. These facilities often have customer relations problems. On the other hand, some plain-looking nursing facilities are able to maintain full census while their competitors struggle.

Kotler and Clarke (1987) consider the personnel of an organization as the 5th P of marketing (the other four being product, price, place, and promotion, as discussed earlier). Clients often judge quality and their satisfaction with services by how employees interact with them rather than by the technical quality of services, something that clients generally cannot assess. Customers observe the staff's behaviors and attentiveness to tasks; they evaluate the staff's responsiveness to problems; they notice whether the employees are friendly and cheerful; and they rely on the staff for information on their loved one's condition. When they visit the facility, family members also notice how other patients are treated. Family members use such clues to form opinions about the facility's reliability and dependability because they cannot be at the facility all the time. Negative observations create psychological stress for the potential customers, which dilutes their perception of value.

Following are some suggestions for building better customer relations:

- *Acknowledgement and helpfulness.* Associates should greet and smile when they pass family members and other visitors. The receptionist should acknowledge with a cheerful greeting anyone who enters the facility and inquire how they can be assisted. Kotler and Clarke (1987) point out that the airlines are known to run all flight attendants, sales agents, and other staff members who have customer contact through "smile school." In the hospitality industry, employees are trained in customer relations and client interactions. Nursing facilities must do the same.

- *Empathy and compassion.* Associates should be trained to understand customer needs and feelings and in how to pay individualized attention to clients. True compassion requires associates to "be in the customer's shoes" and imagine what the other person must be going through.

- *Contact and communication.* Regular contact and factual updates on the patient's condition build trust. When family members are informed about how the patient is doing, these family members must also be notified as to what the staff are doing to address the patient's needs. Timely follow-up by associates on questions and concerns raised by family members is critical. Professional staff members should not merely inform, they must also educate clients so that expectations are maintained at a reasonable level without making it sound that staff members are giving excuses. This education should include explanations of why certain expectations may be unreasonable. Expectations should be discussed in the context of the facility's operational policies and procedures and quality standards.

## Promotion and Public Relations Tools

The main objective of a promotion and public relations campaign is to position the nursing facility in the marketplace and to build and maintain a positive image of the facility through effective communication. Promotional efforts are targeted at would-be customers. Public relations or community relations encompass a broader function: they are directed at other key stakeholders and the community at large. Examples of these stakeholders include the facility's associates, community health care agencies, physicians, the local media, legislators and other public officials, and any other agencies the facility considers to be desirable exchange partners. Promotion and public relations work hand-in-hand, and many of the promotional tools can also be used for public relations.

Promotional and public relations goals can be accomplished by using a variety of tools. Developing a uniform strategy, however, is essential in order to communicate the same message through several different media. The NHA should establish a budget for promotional activities and should also allocate resources for activities such as advertising, printing informational materials, and public relations programs. The NHA should also decide which channels of communication will be the most cost effective in achieving the promotional goals. An undertaking is cost effective when the benefits achieved are greater than the costs incurred; a facility's cost effectiveness can be determined by how well the facility does in its efforts to achieve its goals in census development. The facility's

budget and resource allocation may also depend on whether the facility considers that the expertise of a professional marketing firm or a public relations firm is necessary.

## Advertising

*Advertising* includes all forms of paid, non–face-to-face communication with a target audience. Advertising uses an identified sponsor. Media such as newspapers, radio, and television are the primary vehicles of advertising and are considered the most effective vehicles of advertising. But using them is more expensive than using telephone directories, billboards, or the Internet. Advertising incurs investments for which the paybacks are not always known, and advertising's effectiveness can be determined only by how much progress the facility makes toward certain measurable outcomes, such as an increased number of inquiries.

The advertising message needs to be carefully crafted. An ideal message encompasses the AIDA framework: It gets *attention,* holds *interest,* arouses *desire,* and obtains *action.* The problem, of course, is that ascertaining these attributes is difficult without extensive field testing, which is expensive. However, the NHA can use some innovative approaches, such as testing the message using a focus group consisting of family and staff members. Extensively used in marketing research, a *focus group* consists of about 8 to 12 people who participate in an unstructured session with a skilled moderator to discuss their thoughts and feelings about an issue, an organization, or a service.

The advertising message must include a selling line. A *selling line* is a carefully crafted brief message used in advertising to interpret the facility's positioning statement. The selling line should contain the benefits sought by individuals who make the buying decision (Luther, 2001). Yet advertised messages must be free from any misleading statements or claims that may be construed as warranties or promises about clinical outcomes or the quality of care (Becker, 2001). Some basic information must be included in all advertisements and printed on all promotional materials. For example, all advertisements and promotional materials must contain the facility's name, logo, street address, location, telephone number, and Web address.

## Publicity

The term *publicity* refers to nonpaid communication of information about the facility and its services, and it plays an important role in the facility's promotion and public relations strategy. The fact that the facility does not pay for publicity distinguishes publicity from advertising, and it should therefore be used as a primary channel of promotion. Getting free publicity in the local media is not as difficult as it may sound. Opportunities for publicity can be categorized into three main areas:

- Announcements.
- Human interest stories.
- News events.

### Announcements

The media play an important public service informational role, and members of the media are frequently looking for information that would be of interest to the general public. Announcements for programs such as health fairs, health screenings, and educational seminars are accepted without charge by many community newspapers and radio stations.

### Human Interest Stories

Human interest stories and follow-up reports on various events are also of interest to the community. Examples include noteworthy events in the lives of certain residents in the nursing home; substantial fund-raising efforts organized by the facility or carried out in collaboration with other local agencies to support foundations such as the American Heart Association, the Alzheimer's Association, or the Arthritis Foundation; celebration of a landmark anniversary of the facility; or a celebrity's visit to the facility. Brennan (1981) reported on examples of numerous human interest stories published in local newspapers across the country. Some notable stories included residents participating in yoga classes, nursing students training at a local nursing home, a family reunion that included five generations, a resident who served as an altar boy at the local Catholic church, and residents featured in an Easter parade.

### News Events

News events featuring the facility, its staff, or residents should be transmitted to the local media. Examples include the facility's outstanding performance on the certification survey, accreditation by the Joint Commission, appointment of a new administrator, ground breaking for a new facility, or ribbon cutting for a new service.

## Personal Contact

An extremely important part of a facility's promotional strategy is the facility's *personal contacts* with referral agents. *Referral agents* are professionals in the community who are in a position to influence prospective clients about choosing a facility. Regular personal contact with physicians and hospital discharge planners is critical because these professionals are often consulted by families when they place a loved one in a nursing facility. Personal contact is established when the administrator or other key personnel make presentations before community groups, such as the Rotary Club or a women's auxiliary. Personal contact can be effectively combined with disseminating promotional materials such as business cards, facility brochures, or photo albums.

## Promotional Materials

Brochures, business cards, newsletters, photo albums, videos, DVDs, and websites are commonly used as *promotional materials.* The quality and content of these materials must be developed with the aim of accomplishing the facility's positioning goals. For instance, positioning high-end services by using an ordinary black-and-white brochure would be counterproductive. On the other hand, a simple facility located in a rural area and known mainly to its local population need not spend money on developing a costly brochure.

In highly competitive markets, different types of promotional materials are necessary, and each one is designed to serve a different purpose. An administrator who meets a physician in the nursing facility's hallway for the first time will give the physician a business card. An administrator will also hand a business card to the receptionist when making a personal call to a physician's office. Brochures are used in a variety of ways: they are included in the packet of information that is handed to prospective clients during the preadmission inquiry; they are kept in the facility's lobby to be picked up by visitors; they are left with hospital discharge planners to be handed out to prospective clients; and they

can be distributed to the public during events such as health fairs. The facility's newsletter is a vehicle for regular communication with the associates, current residents and their families, and key stakeholders. Photo albums are left with key referral agents such as physicians and hospital discharge planners to use in promoting the facility's services to prospective clients. Video cassettes or DVDs can be used with likely prospects. Especially when the patient or the spouse cannot personally visit the facility, a video or DVD can be very effective in showing the facility's living environment. The video or DVD can also be effectively used during speaking engagements to supplement an oral presentation. Use of websites is now common; Web pages can be designed to create a virtual facility tour, using action photographs that include people engaged in various activities. For privacy reasons, obtain written consent for taking and using photographs of people, and avoid identifying individuals in photographs (Miller & Hutton, 2000).

## Event Promotion

*Event promotion* is accomplished by organizing programs and special events at the facility—programs and events to which the community is invited. This strategy serves two main purposes: (1) it can, depending on the type of event, generate free publicity, often both before and after the event; and (2) it creates promotional opportunities by letting key stakeholders and the public see first-hand what the facility is like. Certain events are targeted at specific stakeholder groups, such as a reception for physicians, which may also include social workers and nurses from surrounding hospitals; a special event for nursing students from area colleges; or an event to honor community volunteers. Other events include wider audiences. An open house in conjunction with the dedication of a new facility or a new addition attracts interested audiences. A facility's landmark anniversaries, such as the 5th and the 10th, present excellent opportunities for special celebrations to which the local community should be invited.

## For Further Thought

1. How would you develop a marketing strategy at the beginning stages of planning a new facility?
2. How would you formulate a marketing strategy for a facility that is experiencing a loss of market share?
3. What information will you include in a promotional brochure for a nursing facility?

## For Further Learning

American Marketing Association
   http://www.marketingpower.com/
American Advertising Federation: Trade association of the advertising industry
   http://www.aaf.org/

## REFERENCES

American Marketing Association. 1995. *Dictionary of Marketing Terms,* 2nd ed., ed. P.D. Bennett. Chicago: American Marketing Association.

Becker, S. 2001. *Health Care Law: A Practical Guide,* 2nd ed. Newark, NJ: Matthew Bender & Company.

Bovée, C.L., et al. 1995. *Marketing,* 2nd ed. New York: McGraw-Hill.

Brennan, J. 1981. *Public Relations Can Be Fun and Easy Especially for Nursing Home People.* Washington, DC: American Health Care Association.

Czinkota, M.R. 2000. *Marketing: Best Practices.* Fort Worth, TX: The Dryden Press.

Drucker, P.F. 1974. *Management: Tasks, Responsibilities, Practices.* New York: Harper & Row, Publishers.

Engel, J.F., et al. 1994. *Promotional Strategy: Managing the Marketing Communications Process,* 8th ed. Chicago: Richard D. Irwin.

Kotler, P. 1991. *Marketing Management: Analysis, Planning, Implementation, and Control,* 7th ed. Englewood Cliffs, NJ: Prentice-Hall.

Kotler, P. 2000. *Marketing Management: The Millennium Edition.* Upper Saddle River, NJ: Prentice-Hall.

Kotler, P., & Andreasen, A.R. 1996. *Strategic Marketing for Nonprofit Organizations,* 5th ed. Upper Saddle River, NJ: Prentice Hall.

Kotler, P., & Clarke, R.N. 1987. *Marketing for Health Care Organizations.* Englewood Cliffs, NJ: Prentice Hall.

Luther, W.M. 2001. *The Marketing Plan: How to Prepare and Implement It,* 3rd ed. New York: American Management Association.

Macknick, F.J. 1998. Two takes on facility marketing. *Nursing Homes Long Term Care Management* 47, no. 10: 70–72.

Majaro, S. 1993. *The Essence of Marketing.* New York: Prentice Hall.

McKenna, R. 1991. *Relationship Marketing: Successful Strategies for the Age of the Customer.* Reading, MA: Addison-Wesley.

Miller, R.D., & Hutton, R.C. 2000. *Problems in Health Care Law,* 8th ed. Gaithersburg, MD: Aspen Publishers.

O'Malley, J.F. 2001. *Healthcare Marketing, Sales, and Service.* Chicago: Health Administration Press.

# Chapter 18

# Effective Budgeting and Financial Controls

## What You Will Learn

- Financial management is essential for making vital resources available to the organization. Budgeting and financial control are the two main functions of financial management.

- Financial management begins by understanding the organization's profitability. Additionally, the nursing home administrator must have detailed reports to monitor the facility's operations and make decisions.

- Variances between what has actually happened and what was planned in the budget are useful for managing revenues and controlling costs.

- Revenue management is based on two main factors: maintaining expected census levels and achieving the expected payer-mix of patients. Because of wide variations in the amount of reimbursement from various payers, simply achieving the census targets is not likely to realize the budgeted revenues.

- Cost control begins with an understanding of fixed, variable, and semi-fixed costs. These differences help identify controllable and noncontrollable costs.

- The administrator generally has more control over the hours of labor than over wages. To be useful tools, the labor-hour report and the labor-cost report should use variance analysis for monitoring labor costs.

- Three main techniques—variance analysis, accounts payable report, and inventory management—are used to control nonlabor expenses.

- Management of accounts receivable is critical for cash flow. Procedures are necessary to prevent lost revenues and to minimize write-offs. The collection cycle is a measure of efficiency in collecting the receivables.

> • Budgeting involves making projections for the next fiscal year on the basis of reasonable assumptions. Revenues, labor costs, and other expenses are budgeted in that order. Operating margin indicates the organization's profit goal.

## Financial Management and Its Importance

A good understanding of financial management is a necessary qualification for any health facility administrator. Financial management is a critical administrative function that is essential for ensuring a nursing facility's success over the long run. Although financial management is directly associated with the "managing a business" aspect of the administrator's responsibilities (see Chapter 15), financial management also affects the organization's ability to maintain patient care standards; deliver value; manage the open systems; and carry out other vital functions such as marketing, staff development, and quality improvement. A nursing facility's vital resources are controlled and conserved through effective financial management.

Financial management encompasses two classical functions of management: planning and controlling (see Chapter 15). Financial planning incorporates two types of decisions:

1. What future financial objectives are desirable and achievable?

2. What resources are needed and how will they be allocated so that the objectives are achieved?

Such a process of financial planning is called *budgeting*. Once formulated, the *budget* becomes a tool for exercising financial control. It sets expectations, which become

financial objectives that the nursing home administrator (NHA) is responsible for achieving. Managers exercise financial control when they compare the actual operating results against the budget, identify unacceptable variances, evaluate reasons for the variances, and take appropriate corrective action. Besides the planning and control functions just described, financial management also includes controlling cash and other assets such as food and supplies inventories.

The planning and control functions associated with budgeting and financial management call for managerial decision making. Sound decisions require good information. Hence, effective financial management is driven by well-designed systems for analyzing information and reporting on the organization's performance; such systems facilitate budgeting and control processes and help administrators keep track of cash and inventories. One basic financial information system is the accounting system. Accounting is a professional field in its own right. The NHA does not need to be an accountant, but he or she must be able to understand the basic accounting statements produced by the accounting system. A well-designed financial information system does more than just simple accounting. The system must enable the NHA to formulate an annual budget. It should also produce various reports to help the NHA understand and manage the financial performance of the facility.

# Accounting and Financial Statements

Accounting, more precisely called *financial accounting*, entails recording all financial transactions and preparing standard reports known as financial statements. Each financial transaction is recorded following the well-established double-entry system of debits and credits, and a set of standards called *generally accepted accounting principles (GAAP)*. Examples of common financial transactions include revenues derived from providing services; purchases of food, supplies, and other items; expense for salaries and wages; receipts of cash; and payments by cash or check. Most of these routine transactions are recorded by the nursing home's bookkeeping personnel. In addition to the recording of routine transactions, which a bookkeeper can generally handle, a professional accountant generally makes additional financial entries such as those pertaining to lease or rental arrangements, loans, tax payments, depreciation of assets, and income from investments. Generally, at the end of a specified period, all the financial transactions for that period are summarized in three main types of financial statements: the income statement, the balance sheet, and the cash flow statement. As discussed in subsequent sections, these statements provide concise information on the facility's profitability as well as its economic resources and obligations.

## The Income Statement

The income statement is also sometimes called the operating statement, the profit and loss statement, or the P&L. Exhibit 18–1 provides an example of an income statement. The *income statement* furnishes a summary of revenues, expenses, and profitability for a giv-

**Exhibit 18–1**  XYZ Nursing Care Facility Income Statement for Year Ended 2008

| | |
|---|---:|
| Net patient revenues: | |
| Private pay | $1,395,540 |
| Private insurance | 132,030 |
| Medicaid | 1,858,490 |
| Medicare | 943,160 |
| Veterans contract | 74,600 |
| Total net patient revenue | $4,403,820 |
| Other service revenues | 262,120 |
| Rental income | 8,040 |
| Income from investments | 43,620 |
| Total revenue | $4,717,600 |
| | |
| Operating expenses: | |
| Administrative salaries | $182,740 |
| Advertising and promotion | 14,400 |
| Other administrative | 12,240 |
| Nursing salaries | 2,294,950 |
| Medical supplies | 511,910 |
| Equipment rental | 26,400 |
| Dietary salaries | 300,370 |
| Raw food | 147,020 |
| Dietary supplies | 26,400 |
| Dietary chemicals | 25,700 |
| Environmental service salaries | 274,460 |
| Environmental supplies | 38,160 |
| Social services salaries | 42,900 |
| Activity salaries | 75,220 |
| Activity supplies | 5,040 |
| Contracted services | 194,290 |
| Fees | 46,210 |
| Utilities | 53,670 |
| Depreciation | 93,650 |
| Provision for bad debt | 70,230 |
| Other expenses | 23,400 |
| Total expenses | $4,459,360 |
| | |
| Operating income | $258,240 |
| Provision for income taxes | 77,470 |
| Net income (loss) | $180,770 |

en period, such as a month, a quarter, or a year. It has three main sections. The first section is a listing of the revenue derived from each payer source and the total revenue. The second section lists various expense line items such as salaries, supplies, raw food, utilities, and advertising. The third section consists of operating income, income taxes, and net income. For nonprofit and public facilities that do not pay income taxes, operating income equals net income. In general, net income or net profit equals total revenue minus total expenses (although shown separately on the income statement, income tax is actually an expense). Thus, the income statement provides valuable information on the profitability of an organization. By identifying revenues by each payer source and by identifying expenses by each type of expense, the income statement provides a summary of how the bottom-line profit was derived. On the other hand, if total expenses exceed total revenue the result is a net loss.

The income statement is of primary importance to the NHA. The balance sheet and the cash flow statement are important to corporate officers and owners.

## The Balance Sheet

A *balance sheet* summarizes the financial position of a business organization at a given date, such as the last day of a month or the last day of a year. A balance sheet has two sections:

1. A summary of all the *assets* or economic resources of the facility appears in the section on the left or at the top (based on how one chooses to lay out the balance sheet). Total assets constitute the financial value of everything the facility owns.

2. The right-hand or bottom section of the balance sheet contains two subsections: liabilities and equity. *Liabilities* constitute the facility's economic obligations or debts. Total liabilities constitute the financial value of everything the facility owes to other entities. *Equity*, which is also called owners' equity or stockholders' equity, represents the interests or rights of the owners in a for-profit corporation. In a nonprofit organization, no ownership interest exists. Therefore, *net assets* is the term used by nonprofit organizations for the equity portion of the balance sheet.

According to the fundamental accounting equation, total assets equal the sum of total liabilities and equity (or net assets). Thus, the two main sections of the balance sheet are exactly balanced. See Exhibit 18–2 for an illustration of the balance sheet.

## The Cash Flow Statement

The *cash flow statement* is a summary of transactions that increase or decrease cash during a given period, such as a month, quarter, or a year. It identifies the sources of incoming cash and the uses of outgoing cash. Preparing a cash flow statement is necessary because businesses commonly use an accounting method called *accrual-basis accounting*, a method in which revenues and expenses do not match cash inflows and outflows. Revenue is recognized at the time services are rendered although the bulk of payments for those services is received at a later date from various payers. Similarly, expenses are booked as they are incurred, even though payments to vendors are generally made at a later date. Certain expenses, such

**Exhibit 18–2** XYZ Nursing Care Facility Balance Sheet on December 31, 2008

| Assets | | Liabilities and Equity | |
|---|---|---|---|
| **Current Assets:** | | **Current Liabilities:** | |
| Cash | 62,350 | Accounts payable | 44,170 |
| Accounts receivable | 981,260 | Accrued salaries | 32,140 |
| *Less allowance for bad debts* | 70,230 | Current maturities of | |
| Inventories | 57,600 | long-term debt | 41,330 |
| Prepaid expenses | 24,400 | Long-term debt | 13,364,390 |
| | | *Less current maturities* | 41,330 |
| Land, buildings, and equipment | 23,670,190 | | |
| *Less accumulated depreciation* | 8,521,260 | Total Liabilities | 13,440,700 |
| Other assets | 258,990 | Equity | 3,022,600 |
| Total Assets | $16,463,300 | Total Liabilities and Equity | $16,463,300 |

as advertising and insurance, may be prepaid for a whole year. In such a case, a cash outflow would occur at the beginning of the year, but the expense would be spread out over the entire year.

Note that cash flow is not an indicator of profitability. Cash flow is, however, an important measure of an organization's financial health. A positive cash flow—in which inflows exceed outflows—means that the nursing home has the ability to meet its cash obligations in a timely manner. The facility must have cash to pay the employees on every payday, make payments to vendors according to the terms of credit, make lease payments for building and equipment, and pay loan installments to banks—to name some examples. An organization can face serious financial trouble if it does not have adequate cash to meet such financial obligations when they are due.

# Management Reports

The three types of financial statements just discussed do not provide all the information that managers need to control facility operations. The administrator and department managers need detailed reports that can help them monitor the facility's operations and make decisions. *Management accounting* is the term used for the process of preparing reports considered useful for management control and decision making. Several types of routine management reports may be prepared for the NHA and department managers. Corporate officers also routinely review such reports to evaluate operations. In addition to routine reports, certain nonroutine reports may be necessary from time to time. For example, a *pro forma* report that forecasts anticipated patient days, expected revenues, and anticipated expenses is often necessary before a facility launches a new service. Such a report can help management decide whether the facility should commit the resources to develop the new service that is being considered.

Financial accounting systems are standardized, and the format of financial statements varies little among different nursing home organizations. Management accounting systems, on the other hand, can have a great deal of variation. The number and types of management reports, as well as their usefulness, depend on the level of sophistication of the financial information systems. Because no standards exist in management accounting, the format of management reports and the level of detail also vary from one organization to another.

Routine management reports furnish an analysis of operational information. Because the income statement and the balance sheet are summary statements, they lack the details necessary for managing revenues, controlling costs, and monitoring accounts receivable.

# The Technique of Variance Analysis

*Variance analysis* is an examination and interpretation of differences between what has actually happened and what was planned in the budget (Gapenski, 2002). A *variance* is the difference between an actual (realized) numeric value and a budgeted (expected) value. Variances pinpoint deviations from the budget, and they enable the NHA to monitor the facility's profitability.

The technique is used for managing revenues and for controlling costs. Negative variances signify that the actual results are worse than what was projected in the budget, and such results threaten the expected profitability. Negative variances require follow-up, particularly in areas in which costs are controllable. Such controllable areas are those areas of the operation in which management intervention to reduce costs would not jeopardize quality or violate regulations. For example, labor hours cannot be cut below the minimum staffing levels established by regulations or cut below the number of staff hours necessary for meeting patients' needs, whichever is higher. Hence, negative variances require careful evaluation and judicious action. Variance analysis and other types of management reports are discussed later in greater detail.

# Managing Revenues

Management of revenues is based on two factors:

- *Maintaining expected census levels. Census* means the number of patients in a facility on a given day. Each day spent by a patient in the nursing facility is called a patient day. Hence, patient days over a period represent the cumulative number of days spent by all patients. *Patient days*, also referred to as *days of care*, amount to a cumulative census over a specified period. *Average daily census* is the average number of patients per day over a specific period of time such as a week, a month, or a year. It is calculated by dividing the total patient days over a period by the number of days in that period (Table 18–1).

- *Achieving the expected payer-mix of patients. Payer-mix* is also called census-mix. It is the mix of patients by payer type, such as Medicaid, Medicare, or private pay. Table 18–2 illustrates the payer-mix for a facility, which is also graphically illustrated in Figure 18–1.

**Table 18–1** Days of Care and Average Daily Census for a 7-day Period

| Day | Daily census |
| --- | --- |
| Day 1 | 121 |
| Day 2 | 119 |
| Day 3 | 118 |
| Day 4 | 117 |
| Day 5 | 120 |
| Day 6 | 118 |
| Day 7 | 120 |
| **Patient days** | 833 (Total census of days 1 through 7) |
| **Average daily census** | 119 (833 / 7) |

**Figure 18–1** Payer-mix for 2008

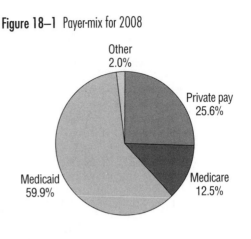

The objective of census management is to keep the facility's beds filled. Having more patients in the facility generally translates into more revenue. But simply having more patients is not always enough for achieving revenue targets. A facility may maintain or exceed its expected census levels and yet experience revenue shortfalls because of wide variations in the amount of reimbursement from the various private and public sources of financing. Medicaid generally maintains the lowest reimbursement rates. Private-pay charges, which are established by the facility, are generally the highest. Exhibit 18–3 illustrates the effect of payer-mix on revenues. Notice that the facility has actually met its budgeted patient days target of 3,472 and its budgeted 88.9 percent occupancy rate in the month of October. However, shortfalls (indicated by negative variance signs) in achieving targeted private-pay and private-insurance patient days have resulted in a

**Table 18–2** Payer-mix for the Year 2008

| Pay type | Patient days | Payer-mix |
| --- | --- | --- |
| Private pay | 10,998 | 25.6% |
| Medicare | 5,370 | 12.5% |
| Medicaid | 25,695 | 59.9% |
| Other | 861 | 2.0% |
| TOTAL | 42,924 | 100.0% |
| Average daily census | 117.6 | |

**Exhibit 18–3** Payer-mix and Revenue Report for Month of October, 2008

Available beds: 126

| | Budget | | | | | Actual | | | | | Variance | | |
|---|---|---|---|---|---|---|---|---|---|---|---|---|---|
| | Patient days | % | Rates | Revenue | | Patient days | % | Rates | Revenue | | Patient days | Rates | Revenue |
| Private pay | 903 | 26.0% | $196.55 | $177,430 | | 854 | 4.6% | $196.55 | $167,854 | | −49 | $0.00 | −$9,576 |
| Private insurance | 104 | 3.0% | 156.00 | 16,249 | | 73 | 2.1% | $156.00 | 11,388 | | −31 | 0.00 | −4,861 |
| Medicaid | 1,805 | 52.0% | 136.00 | 245,540 | | 1,885 | 54.3% | $136.00 | 256,360 | | 80 | 0.00 | 10,820 |
| Medicare | 521 | 15.0% | 182.00 | 94,786 | | 526 | 15.1% | $182.00 | 95,732 | | 5 | 0.00 | 946 |
| Veterans contract | 139 | 4.0% | 170.00 | 23,610 | | 134 | 3.9% | $170.00 | 22,780 | | −5 | 0.00 | −830 |
| TOTALS | 3,472 | 100.0% | $160.60 | $557,614 | | 3,472 | 100.0% | $159.59 | $554,114 | | 0 | −$1.01 | −$3,500 |
| Average daily census | 112 | | | | | 112 | | | | | 0 | | |
| Occupancy rate | 88.9% | | | | | 88.9% | | | | | 0.0% | | |

Note: Occupancy rate = Average daily census / Available beds revenue shortfall of $3,500 for the month. Notice that the actual payer-mix produces an average reimbursement rate of $159.59, which is $1.01 lower than the average budgeted rate of $160.60 for each patient day, and is also a negative variance.

One way to eliminate the revenue shortfall in this case is to increase the overall census by 22 patient days for the month. In this case, 22 patient days times the average reimbursement rate of $159.59 per patient day equals $3,511, which is sufficient to cover the revenue shortfall. Another way to achieve the revenue objective is to realize higher reimbursement rates than the rates projected in the budget. Higher reimbursement rates, however, are often difficult to achieve because the NHA has little or no control over third-party reimbursement rates. For a substantial number of patients, the rates are established by third parties such as Medicaid and Medicare. Private-pay rates are under management's control, but market factors such as competition from other facilities often limit the administrator's ability to unilaterally raise private-pay rates.

# Controlling Costs

Cost control requires an understanding of three main types of costs: fixed, variable, and semi-fixed (also called step-fixed or step-variable). The three types of costs operate differently within a certain **census range**, which is an anticipated range of patient census. The generic term used in cost accounting for a range of volume or activity such as census is "relevant range." Associating costs with a census range is central to controlling costs without jeopardizing quality of care or demoralizing the associates with staffing shortages. When the concept of census range is employed in planning expenditures, cost expectations are established for an anticipated range of the facility's patient census. A census range should be used because no one can exactly predict the census for a future time.

## Types of Costs

The nature of a particular type of cost can be evaluated on the basis of its relationship to a change in the facility's census. Suppose that costs are being budgeted for a census range of 108 to 116 patients. Some costs would remain unchanged, regardless of whether the facility has 108 or 116 patients. Costs that do not vary with the number of patients within the census range are called *fixed costs*. Fixed costs are noncontrollable. For example, regardless of whether the facility has 108 or 116 patients, the facility must still have the same number of RN hours per day (Figure 18–2). Administrative costs, telephone and utilities, rent or lease costs for the building, and maintenance and repairs are other examples of fixed costs.

*Variable costs*, on the other hand, vary with the change in the number of patients within the census range. For example, if the cost of raw food is $4.00 per patient per day, the food cost would be $432 per day when the facility has 108 patients; it will be $464 per day when the census is 116. Other costs that are considered variable include medical and nursing supplies, dietary supplies, temporary labor, linens, and laundry chemicals. Note that for variable costs, the variable cost rate (also known as the cost per unit) remains constant. The variable cost rate is expressed as a per-patient-day cost (PPD cost), which is a constant amount per patient per day. In the food cost example, the PPD food cost remains constant at $4.00. To get the total food cost, the PPD cost is multiplied by the number of

**Figure 18–2** RN Hours within a Census Range of 108 and 116

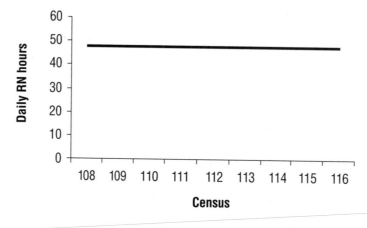

patients. The total variable costs are controllable. Suppose the facility has been operating with a daily census of 114, and the census drops to 110. The facility must reduce its spending on food from $456 per day to $440 (Figure 18–3), even as the PPD cost remains constant at $4.00. This cost control technique is not applicable to fixed costs discussed earlier.

The third category consists of semi-fixed or step-variable costs. **Semi-fixed costs** remain fixed within parts of the census range; they rise or fall for another part of the cen-

sus range. Semi-fixed costs are generally encountered in paraprofessional labor hours, such as certified nursing assistant (CNA) hours. The example illustrated in Figure 18–4 assumes that CNAs are scheduled in eight-hour increments. In this example, 360 hours of CNA time is scheduled even though the census may vary between 108 and 110; 368 hours are scheduled when the census increases to 111; an additional eight hours are scheduled only when the census reaches 114. Like variable costs, semi-fixed costs are also controllable. But unlike variable costs, semi-fixed

**Figure 18–3** Food Cost Within a Census Range of 108 and 116

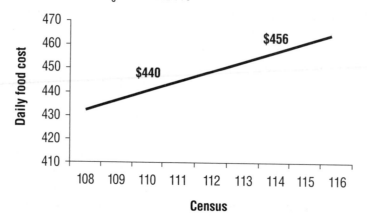

costs are not controllable for minor fluctuations in census. The example given here assumes that CNAs are assured work for a full shift unless the census drops by three patients, such as from 116 to 113 or from 113 to 110. Depending on management policy, some facilities may treat semi-fixed costs as variable costs. Semi-fixed labor costs can be treated as variable costs, especially when a facility is able to employ adequate part-time associates who may be called in as needed. Some facilities that do not have this flexibility still treat these costs as variable; thus, a CNA is sent home without completing a full shift if the census drops by as little as one patient. Such a practice can be demoralizing for the associates and contribute to other problems such as absenteeism and turnover. In the long run, relatively small upfront cost savings may actually end up costing the facility much more.

## Controlling Labor Costs

Labor costs have two components: hours of labor and dollars spent on labor. Hours of labor have a direct effect on labor dollars. But labor dollars are also affected by average wages paid to the associates. Wages are governed by a facility's wage policies. Competitive pressures may also influence how much a facility may have to pay to hire and retain qualified associates. Hence, the NHA may have more control over the hours of labor than over total dollars spent on wages and salaries.

Labor costs and other expenditures are controlled using the technique of variance analysis mentioned earlier. Cost control begins with the budgeted figures being adjusted to reflect changes in census. Exhibit 18–4 presents a labor hour report for a particular nursing unit within a facility. Similar reports would be prepared for other nursing units and departments such as food service, housekeeping, and laundry. A report will also be prepared for the entire facility. A labor hour report is generally produced every pay period. This report shows budgeted hours, actual hours, adjusted budget hours, and the variance between the adjusted budget and the actual hours. The budgeted hours in this example were based on 532 patient days for the pay period. However, the facility's actual patient days were 504. Therefore, for determining the variances, the budgeted hours must

**Figure 18–4** Nursing Assistant Hours within a Census Range of 108 and 116

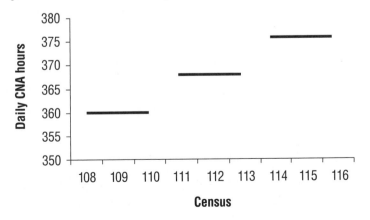
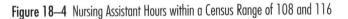

Exhibit 18—4

**Labor Hour Report**
**Pay period: October 11, 2008—October 24, 2008**
**Department: Nursing (Unit B)**

Patient days
| Budget | Actual |
|--------|--------|
| 532    | 504    |

| | Budget | | | | Actual | | | | Adjusted budget | | Variance | |
|------|------------------|-------------------|-----------------|--------------|------------------|-------------------|----------------|--------------|----------------|------|-------|-------|
| | Regulars Hours | Overtime Hours | Totals Hours | PPD Hours | Regular Hours | Overtime Hours | Total Hours | PPD Hours | Total Hours | PPD | Total | PPD |
| RN | 224 | 0 | 224 | 0.42 | 224 | 4 | 228 | 0.45 | 212 | 0.42 | −16 | −0.03 |
| LPN | 332 | 4 | 336 | 0.63 | 318 | 0 | 318 | 0.63 | 318 | 0.63 | 0 | 0.00 |
| CNA | 1,762 | 30 | 1,792 | 3.37 | 1,710 | 28 | 1,738 | 3.45 | 1,698 | 3.37 | −40 | −0.08 |
| Total | 2,318 | 34 | 2,352 | 4.42 | 2,252 | 32 | 2,284 | 4.53 | 2,228 | 4.42 | −56 | −0.11 |

be adjusted for the lower actual census. The actual census is seldom the same as the census that was budgeted. An adjusted budget, which is also called a *flexible budget,* is derived by applying budgeted PPD hours to the actual patient days. Hence, in a **flexible budget**, the budgeted costs are raised or lowered to reflect the actual census. For example, in Exhibit 18–4, the total labor hours under the "adjusted budget" column have been calculated by multiplying the budgeted 4.42 PPD total hours by the actual census of 504. A flexible budget extrapolates budgeted variable costs to reflect actual patient days.

*Flexible budget = Budgeted PPD hours (or costs) × Actual patient days*

Most accounting and finance software programs treat labor hours as variable costs rather than fixed or semi-variable costs. Nevertheless, computer-generated labor hour reports are useful in pointing out the variances. In Exhibit 18–4, the negative variance of 16 hours for RNs indicates overstaffing, but if RN hours are treated as a fixed cost, the variance can be ignored. On the other hand, RNs have incurred four hours of overtime that was not budgeted, and this overage calls for follow-up to determine whether this overtime was avoidable. It can be seen that four hours of overtime budgeted for LPNs was not used. It is possible that there was a trade-off between LPN and RN overtime, but RN wages are higher than those for LPNs, so this difference would negatively affect the labor dollars, as is apparent from Exhibit 18–5. The budgeted overtime costs for LPNs were $88 for four hours of overtime. For the same four hours of overtime, the actual costs for RNs amounted to $106. In such a case, the NHA should decide whether circumstances warranted swapping overtime hours.

In Exhibit 18–5, the labor-hours shown in Exhibit 18–4 have been converted to dollar costs using the hourly wage rates. For variance analysis, a flexible budget (adjusted budget) is formulated to reflect budgeted dollar costs adjusted for the lower patient day total of 504. Notice in Exhibit 18–5 that even though RN costs are considered fixed, the negative cost variance of $382 is excessive because the hourly rate has been exceeded by $0.47 per hour. The nonbudgeted overtime is partially responsible for the overage. However, the NHA can evaluate the portion of overage attributable to the overtime incurred and the portion attributable to other causes. The portion attributable to other causes is $0.32 per hour (the $17.63 hourly rate under Actual Regular Costs minus the $17.31 hourly rate under Budgeted Regular Costs). This variance could be the result of market competition that may have become more intense since the budget was finalized. To hire or retain qualified RNs, the facility may have had no choice but to pay higher wages. The remaining $0.15 of the $0.47 variance in hourly rate is attributable to overtime (the $17.78 hourly rate under Actual Total Costs minus the $17.63 hourly rate under Actual Regular Costs).

In Exhibit 18–5, the LPN costs are better by $46 than the budgeted costs, a positive cost variance. Even though there is zero variance for LPN hours, cost savings have been realized because of a positive variance of $0.13 in the hourly rate—mainly because no overtime was incurred even though it was budgeted. CNA costs appear to be problematic; these costs have a negative variance of $266, even though the variance for hourly rate is positive by $0.04. As shown in Exhibit 18–4, CNA hours have been exceeded by 40, which amounts to an average of 2.9 hours per day during the pay period. The administrator

Exhibit 18–5

**Labor Cost Report**
**Pay period: October 11, 2008–October 24, 2008**
**Department: Nursing (Unit B)**

Patient days

| Budget | Actual |
|---|---|
| 532 | 504 |

| | Budget | | | | | | Actual | | | | | | Flexible Budget | | Variance | |
|---|---|---|---|---|---|---|---|---|---|---|---|---|---|---|---|---|
| | Regular Costs | | Overtime Costs | | Total Costs | | Regular Costs | | Overtime Costs | | Total Costs | | Total Costs | | Total Costs | |
| | Dollars | Hourly rate | Dollars | Hourly rate | Dollars | Hourly rate | Dollars | Hourly rate | Dollars | Hourly rate | Dollars | Hourly rate | Dollars | Hourly rate | Dollars | Hourly rate |
| RN | $3,877 | $17.31 | $0 | $0.00 | $3,877 | $17.31 | $3,949 | $17.63 | $106 | $26.45 | $4,055 | $17.78 | $3,673 | $17.31 | –$382 | –$0.47 |
| LPN | 4,864 | 14.65 | 88 | 21.98 | 4,952 | 14.74 | 4,646 | 14.61 | 0 | 21.92 | 4,646 | 14.61 | 4,692 | 14.74 | 46 | 0.13 |
| CNA | 14,184 | 8.05 | 362 | 12.08 | 14,546 | 8.12 | 13,714 | 8.02 | 337 | 12.03 | 14,051 | 8.08 | 13,785 | 8.12 | –266 | 0.04 |
| Total | $22,925 | $9.89 | $450 | $13.24 | $23,375 | $9.94 | $22,309 | $9.91 | $443 | $13.83 | $22,752 | $9.96 | $22,151 | $9.94 | –$601 | –$0.02 |

should investigate this variance further. What must be determined is whether managers in the nursing department had the flexibility to schedule part-time staff or whether the excess staffing was the result of a policy of assuring a full shift to the CNAs who come to work as scheduled. In spite of the influence of such factors, the fact remains that Nursing Unit B has exceeded its labor budget by $601 during the given pay period. To prevent ongoing budget shortfalls, the facility must build census or reduce costs.

# Controlling Nonlabor Expenses

A facility's basic approach to controlling expenses—such as food, supplies, and linens—is also based on variance analysis. However, other types of monitoring and control methods are also used, and these methods are discussed in this section. The technique of variance analysis for expenses is very similar to what was discussed earlier. Exhibit 18–6 presents the expense summary for the food service department. This summary contains variances for the month of October and for the year-to-date totals for 10 months of the year. Although the flexible budget is not shown, the variances are derived from a comparison of the actual expenditures against a flexible budget. As usual, the flexible budget is calculated by multiplying the budgeted PPD costs by the actual patient days. Labor costs for supervisory personnel are considered fixed costs, so a negative variance is produced when the actual patient days are below budget. Similarly, the negative variances for labor cost for operational staff may be ignored if these costs are considered fixed. Details of labor hours and labor costs for the food service department will appear very similarly to nursing labor hours and costs shown

earlier. In Exhibit 18–6 the variance for raw food cost is very small and can be ignored; expenditures for chemicals and small equipment are better than budget; food service supplies, however, require further investigation.

## Accounts Payable Report

Expenses should also be monitored by looking at an accounts payable report. This report is generally produced weekly, and it lists all the *accounts payable*—money owed to vendors from whom goods, supplies, and services have been purchased on credit—processed by the facility's bookkeeper. The report shows the date when an invoice was processed, the name of the vendor, and the amount paid. Reviewing this report each week may bring to attention anything that may appear out of place.

## Inventory Management

Inventory management is an important tool for controlling expenses. Receiving and inventory control procedures for food items were discussed in Chapter 12. Similar procedures must be adopted for other inventoried items. As an example, a linen inventory control system is presented in Exhibit 18–7. Such a system serves two main purposes: (1) it ensures that the facility always has adequate linens available to serve patients, and (2) it provides a mechanism for linen cost control.

The first of these objectives is achieved by establishing adequate par levels, as discussed in Chapter 13. The second objective of linen cost control is achieved by instituting inventory control systems discussed in Chapter 12. In the perpetual inventory system for linens, the closing inventory at the end of a month equals the beginning inventory (what was on hand at the first of the

Exhibit 18–6

## Expense Summary—Food Service Department
## Month of October 2008

**Patient days**

|  | Month | | Year to date | |
|---|---|---|---|---|
|  | Budget | Actual | Budget | Actual |
|  | 3,472 | 3,286 | 34,564 | 33,423 |

| | Month | | | | Year to date | | | | Variance | |
|---|---|---|---|---|---|---|---|---|---|---|
| | Budget | PPD | Actual | PPD | Budget | PPD | Actual | PPD | Month | Year to date |
| Labor: | | | | | | | | | | |
| Supervisors | $3,835 | $1.10 | $3,835 | $1.17 | $38,350 | $1.11 | $38,350 | $1.15 | –$205 | –$1,266 |
| Operational staff | 13,690 | 3.94 | 13,367 | 4.07 | 136,900 | 3.96 | 134,978 | 4.04 | –410 | –2,597 |
| Raw food | 13,888 | 4.00 | 13,264 | 4.04 | 136,873 | 3.96 | 132,420 | 3.96 | –120 | –65 |
| Chemicals | 1,121 | 0.32 | 1,012 | 0.31 | 11,060 | 0.32 | 10,068 | 0.30 | 49 | 627 |
| Food service supplies | 1,296 | 0.37 | 1,346 | 0.41 | 12,789 | 0.37 | 13,323 | 0.40 | –119 | –956 |
| Small equipment | 215 | 0.06 | 180 | 0.05 | 2,150 | 0.06 | 1,956 | 0.06 | 23 | 123 |
| Total cost | $34,045 | $9.81 | $33,004 | $10.04 | $338,122 | $9.78 | $331,095 | $9.91 | –$783 | –$4,135 |

**Exhibit 18–7**  Linen Inventory on October 31, 2008

| | Par levels | On hand | Purchases | Discards | Closing inventory | Physical count | Over/ (short) | To replenish | Replenishment cost | |
|---|---|---|---|---|---|---|---|---|---|---|
| | | October 1 | | | October 31 | October 31 | | | Unit cost | Total cost |
| Bath towels | 384 | 412 | 0 | 17 | 395 | 406 | 11 | | $1.72 | |
| Hand towels | 636 | 507 | 120 | 0 | 627 | 611 | −16 | 25 | $0.90 | $22.50 |
| Wash cloths | 1,260 | 966 | 300 | 0 | 1,266 | 1,009 | −257 | 251 | $0.39 | $97.26 |
| Bed sheets | 504 | 478 | 36 | 14 | 500 | 500 | 0 | 4 | $4.15 | $6.60 |
| Pillow cases | 252 | 276 | 0 | 6 | 270 | 268 | −2 | | $1.37 | |
| Blankets | 252 | 162 | 0 | 11 | 151 | 154 | 3 | 98 | $7.80 | $744.40 |
| Bedspreads | 192 | 178 | 0 | 4 | 174 | 174 | 0 | 18 | $9.60 | $352.80 |
| Mattress pads | 192 | 230 | 0 | 2 | 228 | 224 | −4 | | $6.85 | |
| | | | | | | | | Total Replenishment Cost | | $2,233.56 |

month, which is the closing inventory from the previous month) plus purchases, minus discards:

*Closing inventory at the end of a month =*
*Beginning inventory + Purchases – Discards*

The system requires that the person in charge of linens maintain a record of items discarded because of thinning, fading, and tearing. Periodically, a physical inventory should be taken by counting each linen item. Because linens are constantly in circulation, the facility should develop a procedure for counting all linens throughout the facility. A suitable time for taking a physical inventory is when patient care activities have slowed down, generally in late afternoon or during the night. At a given time, the nursing staff should count all linen items in patient rooms, bathrooms, linen carts, and storage closets on nursing units. At the same time, all soiled linens should be removed to the laundry for washing. These soiled items are counted as they come out of the laundry processing area for folding and storage. Before this count, all items that were processed in the laundry and linens in the main storage room should have been counted. Following this method should produce a fairly accurate count, although there will always be some minor discrepancies. The "over/(short)" column in Exhibit 18–7 shows such discrepancies. For example, the overage of 11 bath towels and shortage of 16 hand towels may be attributed to a miscount, such as counting some hand towels as bath towels. On the other hand, a shortage of washcloths is more significant if the counting was accurate. Such variances in a given month should not cause any alarm, but shortages occurring month after month indicate pilferage or other misuse. The column "to replenish" is the difference between "physical count" and "par levels." This replenish amount shows the number of additional linens the facility must purchase to bring the counts up to par levels. According to Exhibit 18–7, the greatest need is to purchase additional blankets. The NHA should place an order in November to purchase eight dozen blankets. If the budget allows it, the NHA should also purchase 18 bedspreads in November. The last column in Exhibit 18–7 provides the total cost of bringing current inventory to par levels.

## Managing Receivables

*Accounts receivable* are amounts due from patients and from third-party payers for services that the facility has already provided. Receivables are revenues that have yet to be collected. The income statement, discussed earlier, records all revenues regardless of whether the facility has actually received payment for the services it has performed. A facility that may be profitable on paper may experience serious financial difficulty if the booked revenues remain uncollected. Collecting receivables is critical for maintaining adequate cash flow. Therefore, managing accounts receivable is one of the critical elements of cash management, which is vitally important for the long-term survival of the facility.

Accounts receivable management has three objectives (Cleverley & Cameron, 2002):

- Minimize lost charges and reimbursement.
- Minimize write-offs for uncollectible accounts.
- Minimize the accounts receivable collection cycle.

## Minimizing Lost Charges and Reimbursement

The term *charge* means a fee that is established by the nursing facility for a particular service or product. The key phrase in this definition is "established by the facility." In contrast, *reimbursement* is the fee established by a third-party payer, such as Medicaid, Medicare, or a managed care organization. As discussed earlier, the NHA has little or no control over third-party reimbursement rates. The NHA generally has more control over the charges the facility establishes for basic *per-diem* (patient day) room-and-board rates and for ancillary services and supplies.

To minimize lost charges and lost reimbursement, the nursing facility must have a census tallying system to accurately account for all patients in the facility at midnight each day. A *midnight census report* is completed by the nurse in charge on the night shift. This report should be verified by the director of nursing the following morning. The midnight census report is forwarded to the facility's business office, where this report is used for calculating daily revenues for all patients by their respective payer types. Such daily revenue accounting forms the basis for producing monthly bills for each payer. Without adequate controls over daily census accounting, some revenues would be lost.

Charges other than room-and-board include ancillaries, such as rehabilitation therapies and medical supplies. Most third-party reimbursement rates are now all-inclusive. An *all-inclusive rate* is a bundled fee that includes, in a single rate, all services and supplies furnished to a patient. For private-pay patients, however, ancillary items are billed in addition to the basic room-and-board fee. To capture ancillary charges for private-pay patients, the facility must maintain adequate procedures to record all ancillary services and supplies used by each patient. For example, each time a supply item such as a catheter is used, a voucher should be filled out.

## Minimizing Write-offs

The accounting term for write-offs is "bad debts." Bad debts represent legitimate revenues, and the facility is entitled to get paid for the services it has already provided. For various reasons, however, the facility is not able to collect all the monies it is owed. After several attempts to collect such outstanding accounts, these accounts are declared uncollectible and are called bad debts. So, a *bad debt* is an amount that is legitimately owed to the facility but is deemed uncollectible.

Billing errors are the most common reason for which third-party payers reject claims for payment. In other instances, a payer may request evidence for services delivered. In either case, if the facility fails to do adequate and timely follow-up and the dispute over payment remains unresolved, a claim will eventually turn into a bad debt. To minimize such problems, the facility's personnel must thoroughly understand the rules established by each third-party payer. The facility must maintain updated Medicare and Medicaid manuals for reference purposes, and all new personnel must be adequately trained to comply with all rules that pertain to payment. Compliance with rules and regulations and maintenance of appropriate documentation in the medical records are critical to billing and collections.

Although third-party payments constitute the largest component of accounts receivable, the facility must also institute procedures for billing and collecting accounts due from private sources. Deductibles and coinsurance, discussed in Chapter 7, are to be paid privately by the patient. Most nursing home patients have a *responsible party* handling the patient's private financial affairs. Complete information on each patient's designated responsible party, such as a spouse or relative, must be obtained at the time of admission. When the patient is admitted, the responsible party is also asked to sign a statement that he or she, as the responsible party, assumes the responsibility to pay all amounts that the patient must pay privately. At the time of admission, the facility should also furnish a copy of the facility's credit and collection policy to the responsible party.

Timely billing and follow-up are critical for collecting private monies. The facility must institute collection policy and procedures to be followed by its administrative personnel. The collection policy should outline at what point a collection call should be made, at what point a letter should be sent to demand payment, and at what point an account should be turned over to a collection agency. The policy should also outline at what point and under what circumstances the organization writes off accounts as bad debts (Nowicki, 2001). The decision to write off uncollectible amounts is made jointly by the administrator and corporate officers (for facilities affiliated with hospitals or multifacility chains) after evaluating each account that falls within the policy criteria for a bad debt. As a rule of thumb, after various collection efforts have been made and an account still remains uncollected for a year, it should be written off as a bad debt.

## Minimizing the Collection Cycle

Apart from following procedures to monitor and collect receivables, it is equally important for a facility to establish standards for collection and to determine whether accounts are being collected in a timely manner. An essential tool for monitoring receivables and evaluating performance is called an "aging schedule," also known as an "aging report." An *aging schedule* provides a breakdown of each patient's account by showing the length of time that various amounts within the account have been outstanding. Exhibit 18–8 provides an illustration of an aging schedule. Notice that this exhibit shows the amounts due from each payer type and the age of each amount due. This exhibit also provides totals for the entire facility, and it shows the percentage of the total receivables that have been outstanding in each age category.

The collection cycle for accounts receivable is measured in terms of the *collection period*, which is also called "days' revenue outstanding" or "days in accounts receivable." This measure indicates the number of days' worth of revenue that is in accounts receivable, which also indicates the average number of days it takes to collect patient revenues. Hence, the collection period evaluates how quickly a facility is able to bill and collect its revenues. This measure should be calculated at the end of each month using year-to-date data. The calculation is as follows:

$$\text{Collection period} = \frac{\text{Total accounts receivable}}{\text{Revenue/Days in period}}$$

Exhibit 18–8 shows that the receivables constitute 63.2 days' worth of patient revenues. This result is derived by plugging the year-to-date patient revenue of $5,205,696 (not shown) and the 304 days in the period from January through October into the preceding formula. The NHA and governing board should decide whether 63.2 days is an acceptable collection period or whether a shorter period ought to be the standard.

Exhibit 18–8  Aging Schedule on October 31, 2008

| Patient name | | 0–30 days | 31–90 days | 91–120 days | over 120 days | Total Outstanding |
|---|---|---|---|---|---|---|
| Adam, B | Private | 920 | 103 | | 1,354 | $2,377 |
| | Medicare | 3,395 | 972 | | | $4,367 |
| | Medicaid | | 2,049 | | 374 | $2,423 |
| | Other | | | | 127 | $127 |
| | | | | | | $9,294 |
| Blake, C | Private | 858 | 143 | | | $1,001 |
| | Medicare | | | | | $0 |
| | Medicaid | | | | | $0 |
| | Other | 3,579 | | | | $3,579 |
| | | | | | | $4,580 |
| Cooper, D | Private | | | 684 | | $684 |
| | Medicare | | | | | $0 |
| | Medicaid | 2,894 | 320 | | | $3,214 |
| | Other | | | | | $0 |
| | | ......... | ......... | ......... | ......... | ......... |
| Total receivables | | $708,865 | $218,612 | $41,125 | $112,553 | $1,082,237 |
| | | 65.5% | 20.2% | 3.8% | 10.4% | |
| | | | | | Collection period | 63.2 days |

# Budgeting

As stated earlier, the budget ties together operational planning and control functions. Budgeting is the planning phase that involves detailed plans expressed quantitatively in dollar terms; these plans specify how revenues will be generated and what resources will be used during a specified period (Gapenski, 2002). The control phase of the budget is used for the purpose of managing revenues and controlling costs using variance analysis, as discussed earlier. This section focuses on the planning phase of preparing a budget.

An operating budget combines forecasts for revenues and expenses. Its format is like that of an income statement. The operating budget is generally prepared for an entire fiscal year, and the planning process for this budget often begins three to four months before the current fiscal year ends. The fiscal year is established by the governing board. The fiscal year may or may not coincide with the calendar year, but generally it does.

Budgeting involves making projections for the next fiscal year on the basis of some reasonable assumptions. Throughout the budgeting process, this question must be asked: "What can we reasonably expect to achieve?" Answers to this question should incorporate all known variables, such as any foreseeable changes in market competition; trends in the local economy; anticipated Medicare and Medicaid reimbursement rates based on economic and political factors; local labor market conditions for nursing and other personnel; general inflation for consumer products; and results expected from implementing any new strategies, such as a refocused marketing plan or major renovations. Using such assumptions, the NHA must first forecast anticipated census volume by pay type. Projections are also needed for private-pay

charges, reimbursement rates from third parties, staffing requirements, wage and benefit costs, and nonlabor expenses.

The assumptions just mentioned are applied to some base of reference. A reasonable base to use is what the facility has accomplished in the current fiscal year so far. Current data are often compared with the previous year's performance data. Using all this information, managerial judgments are made regarding reasonable projections for the next fiscal year. The budgeting process is greatly facilitated by developing budget worksheets. The worksheets include all major pieces of information on which the budget projections are based.

## Budgeting Revenues

The basic equation for a facility's revenue is $R = Q \times P$, where $R$ is revenue, $Q$ is quantity (census), and $P$ is price (charge or reimbursement rate). A sample of a worksheet for census forecast is presented in Exhibit 18–9. The first two sections of this exhibit contain historical and current data for 2008 and 2009. Note that at the time the budget projections for 2010 were made, the census data for 2009 were available only for the period until and including the month of October. The assumptions made for the 2010 projections have been noted on the worksheet. A similar worksheet (not shown) is used for projecting per-diem rates, and patient revenues are calculated using the revenue formula just presented. Budgeting software programs calculate the revenues automatically as the census and per-diem rates are entered into the computer. Finally, estimates for ancillary revenue and other revenues, such as income from investments or rental fees, should be added to the budget to arrive at the total revenue figure.

Exhibit 18—9  Census Projection Worksheet for 2010 budget

| | Jan | Feb | Mar | Apr | May | Jun | Jul | Aug | Sep | Oct | Nov | Dec | Year |
|---|---|---|---|---|---|---|---|---|---|---|---|---|---|
| **2008 Average daily census** | | | | | | | | | | | | | |
| Private pay | 27.8 | 28.1 | 29.1 | 28.5 | 27.7 | 28.0 | 28.0 | 27.0 | 26.6 | 24.7 | 23.4 | 24.0 | 26.9 |
| Private insurance | 2.2 | 2.2 | 2.4 | 2.4 | 2.5 | 2.3 | 2.1 | 3.0 | 2.0 | 3.0 | 4.0 | 4.0 | 2.7 |
| Medicaid | 59.6 | 59.2 | 59.9 | 62.9 | 61.8 | 63.4 | 63.9 | 63.1 | 64.8 | 65.2 | 65.7 | 63.2 | 62.7 |
| Medicare | 13.4 | 13.6 | 15.6 | 14.9 | 16.1 | 16.3 | 16.6 | 16.0 | 16.8 | 16.2 | 14.7 | 13.8 | 15.3 |
| Veterans contract | 4.0 | 5.0 | 5.5 | 5.5 | 4.5 | 3.5 | 3.5 | 3.0 | 2.0 | 2.0 | 1.0 | 0.0 | 3.3 |
| Total | 107.0 | 108.1 | 112.5 | 114.2 | 112.6 | 113.5 | 114.1 | 112.1 | 112.2 | 111.1 | 108.8 | 105.0 | 110.9 |
| Occupancy rate | 84.9% | 85.8% | 89.3% | 90.6% | 89.4% | 90.1% | 90.6% | 89.0% | 89.0% | 88.2% | 86.3% | 83.3% | 88.0% |
| | | | | | | | | | | | | | |
| **2009 Average daily census** | | | | | | | | | | | | | |
| Private pay | 22.4 | 23.1 | 24.1 | 23.5 | 23.7 | 24.2 | 26.0 | 27.0 | 26.6 | 27.5 | | | 24.8 |
| Private insurance | 2.2 | 2.2 | 2.4 | 3.4 | 4.5 | 2.3 | 2.1 | 3.0 | 2.0 | 2.4 | | | 2.6 |
| Medicaid | 62.6 | 61.2 | 59.9 | 62.9 | 61.8 | 65.4 | 63.9 | 63.1 | 64.8 | 60.8 | | | 62.6 |
| Medicare | 13.4 | 13.6 | 14.6 | 13.9 | 16.1 | 15.2 | 16.6 | 16.0 | 16.8 | 17.0 | | | 15.3 |
| Veterans contract | 2.0 | 2.0 | 1.0 | 1.0 | 0.0 | 0.0 | 3.5 | 3.0 | 2.0 | 4.3 | | | 1.9 |
| Total | 102.6 | 102.1 | 102.0 | 104.7 | 106.1 | 107.1 | 112.1 | 112.1 | 112.2 | 112.0 | | | 107.3 |
| Occupancy rate | 81.4% | 81.0% | 81.0% | 83.1% | 84.2% | 85.0% | 89.0% | 89.0% | 89.0% | 88.9% | | | 85.2% |

(continues)

**Exhibit 18–9** Census Projection Worksheet for 2010 budget (Continued)

| | Jan | Feb | Mar | Apr | May | Jun | Jul | Aug | Sep | Oct | Nov | Dec | Year |
|---|---|---|---|---|---|---|---|---|---|---|---|---|---|
| **2010 Average daily census projections** | | | | | | | | | | | | | |
| Private pay | 26.0 | 26.0 | 28.0 | 29.0 | 30.0 | 30.0 | 31.0 | 31.0 | 31.0 | 31.0 | 30.0 | 30.0 | 29.4 |
| Private insurance | 2.6 | 2.6 | 2.6 | 2.6 | 2.6 | 2.6 | 2.6 | 2.6 | 2.6 | 2.6 | 2.6 | 2.6 | 2.6 |
| Medicaid | 58.0 | 58.0 | 60.0 | 60.0 | 62.0 | 62.0 | 62.0 | 62.0 | 62.0 | 61.0 | 59.0 | 59.0 | 60.4 |
| Medicare | 17.0 | 18.0 | 18.0 | 19.0 | 19.0 | 19.0 | 20.0 | 20.0 | 20.0 | 20.0 | 20.0 | 20.0 | 19.2 |
| Veterans contract | 2.0 | 2.0 | 0.0 | 0.0 | 0.0 | 0.0 | 0.0 | 0.0 | 0.0 | 0.0 | 0.0 | 0.0 | 0.3 |
| Total | 105.6 | 106.6 | 108.6 | 110.6 | 113.6 | 113.6 | 115.6 | 115.6 | 115.6 | 114.6 | 111.6 | 111.6 | 111.9 |
| Occupancy rate | 83.8% | 84.6% | 86.2% | 87.8% | 90.2% | 90.2% | 91.7% | 91.7% | 91.7% | 91.0% | 88.6% | 88.6% | 88.8% |

Assumptions:

1. The previous administrator resigned in November 2008. The facility was without a permanent administrator for two months. It is assumed that a temporary drop in census occurred in early 2009 due to this change.

2. A new marketing strategy aimed at private-pay clients was implemented in September 2009. It is assumed that private-pay census will be slightly higher in 2010.

3. The VA contract will not be renewed once the existing VA patients are discharged.

4. Contract with a new rehab company is expected to increase Medicare census.

# Chapter 19

# Effective Quality and Productivity Management

## What You Will Learn

- A common misconception is that quality and productivity are not compatible. However, productivity and quality are interrelated.
- Quality is a multifaceted concept. Services delivered must be consistent, timely, uniform across the patient population, and dependable. Both quality of care and quality of life must address the patients' holistic needs and promote desirable outcomes.
- Both technical quality as well as consumer-defined quality must be evaluated. Evidence-based protocols standardize clinical processes, decrease care variability, and improve outcomes.
- Three domains of quality—structure, process, and outcome—are equally important in driving quality improvement. The use of clinical pathways can promote teamwork, produce higher quality, and reduce costs.
- Nursing home regulations have been necessary and have been instrumental in improving quality. However, quality improvement must go beyond regulatory compliance.
- Once the basic structural and process elements are in place, the focus of measurement must be on outcomes. A number of nursing home consumer satisfaction surveys are now available. Scores must be evaluated in relation to some standard. Quality-of-life measures have also been developed.
- Continuous quality improvement is based on six principles: meeting customer needs must be at the forefront, management must seriously engage in building a culture of quality, quality improvement is data driven, all departments of the nursing home must be involved, interdisciplinary teamwork is necessary, and continuous learning must be part of the culture.

- According to the work of quality pioneer W. Edwards Deming, value must be created to compete in the market; inspections are a tool for information gathering, not for improving quality; quality improvement systems should be used to identify process problems, not to blame workers; cooperation rather than competition should be promoted among departments; posters and slogans do not improve quality; and work quotas are counterproductive.
- The Wellspring model has demonstrated that quality can be improved by rigorous staff training, implementation of best practices, data-driven measurement, and staff empowerment.

## Some Common Misperceptions

Efficiency, productivity, and quality improvement are often regarded as isolated and even contradictory concepts. When the words "efficiency" and "productivity" are mentioned, some people instinctively equate those words with "doing more with fewer resources." Nursing home personnel have a tendency to presume that improved efficiency means working harder, doing more in less time, and constantly rushing to meet patients' needs. It is also assumed that quality suffers when greater efficiency is required and that an organization may achieve higher quality or greater efficiency, but not both. Years of research and experience in various industries, however, have demonstrated that such ideas are flawed.

Modern methods of improving quality and productivity were developed in manufacturing industries. Service organizations, in general, lagged behind the manufacturing sector in implementing these methods. Hospitals, nursing facilities, and other health care organizations were even slower than other service providers in adopting the concepts and methods of quality improvement. First, health care managers were skeptical that quality could be improved. Second, they were skeptical that quality and productivity could both be improved without compromising the other. Increasingly, however, health care managers have realized that quality and productivity can indeed be managed and that effectively managing these areas can provide a competitive edge to health care delivery organizations.

Through quality management, American medical care delivery has achieved some incredible accomplishments. The average length of stay in hospitals has been drastically reduced, and a great deal of patient care has shifted from full-service hospitals to less expensive sites such as outpatient surgery centers and rehabilitation hospitals. These changes occurred while some experts were predicting that quality of medical care would suffer. But the dire consequences these experts predicted never materialized.

## Productivity and Quality

For all practical purposes, *productivity* and *efficiency* are used as synonymous terms. Measuring productivity and efficiency means taking into account the cost of inputs used in the production of certain outputs. Delivery of patient care is particularly labor intensive, which means that people have to provide hands-on services that, in most instances, cannot be taken over by technology. Hence, improving productivity is challenging in the health care industry.

Although productivity is often viewed as physical outputs produced in exchange for certain quantified inputs, a sole focus on physical outputs can actually be counterproductive. The notion of outputs must incorporate the quality of the outputs produced, not merely the quantity of outputs.

$$Productivity = \frac{Outputs}{Inputs}$$

$$\begin{array}{l} Productivity \\ enhancement \end{array} = \frac{Desired\ quality}{Minimization\ of\ resource\ inputs} \quad (1)$$

$$or$$

$$\frac{Maximized\ quality}{Unit\ of\ resource\ inputs} \quad (2)$$

For simplicity, *outputs* in a nursing facility are collectively called *patient care*. These outputs encompass the quality of all clinical, social, and residential structures, as well as the various patient care delivery processes such as social services; medical care, nursing, and rehabilitation; recreation and activities; dietary services; plant and environmental services; and administrative and information systems. Productivity is enhanced when the most desirable outputs are produced at the least cost for these services.

Productivity and quality are interrelated. According to current management thought, improved quality can lead to improved efficiency and vice versa. From this perspective, ***productivity*** is defined as maximization of quality for each unit of resources used in delivering health care. Accordingly, productivity can be expressed as "desired quality at the lowest possible cost" (equation 1) or as "highest possible quality for a given cost" (equation 2) (Palmer, 1991, p. 12). Measuring productivity therefore requires assessing how effectively a nursing facility's resources are used in delivering patient care services. ***Inefficiency***, on the other hand, reduces the opportunity for quality at a given level of resources (Griffith & White, 2002). In other words, when resources are deployed without enhancing quality, the use of such resources is inefficient.

To borrow language from the manufacturing industry: "It takes just as many resources to make a bad product as it does to make a good one" (Evans & Lindsay, 1993, p. 30). In a nursing home, delivering poor patient care would still require the same level of resources as it would to deliver good patient care. In fact, the cost of poor quality can be very high. In the long run, the cost of poor quality may actually far exceed the cost of producing high-quality service. Just think of the many costs associated with low quality. Direct costs can include fines and penalties imposed by regulatory agencies, legal costs incurred in defending against lawsuits, and payment of legal settlements. Indirect costs can have a long-term negative effect on the facility from the erosion of trust in the community, followed by declining reputation, inability to sustain exchange relationships with community partners, and a drop in patient census. Other indirect costs may include increased staff turnover and absenteeism. Costs associated with investigation of complaints are also indirect costs of poor quality.

Finally, productivity requires that quality be managed. Quality improvement is an investment that calls for resources. These resources are wasted if the focus of quality improvement is on the wrong components. On the other hand, appropriately managed quality improvement should enhance the profitability of a nursing facility. Various studies have shown that nursing homes that produce quality services are able to lower their costs for delivering patient care because quality improvement often improves processes of care as well as productivity. Even when higher costs are incurred by increasing hours for RNs in relation to other staff, an indirect inverse effect on overall costs is observed through the positive effect of these extra RN hours on outcomes of care (Weech-Maldonado et al., 2003). A higher skill-mix can lead to a reduction in overall costs because of better health outcomes and improved efficiency. For example, through a higher skill-mix, care-related problems can be addressed more promptly, better direction can be given to paraprofessionals, and regulatory and legal sanctions can be avoided through improved care.

The Institute of Medicine (IOM) also concluded that there was little relationship between quality of nursing home care and Medicaid reimbursement policy. Some facilities provided excellent care at the same Medicaid payment rate and with the same payer-mix as other facilities in the same geographic area that provided substandard care. In essence, paying more to nursing homes will not guarantee higher quality, because many determinants of quality—such as staff attitudes, motivation, efficiency, administrative philosophy, and managerial skills—do not require additional expenditures and are not significantly related to costs (IOM, 1986; IOM, 2001).

# What Is Quality?

Quality is a multifaceted concept. *Quality* in a nursing facility can be defined as the consistent delivery of services that maximizes

the physical, mental, social, and spiritual well-being of all residents, produces desirable outcomes, and minimizes the likelihood of undesirable consequences. Notice that delivery of quality care in the nursing home has four essential components: consistency, holistic well-being, desirable outcomes, and prevention of undesirable consequences. Quality is compromised when lapses occur in any one of these four areas.

## Consistency

The word *consistency* signifies four characteristics that apply to all services described in Part III:

- Continuity.
- Regularity.
- Uniformity.
- Reliability.

*Continuity* means that quality must be consistently delivered over time. Variations from one day to another must be kept to a minimum. In practical terms, continuity means that the facility should, among other things, be just as clean on the weekend as it is on a weekday and that the food served should taste just as good at supper as it does at lunch.

*Regularity* means timeliness. Regularity emphasizes timely attention to patient needs. Examples of regularity in a facility include regular bed checks for incontinent patients, prompt response to call signals from patients who need staff attention, and timely attention to situations that require the intervention of social services.

*Uniformity* is sustained delivery of quality not only over time but also across the patient population within the facility. Uniformity means delivering the same caliber of services to all patients regardless of their pay status, race, or any other characteristics.

*Reliability* is the acid test of consistent quality. Reliability is achieved when quality becomes a part of an organization's culture. Reliability is achieved when a facility's associates can deliver uncompromised quality when no one is watching, because management and family members cannot be in the facility all the time to ensure this uncompromised quality. Trust and dependability are built when family members can be free from undue worry about the total well-being of their loved ones.

## Holistic Well-Being

In the nursing home, quality must be based on the holistic concept of health and well-being, described in earlier chapters. This concept emphasizes the well-being of every aspect of what makes a person whole and complete. A holistic approach requires providing services that meet the patient's physical, mental, social, and spiritual needs. Hence, quality includes much more than clinical care. It must also emphasize all aspects of quality of life. Quality of life has become a vital component of the Requirements of Participation for SNF or NF certification of nursing homes (see Exhibit 6–1 in Chapter 6). As explained in Chapter 6, periodic inspections have been established for the purpose of monitoring compliance with certification standards and for noting violations of those standards. However, when quality is actively pursued, a facility will take steps to maximize the quality of life for every resident in addition to ensuring the highest levels of medical and nursing care.

## Desirable Outcomes

An *outcome* is an actual result obtained from medical, nursing, and other clinical interventions. An increase in positive outcomes indicates that quality has improved. For example, quality is improved when a greater number of patients than before undergo rehabilitation therapy after orthopedic surgery and return home, when there is notable progress with the healing of pressure ulcers that were present when patients were admitted, and when patients are weaned off urinary catheters. On the flip side, incidence of pressure ulcers acquired in the facility, prevalence of falls or injuries, frequency of infections, and occurrence of health-threatening weight loss or dehydration are indicators of negative quality outcomes.

## Prevention of Undesirable Consequences

An important aspect of quality is the system a nursing facility implements to prevent negative outcomes—and how effectively that system is actually used and monitored. Such negative outcomes as accidental deaths and injury from negligence can have catastrophic consequences. Waiting for negative outcomes to occur is obviously not the desirable approach. Clinical errors, lapses in safety, unsanitary conditions, and untimely maintenance and repairs do not always produce negative consequences, but they often have the potential to cause harm. For example, a patient smokes unsupervised in a smokers' lounge. Even though nothing happens, the situation is really not as innocuous as it may appear. What if the patient was severely burned or a section of the building had caught fire? The potential devastation is unimaginable.

# Technical and Consumer-Defined Quality

The preceding description of quality can be called *technical quality*, which deals essentially with clinical factors. The level of a facility's technical quality depends on its clinical structures, its processes and practices, and the technical competence of its health care professionals. The quality of technical performance is evaluated against best practice standards that can be achieved given current scientific knowledge and technology in long-term care delivery (Donabedian, 1995). Generally speaking, technical quality is evaluated through expert assessment. However, increasingly, evidence-based practices are being used as a means of reducing inappropriate clinical care and improving patient outcomes (Berlowitz et al., 2001). These evidence-based practices, also referred to as ***best practices***, have been standardized in the form of *clinical practice guidelines,* which are protocols designed to help practitioners make appropriate health care decisions for specific circumstances (Field & Lohr, 1990). The American Geriatric Society and the American Medical Directors Association (AMDA) have developed practice guidelines for the care of the elderly patient. The AMDA has also developed training tools on how to implement the guidelines. The Agency for Healthcare Research and Quality has produced clinical practice guidelines for management of urinary incontinence, prevention of pressure ulcers, treatment of pressure ulcers, post-stroke rehabilitation, and pain management for cancer patients. The underlying premise of evidence-based protocols is that standardizing work processes decreases variability in care delivery and improves outcomes (Finch-Guthrie, 2000). However, implementation of standardized guidelines has been challenging in nursing homes because care delivery in nursing homes requires interdisciplinary decision making, and as much as 70% of the care is provided by paraprofessionals who have little formal training. Hence, training of associates is critical to improving quality.

The direct consumers of long-term care (i.e., patients and family members) seek technical quality, but they are not equipped to evaluate it because their observations alone cannot assess the level of clinical quality. Yet consumers do form impressions about a facility's level of quality. Consumers' impressions about quality can be called *consumer-defined quality.* These impressions are based on their personal observations and experiences, what they may hear from other family members, and how the facility's staff interacts and communicates with them. Also, consumers are better able to assess quality-of-life factors than technical quality. Their impressions are also influenced by the aesthetics of the physical premises, cleanliness and comfort, food, activities, staff attitudes, interactions with management, and the facility's accommodation of individual needs and preferences.

It is possible for consumer-defined quality to actually be at odds with a facility's technical level of quality. In general, consumers seek more than technically correct health care. They seek humanistic qualities as well as technical competence (Palmer, 1991). Staff interaction with the patient and family, listening for signs of distress, responsiveness, timely exchange of information, respect, empathy, honesty, and sensitivity are key elements of the exchange relationship between the facility and its clients.

Evaluation of total quality must incorporate both the technical side and the consumer side. Client satisfaction has been increasingly recognized as a desirable outcome in various health care delivery settings. Customers' perspective, determined by both residents and family members, is now considered an important element of nursing home quality. This perspective can point to such interpersonal aspects as communications and staff attitudes.

## Framework of Quality

The management of quality requires an understanding of the framework to guide the improvement of organizational quality. This framework has been credited to the work of Avedis Donabedian (1919–2000). He proposed three domains in which health care quality should be examined: structures, processes, and outcomes. All three domains are equally important in driving quality improvement, and they are closely linked in a hierarchical manner (see Figure 19–1); structures influence processes, and both structures and processes together influence outcomes. Structures and processes in long-term care are shaped by regulations; other changes in the external environment such as new technology, social and cultural change, ecological forces (new infections, antibiotic-resistant

**Figure 19–1** Framework of Quality

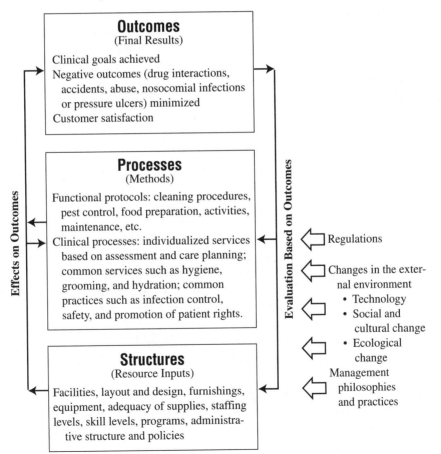

strains of bacteria, natural events, etc.); and management philosophies and practices.

## Structures

*Structure* provides the necessary foundation without which quality patient care cannot be delivered. In that sense, structure is where quality begins; it is the foundation of quality. Structural criteria refer to the availability of resources, such as facilities, equipment, staffing levels, staff qualifications, programs, and the administrative structure (McElroy & Herbelin, 1989). Space, building layout, furnishings, modern equipment, adequate supplies, trained associates, staffing levels and skill-mix, minimum absenteeism and turnover, and facility policies constitute structural elements of quality. The structural elements determine a nursing home's capabilities to deliver an adequate level of care. Inadequate structural quality would negatively affect processes and outcomes.

## Processes

*Processes* are methods designed for producing desired outputs and the application of those methods to actually produce desired outcomes. Processes entail staff functions, timeliness, accuracy, following established protocols, observation, and taking appropriate action to counter negative observations. Each department of the nursing facility must establish functional protocols to aid in the achievement of the process elements of quality. Examples of such protocols include clinical practice guidelines; quality improvement program; cleaning and sanitizing procedures; pest control; food purchasing, storage, production, and service; building and equipment maintenance procedures; and activities and recreational programming.

The quality of nursing home processes is governed by achieving excellence in the delivery of services that can be classified into three categories: individualized services, common services, and common practices.

## Individualized Services

As pointed out in some of the earlier chapters, patient assessment is the cornerstone on which clinical processes (such as plan of care and the delivery of services) are based to meet individual needs. Individualized care plans establish clinical expectations that guide the delivery of individual care such as administration of medications, nursing treatments, rehabilitation therapies, social interventions, recreational support, special diets, and assisting the patient with activities of daily living (ADLs). An innovative care planning and care management technique that has been successfully employed in hospitals is clinical pathways; use of this practice is now spreading to other health care settings. A *clinical pathway* is a care-planning tool that outlines important aspects of care necessary for meeting specific outcomes. Pathways are designed for the typical patient from a designated population, such as a patient who has undergone a hip replacement. The pathway is a predeveloped flowchart that plots interdisciplinary assessments, interventions, and expected outcomes along a timeline (Finch-Guthrie, 2000). Clinical pathways promote multidisciplinary teamwork because pathway planning requires input from all disciplines and because team interaction is necessary as care delivery progresses along the timeline. The ultimate objective of clinical pathways is to promote clinical quality while at the same time reducing utilization of resources. As an example, pneumonia is one of the most frequent reasons for transferring residents to a hospital

(Loeb et al., 1999). Hospitalization of nursing home patients with pneumonia presents multiple health risks. Hospitalization is also very costly. A clinical pathway developed by Loeb et al. (2006) and tested in 22 Canadian nursing homes showed that of the 680 patients in the study, only 10% in the clinical pathway group were hospitalized compared with 22% among the patient group without the use of the clinical pathway.

## Common Services

The second category, common services, consists of routine functional protocols that apply to all patients unless contraindicated in the care plan. Examples include daily hygiene and grooming, scheduled shower or bath, hydration, bedding change, and clean towels. Other types of common services include accurate billing, timely and complete medical records, communication with family about the patient's status, and notification to physicians. Although the nature of these services is common to all patients, their application is individualized.

## Common Practices

The third category, common practices, includes infection control, quality improvement, environmental cleanliness and comfort, safety and security, respect and dignity, privacy, and active promotion of patient rights. Protocols for common practices should ensure that certain practices are consistently followed to meet the basic needs of the entire patient population in the nursing facility.

## Outcomes

*Outcomes* are the final results obtained from using the structure and processes of the facility. Primarily, clinical outcomes are evaluated against individualized care plans to determine whether preestablished treatment and intervention goals have been met. Other outcomes include elements outside the plan of care and focus mainly on preventing negative incidents such as drug interactions, accidents, alleged abuse, infections, and facility-acquired (nosocomial) pressure ulcers. In almost all cases, outcome issues can be addressed only by a retrospective evaluation of structures and processes and by taking appropriate corrective action.

# Regulatory Minimum Standards

Historically, quality in nursing facilities has been defined by standards established for participation in the Medicare and Medicaid programs. Nursing home inspections conducted by the states, known as the *survey process*, have been used to ascertain compliance with certification standards (see Chapter 6). Compliance with these standards has been widely used as a proxy for quality.

In 1975, the federal Office of Nursing Home Affairs concluded that certification standards in place at the time had focused mainly on the structural elements of nursing homes. It meant that compliance with existing standards indicated only that the facility had the capacity to provide quality care but did not necessarily deliver it. In 1986, the Institute of Medicine produced a landmark study, *Improving the Quality of Care in Nursing Homes*, which concluded that the care provided in the nation's nursing homes was grossly inadequate. This report led to further regulatory changes and the institution of more stringent standards for certification.

Over the years, quality of care in nursing homes has improved, mainly in response to the enforcement of regulatory standards. The survey process, however, has had three major limitations:

1. Regulations establish only minimum standards of quality.
2. Nursing facilities cannot be monitored on a continuous basis by regulatory agencies.
3. There are wide variations in survey results, despite the government's efforts to standardize the process and train its surveyors.

To address some of these concerns, a Quality Indicator Survey (QIS) has been developed by the Centers for Medicare and Medicaid Services (CMS). The program is being phased in gradually. Nursing facilities can use the QIS process to improve their quality of care.

According to the Requirements of Participation, nursing facilities must establish a *quality assessment and assurance committee.* The committee must include the director of nursing, a physician, and at least three other members of the facility's staff. Some major nursing home corporations have based their quality assurance programs on the certification standards, and these corporations internally monitor compliance more frequently than federal regulators do. However, quality improvement should go beyond the federally established minimum standards.

## Measurement and Evaluation of Quality

Quality cannot be improved without measuring it. Measurement requires collection of meaningful data, analysis of the data, and comparison of the data to objective benchmarks of quality. The measurement and evaluation of quality are geared to pinpoint deficiencies so that corrective actions can be undertaken to improve quality.

### Focus on Outcomes

Although structure, process, and outcome data all have a place in measurement of quality, the focus of measurement must be on outcomes. Structural measures only serve to establish a baseline to ensure that staff, facilities, equipment, and organizational features meet at least the minimal necessary conditions for delivering good care (Palmer, 1991). Process measures evaluate methods and practices intended to maintain or improve quality. Outcomes, however, define whether quality goals are being met. Once the basic structural and process elements are in place, the focus of measurement must be on outcomes, which can indicate both positive and negative results. When anticipated results are not achieved, administrators must reexamine the structures and processes to determine where the breakdown occurred and what actions should be undertaken to prevent future failures.

Quality measurement can be illustrated by using the simple example of a meal tray delivered to a patient who requested to have the noon meal in her room. Placing the meal tray before the patient is the main outcome, without which the output would be zero, a total failure of quality. But, assuming that a meal tray is delivered, other attributes of this output—such as timeliness of delivery, conformance of the food items placed on the tray with the patient's diet, compliance with the patient's prior indications of likes and dislikes regarding choice of food items, the quantity of food served, temperatures of the hot and cold items, the amount of food actually eat-en by the patient, and the patient's level of satisfaction with the meal—must be evaluated. Each of these attributes is measurable, so a composite score can be used to quantify the level of quality.

## Measuring Customer Satisfaction

Customer satisfaction is an outcome that characterizes consumer-defined quality. Like technical quality, customer satisfaction can also be measured. Customer satisfaction is best assessed through a satisfaction survey—called a *survey instrument*—completed by patients and their surrogates. It is critical, however, that the reliability and validity of the survey instrument be established in order to get meaningful information about customer satisfaction. **Reliability** is the extent to which the same results occur from repeated applications of a measure under identical conditions. Reliability deals with the precision of measurement. Unless a survey instrument delivers reliable results, the results obtained by surveying customers at repeated intervals, such as every year, cannot be compared. For example, if in year 1 of the survey a facility scored a 7 on a scale of 1 to 10, and in year 2 the same facility scored a 7.5, improvement in customer satisfaction can be inferred only if the instrument used to assess satisfaction had a high degree of reliability. The **validity** of a survey instrument denotes the extent to which the instrument actually measures what it purports to measure. Reliability in itself does not ensure that a measure is valid. An instrument can have very high reliability, but if it has poor validity, the results become useless. For example, if a survey instrument measures customers' satisfaction with factors other than those associated with the facility's services, such as satisfaction with location, geographic access, and opinions of

friends, such an instrument will be useless in helping the facility improve satisfaction by improving the facility's services. Appropriate measurement instruments can be designed by health care researchers.

Satisfaction implies subjective quality in the form of judgments by individuals about their experiences with a service. Individually rated responses from consumer surveys are consolidated to determine an overall score of customer satisfaction. Such aggregated scores derived from all the responses to a survey provide an estimate of the average perceived quality (Lawton, 2001). When necessary, survey results can be supplemented with other approaches such as focus groups, particularly when further clarification or additional information is needed. Research has demonstrated that there is a high degree of correlation between subjective assessments of satisfaction and key outcomes.

A number of nursing home consumer satisfaction surveys are now available. Several states are using such surveys. Many of these instruments have undergone extensive development and testing. Separate survey instruments should be used for nursing home residents and their family members. For nursing home residents, a survey administered by an interviewer is likely to produce more objective results than one that the resident fills out independently. Interviewer-administered resident satisfaction surveys have been developed by NRC Picker, Rutgers University, and Vital Research. Several instruments are also available for self-administered family satisfaction surveys (Moore et al., 2004).

## Evaluation and Interpretation

Once outcomes have been measured, the results must be interpreted. For instance, a numerical score is meaningless unless its relevance is clearly established. Such interpretation of measurements in this context is called *evaluation*. The goal of evaluation is to transform numerical scores into meaningful information that would be useful for improving quality. Evaluation is always done in relation to some benchmark. A benchmark can be anything that management considers acceptable. For example, staff turnover is an inverse and indirect measure of quality; a high score indicates low quality of human resource and leadership practices, and vice versa. Suppose a given nursing home has an annual turnover rate of 30% for licensed nurses. This measure is not very helpful unless it can be interpreted in relation to some benchmark such as nurse turnover rates in the nursing home industry or within a multifacility corporation or a target established by the administrator and the governing board.

## Measuring Quality of Life

For nursing home residents, quality of care and quality of life (QoL) are closely intertwined. Only recently have measures of QoL been developed and tested, mainly through research projects undertaken at the University of Minnesota under the direction of Rosalie Kane (Kane, 2001). These measures are shown in Exhibit 19–1 for illustrative purposes only. The questions are intended to be used for interviews in which nursing home residents, including those with mild to moderate cognitive impairment, are asked the actual questions in each of the 11 domains. Although the implementation of these measures has been difficult, they provide an understanding of the domains that must be addressed to improve quality of life.

## Quality Improvement

The current focus in health care is on *continuous quality improvement (CQI)*, which is an ongoing undertaking to improve quality throughout the nursing facility. Also called total quality management (TQM), quality improvement requires total effort involving all associates in the organization. Quality improvement in long-term care embodies six basic principles (adapted from Evans & Lindsay, 1993) that form the framework for CQI:

- A facility can be successful only by understanding and fulfilling the needs of customers.

- Leadership in improving quality is the responsibility of the nursing home administrator, with full support from the governing board. Leaders must work toward establishing a culture of quality.

- Statistical evaluation using factual data is the basis for CQI.

- All departments within the facility must implement CQI.

- Problem solving and process improvement are best performed by interdisciplinary (or multidisciplinary) work teams.

- Continuous learning, training, and education are the responsibility of everyone in the organization, but these activities require support from the top.

## Meeting Customer Needs

Quality management is primarily based on understanding who the customers are. Here, the term *customer* is used in a broad sense as any entity that receives the product of a transaction. Patients and their families are commonly regarded as customers, and rightly so.

**Exhibit 19–1** Quality of Life Measures (illustrative only)

---

**Domains, their definitions, and questions for assessing each domain**

Note: Depending on the resident's ability to respond, the questions are assessed according to a 4-point scale (often, sometimes, rarely, never) or a dichotomous scale (mostly yes, mostly no), except for the first two questions in the Meaningful Activity scale.

**A. Physical comfort.** Residents are free from pain, uncomfortable symptoms, and other physical discomforts. They perceive that their pain and discomfort are noticed and addressed by the staff.

    1. How often are you too cold here?

    2. How often are you so long in the same position that it hurts?

    3. How often are you in physical pain?

    4. How often are you bothered by noise when you are in your room?

    5. How often are you bothered by noise in other parts of the nursing home, for example, in the dining room?

    6. Do you get a good night's sleep here?

**B. Functional competence.** Within the limits of their physical and cognitive abilities, residents are as independent as they wish to be.

    1. Is it easy for you to get around in your room by yourself?

    2. Can you easily reach the things that you need?

    3. If you are anywhere in the nursing home and need a bathroom, can you get to one quickly?

    4. Can you easily reach your toilet articles and things that you want to use in your bathroom?

    5. Do you do as much to take care of your own things and your room as you can and want?

**C. Privacy.** Residents have bodily privacy, can keep personal information confidential, can be alone as desired, and can be with others in private.

    1. Can you find a place to be alone if you wish?

    2. Can you make a private phone call?

    3. When you have a visitor, can you find a place to visit in private?

    4. Can you be together in private with another resident (other than your roommate)?

    5. Do the people who work here knock and wait for a reply before entering your room?

**D. Dignity.** Residents perceive their dignity is intact and respected. They do not feel belittled, devalued, or humiliated.

    1. Does the staff here treat you politely?

    2. Do you feel that you are treated with respect here?

    3. Does the staff here handle you gently while giving you care?

    4. Does the staff here respect your modesty?

    5. Does the staff take time to listen to you when you have something to say?

---

*(continues)*

**Exhibit 19–1** Quality of Life Measures (illustrative only) (Continued)

**E. Meaningful activity.** Residents engage in discretionary behavior that results in self-affirming competence or active pleasure in the doing of or watching of an activity.

1. Do you get outdoors: As much as you want? Too much?
   Too little?
2. About how often do you get outdoors?
3. Do you enjoy the organized activities here at the nursing home?
4. Outside of religious activities, do you have enjoyable things to do at the nursing home during the weekend?
5. Despite your health condition, do you give help to others, such as other residents, your family, people at this nursing home, or the outside community?
6. Do the days here seem too long to you?

**F. Relationships.** Residents engage in meaningful person-to-person social interchange with other residents, with the staff, or with family and friends who live outside the nursing home.

1. Is it easy to make friends at this nursing home?
2. Do you consider that any other resident here is your close friend?
3. In the last month, have people who worked here stopped just to have a friendly conversation with you?
4. Do you consider any staff member to be your friend?
5. Do you think that *(name of the facility)* tries to make this an easy and pleasant place for families and friends of residents to visit?

**G. Autonomy.** Residents take initiative and make choices for their lives and care.

1. Can you go to bed at the time you want?
2. Can you get up in the morning at the time you want?
3. Can you decide what clothes to wear?
4. Have you been successful in making changes in things that you do not like?

**H. Food enjoyment.** Residents enjoy meals and food.

1. Do you like the food at *(name of the facility)*?
2. Do you enjoy mealtimes at *(name of the facility)*?
3. Can you get your favorite foods at *(name of the facility)*?

**I. Spiritual well-being.** Residents' needs and concerns for religion, prayer, meditation, spirituality, and moral values are met.

1. Do you participate in religious activities here?
2. Do the religious activities here have personal meaning for you?
3. Do you feel your life as a whole has meaning?
4. Do you feel at peace?

*(continues)*

**Exhibit 19–1** Quality of Life Measures (illustrative only) (Continued)

**J. Security.** Residents feel secure and confident about their personal safety, are able to move about freely, believe that their possessions are secure, and believe that the staff has good intentions. They know and understand the rules, expectations, and routines of the facility.

　　1. Do you feel that your possessions are safe at this nursing home?

　　2. Do your clothes get lost or damaged in the laundry?

　　3. Do you feel confident that you can get help when you need it?

　　4. If you do not feel well, can you get a nurse or doctor quickly?

　　5. Do you ever feel afraid because of the way you or some other resident is treated?

**K. Individuality.** Residents express their preferences, pursue their past and current interests, maintain a sense of their own identity, and perceive they are known as individuals.

　　1. Taking all staff together, nurses, aides and others, do staff members know about your interests and what you like?

　　2. Do staff members know you as a person?

　　3. Are the people working here interested in your experiences and the things you have done in your life?

　　4. Does the staff here take your preferences seriously?

　　5. Do residents here know you as a person?

　　6. Are your personal wishes and interests respected here?

*Source: Quality of life scales for nursing home residents* (December 2001). CMS project: Measures, indicators, and improvement of quality of life in nursing homes. Study Director: Rosalie A. Kane; CMS Project Officer: Mary Pratt; CMS Co-project Officer: Karen Schoeneman. Used by courtesy of Rosalie A. Kane, Division of Health Services Research and Policy, School of Public Health, University of Minnesota.

There are other customers, however, who may not receive the end product, but have a vested interest in the quality of the products. Griffith and White (2002) referred to them as *customer partners.* Customer partners or external customers are the stakeholders. They include payers (Medicaid, Medicare, managed care organizations, and other insurers), regulatory agencies (state departments of health, agencies on aging, local health and fire departments, and the Joint Commission for Accreditation of Healthcare Organizations), and referral agencies (hospitals, physicians, and others). A nursing facility also has *internal customers,* which include all personnel who receive information, services, or other professional support from fellow employees. To deliver what external customers expect, these internal customers have to depend on each others' outputs (Bradley & Thompson, 2000). Attending physicians, for example, rely on information and support from the facility's nursing staff, and these physicians should be regarded as critical internal customers. The same attending physicians can also be regarded as external customers when they refer patients to the facility. Certified nursing assistants (CNAs) need the support of professional nurses, and nurses in turn often rely on the CNAs to report problems or changes in a patient's condition.

Quality cannot be improved without a strong commitment on the part of all associates to meet the needs and expectations of all customers. Also, the requirements of internal customers should be linked to those of the external customers. If an internal requirement does not in some way help meet external customer requirements, then its value should be questioned (Gaucher & Coffey, 1993).

## Leadership and Culture

Commitment, leadership, and support from top management play a vital role in establishing the overall tone for CQI. Empirical evidence demonstrates that success in CQI implementation is strongly associated with the commitment and culture of top management. In organizations characterized by top management commitment, turnover at key top-level positions is low, the associates view top management as strong advocates of CQI, leaders are open minded and communicative, leadership styles are participatory and team oriented, and top managers demonstrate a clear understanding of CQI principles (Parker et al., 1999).

Top managers must first understand the concepts of CQI and then become knowledgeable about the tools, processes, and methods necessary for quality improvement (Baird et al., 1993). Commitment to CQI includes allocation of required resources. Top managers should then set goals and plans for implementing principles and practices for quality. Top managers must be committed to involving all associates by providing proper

training and a reward system for accomplishing quality goals (Evans & Lindsay, 1993).

Most experts agree that quality improvement occurs in an organizational culture that values quality. On the other hand, one of the key barriers to change is the conscious or unconscious retention of old beliefs and actions that discourage innovation, creativity, empowerment, or other components of CQI (Gaucher & Coffey, 1993). Once a CQI program is under way, both managers and workers should be prepared to accept failures along the way. However, patience and perseverance are necessary. Fear of failure only stifles innovation.

Management must seriously engage in building a culture of quality. A CQI culture has the following characteristics (Parker et al., 1999):

- CQI is not viewed as a distinct initiative, but as an everyday part of each associate's job.

- Morale is high, and staff turnover is low.

- Associates have a strong sense of pride in the organization.

- Communication is open, and risk taking is rewarded.

- Change is readily accepted.

- Strong team orientation is apparent.

Organizational culture can change only gradually over time. Management must continually emphasize to its associates that quality remains a top priority; otherwise, the organization risks losing the commitment of the associates (Evans & Lindsay, 1993). Relatively short tenures of nursing home administrators and other key personnel disrupt the cultural continuity that is so essential for CQI. Job-hopping administrators never get to understand the facilities they manage for short durations. Such administrators do a great disservice to the patients and to their profession because follow-through over time is necessary for building quality and productivity. A culture of quality is built over time with staff stability and consistency. This culture requires empowering leadership that is open to the ideas of others. Managers share organizational power by giving autonomy and discretion over tasks to the associates; they build relationships by coaching and mentoring; they use rewards and recognition to change behaviors that would otherwise stifle quality improvement (Gaucher & Coffey, 1993).

## Data-Driven Process Improvement Cycle

Quality improvement is anchored on a quantitative approach in which data and measurements are used to evaluate the current state of quality, improve processes, and track progress. The Deming cycle, named after W. Edwards Deming (1900–1993), is used to focus on improving processes that would result in improved outputs. It involves four steps: plan, do, study, and act (PDSA). The PDSA cycle is a continuous improvement cycle (Figure 19–2) that can be applied to any process, using data to identify key process problems.

**Figure 19–2** The PDSA Cycle

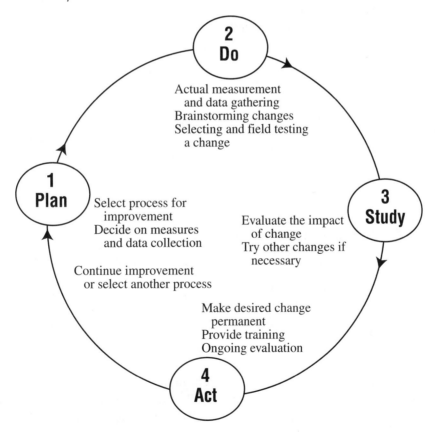

## Plan

The "plan stage" consists of studying the current situation, gathering appropriate data, and planning for improvement. The plan stage focuses on uncovering quality problems and selecting a specific area for improvement. Initially, it may be best to address small-scale problems that would facilitate learning the PDSA process and build the confidence of associates in applying this process. If benchmarks or standards are available, variations are measured to determine how much current outcomes deviate from the standards. Decisions are made about what type of ongoing measurements or data collection are needed. For example, CNAs who serve meals to residents may report frequent diet errors, but only data collection can provide quantitative information on the number and types of errors to indicate the extent of the problem.

Once the PDSA system is learned, the selection of topics should be driven by priorities in addressing areas where outcomes are less than acceptable. Improvement in patient care should outweigh all other goals of a quality improvement program. Answering certain questions can help focus on the most important topics (Vitale & Vengroski, 1993): Does the problem interfere with the delivery of quality care? Is it a high-risk concern? Will the benefit of improved outcomes outweigh the cost of monitoring and correcting the problem? Is the problem common enough to warrant the effort and cost to solve it? Can the problem be solved with available financial and human resources?

## Do

The "do stage" involves actual measurement and data gathering. Sources of data may be the facility's own internal records and information systems, special surveys, logs, check-sheets, or observational studies. The data can be charted using flow diagrams, cause-and-effect diagrams, and various types of statistical charts. Charting provides a clear understanding of the process to be improved because the charts help visualize trends and the magnitude of deviations from acceptable standards. Charts and diagrams can also help pinpoint critical elements that can be improved. Changes are then discussed and implemented on a small-scale trial basis. In the previous example, tray accuracy studies can be a useful diagnostic tool for evaluating the quantity and seriousness of diet errors, both from the standpoint of quality of care and quality of life (Dowling & Cotner, 1988). Such studies may also point to where in the process the breakdowns occur. In the "do stage" of the PDSA cycle, a critical step in the process where the breakdown occurs is chosen for testing an intervention that could alleviate the breakdown. For example, in the meal delivery system, a checker may be assigned at the end of the tray line to check all items on the meal trays against diet cards for individual patients.

## Study

The "study stage" requires an evaluation of the changes that have been made in a selected process and the effect of those changes on quality improvement. This stage requires ongoing data collection to determine the effectiveness of implemented changes, and the extent of improvement. If the changes do not produce at least some improvement, other changes should be discussed, tried, and tested. In the meal tray example, ongoing data collection will tell whether the change results in reducing diet errors and whether the change should be made permanent.

## Act

The "act stage" deals with implementing a change after the value of that change has been confirmed. New practices are institutionalized by training all associates who are affected by the changes and by communicating, updating policies and procedures, and monitoring to ensure that the improved methods become routine.

The PDSA process is repeated to further improve the same process, if outcomes show the need for additional improvement, or to address a different area of concern. Ongoing use of the PDSA cycle produces continuous improvement in quality.

## Encompassing All Departments

CQI must focus on all departmental functions in the facility. Because the main functions of the different departments are interdependent, total quality can only be achieved by applying CQI to every function. CQI requires scrutiny of interdepartmental communications, process interlinkages, and horizontal coordination among the various organizational units, all in the context of meeting the expectations of internal and external customers.

## Interdisciplinary Work Teams

The interdependency of functions in a facility underscores the need for an interdisciplinary approach to quality improvement. A team approach to quality improvement is likely to make the process unbiased, systematic, and thorough. The team approach can be accomplished by formulating a quality improvement committee composed of associates representing every discipline. Under the leadership of the administrator or a consultant, the composition of the committee should change as new quality issues are addressed. As different associates get the opportunity to be on the team, the team becomes a mechanism for building a culture of quality in the organization, in training associates, and in building a sense of ownership in quality improvement. Once the CQI is well established, more than one team can work on different quality improvement projects.

Hiring a consultant may be necessary for CQI, especially when a facility initiates a CQI program. The consultant can evaluate the cultural aspects of the organization that could pose barriers to the success of a CQI program. When substantial barriers are foreseen, the administrator is in a better position to develop a strategy for gradual change. The consultant can also be instrumental in training associates at all levels as well as senior management. Such organization-wide training is how CQI programs are almost always formally begun. Training is necessary to reach a common understanding about CQI, clarify goals, and establish reasonable expectations.

## Continuous Learning

A well-developed CQI program involves the participation of associates at all levels of the organization. Continuous learning then becomes institutionalized alongside continuous improvement of quality as associates discover improved methods and play a role in implementing them. The results of PDSA cycles should be shared with all affected associates. In an interdisciplinary environment, associates get to better understand how their actions affect the work of others and how their actions, in turn, affect the expectations and satisfaction of both internal and external customers.

# Quality Culture

The end result of CQI is the emergence of an organization-wide culture of excellence. When quality is institutionalized, it produces an organizational culture that retains and attracts like-minded associates who are dedicated to delivering excellence. In such an environment, all associates receive social and psychological gratification by knowing that because they have chosen to put excellence first and foremost, others are better off. Management recognizes the contribution of the associates by expressing appreciation in various forms, including financial rewards. The reward system is designed so that it promotes cooperation and team effort, not envy and competitiveness. As such, the reward system does not exclude any member of the organization. Finally, such a nursing facility gains a community-wide reputation for excellence that is recognized by all external exchange partners. But, even at this stage, facility management continues to seek ways to improve structures, processes, and outcomes. Management ensures the satisfaction of customers through a firm commitment to never-ending improvement in quality.

In studying the ongoing pursuit of quality, some thoughts from Deming are noteworthy. Deming is counted among the greatest pioneers of the quality improvement movement. Many books on CQI have reproduced, in one form or another, his 14 principles of quality improvement. These principles are directed at management attitudes and actions, because Deming believed that quality breakdowns were attributable to management, not workers. Much of the earlier discussion in this chapter incorporates these principles. The following thoughts summarize the remaining pertinent requirements that are also necessary for building a culture of quality in nursing facilities:

- Create constancy of purpose toward improvement of product and service, with the aim to become competitive in the market. A facility must create value to remain ahead of the competition. Because

$$Value = \frac{Quality}{Cost},$$

cost reduction efforts that reduce quality are likely to decrease value. On the other hand, improving quality may increase cost somewhat, but value is enhanced to a greater extent than costs are increased (Lighter & Fair, 2000). Hence, CQI efforts should aim to increase both quality and productivity.

- Cease dependence on inspections to improve quality. Eliminate the need for inspections on a mass basis by building quality into the product (service) in the first place. Inspection should be used as an information-gathering tool for improvement, not as the principal tool for quality control (Evans & Lindsay, 1993).

- Drive out fear so that everyone may work effectively for the organization. Fear may promote short-term gains, but longer-term accomplishments are less likely, because workers spend more time inventing ways of avoiding difficult situations than finding methods of improving output. Empowerment rather than threats should be used to motivate employees (Lighter & Fair, 2000). CQI should be used to find process problems, not to assign blame to workers. Otherwise, they would spend their time covering up problems for fear of being blamed for problems.

- Break down barriers between departments. Internal competition for raises, performance ratings, and recognition can be counterproductive. Incentives associated with CQI should promote cooperation and teamwork, not competition.

- Eliminate slogans and exhortations. Posters and slogans assume that all quality problems are attributable to people. They overlook the fact that most quality problems are systemic and cannot be improved through posters, slogans, or the wearing of happy-face buttons. Attacking problems rather than workers, understanding the causes of problems, and using statistical thinking and training to improve processes are necessary for achieving higher quality.

- Eliminate quotas. Standards and quotas that workers are often held to are generally used punitively. These standards and quotas are born out of short-term perspectives and create fear. A quota, such as requiring each CNA to take sole responsibility for a predefined number of patients, promotes short-cuts in quality in order to reach a numerical goal. Once numerical goals are achieved, there is no incentive to continue production or to improve quality. When these standards are not achieved workers become frustrated and resentful (Evans & Lindsay, 1993).

- Remove barriers to pride in workmanship. Hourly workers such as CNAs, housekeepers, dishwashers, and laundry workers are often treated by management as commodities. Pride in workmanship can be achieved through teamwork and continuous improvement strategies when workers are treated as valuable resources, not as commodities. According to Dem-

ing, there are three categories of employees: most work within the system, some are outside the system on the superior side, and others are outside the system on the inferior side. While superior performers should receive special compensation, inferior performers need extra training or should be replaced (Evans & Lindsay, 1993).

# The Wellspring Model

The Wellspring Model was created by Wellspring Innovative Solutions Inc. Implemented in 1994, the Wellspring Model has been used by an alliance of 11 nonprofit nursing homes in Wisconsin. Participants have been driven by the mission to improve the well-being of residents through quality improvement.

The Wellspring Model was derived from published research on workforce issues and management practices and on the effect of those issues and practices on the quality of patient care in nursing homes. The program is highly focused on using clinical modules that represent evidence-based best practices and on empowering associates. Wellspring has developed specific training modules for general issues of the older adult, incontinence care (elimination), nutrition, fall prevention, skin care, well-being, palliative care, and leadership.

Participating facilities pool their resources to employ a geriatric nurse practitioner (GNP) and to pay for staff training and data analysis. Managers as well as associates are trained in the clinical modules and on data collection. The training sessions are organized at a centralized location. The GNP is involved in clinical training, support, and reinforcement in all facilities. The management staff learns to adopt a coaching and mentoring style. Each facility has a designated nurse coordinator, who coaches the associates on implementing clinical modules. Associates are permanently assigned to teams responsible for rendering care to the same residents, an approach that fosters collaboration (Manard, 2002). All associates participate in decisions that affect their work and the care of residents they serve. Permanent resident assignments enable the associates to get to know the residents with whom they work on a daily basis. Some of these facilities have also turned over staff scheduling to the teams (Reinhard & Stone, 2001).

The Wellspring program also provides an example of how the principles of CQI can be applied to achieve higher quality by integrating top management commitment, organization-wide participation, organization of the associates into self-managed work teams, and data-driven methods for quality improvement. The project has successfully demonstrated that quality can be improved without increasing costs of input, thus dispelling the notion that quality can only be produced at higher cost. By forming a consortium, participating facilities realize cost savings through collaboration, resource sharing, and common learning. A study by Stone et al. (2002) reached the following conclusions:

- Rates of staff turnover were lower and increased more slowly than in comparable nursing homes in Wisconsin within the same time period.

- Wellspring facilities improved their performance on the federal survey.
- Generally, Wellspring facilities had lower costs than the comparison group.
- There is evidence that associates were more vigilant in assessing problems and took a more proactive approach to resident care, although clear evidence of improvement in clinical outcome, using minimum data set (MDS) quality indicators, could not be documented.
- Observational evidence and interview results indicated a better quality of life for residents and an improved quality of interaction between residents and staff.

The Wellspring Model has been replicated in some other states. According to 2005 information available on the organization's website, there were two alliances in Wisconsin, one in the Carolinas, and one in Maryland and District of Columbia.

The long-range answer to improved quality lies in a clear understanding of what quality is and the adoption of well-recognized principles and methods of quality improvement. These initiatives must come from nursing home leaders. Public policy, on the other hand, must support outcomes research to help develop and use evidence-based guidelines for patient care delivery.

## For Further Thought

1. Introducing a CQI initiative into a nursing facility is often associated with start-up costs, which in some instances may be quite substantial. For example, adopting the Wellspring program may cost $50,000 or more. What other direct or indirect costs may be associated with the adoption of CQI?

2. How would you evaluate whether spending a substantial amount of money on CQI is worth it?

3. As the administrator of a skilled nursing facility, how would you determine whether the facility is ready for CQI adoption?

---

## For Further Learning

The Wellspring Program (Wellspring Innovative Solutions Inc.)

http://www.wellspringis.org

---

## REFERENCES

Baird, R., et al. 1993. The implementation of total quality. In A.F. Al-Assaf and J.A. Schmele (eds.). *The Textbook of Total Quality in Healthcare* (pp. 91–101). Delray Beach, FL: St. Lucie Press.

Berlowitz, D.R., et al. 2001. Clinical practice guidelines in the nursing home. *American Journal of Medical Quality* 16, no. 6: 189–195.

Bradley, M.G., & Thompson, N.R. 2000. *Quality Management Integration in Long-Term Care.* Baltimore: Health Professions Press.

Donabedian, A. 1995. The quality of care: How can it be assessed? In N.O. Graham (ed.). *Quality in Health Care: Theory, Application, and Evolution* (pp 32–46). Gaithersburg, MD: Aspen Publishers.

Dowling, R., & Cotner, C. 1988. Monitor of tray error rates for quality control. *Journal of the American Dietetic Association* 88: 450–453.

Evans, J.R., & Lindsay, W.M. 1993. *The Management and Control of Quality.* St. Paul, MN: West Publishing.

Field, M.J., & Lohr, K.N. 1990. *Clinical Practice Guidelines: Directions for a New Agency.* Washington, DC: National Academy Press.

Finch-Guthrie, P. 2000. Care planning for older adults in health care settings. In R.L. Kane and R.A. Kane (eds.). *Assessing Older Persons: Measures, Meaning, and Practical Applications* (pp. 406–437). New York: Oxford University Press.

Gaucher, E.J., & Coffey, R.J. 1993. *Total Quality in Health Care: From Theory to Practice.* San Francisco: Jossey-Bass Publishers.

Griffith, J.R., & White, K.R. 2002. *The Well-Managed Health Care Organization,* 5th ed. Chicago: Health Administration Press, and Washington, DC: Association of University Programs in Health Administration.

IOM. 1986. *Improving the Quality of Care in Nursing Homes.* Washington, DC: National Academy Press, Institute of Medicine.

IOM. 2001. *Improving the Quality of Long-Term Care,* eds. G.S. Wunderlich and P.O. Kohler. Washington, DC: National Academy Press, Institute of Medicine.

Kane, R.A., et al. 2001. *Quality of Life Scales for Nursing Home Residents.* CMS project: Measures, indicators, and improvement of quality of life in nursing homes. Unpublished manuscript.

Loeb, M., et al. 1999. Risk factors for pneumonia and other lower respiratory tract infections in elderly residents of long-term care facilities. *Archives of Internal Medicine* 159, no. 17: 2058–2064.

Loeb, M., et al. 2006. Effect of a clinical pathway to reduce hospitalizations in nursing home residents with pneumonia. *Journal of the American Medical Association* 295, no. 21: 2503–2510.

Lighter, D.E., & Fair, D.C. 2000. *Principles and Methods of Quality Management in Health Care.* Gaithersburg, MD: Aspen Publishers.

Lawton, M.P. 2001. Quality of care and quality of life in dementia care units. In L. Noelker and Z. Harel (eds.). *Linking Quality of Long Term Care and Quality of Life* (pp. 136–161). New York: Springer.

Manard, B. 2002. *Nursing Home Quality Indicators: Their Uses and Limitations.* Washington, DC: Public Policy Institute, AARP.

McElroy, D., & Herbelin, K. 1989. Assuring quality of care in long-term care facilities. *Journal of Gerontological Nursing* 15, no. 7: 8–10.

Moore, T., et al. 2004. *Maryland Nursing Home Consumer Satisfaction: Recommendations Report—Final.* Abt Associates Inc. Retrieved March 2009 from http://mhcc.maryland.gov/longtermcare/recomfinalrpt.pdf.

Palmer, R.H. 1991. Considerations in defining quality of health care. In R.H. Palmer, A. Donabedian, and G.L. Povar (eds.). *Striving for Quality in Health Care: An Inquiry into Policy and Practice* (pp. 3–58). Ann Arbor, MI: Health Administration Press.

Parker, V.A., et al. 1999. Implementing quality improvement in hospitals: The role of leadership and culture. *American Journal of Medical Quality* 14, no. 1: 64–69.

Reinhard, S., & Stone, R. 2001. *Promoting Quality in Nursing Homes: The Wellspring Model.* New York: The Commonwealth Fund.

Stone, R., et al. 2002. *Evaluation of the Wellspring Model for Improving Nursing Home Quality.* New York: The Commonwealth Fund.

Vitale, B.A., & Vengroski, S.M. 1993. *Quality Assessment and Improvement in Long-Term Care: A Continuous Process.* Philadelphia: F.A. Davis.

Weech-Maldonado, R., et al. 2003. Does quality of care lead to better financial performance? The case of the nursing home industry. *Health Care Management Review* 28, no. 3: 201–216.

# PART V

## Case Studies

This section contains 12 cases that represent a variety of situations and challenges that nursing home administrators are likely to encounter in their careers. The cases have been developed specifically to supplement materials in this textbook. Each case narrative is followed by questions that require application of the materials learned and provoke further thought to make the student reason beyond what may be discovered in a textbook. Following is an overview of the cases:

- *Case 1: A Central American Immigrant Couple.* An elderly immigrant couple has been living with their son's family for a number of years. Changes in their circumstances require the family to make arrangements for the parents' long-term care needs. Is a nursing home appropriate?

- *Case 2: A Legal and Ethical Dilemma.* A lady who lived independently until she was 87 years old now has to live in a nursing home. She suffers from depression and dementia. The lady's son, an attorney, has threatened the facility with a lawsuit for failure to comply with his mother's alleged request to withhold food so she can die a quick death. The

matter is before the ethics committee for deliberation. What are the patient's rights?

- *Case 3: Abusive Spouse.* The wife of a 72-year-old nursing home resident has been accused of patient abuse. Is this really abuse?

- *Case 4: Advance Directives.* A young head trauma patient has been transferred back and forth between the nursing facility and the hospital. The court-appointed legal guardian is uninvolved. How can advance directives be obtained?

- *Case 5: Wound Care at Mountainview Nursing Center.* For an 83-year-old resident who has various chronic comorbid conditions, his daughter has the power of attorney. She does not go along with medical advice to amputate the patient's gangrenous leg. One day maggots are discovered in the wound. What are the legal implications of the nursing care the patient had received?

- *Case 6: Implementing Culture Change in Food Service.* The governing board of a four-story, 32-year-old nursing home has authorized funds to construct household-style kitchen and dining facilities on each floor. Current plans call for closing the existing kitchen, yet the facility must continue to serve meals to the residents. How can this be accomplished?

- *Case 7: Evacuation of Angel Care Center.* Hurricane Rita was approaching. Some residents were relocated, but about half had to be evacuated. Evacuation of nursing homes was not on the local government's evacuation plan. A day before the mandatory evacuation, the administrator learned that contracted transportation would not be available for taking the residents to a retreat center located 120 miles away. Last-minute pleas for help came through, but numerous problems were encountered. What lessons can be learned?

- *Case 8: Tug-of-War with the Director of Nursing.* A rookie administrator ends up creating tensions with the Director of Nursing. How can such conflicts be managed?

- *Case 9: Corporate Compliance at Mid-Atlantic Care Centers.* Five minority employees of a chain-affiliated nursing facility file a lawsuit over compensation issues triggered by the involvement of the vice president of operations. Which conditions of corporate compliance were

broken, and what should be the appropriate role of governance?

- *Case 10: Chapel Square Health Care Center: Workforce Diversity.* An inner-city unionized nursing home has a history of staff-related issues. The changing inner-city social environment and a workforce that has become culturally diversified pose serious challenges for a new administrator. The problems appear to be insurmountable. Is there a way out?

- *Case 11: Start-up of Blissful Gardens.* A new long-term care center that will have a small number of independent living apartments and a small skilled nursing facility is under construction. The executive director needs to define the mission, plan to hire management personnel, prepare a marketing plan, and think about future profitability. Can this operation be profitable by the end of its second year?

- *Case 12: Implementation of the Wellspring Model.* Administrators participating in a Wellspring alliance share their experiences about culture change. Some associates in one of the participating facilities express their opinions. What can be the underlying causes when a good program does not seem to work?

# Case 1

## A Central American Immigrant Couple

Rosa and Jaime Sanchez immigrated to the United States from a Central American country 18 years ago when they were in their early-60s. A son and a daughter were already living and working in the United States when they arrived. Rosa and Jaime lived with their son, Jorge, his wife, Maria, and two small children in a two-bedroom apartment. To make ends meet, Rosa found work in the laundry of a nearby motel, and Jaime took the night janitor's position at the local boys' club. Rosa had hypertension, which she controlled with medications obtained at a nearby community health center. Jaime was an insulin-dependent diabetic and had to pay for most of his medical expenses.

Two years after the arrival of her in-laws, Maria gave birth to another child. During the next six years or so, Rosa and Jaime learned barely enough English to become U.S. citizens. During this time, Jorge and Maria purchased a modest three-bedroom home, and the parents occupied one of the bedrooms. During this time, Rosa and Jaime had to stop working because of old age and declining health. Without a source of income, they qualified for Supplemental Security Income (SSI) and Medicaid. Most of the SSI income was handed over to the son for their room-and-board expenses. Medicaid covered their medical expenses.

Starting at age 71, Jaime suffered several mini-strokes. His blood sugar had not been well controlled. He also developed glaucoma in one eye and was barely able to see with that eye. The son and his wife both had full-time jobs. Before, Rosa was able to spend a lot of time taking care of her grandchildren, but now her husband required more attention. He needed assistance with bathing. He also needed insulin injections and blood sugar monitoring three times a day. Their daughter, who lived with her family about 15 miles away, came over and provided help periodically.

Jaime is now 77 years old. Two years ago, he fell and injured one of his ears. He has lost 75% of his hearing in that ear. Fortunately, he did not sustain any fractures. He wears a hearing aid in the other ear. Recently, he complained of declining eyesight in the good eye. An eye exam showed signs of macular degeneration. Rosa does not have the level of strength she once had to take care of Jaime. Both Jaime and Rosa use canes for walking because of some limitations in mobility.

Jaime and Rosa's grandchildren are grown. They need more space in their home and time to devote to their studies. Jorge and Maria show some level of frustration because they are unable to devote the necessary time to take care of Jorge's elderly parents. The parents have suggested that they don't have the money to go to an assisted living facility, but perhaps they can qualify for care in a nursing home. Jorge, Maria, and Jorge's sister have come to realize that the parents need to move out, but they don't know where to turn.

Jorge calls a nursing home located six miles from his home and makes an appointment to see the administrator.

## Assignment

1. On the basis of the information given in the case, assess Jaime and Rosa's current long-term care needs.

2. What type of living and care arrangement would you recommend?

# Case 2

## A Legal and Ethical Dilemma

CONTRIBUTED BY ALAN S. WHITEMAN, PhD, FACMPE, AND LISA E. SLINEY, MS, LNHA

## Background

Mary Evelyn Greene, who has memory impairment, lives in a private room at Shady Brook Skilled Nursing Facility, located in a beautiful suburb of a major metropolitan city. She has resided at Shady Brook for the past 18 months. Before moving into Shady Brook, Mrs. Greene lived independently in her own home with assistance from a private-duty nursing assistant and a housekeeper. She and her husband had resided together in this home for more than 50 years. Mrs. Greene is 89 years old and suffers from several health problems associated with aging.

Mrs. Greene has one son, David Greene. David has the power of attorney to handle his mother's health care and other personal affairs. David works as a trial attorney in one of the city's largest and most prestigious law firms. He owns a large home in an upscale neighborhood and works hard to put two of his children through college and another one through medical school. His home is about an hour's drive from his workplace and about 20 minutes from Shady Brook. David's wife Barbara has never been close to her mother-in-law and has not shown much interest in her care. Hence, caring for his mother has become a major responsibility for David, and he is having a difficult time dealing with her declining health and the onset of mild dementia. It is becoming increasingly more difficult for David to leave his law practice or the court room to deal with issues related to his mother.

Mrs. Greene's husband was a very successful land developer who left her with a very large estate, which meets all of her financial needs. After her husband passed away, Mrs. Greene decided to remain in her home. She was able to maintain her independence until she was 87 years old, when she began to show signs of dementia. Shortly thereafter, David moved her to Shady Brook. David also hired a part-time "sitter" to keep her mother company because she was too weak to go out of her room on her own. Mrs. Greene seems to enjoy the sitter's company and likes the attention she gets.

Upon entering Shady Brook, Mrs. Greene became depressed over losing her independence, her home, and a growing frustration with forgetfulness. She gradually lost her appetite, and her desire to eat continued to decline. On the other hand, Mrs. Greene seems

Dr. Whiteman is Associate Dean, Division of Health Management Programs, College of Health Sciences, Barry University.

Ms. Sliney is Executive Director, St. Andrews North in Boca Raton, Florida, and is a doctoral candidate.

to enjoy the smell of certain foods. The associates monitor and document her food intake and her facial expressions when she is offered different foods. Mrs. Greene is particularly fond of Susan Brown, a certified nursing assistant (CNA), who sits with her and helps Mrs. Greene with whatever little she can eat. When this occurs, her appetite shows some improvement. Mrs. Greene also responds well to volunteers who carry out activities at the facility.

## Frustrated Family Member

Mrs. Greene has become too weak to eat on her own. When no one is feeding her, she leaves most of her food on the tray. Recently, she has sustained a weight loss of more than five pounds per week. Her plan of care needs to be reevaluated, and her situation needs immediate attention.

David has been visiting his mother quite regularly. Recently, however, his visits have become less frequent, generally two to three times per week. The associates who work on Mrs. Greene's nursing unit have reported some changes in David's attitude. At one time he became angry with his mother, raised his voice, and spoke to her as if she were a bad child. Although no one was present in Mrs. Greene's room at the time, the associates working at the nursing station heard David's loud voice. When the charge nurse went into Mrs. Greene's room to find out why David was angry, David told her that it was none of her business. On David's subsequent visits, the associates observed that Mrs. Greene would become agitated during David's visits. These issues were brought to the charge nurse's attention, and they were documented in the patient's medical record.

## The Dilemma

One day David approached the charge nurse and exclaimed that his mother had expressed that she wished to die. On his next two visits, David also told the CNAs that his mother's desire was not to eat anything so she could just die a quick death. This was the first time the CNAs had heard that Mrs. Greene had expressed a desire to die. The associates also believed that Mrs. Greene appeared to be happier when David was not there.

Before the week was over, David came into the facility early in the morning on his way to work. He handed a sealed envelope to the incoming charge nurse on the day shift. The envelope was addressed to Betty Wright, Shady Brook's administrator. David said to the charge nurse, "I have been telling you people that my mother wishes a speedy death. Tell your administrator that I will be filing a lawsuit if my mother's wishes are not carried out." David left without visiting his mother.

Betty Wright decided to place the issue on the ethics committee's agenda for that same afternoon. As a safeguard, Betty also notified the facility's liability insurance carrier of the potential legal action.

## Meeting of the Ethics Committee

That afternoon, Betty met with members of the ethics committee: chaplain, medical director, director of nursing, charge nurse, social worker, two CNAs, and the local ombudsman. Betty began the meeting with these remarks: "The man's mother has been declining rapidly and eats very little. He wants his mother to die rather than prolong her suffering. I have learned that the son is the heir to his mother's estate, and my overall concern is my trust in his decision or his motives. I think he needs the money to pay for the college expenses for his three children. Although it is not uncommon for some residents to be ignored by family after they are admitted, it is rare that they express the wish to enable the death of a rel- atively healthy person." The ethics committee is faced with the issue of what is legally and ethically appropriate. The committee deliber- ates on whether or not to comply with David's request to withhold food—and the threat of a lawsuit.

## Assignment

1. In a sentence or two, identify the main issue.
2. Outline the facts pertaining to this issue.
3. Identify alternative solutions that the ethics committee might consider.
4. What may be the consequences of the alternatives you have proposed in question 3? Discuss the consequences from the perspectives of (a) Mrs. Greene and (b) Shady Brook.
5. Discuss the alternatives from the standpoint of the patient's rights.
6. What will be your recommendation to the ethics committee?
7. In their deliberations, should the committee members take into consideration Betty's comment that Dave needs the money to educate his children?

# Case 3

# Abusive Spouse

THE ASSISTANCE OF ANTHONY UGHETTI, NHA, IN DEVELOPING THIS CASE IS GRATEFULLY ACKNOWLEDGED.

Sid Hollister, a 72-year-old male patient with Parkinson's disease and dementia, was admitted to Golden Gate Nursing Center. The attending physician ordered a pureed diet, and the patient had a G-tube for enteral feeding. Mr. Hollister occupied a private room, located right across from the nursing station.

Mrs. Hollister, the patient's spouse, made it a point to visit the facility every day, particularly at meal times. As time progressed, she seemed to spend more and more time in the facility. Although the posted visiting hours were from 6:30 a.m. to 8:30 p.m., Mrs. Hollister often stayed in the facility until late at night. The associates observed behaviors that led them to think that Mrs. Hollister carried a lot of frustration and dissatisfaction, but she never expressed any complaints. From time to time, she would make comments such as, "I can't leave him alone here; something will happen to him." "There is never any help around here." She constantly felt that she needed to be involved with Mr. Hollister's care. She would assist him with eating. She kept a washcloth to wipe off the drooling saliva from the patient's face. She even started directing his care regarding bathing and toileting.

One January day during the lunch meal, Mrs. Hollinger was in the room feeding the patient. A nurse observed that Mrs. Hollinger was forcing the patient's mouth open. Her hand was lifted up, and she allegedly slapped the resident on the left cheek. The staff immediately removed the spouse from the patient's room. The DON and the police were notified. A police report on domestic violence was registered. The facility also completed its internal incident report, and another incident report was sent to the state Department of Health.

From this point on, Mrs. Hollinger was barred from the facility. After she complained about her right to be in the facility, the social worker notified her that she could be in the facility as long as she was supervised. A meeting was held in the facility that included the local ombudsman, a representative from adult protective services, and the corporation's risk management representative. An understanding was reached that the facility would monitor Mrs. Hollinger's conduct during her visits to the facility.

There were no further incidents. In April, John Shull was appointed as the administrator. At 7:30 a.m. when John came to work one day in July, a CNA approached him and informed him that she saw Mrs. Hollinger hit her husband on the face. The alleged incident had occurred during breakfast in the patient's room. The wife admitted and said, "I was giving him a glass of water, and he clamped his teeth down on it. I had to smack his face a bit to make him let go. This is not abuse." Upon examination by a nurse, it was found that no injuries were sustained by the patient.

## Assignment

1. Should the latest incident in July be regarded as patient abuse or not? See Exhibit CS3–1.

2. How would you go about investigating and documenting the incident? See Exhibits CS3–2 and CS3–3.

3. Suppose this is patient abuse, what further action would you take?

**Exhibit CS3–1** Definition Diagram—Abuse

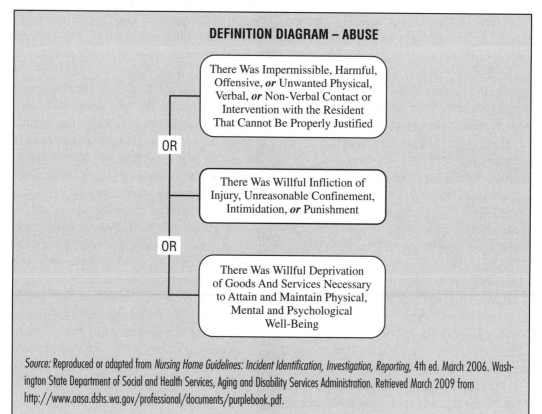

**DEFINITION DIAGRAM – ABUSE**

There Was Impermissible, Harmful, Offensive, *or* Unwanted Physical, Verbal, *or* Non-Verbal Contact or Intervention with the Resident That Cannot Be Properly Justified

OR

There Was Willful Infliction of Injury, Unreasonable Confinement, Intimidation, *or* Punishment

OR

There Was Willful Deprivation of Goods And Services Necessary to Attain and Maintain Physical, Mental and Psychological Well-Being

*Source:* Reproduced or adapted from *Nursing Home Guidelines: Incident Identification, Investigation, Reporting,* 4th ed. March 2006. Washington State Department of Social and Health Services, Aging and Disability Services Administration. Retrieved March 2009 from http://www.aasa.dshs.wa.gov/professional/documents/purplebook.pdf.

**Exhibit CS3-2** Responsibility Table

This table serves as a tool to help providers in understanding responsibilities to protect, investigate, report, and prevent abuse, neglect, exploitation, and misappropriation of resident properly.

|  | **Nursing Home Responsibilities** |
|---|---|
| Protection | • Safeguard resident(s) from further incident reoccurrence<br>• Treat all consequent ill effects experienced by resident(s)<br>• Provide first aide or emergency medical attention to address any sustained injuries and/or medical/mental problems<br>• Implement facility administrative decisions (e.g., suspension or reassignment of staff during investigation, if necessary) |
| Investigation | • Conduct Phase I investigation within 24 hours<br>• Follow up with Phase II investigation if cause and/or reasonable cause undetermined |
| Reporting | • Log in state reporting log abuse, neglect, superficial/substantial injuries of unknown source, misappropriated property<br>• Notify State Hotline of allegations within 24 hours<br>• Notify Administrator immediately of allegations<br>• Notify police of suspect crminal activity |
| Prevention and Corrective Action | • Resolve cause<br>• Prevent re-occurrence of incident (e.g., revise plan of care, disciplinary action, education, training, revision of principle/procedure)<br>• Engage facility administrative decisions<br>• Report all suspect incidents of abuse, neglect, exploitation, or misappropriated property |

*Source:* Reproduced or adapted from *Nursing Home Guidelines: Incident Identification, Investigation, Reporting,* 4th ed. March 2006. Washington State Department of Social and Health Services, Aging and Disability Services Administration. Retrieved March 2009 from http://www.aasa.dshs.wa.gov/professional/documents/purplebook.pdf.

**Exhibit CS3–1**  Definition Diagram—Abuse

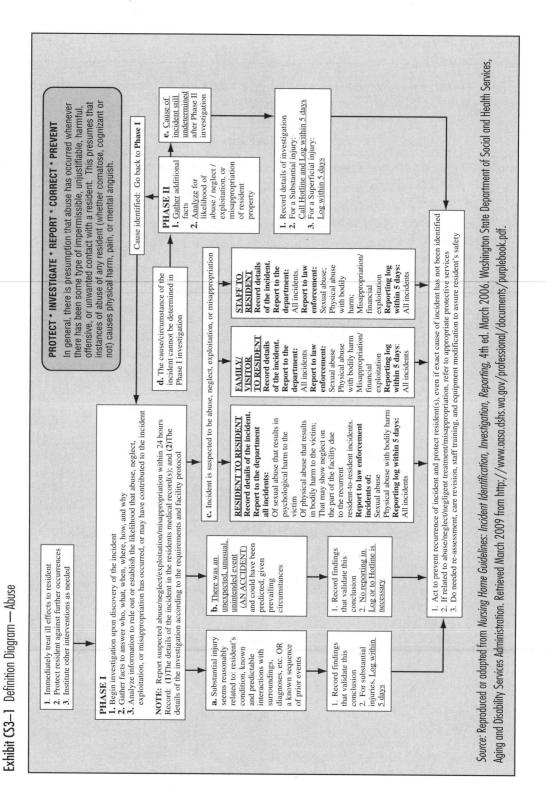

*Source:* Reproduced or adapted from *Nursing Home Guidelines: Incident Identification, Investigation, Reporting,* 4th ed. March 2006. Washington State Department of Social and Health Services, Aging and Disability Services Administration. Retrieved March 2009 from http://www.aasa.dshs.wa.gov/professional/documents/purplebook.pdf.

# Case 4

---

# Advance Directives

THE ASSISTANCE OF PATRICK CLAUDIUS, MD, IN DEVELOPING THIS CASE IS GRATEFULLY ACKNOWLEDGED.

An 18-year-old male patient was admitted to Greenfields Nursing Home, South Carolina, from another skilled nursing facility located in North Carolina. The patient was moved to South Carolina because he qualified for Medicaid in that state. The patient stayed at Greenfields for 12 years until his death at the age of 30.

The patient had sustained a serious head injury in an auto accident at the age of 15. As a result of this injury, the patient became comatose. He remained in a persistent vegetative state and had a G-tube for enteral feeding. However, the patient's overall condition was stable. He received maintenance rehabilitation for severe contractures in hands, arms, and feet. The patient also received regular sensory stimulation.

The patient had fevers off and on in the range of 100° F to 102° F. His fevers were most likely to be secondary in nature because most other causes, such as infections, were excluded. The nursing staff was able to control the fevers using ice packs and alternate administration of Tylenol and Motrin. At times, however, he would have episodes of urinary tract infection. He was also hospitalized with recurrent aspiration pneumonia. He began running fevers as high as 106° F. Sputum and urine cultures showed the presence of methicillin-resistant *Staphylococcus aureus* (MRSA) infection. Sometimes, severe infection required hospitalization in the intensive care unit. Intermittently, the patient had to be placed on a ventilator.

Shortly after the auto accident, the patient's mother abandoned him. The mother is the one who caused the accident that resulted in this patient's severe head trauma; she was driving the vehicle in a state of intoxication. The patient had no family contact whatsoever. The court appointed the Department of Social Services as the patient's legal guardian. The Department of Social Services, however, was uninvolved in his care and did not give any directives regarding continuity of treatment. The patient eventually died of natural causes.

---

# Assignment

1. Should the patient have been referred to hospice care?
2. The patient went into coma at the age of 15 and had no advance directives. What role would advance directives have played in this case?
3. How might Greenfields Nursing Home be able to obtain advance directives in a similar situation?

# Case 5

## Wound Care at Mountainview Nursing Center

THE ASSISTANCE OF PATRICK CLAUDIUS, MD, IN DEVELOPING THIS CASE IS GRATEFULLY ACKNOWLEDGED.

Subsequent to his discharge from a local acute care hospital where he had received treatment for pneumonia, Jim Harris was admitted to Mountainview Nursing Center five years ago. Mr. Harris was 83 years old. According to the minimum data set (MDS) assessment, the patient had various chronic comorbid conditions. These conditions persisted over a period of two years while Mr. Harris was a patient at Mountainview. The patient was eventually discharged to an acute care hospital and never returned to Mountainview.

Mountainview is a 112-bed dually certified nursing care facility affiliated with a for-profit multifacility chain. The nursing home is located in a rural county with a population of 27,000. The median household income in the county is $32,900. Approximately 64% of the adults over the age of 25 have completed a high school education; 10% of the adult population have finished a bachelor's degree or higher.

Mr. Harris's daughter, Nancy, had the power of attorney for the patient's medical treatment. Nancy visited the facility regularly and did not express any notable concerns with her father's care at Mountainview.

## Medical and Nursing Evaluations and Treatments

### Diagnoses at the Time of Admission

- Diabetic gangrene of the foot (heightens the risk for septicemia).
- Peripheral vascular disease (causes poor healing of wounds).
- Congestive heart failure (poses high surgical risk).
- Depression.
- Short-term memory loss.
- Dysphagia (increases the risk of nutritional deficiency).
- Unsteady gait; a walker was used for ambulation.

### Main Observations

The patient had a vascular (ischemic) ulcer.* Necrosis of the tissues had set in, the wound was infected, and purulent discharge was observed.

_____
*An open wound that results from poor blood circulation.

535

## Treatments

The wound's dressing was to be changed once a day, and Accuzyme, a topical medicine, was to be applied with each dressing change. Protein supplements, zinc supplement, and multivitamins were ordered to promote healing of the wound. The patient needed insulin for diabetes.

In addition to daily dressing change, the wound was measured once a week. The patient was also referred to a specialized wound care center located 45 minutes away from Mountainview. The patient received wound care once a month at the wound care center. At Mountainview, Mr. Harris also received intermittent physical therapy to promote circulation and speech therapy for dysphagia.

While the patient was in the hospital, before his admission to Mountainview, a Doppler study was conducted to evaluate arterial circulation in the leg. The test showed a severe blockage in the leg. Consultation with a vascular surgeon was recommended. However, Nancy refused the consultation on grounds that surgery presented too great a risk given the patient's medical condition. Nancy also refused the insertion of a G-tube through which the patient could ingest specialized nutritional formulas.

A general surgeon had recommended amputation of the leg because of the gangrene. Nancy considered this to be too drastic a measure and did not opt for it. The surgeon as well as the patient's attending physician had discussed with Nancy the risks and benefits of leg amputation versus non-surgical treatments. According to medical opinion, amputation presented the least risk. However, Nancy had anticipated that over time her father's wound would heal. As time progressed, Nancy showed growing frustra-tion that the wound was not healing. Although some progress would be noted at times, it would be followed by deterioration. The ups and downs in the healing process persisted.

## Incidents and Outcomes

In the final 30 days of the patient's stay at Mountainview, the patient sustained a fall from wheelchair to floor. Mr. Harris did not have a history of falls even though his gait was unsteady. A restraint was not recommended and was not used. When the patient was in a wheelchair, the nursing staff used a personal alarm that would alert the staff to any forward movement or leaning from the wheelchair. However, by the time the staff came to see what had happened, the fall had already occurred. The nurses did not notice any injuries from the fall, but the patient was sent to the hospital for evaluation. Within two weeks of the fall, the patient developed pneumonia and was hospitalized, but he returned to Mountainview within three to four days.

One morning a nurse found that the dressing had slipped from the wound. At times the patient was agitated. Hence, the nurse believed that the patient may have kicked off his dressing while he was agitated. On closer examination, the nurse saw maggots in the wound. The wound was cleaned with saline solution, and the dressing was changed. In the afternoon, maggots were found again. In accordance with nursing protocols, Nancy was informed, and the medical director, who was also the attending physician for this patient, was notified. The patient was transferred to the hospital's emergency room.

The patient never returned to Mountainview. Three months later, the facility was informed that it was named as the defendant in a lawsuit. Mountainview's corporate office settled the lawsuit out of court for an undisclosed amount.

---

## Assignment

1. Evaluate the legal implications of the nursing care that Mr. Harris received while a patient at Mountainview Nursing Center.

2. Would a physical restraint be appropriate to prevent falls in this situation?

3. Discuss the care of Mr. Harris from the standpoint of his rights as a patient.

4. In this situation, how would you ensure that the patient's own wishes are carried out?

5. Why do you think the nursing home corporation settled this case out of court? Would you have let the litigation proceed through the court system? Do you think the facility would be held liable?

6. It was assumed that the patient's agitation caused the dressing to dislocate. Could the facility have done anything to prevent that?

7. What actions would you take to assess and improve infection control practices in the nursing home following Mr. Harris's discharge?

8. In this case, Nancy refused the insertion of a G-tube. In a patient who has dysphagia, medical problems such as aspiration, pneumonia, and choking can occur. Can the facility take any proactive steps to protect itself against a charge of negligence?

# Case 6

---

# Implementing Culture Change in Food Service

CONTRIBUTED BY JULLET DAVIS, PhD, AND PAUL DAVIS

City Nursing Home (CNH) is a nonprofit, independent, 200-bed facility located outside a major city in the western United States. The community has a population of nearly 150,000 with a high rate of poverty. CNH has a current occupancy rate of 97%, which is significantly higher than the state and national averages. CNH is ranked highly on Medicare's 19 quality indicators (Table CS6–1), but the facility had 8 deficiencies cited on its certification survey when it was inspected about a year ago (Table CS6–2). The four-story building was opened 32 years ago and has maintained an excellent reputation for delivering quality patient care. Staff stability in a community that offers relatively few jobs has been one of the main factors that has contributed to the quality of care. The facility trains its own certified nursing assistants (CNAs). With less turnover compared with the industry, and having a pool of trained CNAs to fill vacancies, the facility maintains above-average staffing levels. The facility also takes pride in having its own in-house rehabilitation therapy staff. Ms. Morehouse has been the administrator of CNH for the past 12 years.

For its current strategic plan, the governing board has approved adoption of culture change mainly through self-managed work teams in nursing services and the implementation of family-style dining. Implementation of this plan would require both structural and process changes. The existing kitchen is located in the basement of the building, and the main dining room is on the first floor. Using an elevator, food is transported in carts with hot and cold compartments. CNAs pick up the meal trays with pre-portioned food straight from the food carts, check the resident's name against the meal card on each tray, and place each tray in front of the resident. While the service is efficient, its appeal is very institutional. Also, residents and families have been generally satisfied with the meals. One main issue in the past few years has been three leg injuries that the food service associates sustained while transporting the heavy carts. One of the injuries was serious enough to keep the associate away from work for four months. Shortly after returning to work, that associate resigned to take a job at the local McDonald's. One year, the kitchen sustained some

Dr. Davis is Associate Professor of Health Care Management, Management and Marketing Department, University of Alabama.

flooding after heavy spring rains and had to be closed down for almost two weeks. Food services were temporarily contracted out.

Ms. Morehouse and the board worked together to engage the architectural firm of Caplin & Reese. The firm has had some experience with modern architectural designs for nursing homes. Considering the financial resources and other logistical issues, the facility would redesign its kitchen and dining areas in three to four phases. It is anticipated that over the next few years, each floor will have its own family-style kitchen and dining area. CNH is now in the early planning stage, having recently formed the Food Services Planning Committee.

The Planning Committee met two weeks ago, and Ms. Morehouse is reviewing the minutes from that meeting:

---

### Minutes from the Planning Committee Meeting

Present: Ms. Morehouse, administrator; Mr. Hassan, finance and admissions coordinator; Mr. Washington, food services director; Ms. Laird, director of nursing; Ms. Smith, rehabilitation supervisor; Mr. Keith, construction representative; Mr. Morgan, designer; Mr. Welbourne, contractor; Ms. Reese, architect.

The meeting started at 9 a.m.

Ms. Morehouse began with introductions of those present. She explained that culture change in the nursing home industry was going to gain momentum and, if traditional facilities did not adapt to changing consumer expectations, they would not be able to compete. Hence, the governing board had authorized a long-range plan to implement certain structure and process changes. Modification of current dining arrangements was part of this long-range plan. Ms. Morehouse then opened the meeting for comments and questions from those present.

Mr. Washington, who has been employed at CNH for almost 20 years, explained the existing food service procedures. The kitchen is located below ground. He acknowledged that this layout was not uncommon when the facility was built, but the location is dark and damp according to current standards. The flooding about six years ago was like a nightmare. A large amount of food had to be discarded because of spoilage and the risk of contamination. An outside cleaning company had to be hired, and even then it required a lot of staff overtime to bring the kitchen into operation again. The residents were used to having home-cooked meals, and there was a lot of dissatisfaction with the food that was catered in. Mr. Washington fully supported the idea of moving the kitchen out of the basement, but he was not quite sure how the staffing for the four smaller kitchens would have to be planned. But, then, that was still a few years away!

Ms. Morehouse stated that the main purpose of today's meeting was to discuss the first phase of the project. This phase would be completed in two stages. In the first stage, the existing basement kitchen will be converted to a larger food storage and dishwashing area than what currently existed. A temporary kitchen would be built on the first floor. In the second stage, a household-style kitchen would be constructed by taking space from a portion of the current dining room on the first floor. She noted that during today's meeting, the designers would begin discussion of their plans for this phase of the project.

Mr. Hassan expressed some misgivings about this arrangement. He stated that he was not convinced that building a kitchen on every floor was the best use of financial and human resources. He noted that the first phase of the project

---

*(continues)*

alone would cost roughly $1,000,000. He also mentioned that other than the first floor, the other three floors simply did not have the space for a kitchen area.

Mr. Washington responded that the current arrangement was outdated and that elimination of food carts would be a big plus for the facility. But, he agreed that availability of space on the remaining three floors was a problem and he was not sure what would be the best solution.

Ms. Laird stated that she was excited about the project. The aromas from meal preparation on the floors would create a homelike environment in the facility. Some of the residents could even help out and do minor chores in the kitchens if they so desired.

Ms. Morehouse suggested that they discuss Mr. Hassan's concerns at a later date since the board had already approved the construction budget for the first phase. She asked for an update from Mr. Morgan, Mr. Welbourne, and Ms. Reese.

Mr. Welbourne informed the group that his team was ready to begin both the remodeling of the basement to create food storage and dishwashing areas. At the same time, construction of a temporary kitchen on the first floor would begin. He said that it would take about five months to complete this project. Once the basement and the temporary kitchen renovations were completed, a portion of the dining room would be blocked off to begin construction of the new household-style kitchen. He estimated that this stage would take an additional three months.

Ms. Morehouse informed the group that therapy services would be moved and the temporary kitchen would be placed in that space.

Ms. Laird questioned how noise, dust, security, and other potential disruptions would be handled during the construction. Mr. Welbourne said these considerations have been included in his plans, and he furnished some details. He requested that Ms. Laird should provide him with a list of any resident-related concerns and he would address those concerns before the next meeting.

Ms. Smith said that she had become aware of some resident-related concerns. She stated that rehabilitation was using a large open area that has also been used as a multipurpose space for activities such as church services, meetings, games, parties, etc. She added that the activity director was upset that once the kitchen was moved to this location, the space would be too small to accommodate all of the residents. Mr. Welbourne suggested that perhaps activities could temporarily take place on the floors or in the residents' rooms. Ms. Smith expressed concern that the residents may be isolated in their rooms. Ms. Morehouse stated that a solution to this would need to be explored.

Ms. Reese and Mr. Morgan jointly presented the completed designs. Ms. Morehouse asked about the color scheme and overall kitchen aesthetics. Ms. Reese responded that her plan was to use colors consistent with the current facility color scheme given that the facility had been repainted less than a year ago. Ms. Morehouse said that the proposed color scheme would not be consistent with culture change. She offered to provide Ms. Reese with information on appropriate color schemes and other aesthetics consistent with culture change. Mr. Morgan explained that the kitchen would be equipped with commercial-style fixtures and appliances. He further stated that he was concerned that it sounded like the facility wanted something other than an institutional-type kitchen. Ms. Morehouse agreed that the kitchen fixtures and appliances needed to be chosen with the household model in mind. She asked if it would help if she provided him with

*(continues)*

some information detailing what type of fixtures and appliances would be appropriate for this style of kitchen. Mr. Morgan said he would welcome this information and attempt to make appropriate modifications with the understanding that all items must still meet NFPA and Life Safety Code regulations.

Ms. Morehouse asked whether there were any other concerns from anyone. Mr. Washington wanted to know whether the temporary kitchen on the first floor would be sufficient to prepare meals for 200 residents. Mr. Welbourne replied that the temporary kitchen was not meant for cooking that many meals. He said that the main use of the temporary kitchen would be for heating and serving meals, but it would not be equipped to prepare meals on a large scale. Mr. Washington stated that because the facility is required to provide hot meals, he would have to research other options. He further stated that because the kitchen staff would not be cooking meals during the building stage, each member of the kitchen staff would need new task assignments, because their essential jobs would change. The cooks, for example, would need new assignments because they would not be involved in meal preparation. Ms. Morehouse requested a report from him on the new task assignments.

Ms. Smith stated that while she understood the reason the current therapy location was chosen for the temporary kitchen, her staff was not happy with the idea of moving. She further stated that the residents would need to be prepared for moving to a new location to receive therapy. Ms. Morehouse replied that she understood these challenges and would work with Ms. Smith to address staff and resident concerns.

The meeting adjourned at 11:30 a.m.

Following the meeting, Ms. Morehouse jotted down a list of things to do. As she pondered over it further, she was convinced that culture change was necessary, but wondered whether alternative plans should be explored.

## Assignment

1. In a brief memo to the members of the Planning Committee, outline the main advantages of implementing household-style meal service.

2. In the context of this case, do a SWOT analysis outlining the facility's strengths and weaknesses in relation to external opportunities and threats with the objective of informing members of the governing board on the value of their strategic decision.

3. Provide specific responses to the concerns expressed by the members of the Planning Committee.

4. What alternative plans should Ms. Morehouse consider?

**Table CS6–1** Medicare Quality Measures for City Nursing Home

| Quality Measures | City Nursing Home (%) | State Average (%) | National Average (%) |
|---|---|---|---|
| Long-stay residents given influenza vaccination during the flu season | 100 | 92 | 90 |
| Long-stay residents who were assessed and given pneumococcal vaccination | 100 | 94 | 87 |
| Long-stay residents whose need for help with daily activities has increased | 19 | 12 | 15 |
| Long-stay residents who have moderate to severe pain | 0 | 2 | 4 |
| High-risk long-stay residents who have pressure sores | 15 | 14 | 12 |
| Low-risk long-stay residents who have pressure sores | 0 | 2 | 2 |
| Long-stay residents who were physically restrained | 0 | 3 | 4 |
| Long-stay residents who are more depressed or anxious | 8 | 10 | 14 |
| Low-risk long-stay residents who lose control of their bowels or bladder | 50 | 52 | 50 |
| Long-stay residents who have/had a catheter inserted and left in their bladder | 2 | 4 | 6 |
| Long-stay residents who spend most of their time in bed or in a chair | 0 | 2 | 4 |
| Long-stay residents whose ability to move about in and around their room got worse | 17 | 11 | 12 |
| Long-stay residents with a urinary tract infection | 3 | 7 | 9 |
| Long-stay residents who lose too much weight | 8 | 8 | 9 |
| Short-stay residents given influenza vaccination during the flu season | 100 | 84 | 80 |
| Short-stay residents who were assessed and given pneumococcal vaccination | 100 | 87 | 80 |
| Short-stay residents with delirium | 0 | 1 | 2 |
| Short-stay residents who had moderate to severe pain | 0 | 15 | 19 |
| Short-stay residents with pressure sores | 21 | 19 | 16 |

**Table CS6–2** Survey Deficiencies

| Deficiency Category | Survey Date | | |
|---|---|---|---|
| | Current Complaint Reporting Period: July–September | One Year Ago Complaint Reporting Period: July–June | Two Years Ago Complaint Reporting Period: July–June |
| Mistreatment | 2 | 0 | 0 |
| Quality care | 2 | 3 | 1 |
| Resident assessment | 1 | 0 | 0 |
| Resident rights | 1 | 0 | 0 |
| Nutrition and dietary | 2* | 1** | 0 |
| Pharmacy service | 0 | 0 | 0 |
| Environmental | 0 | 3 | 2 |
| Administration | 0 | 2 | 1 |
| Reported between inspections | 0 | 0 | 0 |
| Total number of health deficiencies for this nursing home | 8 | 9 | 4 |
| Average number of health deficiencies in the state | 6 | 6 | 6 |
| Average number of health deficiencies in the United States | 9 | 9 | 9 |

*Inspectors determined that the nursing home failed to:
1. Provide food in a way that meets a resident's needs.
2. Store, cook, and give out food in a safe and clean way.

**Inspectors determined that the nursing home failed to:
1. Store, cook, and give out food in a safe and clean way.

# Case 7

# Evacuation of Angel Care Center

Hurricane Rita made landfall on the morning of September 24, 2005, as a category 3 hurricane on the Saffir-Simpson scale. The storm caused significant damage in Texas and Louisiana. In the days preceding landfall, Rita's strength increased to a category 5 with winds of 175 mph, and landfall was projected at that time anywhere from Matagorda Bay to the Freeport/Galveston Bay in Texas. Eventually, however, Rita turned to the east. Although the bay areas were spared from the main wrath of the storm, strong winds damaged power lines, trees, many homes and businesses, and public utility facilities.

In 2005, the county's population was estimated to be 3.7 million, making it the most populous county in Texas and the third most populous county in the United States. The county is split into four geographical divisions called precincts. Each precinct elects a commissioner to sit as a representative of the precinct on the commissioner's court and also for the oversight of county functions in the precinct. The county's southern section is located in surge zone 1. As a result of Hurricane Rita, the county was formally declared a federal disaster area. It gave the county residents access to federal funds for cleanup and restoration.

## The City Government

The state government has delegated to local governments at the county and city levels the responsibility for disaster planning and civil assistance. The city's standing plan requires safe shelter in place (no evacuation) in the event of a category 1 or category 2 hurricane. In the event of a more severe storm, the city government would decide whether or not evacuation would be mandated.

On the afternoon of Monday, September 19, city government officials, emergency management personnel, and police and fire chiefs began meeting to discuss preparations for the storm. The State Operating Center in Texas was briefing local governments on the status of the storm and the state's preparations. On the basis of these updates, the city government issued a press release warning that the storm was intensifying and that preparations should be under way to include possible evacuation if advised to do so. The local health department and the Emergency Management Services (EMS) staff began contacting special needs facilities to advise them of the approaching storm and to ascertain whether the facilities had evacuation plans in place. Also on September 19, the Texas Department of Aging and Disability Services faxed a letter to all nursing homes in the state. In the letter, the department implored the facilities to review their disaster plans and to be prepared to implement the plans as necessary (Exhibit CS7–1).

City government officials continued to meet on Tuesday, September 20. At this point, a local school district also joined the meetings to discuss the use of school buses in case an evacuation was ordered. One city government official met with officials in an adjoining county to learn about their emergency plans. Later during the day, city government officials met with industry representatives and hospital representatives. At 6:15 p.m., the local government issued a voluntary evacuation advisement for the general public. In addition, a mandatory evacuation order was given for residents with special needs such as those with physical and mental disabilities.

## Angel Care Center

### The Facility and Its Organization

Angel Care Center (ACC) is a 105-bed nursing facility that is affiliated with a Christian denomination. All the beds are certified for Medicare, and 68 of the beds are dually certified. The facility was built in three stages. The original section was constructed during the 1960s, and now has 51 rooms that offer private accommodations and 10 beds in 5 double rooms. A 26-bed wing was added sometime in the 1970s. Two more wings, one to accommodate services such as laundry, maintenance, and storage, and the other providing 18 beds, were built in 1987–1988.

The administrator, Marsha Gabel, who has the title of executive director, has been with ACC for 18 years. Marsha obtained her NHA license in 1980. She joined ACC in 1987 as the facility's assistant administrator, and was named executive director in 1992. She has an undergraduate degree in behavioral sciences. Before Hurricane Rita, Marsha had no experience in the evacuation of nursing home residents.

Exhibit CS7–2 shows the facility's organizational chart. A risk manager's position is somewhat unique to ACC. Exhibit CS7–3 summarizes the main responsibilities of this position. The risk manager, Frances Cummings, who is a registered nurse (RN), had been employed with ACC for 2 years. Frances had prior experience with evacuation of nursing home residents. Susan Andrews, the director of nursing (DON), had 10 years of experience and had been with ACC for 3 years.

### Mission Statement

Angel Care Center provides a retirement home for older adults where they will feel secure, receive high-quality care, and enjoy the company of others in a loving and Christian environment.

Angel Care Center is a not-for-profit organization that strives to operate efficiently and charges rates that reflect the full cost of care. In recognition of its charter to serve all, Angel Care Center has a program to provide some financial assistance to those who cannot pay the full cost of their care.*

### Disaster Planning

In fall 1998, the air-conditioning unit located above one of the patient care wings of the facility burned out. At around 2:00 a.m., the staff noticed smoke odors in that wing and in two other adjoining wings. Although the fire alarm was not pulled, the local fire department was called. The charge nurse on duty, a licensed vocational nurse (LVN), decided that the affected wings had to be evacuated.

---

*Financial assistance includes providing the difference between the full cost of care and whatever payments may be provided by Medicaid for residents who qualify for that program.

Exhibit CS7–1

COMMISSIONER
James R. Hine

**TEXAS**
Department of Aging
and Disability Services

September 19, 2005

Dear Provider:

As you are aware, another tropical storm is expected to enter the Gulf of Mexico this week and strengthen, threatening the Texas Coast. In anticipation of this, we are asking that you ensure your preparations for a storm are in place.

State regulations require that all facilities have written emergency preparedness plans that provide specific procedures to respond to disasters such as severe weather. Please review your plans and ensure that you and your entire staff are prepared to implement such plans if necessary.

In an event of an evacuation is ordered, critical items in your plan include transportation arrangements to move residents, and emergency healthcare back-ups, including dialysis treatments for patients who require this. You should contact the entity(ies) that will be providing the transportation and the locations to which residents are to be evacuated to ensure they are prepared to transport and receive your residents. Check to be sure those sites will have food and supplies for your residents, or be prepared to take some with you.

Other important considerations are your plans to assure necessary supplies and equipment are available should your facility be left without power, or delivery of supplies.

We will be contacting you for more detailed information as landfall is identified. If we can provide assistance to you, please contact one of our program managers:

| | |
|---|---|
| Valerie Collins, Geriatric/Assisted Living Facilities | 713-767-2305 |
| Mark Kendall, Geriatric/Assisted Living Facilities | 713-767-2363 |
| Carolyn Kirkwood, Geriatric/Assisted Living Facilities | 713-767-2303 |
| Carol K Wright, Geriatric/Assisted Living Facilities | 713-767-2301 |
| Larry Beauvais, Life Safety Code | 713-767-2293 |
| Kay Smith, ICF/MR Facilities | 713-767-2292 |
| Marline Boyd, HCSSA Agencies | 713-767-2067 |

Sincerely,

Brenda McCoy, Regional Director
Region 06, Houston

BMC:sam

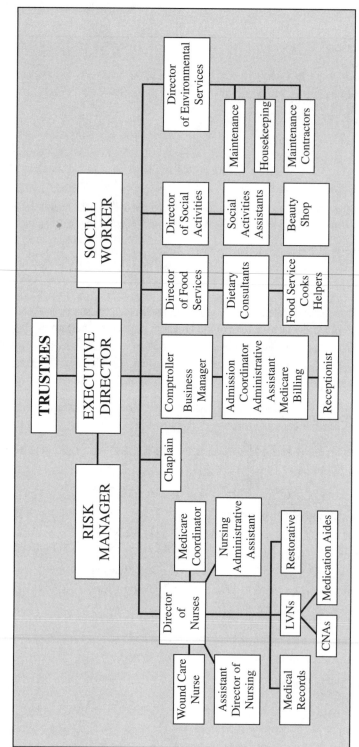

**Exhibit CS7–2**

**Exhibit CS7–3**  Risk Manager: Frances Cummings, RN

The position reports to the Executive Director and has the following main responsibilities:

- Quality improvement. The individual heads the Quality Assurance Committee. A subcommittee meets weekly to evaluate and discuss patient care quality issues, such as pressure sores, weight variations, falls, medication use, infection control, hydration, family satisfaction surveys, and state inspection survey findings.
- Review all resident-related incident and accident reports. Perform investigations and follow-ups.
- Follow up on complaints from family members.
- Make regular building rounds to identify potential hazards.
- Staff in-service and training.
- Prepare for state inspection surveys, with subsequent involvement during the survey process.
- Coordinate annual risk assessment. An external private company does annual site visits for risk assessment.

Approximately 20 residents were evacuated outside the building in wheelchairs and geriatric chairs. The residents were brought back into the facility when the fire department declared an all clear. ACC experienced no other incidents until Hurricane Rita.

The facility had a disaster plan (The section on evacuation has been reproduced in Exhibit CS7–4). On September 19, Marsha Gabel began planning for a possible evacuation of the 104 residents present in the fa-

cility. As early as July 2005, Marsha had entered into a transportation contract with Coach USA. The contract required Coach USA to provide two 55-passenger buses to transfer residents to a designated location during an emergency and to transport the residents back to the facility after the emergency was over. Services of Coach USA were subject to the availability of equipment and drivers (Exhibit CS7–5).

**Exhibit CS7–4**  Angel Care Center Disaster Plan (Section of Evacuation)

**I. Fire Evacuation**

A. There are two basic types of evacuations:

1. *Safe-area evacuation:* A safe-area evacuation will be done when the fire is located and affecting only one area while not endangering the nursing home as a whole. If this type of evacuation is ordered, personnel will evacuate residents to other areas within the facility.
2. *General evacuation:* A general evacuation will be done when the building is endangered by a major fire. If this type of evacuation is ordered, residents will be evacuated by following the fire plan or the bulletin board in your work area.

*(continues)*

**Exhibit CS7—4** Angel Care Center Disaster Plan (Section of Evacuation) (Continued)

B. In the event of an evacuation, it is the responsibility of the Director of Nursing and/or Assistant Director of Nursing and Charge Nurses to ensure that all residents are evacuated in a proper and orderly manner with their medications.

Call the Civil Defense to provide transportation in moving the residents if the facility must be evacuated.

C. Residents are evacuated to their families, Jordan Care Nursing Center in Houston, or other facilities as deemed necessary.

D. There are three basic categories of residents to be evacuated:

1. *Ambulatory:* They and visitors should be led in groups in accordance with the type of evacuation ordered. Have them walk out the nearest exit. If residents are slow ambulating, use wheelchairs. They should go directly to the area specified by the Administrator. DO NOT LEAVE RESIDENTS WITHOUT GUIDANCE FOR FEAR OR PANIC. DO NOT LET ANY RESIDENT RE-ENTER THE BUILDING TO GET ANYTHING. KEEP RESIDENTS WARM.

*[Note: The remaining two subsections are missing in the original plan]*

E. Be alert to the following:

1. Note the possible sources of danger, such as crumbling walls, broken glass, and water mains.
2. Don't try to drag a person away from a live wire unless you have insulated material (thick rubber gloves). Make sure the material is dry. If you know where the circuit breaker is, TURN OFF FIRST.
3. Don't move a resident unless it is to remove her/him from immediate danger.
4. If testing for an electrical short, use the back of your hand; never use the palm of your hand.

**II. Other Emergencies**

A. *Storms:* Nurses and aides should check all resident rooms when there is evidence of an approaching storm to secure all windows and to reassure the residents.

B. *Hurricane:* HURRICANE WATCH (does not mean that hurricane conditions are imminent, but there is a real possibility that a hurricane will threaten the area within 24 hours).

The administrator will call a meeting of Department Heads to begin checking the following:

(a) Transistor radios and flashlights with spare batteries.
(b) Nonperishable foods, canned goods, and water containers.
(c) Make arrangements for materials such as boards, lumber, and tape for boarding up windows and other glass openings.
(d) Move or tie down movable objects, garbage cans, boards, signs, etc.
(e) Check the supply of special items such as emergency medicines, drinking water, etc.
(f) Monitor progress of the storm by radio or television.

C. HURRICANE WARNING (means that hurricane conditions are expected within 24 hours).

*(continues)*

**Exhibit CS7—4** Angel Care Center Disaster Plan (Section of Evacuation) (Continued)

*TAKE THE FOLLOWING ACTIONS IMMEDIATELY:*

Department Heads will meet to finalize plans and take the following steps:

(a) Board up large windows. Tape may help against shattering.

(b) Move all loose objects from outside.

(c) Fill containers with water.

(d) Warn residents to stay indoors on downwind side of the house away from windows and glass doors. The strongest winds will come from somewhere between north and southeast directions.

(e) Beware of the eye of the hurricane. Do not be fooled by a lull in the wind because high winds may return from the opposite direction.

(f) Administration or a designated representative will attend meetings of the city's Emergency Management Center to obtain information and updates, and coordinate evacuation plans if deemed necessary.

(g) If the hurricane is a category 3 or 4, the roster of residents will be evaluated to determine those who can be cared for by their families for the duration of the hurricane and until all clean up etc. has been completed. Nursing staff will prepare medications and/or other supplies if necessary. Housekeeping will pack belongings for approximately one week. If the hurricane is a category 5 or greater and total evacuation is deemed necessary, arrangements will be made by the Administrative Staff for the removal of heavy-care residents (Schroeder Ambulance Service has a stretcher ambulance than can carry at least two residents).

### III. Evacuation

The city's Emergency Management Center (EMC) has advised: In case of a hurricane, the residents of Angel Care Center will NOT be evacuated unless deemed necessary by the EMC. If evacuation becomes necessary, the facility will make arrangements for lodging and transportation. Staff will be requested to accompany the residents. Compensation will be provided to those assisting.

A. *Tornado:* If complete evacuation is not deemed advisable, remove all residents in their beds and simply roll beds out of the rooms to corridor areas. Keep some windows partially open on the opposite side from the direction of tornado to avoid creating a vacuum in the building.

B. *Explosion:* In the event of an explosion in one of the nearby petrochemical plants that causes damage to the facility and/or injury to the residents, ALL OFF-DUTY PERSONNEL are to report to the facility as soon as possible.

### IV. Responsibilities of Personnel Not Assigned to a Station

In the event of a fire or disaster, the following units shall first secure their own work areas and then report to the location of the fire or disaster to aid in the removal of residents from that area:

Office personnel

Dietary personnel

Social and activity personnel

Beauty shop personnel

Restorative nursing personnel

Laundry personnel

*(continues)*

**Exhibit CS7–4** Angel Care Center Disaster Plan (Section of Evacuation) (Continued)

---

### V. Transferring of Medical Records

In the event of an evacuation of Angel Care Center, the Director of Environmental Services, aided by the Secretary, shall be responsible for transferring medical records to the designated location.

---

**Exhibit CS7–5** Contract with Coach USA

---

July 14, 2005

Re:   Angel Care Center
        1800 Sherman Avenue

This letter is to confirm our telephone conversation on July 14, 2005. It is agreed that Coach USA will provide emergency transportation for the above facility. The service would involve two 55-passenger buses transferring residents to and from designated location. Service will be supplied on an as-needed basis and is subject to availability of equipment and drivers. It is understood that the above facility would pay Coach USA based on established hourly commercial rates or mileage charge, whichever is greater.

Thank you for choosing Coach USA.

Signed (Jim Jacobs)
Sales Representative

Price Rates
Mon–Thu                  $425.00 (5-hour minimum)
Fri–Sun                    $500.00 (5-hour minimum)
$85.00 for each additional hour

Day Rates Mon–Thu      $880
Day Rates Fri–Sun        $950

$3.00 per mile live miles
$1.85 per dead head mile

Susan Andrews and Frances Cummings began planning how patients would be evacuated. Marsha and the department managers shared the responsibility of calling all families to find out which families would take their loved ones with them. During the phone calls, comments such as "it's your responsibility," "I can't handle my daddy," and "there is no way I can take care of my mother" were frequently heard. But, others wanted to take their loved ones with them. Marsha also tried to find empty beds in nursing homes around the area.

Before ACC had to evacuate, 54 residents went with their family members, leaving 50 in the facility. Only the medications and directions for medication administration accompanied the 54 residents who went home. Another 8 residents were transported to a skilled nursing facility located 120 miles away. These patients were designated as "special care residents" and were evacuated by private ambulances. Exhibit CS7–6 provides information on the medical conditions of these patients. Medications and medical records accompanied these patients. ACC

**Exhibit CS7–6** Special Care Residents

**Resident A**

Chronic pulmonary disease; end-stage renal disease; diabetes; congestive heart failure; oxygen dependent.

**Resident B**

Atherosclerotic cardiovascular disease; atrial fibrillation; congestive heart failure; dependent for all ADLs; oxygen dependent.

**Resident C**

Severe chronic obstructive pulmonary disease; morbid obesity; history of respiratory failure; oxygen dependent; steroid dependent.

**Resident D**

Cerebral vascular accident; chronic obstructive pulmonary disease; congestive heart failure; morbid obesity; dependent for all ADLs; intermittent oxygen use; at risk of decompensation.

**Resident E**

Renal insufficiency; congestive heart failure; morbid obesity; dependent for all ADLs; needs to be positioned at a 30-degree angle for proper breathing.

**Resident F**

End-stage renal disease; atherosclerotic cardiovascular disease; congestive heart failure; dementia; uses Foley catheter; dependent for all ADLs.

**Resident G**

Cerebral vascular accident; dementia; diabetes mellitus; gastro-intestinal tube feeding.

**Resident H**

Atherosclerotic cardiovascular disease; chronic obstructive pulmonary disease; cerebral vascular accident; dementia; gastro-intestinal tube feeding.

became responsible for evacuating the remaining 42 residents. In preparation for the evacuation, ACC procured extra medications, drinking water, and skin and wound care products.

On learning about the city's orders for a mandatory evacuation, Marsha contacted Coach USA to obtain the services of two buses. She did not get a firm commitment from the bus company. Coach USA told her that the company had no drivers available at that time. Marsha hoped that Coach USA would have the buses and drivers available on Wednesday, September 21, when the facility must evacuate. The local government was unable to furnish transportation. Other nursing homes in the area were in a similar bind.

Marsha recalled that she knew Mr. Spicer who was the executive director of a large retirement/nursing home complex located about 200 miles away. On the 20th, as a back-up plan in case Coach USA would not come through with their services, Marsha called Mr. Spicer with a desperate plea for help.

## The Evacuation

On September 21, Coach USA was unable to provide the much-needed buses. Fortunately, Mr. Spicer was ready, along with three of his staff, to make the 200-mile trip to ACC. Mr. Spicer and his team brought with them a 21-passenger van, a 16-passenger van equipped with a wheelchair lift, and a pick-up truck. They reached ACC at 7 p.m., after spending more than 6 hours on the road, a trip that normally should take about 3½ hours. A nursing facility in Houston, which did not have to evacuate, was also able to provide a bus and a van. Evacuated residents would be trans-

ported 120 miles away to a furnished two-story retreat center. The center had motel-like accommodations that included kitchen, dining, and laundry facilities.

## On the Move

At around noon on September 21, the bus obtained from the Houston facility left ACC with eight residents and five staff members. Medical records, medical equipment, nursing supplies, and some of the personal belongings of these residents were also dispatched at the same time. The trip to the retreat center took about two hours. Frances Cummings arrived at the center to do some basic preparations for patient care.

By 8 p.m. on September 21, the remaining 34 residents were evacuated and loaded on the two vehicles furnished by Mr. Spicer. One van was filled with 34 wheelchairs. Medical records, medications, supplies, oxygen cylinders, and one bag of personal belongings for each resident were also loaded. A cooler with ice, nutritional drinks, and drinking water were carried. The dietary department packed sandwiches for the trip that was anticipated to take about three to four hours. A convoy of nine vehicles that included six personal vehicles belonging to the staff set out for the retreat center shortly after 8 p.m.

By this time, the main highways had become clogged with traffic. Vehicles on all evacuation routes were moving at a crawling pace, at times standing still for long periods of time. Only emergency vehicles were permitted to use the highway lanes going in the opposite direction. The outside temperature was 100° F, but all vehicles were equipped with air-conditioning. People in different vehicles communicated with each other using walkie-talkies.

## The Transportation Ordeal

One of the drivers heard someone say, "She's vomiting on me, she's vomiting on me; make her stop." A certified nursing assistant (CNA) on board did the best she could using the wipes and water available on the van. The same thing was heard again. There were no empty seats to move anyone, nor a good way to clean the residents. Residents would slide forward in their seats as brakes were applied, and the staff would assist them back into their normal sitting positions. Around midnight, this van developed transmission trouble. A message was relayed on the walkie-talkies to pull off the highway at the next exit. Pulling into a commercial parking lot, the driver shut off the engine, got out, and noticed that transmission fluid was pouring out underneath the vehicle. The 17 residents on this van had to be moved, in most cases physically lifted using bed sheets, to the remaining vehicles. To make room for the passengers, some of the equipment had to be jettisoned. The convoy of eight vehicles had to get back on the highway, but the Department of Public Safety was not available to help.

The convoy managed to get back into traffic despite numerous disabled cars that blocked the highway shoulders. By this time, the traffic was moving even slower. Earlier it took 16 minutes to cover a half mile; now it was taking 26 minutes. The concern for the residents' well-being was on the rise because the residents had been on the vehicles for at least eight hours.

It was around 4 a.m. on September 22 when the engine of the second passenger van stopped. The alternator was not running fast enough to keep the battery charged. After the vehicle was given a jump start in blocked-up traffic, the driver had to get off at the next exit. This vehicle also started spewing transmission fluid and could go no further. To remain stranded was not an option.

To add to the ordeal, the van carrying patient care supplies got separated from the ones carrying the passengers. Another main challenge encountered was how to keep the residents cleaned and changed on the vehicles. Even if this could be done, privacy would be an issue.

## At the Retreat Center

The trip to the retreat center took more than 18 hours. Residents were exhausted and dehydrated. But, fortunately, no lives were lost. Susan Andrews took charge of accommodating the patients and ensuring continuity of care.

Before leaving ACC, things had to be packed in a hurry. The cardboard boxes were not sturdy enough to hold the weight of the medical records. Some records did not stay together. Wheelchair footrests and other accessories that were taken apart to save space also got mixed up. Some of the patients' articles of personal clothing were misplaced. There was a shortage of skin care products and other supplies.

Some supplies were purchased at a local Wal-Mart store. A triage system was instituted to address patient care needs. During the trip, eight residents had developed stage I and II pressure sores. Skin care, care for urinary incontinence, hydration, and assistance with feeding were high priorities. One resident had a tendency to wander outside. Others showed signs of general confusion and anxiety. Television programming was mostly about the hurricane and the damage it was causing.

Most staff employed at ACC could not go to the retreat center; many had their own families to attend to. Associates who went to the retreat center included 2 RNs (Susan Andrews and Frances Cummings), 2 LVNs, 16 CNAs (including 1 certified medication aide), and 7 others. To some extent, staffing pressures were relieved because the retreat center had cooks available to handle the cooking and meal services. The retreat center had a supply of linens, but it was not adequate to meet the needs of nursing home patients. Frequent washing of linens became necessary.

At first, the staff members were overwhelmed. They were themselves tired and stressed. Patient care was chaotic until things could be better organized. However, overall staff morale was high. Susan Andrews organized the staff to work in pairs. Once basic routines were set up, shifts were assigned so staff could rotate and get some relief.

# The Aftermath

The hurricane caused severe destruction in southern Texas. However, before landfall, the storm had veered to the east, and ACC was spared any damage. On September 26, families started bringing patients back, and the facility began resuming normal operations.

In retrospect, lack of good transportation and shortage of staff were the two most critical problems experienced. Yet, one staff member remarked, "If I have to do this again even without any extra pay, I would do it." Marsha Gabel thought that the local government should do better disaster planning. However, in the aftermath of Hurricane Rita, neither city nor county officials have contacted ACC with plans for any future eventualities.

## Assignment

1. Review Angel Care Center's contract with Coach USA (Exhibit CS7–5). What recommendations can you make to improve this contract?

2. When the second van carrying passengers became disabled, to remain stranded was not an option. What options would there be to complete the trip to the retreat center?

3. On a trip that lasted more than 18 hours, at least some patients would require cleaning and changing. How could such care be provided while on the move?

4. What would you do to relieve fear and anxiety among the residents after they have been moved to a temporary shelter, such as the retreat center in the case?

5. What human resource policies would you recommend to improve staffing under the type of circumstances described in the case?

6. Review Angel Care Center's evacuation plan (Exhibit CS7–4). What recommendations can you make?

7. What actions can the facility's administrator take to work more closely with the city and county governments to prepare for any future eventualities?

# Tug-of-War with the Director of Nursing

THE ASSISTANCE OF ANTHONY UGHETTI, NHA, IN DEVELOPING THIS CASE IS GRATEFULLY ACKNOWLEDGED.

Tim Wagner worked as a physical therapy assistant (PTA) for 17 years, and for a year tried the position of director of sales and marketing at a 120-bed skilled nursing facility (SNF). While holding a full-time PTA position, Tim also enrolled at a local university and completed a bachelor's degree in health services management. Upon graduation, Tim accepted the position of clinical liaison for special projects with Lippert Healthcare Inc., a privately owned multifacility chain that operated 10 skilled care facilities. Tim's main responsibilities included assisting the 10 nursing homes with recruitment of therapy staff; development of therapy staff; optimizing utilization of therapy services to maximize revenues, clinical outcomes, and staff productivity; and assisting in the development of programs such as fall prevention, restorative care, and wound care. The nursing home corporation also utilized Tim as interim rehab manager whenever a need arose in one of the chain's facilities. Tim used his clinical background to his advantage and applied what he learned in his health services management program. He performed exceptionally well in this position. However, his main ambition after graduating with a bachelor's degree was

to become a nursing home administrator (NHA). His goal was realized when Lippert Healthcare appointed Tim to be the administrator of Cloverleaf Nursing Center, a 90-bed SNF located in a small town of approximately 33,000. Lippert's corporate officers told Tim, "Since you want to be an administrator, we will put you at Cloverleaf. The management staff here is stable. It will be a place where you can learn and grow."

## Previous Administrators

### Joe Atkins

At Cloverleaf, Tim replaced Joe Atkins, who had managed the facility for approximately a year and a half. Joe was transferred within the chain to manage another nursing home that needed an experienced administrator. During the interim period of two months after Joe was moved to another city and Tim came to Cloverleaf, the director of nursing (DON), Claudia Moore, functioned as the interim administrator. Claudia had been employed at Cloverleaf for nine years. She had been the DON for a year and a half, and was a charge nurse for more than seven years before that. She had no desire to become a licensed NHA.

Joe was in his mid-40s. He had a master's of science degree in community health nursing, had been a DON, and had five years of experience as NHA. Although Joe was regarded as a people-oriented person, he would become confrontational if he disagreed with a subordinate and would assign personal blame when something did not go well. From time to time, he would have mood swings. As one department manager described it, "One day he would be all happy and everything would go well; the next day he would be chewing people out." At times, he would burst out, "I say you do this, and you will do it now." Apart from periodic episodes like these, Joe had given a free rein to most of his department managers, but he also favored some managers over others. He had formed an "inner circle" of his favorite managers that included the DON, the dietary manager, the human resource director (who worked three days a week), and the maintenance man. Not part of this inner circle were the business office manager, the social worker, the activity director, and the rehabilitation manager (who worked part time). People in the inner circle generally assembled for lunch in the DON's office, would go out to eat together, or go for a drink or two after work; on some occasions, they would be invited to Joe's home for some partying.

## Margaret Bond

Before Joe, Cloverleaf's administrator was an older female, Margaret Bond. She had managed this facility for a number of years. Ms. Bond had a passive personality. She spent most of her time in her office and was not seen much out on the floors.

Before coming to Cloverleaf, Ms. Bond was the administrator of a 35-bed facility, where she had fostered a family-like working environment with her staff. This facility closed down, and she was hired as the administrator at Cloverleaf. She brought with her the business office manager, the DON, and the facilities manager who was in-charge of all plant and environmental services. Those who had worked with Ms. Bond described her as "motherly" and "cliquish." The assistant director of nursing (ADON) sometimes felt that the DON received preferential treatment from Ms. Bond for things such as requests for time off. The facilities manager would spend an inordinate amount of time in Ms. Bond's office while the work often did not get done. Ms. Bond had a pet name for the facilities manager, but other staff sometimes felt demeaned by her.

One day Ms. Bond sustained a broken hip in the nursing home. She took a long leave of absence and subsequently went on permanent disability leave. During her absence, Lippert's corporate officers visited the facility after a negative annual inspection by the state's Department of Health, and they terminated the DON and the facilities manager for unsatisfactory performance. This is when Joe Atkins was brought in as the administrator.

## The Upset DON

Thirty-one-year-old Tim obtained his NHA license and was so glad to have gotten a foot-in-the-door at this 90-bed facility. But shortly after settling into his new position, Tim felt as if there was a tug-of-war between him and Claudia Moore, the DON. Tim thought that this situation was prompted by some recent incidents.

## Ruffie Jacob

A patient, Ruffie Jacob, was admitted from the local hospital at around 6 p.m. on a Thursday. The hospital's policy did not allow them to send medications with a discharged patient. Intravenous Vancomycin (prescribed for severe infections) to be administered twice daily was one medication the patient was on. Cloverleaf had a contract with a local pharmacy, but the pharmacy did not have IV Vancomycin in stock. The patient had to miss a dose Thursday night. Tim learned about it the next morning and found that even at that time the medication had not arrived. Tim became concerned and went to check with Claudia, who responded, "I have got it under control, don't worry about it. I am dealing with the pharmacy." That afternoon Tim felt that he had to transfer the patient to the hospital, but Claudia overruled his decision. The medication came in at around 5 p.m. on Friday. On Sunday, the patient expired. Tim was very uncomfortable that it could become a potential legal issue. He informed the corporate officers, including the legal officer, who advised Tim to contact the medical director and explain the circumstances. On Monday morning, the medical director asked Claudia about the incident. After her meeting with the medical director, Claudia approached Tim and said, "Why did you make such a big deal of it? I had it under control." Tim explained that he had to inform the corporate officers about the potential liability, and the corporate officers had asked him to contact the medical director.

## The Supply Clerk

Nancy is both the central supply clerk and the van driver for Cloverleaf. She filled out a request for a day off and presented it to Tim in person. Tim granted her the time off. The day Nancy was off, Claudia approached Tim and asked, "Where is Nancy?" Tim explained that since Nancy reported to him, he had granted her request for a day off. Claudia was not pleased, and asked, "Why are you doing this to me? Nancy is my employee."

## The Night Rounds

Tim realized that it was important for him to make rounds of the facility unannounced on some weekends and nights. Once he dropped in at 2:00 a.m. for a surprise visit. Claudia told Tim the following day that a CNA, whom she did not name, felt that people were not being trusted, and that the CNA was going to turn in her resignation. "Why don't you trust us? Why do you have to check up on us?" Claudia demanded. Tim replied, "It is not a question of trust. I just need to get to know the operations and the night people." The next time Tim came in during the night shift, he told the staff, "I am not here to check up on you. I am just here to check the building."

## The PPS Meeting

Responsibilities in the nursing department were shared by three managerial personnel: the DON, the ADON, and the resident assessment coordinator. Corporate policy required the facility to have a daily PPS (prospective payment system) meeting in the morning. The meeting was meant to serve several purposes: review the clinical condition of patients; agree on the resource utilization group (RUG) categories; and share information on clinical progress, therapies, and discharge planning. During this period, the facility was in the process of filling the resident assessment coordinator's position. In the interim, Claudia was handling the minimum data set (MDS). She had a lot of catching up to do. Tim was concerned about the annual survey, which could take place any day. He was not sure whether Claudia had a firm grip on keeping the assessments and care plans current. In the PPS meetings, Tim noticed that information was often missing. Tim thought that Claudia was perhaps overwhelmed with the increased workload. Tim had also observed that certain clinical systems were getting neglected. So, one day Tim decided to take over the PPS meetings. He thought he could help relieve some of the pressures Claudia was experiencing. Claudia, however, was not pleased. She approached Tim and asked him, "Am I not doing my job here? Am I not meeting your expectations?"

## Assignment

1. Using the leadership models described in the textbook, describe the leadership styles of Joe Atkins, Margaret Bond, and Tim Wagner.

2. Was it appropriate for Tim Wagner to intervene in the situation concerning Ruffie Jacob? Explain why or why not.

3. Did the DON have Mr. Jacob's situation under control? What should have been done?

4. Was it appropriate for Tim to grant Nancy the day off? Explain why or why not.

5. Should a nursing home administrator visit the facility on weekends and nights? How should such visits be approached?

6. Was it appropriate for Tim to take over the PPS meetings? Explain why or why not.

7. Why do you think the tug-of-war existed? How should Tim manage the conflict he has with the DON?

# Case 9

# Corporate Compliance at Mid-Atlantic Care Centers

CONTRIBUTED BY PAUL R. WILLGING, PhD

Dave Short had been vice president for operations at Mid-Atlantic Care Centers, a mid-size nursing home chain headquartered in Baltimore, for 22 years . . . and a good one, he thought! While having a genial personality, Dave worked "by the book," despite his willingness to accommodate the particular needs and preferences of staff throughout the company's seven facilities. With the corporation's director of human resources, who reported to him, he had established personnel policies that he thought were among the most enlightened in the profession. He recognized that associates were best served within an environment that emphasized corporate culture as much as its bottom line, and he went out of his way to make sure that Mid-Atlantic's corporate culture was conducive to staff satisfaction and retention. In short, Dave felt that he was an enlightened as well as a sensitive manager who didn't let bureaucratic considerations interfere with employee morale.

Dave was taken by surprise when he received word that five minority employees in one of the company's facilities had initiated a multi-million-dollar lawsuit against Mid-Atlantic for racial discrimination. Dave's reaction to the litigation alternated between anger and disappointment. Dave knew each of the plaintiffs. In his opinion, all five were marginal at best and had been given every opportunity to succeed. He felt that they had been treated with the utmost respect, and he personally had been more than accommodating to what he felt were serious inadequacies in their work output. And now his sense of fair play was being rewarded with litigation! As Dave looked at the events leading up to this state of affairs, his anger only grew.

Dr. Willging is Associate Director, Division of Geriatric Medicine, Johns Hopkins University School of Medicine. He was president of the American Health Care Association from 1983–1999 and president of the Assisted Living Federation of America from 2002–2003.

# The Issues

## Compensation Policies

In working "by the book," Dave had tried to make sure the policies were state of the art. Salaries and benefits were clearly laid out in policies developed by one of the nation's pre-eminent human resource consultants. Each job in the corporation was analyzed and compared with similar positions across the country, adjusted for local peculiarities, and ultimately tied to a salary range. The range was a product of management and budgetary considerations with an emphasis on keeping Mid-Atlantic competitive in a very difficult job market.

## Staff "Buy-In"

At least once a year, Mid-Atlantic's staff compensation policies were explained at department head and staff meetings in each of its facilities. While the salary ranges for all jobs were established on the basis of the company's desire to be competitive in the nursing home market, they were flexible enough to allow considerable discretion within each range to reward associates according to their performance. When questioned by some associates, explanations were given about the need to have upper limits to any job's compensation just as there had to be lower limits, and there had to be penalties when job performance was not deemed sufficient to warrant even the lowest level of compensation. As Dave explained at each staff meeting, failure to meet even minimal job expectations was a question of retention, not compensation.

## Communication

Dave liked to think that he had an open-door policy. Anyone with a problem was welcome to come in and discuss it with him, assuming it had first been discussed with a department head and/or facility administrator. The five litigants had been afforded more than one such opportunity. In fact, those five had been targeted for termination by their respective department heads long before they initiated the lawsuit. But, when the facility sought approval from Dave to terminate them, he put the adverse action on hold. In discussions with the facility's administrator, Dave suggested that their respective supervisors "work both with and around them" to help them improve their performance. In the meantime, their compensation would be put on hold until satisfactory performance was achieved. It was the hold on their compensation that had earlier prompted these five associates to request a meeting with Dave.

The meeting did not go particularly well. What the five associates viewed as inconsistent application of compensation policy, Dave saw as an example of his willingness to be flexible in dealing with associates. None of the five were deemed to be performing at a level consistent with even the lowest levels of their given salary ranges. Yet, rather than taking action to terminate them as the policy suggested (and both department heads and the facility administrator recommended termination), Dave had chosen to take a more sensitive approach, one designed to display his willingness to accommodate employee needs. Dave's actions reflected his strong inclination to make "personnel" decisions "personal," as he liked to put it.

At one point, the discussion became so heated that the five associates suggested that an outside, unbiased party be brought in to provide an independent assessment of the equitable application of staff compensation policy. The call for an independent audit, the five argued, was buttressed by their contention that only minority employees in the facility were paid beneath their salary ranges. The suggestion of racial overtones only hardened positions on both sides of the discussion.

## Problem Verification

Given his own willingness to discuss any issue with staff, Dave saw little need to waste his and his associates' time by further reviewing an issue with which he was intimately familiar. In his own heart, Dave knew that while no one was perfect, there was not even a hint of racism reflected in corporate policies and their application. While the minority status of the five litigants was coincidental, it was only that—coincidental. Dave also knew that his decisions had been in the best interest of the employees themselves. Dave thought had he not been kind-hearted, these employees would be unemployed and unlikely to find jobs that would pay what they were getting from Mid-Atlantic.

Consequently, it seemed a waste of time to have an external party review what were already well-documented actions within the company. After all, the process that led to the recommendation to discharge these employees had been appropriately documented in accordance with the company's personnel procedures. The employees had been made aware of their failure to perform. They had been provided specific standards of acceptable performance and given more than sufficient opportunity to improve. Dave's explanation of company policy had made it clear to them that the alternative option open to him was termination. Surely this was little more than a scam on the part of these employees and their attorney, and really shouldn't be offered the luxury of yet another review. Dave saw an independent audit as just that—a luxury that Mid-Atlantic could

ill afford. Dave viewed the reliance on any outside resources as a flagrant misappropriation of scarce facility resources. Nor were there any obvious solutions that might stem from an external audit. The aggrieved associates might be brought up to their established salary ranges, but that would simply be rewarding poor performance. They could be discharged, but at this stage in the game such action would appear retaliatory. Best to leave well enough alone and let the courts do their own independent audit.

## The Final Outcome

Dave's disinclination to spend dollars on outside resources was overturned by Mid-Atlantic's president and chief executive officer (CEO) when it became clear that the five employees were not interested in further discussions with Dave. In the face of the impending lawsuit, the CEO engaged external labor counsel. The counsel wasted little time before advising the CEO that this particular case was a "loser." And this was not just because a jury reflecting Baltimore's racial complexion would not be sympathetic to Mid-Atlantic's defense. "Coincidental" or not, it would be tough to explain why the company's compensation policies appeared to disproportionately affect minority employees, at least in this one facility. As it turned out, the case never went to trial because the company settled out of court.

Of much greater significance, however, was the fact that Dave's actions violated several of the principles of effective corporate compliance. Had the case gone to trial, the most effective defense would have been the argument that Mid-Atlantic had done nothing more than consistently apply its own long-standing, well-documented, and generally accepted company policies.

## Assignment

1. Explain which of the seven conditions of corporate compliance were violated by Dave Short.

2. How might he have circumvented the problems he faced?

3. How could he best balance his desire to accommodate particular associate needs with his responsibility to the corporation as a whole?

4. What should be the appropriate role of governance in this case?

# Case 10

# Chapel Square Health Care Center: Workforce Diversity

CONTRIBUTED BY JEFFREY A. KRAMER, PHD

## Historical Background

Chapel Square Health Care Center, a skilled nursing facility, is one of a decreasing number of inner-city nursing homes still operating in New Haven, Connecticut. Once a thriving New England city, New Haven has been hard hit by intense poverty, rising crime rates, and an exodus of the middle class to the suburbs. Chapel Square was built in an era when elderly people requiring institutional long-term care (LTC) intentionally sought out nursing homes in New Haven. Chapel Square was built in 1977 by John Stearns, a long-term care facilities developer who foresaw a need for LTC beds in the heart of urban areas. In the 1970s, he invested heavily in nursing home ventures throughout northeastern United States. Chapel Square was one of nine facilities he built during this period, and one of the first to become unionized.

Chapel Square originally had 180 beds, providing both skilled and intermediate care. From the late 1970s to the mid-1980s, occupancy was typically close to full capacity. As competition grew, Chapel Square expanded its patient base beyond geriatric care

to ensure high occupancy rates. The facility began admitting mentally retarded/developmentally disabled (MR/DD) patients who were being moved out of state facilities. Hence, the facility's primary mission of caring for the elderly was gradually compromised for the sake of guaranteed reimbursement and filled beds. This strategy provided short-term profitability—but had long-term repercussions.

During the 1990s, Chapel Square experienced a significant decline in demand. The mixed-resident population alienated geriatric patients' interest in the facility. Neighborhood decline had become noticeably worse, with crime and drugs becoming more prevalent. In addition, a dwindling pool of private-pay patients intensified competition from other facilities that also struggled to keep their beds filled and attract private-pay patients. Many started specialized services such as subacute care and rehabilitation programs, obtained accreditation by the Joint Commission on Accreditation of Healthcare Organizations (JCAHO), or followed other strategies to differentiate themselves from their com-

Dr. Kramer is Director, Programs in Healthcare Management & Insurance Studies, School of Business, University of Connecticut.

petitors. Further, the physical plant of Chapel Square had deteriorated to the point where it affected the ability to recruit patients and staff and jeopardized compliance with state and federal regulations.

## Renovations and Expansion

The problems associated with a deteriorating physical plant, declining census, diversified patient mix, and cuts in reimbursement became more pronounced during the 1990s. Desperately trying to stay afloat, Chapel Square launched an ambitious construction program. The project included extensive renovation of the existing structure and major expansion that added 60 skilled nursing beds. The rationale was that additional beds in a new wing would enhance Chapel Square's declining reputation, attract more private-pay residents, and introduce economies of scale. The original intermediate beds were converted to skilled beds. While the financial risks associated with the project were considerable, it was viewed as a last resort plan for long-term survival of the facility. Renovations and construction of the new wing were completed in 1996. During this time, Chapel Square was also successful in relocating all of its MR/DD population to community-based providers. An aggressive marketing campaign was launched to highlight Chapel Square's new focus on geriatric services and its modern facilities.

## Management Challenges

During this period, facility ownership and management changed several times. While the facility remained proprietary, several owners had experimented with various management approaches at Chapel Square.

Throughout its history, the facility had been led by several well-intentioned—but minimally effective—administrators, contracted management services, and management teams. Shortly after construction on the new addition was completed, a new administrator, Ketty Hansen, was hired to "turn things around."

Hansen was not discouraged by the problems Chapel Square presented. She had worked in a number of inner-city facilities and was accustomed to the challenges of managing problem-plagued facilities. She was pleased by the physical plant improvements. Almost immediately she identified three major, interrelated problems that needed prompt attention if Chapel Square was to survive and prosper: an exceptionally low private-pay census, a poor reputation for quality, and an ethnically diverse and unionized workforce.

By this time, declining private-pay census had become a national trend. Despite its aggressive marketing campaign, Chapel Square could not fully shake its prior reputation for the mix of patients it served. On the other hand, the facility did have some success in attracting geriatric residents.

At the turn of the new century, the facility housed a diverse resident population in terms of ethnic distribution, with a patient mix of approximately 30% Caucasian, 30% African American, 30% Hispanic, and 10% from other ethnic backgrounds. The facility also remained heavily dependent on Medicaid reimbursement. Its payer mix was 1% private pay, 5% Medicare, and 94% Medicaid. The overall occupancy rate was 70%, which did not enable the facility to reach a reasonable level of profitability. The low occupancy rate and heavy dependence on Medicaid were pressing problems that required Hansen's immediate attention.

Chapel Square's reputation for low quality also required immediate attention. Its inner-city location did not help the situation, and the many survey deficiencies the facility had received over the years only made a bad situation worse. On several occasions, regulators had to threaten the facility's management with decertification, that is, expulsion from the Medicare and Medicaid programs. While candidly admitting to herself and her department managers that the facility deserved its current reputation, Hansen recognized that measures were needed to reverse these impressions.

When Hansen was first offered the administrator's position, she knew that Chapel Square was unionized and had a diverse workforce. Having worked in unionized facilities before and having established a good rapport with union leaders, she had earned a reputation over the years for managing human resources successfully, even under exceptionally adverse conditions. However, she quickly discovered an unprecedented level of dysfunctional behavior among the Chapel Square staff. Recognizing its overall negative impact on what she was trying to achieve, she immediately set to work to address these problems.

## Operational Issues

Hansen had observed a number of shortcomings that she felt contributed to the poor quality care. Basic supplies were lacking to the point where care was compromised. The facility was critically short on bed linens. The staff's prevailing attitude about supplies was, "We're not going to get them, so why bother even asking."

There was a desperate need to change ingrained staff behaviors that had become the hallmark of this facility's operational philosophies. Historically, employees had felt abused by management, and over time, a sense of complacency had resulted. Simply put, Chapel Square had become a facility without a spirit. Staff's complacency about quality of care only made matters worse. Staff's apathy would be quickly picked up by newly hired staff. It seemed that the facility was stuck in a rut. Hansen was appalled that the facility was dirty and that the nursing staff was poorly trained and not capable of meeting patients' nursing needs. Verbal abuse of residents by staff was a regular occurrence. The dietary department used only two menus, alternating them weekly.

Unionized positions at Chapel Square were typically paid $3 to $4 more per hour than at other facilities, helping to ensure a steady flow of job applicants. In past negotiations, management had agreed to union demands to avert lengthy and damaging strikes. High salaries raised costs, but did not improve performance. Paltry increases in Medicaid rates had made union wages unsustainable for the longer term.

## Workforce Diversity

Chapel Square's staff reflects the "melting pot of America." It is dominated by three major immigrant groups: West Indians, Hispanics, and East Indians from southern Asia. West Indians are the largest group, representing 50% of the licensed nursing staff, the majority of nursing management, 50% of the housekeeping department, 75% of certified nursing assistants (CNAs), and the entire dietary department. They are primarily from Jamaica and Haiti. Members of the Hispanic group come mainly from Cuba, Puerto Rico, and Costa Rica. They, too, represent a significant proportion of the overall staff, with 35% of the licensed nurses, 24% of CNAs, 50% of housekeeping staff, and the entire maintenance staff. The third largest group, East Indian, is spread throughout the facility without large representation in any given department. Other ethnic and national groups adding to the diverse workforce consist of Africans, Caucasians, African Americans, and Chinese.

Hansen's assessment of her facility's workforce took on great importance as she sought to initiate improvements. She viewed the staff as a dysfunctional family, with multiple communication barriers resulting from ethnic and cultural differences. New staff often came from the ethnic networks of current Chapel Square staff. Many workers were members of large extended families that had immigrated to the United States in recent years. While this made for easy recruitment, it also tended to divide staff along ethnic lines. Intra-staff communication was essentially nonexistent.

During her first few months at Chapel Square, Hansen observed pronounced differences in behaviors and characteristics that existed among the groups, including levels of education, cultural values, participation in facility management, and communication styles. The large ethnic groups tended to have hierarchical structures reinforcing differences among the nationalities. For example, among the West Indians, a class system seemed to exist that placed Jamaicans above Haitians and other West Indians. The Hispanic hierarchy tended to value Cuban workers over Costa Ricans and Puerto Ricans. East Indians lacked a hierarchical structure; a characteristic that Hansen found surprising given the rigid caste system in their home country. East Indians, however, were often the most distant group, rarely interacting with other nationalities in the work setting.

Varying levels of education also seemed to strain relationships. Jamaicans and Africans were typically the most highly educated. It was not unusual for the CNAs from these nations to hold master's degrees, because recent immigrants were often unable to secure other jobs. Hispanics usually had less formal education, and this often adversely affected relationships with other staff. Caucasians and Indians were usually well educated, although this too varied considerably.

Hansen recognized that cultural, religious, educational, language, and economic differences among the various nationalities were affecting patient care and facility operations. Communication problems were widespread, and little was being done to resolve the confusion they created. For example, Jamaican CNAs would talk to Jamaican nurses, but not to Hispanic nurses. Most West Indians, Hispanics, and East Indians would not communicate with African nurses. In general, the staff did not seem to communicate well with either their superiors or their subordinates. Communication linkages were further strained by each group's preference to communicate in their native language, even if they had fluency in English.

The management staff at Chapel Square was mostly Caucasian. Ketty Hansen and her assistant administrator, Bob Manning, were Caucasian, as were all the department heads. Of the 13 charge nurses, there were 6 West Indians, 1 African, and 2 African Americans.

To bring about change, Hansen started by replacing a couple of the existing department heads in an effort to replicate the ethnic mix of the facility's staff. She also identified informal leaders among the staff, representing various ethnic groups, to help work on the communication problems. These leaders served as interpreters during meetings and tried to help overcome cultural barriers. They understood the need for change and played an important role in facilitating the process.

While this approach was marginally effective, the unevenness of the leaders' dedication to the proposed changes limited its impact.

Other approaches were also tried to improve communication within the facility. Small-group training programs were developed to promote attitudinal changes. Outside consultants were brought in with packaged training programs to improve staff communication, but the results were disappointing. Hansen also began to emphasize a more informal management style that took into account the unique characteristics of the facility. She spoke frequently of a team orientation and spent considerable time with her management staff reinforcing concepts of team building and group consensus.

## Management's Dilemma

Despite these efforts, there was little progress in improving attitudes. Hansen and her management staff became increasingly convinced that the communication problems were more a result of cultural differences than anything else. Hansen noticed that not all groups were equally receptive to the changes being implemented. East Indians accepted the changes without much resistance. Hispanics and Haitians, who had the least developed English skills, were not as responsive and posed a more difficult challenge.

After several frustrating months of trying to improve internal communications, Hansen formed a Cultural Awareness Committee. The committee was comprised of representatives from all major groups in the facility. Special attention was given to selecting members who were both respected by their fellow workers and had demonstrated a willingness to improve the quality of the facility's patient care and overall performance.

Hansen asked the committee to develop activities for the staff that may help overcome cultural barriers.

Hansen had hoped that her actions would lead to positive results. Occupancy had remained relatively stable at 70%, and the facility seemed unable to shed its "poor-quality" reputation. But, Hansen feared that unless this image could be changed, the facility would lose market share. The corporate officers, while supportive of the management staff, were also losing patience. Without improvements in the financial performance, the possibility of selling the facility or declaring bankruptcy could not be ruled out.

Hansen worked with the Cultural Awareness Committee during the next few weeks to help participants develop their agenda. She reinforced the notion that the committee should plan activities whereby "each group could be proud of its own culture, but understand and appreciate other cultures." The first idea that surfaced was for a mini-exhibition that would include exhibits from each cultural group. This idea was rejected, however, because some committee members felt it would lead to further isolation rather than facilitate understanding. After much deliberation, the committee finally endorsed the idea of a Cultural Day to include special attire and foods from the many ethnic and cultural groups. While not significantly different from the first idea, the committee was enthusiastic. And, while she remained somewhat skeptical, Hansen supported the idea.

As Cultural Day approached, Hansen continued to work on several different fronts. She met regularly with the Cultural Awareness Committee and made sure they had ongoing input and support from the management staff. She visited each patient care unit almost daily, getting to better know and understand the staff, residents, and families.

She also informally met with many members of the staff to solicit their opinions about how to improve the facility and its image.

On a separate track, Bob Manning was assigned to monitor Chapel Square's adherence to certification regulations. He responded with a "certification watch," which simulated the inspection process. Finally, realizing that additional steps were needed, Hansen called together her management staff. She asked them to begin work on a long-term strategic plan to improve communication among the facility's ethnic and cultural groups. It was hoped that this would lead to improvements in patient care and ultimately improve the facility's reputation in the community. A draft document outlining their ideas was to be submitted to her for initial review. They began to work on this arduous task the following day, aware of the many obstacles facing them.

## Assignment

1. Identify the underlying issues in this case.

2. What do you believe would be the most effective strategies for resolving these issues?

3. Was it a good decision by Hansen to replace a couple of department heads in an effort to replicate the staff's ethnic mix?

4. Do you support Hansen's efforts to date? Should the facility's owners instead appoint an administrator from an underrepresented group? Would this make a difference? What other initiatives do you think Hansen should undertake to bridge the cultural differences among the staff?

5. What early indicators might suggest that progress was being made, supposing that some of your recommendations in question 4 were successful? What metrics and measures would you use?

# Case 11

---

# Start-up of Blissful Gardens

CONTRIBUTED BY CINDY K. MANJOUNES, MHA

Blissful Gardens is a new long-term care (LTC) and independent living facility set to open its doors to the first residents in approximately a year. The facility is located in the outskirts of St. Louis, Missouri, a major metropolitan area. In the state of Missouri, an LTC facility cannot be licensed without certificate of need (CON) approval. Necessary permissions have been obtained, and construction has begun.

## Building and Facility Plans

Blissful Gardens will have two separate buildings that will be joined by a central atrium and a section that will house administrative offices, a dining room, a piano lounge adjoining the dining room, and an arts and crafts room. One of the buildings will have three stories with 12 one-bedroom apartments for independent living. Each apartment will have its own private bathroom and a kitchenette. The building will be constructed as a "green facility," making use of many recycled materials for construction and also many energy conservation and efficiency devices. At least some of the trash will be recycled. Each

apartment will have security features, including pull cords to summon help when needed. At an additional fee, the residents will have the choice of having two or three daily meals in the main dining room. Residents will need to furnish the apartments with their own furniture, linens, and other furnishings. High-speed Internet connections and TV cable will be available for an additional fee in the individual apartments. There will also be a lounge area with a big-screen TV with full cable access and comfortable seating for group TV viewings. A separate common room will have four computers with printers provided by the facility for the residents' use. Once-a-week housekeeping services will be included in the monthly rent. Laundry service will be available for an added fee, or the residents will have the option to do their own washing and drying in an on-premise laundry.

The second building will be single-story with the capability to house 24 residents who require substantial assistance with ADLs and clinical interventions. The facility has a nested single-room design with six "neighborhoods." Two of these neighborhoods will be used for Alzheimer's care. In the Alzheimer's unit, the decorations will be brightly colored

---

Professor Manjounes is Assistant Professor, Faculty Advisor, and Department Chair of Health Management and Gerontology Programs, Lindenwood University.

and cheery. The rooms will all be painted a light tan with white ceilings and baseboards. The curtains will be either bright blue or green, and the tiled floor will be tan and blue. The residents and their families will be encouraged to hang family pictures on the walls or other artwork of their choice. Each room will be furnished with a bed, a lift chair, a small table, and two straight-back chairs. The hallways will be decorated with black and white pictures of many historical places and events in the St. Louis area.

Blissful Gardens will have a 20-seat bus to provide shuttle service once a week to the grocery store, Wal-Mart or Target, the movie theatre, and some local restaurants. Other local entertainment outings at various local attractions will also be scheduled. Residents will reserve their seats for these outings in advance.

## Current Operations and Plans

Ms. Remedios has been recently hired as the executive director (ED) of the entire facility. The board of directors had established a strict set of minimum requirements when they began their search for an ED:

- A master's degree in gerontology or related discipline.
- Current nursing home administrator's license.
- A minimum of 10 years' experience in the long-term care field, with a progression of management responsibilities.
- Criminal background clearance.

Construction of the facility is about one-third complete. Ms. Remedios and a secretary currently occupy a temporary office space in a strip mall approximately one mile from the construction site.

The board has been meeting twice a month. Board members have been mainly focused on timely progress of the facility's construction. Ms. Remedios now visits the construction site once or twice a week, meets with the contractor, and discusses progress with the board. The board has asked her to begin marketing and staff recruitment efforts. The goal is to recruit an experienced director of nursing within the next five to six months so the facility can begin planning for Medicare and Medicaid certification. In addition, all department head positions should be filled two months before the facility opens. The department heads will be heavily involved in recruiting and training qualified associates. The goal is to have adequate staffing in all areas to serve the facility's residents at 25% capacity when it opens its doors.

An entrepreneur is the primary contributor for the start-up of the facility, which will be operated as a for-profit venture. The entrepreneur chose the name, Blissful Gardens, in honor of her late mother, Mrs. Hatbliss, who was an avid gardener and left behind a fairly substantial estate. Part of the proceeds from the estate was designated to fill some need in the local community. Before she passed away, Mrs. Hatbliss was in a local nursing home, and the family did not have good experiences with the care she received before she passed away. Hence, the daughter decided to dedicate the funds to develop a resident-friendly, yet sophisticated and top-notch facility where people would not only feel comfortable and valued, but they would also receive the best services and care available in the community. According to the philosophy expressed by the board of directors, "resident friendly" means that the facility will provide the comforts of one's own home and the associates will help nurture the residents so that each individual can continue to enjoy their golden years and realize self-fulfillment. To maintain high standards, the independent living section will be 100% private pay, and the goal is to have 75% private-pay residents in the nursing center.

# Board Composition and Funding

The eight-member board has the following composition:

- Chairman of the board: a local board-certified internist with experience in geriatrics: Mrs. Hatbliss was his patient for many years.
- Financial adviser: the president of a local bank.
- The chief executive officer of a local manufacturing business.
- The chief operating officer of a managed care organization.
- Legal counsel: a lawyer with a prestigious local law firm.
- Two local well-known small-business owners.
- A retired school superintendent.

The estate of Mrs. Hatbliss provided $2 million. Total start-up costs have been estimated to be between $3.2 and $3.5 million. The board has secured a loan of $1 million from a local bank, with a line of credit approved for another $500,000. Local businesses will be solicited for donations for some of the equipment. Plaques will be placed on the walls to recognize such donations.

# Market Area and Competition

There are four medical systems located within 15 miles of Blissful Gardens. Two of the hospitals have their own LTC facilities. These hospital-operated facilities, with a total of 22 beds, present the only competition in the immediate area. One of these facilities, located 5 miles away, recently came under scrutiny for reported health and safety violations. The media aired some unfavorable stories. The other hospital facility is 12 miles away and is running at full capacity with a waiting list.

The local community is ethnically diverse and has a stable economy because of its proximity to St. Louis. Most of the people settled in this area are either retired or are middle-aged, the median age of population being 52. The average household income in the area is $100,000. New businesses have been steadily opening up in the area. A new shopping mall is being built approximately eight miles from Blissful Gardens. A new condominium community, about seven miles away, opened six months ago.

# Main Goals

The facility's utilization is projected to be at 50% capacity six months after opening and at 75% by the end of its first year of operation. To achieve this goal, a relationship must be established with the two hospitals that do not have their own LTC facilities. The board anticipates that the facility will start turning a profit by the end of its second year of operation. One of the board members is a good friend of the owner of a local talk radio station, who could be tapped to help promote the facility.

The board assigned Ms. Remedios several tasks to complete and report back.

**Assignment**

1. Develop a mission statement for Blissful Gardens.

2. One of the first tasks Ms. Remedios must undertake is to prepare a recruitment plan to hire management personnel. Outline your plan. Justify each position, and provide the main qualifications these individuals must possess. Include their salaries.

3. Prepare a marketing plan for Blissful Gardens.

4. Assuming that the facility will open on January 1, prepare a budget for the first year of operation. Can this operation be profitable by the end of its second year?

# Case 12

## Implementation of the Wellspring Model

THE ASSISTANCE OF LYNN BINNIE, NHA, IN DEVELOPING THIS CASE IS GRATEFULLY ACKNOWLEDGED.

Lou Baker joined the Wellspring consortium 6 years ago. Making the transition from a traditional nursing facility to the Wellspring model of cultural change has presented many challenges. A consortium of 8 nursing homes that Fair Park Nursing Center first became a part of disbanded within 3 years of its formation. Administrators who left the alliance felt that they could accomplish just as much on their own without having to be affiliated with the Wellspring program. For the past 3 years, Fair Park has been a member of another alliance that comprises 8 facilities scattered throughout the state. Mr. Baker observes that members of this second alliance are less critical of the Wellspring program unlike members in the first alliance that had failed to hold together. However, there is a feeling that this group may think more highly of the program than what it actually has delivered. The group may be more focused on bonding than on the accomplishment of results. Minutes of one Alliance meeting (Exhibit CS12–1) are representative of the meetings that members of this alliance hold every month.

## Fair Park Nursing Center

Fair Park is a 90-bed skilled nursing facility that is part of a nonprofit corporation which also operates assisted living services and independent living apartments on the same campus. Mr. Baker is the administrator of the nursing center, and reports to the corporation's CEO. He has been with Fair Park for 9 years. He holds a bachelor's degree in business administration and has 24 years of experience in managing retirement living and SNF operations.

**Exhibit CS12–1** Minutes

### Wellspring Alliance

In Attendance: Steve Sanders, Jim Tangle, Tom Renfrew, Kathy Hogden, Lynn Bennick, Michael Borgen, Lou Baker, Colleen Davis

**Agenda** reviewed, and two items added.

**Minutes** of the alliance's previous meeting were approved as written. There was no financial report other than discussion that monthly dues would begin soon (as forecasted by Mike). Plan to establish the amount of dues at the next meeting.

**Group purchasing of insurance**—Steve followed up with two sources. Group purchasing of health insurance (almost everyone knows) is not an option. Group purchasing of property and liability insurance is an option according to his sources. Steve is waiting for further information from both sources. Following discussion, it was requested that each facility come prepared to the next meeting to say 'yea' or 'nay' to their support of the alliance proceeding with getting group quotes.

**Next alliance meeting**—Location will be Fair Park at 10:30 a.m. Our annual schedule shows that each facility would bring their Building and Grounds Managers and Human Resources Directors to the June meeting so that they can have break-out meetings of their own. Each facility needs to check with those individuals ASAP to be sure they have this date on their schedule. Email Lou ASAP with number of people coming from your facility, and with possible topics they would like to discuss. Topics may include Life Safety Code surveys, and paid time off policies, etc.

**Staff Time Off question**—Lou asked whether anyone has experienced this: Staff of other nationalities just up and wanting a month or two off in the summer—to return to their homeland—and think it deplorable when we take issue with that request. No one had much experience with this. Lou said it's happened there a few times over the years. Most felt that requiring a leave of absence would be justified.

**Nurse Practitioner Report**—There was none.

**V.A. Medications**—Lynn asked for feedback on requests for this. Steve's local pharmacist agreed to package them in unit dose, which made the admission possible. Tom raised the issue of immediate availability of medications should Doctor's orders change. All agreed that a facility has the right (in its policies) to set requirements for pharmacy suppliers, such as 'must be packaged in such-n-such way,' and have 24-hour availability, etc.

**Kim Wishard**—Michael said that at the last minute it was determined that this would be a good day for Kim (the newly-hired GNP for the alliance) to meet several people. So Kim is meeting right now with coordinators and DONs. However, Kim's first official day will be a week from today.

Michael handed out copies of the 'Letter of Understanding,' and of the 'Independent Contractor Agreement.' He clarified the hours as stated in the 'Letter of Understanding.'

Motion approved to ratify the two documents with the understanding that in the event of a discrepancy between the two, the 'Letter of Understanding' would take precedence. Following further discussion about Kim's orientation and work, Kathy volunteered to offer her facility as a 'home' base from which Kim could work so she could utilize the copier, and do mailings, etc.

**(Lunch Break)**

(continues)

**Exhibit CS12–1** Minutes (Continued)

Meeting continued with Wellspring coordinators and DONs. Discussed Kim's orientation. She said she would be working Mondays and Fridays at her current job, and would be available Tuesdays, Wednesdays, and Thursdays for our alliance. She has her own fax and scanner and uses email a lot.

**Kim would like brochures of each of our facilities.** Members should send those to her. A schedule of this year's alliance meetings has been given to her. She also has a copy of the coordinators' schedule of conference calls, modules, and follow-up dates. Michael has already provided Kim with the alliance directory. Colleen will email Kim the directory of coordinators and DONs.

As for Kim's schedule of visits, it was emphasized that visits should be monthly (or every other month if travel/distance is an issue—with longer days dedicated). Kim would prefer to set that original visit schedule. She will be at the Elimination Module on the follow-up day. She will also be at the alliance's next meeting at Fair Park.

Colleen asked the alliance members whether we would approve of them lining up an educational speaker for the Elimination follow-up day. Following discussion it was determined such a speaker would be unnecessary as discussion and reporting would pretty much fill the day.

It was also asked whether module training and alliance meetings could be on the same day. Tom said that previous attempts at this were not effective, as coordinators and the GNP had preferred to network among themselves during lunch at module training sessions. So, such coordination will not be pursued.

Meeting Adjourned at 4 p.m.

# The Wellspring Model

## The Seven Elements

Seven elements are at the heart of the Wellspring model. Effective implementation of each is regarded as critical to the program's success:

1. The Alliance which comprises a consortium of member facilities that collaborate with each other and share information, particularly information pertaining to clinical and other operational outcomes.

2. Training modules that cover clinical areas such as incontinence care (elimination), nutrition, fall prevention, skin care, and palliative care. An additional module on leadership is used for training facility associates in leadership positions connected with the implementation of the modules in the nursing facilities. The modules have been developed by Innovative Solutions Inc. (www.wellspringis.org) and are based on evidence-based best practices. The Wellspring Institute provides training at a central location by nationally recognized experts.

3. Care Resource Teams are formed within each facility. Each team focuses on 1 or 2 clinical modules. The teams are multidisciplinary; for

example, a housekeeper may serve on the skin care team. Associates volunteer and choose which care team they will serve on. All associates in a facility—CNAs, maintenance personnel, activity staff, office staff, and social workers—are encouraged to serve on one team or another. Each team selects its own chair or leader who generally holds a supervisory position in the facility. Because of the training received at the Wellspring Institute and further skill development that may occur through ongoing communication with their counterparts in other facilities within the alliance, the teams are seen as experts within the facility on the clinical care modules they represent. Each Care Resource Team meets monthly within its own facility to discuss problems and issues with the implementation of the modules and compliance with the best practices as defined by the modules. All but one module, the Leadership module, cover clinical areas. Training in the Leadership module is specifically designed for the leader of each Care Resource Team.

4. Facility-based Wellspring Coordinator is an RN, and is often the nurse responsible for in-service education or quality improvement (QI) in the facility. His or her main job is to coordinate and facilitate the work of Care Resource Teams. The coordinator attends all training modules at the Wellspring Institute, and also attends quarterly meetings for collaboration and networking with other coordinators.

5. A geriatric nurse practitioner (GRP) is assigned to each alliance. A GNP is an RN who has received advanced training, generally at the Master's level, in health care issues pertaining to the elderly. In the Wellspring program, the GNP periodically visits each facility within an alliance to provide training and reinforcement. The facility's Wellspring Coordinator also keeps in telephone contact with the GNP at least once a month.

6. Data collection and analysis are a key component of quality measurement. Care Resource Teams collect the data within their own facility. Facilities forward the data to a contracted data analyst who aggregates the information and prepares summary reports.

7. The cultural change espoused by the Wellspring model calls for a management philosophy based on staff empowerment in which routine decision making shifts from supervisors to front line caregivers.

## Direct and Indirect Costs

Membership in Wellspring requires a one-time licensing fee ($20,000 in 2007). A monthly fee of $600 is paid to Wellspring Solutions Inc. for data analysis, yearly resident/family satisfaction surveys, and training provided by the Wellspring Institute. Each facility pays an additional $700 a month for the GNP's services. Indirect costs associated with the program include hourly pay, lodging, and meals when staff members go to the Wellspring Institute, travel costs for monthly alliance meetings, and the purchase cost of any special equipment. For example, an ultrasound bladder scanner (cost approximately $8,000) is recommended to be used in the Incontinence module to measure residual urine.

## Opinions and Experiences of Alliance Administrators

In one Wellspring alliance, member administrators candidly spoke about their experiences and expressed their opinions:

1. "For many of us, geography presents a big challenge," one alliance member stated. Facilities take turns hosting the monthly alliance meetings. Counting travel time, administrators spend one long day each month. Some alliance meetings involve other staff who must also devote a full day away from their jobs. Staff travel also presents potential liability for the facilities in the event of an accident or some other unforeseen incident. Geography may also have been a factor in the dissolution of the alliance that Fair Park had first joined. Most of these facilities were located relatively close to each other, which created skepticism among the alliance members about openly sharing information. Since these facilities could possibly be competing against each other, the administrators were reluctant to share sensitive information about their operations. Before leaving the alliance, one administrator had stated, "We were promised more than what we got from the program. We were told we would save money on staff turnover and incontinence supplies." When this alliance broke up, the GNP was hired away by a small chain of three facilities.

2. Another administrator remarked, "I decided to join Wellspring when a CNA stood up before a microphone and described how a 100-year old incontinent resident became continent again. But, I have become somewhat pessimistic after observing that Wellspring corporation talks about empowerment of staff, but does not practice it at the corporate level. They simply told us that Incontinence was the first module we had to go through; there was no discussion about it. We were also told that the MDS would have to be done in 15 minutes. I felt that there was too much control. Also, it was mandated that to join the Wellspring program, a facility had to be nonprofit."

3. "Because our board of directors was convinced, we were in," said one administrator. Another pointed out, "My CEO was sold on the program, and I had to be in. There was no "buy in," just a verbal consent from my department managers. We are still with the program because of the CEO's ongoing commitment to a systematized QI process." "Yeah," responded another, "Getting the staff to buy into this program has been a real challenge." Another administrator interjected that compared to other facilities, the ones participating in Wellspring already had higher staffing levels, commitment to quality, and a mission centered on patient care. "We very likely already had a higher level of quality in our facilities," said another.

4. "My staff reacted quite negatively to the idea of empowerment. Their reaction was, 'You are not paying me

to do that. Our jobs are going to change.' The extensive data collection became overwhelming; it was quite an interruption to the normal work flow. We were not given much training on how to collect data."

5. "It has been hard to get a handle on quantifiable results. A lot of uncertainty still prevails about the value of all the data. There have been only some minor victories in incontinence, but no dramatic changes have been noted."

6. "One problem continues to this day: There is no nurturing of the Care Resource Teams. At first they are quite enthusiastic, but then there is a fall off. Consistency in the composition of these teams has also been difficult to maintain; voluntary participation does not seem to occur; commitment and passion are often lacking; and the non-nursing staff often feel out of place in making a legitimate contribution to the quality of clinical care."

7. "Value is lost when administrators don't know what is being accomplished. The GNP is supposed to go over the outputs of the QI analysis, interpret the results, and suggest changes. However, the alliance has not had a GNP for the past year and a half or longer. One has just been recruited. She is getting oriented to the alliance and the member facilities. Besides, GNPs do not have the qualifications or training in teambuilding."

8. "In our facilities, 'Wellspring' and 'empowerment' have become 'dirty words.' Staff reacts negatively to them. We have replaced use of the term 'Wellspring' with 'best practices.'"

## Comments from Staff at Fair Park
### Certified Nursing Assistants

1. "I have worked at Fair Park for 13 years. I am on the Care Resource Team for Nutrition/Hydration. Mostly, just the nursing staff has joined this team. My initial reaction when we first started Wellspring 6 years ago was that it was a new thing and it would create more work for nursing. A change in attitude was necessary, but we are still changing the attitudes. They started recording how much fluid the patients were drinking (fluid intake) and also everybody's diet was recorded. We started concentrating on people who were losing weight. Before we used to look at all people. This is a bad thing in my opinion. The squeaky wheel is getting the grease."

2. "There has been no change in management practices and no change in decision making at the CNA level. We are told, 'Ok, you and your partner work with these patients,' but it has always been that way."

3. "I have worked here for 4 years. Wellspring is fine. There have been no problems. It helps me learn, develop my skills, and become a better CNA."

4. "I have been here for over 6 years. I have just joined the team on Elimination. There are 10 people on this team, but only 4 or 5 come to each monthly meeting. I think I now get more respect as a CNA. It is a good program, but it has created more paperwork. Now I see that the amount of paperwork is being reduced because we are concentrating on at-risk patients."

## Wellspring Coordinator

"I have 30 years of experience in long-term care nursing. At Wellspring meetings, we learned how we would be doing things; they would teach us the best practices. But, there was a lot of negativity right from day one. I feel that the program was not portrayed correctly. All the department managers should have been brought on board. It was tried, but they did not go along with it. They felt that an outsider was coming in to tell them what to do.

"Only a few team members come to the monthly meetings; others do not seem to care. Also, many employees cannot go to Wellspring Institute for training in modules because of their family situations.

"I think it's a good program, but people are not receptive. Their attitude is, 'We are doing fine.' They are given the information, but it does not always get done. People come back from module training all psyched up, but there is no follow through because nobody is held accountable. Then it all falls back on my shoulders.

"The modules don't get implemented because staff members have to work with people from other departments. Also, we have a lot of long-term employees; it is difficult for them to accept change. The main frustration is felt in the nursing department because they feel they have to do extra work. Nurses have also become cynical. Even when nursing home regulations call for more paperwork, the staff thinks it is Wellspring requiring them to do more."

## Department Managers

"Most staff members are indifferent because they haven't seen any worthwhile change. The pain management and behavioral mod- ules have excellent participation because they can see the changes. Participants in these modules are quite enthusiastic about the benefits of Wellspring. On the other hand, participation in the incontinence and falls modules are quite a different story. We are lucky if out of 10 participants, 1 shows up at the monthly meetings. The reason is people cannot see any changes; the data do not show improvements in falls or incontinence. Besides, the training sessions have become repetitious; there is little if any new information even though each module training session is repeated only every 2 years or so."

"One GNP was great about getting everybody together to discuss issues, but she came here only once, mainly because of the distance. If I have my say, I would get out of Wellspring; there is very little "buy in" from the staff, and they are not behind the program. Out of 8 or 9 department managers, only 1 or 2 really support the program."

"Non-nursing staff resist going to the training sessions. They come back and say, 'Why did I have to go to that?' Administrators meet once a month, but we don't know what has come out of it."

## Conclusions of a Research Study[1]

The Commonwealth Fund supported a 15-month evaluation of Wellspring conducted by a team of researchers who used a multi-faceted methodology: site visits; interviews and focus groups with staff, residents, and families; participant observation; and analysis of secondary data from diverse sources.

[1]Excerpted from Stone, R.I. et al. 2002. *Evaluation of the Wellspring Model for Improving Nursing Home Quality*. New York, NY: The Commonwealth Fund. Retrieved March 2009 from: http://www.cmwf.org/usr_doc/stone_wellspringevaluation.pdf

Site visits of the 11 facilities in the charter alliance (all were located in Wisconsin) were conducted from November 2000 through May 2001. Quantitative findings pertain to comparisons between selected time periods prior to the implementation of the Wellspring model (1994–1995) and selected time periods after the model had been implemented (1999–2000). Wellspring was founded in 1994 and became fully operational in 1998. However, in the analyses, there is some inconsistency in the use of the pre-Wellspring and post-Wellspring time periods.

Following is a summary of the findings of this research:

## Qualitative Findings

For the most part, the training modules were well-developed and up-to-date in terms of their clinical content. However, one exception to this positive finding was the Management (Leadership) module, which appeared to be disorganized and vague and needed a major overhaul. The attendance at the module training sessions was generally very good, but facilities sometimes did not send individuals representing all levels and on other occasions failed to send individuals who could be the most successful implementers of the training ideas back in the facility.

There were varied opinions from facility staff and administration about the involvement of the GNP in troubleshooting and providing ongoing support to the facilities. As for the Wellspring Coordinators, on the whole, they approached their jobs with a serious and strong commitment to the model. However, in some cases they felt frustrated by various types of barriers.

The researchers found quite a bit of variation in how the Care Resource Teams functioned. Some were well organized, diverse across levels and disciplines, active in maintaining their schedule of meetings, and active in data collection. However, it was rare to see all these characteristics present in all the teams in a facility. There were several facilities where the teams were barely functional. For the most part, the greatest difficulty seemed to be keeping up the initial momentum generated by the module training. Scheduled monthly meetings and attendance at them often would fall off after a period of time.

The researchers concluded that in its supportive role the Alliance had served with distinction and success, but greater effort would be needed for Wellspring to move into the next stages of its evolution. Despite the strong supportive role of the Alliance, the problems that arose at some points required a stronger management and accountability function than the Alliance was able to muster. Its governance structure resembles a confederacy more than a strong management body.

Of all the elements in the Wellspring model, the data collection function was found to be the least well implemented and most problematic. Although considerable resources have been invested in data collection and analysis, almost universal confusion existed in the facilities about the purpose, meaning, and structure of the data. In most facilities, data collection was sporadic at best, and it was rare that a facility made substantial use of the data internally.

## Quantitative Findings

The researchers reported that between 1995 and 1999, the retention rate for all Wellspring nursing staff increased from 70% to 76% while the retention rate for non-Wellspring facilities in Wisconsin dropped from 74% to

68%. To assess the quality of care, the researchers conducted a series of analyses of resident status and change in status using measures that would most likely capture the impact of the Wellspring clinical module training and implementation (incontinence, falls, behavior, physical functioning, nutritional status, restraints, and skin care). Between 1996 and mid-2000, few differences were observed between the Wellspring and the non-Wellspring facilities.

# Wellspring's Future Outlook

Alliance administrators presented their views on the future outlook for Wellspring: "I don't think it will last . . . nationally it will go away mainly because there has been a lack of growth." "Some alliances will continue in one way, shape, or form." "Quality improvement is going to stay in one form or another . . . but, the Wellspring program requires a huge commitment of time and finances." "Wellspring needs a business plan to recruit more facilities; such a plan does not exist."

## Assignment

1. The Alliance is one of the critical elements for success with the Wellspring program. What should be the main objectives of the Alliance?

2. What recommendations can you make to modify the role of the Alliance so that it functions more effectively toward the accomplishment of the objectives you stated in (1)? Be specific in your response and give reasons for your recommendations.

3. Evaluate the pros and cons of the Wellspring model. What suggestions can you make to improve the model?

4. How can accountability be established at the Alliance level? How can this accountability be carried through at the alliance meetings?

5. What can you propose for the Care Resource Teams to function more effectively as teams?

6. As an administrator of a SNF would you join Wellspring? If you were already a member, would you stay with the program or would you be inclined to leave the program? Provide adequate explanations.

7. By its very nature, any kind of change fosters uncertainty and resistance among the members of an organization. As a nursing home administrator how would you plan and implement organizational change such as adopting the Wellspring model?

# GLOSSARY

**Abuse:** (1) Willful infliction of injury, unreasonable confinement, intimidation or punishment with resulting physical harm, pain, or mental anguish to a patient. (2) Fraud committed against a public program such as Medicare or Medicaid.

**Access:** The ability of a person needing services to obtain those services.

**Accounts payable:** Money owed to vendors from whom goods, supplies, and services have been purchased on credit.

**Accounts receivable:** Amounts due from patients and third-party payers for services that the facility has already provided.

**Accreditation:** Accreditation of a nursing facility by the Joint Commission on Accreditation of Healthcare Organizations (JCAHO).

**Accrual-basis accounting:** The commonly used method of accounting in which revenues and expenses do not match cash inflows and outflows.

**Acquired Immune Deficiency Syndrome (AIDS):** AIDS develops when a person infected with the human immunodeficiency virus (HIV) undergoes a breakdown of the immune system and becomes susceptible to serious illness and death from other viruses, parasites, fungi, and bacteria.

**Activities of daily living (ADLs):** The most commonly used measure of disability. ADLs determine whether an individual needs assistance in performing six basic activities: eating, bathing, dressing, using the toilet, maintaining continence, and getting into or out of a bed or chair (transferring). Grooming and walking a distance of eight feet are sometimes added to evaluate self-care and mobility.

**Activity:** Active or passive involvement of patients in any activities, outside the activities of daily living, that provide meaning and personal enrichment.

**Acuity:** The level of severity of a patient's condition.

**Acute care:** Short-term, intense medical care for an episode of illness or injury often requiring hospitalization.

**Acute conditions:** Episodic conditions that require short-term but intensive medical interventions.

**Administrative information system:** Information technology that is designed to assist in carrying out financial and administrative support activities such as payroll, patient accounting, billing, accounts receivables, materials management, budgeting and cost control, and office automation.

**Administrative law:** Rules and regulations formulated by the departments or agencies of the executive branch of government to carry out the intent of statutory law.

**Administrator-in-training (AIT):** An internship with a certified preceptor required for an NHA license in some states.

**Admission agreement:** A contract that spells out the services the nursing home will provide and the cost of those services.

**Adult day care:** A community-based nonresidential service that enables a person to live with family but receive professional services in a daytime program in which nursing care, rehabilitation therapies, supervision, and social activities are available.

**Adult foster care (AFC) homes:** Small, family-run homes licensed to provide room, board, supervision, and personal care to nonrelated adults who are unable to live independently. These neighborhood homes are also called "group homes."

**Advance directive:** A written statement prepared by a competent individual indicating his or her desires for medical treatment in case the patient loses the capacity to make decisions.

**Ageism:** Prejudicial treatment of the elderly based on stereotypes and misconceptions.

**Agent:** Someone authorized to act on behalf of another (a principal); for example, a corporation generally authorizes the nursing home administrator to represent it or to act on its behalf.

**Aging-in-place:** Accommodating the changing needs of older adults while living in familiar surroundings.

**Aging schedule:** Also called an "aging report," it shows the length of time that various amounts within each patient's account have been outstanding.

**Agitation:** Verbal, vocal, and motor activities that are repetitive and outside of socially acceptable norms.

**AIDS:** See *Acquired Immune Deficiency Syndrome.*

**AIT:** See *administrator-in-training.*

**All-inclusive rate:** A bundled fee that includes in a single rate all services and supplies furnished to a patient.

**Allopathic medicine:** Medical approach—as practiced by physicians trained as doctors of medicine (MDs)—that views medical treatment as active intervention to produce a counteracting reaction in an attempt to neutralize the effects of disease.

**Almshouse:** See *poorhouse.*

**Alzheimer's disease:** A progressive degenerative disease of the brain, producing memory loss,

confusion, irritability, and severe functional decline. The disease becomes progressively worse and eventually results in death.

**Ambulation:** Moving about.

**Ambulatory:** Being able to move about.

**Ambulatory care (ambulatory services):** Services that require the patients to come and receive needed services at a community-based location. In a broader context, ambulatory care can be any outpatient service such as a visit to the physician's office or clinic or outpatient surgery.

**Ancillaries:** Services and products, such as rehabilitation therapies, pharmaceuticals, catheters, dressings, incontinence pads, oxygen, etc., that can be billed separately to private-pay patients in addition to the basic room-and-board rate.

**Antisepsis:** Removing or destroying microorganisms.

**Aphasia:** Impaired ability to communicate.

**Apraxia:** A speech disorder in which the tongue, lips, and vocal cords are unable to work together. As a result, the person is unable to say what he or she wants to say.

**Arbitration:** A process in which a neutral third party hears both sides in a dispute and renders a decision that is binding on both parties.

**Area of refuge:** A zone of safety within a building that is protected from the effects of fire and smoke and that provides direct access to an exit.

**Area Agency on Aging:** Agencies established in local communities under the 1973 amendments to the Federal Older Americans Act of 1965 to address the needs of Americans aged 60 and over. Among other services, these agencies assess clients' needs and determine eligibility for services best suited to meet their needs.

**Asepsis:** Absence of harmful microorganisms called pathogens. It refers to the practice of clean procedures, such as hand-washing.

**Assault:** A threatening act in which physical contact need not occur, but the assaulted individual reasonably believes that the aggressor is capable of an imminent physical act. See *battery.*

**Assessment:** The process by which health care professionals attempt to reliably characterize the patient's physical health, functional abilities, cognitive functioning, psychological state, social well-being, and past and current use of formal services.

**Assets:** The financial value of everything a business owns, as shown on the balance sheet.

**Assisted living facility:** A residential setting that provides personal care services, 24-hour supervision, scheduled and unscheduled assistance, social activities, and some nursing care services.

**Associate:** An employee or staff member.

**Audiologist:** A health care professional who is specially trained and licensed to provide direct clinical services to individuals with hearing or balance disorders.

**Autism:** A complex developmental disability that typically appears during the first three years of life and is the result of a brain disorder. It affects the person's social interaction and communication.

**Autonomy:** A cluster of notions that include self-determination, freedom, independence, and liberty of choice and action.

**Average daily census:** The average number of patients per day over a specified period of time such as a week, a month, or a year.

**Baby boomers:** People born between 1946 and 1964. This age group constitutes approximately 70 million Americans who will start retiring around 2010. By 2030, when all the baby boomers will have retired, experts predict that they will severely strain the nation's health care system.

**Bad debt:** An amount that is legitimately owed to the facility, but is deemed uncollectible.

**Balance sheet:** A financial statement that summarizes the financial position (assets, liabilities, and equity) of an organization at a given date, such as the last day of a month or the last day of a year.

**Bargaining unit:** A distinct group of employees who may reasonably be grouped together for the purpose of collective bargaining.

**Battery:** An action in which intentional touching occurs without consent from the other individual. See *assault.*

**Bed-hold:** When a patient is temporarily out of the facility (at a hospital or with family), but the bed is being held and must be paid for.

**Benefit period:** Under Part A of Medicare, it refers to a period of time that begins when a patient is hospitalized for a particular spell of illness and ends when the patient has not been an inpatient in a hospital or has received skilled nursing care in a SNF for 60 consecutive days for that particular spell of illness.

**Best practices:** Evidence-based practices.

**Bill:** A proposed piece of legislation.

**Biophilia:** The human tendency to pay attention to, affiliate with, and respond positively to nature.

**Bioterrorism:** The use of chemical, biological, or nuclear agents to inflict harm on relatively large civilian populations by rogue individuals or groups.

**Board-and-care homes:** Very basic long-term care homes that provide physically supportive dwelling units, monitoring, assistance with medications, supervision, and light care with ADLs, but do not provide nursing care. These facilities are also called "domiciliary care facilities" or "shelter care facilities."

**Board of directors (board of trustees):** See *governing body.*

***Bona fide:*** See *good faith.*

**Breach of contract:** A civil wrong involving the violation of a specific agreement between two parties.

**Budget:** A tool for exercising financial control. It sets expectations that become financial objectives that the nursing home administrator is responsible for achieving.

**Budgeting:** The process of financial planning.

**Bundled rate:** A price that includes all services a patient may require.

**Capitation:** Payment of a predetermined fixed monthly rate per person to include all covered services.

**Cardiologist:** A physician who specializes in the treatment of heart diseases.

**Care plan:** See *plan of care.*

**Case management:** A centralized coordinating function in which the special needs of older adults are identified and a trained professional determines which services would be most appropriate, determines eligibility for those services, makes referrals, arranges for financing, and coordinates and monitors delivery of care to ensure that clients are receiving the prescribed services.

**Case-mix:** Mix of patients with different acuity levels. Patients who are more seriously ill require more intensive use of resources and incur greater cost to the facility.

**Cash flow statement:** A summary of transactions that increase or decrease cash during a given period, such as a month or a year.

**Census-mix:** See *payer-mix.*

**Census range:** Anticipated range of patient census.

**Census:** Number of patients in a facility on a given day.

**Centers for Medicare & Medicaid Services (CMS):** An agency of the federal Department of Health and Human Services.

**Cerebral palsy:** A developmental disability caused by brain damage occurring before or during childbirth.

**Certificate of need (CON):** State laws that require a state planning agency to approve building of a new facility or expansion of an existing one.

**Certification:** (1) Federal authorization required for a facility to admit Medicare and Medicaid patients. (2) A process by which a nongovernmental agency or association recognizes the competence of individuals who have met certain qualifications as determined by the agency or association.

**Certified nursing assistant:** A nurse aide who has completed at least the minimum training required by regulations.

**Channels of distribution:** A marketing term that refers to the mechanisms used for bringing products and customers together to create an exchange.

**Charge:** A fee that is established by the nursing facility for a particular service or product.

**Chemotherapy:** The use of anti-cancer (cytotoxic) drugs to destroy cancer cells. Chemotherapy drugs may be given on their own, but often several drugs are combined.

**Chiropractor:** A licensed practitioner who holds a doctor of chiropractic (DC) degree. Chiropractors treat patients through chiropractic manipulation, which includes manipulation of the spine, physiotherapy, and dietary counseling.

**Chronic condition:** A medical condition that persists over time, is generally irreversible, and can result in complications if left untreated.

**Civil law:** Body of laws governing private legal affairs, such as private rights and duties, contracts, and commercial relations.

**Claim:** A bill submitted to the fiscal intermediary claiming payment for services provided.

**Client-centered care:** See *person-centered care.*

**Clinical information system:** Information technology that is designed to be used by various clinicians to support the delivery of patient care.

**Clinical pathway:** A care-planning tool that outlines in a time sequence important aspects of care necessary for meeting specific outcomes.

**Clinical practice guidelines:** Evidence-based standardized protocols indicated for the treatment of specific health conditions.

**Closed system:** A management approach that emphasizes only the interrelationships between the various internal components of the organization, while the interaction with the external environment is largely ignored.

**Collection period:** Number of days' worth of revenue that is in accounts receivable.

**Collective bargaining:** Good-faith negotiation between a union and management.

**Common law:** Body of legal principles and precedents that have been handed down in the form of court decisions.

**Community advisory board:** Composed of key community leaders, the community advisory board functions as the "eyes and ears" for the facility. Through their influence, the advisory board members can also assist the administrator form meaningful partnerships with community agencies.

**Comorbidity:** The simultaneous presence of two or more health problems.

**Compensatory damages:** Damages awarded by a court to "make the person whole again." Also see *punitive damages.*

**Competent:** In reference to legal competence, a person who is of sound mind and of legal age.

**Complementary services:** Services that are not directly rendered by the facility in which the patient resides, but are necessary to address the total health care needs of a patient. Complementary services are necessary for delivering total care.

**Consideration:** In contract law, something of value promised to another in exchange for something else of value.

**Constitutional law:** Law based on the Constitution of the United States.

**Continuing care retirement community (CCRC):** Also called a life-care community, it is an organization that integrates and coordinates the independent living and other institution-based components of the LTC continuum. Different levels of services are generally housed in separate buildings, all located on one campus.

**Continuous quality improvement (CQI):** An ongoing undertaking to improve quality throughout the nursing facility. It is also called "total quality management (TQM)."

**Continuum of long-term care:** The full range of long-term care services that increase in the level of acuity and complexity from one end to the other—from informal and community-based services at one end of the continuum to the institutional system at the other end.

**Contract:** A legally binding agreement between two or more parties to carry out a legal purpose.

**Controlled substances:** Narcotics, stimulants, depressants, hallucinogens, anabolic steroids, and chemicals that are governed by the Controlled Substances Act (CSA), Title II of the Comprehensive Drug Abuse Prevention and Control Act of 1970. Except as provided under the law, their possession and use are illegal.

**Controlling:** The process of monitoring, evaluating, and correcting.

**Copayment:** An amount an insured must pay out of pocket each time a health care service is used.

**Corporate compliance:** A corporation's accountability to its various stakeholders. It includes compliance with laws, regulations, and ethical standards to "do what is right."

**Corporate law:** Statutes defining the rights and responsibilities of corporations.

**Corporation:** A legal entity that is regarded as separate from its owners.

**Cost–benefit:** Benefits to be derived in relation to costs for a proposal or a program.

**Cost-effectiveness (cost-efficiency):** Cost-effectiveness is achieved when the benefits are greater than the costs incurred.

**Crime:** An offense committed against the general public regardless of whether only one or more individuals have been wronged.

**Criminal law:** A branch of law that defines crimes and provides for their punishment.

**Cross-contamination:** Transfer of disease-causing organisms through contact with a dirty surface, unwashed hands, or insects.

**Cultural change:** The integration of the three elements of person-centered care—clinical care, socio-residential elements, and human factors—along with the enrichment of the environments in which people live and the empowerment of both clients and associates.

**Cultural competence:** Ability of an organization to deliver health care services in accordance with the cultural needs and preferences of the clients.

**Custodial care:** Nonmedical care that includes routine assistance with the activities of daily living (ADLs) but does not include active nursing or rehabilitative treatments. Such care is provided to maintain function because the person's overall condition is not likely to improve.

**Customer:** Any entity that receives the product of a transaction.

**Days of care:** Cumulative census over a specified period of time. Also called "patient days."

**Decision making:** Choosing from among different alternatives.

**Decision support system:** Information technology that provides information and analytical tools to support effective management.

**Deductible:** An amount the patient must first pay each year (or at the beginning of a benefit period for Medicare) before any amount of benefits would be payable by insurance.

**Deemed status:** Medicare rule that a hospital accredited by the Joint Commission on Accreditation of Healthcare Organizations is deemed to have met the Medicare certification criteria.

**Defendant:** A party against whom a lawsuit is brought.

**Deficiency:** A nursing facility's failure to meet any of the standards, as determined by a survey.

**Delirium:** A state of mental confusion that often manifests itself in the form of disorientation, incoherent speech, and physical agitation.

**Dementia:** A generic term that describes progressive and irreversible mental dysfunction that results in complex cognitive decline. These cognitive changes are commonly accompanied by disturbances of mood, behavior, and personality.

**Demographic imperative:** Future growth of one population group at the expense of another group, such as growth of the elderly population while the younger population shrinks.

**Dermatologist:** A specialist physician who treats infections, growths, injuries, and other disorders related to the skin.

**Developmental disability:** Physical incapacity that generally accompanies mental retardation and often arises at birth or in early childhood.

**Dietitian:** Sometimes referred to as nutritionist, a dietitian provides nutritional information and diet-related services to patients.

**Differentiation:** A competitive strategy in which a facility creates distinctive features that allow customers to distinguish the facility's offer from that of its competitors.

**Directed plan of correction:** Measures imposed to bring a facility into compliance with federal certification standards when regulators do not believe that the facility can formulate and implement an effective plan of correction on its own.

**Disability:** A physical or mental impairment that substantially limits one or more of a person's major life activities, according to the Americans with Disabilities Act of 1990.

**Discharge planner:** A social worker employed in a hospital's discharge planning department to facilitate a smooth transfer of patients to an appropriate setting after discharge from the hospital.

**Discharge planning:** A process that includes decisions about when a patient may need to be discharged from the facility and what may be needed to make a smooth transition from one level of care to another or from the facility to living independently.

**Distinct part:** A section of a nursing home that is distinctly certified from the rest of the facility.

**Docket:** An annotated meeting agenda that lists the items to be discussed and also provides some pertinent details and explanations for each item.

**Do-not-resuscitate (DNR) order:** An advance directive in which a person specifies that he or she does not wish to have heartbeat or breathing restored in the event of a cardiac or respiratory arrest.

**Domiciliary care facilities:** See *board-and-care homes.*

**Domotics:** "Smart home" technology.

**Dual certification:** Federal certification that authorizes a facility to admit both Medicare (SNF certification) and Medicaid patients (NF certification).

**Durable power of attorney (DPOA):** A written document that appoints another individual to make decisions on behalf of a patient.

**Dysarthria:** Slurred or unintelligible speech due to muscle weakness or other problem.

**Dysphagia:** Difficulty in swallowing due to a dysfunction in any phase of the swallowing process.

**Economic strike:** A common type of strike by union workers that occurs when the union and management fail to reach an agreement.

**Edenizing:** Changing a nursing home's environment by implementing the principles developed by Eden Alternative, Inc.

**Eden Alternative:** A cultural change that entails viewing the surroundings in facilities as habitats for human beings rather than as facilities for the frail and elderly, as well as applying the lessons of nature in creating vibrant and vigorous settings.

**Effectiveness:** Success in achieving certain output goals.

**Efficiency:** A measure of outputs in relation to the resources used in producing the outputs.

**Elimination period:** In a long-term care insurance plan, the initial waiting period during which LTC services are used but not covered by insurance.

**Emphysema:** A chronic condition characterized by damaged air sacs in the lungs. The resulting reduction of surface area available for gas exchange makes breathing difficult and makes the heart work harder to circulate blood through the lungs. All these changes make less oxygen available to the body.

**Employment-at-will:** A legal doctrine according to which employment is at the will of both the employer and the employee.

**Employment discrimination:** Failing or refusing to hire; discharging or otherwise discriminating against an individual with respect to terms, conditions, or privileges of employment; or limiting, segregating, or classifying employees in a way that it deprives an individual of employment opportunity, training, advancement, or status when such actions are in violation of a law.

**End-of-life care:** Hospice services for the terminally ill.

**Enriched environments:** Also referred to as "enhanced environments," they are physically and psychologically supportive environments that promote positive feelings and harmony, and reduce boredom and stress.

**Enteral feeding:** Delivery of liquid food through a tube directly into the stomach.

**Entrée:** The main dish on a menu.

**Environmental assessment:** A formal analysis and evaluation of environmental trends to understand their potential implications for a facility's long-term success. See *external environment.*

**Environmental scanning:** Using various formal and informal processes to identify, on an ongoing basis, significant trends and events in the external environment.

**Epidemic:** Excessive prevalence of a negative health condition.

**Epilepsy:** A brain disorder in which signals sent by nerve cells become disturbed, causing strange sensations, emotions, convulsions, muscle spasms, or loss of consciousness.

**Equity:** Also called "owners' equity" or "stockholders' equity," it represents the interests or rights of the owners in a for-profit corporation.

**Esophagostomy tube:** A small tube that enters a surgical incision on the side of the neck and is generally removed after each feeding. The tube allows food to enter the esophagus and then flow down into the stomach.

**Ethics committee:** A multidisciplinary forum that is generally called upon to make decisions in the patient's best interest, particularly when legal avenues are not clear-cut.

**Ethnocentrism:** A belief that one's way of life and view of the world are inherently superior to those of others and that they are desirable for others to acquire. It involves judging another's culture as inferior to one's own.

**Evacuation:** Removal of patients and vital equipment from an unsafe area to a safe area during a fire or other emergency situation.

**Evidence-based care:** Delivery of services using best practices that have been established through clinical research.

**Exempt employees:** Salaried workers who are exempt from overtime provisions of the Fair Labor Standards Act.

**External environment:** Social, political, economic, technological, informational, and ecological forces that are external to the organization.

**Extramural services:** Community-based services that are delivered outside a patient's home and require that the patients come and receive the services at a community-based location. Examples include adult day care, mental health outpatient clinics, and congregate meals provided at senior centers.

**False imprisonment:** Unlawful restriction of freedom.

**Family management:** A proactive approach to minimize dissatisfaction and conflict by addressing family members' emotions about placing someone in a nursing home.

**Federal preemption:** Federal laws supersede state and local laws.

**Federalism:** Sharing of powers between the federal and state governments.

**Felony:** Crime of a serious nature that is subject to a jail term of more than one year.

**Financial accounting:** The recording of all financial transactions and the preparation of financial statements.

**Financing:** Means by which patients receiving services in nursing facilities pay for those services.

**Fixed cost:** A cost that does not vary with the number of patients. These costs are noncontrollable.

**Flexible budget:** An adjusted budget in which the budgeted costs are raised or lowered to reflect the actual census.

**Focus group:** A group of about 8 to 12 people who participate in an unstructured session with a skilled moderator to discuss their thoughts and feelings about an issue, an organization, or a service.

**Fraud:** A knowing disregard of the truth that results in harm.

**Gastrostomy tube (G-tube):** A mechanism for delivering nutrition through a tube that passes through a surgical opening in the abdomen and into the stomach.

**General partnership:** A partnership in which there is no limit on the potential liability of the partners.

**Geriatrics:** A branch of medicine that deals with the problems and diseases that accompany aging.

**Gerontology:** An area of knowledge that deals with the understanding of the aging process, the changes accompanying aging, and the special problems associated with aging.

**Good faith:** A legal term that refers to actions that are generally consistent with how a reasonable person would act under similar circumstances.

**Governance:** The act of governing. It refers to trusteeship and stewardship of an organization's resources and capabilities to benefit its stakeholders.

**Governing body:** Also called "governing board," "board of directors," or "board of trustees," it has the ultimate legal responsibility for a facility's operations.

**Green House:** A small freestanding facility designed to house 7 to 10 residents who live together in a homelike setting. Generally, a number of Green Houses are arranged around a central skilled nursing facility that provides support services.

**Grievance:** A formal expression of employee dissatisfaction about some job situation.

**Group homes:** See *adult foster care homes.*

**Group insurance:** Insurance that is made available to individuals through their employers, unions, professional organizations, or consumer organizations such as the AARP.

**Guardian:** Someone who is legally empowered and charged with the responsibility to make decisions in the patient's best interest when the patient is not legally competent to act for him- or herself.

**Handicap:** See *disability.*

**Health screening:** Early detection of health problems through regular exams and tests so that early treatment can be provided to prevent complications and ensuing disability.

**Health policy:** The government's decisions and actions that are intended to achieve certain purposes or goals pertaining to health care.

**Hemodialysis:** A routine treatment necessary for patients whose kidney function has failed. During dialysis, the patient's blood is allowed to flow through a machine with a special filter that removes waste.

**HIV:** See *human immunodeficiency virus.*

**Holistic model:** A philosophy that emphasizes that health care delivery should focus not merely on a person's physical and mental needs, but should also emphasize well-being in every aspect of what makes a person whole and complete.

**Home- and Community-Based Services (HCBS) Waiver:** Enacted under Section 1915(c) of the Social Security Act, the program allows states to offer LTC services that are not otherwise available through the Medicaid program. The latter had authorized payments for institutional care only.

**Home health care:** Delivery of services such as nursing care and rehabilitation therapies to patients in their own homes because such patients do not need to be in an institution and yet are generally unable to leave their homes safely to get the care they need.

**Home telehealth systems:** Use of telecommunication technology for the distance monitoring of patients and delivery of health care with or without the use of video technology.

**Hospice:** A cluster of special services for the terminally ill with a life expectancy of six months or less. It blends medical, spiritual, legal, financial, and family-support services.

**Hostile environment:** Work environment in which behaviors of managers or coworkers create severe stress that interferes with an individual's ability to perform his or her job.

**Hotel services:** Services such as meals, housekeeping, laundry, and maintenance services provided to patients in hospitals and long-term care facilities.

**Human immunodeficiency virus (HIV):** A virus that gradually destroys the body's natural immune system designed to fight infections and disease.

**Human resource:** Associates employed by an organization.

**Human resource management:** The organizational function of planning for human resource needs, recruitment, selection, compensation, development, evaluation, and handling of grievances and labor relations.

**Hydration:** Adequate fluid intake to prevent dehydration.

**Hypertension:** High blood pressure.

**Iatrogenic:** Complications caused by the process of medical care.

**ICF/MR:** A federal certification for an Intermediate Care Facility for the Mentally Retarded.

**Immediate jeopardy:** Noncompliance with a standard that has caused or is likely to cause serious injury, harm, impairment, or death to a resident receiving care in the facility.

**Impasse:** Failure to reach an agreement during collective bargaining.

**Imprest amount:** A fixed amount, such as $400 or $500, which is maintained by periodically replenishing the petty cash that has been used.

**Incident:** Any unexpected negative occurrence involving a patient, associate, or visitor.

**Income statement:** Also called "operating statement: or "profit and loss statement (P&L)," it furnishes a summary of revenues, expenses, and profitability for a given period of time.

**Incontinence:** Inability to control bowel and/or bladder function.

**Incorporation:** Formation of a corporation, which requires filing of articles of incorporation (called a charter or certificate of incorporation in some states) with the proper state authority.

**Indwelling catheter:** A catheter that remains in the bladder to drain urine into a bag.

**Inefficiency:** Deployment of resources without enhancing quality.

**Infantilization:** Treating older adults as children.

**Infection control:** A comprehensive program to prevent the transmission of infections protecting the residents, the staff, and visitors from contracting infections while in the facility.

**Infection control practitioner (ICP):** Generally a registered nurse who is responsible for overseeing the facility's infection control program.

**Infectious waste:** Hazardous waste that can pose health risks from communicable infectious agents.

**Informal care:** Unpaid services provided by family and others.

**Information systems:** Computer-based applications used for transforming raw data into information that can be used in a variety of ways to improve operational efficiencies and the quality of services.

**Informed consent:** (1) The right of a patient to make an informed choice about medical care. (2) Consent by a patient to authorize release of information from his or her medical record based on the patient's understanding of what information will be released and what use will be made of that information.

**Injury:** Physical, financial, or emotional harm.

**Inpatient services:** Health care services provided on the basis of an overnight stay in a facility.

**In-service:** An educational session.

**Instrumental activities of daily living (IADLs):** Activities considered necessary for independent living. IADLs include doing housework, cooking, doing laundry, grocery shopping, taking medication, using the telephone, managing money, and moving around outside the home.

**Integrated health system:** A local or regional health services conglomerate, usually built around a major hospital that offers a range of health care services by linking hospitals, clinics, and managed care organizations.

**Intentional tort:** A willful act that violates the rights or interests of others.

**Interdependence:** A state of living together (symbiosis) in a mutually beneficial relationship.

**Interdisciplinary:** See *multidisciplinary*.

**Interest group:** An organized sector of society, such as a business association, citizen group, labor union, or professional association, whose main purpose is to protect its members' interests through active participation in the policymaking process.

**Internist:** A physician who specializes in treating diseases related to the internal organs of the body.

**Interoperable:** Electronic medical information that is available simultaneously to various health care providers.

**Intimacy:** (1) A person's privacy during visits with family, friends, or counselors. (2) Sexual intimacy. (3) Closeness or proximity of the caregiver to the dependent elder that goes beyond mere familiarity.

**Intramural services:** Community-based services that are taken to patients who live in their own homes, either alone or with family. The most commonly used intramural services include home health care and Meals On Wheels.

**Jejunostomy tube (J-tube):** A surgically placed tube that enters the small intestine for the delivery of specialized nutritional formulas.

**Job-unit contract:** A contract established each time a need arises for infrequent major jobs.

**Joint venture:** A separate organization formed jointly by two or more existing entities for pursuing a common purpose.

**Leadership:** Influencing people to act for certain goals that represent the values and motivations—wants, needs, aspirations, and expectations—of both leaders and followers.

**Learned helplessness:** A psychological state in which patients believe that they can no longer do anything for themselves and must depend on others.

**Liabilities:** Economic obligations or debts.

**Liability:** Potential damages ensuing from legal action.

**Libel:** A written false report intended to defame another person. See *slander.*

**Licensed practical (or vocational) nurse (LPN/LVN):** An LPN or LVN is a professional nurse who has completed a state-approved program in practical nursing, which is generally one or two years in duration, and has passed a national written examination.

**Licensure:** Licensing of a health care facility or a health care professional in accordance with state laws that require that certain conditions be met for the granting of a license.

**Life Safety Code:** Rules and standards developed by the National Fire Protection Association to specify numerous fire safety and other elements of building construction, fixtures, and furnishings that nursing facilities must comply with.

**Limited partnership:** A partnership in which the individual liability of partners is limited to the extent of each partner.

**Litigation:** Legal action brought before a court of law.

**Living will:** An advance directive specifying a person's wishes regarding medical treatment in the event this person becomes incompetent.

**Local area network (LAN):** A LAN links a group of computers to a central server so all LAN users can access the same information.

**Long-term care (LTC):** A variety of individualized and well-coordinated total care services that promote the maximum possible independence for people with functional limitations and that are provided over an extended period of time, using appropriate current technology and available evidence-based practices, in accordance with a holistic approach while maximizing both the quality of clinical care and the individual's quality of life.

**Long-term care facility:** An institution, commonly referred to as a nursing home, that is duly licensed to provide long-term care services.

**Maintenance rehabilitation:** Rehabilitation that is aimed at preserving the present level of function and preventing secondary complications.

**Malice:** Knowingly doing something with the desire to cause harm.

**Malpractice:** Negligence or carelessness in the delivery of services according to accepted standards of care so that harm is caused to the recipient of care.

**Managed care:** An approach to delivering a comprehensive array of health care services to a defined group of enrolled members through efficient management of service utilization and payment to providers.

**Management:** What managers do to maintain an organization and to move it forward. Management is about getting things accomplished on a daily basis.

**Management accounting:** The process of preparing reports considered useful for management control and decision making.

**Management by objectives (MBO):** A system of management that is based on a joint agreement between supervisors and associates on what specific and measurable objectives would be accomplished over a given period of time, at the end of which the supervisors evaluate individual associates on the basis of the accomplishment of these objectives.

**Margin:** See *operating margin.*

**Market segmentation:** The process of dividing a large market into smaller segments in order to identify the target market.

**Marketing:** Actions undertaken to elicit desired responses to some object from a target audience.

**Marketing mix:** The four factors—product, price, place, and promotion (known as the 4 Ps)—that are operationalized to position a facility in the target market.

**Mastectomy:** Surgical removal of a breast.

**MBO:** See *management by objectives.*

**MDS:** See *minimum data set.*

**Meal plan:** The number of meals to be served per day

**Meals On Wheels:** A home-delivered meals service.

**Medicaid:** Also called Title 19 of the Social Security Act, it is a jointly funded federal–state health insurance program for the indigent.

**Medical model:** Delivery of health care that places its primary emphasis on the treatment of disease, relief of symptoms, and intensive use of medical technology, with little emphasis on the promotion of optimum health in a holistic context.

**Medicare:** Title 18 of the Social Security Act to cover health care services for the elderly, certain disabled people, and those who have end-stage renal disease.

**Mental retardation:** Below-average intellectual functioning that is long term and incurable.

**Menu cycle:** A specified period of time, generally three to four weeks, during which the main items on the menus are not repeated. At the end of this period, the same daily menus are repeated in the same order.

**Microorganism:** A living organism that cannot be seen with the naked eye.

**Mid-level providers:** See *nonphysician practitioners (NPPs).*

**Midnight census report:** A report verifying the presence of each patient in the facility during the night.

**Minimum data set (MDS):** A set of standardized screening elements that must be assessed for each patient admitted to a skilled nursing facility.

**Misappropriation of resident property:** Deliberate misplacement, exploitation, or wrongful, temporary, or permanent use of a resident's belongings or money without the resident's consent.

**Misdemeanor:** Crime of a less serious nature than a felony. It is punishable by a jail term of less than one year.

**Mission:** An organization's mission defines its basic purpose and enunciates why the organization exists.

**MR/DD:** See *mental retardation* and *developmental disability.*

**MS:** See *multiple sclerosis.*

**MSBT:** See *multisensory stimulation.*

**Multidisciplinary (or interdisciplinary):** A team approach to problem solving or delivery of care in which all key disciplines, such as nursing, food service, therapy, social work, and activities, participate and make joint decisions.

**Multisensory stimulation (MSS):** Also known as "multisensory behavior therapy (MSBT)," it involves stimulation of all the primary senses—touch, hearing, sight, smell, and taste—through a combined effect of textured objects, soft music, colored lighting, aromas, and favorite foods. Also see *Snoezelen.*

**Multiple sclerosis (MS):** A disorder of the central nervous system (brain and spinal cord) involving decreased nerve function. It involves repeated episodes of inflammation of nervous tissue in certain areas. The inflammation destroys the covering of the nerve cells in that area. The disorder most commonly begins between 20 to 40 years old and is one of the major causes of disability in adults under age 65.

**Musculoskeletal disorders (MSDs):** Injuries or illnesses affecting the connective tissues of the body such as muscles, nerves, tendons, joints, cartilage, or spinal discs.

**Nasoduodenal tube:** A mechanism for delivering nutrition through a tube that passes through the patient's nose and goes down into the duodenum, the first part of the small intestine.

**Nasogastric tube (NG-tube):** A method of delivering nutrition through a tube that passes through the nasal openings, down to the esophagus, and into the stomach.

**Neglect:** Failure to provide to a patient goods and services necessary to avoid physical harm, mental anguish, or mental illness.

**Negligence:** Failure to exercise the degree of care that a reasonable person would exercise in similar circumstances.

**Nephrologist:** A physician who specializes in kidney diseases, kidney transplantation, and dialysis therapy. Nephrology is classified as an internal medicine subspecialty.

**Net assets:** For a nonprofit organization, Net assets = Total assets – Total liabilities.

**Neurological:** Associated with the nervous system.

**NF (nursing facility):** Federal certification that authorizes a facility to admit Medicaid patients.

**NHA:** See *nursing home administrator.*

**Niche marketing:** Concentrating on a single market segment through a high degree of specialization in a particular service.

**Noncertified:** A facility that is not certified to admit Medicare and/or Medicaid patients.

**Nonexempt employees:** Workers who are paid an hourly rate, which must at least equal the minimum wage established under law. Nonexempt employees are also entitled to overtime pay.

**Nonphysician practitioners (NPPs):** NPPs are clinical professionals who practice in many of the areas in which physicians practice but who do not have an MD or DO degree. The two main types of NPPs who practice in LTC settings are nurse practitioners and physician assistants.

**Nonprofit:** A form of ownership in which the entity must serve a charitable purpose in exchange for tax-exempt status. Nonprofit organizations are prohibited by law from distributing profits to any individuals.

**Nonselective menu:** A menu that does not regularly offer a choice of entrées to all residents.

**Nosocomial:** A negative health condition that is caused by the process of health care delivery.

**Nurse aide registry:** A registration system for certified nursing assistants that all 50 states and the District of Columbia maintain. The registries enable facilities to verify the certification status of a nurse aide.

**Nurse practitioner (NP):** NPs are advanced practice nurses who provide health care services similar to those of primary care physicians. Some NPs specialize in geriatrics.

**Nursing home administrator (NHA):** As an agent of the governing body, a full-time NHA is responsible for the day-to-day management of a nursing facility.

**Nutritional screening:** Identifying patients who may be at risk for nutritional problems.

**Occupancy rate:** Percent of total beds occupied.

**Occupational therapists (OTs):** Therapists who provide a broad range of therapies that help patients recover or maintain the daily living and work skills. Their goal is to help patients achieve independence and satisfaction in all facets of their lives.

**Occupational therapy:** Therapies tailored for the adaptive use of the upper extremities for performing various tasks. It can help patients with fine motor skills, adaptive equipment, splints, and other support mechanisms that are tailor-made to facilitate the performance of daily tasks.

**Ombudsman:** A trained professional who works independently with area nursing home residents and their families to resolve concerns they may have about their lives in a facility.

**Oncology:** A medical specialty dealing with cancers and tumors.

**On-line Survey Certification and Reporting (OSCAR):** A database that states are required to maintain. It contains comprehensive information about past and current surveys and complaint investigations.

**Open system:** An approach to management that recognizes the effects of external factors and views internal operations in relation to changes in the external environment.

**Open-call contract:** A contract established with preferred contractors to provide services on an as-needed basis.

**Operating margin:** Total profit (or loss) as a percent of total revenue.

**Ophthalmologist:** A physician who specializes in the treatment of diseases and injuries of the eye.

**Opportunity cost:** Foregone value of time that could have been used for something more productive.

**Optician:** An optical technician who generally holds an associate's degree in opticianry. An optician dispenses and fits eyeglasses.

**Optometrist:** A licensed professional who holds a doctor of optometry (OD) degree and is trained to diagnose and treat vision problems and other eye disorders. They most commonly prescribe eyeglasses and contact lenses.

**Ordinance:** A law passed by a local government, such as a county, city, or municipality.

**Organizing:** Determination of what tasks are to be done, who is to do them, how the tasks are to be grouped, who reports to whom, and where decisions are to be made.

**Orthopedist:** A physician who specializes in correcting deformities of the skeletal system and may surgically repair bones and joints.

**Osteopathic medicine:** Medical approach—practiced by doctors of osteopathic medicine

(DOs)—that emphasizes the musculoskeletal system of the body such as correction of joints and tissues.

**Out of pocket:** Costs to be paid by the recipient of health care services. Main examples are deductibles and copayments.

**Outcome:** An actual result obtained from medical, nursing, and other clinical interventions.

**Outpatient services:** Any health care services that do not require an overnight stay in a facility.

**Package price:** See *bundled rate.*

**Palliation:** Medical care that is focused on relieving unpleasant symptoms such as pain, discomfort, and nausea.

**Par level:** The minimum number of units of an item the facility should maintain in its inventory, including items in circulation and in storage.

**Paraprofessional:** A caregiver who generally does not require a license to practice, and works under the supervision of a licensed professional. Examples include certified nursing assistants and therapy assistants.

**Parenteral nutrition:** Delivering a special liquid nutritional formulation directly into the blood stream, when the gastrointestinal tract is not functioning properly.

**Parkinson's disease:** A progressive disorder of the central nervous system. Clinically, the disease is characterized by a decrease in spontaneous movements, gait difficulty, postural instability, rigidity, and tremor. Parkinson's disease is caused by the degeneration of certain neurons in the brain.

**Partnership:** An association of two or more individuals or organizations for the purpose of carrying out a business for profit.

**Passivity:** A decline in human emotions, withdrawal from interactions with others and surroundings, and a decrease in motor activity.

**Pathogen:** Disease-causing organism.

**Pathological waste:** Human waste that may contain human tissue, blood, or body fluids.

**Patient days:** Cumulative census (number of patients) over a specified period of time. Also called "days of care."

**Patient's bill of rights:** A printed handout listing the rights of patients as residents of a nursing facility. The Patient Self-Determination Act of 1990 requires that patients be informed of their rights.

**Payables:** See *accounts payable*.

**Payer-mix:** Also called "census-mix," it is the mix of patients by payer type, such as Medicaid, Medicare, private pay, etc.

**Per diem:** Per day, such as a per-diem rate of reimbursement.

**Per-patient-day (PPD):** A revenue or cost amount for each patient day.

**Personal care:** Basic assistance with light ADLs and services such as meals and recreation.

**Person-centered care:** A philosophy that integrates physical layout and design with empowerment of the residents, families, and staff. Also called *client-centered care*.

**Physiatrist:** A physician who has specialized in physical medicine and rehabilitation.

**Physical therapist (PT):** A rehabilitation professional who has specialized in the treatment of musculoskeletal disorders (loss of function associated with bones, joints, spine, and soft tissue), neuromuscular disorders (loss of function associated with the brain and nervous system, e.g., stroke), patients recovering from cardiopulmonary problems, and severe wounds. PTs specialize in the restoration of various ADL functions.

**Physical therapy (PT):** Treatments geared toward improving ambulation, range of motion, physical strength, flexibility, coordination, balance, and endurance. It also includes fitting and training patients to use artificial limbs, canes, and walkers.

**Physician assistant (PA):** A trained professional who can perform physical examinations, diagnose and treat illnesses, order and interpret laboratory tests, and make rounds at LTC facilities under the direction of a physician.

**Picketing:** A concerted action by striking union employees in which they patrol the perimeter of a facility displaying placards that call attention to a labor dispute.

**Pilferage:** Small-scale theft of relatively inexpensive items.

**Pioneer Network:** A national organization that began as a grassroots movement of caregivers, consumer advocates, and others who were concerned about the quality of life in nursing homes. The organization advocates cultural change in nursing facilities through educating, sharing of ideas, and forming coalitions with stakeholders such as regulators, ombudsmen, consumers, and care professionals.

**Plaintiff:** Party who brings a lawsuit before a court to seek damages or other legal remedies.

**Plan of care (care plan):** A written plan developed through team participation of various professional disciplines to clearly outline how each identified need of a given patient will be addressed and what specific goals will be accomplished.

**Plan of correction (POC):** The facility's written plan for corrective action to achieve sustained compliance with standards in response to deficiencies cited during a survey.

**Planning:** Defining or clarifying the organization's purpose, establishing objectives, and planning a course of action to achieve those objectives.

**Podiatrist:** A physician who treats patients with diseases or deformities of the feet.

**Policy agenda:** In the public domain, a set of priorities for political action.

**Policymakers:** The term generally applies to legislators and decision makers in legislative bodies and regulatory agencies who become actively involved in crafting laws and regulations to address public issues.

**Poorhouse:** A government-operated institution during colonial and post-colonial times where the destitute of society, including the elderly, the homeless, the orphan, the ill, and the disabled, were given food and shelter, and conditions were often squalid.

**Portion control:** Accuracy in serving food according to pre-established quantities.

**Positioning statement:** In developing a marketing strategy, it describes how the facility should be positioned in the market.

**Positioning:** Staking out a position in the target market.

**Postural hypotension:** A drop in blood pressure when a person changes posture, generally when standing up from a sitting or lying to standing position.

**Preadmission inquiry:** Interaction with the facility's staff during the first visit a potential client makes to get information about the facility.

**Pre-admission Screening and Resident Review (PASRR):** Screening required under federal law to ensure that when people have a mental illness, mental retardation, or developmental disability, they are placed in a nursing home only if they need nursing home care.

**Preceptor:** A nursing home or assisted living administrator who meets prescribed qualifications and has been certified to mentor interns in an administrator-in-training (AIT) program.

**Pressure ulcer:** Also referred to as a "pressure sore" or "decubitus ulcer," it is a localized area of soft-tissue injury resulting from compression between a bony prominence and an external surface.

**Prevalence:** The number of cases of a negative health condition or disease in a given population that are present at a certain point in time.

**Primary care physician:** A physician in general practice, such as family practice, general internal medicine, general pediatrics, and obstetrics and gynecology.

**Primary care:** Basic, routine, continuous, and coordinated medical care rendered by a primary care physician or a mid-level provider such as a physician's assistant or nurse practitioner.

**Principal:** An entity that appoints an agent.

**Privacy Rule:** Standards issued by the Department of Health and Human Services for the protection of patients' personal medical information as directed by the Health Insurance Portability and Accountability Act of 1996.

**Private laws:** Laws that affect an individual, family, or small groups of people.

**Private-pay patients:** Patients in a nursing home who have a personal or private source of funding to pay for the services.

**Productivity:** Maximization of quality for each unit of resources used in delivering health care.

**Program evaluation:** Systematic appraisal of a program to determine whether expected results are being achieved.

**Programming:** Structured methods of delivering needed services.

**Promotion:** Communication system that creates awareness of the product, its features and benefits, and its location of purchase, and also reassures the customer after the purchase has taken place.

**Prospective payment system (PPS):** A method of reimbursement based on case-mix so that facilities incurring a more intensive use of resources for treating more complex conditions are paid more.

**Protected healthcare information (PHI):** Under the provisions of the Health Insurance Portability and Accountability Act of 1996, it is defined as individually identifiable health information that relates to the past, present, or future physical or mental health of, or the provision of healthcare to, a patient.

**Provider:** An organization or individual that delivers LTC services and gets paid for the services delivered.

**Public facility:** A facility owned by the government.

**Public laws:** Laws that affect society as a whole.

**Public policy:** Decisions and actions of the government that are intended to address current and potential issues that the government believes are in the best interest of the public.

**Public relations:** Also called "community relations," public relations is a formal program of communication with external stakeholders and the community at large.

**Publicity:** Nonpaid communication of information about the facility and its services.

**Punitive damages:** Damages awarded in excess of the actual losses suffered by a plaintiff to make a public example of the defendant on the basis of egregious conduct.

**Quality:** Consistent delivery of services that maximize the physical, mental, social, and spiritual well-being of all patients, produce desirable outcomes, and minimize the likelihood of undesirable consequences.

**Quality of care:** Achievement of desirable clinical and satisfaction related outcomes.

**Quality of life:** The total living experience, which results in overall satisfaction with one's life. The integration of social, environmental, and personal factors—including safety, comfort, personal preferences, dignity, interpersonal relations, and pain management—into the delivery of care. These factors are considered just as important and desirable as better health.

*Qui tam relator:* A whistleblower, under the False Claims Act, who has knowledge that a person or an entity is submitting false claims or otherwise defrauding the federal government.

**Reality orientation:** A form of therapy for confused or disoriented individuals that consists of reiteration of the person's identity, orientation to time and place, and reinforcement of consistency in daily routine. Repeated attempts are made to draw the person into conversation, using simple questions, pictures, or whatever may spark their interest.

**Reasonable accommodation:** Actions such as alteration of facilities and the work environment as well as job restructuring to focus on the essential functions, and altering or eliminating nonessential aspects of a job in order to accommodate a disabled employee.

**Receivables:** See *accounts receivable.*

**Reconditioning:** Thorough cleaning of certain areas, particularly patient rooms.

**Referral agents:** Professionals in the community who are in a position to influence prospective clients about choosing a facility.

**Registered nurse (RN):** A professional nurse who has completed an associate's degree, a diploma, a bachelor's degree, or a master's degree in nursing, and has been licensed as a registered nurse.

**Regulations:** Administrative interpretations of statutes, containing details on carrying out the statutes. Regulations carry the force of law.

**Rehabilitation:** The process of delivering the minimal services that maintain the present or highest possible level of function.

**Reimbursement:** (1) Method used by a payer to determine the amount of payment. (2) The amount that is actually paid to a facility on behalf of a patient.

**Reliability:** Reliability of a measurement instrument reflects the extent to which the same results occur from repeated applications of a measure.

**Reminiscence:** Remembering, and in some way reliving past experiences is considered important for emotional well-being. Photo albums, memorabilia, and old news clips can be used as aids.

**Requirements of Participation:** Federal regulations as prescribed by the Nursing Home Reform Act of 1987 for the certification of nursing homes.

**Resident council:** An independent, semi-formal body made up of all residents who are able to participate. The purpose of this forum is to empower the residents so they can have a say in the operations of the facility.

**Resource utilization group (RUG):** A classification system designed to differentiate Medicare patients by their levels of resource use. Medicare uses the RUG categories to determine the per-diem reimbursement rate.

**Respite care:** Any temporary long-term care service (adult day care, home health, or temporary institutionalization) that focuses on giving family caregivers time off while the patient's care is taken over by the respite care provider.

***Respondeat superior:*** Also called "vicarious liability," it is a legal doctrine that holds a corporation liable for the tortious acts of its employees.

**Responsible party:** A person, such as a spouse or relative, who handles a patient's private financial affairs.

**Restorative rehabilitation:** Rehabilitation therapy aimed at regaining or improving function through short-term intensive treatments.

**Restraint:** A device used to restrict a person's freedom of movement.

**Revenue:** Amounts earned by a nursing facility from the delivery of services.

**Reverse mortgage:** A type of loan against the equity in the home.

**Risk adjustment:** A method that accounts for variations in health status to determine the expected consumption of health care resources.

**Risk management:** The identification, analysis, and reduction or prevention of risks.

**Routine contracts:** Contracts for services that are performed on a regular basis.

**Sanitizing:** Reducing microbes to relatively safe levels on an inanimate object.

**Scope:** In the context of a deficiency, the number of patients that are potentially or actually affected as a result of not meeting a standard.

**Secondary disability:** Functional loss of capabilities that were previously unaffected.

**Security audit:** An examination of all physical security measures and potential lapses.

**Selective menu:** A menu that offers a choice between two entrées from which each resident can make a selection.

**Self-managed work team (SMWT):** A group of associates who are together responsible for performing a range of tasks, including scheduling, planning of tasks, and monitoring the team's performance.

**Self-perpetuating board:** A governing body that itself selects new members to succeed the ones who would no longer serve.

**Selling line:** A carefully crafted brief message used in advertising to interpret the facility's positioning statement.

**Semantic differential:** A technique used by market researchers in which people are asked to rate a facility and its competitors on dimensions such as quality, reputation, friendliness of staff, comfort, décor, etc.

**Semi-fixed costs:** Also called "semi-variable costs" or "step-variable costs," these costs remain fixed within parts of the census range.

**Senior center:** A local community center for older adults where seniors can congregate and socialize. Many centers offer a daily meal. Others sponsor wellness programs, health education, counseling services, information and referral, and some limited health care services.

**Sensory stimulation:** Therapy to stimulate the senses in patients with dementia or those in comatose or vegetative states. It may involve use of stuffed animals for tactile stimulation, sounds, taste and smell, or visual stimulation. Also see *multisensory stimulation.*

**Septicemia:** Also called "blood poisoning," septicemia is a rapidly progressing and life-threatening infection due to the presence of bacteria in the blood.

**Severity:** In the context of a deficiency, the extent of actual or potential harm and negative health outcomes as a result of not meeting a standard.

**Sharps:** Any objects that can cut or puncture, such as needles, blades, broken glass, and nails.

**Shelter care facilities:** See *board-and-care homes.*

**Sick-role model:** Proposed by Talcott Parsons, in the sick role the patient is expected to relinquish control to medical personnel and comply with their directions.

**Skill-mix:** The ratio of a particular skill type to the total staff. For example, the ratio of registered nurses, licensed practical nurses, and nursing assistants to total nursing staff.

**Skilled nursing care:** Physician-directed care provided by licensed nurses and therapists. It may include monitoring of unstable conditions; clinical assessment of needs; and treatments such as intravenous feeding, wound care, dressing changes, or clearing of air passages. The patient may also require rehabilitation therapies such as physical therapy, occupational therapy, speech therapy, or respiratory therapy.

**Skilled nursing facility:** A long-term care facility that is equipped to provide skilled nursing care.

**Slander:** An oral false report intended to defame another person. See *libel.*

**Smoke compartment:** A space of 22,500 square feet or less that is protected by fire barriers inside a building.

**SNF (skilled nursing facility):** A long-term care facility certified to admit Medicare patients.

**Snoezelen:** A Dutch term for multisensory stimulation through soft music, aromatherapy, textured objects, colors, and food.

**Social support:** A variety of assistive and counseling services to help people cope with situations that may cause stress, conflict, grief, or other emotional imbalances. The goal is to help people make adjustments to changing life events in their lives.

**Social work designee:** A person who does not possess a bachelor's of social work (BSW) degree but has a related academic degree. In some states, such a person may be employed as a social worker with adequate consultation from a qualified social worker.

**Sole proprietorship:** Single ownership in which the business is not incorporated.

**Speech/language pathologists (SLPs):** Also referred to as "speech therapists," they assess, diagnose, and treat speech, language, and cognitive disorders. They also treat dysphagia.

**Speech/language pathology (Speech therapy):** Therapy focusing on individuals with communication problems, including disorders of speech, language, feeding, and swallowing.

**Spend down:** Spending one's assets and income down to Medicaid eligibility thresholds by incurring medical or remedial care expenses.

**Spina bifida:** A disabling birth defect in which the spine fails to close properly.

**Stakeholder:** Any constituent group that has an interest in what a nursing facility stands for and what outcomes it produces.

**Standard precautions (SPs):** General infection control precautions to be used when delivering hands-on care to any patient, or when handling soiled articles of linen and clothing. It requires the use of gloves, gowns, and masks as necessary to avoid contact with body fluids.

**Statement of position:** In developing a marketing strategy, it describes the existing market position of a facility.

**State survey agency:** Agency responsible in each state to carry out monitoring for compliance with the state licensure standards and the federal Requirements of Participation

**Statute of limitations:** A period prescribed by law within which a legal action can be taken.

**Statutory law:** Statutes passed by various legislative bodies, such as the U.S. Congress, state legislatures, or legislative bodies of local governments.

**Stoma:** An artificially created opening in the body.

**Strategy:** Major decisions that an organization's top managers must periodically make to steer the organization in a direction that is in response to changes in the external environment.

**Strike:** Work stoppage as a concerted effort by unionized employees.

**Stroke:** A sudden interruption in the blood supply of the brain. Most strokes are caused by an abrupt blockage of arteries leading to the brain (ischemic stroke). Other strokes are caused by bleeding into brain tissue when a blood vessel bursts (hemorrhagic stroke).

**Subacute care:** Post-acute services for people who require convalescence from acute illnesses or surgical episodes. These patients may be recovering but are still subject to complications while in recovery. They require more nursing intervention than what is typically included in skilled nursing care.

**Substantial compliance:** A level of compliance with the Requirements of Participation such that any identified deficiencies would pose a risk of only minimal harm to patient health and safety.

**Substitute services:** Other long-term care options that clients may choose from, such as home health care instead of a skilled nursing facility.

**Summary judgment:** Prompt disposition of a legal case without a trial.

**Supplemental Security Income (SSI):** A federal program that provides cash assistance for food, clothing, and shelter to the elderly, blind, and disabled people who have little or no income.

**Support services:** Basic assistive services that may be available in supportive housing units. Services may include meals, transportation, housekeeping, building security, social activities, and outings.

**Supportive housing:** Accommodations in which certain functional and safety features are carefully planned to compensate for people's disabilities to the maximum extent possible in order to promote independence.

**Surveillance:** In the context of infection control, identifying and reporting all cases of infection in the facility and identifying all infected residents and staff.

**Survey:** An inspection to verify compliance with state and federal standards.

**Target market:** Part of the overall market from which the nursing facility will attract customers.

**Temperature danger zone:** The temperature range of 40° F (5° C) and 140° F (60° C) in which food bacteria thrive and multiply rapidly.

**Third party:** A payer other than the patients and their families. Examples of third-party payers are insurance companies, managed care, Medicare, Medicaid, and the Veterans Administration.

**Thriving:** Living life to the full.

**Tort:** A civil wrong other than a breach of contract. Tort may also involve interference with another's rights, either intentionally or otherwise.

**Total care:** Recognizing any health care need that may arise and ensuring that the need is evaluated and addressed by appropriate clinical professionals. When evaluation and treatment are beyond the nursing home's scope of services, referral must be made to an external provider.

**Transfer:** (1) Movement of a patient from one surface to another, such as from bed to chair, or from wheelchair to car seat. (2) Movement of a patient from one facility to another.

**Transitional care unit (TCU):** A skilled nursing unit located within a hospital.

**Transmission-based precautions:** Infection control precautions to follow when caring for patients who have a communicable disease. These precautions are used in addition to standard precautions.

**Undifferentiated marketing:** Also called "mass marketing," it purposefully ignores market segmentation, and targets the aggregate market using the same marketing mix for the entire market.

**Unfair labor practice:** An action declared as illegal under the National Labor Relations Act.

**Union steward:** A unionized employee who works at the facility and officially represents the union on issues involving the labor contract.

**Upcoding:** Billing for services that procure a higher reimbursement than the services actually provided and that should have been billed at a lower rate of reimbursement.

**Utilization:** Actual use of health care that occurs when people needing services have access to them.

**Validation therapy:** A type of therapy in which a person's belief that he or she is actually living in the past is accepted and validated by staff members working with the patient.

**Validity:** The extent to which a measurement instrument actually measures what it purports to measure.

**Value** (singular): The worth that is perceived by each party in an exchange. Value is created when the facility produces benefits that exceed, or at least equal, the inputs brought by outsiders into the exchange.

**Value network:** A total pattern of values received, generated, and distributed through an organization's ongoing relationships with its clients and stakeholders.

**Values** (generally plural): Principles and ideologies held sacred by an organization.

**Variable cost:** A cost that varies with the change in the number of patients.

**Variance:** The difference between an actual (realized) numeric value and a budgeted (expected) value.

**Variance analysis:** An examination and interpretation of differences between what has actually happened and what was planned in the budget.

**Ventilator:** A small machine that takes over the breathing function by automatically moving air into and out of the patient's lungs.

**Vicarious liability:** See *respondeat superior.*

**Vision:** A compelling picture of how an organization will look and function when its main objectives are achieved.

**Vital signs:** Generally, body temperature, pulse rate, blood pressure, and respiratory rate are referred to as vital signs. Any abnormalities in these measures triggers further clinical evaluation.

**Wage garnishment:** Any legal or equitable procedure through which some portion of a person's earnings is required to be withheld by an employer for the payment of a debt.

**Walk-in clinic:** A freestanding outpatient clinic where patients are seen on a first-come-first-served basis without prior appointments.

**Wayfinding:** Features that can help people find their way through a large institution with relative ease.

**Zoonosis:** Transmittal of infections from vertebrate animals to humans.

# INDEX

## A

AAC (Activity Assistant, Certified), 66
AAHSA (American Association of Homes and Services for the Aging), 89
abbreviated standard surveys, 125–126
absenteeism, staff, 426
abuse
  abusive spouse case study and, 529–532
  addressing quality of care, 32–33
  defined, 585
  financing, 163–165
  right to freedom from, 117
access
  controlled by procedural security, 357–358
  defined, 585
  future policy for, 39
  public policy for, 34–35
accessibility standards, 140–141
accidents
  causing admission to LTC, 12
  preventing, 349–350
accommodation, in conflict resolution, 260
accounting, financial
  balance sheet, 473
  cash flow statement, 474–475
  income statement, 473–474
  management accounting vs., 475–476
  overview of, 473
accounting, front office functions
  accounts payable, 372
  billing, accounts receivable, and collection, 373–374

cash receipts and deposits, 376
  overview of, 368
  patient trust fund, 375–376
  payroll and compensation, 368–372
  petty cash fund, 373
accounts payable
  administrative systems, 372
  defined, 585
  monitoring expenses by reviewing report on, 485
  overview of, 372
accounts receivable, 373–374, 585
accreditation, 114, 585
accrual-basis accounting, 474, 585
ACHCA (American College of Health Care Administrators), 89
acquired immune deficiency syndrome (AIDS) patients
  defined, 585
  ecological factors of, 86
  long-term care for, 14–15
  nondiscrimination of, 117
act step, in PDSA improvement cycle, 513–515
Active Disease Diagnosis, MDS 3.0 draft, 184–185
active listening
  communication skills, 259
  conflict resolution, 413–414
activities and recreation, 307–324
  activity department, 309–310
  for dementia patients, 317–318
  for further learning, 323

activities and recreation (*cont.*)
  for further thought, 322
  goals and purpose of, 308–309
  intervention approaches, 315–317
  overview of, 307–308
  program development, 310–315
  program evaluation, 320–321
  program planning and implementation,
    318–320
  references, 323–324
  skills and competencies, 310
  volunteer support for, 321–322
activities of daily living (ADLs), 585
  80% of elderly managing, 254
  assisted living facility providing, 19,
    52–53
  for children and adolescents, 13–14
  CNAs assisting with, 286
  custodial care providers for, 52
  determining level of dependency, 12–13
  for ventilator-dependent patients, 14
Activity Assistant, Certified (AAC), 66
activity calendars, 319–320
Activity Director, Certified (ADC), 66
activity professionals, 66
activity theory of aging, 252–253
acuity
  continuum of LTC and, 15–16
  defined, 585
  determining for LTC, 13
acute care
  for complications from infections in
    LTC, 288
  continuity of after hospitalization, 6
  defined, 585
  Facility Quality Measure/Indicator
    (QM/QI) Report on, 127
  financing, 41
  inpatient rehabilitation facilities for,
    55–56
  MCO partnerships serving post, 162
  medical record content about, 377
  non LTC care services for, 20, 93

PACE program offering, 160
  total care coordination of, 8
acute conditions
  defined, 585
  overview of, 5
  subacute care facilities for, 15, 54–55
ADA. *see* Americans with Disabilities Act
  (ADA)
ADA (American Dietetic Association), 65,
  327
ADA Amendments Act of 2008, 441–442
ADC (Activity Director, Certified), 66
ADEA (Age Discrimination in
  Employment Act), 441
ADLs. *see* activities of daily living (ADLs)
administration. *see also* nursing home
  administrator (NHA)
  assisted living, 59–60
  DON responsibility for, 285
  home health agencies, 59
  overview of, 59
  skilled nursing facilities, 19
  support of staff, 430
  Wellspring model case, 577–580
administrative information systems, 69–70,
  585
administrative law, 102, 585
administrative officer, 394–395
administrative professionals, 59–61
administrative systems, 365–387
  accounts payable, 372
  billing, accounts receivable, and
    collection, 373–374
  business office and its functions,
    366–368
  cash receipts and deposits, 376
  for further learning, 382
  for further thought, 382
  information systems, 378–381
  medical records, 376–378
  overview of, 365–366
  patient trust fund, 375–376

payroll and compensation, 368–372

petty cash fund, 373

references, 382–383

administrator-in-training (AIT), 61, 585

administrators, stability of, 427–428

admission agreement, 105, 585

admissions

handling inquiries about, 367

obtaining funeral arrangements during, 273

orientation and, 267–269

preadmission inquiry, 264–267

ADN (associate) nursing degree programs, 62–63

adolescents, and LTC, 13–14

ADON. *see* assistant director of nursing (ADON)

adult day care

defined, 585–586

LTC insurance covering, 151

overview of, 17

providers, 49–50

state licensing and regulations for, 34

adult foster care (AFC), 52, 586

advance directives

case study, 533–534

defined, 586

and right to self-determination, 115–116

advertising, 466–467

advisory role, medical director, 282

advocacy agencies, linkages to, 92–93

aesthetics

architectural design for, 217–218

implementing culture change in food service, case study, 541

nursing home, 217–218

person-centered care and, 202

AFC (adult foster care), 52, 586

Age Discrimination in Employment Act (ADEA), 441

age of participants, in activity planning, 311

ageism, 253–255, 586

Agency for Healthcare Research and Quality, 502

agenda, meeting, 412

agents, 109, 586

aging

early, in MR/DD patients, 14

inaccurate views of, 253–254

need for LTC for, 13

social workers understanding of, 252

theories of, 252–253

aging report. *see* aging schedule

aging schedule

defined, 586

monitoring receivables/evaluating performance with, 490

overview of, 374

aging-in-place

assisted living facilities lacking capacity for, 34

CCRC living based on, 56–57

defined, 586

home builder certification specialist program for, 68

agitation, 294, 586

AHCA (American Health Care Association), 89

AHIMA (American Health Information Management Association), 376

AIDA framework, 466

AIDS. *see* acquired immune deficiency syndrome (AIDS) patients

AIT (administrator-in-training), 61, 585

alcohol abuse, 442

ALFA (Assisted Living Federation of America), 89

all-inclusive rate, 586

defined, 489

allopathic medicine, 62, 586

almshouse. *see* poorhouses

Alzheimer's patients

defined, 586

insurance benefits for, 57

managing dementia of, 296–297

Alzheimer's patients (*cont.*)
    specialized care facilities for, 19, 56, 206
    startup of Blissful Gardens, case study,
        571–574
    use of pastel colors for, 228
ambulation
    activity program development for levels
        of, 311
    clinical management and prevention, 6
    defined, 586
    fall prevention program for safe, 292
    maintenance rehabilitation for, 301
    physical therapy improving, 300
    skilled nursing facilities handling poor,
        19
    staff support for urinary incontinence,
        295
ambulatory, defined, 586
ambulatory care (ambulatory services)
    community-based services for, 17
    continuum of long-term care for, 16
    defined, 586
AMDA (American Medical Directors
        Association), 281, 502
American Association of Homes and
        Services for the Aging (AAHSA),
        89
American College of Health Care
        Administrators (ACHCA), 89
American Dietetic Association (ADA), 65,
        327
American Geriatric Society, 502
American Health Care Association
        (AHCA), 89
American Health Information Management
        Association (AHIMA), 376
American Medical Directors Association
        (AMDA), 281, 502
American Speech-Language-Hearing
        Association (ASHA), 65
Americans with Disabilities Act (ADA)
    nursing home compliance with, 123

    overview of, 441–442
    standards of accessibility, 140–141
ancillaries, 489, 586
ancillary professionals, 66
ancillary sector, 67–70
announcements (publicity), 467
antibiotics, overuse of, 288
anti-kickback legislation, 94
antimicrobial products, 353
antisepsis, 289, 586. *see* Omnibus Budget
        Reconciliation Act of 1987 (OBRA-
        87)
aphasia, 300–301, 586
apraxia, 301, 586
arbitration, 440, 586
architecture, modern designs, 212–218
    aesthetics, 217–218
    cluster design, 213–214, 216
    nested single-room design, 213, 215, 217
    overview of, 212–213
    startup of Blissful Gardens case study,
        571–574
area agency on aging, 92, 586
area of refuge
    defined, 586
    *Life Safety Code*®, 137
    overview of, 359
    partial evacuation to, 359–360
Artifacts of Culture Change, 221, 233–243
asepsis, 289, 586
ASHA (American Speech-Language-
        Hearing Association), 65
assault, 107, 586
assemble-and-serve, food preparation,
        337–338
assessment
    activity professional skills in, 310, 319
    and care planning, 286–288
    defined, 587
    information systems for, 378–381
    overview of, 286–287
    plan of care and, 287–288

resident assessment coordinator
responsibility for, 283
role in Medicare prospective
reimbursement, 157–158
social worker skills in, 258–259
Assessment Administration, MDS 3.0
draft, 198
assets
defined, 587
Medicaid qualifications, 158
assistant director of nursing (ADON)
nursing organization of, 283
surveying and monitoring infections,
288
tug-of-war with the director of nursing,
case study, 557–560
assisted living facilities
absence of federal
reimbursement/regulation for, 34
administrators of, 59–60
appealing to private-pay patients, 38
clinicians for, 62–65
continuing care retirement communities
based on, 56–57
defined, 587
institutional providers for, 52–53
overview of, 18–19
quality of care not ensured in, 38–39
startup of Blissful Gardens, case study,
571–574
Assisted Living Federation of America
(ALFA), 89
assistive technology, 68
associate, 587
associate (ADN) nursing degree programs,
62–63
attending physicians, 278–279, 300
audiologists, 8, 20, 587
autism, 13, 587
automatic enunciators, 68
autonomy
CNAs trained in preserving, 286

defined, 587
degree of NHA, 394
of patient rights, 114–115
socio-residential environment providing,
209–210
average daily census
budgeting expenses, 495
defined, 587
overview of, 476–478
projection for budget, 493–494
avoidance, as conflict resolution, 260

**B**
baby boomers
creating cultural change, 85
defined, 587
nursing home litigation and, 101
policy for future, 40
bachelor of science (BSN) nursing
programs, 62–63
bachelor of social work (BSW), 66,
251–252
bacterial infection, food-borne illness, 343
bad debt, 489–490, 587
balance sheet, 474, 587
Balanced Budget Act (BBA) of 1997
creating, 27
denial of payment due to abuse of
patients, 118
managed care options of, 58–59
prospective payment system, 34
bargaining unit, 437, 587
battery, 587. *see also* assault
bed-hold, 373, 587
bed-reserve agreement, 163
Behavior, MDS 3.0 draft, 177–178
benchmarks for evaluations, 508
benefit period, 151–152, 587
bereavement counseling, hospice, 8
best practices
clinical practice guidelines, 502
defined, 587

billing system, accounting, 373–374
bills, policymaking, 27, 587
biophilia
    creating enriched environments, 218
    defined, 587
    Eden Alternative, 221–222
bioterrorism, 86, 587
birth-related disorders, and LTC, 13–14
Bladder and Bowel, MDS 3.0 draft, 183
Blake and Mouton, 400–401
blatant (egregious) conduct, 104
bleach solutions, 353
blind receiving, 334
Blissful Gardens, startup case, 571–574
    assignment, 573
    board composition and funding, 573
    building and facility plans, 571–572
    current operations and plans, 572–573
    main goals, 573
    market area and competition, 573
board of directors (board of trustees). *see*
    governing body
board-and-care homes
    as custodial care providers, 52
    defined, 587
    different meanings of, 18
    ombudsman as advocate for, 93
    as residential or personal care homes, 18
Boards of Charities, 29
bona fide. *see* good faith
bookkeeper functions
    accounts payable, 372
    billing, accounts receivable, and
        collection, 373–374
    cash receipts and deposits, 376
    overview of, 366–368
    patient trust fund, 375–376
    payroll and compensation, 368–372
    petty cash fund, 373
boss-subordinate relationship, 414–415
*Bowen v. Duggan*, 34, 48
brain death, 272–273
breach of contract, 104–105, 587

BSN (bachelor of science) nursing
    programs, 62–63
BSW (bachelor of social work), 66,
    251–252
Buddhists, dietary restrictions, 257
budgeting
    defined, 587
    in financial managing, 472
    integrated information networks for,
        379–380
    overview of, 492–496
    startup of Blissful Gardens, case study,
        571–574
buffet, as menu choice, 330
bulk food portioning system, 341
bundled rate, 150, 587
business management, 396–397
business office, 366–368

**C**
CADE (Commission of Accreditation for
    Dietetics Education), 65
calendars, activity, 319–320
call system, nursing station, 207
capital budgeting, 379
capitation, 161–162, 588
CAPS (Certified Aging-in-Place
    Specialist), 68
cardiologists, 588
care delivery, 201–203
care plan. *see* plan of care (care plan)
Care Resource Teams, Wellspring model
    case, 577–578, 580
caregiving technology, 68–69
carpeting, 218
carts, food transportation, 342
case management
    defined, 588
    overview of, 16
    social worker role, 262
case studies
    abusive spouse, 529–532
    advance directives, 533–534

corporate compliance at Mid-Atlantic care centers, 561–564

evacuation of Angel Care Center, 545–556

implementing culture change in food service, 539–544

implementing Wellspring model. *see* Wellspring model implementation, case study

startup of Blissful Gardens, 571–574

workforce diversity: Chapel Square Health Care Center, 565–570

wound care, 535–537, 557–560

case-mix

defined, 588

Medicare rate of reimbursement, 157

stratified sampling method, 127–128

cash flow statements, 474–475, 588

cash receipts, 375, 376

catheters, and urinary incontinence, 294–295

Catholics, cultural accommodations, 256–258

CBO (Congressional Budget Office), 41

CCRCs (continuing care retirement communities), 56–57, 589

CDM (Certified Dietary Manager), 327

census, 479–481, 588

census range, 479–481, 588

census-mix. *see* payer-mix

Centers for Medicare & Medicaid Services (CMS)

certification standards, 112–113

defined, 506, 588

endorsing culture change, 221

establishing Medicare reimbursement rates, 149

implementing laws, 26–27

implementing policy, 27

regulating SNFs or NFs, 124

centralized meal service, 341–343

CEO (chief executive officer), 391–392, 394–395

cerebral palsy, 13, 588

Certificate of Added Qualification in Geriatric Medicine, 281

certificate of need (CON), 111–112, 588

certification

defined, 588

dual, 113, 591

overview of, 112–114

Certified Aging-in-Place Specialist (CAPS), 68

Certified Dietary Manager (CDM), 327

certified home health providers, 48–49

Certified Medical Director, 281

certified nursing assistants (CNAs), 512

certifications, 425

defined, 588

high turnover and absenteeism among, 284

meal service responsibilities of, 327

nursing organization of, 286

as paraprofessional caregivers, 65–66

training programs for, 284

Wellspring model, case study, 580

Certified Therapeutic Recreation Specialist (CTRS), 66–67

Certified Occupational Therapy Assistant (COTA), 64

CFO (chief financial officer), 391

channels of distribution, 460–461, 588

Chapel Square Health Care Center workforce diversity, case study, 565–570

assignment, 570

historical background, 565–566

management challenges, 566–567

management's dilemma, 569–570

operational issues, 567

workforce diversity, 567–568

charge nurses, 285, 588

chemotherapy, 588

chief executive officer (CEO), 391–392, 394–395

chief financial officer (CFO), 391

chief operating officer (COO), 394–395
children
    as clients of long-term care, 13–14
    facilitating intergenerational contact,
        222–228, 315
    LTC promoting functional independence
        of, 9
chiropractors, 20, 588
Christians, cultural accommodations for,
        256–258
chronic condition
    AIDS evolved from terminal illness to,
        14
    defined, 588
    management and prevention of, 6
civil law, 103, 588
Civil Rights Act
    cultural accommodations under, 256
    on nondiscrimination, 117
    on unlawful harrassment, 443
claims, 373, 588
clean-linen processing, 354–355
clear-liquid diets, 338
clerical functions, front office, 368
client-centered care. *see* person-centered
        care
clients
    children and adolescents as, 13–14
    financing. *see* financing and
        reimbursement
    as most important stakeholders, 79
    older adults as, 12
    overview of, 12
    and payments, 81
    as primary exchange partners, 79, 81
    systems model of value exchanges, 90
clinical care
    modern architecture de-emphasizing,
        212, 213
    in person-centered care environment,
        202–204
clinical information, 69, 588
clinical pathways, 504–505, 588

clinical practice guidelines
    defined, 588
    evidence-based care used for, 10
    overview of, 502
clinicians, 61–65
closed systems, 78, 588
Cloverleaf Nursing Center, case study,
        557–560
cluster design
    decentralized meal services, 341
    nested single rooms within, 213–214
    overview of, 213–214
    partial floor plans, 216
CMS. *see* Centers for Medicare &
        Medicaid Services (CMS)
CNAs. *see* certified nursing assistants
        (CNAs)
Coach USA contract, case study, 549, 552,
        554, 556
coaching style, situational leadership,
        401–402
code phrase, fire safety protocol, 358
Cognitive Patterns, MDS 3.0 draft,
        173–175
collaboration (problem solving), in conflict
        resolution, 260
collection
    cycles, 490–491
    overview of, 373–374
collection periods (accounting), 490, 588
collective bargaining, 439, 589
collective representation, 437–438
color, designing, 217–218, 571–572
commercial insurance, 57–58
Commission of Accreditation for Dietetics
        Education (CADE), 65
commitment, in sustainable relationships,
        94–95
common law, 102, 589
communication skills
    activity professionals understanding, 310
    social workers understanding, 259, 263
    workforce diversity, case study, 565–570

community
    connecting facility with, 398–399
    six-point outreach plan to, 91
    support for activity programs, 313
community advisory board, 95, 589
Community Spouse Resource Allowance
        (CSRA), 160
Community Spouse Monthly Income
        Allowance (MIA), 160
Community Spouse Resource Allowance
        (CSRA), 160
community-based residential settings, for
        MR/DD patients, 14
community-based service providers, 48–50
community-based system, of LTC
    expansion of, 35–36
    extramural services, 17–18
    history of financing, 31–32
    intramural services, 17
    overview of, 15–17
    personal care homes as, 18
    policy of prevention, 40–41
    quality of care not ensured, 38–39
    state policy initiatives for, 34
comorbidity
    creating need for LTC, 6
    defined, 589
    geriatric medicine managing, 280
compatibility, 211–212
compensation. *see also* payroll and
        compensation
    case study, 562
    overview of, 369–371
compensatory damages, 104, 589
competent, 105, 589
competitive differentiation, marketing,
        462–463
complementary services, 88, 589
compliance, surveys, 128–130
compromise, as conflict resolution, 260
computerized provider order entry (CPOE),
        69–70
CON (certificate of need), 111–112, 588

concluding interview, admission inquiry,
        266–267
confidentiality, 118–119, 207
conflict resolution
    medical director role in, 280
    NHA role in, 413
    social worker role in, 259–261, 263
confrontation (forcing), as conflict
        resolution, 260–261
congregate housing, 7, 18
Congressional Budget Office (CBO), 41
consideration
    defined, 589
    in legally enforceable contracts, 105
consistency of services, 95, 500–501
constitutional law, 102, 589
constructive confrontation, 414
consumer-defined quality, 502–503
continuing care retirement community
        (CCRC), 589
continuity of services, 95, 500
continuity theory of aging, 252–253
continuity-of-care model, 269–270
continuous quality improvement (CQI)
    all departments implementing, 515
    continuous learning and, 515
    culture of, 10–11
    data-driven process improvement cycle,
        513–515
    defined, 589
    interdisciplinary work teams, 515
    leadership and culture, 512–513
    meeting customer needs, 508–512
    overview, 508
continuing care agreement, 57
continuing care retirement communities
        (CCRCs), 56–57
continuum of long-term care
    defined, 589
    forming linkages along, 91–92
    overview of, 15–16
contract law, 104–105
contract work, 352

contracts
  continuing care, 57
  defined, 589
  legally enforceable, 105
controlled substances, 298–299, 589
Controlled Substances Act (CSA),
  298–299
controlling, 406–407, 589
COO (chief operating officer), 394–395
cook-and-chill or -freeze, food preparation,
  337
cook-and-serve, food preparation, 336–337
cooks, 327
coordination role, social workers, 262
copayments
  defined, 589
  Part A of Medicare, 152
  Part B of Medicare, 154
coping, 7
corporate compliance
  defined, 589
  essence of, 392–393
  Mid-Atlantic care centers, case study,
    561–564
corporate law, 109–111, 589
corporate liability, 107–109
corporations, 110, 589
corrective action, 531–532
cost-benefit evaluation
  defined, 589
  key control system, 358
  of security equipment, 356
cost-effectiveness (cost-efficiency),
  defined, 589
costs
  controlling, 479
  food, 332, 335–336
  implementing Wellspring model, case
    study, 578–579
  labor, 481–485
  types of, 479–481
  using integrated information networks to
    determine, 379–380

COTA (Certified Occupational Therapy
  Assistant), 64
counseling staff, 434
country-club management, 401
CPOE (computerized provider order entry),
  69–70
CQI. *see* continuous quality improvement
  (CQI)
crime, 103, 589
criminal law
  ascribing personal liability, 105–107
  defined, 589
  as example of public law, 102
  overview of, 103
cross-contamination
  defined, 589
  and food-borne illness, 343–344
  preventing in laundry department, 349,
    354–355
CSA (Controlled Substances Act),
  298–299
CSRA (Community Spouse Resource
  Allowance), 160
cultural change, 85, 589
cultural competence
  defined, 590
  diversity and, 255–258
  implementing Wellspring model, case
    study, 575–584
  overview of, 254
  workforce diversity case study, 565–570
culture change
  Artifacts of Culture Change, 233–243
  culture-based diet preferences, 330
  Eden Alternative and, 222–224
  Green House Project and, 224–228
  implementing in food service, case
    study, 539–544
  within internal environment. *see* internal
    environment
  overview of, 220–221
  person-centered care philosophy of, 201
culture of excellence, 516–517

custodial care
  continuing care retirement communities
    based on, 56–57
  defined, 590
  not qualifying for Part A Medicare
    coverage, 153
  out-of-pocket financing for, 150
  providers, 52
customer
  defined, 590
  measuring satisfaction of, 507
  needs, 508–512
  partners, 511
  relations, 465–466
cycle of exchanges, 80–82, 95–96

**D**

daily cleaning, housekeeping, 353
data-driven process improvement cycle,
  513–515
days of care
  defined, 590
  managing census levels, 476–477
  Part A of Medicare benefits, 151
DD. *see* developmentally disabled (DD)
death of patient
  patient trust fund following, 375
  social worker role in handling, 272–273
decentralized meal service, 341
decision making
  defined, 590
  learned helplessness vs., 269
  managerial, 409–411
  meetings for, 412
decision support systems, 70, 590
decubitus ulcers. *see* pressure ulcers
deductibles
  defined, 590
  Part A of Medicare, 152
  Part B of Medicare, 154
deemed status, 114, 590
defamation of character, 107
defendant, 101, 590

deficiencies
  culture change in food service, case
    study, 539, 544
  defined, 590
  enforcement and remedies, 135–136
  *Life Safety Code*© compliance, 136–137,
    140
  Requirements of Participation
    compliance, 128–130
  Statement of Deficiency and plan of
    correction, 130–135
Deficit Reduction Act of 2005, 35–36
delegating style, situational leadership,
  401–402
delegation of authority, 406
delirium
  defined, 590
  managing, 295–296
  misdiagnosing in elderly, 280
delivery system, LTC, 15–19
demand trust, patient funds, 375
dementia
  activities for, 317–318
  AIDS and, 15
  as common mental disorder, 6
  defined, 590
  delirium associated with, 296
  internal environment for patients with,
    228
  intervention approaches for, 316–317
  managing, 296–297
  misdiagnosing in elderly, 280
  physical functional limitations of, 12
  social events for, 212
Deming cycle, 513
demographic imperative, 40, 590
demographics, segmenting markets by,
  453–455
department directors, 62
departmentation, 405–406
dependency
  determining person's level of, 12–13
  infantilization reinforcing sense of, 258

deposits, facility control of, 376
depression
  AIDS associated with, 15
  group activities to alleviate, 315
  nonpharmacologic approaches for, 299
  often undetected and untreated, 6–7
  symptoms and treatment of, 295
dermatologists, 8, 279, 590
developmentally disabled (DD)
  children and adolescents, 13–14
  defined, 14, 590
  specialized care facilities for children, 19
diabetic diets, 338
diagnosis-related group (DRG) prospective
  payment system, 37
diagnostics, by non-LTC services, 20
diet tickets (cards), 342
dietary aides, 327–328
dietary manager, 326–327
Dietary Managers Association (DMA), 327
Dietary Reference Intakes (DRIs), 331
dietary services, 325–346
  cultural accommodations for dietary
    restrictions, 257
  dietary department, 326–328
  evacuation of Angel Care Center case,
    554
  food cost, 335–336
  food production methods, 336–338
  food production planning, 336
  food safety and sanitation, 343–344
  food service principles, 326
  food service systems, 341–343
  food storage and inventory, 333–335
  for further learning, 344–345
  for further thought, 344
  implementing culture change in food
    service case, 539–544
  menu planning, 328–332
  overview of, 325–326
  purchasing food and supplies, 332–333
  references, 345–346

therapeutic diets and nourishment,
  338–340
dietitians, 65, 590
differentiation strategy, marketing,
  462–463, 590
dignity
  CNAs trained in preserving, 286
  infantilization stripping away, 258
  privacy of person as, 211
dining
  experience in Green Houses, 228
  patient experience of, 343
  for patients with dementia, 228
  socio-residential environment providing,
    211–212
directed plan of correction, 135–136, 590
directing style, situational leadership,
  401–402
director of nursing (DON)
  case study, tug-of-war with, 557–560
  organization of, 285–286
  overview of, 283
  responding to urgent service calls, 350
  skills, qualifications and functions,
    283–285
disability. *see also* developmentally
    disabled (DD); mentally
    retarded/developmentally disabled
    (MR/DD)
  activity planning for, 311
  assessing, 12
  compliance with Americans with
    Disabilities Act, 123
  defined, 590
  of employees, 441
  general standards of accessibility,
    140–141
  government-assisted housing for, 51
  legal definition of, 140
disaster planning
  administrator responsibility for, 349–350
  emergency evacuations, 359–360

evacuation of Angel Care Center, case study, 546, 549–553

    fires, 358–359

    overview of, 358

    simulation drills, 360

discharge planners, hospital

    arranging for community-based services with, 38

    defined, 590

    forming linkages with, 93

    personal contact with, 460, 468

    promoting facility's services to, 468

discharge planning, 269–270, 590

disciplining staff, 434–436

discrimination, employment, 440, 561–564

dishwashing procedures, 344

disinfectants, 353

disorientation, wayfinding for, 209

disposables, dietary supplies, 333

disseminator, NHA as, 404

distinct part, 112, 590

disturbance handler, NHA as, 404

diversity, 255–258, 565–570

division of work, 405–406

Dix, Dorothea Lynde, 29

DMA (Dietary Managers Association), 327

DNR (do-not-resuscitate) order, 117, 590

DO (doctor of osteopathic medicine)

    defined, 62

    as medical director, 280

do step, PDSA improvement cycle, 513–515

dockets, 412, 590

doctor of medicine (MD), 62, 280

doctor of osteopathic medicine (DO)

    defined, 62

    as medical director, 280

documentation

    activity professionals skilled in, 310

    of food intake, 339

    medical records providing, 378

risk management and, 416

social workers skilled in, 261

domiciliary care facilities. *see* board-and-care homes

domotics technology, 68, 591

DON. *see* director of nursing (DON)

Donabedian, Avedis, 503

do-not-resuscitate (DNR) order, 117, 590

DPOA (durable power of attorney), 117, 591

DRG (diagnosis-related group) prospective payment system, 37

DRIs (Dietary Reference Intakes), 331

Drucker, Peter, 449

drug abuse, 442

dry storage, food, 334

DTR (registered dietetic technician), 65, 327

dual certification

    defined, 591

    overview of, 113

    Requirements of Participation for, 131–132

*Duggan v. Bowen*, 34, 48

durable power of attorney (DPOA), 117, 591

duty, negligence and, 106–107

dysarthria, 301, 591

dysphagia

    defined, 591

    SLPs treating, 301

    speech/language pathologists treating, 65

**E**

ecological factors, LTC environment, 86

economic factors, LTC environment, 85

economic strikes, 488, 591

Eden Alternative, 222–224, 591

edenizing, 221–223, 591

EEOC (Equal Employment Opportunity Commission), 441

effectiveness, 591

efficiency (productivity), 498–500, 591
egregious (blatant) conduct, 104
elderly
    government-assisted housing for, 51
    history of welfare policies, 29–30
    HIV prevalence in, 14–15
    population growth of, 40
    social worker knowledge of, 252–255
electronic surveillance, 356
elimination period
    defined, 591
    LTC insurance, 58
emergencies
    emergency kit, 299
    planning menus for, 332
    preparing for, 349–350
emphysema, 591
Employee Free Choice Act, 438
employees. *see* staff
employer contributions, 376
employment discrimination, 440, 591
employment laws, 440–443
employment-at-will doctrine, 440–441, 591
enabler, social worker as, 262–263
enabling technology, 68
end-of-life care, 8, 591
enforcement, OBRA-87 regulations, 39
engagement skills
    of activity professionals, 310
    cultural competence requiring, 254
    in social work practice, 258
English Poor Laws, 29
enriched environments, 218–220, 591
enteral feeding, 339, 340, 591
entrance conference, survey process, 127
entrées
    defined, 591
    in menu planning, 329
    prepared by cook, 327
    specializing food trays for, 390
    upscale facilities giving choices in, 330
entrepreneur role, NHA, 404

environment
    external. *see* external environment
    internal. *see* internal environment
environmental assessment
    defined, 591
    environmental domains, 84–86
    environmental proximity, 86–89
    overview of, 82–83
environmental domains, 84–89
environmental safety, 361–362
environmental scanning
    defined, 591
    environmental domains, 84, 86–89
    overview of, 82
environmental services. *see* plant and
        environmental services
environmental technology, 69
epidemics, 291, 591
epilepsy, 591
Equal Employment Opportunity
        Commission (EEOC), 441
Equal Pay Act of 1963, 441
equipment
    obtaining activity program, 312
    preventative maintenance of, 351–352
    safety of maintenance and housekeeping,
        362
equity (balance sheets), 474, 591
ergonomics, and workplace safety, 141
esophagostomy tube, 340, 591
*Estate of Smith v. Heckler* (1984), 32
ethics
    committee, 115, 263–264
    defined, 592
    patient rights founded on, 114–115
ethnicity
    corporate compliance, case study,
        561–564
    cultural competence and, 255–258
    social worker qualifications, 251
    workforce diversity, case study, 565–570
ethnocentrism, 255–256, 592

evacuation, 359–360, 592
evacuation of Angel Care Center, case
    study, 545–556
  aftermath, 556
  assignment, 556
  city government's role in, 545–547
  disaster planning, 546, 549–554
  the evacuation, 554–556
  facility and its organization, 546
  Hurricane Rita and, 545
  mission statement, 546
evaluation of outcomes, 507–508
event promotion, 468–469
evidence-based care
  as component of LTC, 10
  defined, 592
  policy for future, 42
evolution, nursing home environment,
    200–201
exchange relationships, building, 89–95
  clients and payments, 79
  cycle of exchanges, 80–82
  earmarking funds for, 80
  environmental proximity governing,
    87–89
  mission-driven partnerships, 90–95
  open system theory of, 77, 79
  producing outputs, 95–96
  with stakeholders, 79–80
  value-based, 89–90
executive branch of government, 27
exemplary damages, tort law, 104
exempt employees, 369–370, 592
exit conference, survey process, 130
exits, clearly marked, 138
expenses, budgeting, 495
extended surveys, 126
external environment, 77–98
  building exchange relationships, 89–95
  closed and open systems, 78–79
  cycle of exchanges, 80–82
  defined, 78, 592

environmental domains, 84–86
environmental proximity, 86–89
financing and reimbursement. *see*
    financing and reimbursement
focus on outputs, 95–96
for further learning, 97
for further thought, 96–97
legal environment. *see* legal environment
open-system and strategic management,
    82–83
references, 97–98
regulation and enforcement. *see*
    regulation and enforcement
role of governance, 80
stakeholders, 79–80
understanding, 84
extramural services, 17–18, 592

**F**
facilities manager, 348
facility, certification regulations, 113
Facility Characteristics Report, 126
Facility Quality Measure/Indicator
    (QM/QI) Report, 126–127
facility tour, admission inquiry, 266
Fair Labor Standards Act (FLSA)
  classifying exempt/nonexempt
    employees, 369–370
  limits to jurisdication of, 371
  overtime compensation, 370
  overview of, 368–369
falls, causes and prevention of, 291–292
False Claims Act (FCA), 164–165
false imprisonment, 107, 592
Family and Medical Leave Act (FMLA),
    442–443
family management, 271–272, 592
family members
  diversity and caregiving by, 255–258
  enabler role of social worker helping,
    263
  hospice philosophy of, 8

family members (*cont.*)
  involving in activity programs with
    patients, 313
  involving in discharge decisions, 270
  as most important stakeholders, 79
  providing long-term care, 3
  role in aging parents, 254–255
  social worker managing, 271–272
  social worker role in death of, 272–273
family-style meals, 341, 539–544
FCA (False Claims Act), 164–165
Federal Insurance Contributions Act
  (FICA), 372
federal laws, classifying, 101–102
Federal Long-Term Care Insurance
  Program, 57
federal preemption, 101–102, 592
Federal Unemployment Tax Act (FUTA),
  372
federalism, 102, 592
feedback, communication skills, 259
felony
  crime classified as, 103
  defined, 592
  federal fraud and abuse law, 164
FICA (Federal Insurance Contributions
  Act), 372
figurehead, NHA role as, 404
financial accounting, 473–476, 592
financial management
  accounting, 473
  accounts receivable, 488–491
  balance sheets, 474
  budgeting, 492–496
  cash flow statements, 474–475
  importance of, 472
  income statements, 473–474
  management reports, 475–476
  nonlabor expenses, controlling, 485–488
  revenues, managing, 476–479
  variance analysis, 476
financing and reimbursement, 147–198
  for community-based services, 35–36

concluding interview discussing,
  266–267
defined, 148
discharge planning and, 270
fragmentation of LTC, 35
fraud and abuse, 163–165
for further learning, 166
for further thought, 166
future policies for, 39–40
hospital and health system partnerships,
  162–163
importance of, 148–149
managed care, 161–162
Medicaid, 158–160
Medicare, 151–157
Medicare prospective payment system,
  157–158
out-of-pocket, 149–150
overview of, 147–148
private insurance, 150–151
Program of All-Inclusive Care for the
  Elderly, 160–161
public policies for, 34–35
references, 166–167
reimbursement. *see* reimbursement
reimbursement policies to providers, 36
sources of, 148–149
startup of Blissful Gardens, case study,
  572–573
through private insurance. *see* insurance,
  LTC
Veterans Health Administration contacts,
  163
fire alarm system
  activating, 358
  giving notice of false alarms, 359
  *Life Safety Code*®, 139
fire exit doors, with delayed opening, 356
fire planning
  administrator responsibility for, 349–350
  emergency evacuation, 359–360
  emergency evacuation, case study, 546,
    549

fire-resistive construction, 137
overview of, 358
safety plan and steps, 139, 358–359
simulation drills, 360
Fire Protection Association (NFPA),
136–140
Fire Safety Evaluation System (FSES), 140
fixed costs, 479, 592
flexible budgets, 483, 592
floor care, housekeeping, 353
FLSA. *see* Fair Labor Standards Act
(FLSA)
FMLA (Family and Medical Leave Act),
442–443
focus groups (marketing), 466, 592
follow-up, with prospective client, 267
food service. *see also* dietary services
case study, implementing culture change,
539–544
director. *see* dietary manager
documenting patient intake, 339
preventing food poisoning, 343
station, 341–342
forcing (confrontation), as conflict
resolution, 260–261
framework of quality, 503–505
fraud
awarding punitive damages for, 104
defined, 592
financial, 163–165
as intentional tort, 107
frozen foods, 334, 337
FSES (Fire Safety Evaluation System), 140
full-liquid diets, 338
functional activities of marketing, 450–451
functional independence, LTC promoting,
9
Functional Status, MDS 3.0 draft, 181–182
*Fuqua v. Horizon/CMS Healthcare
Corporation*, 104
furnishings
modern architectural design for, 218
nursing station, 207–208

FUTA (Federal Unemployment Tax Act),
372

**G**
GAAP (generally accepted accounting
principles), 473
gastrointestinal tract infections, 288–291
gastronomy tube (G-tube), 340, 592
gender compatibility, 211
general partnership, 110, 592
generally accepted accounting principles
(GAAP), 473
geriatric nurse practitioner (GNP),
Wellspring Model, 517, 578, 582
geriatrics
defined, 592
director of nursing knowledge in, 284
medical director specializing in, 280
policy initiatives for training in, 41
gerontology, 252, 592
glare, minimizing, 217
GNP (geriatric nurse practitioner),
Wellspring Model, 517, 578, 582
goals
leadership involving attainment of, 398
marketing, 451–452
program evaluation involving, 321
good faith, 592
corporate liability and, 108
governance, 389–418
composition of board, 390–391
corporate compliance, case study,
561–564
defined, 592
executive roles, 393–395
function of board, 391–392
for further learning, 417
for further thought, 416–417
managing business aspect, 395–397
managing facility in community and
society, 398–399
managing work and workers, 397–398
in open system management, 80

governance (*cont.*)
  overview of, 389–390, 392–393
  references, 417–418
  role of NHA, 392
  startup of Blissful Gardens, case study,
    572–574
  through effective leadership, 398–403
  through effective management. *see*
    management
  Wellspring model, case study, 575–584
governing body
  defined, 592
  responsibilities of, 80
  startup of Blissful Gardens, case study,
    571–574
government
  federal fraud and abuse laws, 164–165
  health policy made by, 26–27
  housing assisted by, 51
grand master key, 357
green facilities, 571–574
Green House, 224–228, 432, 592–593
grid, severity scope, 129–132
grievances, 439, 593
grieving, in transition process, 7
gross negligence, 104
gross wages, 376
groundskeeping, contracting out, 348
group homes. *see* adult foster care (AFC)
group insurance, 57, 593
guardian, 115, 593

**H**
handicap. *see* disability
hand-washing, 289–290, 343
harassment in work place, 443
hard-surface floorings, 218
hazardous areas, 139
hazardous waste, 360
HCBS. *see* Home- and Community-Based
    Services (HCBS) Waiver
health care delivery system, 20–21

Health Care Fraud and Abuse Control
    Program, 164
Health Conditions, MDS 3.0 draft,
    186–188
health information technology (HIT), 27,
    42
Health Insurance Portability and
    Accountability Act (HIPAA) of
    1966, 118–120, 164
health maintenance organizations (HMOs),
    58
health policy, 26, 593
health screening, 593
Hearing, Speech, and Vision, MDS 3.0
    draft, 172
*Heckler v. Estate of Smith* (1984), 32
hemodialysis, 593
HI (Hospital Insurance) services,
    Medicare, 151–154
hierarchy, of nursing facility, 246–247
high-carbohydrate diets, 338
high-fiber diets, 338
highly compensated employees, 370
high-protein diets, 338
Hill-Burton Act (Hospital Survey and
    Construction Act) of 1946, 30
HIT (health information technology), 27,
    42
HIV. *see* human immunodeficiency virus
    (HIV)
HMOs (health maintenance organizations),
    58
*Hoffman v. St. Joseph's Hospital*, 371
holistic model
  defined, 501, 593
  integrating into LTC delivery, 9, 10
home health agency administrators, 59
home health care
  certified home health providers, 48–49
  clinicians, 62–65
  for continuity of care after
    hospitalization, 6

defined, 593
LTC insurance covering, 151
PPS reimbursement for, 34
subacute type services rendered by, 55
home telehealth systems, 68–69, 593
Home- and Community-Based Services
(HCBS) Waiver
for adult day care, 50
creating, 32
defined, 593
funding, 35–36
for managed care organizations, 162
utilization and, 38
homemaker and personal care service
providers, 49
*Horizon/CMS Healthcare Corporation v.*
*Fuqua*, 104
hospice services
defined, 593
as LTC component, 8, 48
providers, 50
types of agencies, 50
Hospital Insurance (HI) services,
Medicare, 151–154
Hospital Survey and Construction Act of
1946 (Hill-Burton Act), 30
hospitals
continuity of medical care after, 5–6
evolution of, 200–201
health system partnerships with,
162–163
influencing care delivery philosophy,
201–202
linking with non-LTC sector, 93–94
nursing home construction adapted from,
201
use of when necessary, 6
hostile environment, 443, 593
hot water temperature, monitoring, 361
hotel services
ancillary personnel providing, 66
defined, 593

independent or retirement housing
options, 18
housekeeping department
cleaning, reconditioning, and floor care,
353
infection control, 353–354
operations of, 352
overview of, 349
sanitizing, 353
Housing and Urban Development (HUD),
51
human factors
environment of person-centered care,
202–203
maximizing quality of life, 11
person-centered care challenges,
203–205
human immunodeficiency virus (HIV)
defined, 593
ecological factors in nursing homes, 86
long-term care for people with, 14–15
right to nondiscrimination for patients
with, 117
human interest stories (publicity), 467
human resource management, 420–421,
593
human resources
absenteeism, 426
challenges faced by, 422
compensation, 425
counseling, 434
defined, 420, 593
disciplining, 434–436
employment laws, 440–443
functions of, 421
labor relations and, 437–440
performance appraisal, 431–432
planning, 422–424
scheduling, 424
self-managed work teams (SMWTs),
432–433
staff development, 430–431

human resources (*cont.*)
    staff licensure, certification, and
        registration, 425
    staff recruitment, 424–425
    staffing levels in nursing homes, 422–423
    terminating employment, 436
    turnover and retention of staff, 426–430
    unionization and, 437–440
hydration, 293, 593
hypertension, 5, 40, 593

**I**
IADLs (instrumental activities of daily
        living), 13, 594
iatrogenic problems, 280, 593
ICF/MR. *see* Intermediate Care Facility for
        the Mentally Retarded (ICF/MR)
ICP (infection control practitioner), 86,
        288, 594
Identification Information, MDS 3.0 draft,
        168–171
immediate jeopardy, 129, 593
impasse, collective bargaining, 440, 593
impoverished management, 400
imprest amount, 373, 594
*Improving the Quality of Care in Nursing
        Homes*, 505
incentives, private LTC insurance, 36–37
incident
    abusive spouse, case study, 529–532
    defined, 594
    and risk management, 416
    wound care, case study, 536–537
income statements, 473–474, 594
incontinence
    associated with AIDS, 15
    and catheters, 294–295
    defined, 594
    preventing falls by observing, 292
incorporation, 594
independence
    Green House project promoting,
        224–228

independent or retirement housing for,
        18
    LTC services promoting functional, 9
    maximizing quality of life, 11
    measuring IADL, 13
    preference of elderly for, 254
    startup of Blissful Gardens, case study,
        571–574
independent living
    continuing care retirement communities
        for, 56–57
    government-assisted housing for, 51
    overview of, 51
    private-pay housing for, 51–52
    technology enabling, 68
individualized services
    clinical pathways for, 504–505
    LTC tailored to, 8
    person-centered care and, 202, 204
indwelling catheter, 295, 594
inefficiency, 499, 594
infantilization, 258, 594
infection control
    CNAs trained in, 286
    defined, 594
    education in, 290–291
    food safety and, 343–344
    housekeeping operations for, 353–354
    of infectious outbreaks, 291
    minimizing use of indwelling catheters
        for, 295
    overview of, 288–289
    policies and procedures for, 289
    practices of, 289–290
    screening for, 289
    surveillance, 290
    wound care, case study, 535–537
infection control practitioner (ICP), 86,
        288
    defined, 594
infectious waste, 360, 594
informal care
    defined, 594

forming linkages to, 92
long-term care system, 16–17
information
    gathering for surveys, 128
    social worker role as source of, 262
information packet, for prospective client,
        267
information systems. *see also*
        administrative systems
    defined, 594
    development of, 381
    for further learning, 382
    for further thought, 382
    integrated networks, 379–380
    national data, 380–381
    overview of, 378–379
    references, 382–383
    security issues, 381
information technology (IT), 69–70, 86
informed consent, 115, 594
initial interview, admission inquiry,
        265–266
initial tour, survey process, 127
injury, 594
Injury and Illness Report (Form 301),
        OSHA, 143
inpatient rehabilitation facilities (IRFs),
        55–56
inpatient services
    continuum of long-term care for, 16
    defined, 594
    Part A of Medicare covering, 152
inputs, external environment, 80–81
in-service training
    defined, 594
    employee compensation for, 371
    enforcing as remedy, 135
    nursing administration, 283
inspections
    revolving, 351
    survey process. *see* survey process
        (inspections)
Institute of Medicine (IOM) report, 32, 500

institutional providers, 52–57
institutional system of long-term care
    Alzheimer's facilities, 56
    assisted living facilities, 52–53
    categories of, 18–19
    continuing care retirement communities,
        56
    inpatient rehabilitation facilities, 55–56
    intermediate care facilities for mentally
        retarded, 56
    nursing homes, 53–55
    overview of, 15–16
    policy of prevention, 40–41
    quasi-institutional providers, 50–52
instrumental activities of daily living
        (IADLs), 13, 594
insulated tray system, food transportation,
        342
insurance, LTC
    commercial, 57–58
    creating policies, 27
    financial policy for future and, 41
    financing using, 35
    managed care and, 58–59
    private, 36–37
    role of, 57
    state policy initiatives for, 34
    unpopularity of, 148
integrated health system
    challenges to, 203–205
    defined, 594
    overview of, 379–380
intensive nutrition support (tube feeding),
        339–340
intentional torts, 107, 594
interdependence, 254, 594
interdisciplinary. *see* multidisciplinary
interest checklists, 319
interest groups
    averting deregulation of nursing homes
        with, 32
    building support for policy through, 27
    defined, 594

interest-bearing account, patient trust fund, 375

intergenerational appeal, activity programs, 315

interior finish materials, *Life Safety Code*®, 138

Intermediate Care Facility for the Mentally Retarded (ICF/MR)
  certification category, 113
  defined, 19, 593
  overview of, 56

internal customers, 511

internal environment, 199–243
  aesthetics, 217–218
  causes and prevention of falls, 291–292
  challenges to full integration, 203–205
  clinical organization, 205–208
  culture change, Artifacts of Culture Change, 233–243
  culture change, overview, 220–221
  culture change, the Eden Alternative, 222–224
  culture change, the Green House Project, 224–228
  defined, 75–76
  enriched environments, 218–220
  evolution of nursing homes, 200–201
  facility tour for admission inquiries, 266
  for further learning, 229
  for further thought, 229
  modern architectural designs, 212–218
  overview of, 199–200
  patients with dementia, 228
  philosophy of care delivery, 201–203
  references, 229–232
  socio-residential environment, 208–212

Internal Revenue Service (IRS), payroll withholdings, 372

Internet (Web), 70, 86

internists, 594

interoperable, 27, 594

intervention orientation
  for cognitive disorders, 315

program orientation vs., 309
types of, 316–317

interviews
  concluding admission inquiry, 266–267
  initial admission inquiry, 265–266
  social workers skill in, 261

intimacy
  of caregiving relationships, 258
  defined, 594
  need for, 210

intramural services, 17, 594

intrusion alarms, for safety, 356

intuitive decision making, 410

invasion of privacy, 107

inventory control
  of food, 334–335
  of linens, 355
  management of, 485–488
  movable capital assets, 357
  supplies and materials, 357

investigation, nursing home responsibilities, 531–532

invoice receiving, 334

IOM (Institute of Medicine) report, 32, 500

IRFs (inpatient rehabilitation facilities), 55–56

IRS (Internal Revenue Service), payroll withholdings, 372

isolated scope of deficiencies, 129

isolation, counteracting with wholesome interaction, 211–212

isolation precautions, infection control, 290

issues, in policymaking, 27

IT (information technology), 69–70, 86

**J**

JCAHO (Joint Commission on Accreditation of Healthcare Organizations), 114

Jehovah's Witnesses, cultural accommodations for, 257

jejunostomy (J-tube), 340, 595

Jews, cultural accommodations for, 256–258
job duties, exempt employees, 369–370
job-unit contracts, 352, 595
Joint Commission on Accreditation of Healthcare Organizations (JCAHO), 114
joint venture, 595
judicial branch of government, 27

**K**
key control system, security, 357–358
kickback provision laws, 164
Kotler, Philip, 451

**L**
labeling theory, of aging, 253
labor
    costs, 481–485
    crisis in labor force, 40
    markets, 85
    relations, 437–440
labor-saving technology, 69
language, and communication skills, 259
LANs (local area networks), 381, 595
Lao Tse, 398
laundry department
    linen inventory, 355
    microbicidal washing, 354
    operations of, 354
    overview of, 349
    standard precautions, 354–355
law
    civil and criminal, 103
    constitutional, statutory, administrative, and common, 102
    contract, 104–105
    corporate, 109
    federal, state, and local, 101–102
    health care policy as, 26–27
    nursing home litigation and, 100–101
    personal/corporate liability and, 105–109
    public and private, 102–103

purpose of, 100
tort, 103–104
*L.C. v. Olmstead*, 27
leadership
    building cooperation with, 397
    defined, 595
    and governance. *see* governance
    implications of theories, 401–403
    and management, 406. *see also* management
    meaning and purpose of, 398–399
    role of NHA in providing, 392, 404
    situational, 401–402
    tug-of-war with DON case study and, 557–560
    two-dimensional model of, 400–401
    two-model theory of, 399–400
    Wellspring model case study and, 577, 582
leadership and culture, 512–513
learned helplessness, 269, 595
learning, continuous, 515
legal environment
    classification of laws, 101–105
    corporate law, 109
    for further learning, 121
    for further thought, 121
    licensure, certification, and accreditation, 111–114
    nursing home litigation, 100–101
    overview of, 99–100
    patient rights, 114–120
    personal and corporate liability, 105–109
    purpose of laws, 100
    references, 121–122
legal services, of hospice, 8
legislative branch of government, 27
liabilities (balance sheets), 474, 595
liability
    corporate, 107–109
    defined, 105, 595
    personal, 105–107
liaison role, NHA, 404

libel, 107, 595. *see also* slander
licensed practical (or vocational) nurse
    (LPN/LVN)
    defined, 595
    DON responsibility for training, 285
    in LTC settings, 62–63
licensure
    certification vs., 112–114
    defined, 595
    of LTC professionals, 27
    nursing home administrator, 31, 61–62
    overview of, 111–112
    of physicians, 62
    residential care/assisted living
        administrators, 60
    social services, 251–252
    startup of Blissful Gardens case study
        and, 571–574
    state, 124
life expectancy, future policy and, 39–40
life insurance death benefits, 151
*Life Safety Code*® (LSC)
    building requirements, 208–209
    compliance with, 123
    defined, 595
    Green House compliance with, 225
    licensure and, 112
    overview of, 136–140
    written fire safety plan, 358
lifestyle factors, quality of life, 11
lighting
    modern architectural design for, 217
    for patients with dementia, 228
limited partnerships, 110–111, 595
line relationships, 406
linen closets, enclosing, 205–206, 213
linen inventory, 355
Lippert Healthcare case study, 557–560
listening skills
    communication and, 259
    conflict resolution and, 413–414
litigation

corporate compliance at Mid-Atlantic
        care centers case study and,
        561–564
    defined, 100, 595
    nursing home, 100–101
    reliance on medical records during, 378
    wound care case study and, 535–537
living environment, quality of life, 11
living will, 117, 595
local area networks (LANs), 381, 595
local laws, 101–102
lock-up procedures, 356
Log of Work-Related Injuries and Illnesses
        (Form 300), OSHA, 143–144
loneliness, counteracting, 211–212
long-term care facility, 6, 595
long-term care hospitals (LTCHs), 55
long-term care industry, 47–73
    ancillary sector, 67–70
    for further learning, 70–71
    for further thought, 70
    insurance sector, 57–59
    overview of, 47
    professionals, 59–67
    provider sector. *see* providers
    references, 71–73
    scope of, 48
long-term care (LTC), overview of
    clients, 12–15
    defined, 4, 595
    delivery system, 15–19
    holistic approach, 10
    individualized services, 8
    introduction to, 1
    maximizing quality of care, 10–11
    maximizing quality of life, 11–12
    non-long-term health care system, 20
    overview of, 3
    promotion of functional independence, 9
    rational integration with complementary
        services, 20–21
    use of current technology, 9–10

use of evidence-based practices, 10
variety of services, 4–8
well-coordinated total care, 8
long-term care product, 458–459
lost charges, 489
low-fiber diets, 338
LPN/VPN. *see* licensed practical (or
        vocational) nurse (LPN/LVN)
LSC. *see* Life Safety Code® (LSC)
LTCHs (long-term care hospitals), 55

**M**
maintenance department, 348
maintenance man (supervisor), 349–352
maintenance rehabilitation, 301, 595
malice, 104, 595
malpractice cases
    defined, 595
    nursing home litigation, 101
    reliance on medical records, 378
    under tort law, 103–104
managed care organizations (MCOs)
    defined, 595
    financing, 161–162
    hospital and health system partnerships,
        162–163
    Medicare Advantage coverage for, 155
    overview of, 58–59
management, 403–418
    conflict resolution and, 413–414
    controlling, 406–407
    decision making and, 409–411
    defined, 595
    of human resources, 420–421
    leading, 406
    meetings and, 410–413
    NHA guidelines for, 392
    organizing, 405–406
    overview of, 403
    planning and, 405
    relationship with superiors, 414–415
    risk, 414–415

roles within, 403–405
tug-of-war with DON case study and,
        557–560
values and, 408–409
vision, mission and, 407–408
Wellspring model case study and,
        581–582
management accounting, 475–476, 595
management by objectives (MBO),
        431–432, 595–596
management reports (finance), 475–476
managerial grid and leadership styles,
        400–401
MA-PDs (Medicare Advantage
        prescription drug plans), 155
margin. *see* operating margin
margins, budgeted, 496
market segmentation, 452–455, 596
marketing
    advertising, 466–467
    competitive differentiation, 462–463
    customer relations and, 465–466
    defined, 596
    differentiation strategy, 462–463
    event promotion, 468–469
    functional activities, 450–451
    goals, 451–452
    importance of, 448
    long-term care product and, 458–459
    market segmentation, 452–455
    marketing mix, 458
    niche marketing, 463
    organizational attitudes and orientation,
        451
    personal contacts with referral agents,
        467–468
    personal selling (salesmanship),
        463–465
    philosophy of, 448–449
    place (location) of services and, 460–461
    positioning, 456–458
    pricing strategies and, 459–460

marketing (*cont.*)
  promotion objectives, 461–462
  promotional materials, 468
  publicity, 467
  re-construction due to competition, 201
  startup of Blissful Gardens case study
    and, 573
  strategy, 452
  targeting markets, 452, 455–456
  tools for promotion and PR, 466
  undifferentiated (mass) marketing, 462
  using integrated information networks
    for, 380
  value perception and creation, 449–450
marketing mix, 458–462, 596
mass (undifferentiated) marketing, 462
mastectomy, 596
master's degree in social work (MSW),
  251
materials, promotional, 468
MBO (management by objectives),
  431–432, 595–596
MCCA (Medicare Catastrophic Coverage
  Act), 160
MCOs. *see* managed care organizations
  (MCOs)
MD (doctor of medicine), 62, 280
meal breaks for employees, 371
meal plans, 329, 596
Meals on Wheels, 326, 596
means of egress, *Life Safety Code*®, 138
meats, monitoring internal temperatures,
  344
Medicaid
  for assisted living facilities, 53
  billing accounts receivable, 373
  creation of, 30
  defined, 596
  *Estate of Smith v. Heckler* (1984) and,
    32–33
  financing long-term care, 35
  financing using, 158–160
  fraud and abuse by providers, 163–165

  funding adult day care, 50
  funding custodial services, 52
  funding for nursing homes, 30–31
  homemaker and personal care under, 49
  as largest source of funding for LTC
    services, 35
  for managed care organizations,
    161–162
  PACE service financing, 160–161
  Partnership for Long-Term Care program
    and, 36
  patient trust funds, 375–376
  paying copayments after 100 days, 152
  policy for reimbursement to providers,
    36
  as predominant source of financing care,
    148
  total nursing home expenditures using,
    149
medical care, 277–305
  attending physicians, 278–279
  medical director, 279–283
  overview of, 5–6, 277–278
  in skilled nursing facility, 19
medical director
  director of nursing role and, 283
  functions of, 281–283
  in LTC settings, 62
  overview of, 279–280
  personal traits and qualifications,
    280–281
medical model
  defined, 596
  medical services based on, 4
medical records
  content, 377
  evacuation of Angel Care Center case,
    553–554
  functions of medical records clerk, 376
  locating at nursing station, 207
  Privacy Rule, 118–119
  purpose of, 377–378
  staffing, 376

Medicare, 151–157
  billing accounts receivable to, 373
  categories covered by, 151
  creation of, 30
  deemed status rule, 114
  defined, 596
  financing long-term care, 35
  fraud and abuse of, 163–165
  funding for nursing homes, 30–31
  home health benefits under, 48–49
  hospice care under, 50
  managed care organizations under,
      161–162
  PACE service under, 160–161
  Part A (Hospital Insurance), 151–154
  Part B (Supplementary Medical
      Insurance), 154–155
  Part C (Medicare Advantage), 155
  Part D (prescription drug program),
      155–157
  patient trust funds and, 375–376
  payroll withholdings to, 372
  as predominant source of financing care,
      148–149
  prospective payment system, 157–158
  quality measures, 543
  reimbursement to providers, 36
Medicare Advantage, 58–59, 155
Medicare Advantage prescription drug
    plans (MA-PDs), 155
Medicare Catastrophic Coverage Act
    (MCCA), 160
Medicare Prescription Drug, Improvement,
    and Modernization Act (MMA),
    155
Medicare+Choice program, 58–59
medications
  accessibility from nursing station,
      207–208
  controlled substances, 298–299
  emergency kit, 299
  evacuation of Angel Care Center case
      study and, 553–554

iatrogenic problems in elderly from,
    280
  Part A Medicare benefit for, 154
  pharmacy services for, 297–298
  psychotropic drugs, 299
Medications, MDS 3.0 draft, 193
meetings, management, 410–413
memorabilia, patient autonomy and, 210
mental distress, intentional infliction of,
    107
mental health care
  holistic approach, 10
  managing, 295–297
  by non-LTC services, 20
mental health services, LTC
  CNAs assisting with, 286
  as component of LTC, 6–7
  policy for future, 42
  in skilled nursing facility, 19
mental retardation
  defined, 596
  leading to developmental disability, 14
  specialized care facilities for, 19
mentally retarded/developmentally disabled
    (MR/DD). *see also* developmentally
    disabled (DD)
  children and adolescents as, 14
  intermediate care facilities for. *see*
      Intermediate Care Facility for the
      Mentally Retarded (ICF/MR)
  long-term care for people with, 14
  workforce diversity case study, 570
mentoring of staff, 428–429
menu cycle, 330, 596
menu planning
  meal plans, 329
  menu choice, 329–330
  menu cycle, 330
  menu development, 330–332
  overview of, 328–329
  purchasing food and supplies, 332–333
  standardized recipes and portions, 332
metabolism, in elderly patients, 281

methicillin-resistant Staphylococcus aureus (MRSA), 288

MIA (Monthly Income Allowance), Community Spouse, 160

microbicidal washing, laundering process, 354

microorganisms
  defined, 596
  infection control, 289, 353–354
  microbicidal washing in laundering, 354

middle-of-the-road management, 401

mid-level providers. *see* nonphysician practitioners (NPPs)

midnight census report
  as basis for daily charges, 373
  defined, 596
  minimizing lost charges and reimbursement, 489

mild dementia, 296

Minimum Data Set (MDS)
  defined, 596
  offsite survey preparation using, 126–127
  patient assessment and reimbursement, 157–158
  using information systems for, 378–381

Minimum Data Set (MDS) 3.0 draft, 168–198
  Active Disease Diagnosis, 184–185
  Assessment Administration, 198
  Behavior, 177–178
  Bladder and Bowel, 183
  Cognitive Patterns, 173–175
  Functional Status, 181–182
  Health Conditions, 186–188
  Hearing, Speech, and Vision, 172
  Identification Information, 168–171
  Medications, 193
  Mood, 175–176
  Oral/Dental Status, 189
  overview of, 158
  Participation in Assessment and Goal Setting, 197

  patient assessment and care planning using, 286–288
  Preferences for Customary Routine and Activities, 179–180, 310
  Restraints, 196
  Skin Conditions, 190–193
  Special Treatments and Procedures, 194–196
  Swallowing/Nutritional Status, 188–189
  Therapy Supplement for Medicare PPS, 197

minimum wage, 370

misappropriation of resident property, 117–118, 596

misdemeanors, 103, 596

mission
  accomplishing, 407–408
  board responsibility to review, 391
  defined, 596
  evacuation of Angel Care Center case study and, 546
  startup of Blissful Gardens case study and, 571–574

mix, marketing, 458

MMA (Medicare Prescription Drug, Improvement, and Modernization Act), 155

mobility, assistance with, 9

moderate dementia, 296

modified diets, 338–339

modified five-meal plan, 329

Money Follows the Person, 35

monitor role, NHA, 404

monitoring system, for physical security, 356

Monthly Income Allowance (MIA), Community Spouse, 160

Mood, MDS 3.0 draft, 175–176

Moss Amendments of 1968, 31

movable capital assets, tagging and inventorying, 357

MR/DD. *see* mentally retarded/developmentally disabled (MR/DD)

MRSA (methicillin-resistant Staphylococcus aureus), 288
MSW (master's degree in social work), 251
multidisciplinary
defined, 596
overview of, 279
work teams, 515
multi-drug resistant organisms (MDROs), 288
multiple sclerosis (MS), 596–597
multisensory behavior therapy (MSBT), 316–317, 596
multisensory environment (MSE), 317
multisensory stimulation (MSS), 316–317, 596
musculoskeletal disorders (MSDs), 141–142, 597
music, and dementia, 318
Muslims, cultural accommodations for, 256–258

**N**
NAB (National Association of Long Term Care Administrator Boards), 60–61
nasoduodenal tube, 340, 597
nasogastric tube (NG-tube), 340, 597
National Association of Long Term Care Administrator Boards (NAB), 60–61
National Certification Council for Activity Professionals (NCCAP), 66, 309
National Clearinghouse for Long-Term Care Information, 37
national data, comparing, 380–381
National Labor Relations Act (NLRA), 437
National Labor Relations Board (NLRB), 437
natural disasters, 86. *see also* disaster planning
natural lighting, 217
nature-related activities
in Eden Alternative projects, 222–224
in enriched environments, 218–220
in Green House projects, 224–228

for patients with dementia, 228
theory of biophilia, 218
NCCAP (National Certification Council for Activity Professionals), 66, 309
needs, segmenting markets by, 453–455
negative outcomes, preventing, 501
negative variances, 476
neglect, 117, 597
negligence
ascribing personal liability as, 106–107
defined, 597
wound care case study and, 535–537
negotiation, in conflict resolution, 414
negotiator role, of NHA, 405
nephrologists, 279, 597
nested single rooms, 213–217
net assets, 474, 597
neurological disease
bed sores in elderly from, 293
defined, 597
disability in young adults, 14
news events, publicity, 467
NF. *see* nursing facility (NF)
NFPA (Fire Protection Association), 136–140
NG-tube (nasogastric tube), 340, 597
niche marketing, 463, 597
night lights, 217
1915(c) HCBS waivers, 32, 53
NLRA (National Labor Relations Act), 437
NLRB (National Labor Relations Board), 437
noncertified
defined, 597
nursing home facilities, 113–114
nonexempt employees
classifying, 369
defined, 597
overtime compensation for, 370
nonlabor expenses, controlling, 485–488
non-long-term health care system
defined, 3
linking with, 93–94

non-long-term health care system (*cont.*)
  needed by long-term care patients, 20
  policy initiatives for adoption of HIT, 42
  rational integration of long-term care
    and, 20–21
  well-coordinated total care interfacing
    with, 8
nonphysician practitioners (NPPs)
  defined, 597
  overview of, 63
nonprofit
  corporate law for private facilities,
    109–110
  defined, 597
nonselective menus
  defined, 597
  overview of, 329
nosocomial infections
  defined, 597
  surveillance for, 290
notification system, for receptionist, 367
nourishments, and food intake, 339
nurse aide registry
  banning abusive nurse aides, 118
  defined, 597
nurse aide registries, 425
nurse aide training, 429
nurse practitioners (NPs)
  defined, 597
  overview of, 63
nursing, in LTC settings, 62–63
Nursing assistant certification programs,
    424
nursing assistant (nurse aide) program, 283
nursing facility (NF)
  certification, 112–114
  CMS regulation of, 124
  defined, 597
  out-of-pocket financing for, 151
  PASRR screenings before admission to,
    264
  quality of life for, 501

Requirements of Participation for,
    131–132
nursing home administrator (NHA), 421
  defined, 597
  as director of nursing, 283
  effectiveness of, 395–396
  flat hierarchical structure of, 246–247
  leadership. *see* leadership
  licensing of, 31
  management. *see* management
  managing business aspect, 396–397
  managing facility in community and
    society, 398–399
  managing work and workers, 397–398
  as member of board, 391
  overview of, 61–62
  relationship with board, 391–392
  responsibility for safety, 349–350
  role of, 392–395
  shortage of, 41–42
  tug-of-war with DON case study and,
    557–560
  for urgent service calls, 350
  Wellspring model case study and,
    575–584
Nursing Home Compare, 380
Nursing Home eTool, 142
Nursing Home Reform Act of 1987
  certification and, 112
  overview of, 33–34
  PASRR screenings, 264–265
  role in regulatory oversight, 124
nursing services
  administration of, 283
  Director of Nursing and, 283–285
  falls and fall prevention, 291–292
  infection control, 288–291
  mental and cognitive disorders, 295–297
  organization of, 285–286
  overview of, 283
  patient assessment and care planning,
    286–288

pharmacy services, 297–299
pressure ulcers, 292–294
relating to medical director, 278–283
urinary incontinence and catheters, 294–295
use and misuse of physical restraints, 294
working with attending physicians, 278–279
nursing stations
cluster design for, 213
furnishings, 207–208
location of, 206–207
staffing of, 207
nursing units, 205–206, 213
nutrition. *see also* dietary services
managing for elderly patients, 280–281
menu development based on, 330–331
therapeutic diets and, 338–339
treating pressure ulcers through, 293
with tube feeding, 339–340
nutritional screening, 328, 597

**O**
OAA (Old Age Assistance), 29–30, 200
occupancy rate, 477, 597
Occupational Safety and Health Act of 1970, 142–143
Occupational Safety and Health Administration (OSHA)
overview of, 141–142
recordkeeping requirements, 143–144
standards and enforcement, 142–143
workplace safety rules, 123–124
occupational therapists (OTs)
defined, 597
evaluating food intake problems, 339
overview of, 64
restorative rehabilitation of, 300
occupational therapy, 300, 597
odor control, training in, 206
Office of Nursing Home Affairs, 505

offsite preparation, survey process, 126–127
Old Age Assistance (OAA), 29–30, 200
Older Americans Act of 1978, 92
*Olmstead v. L.C.*, 27
ombudsman
defined, 597–598
forming positive linkages with local, 92–93
offsite surveys using reports from, 127
Omnibus Budget Reconciliation Act of 1987 (OBRA-87)
on activity programs, 309–310
controversy surrounding, 39
impact of, 33–34, 38
oncology, 20, 86, 598
ongoing upkeep, 351–352
On-line Survey Certification and Reporting (OSCAR), 380–381, 598
open system
defined, 598
management, 78–79
requiring strong governance, 80
and strategic management, 82–83
open-call contracts, 352, 598
operating margin, 496, 598
operational budgeting, 379
ophthalmologists, 598
opportunity cost, 460, 598
opticians, 20, 598
optometrists, 8, 20, 88, 598
oral supplements, 338–339
Oral/Dental Status, MDS 3.0 draft, 189
ordinances, 102, 598
organizational attitudes/orientation, marketing, 451
organizing tasks, 405–406, 598
orthopedists, 598
OSCAR (On-line Survey Certification and Reporting), 380–381, 598
OSHA. *see* Occupational Safety and Health Administration (OSHA)

osteopathic medicine, 62, 598
OTs. *see* occupational therapists (OTs)
Out-of-pocket, 149, 598
outcomes (final results)
   defined, 598
   framework of quality, 503
   improved by dining experience, 343
   program evaluation involving, 321
   regulatory minimum standards, 505–506
   wound care case study and, 536–537
outdoor spaces, socializing in, 212
out-of-pocket financing, 149–150
outpatient services, 154–156, 598
outputs (patient care)
   board overseeing facility, 392
   completing cycle of exchanges, 95–96
   efficiency and, 499
   production of, 81
   returns to environment, 81–82
outreach plan, six-point, 91
oversight, role of medical director,
   281–282
overtime compensation, 370
ownership, types of, 109–111

**P**

PA (physician assistant), 63, 599
PACE (Program of All-Inclusive Care for
   the Elderly), 160–161
package price. *see* bundled rate
painting, ongoing upkeep, 348–349, 352
palliation
   for advanced dementia, 297
   defined, 598
   hospice emphasis on, 8
   maximizing quality of life, 11
par level, 355, 598
paraprofessionals
   custodial services by, 52
   defined, 598
   maintenance rehabilitation by, 301
   overview of, 65–66
parenteral nutrition, 340, 598

parking areas
   adequately lit for safety, 356
   ongoing upkeep of, 352
Parkinson's disease, 598
Part A (Hospital Insurance) services,
   Medicare, 151–154
Part B (Supplementary Medical Insurance)
   services, Medicare, 155–156
Part C (Medicare Advantage), 155
Part D (prescription drug program),
   Medicare, 155–157
partial evacuation, 359–360
Participation in Assessment and Goal
   Setting, MDS 3.0 draft, 197
Partnership for Long-Term Care program,
   36–37
partnerships
   customer, 511
   defined, 598
   mission-driven, 90–95
   private for-profit facilities, 110
PASRR (Pre-admission Screening and
   Resident Review), 264–265, 600
passivity
   activity program to stimulate, 315
   defined, 598
   in dementia patients, 317
pathogens
   defined, 598
   infection control practices, 289, 353–354
pathological waste, 360, 598
patient assessment. *see* assessment
patient call signals, nursing stations, 207
patient care (outputs), 499
patient days
   calculating food costs, 335, 340
   controlling labor cost, 481–484
   controlling nonlabor cost, 485–486
   defined, 599
   maintaining expected census levels,
   476–479
patient rights, 114–120
   board policies for, 392

freedom from abuse, neglect, and misappropriation of property, 117–118

nondiscrimination, 117

privacy and confidentiality, 118–120

punitive damages for blatant disregard of, 104

self-determination, 115–117

The Patient Self-Determination Act of 1990, 115–117

patient trust fund, 375–376

patient's bill of rights, 115–116, 599

payables. *see* accounts payable

payer-mix, 476, 599

payments, and clients, 81

payroll and compensation

administrative systems, 368–372

exempt and nonexempt employees, 369–370

limits to FLSA jurisdication, 371

overtime compensation, 370

overview of, 368–369

withholdings, 371–372

PDPs (prescription drug plans), Medicare, 155–157

PDSA (plan, do, study, act) improvement cycle, 513–515

pellet system, food transportation, 342

people-focused, leadership as, 398–399

per-diem rate, 373–374, 599

performance appraisal, of staff, 431–432

periodic planning, NHAs, 405

per-patient-day (PPD), 332, 599

perpetual inventory system, food, 335

PERS (personal emergency response systems), 68

person, privacy of, 211

personal biases, in decision-making, 410

personal care, 18, 599

personal contacts, with referral agents, 467–468

personal domain, socio-residential environment, 208–211

personal emergency response systems (PERS), 68

personal liability, 105–107

personal selling, 463–465

personality traits

activity professionals, 310, 313

front office personnel, 366–368

person-centered care

challenges of, 203–205

creating environment, 202–203

defined, 599

enriched environments integrating, 219–220

philosophy of, 201

reducing psychotropic drug use, 299

pest control, food sanitation, 343

petty cash funds, 373, 375

pharmacies

accessibility of pharmaceuticals room, 207–208

long-term care, 67

services of nursing facilities, 297–299

PHI (protected healthcare information), 118–119, 600

PHPs (Prepaid Health Plans), 58

physiatrists, 63–64, 599

physical dimension, holistic approach, 10

physical inventory, food, 335

physical restraints, 294

physical security, 355–356

physical therapist (PT)

defined, 599

overview of, 64

restorative rehabilitation function of, 300

physical therapy assistant (PTA), 64

physical therapy (PT), 300, 599

physician assistant (PA), 63, 599

physicians

attending, 278–279

linking with non-LTC sector, 93–94

in LTC settings, 62

as medical directors, 279–283

physicians (*cont.*)
  nursing home litigation and, 101
  pronouncement of death by, 273
picketing, 440, 599
pilferage
  defined, 599
  inventory management and, 488
  inventory of food and, 335–336
  inventory of linens and, 355
  procedural security to prevent, 357
Pioneer Network, 221, 599
place (location) of services, 460–461
plaintiff, 101, 599
plan of care (care plan)
  Care Resource Teams in Wellspring
    model case study, 577–578
  defined, 599
  DON responsibility for, 284
  individualized, 8
  integrating safety concerns, 209
  overview of, 287–288
plan of correction (POC), 130, 132–135,
    599
plan step, PDSA improvement cycle,
    513–515
planning
  defined, 599
  management functions, 405
  meetings, 412
plant and environmental services, 347–363
  environmental safety, 361–362
  fire and disaster planning, 358–360
  function and objectives, 348
  for further learning, 362
  for further thought, 362
  housekeeping operations, 352–354
  laundry operations, 354–355
  maintenance operation, 350–352
  organization of environmental services,
    348–350
  overview of, 347
  references, 362–363

  security operations, 355–358
  waste management, 360–361
plate waste, addressing, 339
POA (power of attorney), 117
POC (plan of correction), 130, 132–135,
    599
podiatrists, 8, 20, 88, 599
police patrol, 356
policy, 25–46
  advisory role of medical director, 282
  collection, 374
  current state of, 34–38
  DON responsibility for, 284–285
  established by board, 391–392
  forms and sources of, 26–27
  for further learning, 43
  for further thought, 42
  future of, 39–42
  guiding NHA management, 392
  history of financing community-based
    services, 31–32
  history of welfare policies, 29–30
  infection control, 289
  level 4 of environmental proximity,
    88–89
  making, 28
  overview of, 25–26
  politics and, 28–29, 85
  references, 43–46
  risk management, 416
  security, 356
  shaping long-term care industry, 48
policy agenda, 85, 599
policymakers, 27, 599
politics, 28–29, 85
poorhouses
  defined, 599–600
  evolution of nursing homes, 200
  history of welfare policies, 29–30
portion control, 342, 600
positioning (marketing), 456–458, 600
positioning statement, 453, 458, 600

positive distractions, 220
post-survey revisit, 126
postural hypotension, 292, 600
power of attorney (POA), 117
PPD (per-patient-day), 332, 599
PPS. *see* prospective payment system
    (PPS)
practical nurse. *see* licensed practical (or
    vocational) nurse (LPN/LVN)
preadmission inquiry
  defined, 600
  engaging family members, 271
  overview of, 264–267
  receptionist role, 367
Pre-admission Screening and Resident
    Review (PASRR), 264–265, 600
preceptor, 61, 600
preferences
  determining LTC services received, 5
  segmenting markets by, 453–455
Preferences for Customary Routine and
    Activities, MDS 3.0 draft, 179–180
Pregnancy Discrimination Act of 1978, 441
Prepaid Health Plans (PHPs), 58
prescription drug plans (PDPs), Medicare,
    155–157
President of the United States, policy
    making, 27
pressure ulcers, 281, 292–294, 600
prevalence, defined, 600
preventative maintenance, 350–352
prevention
  policy for future, 40–41
  responsibilities for, 531–532
pricing strategies, marketing, 459–460
pride in workmanship, 517
primary care
  defined, 600
  physician, 600
  provided by non-LTC services, 20
primary exchange partners, 89–90
primary proximities of organization, 84, 87

principal, 109, 600
privacy
  CNAs trained in preserving, 286
  invasion of, 107
  maximizing for quality of life, 11–12
  medical record information, 378
  nested single rooms and, 213–217
  of person, 211
  person-centered care and, 202
  right to, 118–119
  socio-residential environment providing,
    210–211
  of space, 210
  of time, 210–211
Privacy Rule, 118–120, 600
private financing
  LTC insurance, 150–151
  nursing homes re-constructed due to,
    201
  out-of-pocket, 149–150
  total nursing home expenditures using,
    149
private for-profit facilities, 110–111
private insurance, 149–151
private laws, 102–103, 600
private policy, 26
private-pay clients
  certification regulations, 114
  defined, 600
  enhanced and upgraded environments
    for, 206
  housing, 51–52
  selective menus for, 330
private-pay housing, 51–52
pro forma reports, 475
problem-solving
  conflict resolution, 260
  meetings, 412
procedural security, 357–358
processes (methods), 503–504
product, long-term care, 458–459
production, food, 336–338

productivity (efficiency)
  defined, 600
  managing, 397–398
  and quality, 498–500
professional duties, of exempt employees, 370
professionals, long-term care industry, 59–67
  administrative, 59–61
  ancillary, 66
  clinicians, 61–65
  paraprofessional caregivers, 65–66
  social support, 66–67
profits, 95–96
program evaluation, 320–321, 600
Program of All-Inclusive Care for the Elderly (PACE), 160–161
programming, 309–313, 600
promotion
  defined, 600
  event, 468–469
  materials for, 468
  objectives of, 461–462
prosecution, in civil and criminal law, 103
prospective payment system (PPS)
  defined, 600
  home health care and, 34
  subacute/rehabilitation markets and, 37
  tug-of-war with DON case study and, 559–560
protected healthcare information (PHI), 118–119, 600
protection, responsibilities for, 531–532
providers. *see* service providers
psychotropic drugs, 299
PT. *see* physical therapist (PT)
PT (physical therapy), 300, 599
public domain, socio-residential environment, 211–212
public facility, 109, 600
Public Housing program, 51
public laws, 102, 600

public policy
  created by administrative bodies, 27
  defined, 600
  enforcing, 100
  historical perspectives, 29–35
  overview of, 26
public relations, 466, 601
publicity, 467, 601
punitive damages, 104, 601

**Q**

QCIs (Quality of Care Indicators), 125
QIS (Quality Indicator Survey), 125, 506
quality, defined, 601
Quality Indicator Survey (QIS), 125, 506
quality of care
  defined, 601
  evidence-based practices improving, 42
  historical efforts addressing, 32–33
  integrated information networks for, 380
  maximizing, 10–11
  Medicare measures for, 543
  person-centered care and, 202–203
  regulation for, 38–39
  Wellspring model case study and, 578, 580, 583
Quality of Care Indicators (QCIs), 125
quality of life
  activities promoting. *see* recreation and activities
  defined, 601
  integrated information networks for, 380
  integrating into LTC delivery, 9
  integrating need, 205
  maximizing, 11–12
  OBRA-87 lacking data on, 39
quality of service
  consumer-defined, 502–503
  culture of excellence, 516–517
  defined, 500
  framework for improving, 503–505
  fundamentals of, 500–501

measurement and evaluation of, 506–508
quality of life (QoL), measuring, 508
regulatory minimum standards, 505–506
technical, 502
Wellspring Model, 517–518
quasi-institutional providers, 50–52
*qui tam relator* (whistleblower), 164–165, 601
quotas, eliminating, 517

**R**
RACE acronym, fire-protection, 358–359
RAI (Resident Assessment Instrument), 38, 157–158
range, census, 479
RAPs (Resident Assessment Protocols), 287
rational decision making, 410
rational integration with complementary services, LTC, 20–21
RC/AL (residential care/assisted living) administrator, 61
RD (registered dietician), 65, 327, 328
reality orientation, 316, 601
reasonable accommodation, 442, 601
receivables, 488–491. *see also* accounts receivable
receiving methods, food and supplies, 333–334, 336
receptionists, 367–368
recipes, standardized, 332–333
recognition, of activity director volunteers, 322
reconditioning, 353, 601
recordkeeping requirements, OSHA, 143–144
recreation and activities, 307–324
activity department, 309–310
for dementia patients, 317–318
for further learning, 323
for further thought, 322
goals and purpose, 308–309

intervention approaches, 315–317
overview of, 307–308
program development, 310–315
program evaluation, 320–321
program planning and implementation, 318–320
references, 323–324
skills and competencies, 310
volunteer support, 321–322
recruiting health personnel, 425
references, internal environment, 229–232
referral agents, 467–468, 601
referrals, initial admission interview, 265–266
refrigeration, 334
registered dietetic technician (DTR), 65, 327
registered dietician (RD), 65, 327, 328
registered health information administrator (RHIA), 376
registered health information technician (RHIT), 376
registered nurse (RN)
defined, 601
director of nursing qualifying as, 283
in LTC settings, 62–63
nursing organization using, 285–286
pronouncement of death by, 273
as resident assessment coordinator, 283
regularity of services, 500
regulation and enforcement, 123–145
averting deregulation of nursing homes, 32
defined, 601
for further learning, 144–145
for further thought, 144
general accessibility standards, 140–141
history of nursing home, 31
*Life Safety Code*®, 136–140
OSHA and workplace safety, 141–144
oversight, 124–125
overview of, 123

regulation and enforcement (*cont.*)
  person-centered care constraints,
    204–205
  protective purpose of, 100
  purpose of, 124
  references, 145
  Requirements of Participation, 125
  surveys and. *see* survey process
    (inspections)
regulatory minimum standards, 505–506
rehabilitation
  activities vs., 308–309
  CNAs assisting with, 286
  defined, 601
  hospitals. *see* inpatient rehabilitation
    facilities (IRFs)
  maintenance, 301
  nursing homes in 1980s performing, 37
  objectives of, 300
  Part A Medicare benefits for skilled, 153
  professionals for, 63–64
  restorative, 300–301
Rehabilitation Act of 1973, 117
reimbursement. *see also* financing and
    reimbursement
  aspects of, 148
  CMS establishing rates of Medicare, 149
  defined, 489, 601
  Medicare prospective payment system,
    157–158
  to providers, 36
relationship orientation, 400
reliability
  defined, 601
  of services, 501
  of survey instruments, 507
religious observances, 256–258
reminiscence therapy, 316, 318, 601
repeating, as communication skill, 259
reports
  account payable, 485
  management, 475
  midnight census, 489

nursing home responsibilities, 531–532
OSHA recordkeeping requirements,
  143–144
representative role, of medical director,
  282–283
Requirements of Participation
  controlling compliance with, 407. *see
    also* survey process (inspections)
  defined, 124, 601
  standards of quality, 125
resident assessment coordinator, 283
Resident Assessment Instrument (RAI), 38,
  157–158
Resident Assessment Protocols (RAPs),
  287
resident council, 93, 245, 601
Resident Level QM/QI Report, 127
resident sample, survey process, 127–128
residential amenities
  as component of LTC, 7–8, 18–19
  in skilled nursing facility, 19
  state-level policymaking for, 34
residential care/assisted living (RC/AL)
  administrator, 61
residential homes, for light assistive care,
  18
resource allocator, NHA role as, 404–405
resource utilization groups (RUGs)
  defined, 601
  Medicare classification system,
    158–159
  tug-of-war with DON case study and,
    559–560
respiratory tract infections, 288–291
respite care, 18, 601–602
respondeat superior, 99, 108, 602
responsible parties, 490, 602
restorative rehabilitation, 300–301, 602
restraints
  defined, 602
  overuse of psychotropic drugs as
    chemical, 299
  use and misuse of physical, 294

Restraints, MDS 3.0 draft, 196
rethermalization carts, food, 342–343
retirement centers, 18, 51–52
returns to environment, 81–82
revenues
    budgeting, 492–494
    defined, 602
    managing, 476–479
reverse mortgages, 149, 602
revolving inspections, 351–352
RHIA (registered health information
        administrator), 376
RHIT (registered health information
        technician), 376
risk adjustment, 161–162, 602
risk awareness profiles, 319
risk management
    defined, 602
    evacuation of Angel Care Center case
        study and, 546, 548–549
    overview of, 416
RN. *see* registered nurse (RN)
Robert Wood Johnson Foundation, 36, 228
routine checks, 351
routine contracts, 352, 602
routine repair work, 350
RUGs. *see* resource utilization groups
        (RUGs)

**S**

safety. *see also Life Safety Code*® (LSC)
    CNAs trained in, 286
    contrasting color and, 218
    environmental, 361–362
    fall prevention, 292
    food sanitation and, 343–344
    functions, 349–350
    for patients with dementia, 228
    socio-residential environment providing,
        208–209
    supportive housing for LTC and, 7–8
    technology, 68
sandwich generation, 85

sanitizing
    defined, 602
    food safety and, 343–344
    housekeeping operations for, 353
    training staff in methods of, 206
Schedules I through V, Controlled
        Substances Act, 298–299
scheduling, of activity programs, 314–315,
        319–320
scope
    defined, 602
    of noncompliance, 128–130
screening, preadmission, 264–265, 289
secondary disabilities, 311, 602
secondary exchange partners, 79, 90
secondary proximities of organization, 84,
        87
secretarial functions, front office, 368
Section 202 Supportive Housing for the
        Elderly program, 51
Section 8 program, 51
Section 811 Supportive Housing for
        Persons with Disabilities, 51
security
    integrated information networks and, 381
    physical, 355–356
    procedural, 357–358
    socio-residential environment providing,
        208
security audit, 356, 602
segmentation of markets, 452–455
selective menus, 330, 337, 602
selective specialization strategy, marketing,
        456
selective specialization, target marketing,
        456
self-determination, right to, 115–117
self-esteem, promoting. *see* recreation and
        activities
self-managed work teams (SMWTs),
        432–433, 602
self-perpetuating boards, 390–391, 602
selling lines, marketing, 466–467, 602

semantic differential technique, 457, 602

semi-fixed costs, 480–481, 602

senior centers, 17–18, 602

sensory stimulation
  defined, 602
  means of providing, 316
  multisensory stimulation, 316–317

septicemia, 602

service calls, urgent, 350

service providers
  community-based, 48–50
  defined, 600
  as important stakeholders, 79
  institutional, 52–57
  overview of, 48
  policy for reimbursement to, 36
  quasi-institutional, 50–52

services, common, 505

services, LTC
  characteristics of, 4
  defining, 4
  extended period of care, 9
  for functional independence, 9
  holistic approach, 10
  hospice, 8
  individualizing, 8
  maximizing quality of care, 10–11
  maximizing quality of life, 11–12
  medical care, 5–6
  mental health, 6–7
  organization and delivery of, 245–247
  residential amenities, 7
  social. *see* social services
  total care, 8
  use of current technology and, 9–10
  use of evidence-based practices, 10
  variety of, 4–8

Seventh-day Adventists, 256–258

severe dementia, 296–297

severity, 128–129, 602

sexual intimacy, 210, 254

shared service agreements, 163

sharps, 360, 602

shelter care facilities. *see* board-and-care
  homes

short-range planning, NHA function, 405

short-term LTC, 12

sick-role model
  conceding autonomy in, 209
  defined, 602
  person-centered care and, 202–204
  philosophy of, 201–202

simulation drills, fire, 360

single-offer mass-market coverage, 456

single-segment concentration, marketing,
  456

situational leadership, 401–402

skilled nursing care, 5–6, 603

skilled nursing facility (SNF)
  certification category, 112–114
  CMS regulation of, 124
  in continuing care retirement
    communities, 56–57
  defined, 603
  evacuation in Angel Care Center case
    study and, 553
  hospital and health system partnerships,
    162–163
  in long-term care hospitals, 55
  long-term care industry and, 53–54
  Medicare PPS benefit for, 157–158
  organizational chart for, 246–247
  out-of-pocket financing for, 151
  overview of, 19
  Part A Medicare benefit for, 151–154
  quality of life for, 501
  Requirements of Participation for,
    131–132
  in transitional care units, 55

skill-mix (staffing levels), 423, 602–603

Skin Conditions, MDS 3.0 draft, 190–193

skin conditions, pressure ulcers. *see*
  pressure ulcers

slander, 603

sleep disorders, of aging, 253–254, 318
SLPs. *see* speech/language pathologists
(SLPs)
SMI (Supplementary Medical Insurance)
services, Medicare, 154–155
smoke alarms, *Life Safety Code®*, 139
smoke compartments
defined, 603
*Life Safety Code®*, 137, 139
procedures during fire, 359
smoke inhalation, death from, 359
smoking, *Life Safety Code®* and, 139
SMWTs (self-managed work teams),
432–433, 602
SNF. *see* skilled nursing facility (SNF)
Snoezelen, 316–317, 603
social dimension, holistic approach, 10
social factors, and LTC, 84–85
Social Security Act
federal fraud and abuse law, 164
history of welfare policies, 29–30
impact of Medicare and Medicaid,
30–31
payroll withholdings, 372
Title 18 of. *see* Medicare
Title 19 of. *see* Medicaid
Social Security Amendment of 1975, 31
social services, 249–275
activities vs., 308–309
as component of LTC, 7
death and terminal illness, 272–273
department qualifications, 251
department staffing, 250–251
discharge planning, 269–270
diversity and cultural competence,
255–258
family management, 271–272
for further learning, 274
for further thought, 273
of hospice, 8
interviewing skills, 261
knowledge of aging and elderly, 252–255

overview of, 249–250
Part A Medicare benefit for, 154
preadmission inquiry, 264–269
professionals, 66–67
references, 274–275
resident council, 270–271
roles, 261–264
in skilled nursing facility, 19
skills and competencies, 258–261
Social Services Block Grants, 31, 53
social work designee, 251, 603
socializing
cluster design facilitating, 213
socio-residential environment providing,
212
socio-residential environment
autonomy, 209–210
compatibility, 211
dining, 211–212
overview of, 208
of person-centered care, 202–205
privacy, 210–211
safety, 208–209
security, 208
socializing, 212
wayfinding, 209
soft tissue infections, 288–291
soft-surface floorings, 218
software programs, 379
soiled-laundry sorting, 354–355
sole proprietorship, 111, 603
space
activity planning in allotted, 311–312
need for privacy of, 210
Special Treatments and Procedures, MDS
3.0 draft, 194–196
specialized care facilities, 19, 20
speech/language pathologists (SLPs)
addressing swallowing problems, 339
defined, 603
overview of, 65
restorative rehabilitation of, 300

speech/language pathology (speech therapy), 300–301, 603

spend down, 159–160, 603

spina bifida, 13, 603

spiritual dimension, holistic approach, 10

spokesperson role, NHA, 404

sponsorship agreement, 162–163

SPs (standard precautions), infection control, 290, 603

SSI (Supplemental Security Income), 376, 604

*St. Joseph's Hospital v. Hoffman*, 371

staff

activity department, 309–310, 312–313

administrative support of, 430

cluster design decentralizing, 213

development of, 430–431

dietary department, 326–327

DON responsibility for, 284

as important stakeholders, 79

integrated information networks for, 379

levels in nursing homes, 422–423

licensure, certification, and registration, 425

medical director teaching, 282

medical records, 376

mentoring of, 428–429

nursing station, 207

recruitment of, 424–425

retention and turnover of, 426–430

selection of, 428

social services, 250–252

training technology for, 69

turnover decreases due to edenizing, 223–224

stakeholders

defined, 603

meetings with external, 413

organizations benefiting from, 79–80

standard precautions (SPs), infection control, 290, 603

standard surveys, 125–130

standardized recipes, 332–333

standards of care, 281–282

staph infections, 288

startup of Blissful Gardens, case study, 571–574

state laws, classifying, 101–102

State Operations Manual, 125–130

State Survey Agency, 124–125, 603

Statement of Deficiency, 130, 132–135

statement of position, 453, 458, 603

statements

cash flow, 474–475

income, 473–474

patient trust fund, 375

statute of limitations, 377, 603

statutory law, 102, 603

step-variable costs, 480–481

stereotyping

avoiding aging, 252–255

avoiding cultural, 255

stimulation

activity programs for, 315

need for environmental, 220

stoma, 153, 603

storage

food, 334–335

state laws for medical records, 377

strategic planning, 82–83, 405

strategies

defined, 603

marketing, 452, 462–463

strategic management, 82–83

strikes, 440, 603

strokes, 603

structures (resource inputs), 503–504

study step, PDSA improvement cycle, 513–515

subacute care

defined, 604

facilities for, 19, 54–55

hospital and health system partnerships for, 163

need for, 15

nursing homes in 1980s performing, 37

Part A Medicare benefits for, 152–153
  specialized nursing units for, 206
substantial compliance, 125, 604
substitute services, 87–88, 604
Summa Health System, 163
summary judgment, 106, 604
Summary of Work-Related Injuries and
      Illnesses (Form 300A), OSHA, 144
sunlight, 217
Supplemental Security Income (SSI), 376,
      604
Supplementary Medical Insurance (SMI)
      services, Medicare, 154–155
supplies
  activity program, 312
  procedural security for theft of, 357
  purchasing dietary, 332–333
support services
  defined, 604
  for residential amenities, 7
  support groups, for family members,
    272
supporting style, of situational leadership,
    401–402
supportive housing, 7–8, 604
Supreme Court, 102
surrogates, providing long-term care, 3
surveillance
  defined, 604
  for nosocomial infections, 290
survey process (inspections)
  common services, 505
  defined, 124, 604
  enforcement and remedies, 135–136
  example of, 544
  instruments, 507
  overview of, 125
  plan of correction, 130–135
  process and protocols for, 126–130
  standard, 125
  types of, 125–126
swallowing problems. *see* speech/language
    pathologists (SLPs)

Swallowing/Nutritional Status, MDS 3.0
    draft, 188–189
SWOT (strengths, weaknesses,
    opportunities, and threats) analysis,
    82–83, 542
system, defined, 78
systems model of value exchanges, 89–90

**T**

tagging, movable capital assets, 357
target market, 452, 455–456, 604
task management, 401
task orientation, two-dimensional model of
    leadership, 400
taxes, payroll withholdings, 371–372
TB (tuberculosis) screenings, 289
TCUs (transitional care units), 55, 604
teaching, role of medical director, 282
team management, 401
technical jargon, 259
technical quality, 502
technology
  caregiving, 68–69
  as component of LTC, 9–10
  enabling, 68
  environmental, 69
  influencing LTC environment, 85–86
  information, 69–70
  information systems, 378–381
  labor-saving, 69
  overview of, 67–68
  safety, 68
  staff training, 69
telephone calls, front office protocols,
    367–368
temperature danger zone, food, 344, 604
terminally ill patients
  death of, 272–273
  end-of-life care. *see* end-of-life care
  hospice services. *see* hospice services
terminating employment, 436
theft, and food cost, 336
Theory X, leadership, 399

Theory Y, leadership, 399–400

therapeutic diets and nourishment, 338–339

therapeutic purpose, of food intake, 326

Therapy Supplement for Medicare PPS, MDS 3.0 draft, 197

third party claims, 374

third party, defined, 604

three-meal plan, 329

thriving, 218, 220, 604

tile, slip-resistant, 218

time, privacy of, 210–211

Title 18 of Social Security Act. *see* Medicare

tools, promotion and PR, 466

tort law

ascribing personal liability in, 105–107

defined, 604

overview of, 103–104

total care, 8, 604

total evacuation, 359–360

total parenteral nutrition (TPN), 340

total quality management (TQM), 508

training

DON responsibility for, 284

Eden Alternative and, 224

food service staff in portion control, 342

in geriatrics, 41

infection control, 290–291

of nurse aides, 429

teaching role of medical director, 282

Wellspring model case study and, 577, 582

transfer, 604

transitional care units (TCUs), 55, 604

transmission-based precautions, 290, 604

transportation systems, food, 342–343

tray service

accuracy, 342

food transportation systems, 342–343

overview of, 341

using food service station, 341–342

trust

social worker qualifications, 251

sustainable relationships through, 94–95

tube feeding, 339–340

tuberculosis (TB) screenings, 289

tug-of-war with DON, case study, 557–560

turnover and retention of staff, 426–430

two-dimensional model of leadership, 400–401

two-model leadership theory, 399–400

**U**

undesirable consequences, preventing, 501

undifferentiated (mass) marketing, 462, 604

unemployment taxes, 372

unfair labor practices, 438–439, 604

uniformity of services, 500–501

union contract administration, 439–440

union dues, payroll withholdings, 372

union steward, 439, 604

unionization, 437–440

unit-dose medication distribution system, 298

unity of command, 406

upcoding, 164, 604

upholstery fabrics, high-tech finishing of, 218

urinary incontinence and catheters, 294–295

urinary infections, controlling, 288–291

utility closets, enclosing, 205–206, 213

utilization

defined, 604

nursing home data on, 37–38

policy for future, 39

public policy and, 34–35

**V**

vacuum cleaners, and infection control, 354

validation therapy, 316, 604

validity, 507, 605
value (singular)
  defined, 605
  partnerships with non-LTC sector based
    on, 93–94
  perception/creation of marketing,
    449–450
  systems model of value exchanges,
    89–90
value network, 89, 605
values (generally plural)
  defined, 605
  developing set of organizational,
    408–409
vancomycin-resistant enterococci (VRE),
    288
variable costs, 479–480, 605
variance, 605
variance analysis, 476, 605
vegetarians, menus for, 331
vendors
  accounts payable to, 372
  food and supply, 332–333
  information system development using,
    381
ventilator, 14
ventilators, 605
vertical openings, *Life Safety Code®*, 137
very severe dementia, 297
Veterans Health Administration (VHA),
    163
vicarious liability. *see* respondeat superior
violations, corporate compliance, 393
vision
  accomplishing, 407–408
  board responsibility to review, 391
  defined, 605
vital signs, 286, 605
vocational nurses. *see* licensed practical (or
    vocational) nurse (LPN/LVN)
volume factor (staffing levels), 423
voluntary payroll withholdings, 372

volunteer support, activity programs,
    321–322
VPN. *see* licensed practical (or vocational)
    nurse (LPN/LVN)

**W**
wage garnishment, 372, 605
waiver services, 32
walk-in clinic, 605
waste management, 360–361
wayfinding, 209, 605
Web (Internet), 70, 86
weekly cleaning, housekeeping, 353
weight loss, and AIDS, 15
weighting factor, staffing levels, 423
welfare policies, 29. *see also* Medicaid
Wellspring Model, 517–518
Wellspring model implementation, case
    study, 575–584
  assignment, 583
  comments from staff, 580–581
  comments/opinions of Alliance
    administrators, 579–580
  conclusions of research study, 581–583
  direct and indirect costs, 578–579
  Fair Park nursing center, 575–576
  future outlook, 583
  minutes from meeting of Alliance,
    576–577
  overview of, 575
  seven elements of, 577–578
wet-mopping, and infection control, 354
whistleblower (*qui tam relator*), 164–165,
    601
widespread scope, deficiencies, 129
window treatments, modern, 217
withholdings, payroll, 371–372, 376
work order system, routine repair work,
    350
workforce
  Chapel Square Health Care Center
    diversity case study, 565–570

workforce (*cont.*)
  managing, 397–398
  policy initiatives for shortage of LTC, 41–42
  working conditions, 429
wound care case study, 535–537
write-offs, 489–490
written procedures, inquiries, 265

**Y**
young adults, LTC for, 9, 14

**Z**
zoning laws, policies for LTC facilities, 27
zoonosis, 224, 605